Roads to Gettysburg

BY JOHN W. SCHILDT

McCLAIN PRINTING COMPANY
PARSONS, WEST VIRGINIA 26287

1978

Cop. 1

Standard Book Number 87012-295-9
Library of Congress Card Number 78-1137
Printed in the United States of America
Copyright ©1978 by John W. Schildt
Chewsville, Maryland
All Rights Reserved

To my uncle, Raymond E. Staley, who first took me on the Roads to Gettysburg and the wonderful folks at Bethel Church, Chewsville, Maryland.

CONTENTS

Acknowledgments xi

Introduction xiii

I   Along the Rappahannock 1

II   After Chancellorsville 15

III   June Week, June 1-7 27

IV   Lee Moves Northward, June 8-11 36

V   A Long Weekend, June 12-15 45

VI   Hot and Dusty Days, June 16-23 97

VII   Crossing the River, June 24-25 180

VIII   Chambersburg and Carlisle 223

IX   The Clustered Spires of Fredericktown 271

X   A June Sabbath 290

XI   The Commanders 341

XII   A Rainy Monday 357

XIII   The Last Day of June 400

XIV   The First Day of July 449

XV   Gleanings 518

Epilogue 535

Notes 537

Bibliography 569

Index 579

ILLUSTRATIONS

Along the Rappahannock at Fredericksburg 9
Confederate infantry crossing at Williamsport 88
Gum Springs 107
Manassas—familiar territory 116
Another view of the Williamsport crossing 129
Alarm in Harrisburg 130
The Potomac at Shepherdstown 133
Ferry Hill House 134
Aldie 141
Oliver O. Howard 142
The Monocacy Aqueduct 155
Difficulties along the way 170
Jubal Early 171
John Gordon 171
A new flag over Chambersburg 184
Lee and Longstreet cross the Potomac 186
Robert Rodes 189
Dorsey Pender 194
The canal at Edwards Ferry 200
Edwards Ferry today 206
Col. Elijah White 238
John Buford 253
On the banks of the Susquehanna 304
Capture of wagon train 323
Prospect Hall—where the command changed 325
The spires of Burkittsville 325
Richfield—the cavalry camp 325
George A. Custer 325
Gen. John Reynolds 331
Worman's or Wormer's Mill 337

Center Square in Hanover 337
The Old Toll Gate House 395
The Eagle Hotel in Gettysburg .395
An observation post—Hanover—
     Saint Matthew's Lutheran Church 432
Hanover Junction 433
The Central Hotel in Hanover 433
Union Mills 435
Moritz Tavern 442
George G. Meade 444
Saint Joseph's in Emmitsburg 476
Winfield Scott Hancock 488
John Sedgwick 513
The Greek Cross 513
Along the Roads to Gettysburg .535

MAPS

Lee moves North 54
The Union First Corps advances 101
The Confederate approach 163
Roads to Gettysburg 183
Chambersburg in 1863 191
The situation, June 24. 197
Early's route 236
Route of Hancock's corps 278
Wrightsville 305
Reynolds moves toward Gettysburg 403
The First and Eleventh corps, June 29-30 410
Route of the Third and Twelfth corps 423
Another look at Hancock's route 436
The situation on June 30 440
The march of Robert Rodes 469
The route of the Fifth Corps 494
The marches of the Sixth Corps 506

ACKNOWLEDGMENTS

A book can not be published without the assistance of many folks. First of all, a writer draws from sources already in existence. So to all the publishing companies and authors listed in the bibliography we extend our gratitude. A special thanks is given to the Louisiana State University Press for permission to use the excellent maps found in *Here Come the Rebels.* Our gratitude is extended to the University of North Carolina for permission to quote from the papers of Dorsey Pender and William Pendleton, and to Yale University for permission to use the letters of General Webb.

Garnet Jex of Arlington was most kind in permitting his paintings to be used on the cover and in the book. He is widely known in art circles, having attended the Corcoran Gallery and graduating from George Washington University School of Fine Arts.

Russell Brechbill of Chewsville did most of the photography. Dr. David Sipes of Waterford, Virginia, obtained pictures of Gum Springs and Edwards Ferry, and Cedric Smith took pictures in Frederick. The Lane Studio in Gettysburg supplied the picture of General Sedgwick, while the Carlisle Camera Shop copied maps in the unit histories at Carlisle.

The Honorable Edward S. Delaplaine of Frederick was a great help in tracking down dates and places. He also supplied materials from his series on Meade dealing with the change of command. John Winters, a walking Civil War encyclopedia, was very helpful.

John Slonaker and his staff at the United States Military Institute at the Carlisle Barracks were most gracious and helpful. They Xeroxed materials, supplied leads, and were outstanding. Dr. Richard Sommer was also helpful.

John Divine and Henry Raymond provided encouragement and help. We can not say enough about their aid.

To Carol Bland, Dorothy Winkler, George Smith, and those at McClain Printing Company, we also say "thank you" for helping to make this book possible.

INTRODUCTION

The Bible says, "Remember the days of old and consider the years of many generations."[1] This we try to do in *Roads to Gettysburg*. Those days of June and July in 1863 belong to a different era. Life was not so simple then. Getting to Gettysburg required a great effort. My grandmother who was born in 1884 vividly remembers making an all-day trip in a spring wagon from New Midway, Maryland, to Fairfield, Pennsylvania. The armies of Northern Virginia and the Potomac moved by foot, wagon, and horse over 150 miles on dirt roads to Gettysburg.

There were no radio and television stations in 1863. In fact, there was very little mass media. But thirty million Americans were caught up in a war and an issue that divided a nation. In June and July the struggle crossed the Potomac, wound through Maryland, and reached a climax on the fields of Gettysburg.

I first saw the light of day within a few yards of the route of the Union Third and Twelfth corps, plus Generals Meade and Farnsworth's cavalry. Then I lived for twenty-five years in another town along the route of these units, Walkersville, Maryland. I did not realize that the Union First and Eleventh corps marched to Gettysburg two miles west of my hometown, nor did I realize that the Second and Fifth corps took the road through Ceresville, two miles to the east. During my boyhood, we constantly traveled the roads taken by men in blue on the way to Gettysburg.

Then came college in Shepherdstown, and weekly travel over the route of A. P. Hill's Confederate units, and once again the Union First, Third, and Eleventh corps as they concentrated near Middletown to protect the flank of the Union army.

Marriage and service in Pennsylvania came next. Our daughter was born in Chambersburg, just yards from Lee's headquarters, and the route of the bulk of the Confederate army as it moved toward Gettysburg. Several times each week I went through the Chambersburg square where Richard Ewell raised the Confederate flag, and where Lee and Hill met and made the decision to move to Gettysburg.

As I worked on this book, I traveled the Union and Confederate routes from Fredericksburg, Virginia, to the Potomac and through Maryland to Pennsylvania. I could almost visualize the long blue and gray columns, moving in ninety-degree heat, and drenching rain.

The story of the battle has been told and retold. And we will not forget what they did on the fields of Gettysburg. But the story of how they got to Gettysburg and what it was like getting there is full of human interest, suffering, and inspiration. For me it meant seeing new places, meeting new persons, and learning about those who have gone home, as I read their accounts and memories. *Roads to Gettysburg* is an epic story of bravery and endurance. I trust the reader will appreciate the efforts and memories of those in blue and gray who marched to Gettysburg, and those who lived in the towns and villages on the Roads to Gettysburg.

I

ALONG THE RAPPAHANNOCK

On Tuesday, May 5, 1863, the Virginia sky became cloudy and dark. About 3:00 P.M. the rain started to fall.[1] At first it was only a shower, then it fell in torrents. Rifle pits were filled with water. The soaked men bailed water until their backs stiffened. Roads became virtually impassable.

But in the midst of the storm Joseph Hooker, commanding the Union Army of the Potomac, gave the order to retreat from the Chancellorsville battleline. The corps commanders were shocked. They could not believe the order. The army had come to Chancellorsville in high hopes. Hooker had issued inspiring messages saying what he was going to do to the Confederates. However, Lee and Jackson had a surprise for him. And in the hour of opportunity, without committing half of his army, Hooker panicked. In a way the rain was fitting. The storm marked the end of yet another sad story in the leadership in the Army of the Potomac.

The Rappahannock rose rapidly from the downpour and the ensuing flash flooding. Many Union soldiers, anxious to fight, hoped the pontoons at United States Ford would be swept away. But despite the rising water and the stormy weather, the pontoons stayed in place. So the men, mules, and wagons plowed through the mud and slid over the slippery roads.

Morale was low. The men had endured days of fatigue and hardship. For what? Would they never get a leader? Alexander Webb said, "God pity our army."[2] John Gibbon remarked, "I have lost all confidence in him (Hooker)."[3] Many felt the same way. Hooker had been so popular. Now his

1

troops treated him coolly, almost as if to say, "We have no further use for you."[4]

A cloud hung over the army. Officers and men tried to find someone to place the blame and frustration upon. Darius Couch and Henry Warner Slocum were very outspoken in their criticism of Hooker.[5] Couch, commanding the Second Corps, went so far as to say he could no longer serve under Hooker.[6] George G. Meade and John Fulton Reynolds agreed with the commanders of the Second and Twelfth corps, but were not as outspoken in their criticism.[7]

Lincoln was also upset. He knew a battle had occurred at Chancellorsville, but received no dispatches until May 3. Then it was just a word from Daniel Butterfield, Hooker's chief of staff, saying Hooker and Lee were engaged in battle. On Sunday, the third, Hooker finally sent a telegram which was quite evasive, saying a battle had occurred resulting in "no success to us."[8] He also criticized part of his army for not coming to his aid. He seemed confused.

On May 6 came the news that Hooker had recrossed the Rappahannock. President Lincoln turned white when he received the telegram. He walked back and forth with his hands clasped behind him saying, "My God, my God, what will the country say? What will the country say?"[9]

Badly shaken by the news, and with the knowledge that like the other commanders of the Army of the Potomac, Hooker too had failed, Lincoln and Halleck left Washington at 4:00 P.M. on the sixth to visit Joe Hooker. The general's days were numbered.[10]

Arriving at Hooker's camp north of the Rappahannock, Lincoln and Halleck spent several hours talking with Hooker. He wanted to know the condition and morale of the army after the latest in the long series of defeats. So Mr. Lincoln summoned the corps commanders to a conference at Hooker's headquarters. The generals thought Lincoln would ask questions about their feelings toward Hooker and the conduct of the battle.[11] But the president said nothing.

As a result, some of the generals were all in favor of sending a delegation to Lincoln asking for Hooker's removal. They decided against this channel largely because George

2

Meade refused to go along with the idea. Some of the corps commanders did go to Lincoln and vent their feelings.

At first Lincoln thought it was just army griping. But after his return to Washington, a stream of visitors kept coming for two weeks complaining about Hooker. These were both military and civilian. As the complaints mounted, Lincoln had less and less confidence in Hooker's ability to lead the army.

Rumors flew thick and fast. The story got out that John Reynolds was in line for the task. Reynolds would have been a good commander. At forty-two he was in the prime of life. Twenty-six of those years had been spent in military service, including two wars and numerous Indian campaigns. His ability was recognized when he was appointed commandant of cadets at West Point. When the Civil War broke out, Reynolds commanded a brigade, division, and now in 1863 the First Corps.

Along the Rappahannock Reynolds thought about the rumor. If he could lead the army without dictation from Stanton and Halleck and the others in Washington, the job would be a great honor and responsibility. But he doubted whether the politicians would follow a "hands off policy."

Wanting no part of amateur politicians and armchair generals, Reynolds went to Washington in late May. He discussed with Mr. Lincoln the command of the army. He told the president he did not want to be considered unless given "complete freedom to plan and fight his own battles in his own way."

On June 2 Ellie Reynolds and some friends in Baltimore attended a concert. When they returned home there was brother John sitting in the parlor reading. He related that he had been in Washington visiting with the president. According to her story, John said he had been offered the command of the Army of the Potomac, but had declined because the president could not promise him freedom in the field.[12]

Thus there was grumbling and unrest in Washington and along the Rappahannock among the politicians and the brass. But let's look at a few units of the men in the field, the rank and file of the army.

With the Union troops who had been in action at Chancellorsville, there was a double portion of sadness. Once again the enemy had been victorious, and many of their comrades had fallen. The story of the Twenty-seventh Indiana Infantry is characteristic of many in the army along the north bank of the Rappahannock in May of 1863.

Chancellorsville was exceptionally hard on the Twenty-seventh Indiana. When the men returned to their bivouac area and the company streets, they found that in some cases, entire companies had been wiped out, as well as complete mess units. A lot of the huts had but one or two occupants. Several companies had no commissioned officers. Kind and thoughtful friends of two years of campaigning had·"given their last full measure of devotion" at Chancellorsville. When some companies turned out for morning roll call, they looked like morning guard details.[13]

Edmund Brown of Company C writes:

> A loss sadly noticed at the time, and one which never ceased to be felt, was the breaking up of the glee club of Company C. . . . They used to sing "Louisiana Low Lands Low" "Old Kentucky Home," and other sentimental songs, as well as the standard patriotic songs of the time, in a delightful way. Many pleasant hours had been passed in camp listening to their sweet singing; while the weariness of many a toilsome march had been relived or forgotten, under the spell of some ringing song.[14]

The Army of the Potomac:

> appeared to be all torn up, abnormally restless, full of foreboding and anxiety. . . . We had met with a most inexcusable, and therefore most discouraging defeat. Neglect and incompetency we had been the victims of before. This time thousands of the best soldiers, the bravest of men and the purest of patriots had been sacrificed by outrages and criminal worthlessness.[15]

It is easy to see why the soldiers felt this way. After all, if your comrades are killed and wounded due to poor leadership, such feelings are natural.

For some reason, the men of the Twenty-seventh Indiana felt unappreciated. But "after Chancellorsville," a review was held and this time the men from the Hoosier State felt at home and accepted. From General Slocum, commander of the Twelfth Corps, on down the line there was praise for the men from Indiana. "Pap" Williams turned to Slocum and said, "That's a fighting regiment for you."[16]

Although the pickets were friendly, at times there was sporadic rifle and cannon fire "Along the Rappahannock." Rumors flew fast and furious when the sounds of gunfire were heard. Sometimes the stories had Hooker south of the Rappahannock with Lee at his mercy, or else Lee was north of the river with all the odds against Hooker.[17]

Civilians from the North and government leaders came to visit the campsites. Some came looking for their sons and husbands who had fallen or who were hospitalized. As they talked about the future, some at least agreed with Edmund Brown of Indiana; thinking that:

> The Southern leaders were so inflated by it (Chancellorsville) that it gave them wild and unreasonable visions conquest and tribute. This, in turn, gave the people of the North another rude but much needed awakening from their apathy concerning the spirit and aims of the insurgents, and afforded the Army of the Potomac another chance to grapple with its opponents under more favorable conditions.[18]

For nearly six weeks there at Stafford Court House, the Twenty-seventh Indiana, tried hard to pull itself together again, "and to take up the broken threads of army life."[19]

It wasn't as bad with all the units. Many of the units went into camp on the site of their own or other regimental campsites, occupied during the winter of 1863 along the Falmouth to Ford line. For a brief while, some such as the Fourth Ohio of the Second Corps used old log huts constructed in January and February.[20]

Then when the weather cleared they moved to a place where there was a woods for shade and good water. "Two shelter-tents, stretched over a stick, supported by two uprights, constituted the dog tent; sometimes these tents were secured by two guns with bayonets 'fixed' and run into the ground some four feet apart."[21]

> Spring had come; the songsters made the woods ring; many were the men that wandered off alone to write to loved ones, to read or meditate; congenial companions would stroll away, talk over plans and prospects, until they found themselves beyond the picket's post;

5

pickets had good times basking in the sun, the outpost as well as the reserve, watching for the officer of the day as much as for the enemy; down at the river (the Rappahannock) there was a suspension of hostilities; while men waded the river to exchange coffee and tobacco, and get the latest news. In camp men were reading, writing, sleeping, or discussing the probabilities. Duties were easy; there was plenty to eat and to wear; the regiments were reinforced from the well ones that had returned from the hospitals; bushels of mail came each day for the brigade; . . . There was occasionally the too free use of the "commissary" and "stomach bitters" which with the "meerschaum pipe" drove dull care away from those who got enough wages to enable them to afford such luxuries. Taken altogether the camp out in grove was happy, and not very anxious for a forward movement.[22]

Such was life for the Fourth Ohio in camp along the Rappahannock in May 1863.

Things went rather well for the Twenty-fourth Michigan along the Rappahannock. On May 7, the troops from the Wolverine State marched through Falmouth to within a mile and half of White Oak Church. They "camped on a knoll in an old orchard on the Fitzhugh estate, near the crossing of the same name."[23] It was a good spot, well supplied with wood and water. The soldiers named it "Camp Way," after the regimental chaplain.

After ten days of marching and skirmishes, camp life was a welcome change. Company streets were laid out. Evergreen boughs were brought in from the Virginia forests to form walks and arbors. In the evening the men gathered around their campfires and swapped war stories, each trying to seem braver or more dramatic than his comrades.[24]

The Twenty-fourth Michigan was on historic ground. According to the regimental historian, the Fitzhugh estate was the scene of George Washington hatchet and cherry tree incident. Supposedly near the farm, young George had tried to throw a stone or coin across the Rappahannock. The soldiers from Michigan tried it too. But they were not very successful, causing them to believe that young George's truthfulness or athletic ability was questionable.[25]

The once beautiful buildings of the estate were falling into ruin, and the gardens, so productive at one time were now growing up in weeds and briers.

6

Sunday evening the chaplains of the First Corps tried to hold services. But they had competition. More went to the game of chuck-a-luck than to divine services. Colonel Robinson thought this was unfair as "church runs only once a week, but the game goes on daily." Six squares were marked off on a board, blanket, or on the ground. One player represented the banker, the other the venturer. The latter selected a number and rolled the dice in an effort to win money placed on a number on the board or blanket.[26]

On the night of May 14, the Twenty-fourth went on picket duty. The men in gray across the river were very friendly and the soldiers from the North and South carried on a continuous conversation. Often the pickets swam to the middle of the Rappahannock and exchanged coffee and tobacco. "They had only rye coffee and no sugar. Eggs cost them $3.50 per dozen."[27]

Returning from picket duty the next morning, the soldiers found Senator Chase from Michigan and Senator Wade from Ohio in the bivouac area. The men felt they were trying to find what went wrong at Chancellorsville. Both of them were from the committee on the Conduct of the War.

Two weeks of comparative ease went by amidst the "greenfields, fine groves and stately oaks." One day an abandoned yoke of oxen were brought into the camp and used to haul fuel and water for the men of the Twenty-fourth. A few weeks later, just before hitting the Roads to Gettysburg, they were killed for beef.[28]

On the twenty-first of May the Iron Brigade was sent on an expedition to King George and Westmoreland counties east of Fredericksburg. The purpose was to clear the Northern Neck of Confederate troops. They found slightly more than fifty Confederates, five hundred horses and mules, a thousand slaves of all ages, and lots of corn and bacon. This made the trip worthwhile. Returning from their mission, they saw the birthplace of George Washington. Only a chimney and a stone overgrown with weeds saying "Here was born George Washington, February 11, 1732," marked the spot.[29]

In addition to the two United States senators, other distinguished persons came to visit the Twenty-fourth Michigan,

7

including Governor Blair and his wife. The men were given black hats, the badge of the Iron Brigade.[30]

But all good things must come to an end. And on May 30 surplus baggage was sent to the rear, as well as the sick. Most units went on an alert to be ready to move at a moment's notice. Camp life was becoming a little boresome and monotonous. Soon the quiet along the Rappahannock would end, and almost two hundred thousand men would set out on a journey of over 150 miles on the Roads to Gettysburg.

Naturally all the men in the blue and the gray had their memories. The lads on both sides of the Rappahannock heard the church bells in Fredericksburg ringing on May 10. John Smith of the Nineteenth Maine heard the bells tolling that Sunday. He also heard the funeral dirges played by various bands in the Army of Northern Virginia. All of these were heard on the Union side of the Rappahannock. Smith says, "At the time of his death he was the leader most trusted by the Confederates and most feared by us."[31]

On the twenty-ninth of May, the men of the Nineteenth Maine were paid two months' wages. Smith, a member of Company F, summarizes the feeling, "It is wonderful how having money in the pocket improves the appearance of the soldier. He stands straighter, walks prouder, looks happier, acts more independently and enjoys better health. Money in the pocket still makes a person feel better."[32]

The men of both armies engaged in good-natured fun and horseplay in the off duty hours "Along the Rappahannock." The men of the Fourteenth Connecticut played a joke on their beloved Chaplain H. S. Stevens. The chaplain often went into the woods to meditate, or write letters and his sermons. One day he fell asleep as he was writing. A light-hearted young Connecticut officer came by and placed an empty whiskey bottle on the chaplain's outstretched arm. He spread the word that the Reverend Mr. Stevens was hitting the bottle. Men went out into the woods to see for themselves. The chaplain was astonished when he awoke to see himself surrounded by a horde of staring men. He was the subject of much sympathy. The men said they were sorry he had fallen from the straight and narrow path.[33]

From the banks of the Rappahannock at Fredericksburg, the blue and the gray started on the Roads to Gettysburg.

Francis J. Parker, of the Thirty-second Massachusetts, remembered moving from Aquia Creek to Barnett's Ford on the night of May 29.

... A bright full moon and cool breeze made marching delightful. The way was familiar, the roads fine, and the men, in the best of spirits, laughed and sung as they went. At about midnight this hilarity had subsided, and the little column was jogging sleepily along the way, which wound through a deep wood in the vicinity of Hartwood Church. Suddenly, at a sharp turn of the road, where the moonlight fell bright as day, came a stern call "Halt! who goes there?" and a dozen horsemen, springing from the shadow, stood barring the way, bringing forward their carbines with a threatening click as they appeared. The column, however, not halting, pressed forward into the light, showing the glittering muskets of the men and something of their number. The horsemen seemed to suddenly abandon their purpose, for, without a word of parley, they turned their horses into the woods and slipped past us under cover of the darkness. We recognized them, when too late, as a band of guerillas, and learned more concerning them at the first picket post we met.

During our stay at the fords of the Rappahannock, guerillas harrassed us in various ways, hovering around us, indeed, until we neared the border of Maryland. Now a portion of our wagon train would be run off, and an officer would be spirited away when on outpost duty or riding from one camp to another. Again and again the mail was stopped and rifled, the carrier shot or captured. Indeed, these things became of so frequent occurrence that stringent orders came from headquarters forbidding officers or men straying beyond the limits of their camp guards. Many were the sensational rumors concerning the guerillas and their Chief Mosby. One of our cavalry officers used to say that he never could catch a guerilla, but after a long chase occasionally found a man wearing spurs, engaged in digging a well.[34]

What did they do along the Rappahannock? Strong Vincent kept his men pretty busy according to this order issued on May 20:

GENERAL ORDERS NO. 3.
I. The hours for service and parades of ceremony will be the same throughout the brigade.
II. Each duty will be ordered by its proper call, sounded first by the bugler at these headquarters, and the call at its close will be immediately taken up and repeated by the buglers at Regimental Headquarters.
III. Reveille .... 5:00 a.m.
    Breakfast call .... 5:30 a.m.

10

Sick call .... 6:00 a.m.
Drill call (by company) .... 6:30 a.m.
Recall .... 8:00 a.m.
Assembly of the guard .... 8:30 a.m.
    (The proper Troop will be sounded by the drums of the guard before beating off.)
Dinner call .... 12:00 m.
Drill call (by regiment or brigade) .... 4:00 p.m.
Assembly (for dress parade) .... 6:45 p.m.
To the color .... 7:00 p.m.
    (The proper Retreat will be sounded by the drum corps of each regiment before beating off.)
Tattoo .... 8:30 p.m.
Extinguish lights (taps with drums) .... 9:00 p.m.

IV. Brigade drills will be had on Tuesdays and Thursdays.

V. Saturdays will be given to the men as heretofore for purpose of bathing and washing clothes.

VI. The usual Sunday morning inspection will be by regiment at 10 a.m.

To relieve the monotony, the soldiers of the Union Sixth Corps, and A. P. Hill's corps took turns serenading each other in the evenings, playing patriotic and military songs to each other across the river.

Charles S. Wainwright came from the Hudson Valley of New York, near Hyde Park. His parents were prosperous farmers. He was not anxious to enter the war at first. His father was eighty-five years old and the farm needed attention. Charles was only thirty-four years old in 1861, and as soon as the crops were in, he entered the service of the Union. His friend, Marsena Patrick, thought of a light artillery unit that needed a major and Charles was in business. Reading "Hardee's Tactics" at a camp in Elmira and other places, Charles quickly learned military fundamentals, and went with the First New York Artillery from Elmira to Washington. The trip took fifty hours in dirty boxcars.

The first camp in Washington was also a depressing experience, an open field one mile northeast of the capitol. Rain poured and there was no food. The campfires smoked, sputtered and went out. In Washington, the New York farm boys became soldiers. Wainwright and Henry Hunt pushed for artillery commands in the various corps, instead of leaving everything to the digression of the corps commander. After the commander of the First New York was killed, Charles Wainwright became commander of the artillery of the First Corps and then chief of the Fifth Corps. On the first day at Gettysburg he was to lose eighty-three officers and men, and eighty horses, but he along with the rest of the First Corps was fighting for time.

He kept a journal throughout the war, and mentions that in early June the pickets along the Rappahannock were on "most amiable terms." Three deserters from the Fifth Corps had been granted a two-week reprieve by President Lincoln. Charles had other problems. Some men from Stewart's battery robbed a sutler, burned his tent, and shot at him. Whiskey was the cause, and Colonel Wainwright had difficulty getting enough officers to conduct a general court-martial.[35]

On the thirtieth, the Thirty-second Massachusetts moved on to Kemper's Ford. A big mansion was up on the banks. Mr. Kemper was "away," which meant he was in the Confederate army. Mrs. Kemper, an older daughter, and several small girls composed the household. It was a delightful tour of duty. The soldiers and the Kempers became good friends. The Rebel soldiers across the river were very friendly and often shouted news and greetings. For the Virginia family it was their first exposure to Massachusetts soldiers. But they felt safe and comfortable in their presence.[36]

After Chancellorsville it was camp life for many of the soldiers. For nearly a month time was spent "Along the Rappahannock." The 146th New York changed their campsite from the Henry farm to place on the road from Stoneman's Station to Falmouth and Stafford Court House.

> ... We were situated on a grassy mound and had an extensive view in all directions. On the east the Potomac River was visible at Belle Plain, and to the west we could see far beyond the picket lines. We had very little drilling, but found quite enough to do in policing the camp and picketing. The weather was uniformly pleasant and at times very warm, so that on some days we had all we could do to devise ways and means to avoid liquefaction. Bowers of evergreen twelve feet high and about twelve wide were constructed in front of the officers' tents and they found the shade very acceptable, as there was hardly a tree within a mile of our camp.

12

On the whole, our first impressions of a Virginia summer, gained at this time, were not pleasant ones. Intense heat prevailed. Numerous reptiles and insects which inhabited the meadows and woods all about us frequently invaded the precincts of our camp. All the realm of nature seemed fairly teeming with life. Snakes of all kinds abounded—green, black, yellow, blue, spotted, and striped; long and short; rattlers, moccasins, copperheads, and many others less deadly. Numerous lizards basked in the sun or crept noiselessly about. All sorts of bugs, beetles, and ants crawled everywhere. As an offset to this disagreeable throng there were many beautiful birds—great lazy buzzards circling through the air, hawks shrieking, cardinal-grosbeaks flitting about on trees and bushes, thrushes and catbirds, beautiful specimens of woodpecker, tiny birds of dazzling blue color; in short, hundreds of species. We were entertained with most delightful melodies from the soft-singing thrush, the Virginia mocking bird, and many minor songsters. At night the ominous whip-poor-will piped his melancholy song, which had seemed so strangely sad and lonesome when we heard it that night in the woods at Chancellorsville. In marshy hollows and dismal places "peepers" and other insects kept up an incessant din, and the deep-throated frogs added their booming notes to the doleful chorus.

This section of Virginia in which we were located, just east of the Rappahannock, is one of the poorest in the whole State and had been rendered doubly barren by the ravages of war. But few houses met our view and these were for the most part small and dilapidated. Only here and there did we see a plantation house of any considerable size.[37]

Prior to hitting the Roads to Gettysburg, the Army of the Potomac was visited by a large number of British officers. They had traveled to the Fredericksburg area by way of Canada. Naturally, they were entertained royally by Joseph Hooker. Any excuse for a party was welcomed by him. Many said that "ladies and gentlemen, would not be caught around his headquarters." It was no place for either. The various corps commanders also entertained the British officers, but not with all the trappings.[38]

Winfield Scott Hancock told the British officers that he had a regiment as good as any in the world. This was a pretty strong statement. But the British officers wanted to see this outfit.[39]

The unit in question was the Nineteenth Massachusetts commanded by Lieutenant Colonel Devereux. Hancock sent a note asking for a review and demonstration at 2:00 P.M.

Colonel Devereux had such faith in his men that he did not pass the word along. Instead he waited until he saw Hancock and the British officers coming over the hill. Then he had the bugler sound "The Assembly." The men rushed for their equipment, fell into line, and were all ready when Hancock rode into the bivouac area.

Hancock had been in a sweat. He did not know what to expect. But the Nineteenth was equal to the occasion. When the drill was finished, the British visitors agreed it was one of the best units they had seen. They were amazed. Hancock was happy, and the men from Massachusetts filled with pride.[40]

Around the first of June, the 230 men in the Nineteenth Massachusetts were moved to a high hill overlooking Fredericksburg and the lovely Rappahannock River. The men were glad to get away from the balloon men in the Signal Corps. Observers went up in the balloon to get a look at the Confederate camps. The Rebels responded by lobbing a few shells at the Signal Corps base.[41]

Some of the Union campsites were visited every day by an aged, jovial black. He came dressed in a stovepipe hat, walking with a cane. With him he brought a large basket of pies and cakes. As he approached the tented cities, he called out, "Here's your pies and cakes and apples. Pay me today and I'll trust you tomorrow." Quickly he sold his goodies and left to return the next day.[42]

Hooker felt the men needed a boost in spirits after the Chancellorsville debacle. So he introduced the corps badge. This was to inspire the men and make them proud of their units. The flag of the Second Corps was a trefoil. Red designated the first division, white the second, and blue the third. The Rebels called the headquarters flag of the Second Corps "The Ace of Clubs." It was blue with the large cloverleaf in the center.[43]

II

AFTER CHANCELLORSVILLE

Millions of words have been written, and gallons of ink have been used to describe the battle of Gettysburg. However, years ago, the early 1940s to be exact, two aged ladies sat talking in the little town of New Midway. One lady, the author's great-grandmother, was eighty-nine years old. Her friend was over one hundred years old. Sitting on the porch, these ladies described their memories of feeding the boys in blue as they marched to Gettysburg. They told of hiding their horses and cash. The accounts were fascinating to young ears. Now, years later, the seeds of their conversation has led to the book, *Roads to Gettysburg*.

The conversation which I overheard on a hot summer evening made me wonder, "How did the soldiers get to Gettysburg, and what was it like getting there?" *Roads to Gettysburg* is an attempt to follow the armies from Virginia, through Maryland to Gettysburg. At the same time, these pages make an attempt to tell what it was like to be a member of the invading Confederate Army of Northern Virginia, and how it felt to be a member of the defending Union Army of the Potomac. Just as the aged ladies in New Midway had memories, so did others. Thus we try to tell what it was like in the small towns through which the armies marched in June and July of 1863.

We have heard of Gettysburg. But places like Poolesville, Jefferson, Point of Rocks, Middletown, Cavetown, Mont Alto, Williamsport, Greencastle, Chambersburg, Shippensburg, Carlisle, Heidlersburg, Cashtown, Fairfield, Fayetteville,

Waynesboro, Frederick, Walkersville, Woodsboro, Middleburg, Liberty, Johnsville, Union Bridge, Uniontown, Union Mills, Taneytown, Bridgeport, Mechanicstown, and Emmitsburg are all a part of that epic story. Littlestown, Hanover, Manchester, Frizzellburg, and Two Taverns belong to the list also.

The book covers a relatively small area for those of us who travel the interstate highways in modern cars. Although describing some of the movement from the Fredericksburg, Virginia, area to the Potomac, our main concern is the advance of the Confederates through Washington County, Maryland, and Franklin County, Pennsylvania, to Gettysburg, and the parallel advance of the Union army through Frederick and Carroll counties in Maryland to the Pennsylvania line.

Many of the roads are gone now. One can follow U.S. 11 from the Shenandoah Valley to Harrisburg, Pennsylvania, and travel the route of the Army of Northern Virginia. It is not as fast as I-81 but you have time to look around.

U.S. 15, the route of the Union First Corps, has been modernized in recent years. But at some places you can almost imagine the marching of the long blue lines, and bivouac areas near Emmitsburg. Route 194 through Walkersville and Woodsboro to Taneytown and Littlestown has changed very little. Once again you can almost picture the columns of the Third and Twelfth corps as well as headquarters, Army of the Potomac. But traveling in Carroll County to New Windsor, Uniontown, and Manchester is a real delight. The traffic is light. The landscape is dotted with beautiful productive farms. The towns are picturesque and the people friendly. America of yesteryear with the self-sufficient farmer and the farming village come to life as you travel the Roads to Gettysburg.

After Chancellorsville it was a question of time whether the Confederate Army of Northern Virginia or the Union Army of the Potomac would be the first to launch an offensive. In the past, the Union army hit the Confederates at Bull Run, the Peninsula, Fredericksburg, and then again at Chancellorsville. Then it pulled back to lick its wounds, regroup, and try again. The one exception was the Confederate

16

invasion of Maryland which ended at Antietam. Many of the Confederate soldiers, including Longstreet, were committed to defensive warfare, fighting on their home ground. But with dwindling supplies, loss of manpower, and far less natural resources and railroads than the North, the Confederacy simply could not win with a defensive war policy.

One evening in late May of 1863, Robert Edward Lee sent for his military secretary, Col. Armistead L. Long. In the headquarters tent located along the Rappahannock, close to Fredericksburg, Lee talked of daring plans. His proposal was to pull the Army of Northern Virginia off the Rappahannock River line and march west and north to the Shenandoah Valley of Virginia. From the Winchester area he would proceed north and east into Pennsylvania. This was a daring plan, but the South was fighting against time as well as against Northern manpower and supplies.[1]

Lee knew that it was just a matter of time before Hooker or someone else launched another move on Richmond. Just about every Southern man capable of bearing arms was in the military. So, few more replacements could be expected. Now, before the Union could build up again, was the time to move. Proceeding west and north would clear the Shenandoah Valley and relieve pressure on Richmond.[2]

It was now or never. The life of the Confederacy was at stake. Lee had suggested the movement to Long, and also in a letter to President Davis. The strategy was political as well as military. Mr. Davis agreed with Lee for these reasons:

1. Pressure would be taken off of Richmond, and Shenandoah Valley cleared. But an invasion of the North might relieve the siege of Vicksburg.

2. Confederate conferences in London and Paris were going well again after the setback following Antietam. A big victory in Pennsylvania or near Washington might lead British Prime Minister Palmerston and Emperor Napoleon III of France to recognize the Confederacy. If so, the blockade might be broken. This would permit much needed supplies and money to flow into the South. One or perhaps both countries might even send troops. One wonders what might have happened if Lee would have won at Gettysburg.

3. The people of the North were growing weary of the cost of war. Thousands had already been killed. Young men disabled by the wounds of battle were walking the streets of the cities and villages of the North. The war was not popular. A Confederate victory north of the Potomac might lead to a negotiated peace.

4. Taking the war across the river would ease the drain of Virginia food supplies. In Pennsylvania the army could live off the land and gather the horses of the Northern farmers.

These were the stakes. A nation and democracy hung in the balance, awaiting the outcome.

How did the men in the ranks look upon the decision to carry the war across the Potomac? John B. Gordon, a general in Ewell's corps, says "In the logistics of defensive war, offensive are often the wisest strategy." Voltaire states that "to subsist one's army at the expense of the enemy, to advance on their own ground and force them to retrace their steps—thus rendering strength useless by skill—is regarded as one of the masterpieces of military art."[3]

Lee's invasion of Maryland in 1862, and his move toward Pennsylvania in June of 1863, "sought to force the Union army to retrace its steps."[4] In the process, Lee hoped to outmanuever his family and win a victory.

Both armies had been foraging in Virginia for almost two years. The Shenandoah Valley and Northern Virginia could contribute little more at this point. Gordon says the Confederates looked across the Potomac toward the yellow fields of grain as Israel looked across the Jordan to the Promised Land.[5]

Gordon also felt the best defense of Richmond was to threaten Washington, Baltimore, and Philadelphia. A confederate victory might create a financial panic. So the Army of Northern Virginia took the roads that led to Gettysburg, at the zenith of assurance, filled with boundless confidence, and hoping for ultimate victory.[6]

Douglas Southall Freeman and others have pretty well covered the Confederate advance on the Roads to Gettysburg. Therefore, although telling the Confederate story, more emphasis will be placed on the Union army traveling the

18

Roads to Gettysburg, because that story has been almost nonexistent.

Going on a family trip to a strange area requires a lot of planning and map study. But moving armies of 95,000 men and 73,000 men during a forty-two day (June 3-July 14) campaign calls for extraordinary planning.

The Army of the Potomac was comprised of seven infantry corps, each with its own artillery batteries and supply wagons, one cavalry corps, and an Artillery Reserve of over one hundred guns. Even with everything going almost perfect there could be problems. The wagons could create traffic jams. Crossroads became bottlenecks. A corps of eleven thousand men marching four abreast, closed up and without supply wagons and artillery, made a column from two to three miles long. If the 222 supply wagons, fifty ambulances, and twenty-six guns with their limbers and caissons accompanied the corps, the column stretched out over a ten to eighteen mile distance.[7] Thus it is easy to think of the head of the First Union Corps being in Mechanicstown, now Thurmont, while the last of the wagons would be just leaving Frederick.

Lee had three infantry corps with nine divisions and thirty-seven brigades to move. Like Meade, he had no radio or helicopter to direct the march. Marching men accompanied by horses pulling over three hundred vehicles created clouds of dust. Heat, fatigue, and hunger all added to the problem of moving the men on the Roads to Gettysburg.

The cavalrymen had it a little better. Forty miles was their maximum for the day, thirty was better. Otherwise they could exhaust their mounts.[8]

Today we cover the Roads to Gettysburg with little problem. But in 1863 it was different. Some of us have gone on ten mile walks for hunger. But in 1863 the men in blue and the men in gray marched twenty to thirty miles a day on hot, dusty roads.

It is so difficult for us to imagine men marching a hundred miles. We cannot imagine the heat, the choking dust, and the fatigue. We cannot fathom the rumble of the continuous passing of wagons or the clop-clop of the horses. We can

19

hardly imagine the feelings in the hearts of the people in the towns through which the soldiers passed. But this is all a part of Roads to Gettysburg.

The writer has searched and searched for the bivouac areas. They have been most difficult to find. The official records are scanty in their information. One reads, "We camped in Greencastle." But the question is where at Greencastle? Shopping centers and houses have been built over some of the places. For instance, part of the Fifth Corps camped at Arcadia along the Buckeystown Pike in Frederick County. It is now a large housing development. Houses and a cemetery occupy the site of what was Messersmiths Woods in Chambersburg. A large interstate highway cloverleaf is just in front of the place where Meade replaced Hooker as commander of the Army of the Potomac just prior to Gettysburg.

Troops as they marched often took shortcuts. Sometimes they went across the fields or took parallel roads. This does not seem to be the case with the Union First, Eleventh, and Twelfth corps as they took the Roads to Gettysburg. But it is a real possibility for the other Union corps as they moved through Carroll County. Likewise pickets were thrown out to the front, and some units were assigned to guard the flanks.

In these pages, we make every effort to take you with the men of the blue and the gray as they took the Roads to Gettysburg.

"After Chancellorsville" it was time to hit the roads, "The Roads to Gettysburg." To help the reader see the events of that thirty-day period, we list the highlights of those June days in chronological order.

Tuesday, June 2. President Lincoln confers with John Fulton Reynolds about the command of the Army of the Potomac. Mr. Lincoln has become disenchanted with Joseph Hooker.

Wednesday, June 3. Robert E. Lee sets the Confederate Army of Northern Virginia in motion on the initial steps towards Gettysburg. Part of Longstreet's command left Fredericksburg for Culpeper, Virginia.

Thursday, June 4. Today Richard S. Ewell's Second Corps left the trenches of Fredericksburg for the Culpeper area.

Hooker, on the Falmouth side of the Rappahannock River, was not sure whether it was a diversionary movement, or the beginning of something big.

Friday, June 5. John Sedgwick's Sixth Corps made a probing attack on A. P. Hill's Third Confederate Corps at Franklin's Crossing near Fredericksburg. The rest of Lee's army had left the area. Lincoln, Halleck, and Hooker exchanged ideas on how to counter the Confederate moves.

Saturday, June 6. Hooker continued to probe Lee's position. James Ewell Brown Stuart displayed the Confederate cavalry at Brandy Station in a grand review. A skirmish took place in Berryville, Virginia.

Sunday, June 7. Things were pretty quiet today.

Monday, June 8. The First and Second corps of the Army of Northern Virginia arrived at Culpeper. Stuart held another grand review for General Lee and other Confederate officers.

Tuesday, June 9. Today the greatest cavalry battle in North America occurred. While Stuart was engaged in reviews, the Union cavalry under Alfred Pleasonton crossed the Rappahannock at Beverly Ford and Kelly's Ford. For hours the troopers of the blue and the gray fought each other in charge and countercharge. Stuart was barely able to survive. For the first time in this sector of the war, the Union cavalry proved equal to the Confederate horsemen. This gave them and Army of the Potomac a boost in morale. Stuart lost 523 men, the North lost 866.

Wednesday, June 10. Ewell's Second Confederate Corps left Culpeper. Hooker wanted to move on Richmond, thus forcing Lee to turn back. Lincoln vetoed the idea, saying "Lee's Army, not Richmond is your objective."[9] Citizens of the North gained news of an impending invasion and became alarmed. Darius N. Couch was placed in command of the Department of the Susquehanna. The governor of Maryland called for people to rally against invasion.

Friday, June 12. Ewell's command crossed the Blue Ridge into the Shenandoah Valley and headed toward Winchester, fighting several skirmishes on the way.

Saturday, June 13. The Confederate advance drove in the

21

Union pickets near Winchester, and occupied Berryville. Hooker started his move toward the Potomac River.

Sunday, June 14. The Union high command in Washington urged R. H. Milroy to retreat from Winchester to Harpers Ferry. However, he believed an attack by Lee to be impossible. Late in the day he was overwhelmed by Ewell's forces. The victory was so complete that for the moment, Ewell was hailed as another Jackson. Rodes's division moved from Berryville to capture Martinsburg. A. P. Hill, the last Confederate commander in the Fredericksburg area, slipped away to join the rest of Lee's army.

Monday, June 15. The rout of Milroy became complete as his retreat was stopped at Stephenson's Depot, about four miles north of Winchester. Some Union troops managed to escape to Harpers Ferry. But the Confederates savored the fruits of victory which included twenty-three guns, three hundred loaded wagons, over three hundred horses, and inflicted over four thousand casualties on the North. Robert E. Rodes of the Army of Northern Virginia crossed the Potomac near Williamsport, Maryland. He sent the cavalry on toward Chambersburg. Longstreet began moving into the Shenandoah Valley. Folks in the North, growing tired of the war, pelted recruiting officers with eggs.

The division of Robert Rodes pushed on to the Potomac and crossed the river at Williamsport. There was little or nothing in his front to prevent him from moving at will.

Earlier, Lincoln, almost in desperation formed two new departments; that of the Susquehanna, with headquarters at Harrisburg, under General Couch, and that of the Monongahela, with headquarters at Pittsburgh, under General Brooks.[10]

When the news of the Winchester disaster was received in Washington, Mr. Lincoln, saying that the North was now threatened with invasion, called for 100,000 Militia with Maryland providing 10,000; Pennsylvania, 50,000; Ohio, 30,000; and West Virginia, 10,000. These men were to serve for six months. Governor Seymour of New York offered 20,000 men to help meet the threat, and Governor Andrews of Massachusetts offered "every available man."[11]

By the twenty-first and twenty-second, Ewell's command pushed on to Greencastle. In the meantime, cavalry skirmishes took place at Aldie, Middleburg, and Upperville, on June 17, 19, and 21. Longstreet and A. P. Hill continued toward the Potomac and then crossed into Maryland on June 24.

The Union infantry was concentrated largely in the Leesburg area, with elements of the Second Corps at Thoroughfare Gap.

Then came the day of the great river crossing. The First, Third, and Eleventh corps crossed the river at Edwards Ferry. On Friday, June 26, the Second Corps crossed at midnight followed by the Twelfth and the Fifth corps. Joe Hooker moved toward "the clustered spires of Fredericktown," endeavoring to keep between Lee and the cities of Baltimore and Washington. Robert E. Lee reached Chambersburg and conferred with A. P. Hill at the square.

Confederate cavalry came into Gettysburg from the west, and entered the town about noon. Soon Jubal Early and the butternut infantry arrived, after burning the factory of Thaddeus Stevens, located in Caledonia on the way. Guards were placed around public buildings, stores, and some private homes. Taverns were closed in an effort to keep the men from hitting the bottle.

The next day, the Union Sixth Corps crossed the Potomac while Richard S. Ewell marched into Carlisle and took possession of the United States Army post. Cavalry units threatened the Susquehanna and Harrisburg. Elizah White raised havoc in Hanover Junction. Early moved on toward York. Late in the evening a special train arrived in Frederick bringing Colonel Hardie and the sealed orders relieving Joseph Hooker from command.

During the early hours of the last Sunday in June, Joe Hooker stepped down as commander of the Army of the Potomac. The order came from President Lincoln and Secretary of War Stanton. On a farm southwest of Frederick, George G. Meade took over. Thus the command was changed in "mid stream, on the eve of a crucial battle."

Gordon's command and other Confederate infantry

23

occupied York, Pennsylvania, and pushed on in an effort to capture the bridge over the Susquehanna at Wrightsville. Ewell's men had a great day in Carlisle. They relished the idea of being deep in enemy territory and having the people of a northern city at their mercy. During the day the Union Third Corps marched through Frederick, while Meade brought the Twelfth, and First, and Eleventh to the environs of the town. Late in the evening Lee received word that the Army of the Potomac was across the river and near Frederick. From his headquarters tent east of Chambersburg, he sent orders to Ewell and Early to move toward Gettysburg. Jeb Stuart was busy today also, burning a Union supply depot at Edwards Ferry, and capturing a wagon train near Rockville.

Monday brought more rain, and the southern movement of Ewell from Carlisle, the westward movement of Early from York, while Longstreet started east from Chambersburg. In the ranks of the Army of the Potomac, the First and Eleventh corps hit the road for Emmitsburg. The Third and Twelfth along with Meade and the Artillery Reserve traveled what is now Maryland 194 to Middleburg and Taneytown. The Second Corps marched by Route 26 and other roads to Liberty, and Johnsville to Uniontown, a march of over thirty miles.

The Fifth Corps took the same route as far as Liberty, but then continued straight ahead to Unionville. The Sixth Corps had another long march, going from Hyattstown to New Windsor and beyond. The cavalry of both sides were in the saddle and riding all over the countryside.

The last day in June brought continued marching for some and rest for the others. Each footstep brought the men closer to Gettysburg. And on July 1 the roads came together and the great battle occurred.

The writer was amazed to find so little written on the subject of how they got to Gettysburg and what it was like getting there. Many books contain just a few pages. But this book is an effort to tell the epic story of how nearly 175,000 men marched between 150 to 250 miles to get to Gettysburg.

ARMY OF THE POTOMAC U.S.A.
Statistics as of June 1 and May 1, 1863

The number of officers and enlisted men, cavalry and artillery horses, wagons, and means of transportation in the Army of the Potomac.

Number of officers, men, and means of transportation in each command.

| Date | Command | Number of officers | Number of men | Means of Transportation | | | | | Horses | | Pack Mules |
				Horses	Mules	Army Wagons	Wagons, two horses	Ambulances	Cavalry	Artillery	
1863											
June 1	First Corps	949	14,237	393	2,578	404	6	67	120	543	...
June 1	Second Corps	1,039	14,572	670	2,795	496	7	117	110	455	...
May 1	Third Corps	1,212	20,864	951	2,326	525	13	98	141	1,130	...
May 1	Fifth Corps	1,050	18,324	879	2,621	496	7	166	9	860	...
May 1	Sixth Corps	1,483	26,041	1,001	2,933	557	11	167	159	1,034	...
May 1	Eleventh Corps	621	12,616	1,100	1,549	414	10	83	204	467	216
May 1	Twelfth Corps	530	9,401	897	1,480	365	12	94	102	397	...
May 1	Cavalry Corps	719	11,687	1,085	2,404	313	4	86	12,386	699	...
May 1	Artillery Reserve	51	1,408	489	1,307	291	3	15	1	1,499	...
May 1	Engineer Brigade	83	2,115	757	526	120	2	12	12	...	...
May 1	Patrick's Brigade	138	1,865	67	24	21	1	4	4	...	...
May 1	Headquarters Army of the Potomac*	62	1,031	600	1,085	300	13	19	65	...	...
	TOTAL	7,937	134,161	8,889	21,628	4,302	89	928	13,313	7,074	216

*Including Capt. L. H. Pierce's train.

25

RUFUS INGALLS
Brigadier-General, and Chief Quartermaster,
Army of the Potomac

HEADQUARTERS ARMY OF THE POTOMAC,
June 1, 1863.

	Wagon		Officers and men
First Corps	1	to	37 1/4
Second Corps	1	to	31
Third Corps	1	to	41
Fifth Corps	1	to	35
Sixth Corps	1	to	48 1/2
Eleventh Corps	1	to	31 1/4
Twelfth Corps	1	to	26 1/8
Cavalry Corps	1	to	39 1/8
Artillery Reserve	1	to	4 15/16
Engineer Brigade	1	to	18
General Patrick's Brigade	1	to	91
Headquarters Army of the Potomac	1	to	3 1/2

Average on total, 1 wagon to 32 1/8 officers and men.

One wagon to every 50 men ought to carry 7 days' subsistence, forage, ammunition, baggage, hospital stores, and everything else; 75,000 men = 3,750 wagons. Our transportation now is 4,302, besides ambulances and two-horse wagons.[12]

D.B.

Some stories are repeated in the text for the point of emphasis.

The historian of the 109th Pennsylvania says "every event helping to make up the great historical event of the battle of Gettysburg is important."

He is so correct. Certainly the story of how the men got to Gettysburg and what it was like in the ranks on the hot and dusty, then the wet and muddy Roads to Gettysburg is very important. Thus we have searched the regimental histories, old manuscripts and newspapers, as well as personal accounts to tell the story of June of '63.

III

JUNE WEEK, JUNE 1-7

June Week is a time of graduation and celebration from our service academies. But for men in the blue and the gray, "along the Rappahannock, after Chancellorsville," it was a time of preparation for the moment when they took the Roads to Gettysburg.

Although it was early June, the sun and heat were more like summer than spring. Picket duty was maintained along the Rappahannock. Soldiers continued to joke back and forth. The Twentieth Maine had a new brigade commander, Colonel Strong Vincent.[1] Like his name, he was tall, strong, and well built, with a fine pair of sideburns.

For the Confederates, the food supply was getting very short. Eighteen ounces of flour and four ounces of bacon, often of inferior quality, constituted the Rebel diet. Active men lost weight on this diet because it was a bare 1800 calories per day. Likewise there was little for the horses and mules to eat. The grass had been eaten almost to the soil, and tree limbs chewed up.[2]

The Richmond supply system was far from the best. So Lee realized that it was his task to find food. Thus he looked on the land of milk and honey, Pennsylvania. Lee also knew that an invasion would foil Union plans, take them away from the soil of Virginia, and his men could feed off of prosperous Pennsylvania, instead of seeking to get food and supplies from the barren land of Virginia.

Col. Wilbur Nye, the author of *Here Come the Rebels!*, a study of Ewell's Second Corps during the Gettysburg campaign, is of the opinion that enough credit cannot be given to

27

Lee for what he did for his army after Chancellorsville.[3] During the month of May, "he reorganized the infantry units, reorganized, rearmed, and refitted the artillery; and reorganized, refitted, and augmented the cavalry. He procured enough food to last his men until they could supply themselves in enemy territory, replaced hundreds of broken-down cavalry mounts and wagon train mules, and obtained a substantial supply of artillery ammunition of improved pattern and quality."[4] This he did with very little staff assistance.

Lee was concerned about the growing improvement of the Federal cavalry. At the beginning of the war, the Southern cavalry was superb. But time, and the loss of men and equipment had worn it down. Now the Union cavalry was organized into one corps with three divisions and a reserve all under one commander.

As early as May 11, Lee had ordered Stuart to the Culpeper area to watch the enemy and to graze his horses in the lush fields of clover. This position also enabled Stuart to shield the flank of the Army of Northern Virginia.

Lee was now ready to move cautiously, watching to see Hooker's countermoves. In this manner, he could get back to come between Hooker and Richmond if necessary.

The commanders of the Army of Northern Virginia were ordered to be ready to march at a moment's notice. Rations were cooked and packed in haversacks. Ammunition was issued and the men had orders to keep their canteens filled.

Lee knew the risk of moving northward. However, if Hooker moved South on Richmond, Lee, in the terms of chess, would exchange "queens," or move on Washington. However, as long as he was in Virginia, he could still transport his troops by train from Culpeper to Hanover Court House.[5]

During this first week in June, Hooker had as much problem with his cavalry as Lee was to have at the end of the month. Thirty-nine-year-old Alfred Pleasonton, West Point, 1844, was commander in chief of the Union horsemen. Always immaculate, and looking like a picture book cavalryman, Pleasonton even carried a swagger stick. To his credit, he took care of his men and their mounts, realizing that to cavalrymen, their horses meant as much as the feet of the infantry. He also reorganized the Union cavalrymen, gave the men pride in their units, and made it an aggressive fighting machine. However, on the other side of the ledger, he lacked much when gathering intelligence data. In Hooker's defense, we must say that he was hampered during early June by the lack of detail and accuracy of cavalry reports. Pleasonton seemed to assume that his main job was to cripple the enemy cavalry.

Getting ready for June Week, two divisions of the Army of Northern Virginia marched to Hamilton's Crossing, four miles south of Fredericksburg. The date was May 29. A train was coming bringing their new commander, Richard S. Ewell.[6]

This time, "Old Dick" or "Old Bald Head," as the men called him, had a companion. After a life of bachelorhood, he had taken a wife, the former Lizinka Campbell Brown. His marriage to the former widow was but five days old.

Dick Ewell had a big job trying to take the place of Lee's right arm, "Stonewall" Jackson. No doubt this was on his mind as the train neared its destination. He was no stranger to this fighting outfit. Ewell had served with Jackson in the valley and on the peninsula. At Second Manassas or Groveton, he had lost his right leg above the knee. Now at the age of forty-six, he had married, been confirmed in the Episcopal Church, and assigned to the command of an army corps.

On Saturday, May 30, A. P. Hill and Ewell discussed their roles as commanders of the Second and Third corps. The next day, Ewell and Lee attended church, hearing a fine sermon from Tucker Lacy, chaplain of the Second Corps.[7]

Then as June Week started, June 1 in fact, Lee orally outlined his invasion plans to Longstreet, Ewell and Hill. Culpeper was listed as the first objective. Other plans were flexible depending on what Hooker did. Lee was taking no chances of another lost order.

The Confederates, according to Northern thinking, were flushed with success. They had the utmost confidence in themselves and in Robert E. Lee. They were an army of veterans. They knew how to fight and had proved themselves valiant men.

29

As the freshness of the early summer touched the tent covered hills along the Rappahannock, and tinted the fields of wheat with the amber promise of the approaching harvest, General Lee put his . . . army into motion for the invasion of the North.[8]

It was summertime for the Confederacy too. They were riding the crest of military success. Col. Ridden T. Bennett of the Fourteenth North Carolina felt the Army of Northern Virginia was "as tough and efficient as any army of the same number ever marshalled in this planet."[9]

Henry Heth said, ". . . there was not an officer or soldier in the Army of Northern Virginia, . . . who did not believe . . . that it was able to drive the Federal Army into the Atlantic Ocean."[10]

The *Richmond Whig,* in its exuberance twitted "that an artificial leg ordered some months ago awaits General Ewell's arriving in the city of Philadelphia."[11]

So the long lines of gray and butternut left the Fredericksburg area. They had miles and miles to go on the Roads to Gettysburg. Behind them lumbered the cannon, caissons, and supply wagons.

Longstreet tells us that in essence, Lee's plan was to move north on the right flank of the enemy, with Ewell in advance, and his own corps to follow. The cavalry was to move on the right flank to the east. Hopefully, Hooker would withdraw from Stafford Heights as Stuart threatened his rear.

Tuesday, June 2, Ewell, Lee and other high ranking Confederate officers went to Fredericksburg to scan Union positions across the Rappahannock. Lee thought the Union position was rather firm. There were no indications Hooker was planning anything big.

The hour had struck. Now was the time. So on Wednesday, Lafayette McLaws's division of Pete Longstreet's corps left Fredericksburg. Their destination was Culpeper Court House. The men in gray went south to Spotsylvania Court House to avoid being seen by Lowe's balloons. Then the column turned northwest through the Wilderness to Somerville Ford on the Rapidan. John B. Hood's division, located near Verdiersville, headed for Raccoon Ford.

Wednesday, June 4, Dick Ewell and the Second Corps got

under way, Jubal Early taking the road to Spotsylvania Court House. His men camped for the night between the county seat and Shady Grove Church.

Robert Rodes and Edward Johnson, two of Ewell's division commanders, started on the Roads to Gettysburg on June 5.[12] Ewell struck his headquarters at 8:00 A.M. He followed Rodes. Jed Hotchkiss, Jackson's master map maker, rode alongside of Ewell's carriage and gave him a vivid account of the battle of Chancellorsville. Part of the route that day went right through the battlefield.[13]

The day was warm, dry and dusty. The ruins of the Chancellor mansion were passed. Decaying bodies could still be seen in the bushes. Unburied horses were all over the place. The odor of decay was almost stifling in the heat of that first week in June. Papers, torn and broken equipment, ammunition boxes, and bandages littered the ground.[14] No doubt the men wondered if more such scenes were in store.

Joe Hooker was aware of some of the Confederate activity. But he did not know what Lee was up to. Therefore, he ordered John Sedgwick, commanding the Sixth Corps, to make a reconnaissance in force at Deep Run, south of Fredericksburg.[15] Pontoon bridges were already in place.

Hooker, Halleck, and Lincoln had exchanged letters concerning the movement against Lee. A. P. Hill at Fredericksburg was tempting bait. But Lincoln and Halleck insisted on covering Harpers Ferry and Washington. They also feared that should Hooker attack Hill, then Lee would turn toward Washington from the west, or encircle Hooker at Fredericksburg. All this has been covered in the excellent books by Coddington and Nye.

Lee watched the action from his observation post on Telegraph Hill. The action at Deep Run was spirited, and the Sixth Corps obtained a small bridgehead. But it was not a serious matter. Thus as soon as Lee realized there was no threat, he instructed Ewell to resume the march to Culpeper. His men were able to reach Somerville Ford.

Thus by Saturday, June 6, two-thirds of the Army of Northern Virginia was gone from its camps along the south

31

side of the Rappahannock. Only A. P. Hill and his Third Corps was left to confront the Army of the Potomac.

Hooker knew that something was happening. After all, you don't move fifty thousand men without arousing some suspicion. Charles C. Coffin tells us that some deserters from the Confederate army told "Fightin Joe's" intelligence men that an order from Robert E. Lee had been read to the troops telling them they were to have long marches and hard fighting.[16]

Hooker had other problems. Large groups of visitors came to the Fredericksburg area to see husbands, sons, and brothers. In fact, Hooker sent a note to Secretary of War Stanton, saying: "My army is more in danger of being taken by the women than the rebels. They arrive by the steamboat load."[17]

Hooker had internal problems. Some of his generals were very vocal in their criticism of his conduct at Chancellorsville, while many men in the ranks had lost their faith in the man. Rufus Dawes of the Sixth Wisconsin says bluntly, "General Hooker recrossed the river because he was outgeneraled and defeated."[18]

But Dawes, like other regimental officers, had things to do. While encamped at White Oak Church, he acted as presiding judge over misconduct cases. Dawes fined one soldier for paddling across the Rappahannock and getting whiskey from the Rebel pickets. White Oak Church was just a name. There was no church, just a lovely grove of trees and a pleasant spot. Dawes kept the men busy drilling and parading.[19]

Sometime during this period an event occurred which depicts the humanity and great character of John Fulton Reynolds, commander of the First Corps.

Lt. Col. Thomas Chamberlin of the 150th Pennsylvania had the privilege of knowing John Reynolds. His admiration knew no bounds.

> To those who knew little of him he may at times have appeared stern and unnecessarily exacting; but those who, in the course of their duty were frequently brought near him, and knew him more intimately, soon found that beneath a cold and somewhat haughty exterior was hidden a personality of wonderful attraction, and that

he was not without those traits which inspire friendship and invite confidence. His whole life had been that of a soldier, and, being unwedded, his ruling passion seemed to be devotion to his country and his calling. From the very outset he appeared to grasp the magnitude of our civil struggle, and the prospect of years of conflict and endless flow of blood. . . .[20]

Chamberlin witnessed an act of kindness in April. Reynolds and a group of officers were returning from reviewing Wadsworth's division. In some manner the general crowded a private soldier off the road and down he went over an embankment. Reynolds stopped his horse, dismounted and went to the soldier. He expressed his regret and inquired whether he was injured. Reynolds then pulled out his pocketbook and gave the young man a five-dollar bill.[21]

History is the story of men and events. It is hard to tell whether a man shapes history, or whether history shapes the man. Perhaps it is a combination of the two. In any event, Stephen H. Weed passed a milestone on June 6. That day he received the coveted single star of a brigadier general. Weed was born in Potsdam, New York, and then moved with his family to New York City. He was a bright and gifted young man, graduating from West Point in 1854. He served in the typical posts of the day, seeing service against the Seminoles in Florida, and on army posts in Kansas and Utah. On May 14, 1861, he was promoted to captain in the Fifth United States Artillery. That winter he saw service in Harrisburg, Pennsylvania. At Second Manassas, Weed commanded the artillery of Sykes's division of the Union Fifth Corps. At Fredericksburg and Chancellorsville he commanded all the artillery of the Fifth Corps. Then on June 6 he was promoted to brigadier general in command of the Third Brigade of the Second Division of the Fifth Corps. The brigade consisted of the 140th New York commanded by Colonel Patrick O'Rorke, the 146th New York, the 91st and 156th Pennsylvania.[22]

Weed was only thirty-one years old at the time of his promotion. Tragically, he had less than a month to enjoy his status. He had a date with destiny at a place called Little Round Top. But to get there he had to lead his men on the Roads to Gettysburg.

Alanson A. Haines, chaplain of the Fifteenth New Jersey Volunteers, tells us about June 6 and 7 in the Sixth Corps.

June 6th, at 9 A. M., we marched by our old route to the river and went into the ravine, some twenty rods from the bank, where we passed the night in a pouring rain. The Second Division of our corps had made the crossing of the river at 5 P. M. of the fifth. They met with some opposition and a few losses. Their dead and wounded were carried past us, as we descended to our place of bivouacing.

Sabbath morning, June 7th, we were formed in line at 3.30 o'clock, but did not move far. The day was fair and beautiful, and the storm clouds had all passed away. We held divine service at 9 o'clock, with a full attendance of our men, and with large numbers from adjoining regiments, making a congregation of about one thousand. We were forming at sunset for a second service, when the order came to cross the river. In a few moments knapsacks were packed and tents rolled. At the word of command ten thousand men moved across the little plain, and in long lines over the bridges, and formed by battalions on the opposite bank. There was light enough for the enemy to get the range and send shell into the masses of our exposed troops, but not a shot was fired. Our regiment went up the bluffs and took position as reserved pickets. The brigade was posted behind a swell of ground, with skirmishers thrown out in front. Half stood in position with arms in hand, two hours at a time, until relieved by the other half. Those not on duty lay on the ground sleeping, ready to be roused at the first alarm. It was conjectured that the enemy might have an overwhelming force compared with our two divisions of the Sixth Corps, and that they would open their batteries at daylight and rush upon us, to drive us into the river. We were about 200 yards from the enemy's pickets, and several regiments were making rifle pits and throwing up trenches all the night.[23]

We still have to wonder what might have happened had Hooker been granted permission to attack A. P. Hill along the Rappahannock. Here was a golden opportunity to overwhelm a Confederate unit, and march on Richmond. Had this happened, Lee would have hastened back to Fredericksburg, and the marches on the Roads to Gettysburg would never have occurred. History may have been more kind to Hooker, and less so with Lee. But the masterminds in Washington said "no" to Hooker and the way was clear for the men in gray to head north.

During the seventh, Lee met with Generals Jenkins and Imboden and ordered them to prepare the way for the advance of the main Confederate army into the Shenandoah

Valley. Jenkins was to take his cavalry as far as Strasburg and Front Royal, gathering all the information he could.

Imboden was to move into the upper Shenandoah, into the South Potomac Valley. He was to disrupt Union movements around Romney, and ordered to collect cattle, and hinder railroad traffic between Cumberland and Martinsburg.[24]

As the first week in June drew to a close, Ewell and his staff attended a prayer service held by Chaplain Lacy at Raccoon Ford. Then he rode upstream to watch his men cross at Somerville Ford. Rodes came first as he had camped near the river. Then came Early and Johnson. The men in gray gave their new commander heart cheers. "He took off his cap, rode along the line, and acknowledged the salute."[25] Then it was on to Culpeper. Ewell arrived about 10:00 A.M. Lee was already there, having crossed Raccoon Ford while Ewell was watching his men cross at Somerville Ford.

James Longstreet was also in Culpeper, located a mile southwest of town. Lee established his headquarters at Eastern View, three-quarters of a mile east of Culpeper. Richard S. Ewell in the Cooper home, a mile and a half from town. The location of the generals and the bivouac areas are carefully noted in the diary of Jed Hotchkiss and in the notes of Daniel Grimsley of the Sixteenth Virginia Cavalry.[26]

As the shades of night fell on that Sunday, Lee had his First and Second Infantry corps and all of his cavalry gathered within a mile or two of Culpeper Court House.

IV

LEE MOVES NORTHWARD, JUNE 8-11

The Rappahannock and Potomac rivers played an important role in the story of Gettysburg. Both had to be crossed by the Confederate army, and the latter by the men in blue. Both served as barriers to invasion, the Rappahannock aided in the protection of Richmond, while the Potomac was a formidable barrier against Confederate invasion of the North.

The Rappahannock rises in the Blue Ridge Mountains of Virginia, and flows southeast for 250 miles, before flowing into the Chesapeake Bay. For two years Lee used the river to block Union advances toward Richmond. Now after Chancellorsville, he hoped to use the river to screen his movement northward.

However, both Lee and Hooker had to contend with the fact that there were many places where the Rappahannock could be forded. The primary fords from Fredericksburg northward were Banks', United States, Richards', Ellis', Kemper's, Kelly's, and Beverly. Large bodies of troops and equipment used these fords. But at many other places, small units could cross. The banks were rather steep and difficult. It took a lot of men and equipment to guard the fords. And this presented headaches to both commanders.

Hooker became aware of gray-clad men near Warrenton and sent John Buford to reinforce the Second and Third Cavalry divisions under command of Gen. David M. Gregg. Those units were already at Warrenton.

Hooker spent Sunday night evaluating the reports that John Buford kept sending to him. Whatever Lee had in mind, he would counter. Therefore, Hooker ordered Pleasonton to take all of his cavalry and three thousand infantry, cross the upper Rappahannock, seek out the Confederate force near Brandy Station, and either "disperse or destroy it," along with the trains and supplies. Hooker wanted to disrupt things before they could get started.[1] About eleven thousand men were allotted to Pleasonton for the task. His orders were direct, "seek and destroy the enemy." But the cavalry commander claimed his task was primarily one of gaining information.

Some say rain is a sign of the wrath of God. If that is true, He may have been angry about the Gettysburg campaign. It rained often on the Roads to Gettysburg. It poured on July 4, and showers fell frequently as Lee waited to cross the Potomac after Gettysburg. Benjamin Cook of the Twelfth Massachusetts notes that on June 8, the men weathered three heavy thunderstorms in thirty-six hours.

As the showers fell, Lee wrote to Secretary of War James A. Seddon stating his objective in moving north.

> There is nothing to be gained by this army remaining quietly on the defensive, which it must, unless it can be reinforced. I am aware there is difficulty and hazard in taking the aggressive with so large an army in its front intrenched behind a river where it cannot be advantageously attacked. Unless it can be drawn out in a position to be assailed, it will take its own time to prepare and strengthen itself to renew its advance upon Richmond and force this army back within the intrenchments of the city.[2]

As darkness fell on Monday night, Stuart's camps were sprawled over an area of several miles from Stevensburg to above the spot where the Hazel River flows into the Rappahannock. James Ewell Brown Stuart had no worries. He had great confidence in his men. They had ridden circles around McClellan on two occasions, and had struck fear into Union hearts many times. He was a hero to the Confederacy and to his troopers.

The blue-clad troopers spent Monday night on the other side of the Rappahannock. They made no campfires and maintained silence. They were surprised to find that Stuart had not placed patrols on the high north bank of Beverly

37

Ford. Only the Sixth Virginia guarded the ford on the south bank.

The country near the river was wooded, but near Brandy Station it was more open. East of the station and north of the railroad was a prominent ridge, Fleetwood Hill. As the dawn broke on Tuesday, only white mist could be seen rising from the river. Yet the Virginia cavalrymen felt something was moving in the fog. They were correct. Soon a carbine cracked, the opening shot in one of the greatest cavalry battles ever to occur in America. Then came a lot of noise as Buford's columns splashed into the Rappahannock. The Sixth Virginia was soon pushed aside. Colonel Benjamin Franklin "Grimes" Davis was in the advance with the Eighth New York Cavalry.[3] Davis had been born in Alabama and appointed to West Point from Mississippi. But he remained loyal to the Union, and led a miraculous escape from Harpers Ferry just prior to Antietam.

The tempo of small arms fire increased. The rugged terrain kept the Union forces from a complete breakthrough. At the edge of the woods, one hundred Virginia troopers reformed and charged into the Union ranks. This gained precious moments for the Rebels and alerted the main body. A Confederate officer rode toward Davis. "Grimes" raised his saber in defense and slashed at the gray rider. The Confederate officer shifted in the saddle and fired point blank at Davis. The southern-born officer fell dead.[4] This was a crucial blow to the Union. Pleasonton later said he would have won an overwhelming victory had not Davis been killed.

The stand by the one hundred men of the Sixth Virginia may have made the continuation of the Gettysburg campaign possible. Had they not delayed the Eighth New York, Stuart might have lost his horse artillery, and suffered a severe loss. Other Virginia troopers came up now, many riding bareback and without shirts.

To his credit, Stuart did not panic, but deployed his troops wisely. The fighting lasted until late in the afternoon. Lee came close to losing the initiative before getting started right. The blue-clad troopers gained new confidence and respect in themselves. It was a new ball game. No longer would the

Confederate cavalry dominate the scene. Stuart, who had surprised his opponents so often, had been surprised. It is not our intention to go into great detail about this engagement, merely to show that it was a most important event on the Roads to Gettysburg.

The Union cavalry accomplished their mission. We wonder what might have happened without Confederate infantry support. The blue horsemen discovered that Rebel infantry was indeed in Culpeper. They frustrated temporarily the plans of Lee and Stuart. This action could have prevented Gettysburg too. Charles Coffin writes:

> The struggle around Fleetwood was the making of the Union cavalry and the unmaking of the Confederate. Up to that hour the Union cavalry had been of little account as a distinct arm of the service; but now it became a formidable power, while the Confederate cavalry from that hour, was on the wane.[5]

"The battle," quoted a Richmond newspaper, "narrowly missed being a great disaster to our arms. Our men were completely surprised, and were only saved by their own indomitable gallantry and courage.... The Yankees retired slowly, disputing every foot of ground."[6]

The Union cavalrymen were elated by their achievements, "while the Confederates were astonished at their persistence, bravery, audacity...."[7]

Robert E. Lee must have been dismayed too. From his headquarters at Eastern View, three-fourths of a mile east of Culpeper, he went to the Barbour House one mile west of Brandy to watch the cavalry battle. The moments must have been quite anxious.

By nightfall much of the Confederate infantry was in Culpeper County. Rodes's division was encamped at Chestnut Fork about two and one-half miles north of Culpeper. Ewell's corps, the rest of it, was nearer town on the Sperryville Turnpike. Longstreet had McLaws and Hood on the road between Raccoon Ford on the Rapidan River, and the town of Culpeper.[8]

June 9 was a big day for the Union Second Corps. Darius Couch was relieved from command of the unit by his own request. He simply could not take any more of Joe Hooker.

Winfield Scott Hancock, commanding what had been Richardson's division, took his place. We'll hear of Couch later in the defenses of Harrisburg. But let's take a look at Hancock, called by McClellan "Hancock the Superb."

Couch had been a good leader, the senior corps commander in the Army of the Potomac. But Hancock was to prove even better. A native of Norristown, Pennsylvania, a graduate of West Point, and a veteran of seventeen years of military service, Hancock was well prepared for the Civil War. Particularly valuable was his quartermaster experience in Utah and in Los Angeles. In that city he and his wife shared in a very sad farewell party for the Confederates who felt they had to go with their state.

At Antietam he was ordered by McClellan to take command of Richardson's division of the Second Corps. "Fighting Dick" had fallen wounded at Bloody Lane. The appointment of Hancock was one of the best things McClellan ever did. His name ranks among the top as a division and corps commander.

The troops were happy to have Hancock as their commander. Before the month was over, the appointment was looked upon as providential.

Today, the weary cavalrymen of both armies licked their wounds "Along the Rappahannock," and at Culpeper. Although the Union attack threatened to stop or postpone Lee's movement northward, Ewell's men started marching.

Tuesday, Robert Rodes had moved his infantry toward Brandy Station to support the cavalry. The orders came from Ewell at Botts's place. Rodes came up and then moved on to the Barbour House. There he rested until today when he undertook a ten-mile march to the Hazel River, bivouacking near Gourd Vine Church.[9] Hopefully they could be at Front Royal by Friday.

The objective was Winchester. Ewell had briefed his division commanders in the morning. Lee waited to see if Pleasonton would renew the attack. Once it was apparent that a new attack was not in the offing, he gave the command to Ewell to march. The Old Richmond Turnpike, or the main road from Richmond to Winchester was the route chosen.

The road went from Culpeper to Sperryville, Chester Gap, Front Royal, and thence through Nineveh to Newton where it connected with the Valley Turnpike. Robert Rodes was in the lead. He went as far as Gourd Vine Church. Edward Johnson and Jubal Early went to Woodville. Ewell stayed back at Culpeper in corps headquarters. Jed Hotchkiss busied himself copying a map of the Shenandoah Valley.[10] The day was clear and not so hot. The lush meadows of Culpeper were soon left behind. The march was through pretty countryside, rolling farmlands with patches of woods. In fact, the route of Ewell's corps has not changed much since the summer of '63.

On June 10, Edwin H. Balson of the Ninth Massachusetts Battery died of congestion and fever. He had been sick but a few days.

> He was nineteen years old, an excellent soldier, liked by all officers and men. He was the first one we laid away, and we gave him a comrade's burial. At sunset his remains were laid on a caisson, covered with the flag and drawn by six horses, led by comrades, to the grave under an apple tree, near headquarters. The procession was led by the guard entailed for the day, and a regimental bank of the post, and followed by all the company. "Slowly and sadly we laid him down," and as his remains were lowered, the customary salute was fired from revolvers. The grave was marked by a tablet of red sandstone, well carved and lettered by one of our own men. His remains were afterwards moved to Massachusetts.[11]

So before the men covered the Roads to Gettysburg, a young man had given his all, and a home, a chair and hearts were made empty.

On a lighter note, Major Downs of the battery made a trip to Washington and purchased some Boston crackers and cheese, and other delightful items. Some of the lads in the Ninth Massachusetts had keen noses. They smelled the New England items, and after midnight crept under the tent, "took out the barrel of crackers and cheese, and nothing was seen in the morning of either."[12]

On Thursday, June 11, Ewell's march northward continued. Robert Rodes found the road from Gourd Vine Church to Gaines' Crossroads to be in extremely poor condi-

41

tion, making traveling difficult for man and beast. When he reached Gaines' Crossroads he turned left for a few miles, then north to Flint Hill. As Early was to be in the lead, Rodes waited for his columns, but they did not appear. An hour later, General Ewell came up in his carriage, explaining that the other two divisions had been delayed and had to change routes. Bivouac was to be between Little Washington and Flint Hill. Therefore, Rodes proceeded to Flint Hill, and encamped a mile and a half north.[13]

Jed Hotchkiss noted that "the day was pleasant—dusty, but a shower improved the day. We found the grass, clover and timothy, perfectly luxuriant—a great change from the bare fields of Fredericksburg. The men marched well. Pickett's division came to Culpeper Court House yesterday. Longstreet moved his headquarters toward Amissville. I worked on maps of the Valley."[14]

Near Johnson's Ewell made his headquarters. After supper Johnson, Early, and Rodes came for a progress and information report. Hotchkiss made some suggestions on the routes to be taken.

On this Thursday, Hooker ordered Pleasonton to hold the Rappahannock and Beverly fords, keeping watch on the enemy movements, and using the infantry support if necessary. It was discovered that the Fourth North Carolina Cavalry was on the other side of Kelly's Ford. Pleasonton also reported that Lee was in Culpeper along with most of his infantry.

Trooper Samuel Lay of the Tenth New York Cavalry made his way back to the Union lines, escaping after being captured by the Rebels. "He can give you some information as to the forces between here and there." Thus read Pleasonton's report.[15]

Writing from Boscobel for the commanding general of the Third Corps, Adjutant Hayden gave orders for the First Division of the corps to move at 1:00 P.M. to Bealeton to hold the river from Kelly's to Beverly Ford, relieving the cavalry for duty up the river.[16]

Humphreys's Second Division marched at 6:00 A.M. We think nothing of a twenty-five-mile drive. But on that hot

June day, many of his men covered twenty-six miles on foot, marching through clouds of dust on the Washington and Alexandria Turnpike. The Twelfth New Hampshire reached Kelly's Ford at 5:00 P.M.[17] Two hours later they filed into a field, stacked arms and stretched out. But they had to go on another three miles to Beverly Ford. A notation was made that was to appear many times during the next two weeks, "This was one of the hardest marches ever made by the Army of the Potomac."[18]

Major General Alpheus S. Williams from Detroit was in command of the First Division of the Union Twelfth Corps as it trudged the Roads to Gettysburg in 1863. His letters about the march are very descriptive and full of human interest material. Writing to his daughter on June 16, from Fairfax Court House, he said:

> You will be astonished at my locality, but our changes now are magical. Joseph says "presto" and the change! I doubt if he is any wiser with the operation than some of our traveling magicians. . . . We left Stafford Court House Thursday night (the 11th); marched all night to Dumfries; lay there all the next day and left there yesterday morning at daylight; made a march of twenty-five miles with my division in the hottest, dirtiest day I ever saw and reached here last night. I lost a good many men, I fear, by sunstroke. It was a terrible day and my poor fellows suffered greatly.[19]

Williams, in a later letter, was disgusted by the night march to Dumfries on June 11. His division had just established a good camp when the order came to move on. Of course, that's the way it is in the military. A big task faced him that June evening. Pickets had to be brought in from a four- or five-mile front. Wagons parked in the four-mile bivouac area had to be repacked, and hot, weary men faced the prospect of a long night march. Some of the infantry coughed from the dust stirred up by the mounted orderlies.[20]

The march was in pitch blackness through dense pine thickets. The road apparently was bad enough in the daytime, but almost impossible at night. Several wagons upset and blocked traffic. Staff officers were thrown from their mounts in the gullies, and some wagons upset with their bottoms up. Nothing was left to do but to abandon them.

43

Despite all these "vexations," the division finally reached "the Quantico Creek and pitched our shelter tents on the north side near the antique village of Dumfries."[21]

The armies were now ready for a long weekend of marching and maneuvering. The Third Corps was the first Union organization to go after the Confederates. The next day as the long weekend started, the First, Eleventh and Twelfth corps, under Reynolds, Howard, and Slocum were to move out. On Saturday, Meade's Fifth Corps was to break camp, along with Sedgwick and the Sixth Corps and the Artillery Reserve. General Hancock and the Second Corps, bringing up the rearguard, was ordered to march on Monday the fifteenth at the end of the long weekend.[22]

Alfred Pleasonton was busy with a new plan. Brandy Station apparently revealed to him the need of a new cavalry setup. So he reorganized the cavalry corps with the First Division under John Buford, and the Second under David M. Gregg. Alfred Duffie's small command was absorbed by the other two, with that general assuming command of the First Rhode Island Cavalry.[23]

V

A LONG WEEKEND, JUNE 12-15

Mid-June found both armies on the move, Lee heading northward, with Hooker disengaging himself from the Fredericksburg line. The order had gone out on the eleventh from headquarters near Falmouth. All commands were to be ready to move at short notice. The movements would probably require the greatest mobility. Only allowable items were to be taken on the march. All excess baggage and supplies were to be turned in to the quartermaster.[1]

Yet it seems as though Hooker was in a state of confusion. According to Professor Lowe's balloon reports, the Confederate army was stretched from Fredericksburg to Culpeper along the Rappahannock and Rapidan. He felt that Lee was receiving reinforcements daily. But "in the absence of any specific information as to the objects, movements, and purposes,"[2] Reynolds was ordered to take command of the right wing. Hooker wanted to prevent Lee from making a raid.

John Sedgwick was ordered to withdraw to the north bank of the Rappahannock, and when the mission was completed, Gen. Henry W. Benham was to take up the pontoon bridges.[3] The movement was to be done after dark. It seems that Hooker was as much in the dark as anybody.

Lee knew what he wanted to do, and Hooker was making moves. So this long weekend from June 12 to the fifteenth brought the Union forces on the Roads to Gettysburg, while Lee was able to gain his first objective, the capture of Winchester, and a clear path to the Potomac.

The skill, the planning, and the nerve of Lee stand out during these first two weeks in June. In mid-month, the

45

Army of Northern Virginia stretched from Fredericksburg to within a few miles of Winchester, a distance of one hundred miles. The Confederate army was exposed to a flank attack. However, Lee used the mountain barrier to shield, conceal, and protect his movements. The officials in Washington seemed to be as confused as Joe Hooker. Marsena Patrick was especially critical. Lee was in position to threaten the Shenandoah Valley and Harpers Ferry, the upper Rappahannock and Maryland, as well as Pennsylvania.

This Friday, the First Corps got under way. Crossing Aquia Creek to the Fredericksburg railroad, the troops marched twenty miles to Deep Run, north of the Rappahannock near Barnett's Ford. The sun was scorching and the air was filled with suffocating dust.[4]

This march, and the other marches on the Roads to Gettysburg led the men to appreciate John Reynolds. They had to press on. The enemy was ahead of them. But whenever possible, Reynolds had his staff tell the regiments as they went into bivouac, "You will have time to make coffee if you desire." If the regimental commanders were not told this, no fires were made. Legend has it that the First Corps under John Reynolds, at least, "never built an unused fire."

Reynolds sent his staff ahead on the marches, or many times he went himself, in search of good camping areas for his men. He tried to find places with water and firewood. This was an extra plus factor. Likewise, once the tents were pitched, Reynolds did not have the men move somewhere else, that is, unless an extreme emergency arose. This habit produced considerable grumbling in other units. No wonder. After marching twenty miles or so, setting up camp, making coffee, etc., and then to be told "move on," would be very frustrating. A member of the First Corps said, "We were very fortunate that our general had, not only common sense, but sufficient humanity in his heart to use it."

On this June Friday, the Iron Brigade was formed to watch the execution of a soldier for desertion. Sergeant Sullivan D. Green of Company F, Twenty-fourth Michigan, describes the sad experience:

This day is to witness an impressive and unusual sight. In one of yonder ambulances sits a young man under strong guard whose hours on earth are numbered. The other ambulance carries his coffin. He is going to his execution. Many before him have been pardoned by the president, but he will not be thus fortunate. His case is an aggravated one. He has been tried for three previous attempts at desertion and this time endeavored to pass himself off at the court martial in which he had the folly to give his own name, and place of birth, and also claimed to belong to a rebel regiment of the same number as that to which he really belonged, the Nineteenth Indiana. This led to his recognition by the provost marshal who had a full descriptive list of the prisoner. He was found guilty and sentenced to be shot to death with musketry, in presence of the division, on Friday the 12th day of June inst., between 12 M. and 4 P. M.

At about 2 o'clock the Iron Brigade led the column into a field, preceded by the prisoner sitting on his coffin. In silence, three sides of a hollow square were formed. The coffin was placed upon the ground, the prisoner alighted from the ambulance with the chaplain who held a few moments' converse with the doomed man, knelt and prayed with him, and then withdrew a little distance.

The detail of twelve men who were to execute the sentence were ordered out in line, when General Wadsworth addressed them for a few moments. They received their instructions and moved in single file in front of a line of guards, with loaded musketry, and as the two lines faced each other, the muskets were taken one by one from the guard and passed to the detail for the execution, the officer inspecting the lock to ascertain if it was in good condition. They were then marched in single file in front of the coffin and about ten paces distant.

In the meantime, from a desire of the prisoner, the Chaplain came forward the second time. Some moments were spent in solemn conversation and prayer, both kneeling, and as the very air grew still with the hush of death's angel and each heartbeat of the thousands standing around them seemed measured by minutes, they rose to their feet. The Chaplain spoke a last word commending a fellow-mortal's spirit to God, received his last message, pressed his hand and turned away. The last moment had come.

As the marshal stepped toward him, the prisoner took off his hat, placed it on the ground, and as he turned to his coffin he stood face to face for an instant with his executioners, and beyond them the long lines of his comrades who gave him a last, sad, pitying look. However just and necessary the penalty, there is something in such a moment that can scarcely be felt but once, and that at such a time. He was calm and resigned; moved with steady step to his coffin and sat upon it. He said to the marshal that he would rather not have his arms pinioned or his eyes blindfolded, as he was not afraid of the

47

death he was about to meet, but if it was according to custom he would not object.

He took his last look of earth. Whether his thoughts were there or elsewhere, God only knows. The day was most beautiful, and the summer's sun in its warmest brightness fell around him. The field was green and wavy in its verdure. It was the last. A handkerchief was placed over his eyes, and his arms and legs were bound. Then only, a slight shudder passed through him. His shirt was ripped open and his breast made bare. All was ready. At the command "attention," the usual word of caution or preparation, they were to fire. The hat was lifted—10,000 eyes were strained in one breathless gaze—it was lowered, and many eyes withdrew from the sight that was to follow. The report of arms was heard and a lifeless body fell backward to the dust!

A comrade had died at the hands of his fellow soldiers by the same death he feared to meet in the ranks of patriotism. He had cravenly deserted them in the hour of danger and had now paid the penalty. Better had he died amid the carnage of the deadly field and won a heroic fame; better had he borne a maimed and shattered body through his waning years; better have nobly done his duty and been honored as one of his country's best defenders in her need! The division marched by the corpse, the burial detail struck their spades into the earth; the body limp and bleeding, with four bullet holes through the heart, was placed in the coffin, the column moved forward to the dusty road on its march, and we leave each to his own reflections.[5]

John Storrs looked at the executions a little differently than most.

It was a hard fate, but as even the kind-hearted Lincoln, on appeal, refused to pardon, it must have been necessary. There were the usual terrible formalities. The ready excavated graves, the coffins at their brink, with the wretched prisoners and condemned seated thereon. There was the last convulsive grasp of the chaplain's hand; the long, last look at the sun; the bandaging of the eyes—and the word "fire!" from the lips of the commanding officer and, perforated each with eight bullets, somebody's son, or brother, or father, tumbles over into his box, and the tragedy is ended. Yes, they were deserters, that is true. And for aught we know, good reader, "bounty jumpers." If so, they were, perhaps, rightly served. But suppose that these unfortunates were only a trio of country lads that had been cajoled into enlistment by the recruiting sergeant who gave, as they generally did, the most glowing and picturesque accounts of army life; and suppose that, afterward, experiencing the reality as we have thus far seen the men of the 20th experiencing, a vision of the dear old home fireside on the far away northern hills had flashed upon

48

their vision, and then in a moment of heart-sick despondency and weakness they had decided to make a break for home and liberty,— stop fighting and suffering for others' happiness and look a little to their own? In this land of the free ought they to have been shot to death for the act? Military law answers "yes," and in war time that is the statute of all others that must be paramount, must be obeyed, because in no other way could armies be kept in the field. Without the occasional enforcement of the death penalty for offences of this kind (and the number of cases were proportionately small) the men that after tattoo might decide not to appear at reveille, would, perhaps, leave the faithful sometimes in a sad minority.[6]

What was life like that Friday for the Union First Corps as they changed front? For most of the men it was not a pleasant day. For instance, the Ninth New York was awakened from a sound sleep at the hour of 3:00 A.M. Two hours later they were on the road, heading westward. "The day proved to be one of the hottest the men had ever experienced. . . . Water was scarce, fence rails nearly all gone, so that it was difficult to find wood enough during the short halts . . . to cook coffee."

The Ninth New York covered twenty-two miles on this hot June day. Gratefully they came to a stream late in the evening. Many took time to soak their steaming feet. The cool water felt so good.[7]

The Twelfth Massachusetts marched twenty-five miles in fifteen hours before pitching camp at Rappahannock Station.[8]

The Third Corps also moved this Friday, marching from Hartwood Church to Bealeton. Howard's Eleventh Corps moved from Brooke's Station to Hartwood Church. These are names not readily familiar to the Civil War reader, yet a part of the story of Roads to Gettysburg.

June saw the men in blue and gray up and on the roads very early. It was just 4:00 A.M. on Friday when the Confederate Second Corps started forward. Rodes was in the lead, followed by Johnson and Early. Richard Ewell's carriage caught up with Rodes's column of infantry. This occurred somewhere between Flint Hill and Sandy Hook. The two generals talked in the carriage about Winchester and the attack on Milroy.[9]

49

By 11:00 A.M. the first of the men in gray were entering Front Royal.[10] A jubilant welcome awaited them. The townspeople were expecting them. The pontoons needed for river crossings had arrived the previous day, so the citizens of Front Royal knew they were on the way. But Ewell did not use the pontoons at the Shenandoah. He wanted to get across as quickly as possible. So the men waded the river.

Rodes marched another hour and then halted at Cedarville. During the next three hours his command, followed by Johnson's, filed into the fields. They were joined by sixteen hundred cavalrymen under command of Brig. Gen. Albert G. Jenkins. Early came up and the Confederate generals again discussed strategy.[11] "Old Bald Head" had a surprise for Robert Milroy. Early and Johnson would assault the main Union force in Winchester, while Rodes and Jenkins hit Col. Andrew T. McReynolds's brigade at Berryville. After disposing of this force, Rodes would move on to Martinsburg, wipe out the Union garrison there and proceed north to the Potomac River, crossing and remaining in position near Williamsport. However, Jenkins was to roam north into the Cumberland Valley as far as Chambersburg, collecting horses, sheep, beef cattle and other items, returning them to the Williamsport crossing.

Rodes was a good general. He wanted to get closer to Berryville. Then in the morning, his men would not have far to go. So that afternoon, his command marched to Stone Bridge, Jenkins screening the movement.[12]

As darkness fell that night, Rodes and Johnson were across the Shenandoah within an easy day's march of Berryville and Winchester. Early's command was bringing up the rear.[13]

Milroy was apparently unaware of the advance of the Confederates. At least his superiors did not inform him of their approach. About midnight on June 11, Milroy received a telegram ordering him to "immediately take steps to remove your command from Winchester to Harpers Ferry. You will, without delay, call in Colonel McReynolds and other outposts not necessary for observation at the front."[14]

Milroy protested. He did not want to abandon Winchester. He felt he could hold the city. Schenck wired back, "Make all

50

required preparations for withdrawing, but hold your position in the meantime. Be ready for movement, but await further orders."[15]

No doubt Ewell looked with glee upon his task of capturing Winchester. He and many of his men had served in the area under "Stonewall" Jackson. Quite a few of his officers and men were from the Winchester area. The town had a proud history and was linked to George Washington and Gen. Daniel Morgan. Joseph Johnston, Turner Ashby and Jackson had used Winchester as a base of operations. It was a Confederate town, and the gateway to the Shenandoah Valley.

Winchester was a strategic city. Main roads ran east and west and north and south. Today we know them as Routes 50 and 7 to the west and east, and U.S. 11 north and south. In '63, Winchester was the terminus of a branch of Baltimore and Ohio Railroad running from Harpers Ferry. Small farms surrounded the city as well as some orchards. Factories produced hats and wagons, both sorely needed by the Army of Northern Virginia.

Harpers Ferry could be bypassed, but before crossing the Potomac, Winchester and the valley had to be cleared of men in blue. That was the task before Ewell.

In 1863 Winchester had a population of thirty-five hundred. About seven hundred of these were black, but all were not slaves. West of the town was the home of George Mason, the man sent to England to represent the cause of the Confederacy in that nation. Winchester felt that States' Rights were vital to freedom. And after John Brown's Harpers Ferry Raid, it became a strong center of Southern activity.

Saturday, June 13, was a day of marching for the men in blue, some units moving toward Manassas, and others toward Dumfries. While all of this was happening, Ewell's Second Corps of the Army of Northern Virginia was moving toward Winchester.

The order of march took the First Corps of the Army of the Potomac from Deep Run to Bealeton, now a small village along Route 17. Meade's Fifth Corps was ordered from camp near Banks' Ford toward Morrisville. Sedgwick and the Sixth Corps was ordered from Franklin's Crossing to Potomac

51

Creek. Howard was told to take the Eleventh Corps from Hartwood Church to Catlett's Station. Slocum and the Twelfth Corps marched from near Stafford Court House and Aquia Creek toward Dumfries; at the same time the Artillery Reserve covered the miles from Falmouth to Stafford Court House.

On Saturday night, the Army of the Potomac began the tactical and strategic movement which led them to Gettysburg. That morning Hooker had written to Meade and Reynolds stating that he felt Lee was up to one of two things; either an invasion launched from the Shenandoah Valley, or else a big cavalry raid. The Confederate Infantry might just be at Culpeper to support the cavalry. Before sunset Hooker had the news that Longstreet and Ewell had passed through Culpeper and that Ewell was moving northward. Now Hooker had definitive information as to the whereabouts of Lee. He took immediate steps to counter the Confederate moves. Hooker ordered a quick but orderly withdrawal from the Rappahannock River. We'll look at the Union movements in a moment.

Saturday night, Hooker informed Henry Halleck that he was moving his base of operations from Aquia Creek to a point on the Orange and Alexandria Railroad near Washington. To expedite matters, Hooker divided his army into two wings. The right wing was composed of the First, Third, Fifth, and Eleventh corps. These commands were to proceed to Manassas Junction and link up with the Union cavalry. Alfred Pleasonton was ordered to hold Thoroughfare Gap with the cavalry, a brigade of infantry and a battery of artillery.

The second wing was composed of the Second, Sixth, and Twelfth corps with the Reserve Artillery. Its task was to cover the withdrawal of supplies, from the depots, especially the main one at Aquia Creek. Once the mission was completed, the units were to march to Dumfries, about twenty miles north of Fredericksburg and fifteen miles southeast of Manassas Junction. Hooker had lost the initiative and had to move to counter Lee.

As the Army of the Potomac moved away from Fredericksburg, provision had to be made for those wounded at Chancellorsville. On June 13 the order came to send the wounded and supplies to Aquia Creek for transportation to Alexandria. A large quantity of tents, provisions, and supplies had to be destroyed. Holes were knocked in the ends of barrels of vinegar and molasses. Crackers, rice, sugar and other items went up in smoke. Stocks were broken off rifles and thrown into a nearby creek. But some enterprising members of the Eleventh New Jersey were able to save and hide on their person some bottles of blackberry brandy.[16]

This scene was repeated in all the corps and regimental areas. The quartermasters must have been close to tears to see the destruction.

Moving the wounded was a difficult task. The ambulances used in '63 were not the most comfortable. Soldiers often begged the drivers to put them beside the road so they could die in peace. The jolting and swaying of the wagons was severe. Many of the Union soldiers suffering from fractures or amputations had to be carried by stretchers from near Fredericksburg to Aquia Creek. This was also pure misery.

At daylight on Saturday morning, the Iron Brigade, the First Brigade, of the First Division of the First Corps, marched to Grove Church, halting for one hour at "Cool Spring." Then they tramped to Morrisville, a tiny place with barely a half dozen houses. Orson Curtis was impressed with the fancy names of the towns. "What they lacked in size they made up for with their names." Moving on to Bealeton Station, the men from Wisconsin and Michigan halted for the night two miles beyond at Liberty Church.[17]

Charles Wainwright had the artillery of the First Corps all ready to move by daybreak. However, due to other troops being on the road, they did not move out until 8:00 A.M. Like so many other soldiers he found it very hard to "hurry up and wait." John Reynolds came by, leaving nothing to chance, and suggested that all battery commanders feed any leftover hay. "Hartwood Church" was reached about noon. George Meade's Headquarters were close by as the Fifth Corps had been guarding United States and Banks' fords since the cavalry had moved on. Wainwright and Alexander Stew-

53

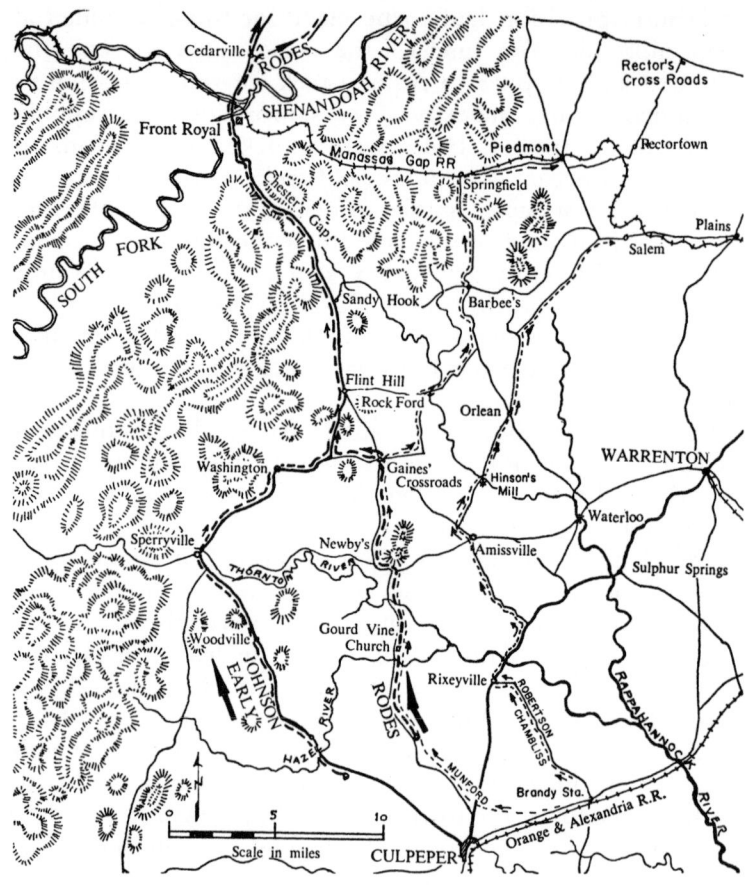

Lee Moves North. Courtesy Louisiana State University
Press from *Here Come the Rebels!*

art Webb had lunch together. Meade and Hooker were not
the best of friends. Meade felt Hooker had done badly at
Chancellorsville. Hooker came to see George one day and the
two of them had a very heated argument. It became so hot
that Webb left the tent.[18]

The thirteenth of June was a better day for Wainwright.
This time he got an early start and reached Bealeton Station
shortly after noon. Camp was pitched in a small woods about

54

one-half mile from the railroad. Charles felt they would be able to stay in the woods for awhile. But he was in for a surprise.

We turn now to the Fifth Corps, commanded in early June by George Gordon Meade. The Fifth moved up the Rappahannock River to guard the fords and crossing places. Meade was very busy supervising this activity. Writing to his wife from above Falmouth on June 6, the general said:

> It has been my opinion for some time that Lee would assume the offensive as soon as he was reinforced to justify him in doing so; but whether he has yet commenced is, I think, not positively settled. Nor have I made up my mind what he will do when he moves.[19]

Three days later in another letter, Meade stated:

> The army is weakened, and its morale not so good as at the last battle, and the enemy are undoubtedly stronger and in better morale. Still, I do not despair, but . . . if they assume the offensive and force us into a defensive attitude . . . our morale will be raised . . . War is very uncertain in its results, and often when affairs look most desperate they suddenly assume a more hopeful state.[20]
> We are now on the "qui vive" to know what the enemy are going to do. I am removed from Hooker's headquarters and know nothing of what is going on, either of plans or surmises. In some respects this is convenient. . . . All we can do is to be on the lookout and ready. Perhaps Hooker may find a chance to assume the offensive and reverse matters as the enemy did at Chancellorsville. This I think would be good luck for us.[21]

Two days later, June 13, the First Corps moved up. John Reynolds stopped by for a visit. He informed Meade that he had been informed that he was being considered for command of the Army of the Potomac. Immediately Reynolds said, "I went to see the President and told him I did not want the command and would not take it."

June the thirteenth took the Twelfth Corps on the road to Brook Station on the Falmouth and Aquia Creek Railroad. The Twelfth Corps had confidence in their leaders. Henry Warner Slocum had a genuine concern for his men. This was expressed many times in many ways. One such event occurred soon after the Twelfth Corps took the Roads to Gettysburg. His command was taking a brief rest. As Slocum and his staff drew near, on horseback, an officer shouted,

"Clear the way." But Slocum said, "Never mind boys, don't get up; my horse is not as tired as you are."[22]

John Boyle of the 111th Pennsylvania felt that Slocum was always considerate of the men. He looked upon him as a handsome man with a slender figure.[23]

John Geary, commanding Second Division, was a man of "imposing presence, more than six feet in height, and powerfully built." He was the first mayor of San Francisco, and territorial governor of Kansas. He was just forty-three in the summer of '63. After the war he became governor of Pennsylvania. George Greene of New York commanded Boyle's brigade. He was older, sixty-one, and a severe disciplinarian, "somewhat abrupt in manner but brave and capable."[24]

Starting at sunrise, Slocum's men marched five miles toward the Potomac River. They found the abandoned winter campsite of another unit. Located on a high hill, the site was ideal. The junk and debris from the other soldiers was gathered up, taken to the edge of the hill and thrown into a ravine. Rubber blankets were used to carry the rubbish.[25]

Bunks were built on poles, eighteen inches off the ground, supported by forks. Pine poles made the bottom of the bed. On top of them was placed the mattress consisting of soft pine boughs. The boughs were called "soldier feathers." Shelter tents were stretched above the bunks. There was a good view, it was a fine military location, and breezes swept over the hill. The twenty-seventh Indiana worked all day to make a nice situation. They were pleased with their efforts. The camp was clean. They were off the ground, and free of dampness.[26]

But as so often happens in the military, their work was all in vain. The men never reaped the benefit of their labors. Beds were made, supper was cooking, and the men from Indiana were looking forward to a good sleep.[27]

Then it happened. The drum started to beat. Hopefully the call would be for routine duty. But no! He beat the "Long Roll." In thirty minutes half cooked meals were swallowed, tents struck, packs placed on the backs of tired men, and "the lovely camp dismantled." And the men from Indiana "started, tired, and sleepy . . . on an all-night's march."[28]

For the men of the Thirteenth New Jersey, "the night was intensely dark. The men stumbled forward half asleep. The light of the burning buildings at Aquia Creek Landing illuminated the sky behind us."[29]

George G. Meade and the Fifth Corps broke camp at 8:00 P.M. Saturday. The 155th Pennsylvania and other regiments moved out in the midst of a heavy thunderstorm, no doubt the same storm that hit Milroy and Ewell earlier around Winchester. No pillar of fire went before them, but their way was lighted by "vivid lightning brightly illuminating the darkness of the roads. . . . At midnight the column reached Hartwood Church and where the troops bivouacked."[30]

The writer of the Fifth Massachusetts Battery has left a tremendous account of the artillery's travel on the Roads to Gettysburg. We begin with June 13. The letters and diaries of the men in the battery, particularly those of Captain Phillips, Lieutenants Scott and Blake, Sergeant Peacock, Corporals Chase and Shackley, as well as the notes of Privates Dyer and Pattison comprise the battery history.

> We left our camp near White Oak Church, Saturday afternoon June 13, 1863, between 4 and 5 o'clock. As we had been expecting to move with the Artillery Reserve for some time, we were all ready, and started out on the road to Stafford Court House. The road was quite good, but dusty. Weather very warm until about 7 p. m., when a thunderstorm came up, but very little rain fell. We of course encountered the usual delays from wagons, teams etc. A short distance before reaching Stafford Court House there was a steep hill, which seemed to have caused most of the delay. Half a dozen wagons, a caisson, and a forge, were tumbled over on either side, but we got up without a halt. We were on the march all night.[31]

Hartwell Osborn of the Fifty-fifth Ohio, Howard's corps states that the weather this Saturday was "warm and the roads very dusty, and there was a painful lack of water."[32]

Chaplain Haines brings us up-to-date on the actions of the Sixth Corps from June 8-13. The men had constructed a line of rough rifle pits during the seventh. These were a mile in length, extending from the bank at Deep Run to the vicinity of the Burnett House.

> We stood in the trenches at 3.30 o'clock of the morning of the 8th. All were in quiet expectation of the sudden uproar that was to

57

come. But the calm was undisturbed, and the bright sun of a beautiful day at length broke upon us without a hostile shot. We were ordered to get breakfast, and soon the little fires showed where our men were occupied in boiling their coffee. After a time the enemy began to annoy us by the bullets of their sharp-shooters, who had posted themselves in some old buildings. One of our batteries shelled the houses, making the shingles and splinters fly and soon dislodging their inmates. In the course of the day the rifle pits were deepened, a lunette fort laid out, and a second line of pits began by the fatigue parties, who were kept constantly at work. No opposing demonstration was made, beyond the occasional picking off of a man by the sharp-shooters, making the others more cautious. We continued shoveling and throwing up earth until the works became very strong, while their riflemen, by their bullets, told us they were observing our actions. This kind of service was continued until we were relieved on Thursday afternoon. We went to the river, where many availed themselves of the privilege of bathing, and were much relieved from the effects of the heat and dust of the past few days. Towards night the enemy's batteries opened upon us; their missiles were harmless, passing but little above us. We were gathering for a prayer-meeting when this firing caused us to disperse.[33]

What was it like for the Sixth Corps on the banks of the Rappahannock on June 13 and 14? Once again, Chaplain Haines of the Fifteenth New Jersey tells us:

At dark on June 13th, six of our companies went out on picket. Soon after, the bridges were covered with hay, and the artillery and most of the infantry south of the river began filing over. The order for our brigade to cross came at 9 o'clock. All the companies, excepting those on duty, marched to the place of crossing. One of the bridges had already been taken up. On the other we crossed in very fair order, moving as rapidly as possible to the opposite shore. Arms were stacked and we were set at work hauling out the pontoons and loading them upon the wagons. Our comrades upon the skirmish line were not called in. After a couple of hours of suspense most of them reached the bank about midnight. Some of the boats had been detained for the purpose of taking them off. All were not so fortunate. Three men were left behind on the river bank and were captured: Privates Fowler, Kent and Sands, from Company K. They had slept in a shelter tent, and were awakened by a Confederate, who put his head inside and wished them "Good morning," with the request to get up and follow him, which they did, though somewhat dazed at their unexpected situation. They were searched and then marched off toward Richmond. When it was morning, some poor fellows came to the water's edge, begging most piteously that a boat might be sent for them. It was too late, and though their sad cry was heard on the air, they were left to their fate, to fall as prisoners into the hands of the enemy. One of them ran up the river several miles, and when day came hid in the bushes. The next night he swam across the river, overtook some Union guards, and a week afterward reported as we were marching.

The whole night was spent in taking up the bridges and getting the boats off, which was not accomplished until the dawn of morning showed our position to the enemy. Our officers were becoming nervous at our exposure, and particularly with the behavior of a Colonel of United States Engineers, who had been drinking, and continually interrupted and delayed the work. At length the last pontoon was drawn from the water, and loaded on its wagon, and we hurried up the bank.[34]

The re-crossing was uninterrupted by any firing from the enemy. They could have greatly annoyed us in our exposed condition. We were in the rear; the rest of the corps had gone on, and was considerably in advance. We reached Stafford Heights, and were then marched quietly to the Lacy House, where we halted about 9 o'clock for breakfast. This house, we were told, was once the residence of Washington's father, and the garden the scene of the cherry-tree hacking. We halted two hours for a much needed rest after the wakefulness and toil of the preceding night. To any not accustomed to such scenes, it would have been a strange sight to see in broad daylight three thousand men sleeping in the sun.

The Captain of Company E reported that Sergeant Scudder had been left behind—having had a leg broken under one of the boats. Four drummer boys volunteered to go back with the Chaplain and bring him off. The videttes at first refused to let them pass, but, after learning their purpose, an officer said, "You take your own risk; all behind us is abandoned to the enemy." A walk of four miles brought them to the man. He was placed on the Chaplain's horse, and painful as the motion was, he rode until they came upon the column again. The heat became intense, and the drummers were so wearied and overcome by it, they had, one after another, to fall behind, careless whether the enemy surprised them or not. The brigade had moved on four miles further, to Potomac Creek, where an ambulance was obtained and the sergeant placed in it. The man was saved, but with great risk to the self-sacrificing boys, who gave us much anxiety, and it was near sunset before all fears for their safety were removed by their appearance.

At 7.30 P. M. there was divine service. It was well attended, considering the weariness of the men, and the exhaustion of mind and body to which they had been subjected. We were prepared for the night, hoping to get a good rest, when the order came at 9 o'clock to fall in, and we marched all night long. Much of our route was over an old corduroy road, whose poles were loose, and we went stumbling and tripping among them with some hazard to limb and life. In the obscurity of night the companies were much intermingled, and one regiment crowded in upon another. Yet hour after hour we were pressing on.[35]

The Confederates were up bright and early, at 4:30 to be exact. "Dick" Ewell was not about to lose any time. Winchester was his objective, and the sooner he took it the better. Three days' rations had been cooked the night before, so there was no delay. Colonel Nye tells us that the Confederates rarely pitched tents while marching in warm weather. So all they had to do was roll up their blankets, make a quick trip to the latrine, and eat a bite. Then the men in gray were on the Roads to Gettysburg, with the first stop, Winchester.

General Ewell was in good spirits. Like many others in all wars, it seems as though the proximity of combat makes the adrenalin flow faster. Ewell even got out of his carriage and called for his horse. However, when the horse tried to jump a rail fence, Ewell fell heavily to the ground. He tried to make light of the fall, but his staff could see that the general was hurting.[36] But he continued to act like Jackson. In light of future events one has to wonder what happened to the man who was moving on Winchester like another Jackson.

It is not our purpose to describe the fighting in detail. That has already been done in *Here Come the Rebels!* and other books. By noon, Johnson's division reached a point within two miles of Winchester. Early was also attacking south of town, having marched from Nineveh to Newtown, and then up the valley pike through Kernstown.[37] By nightfall, the men in gray were in place along Abrams Creek. A heavy thundershower made sleeping rough.

Robert Rodes also started early. He had hoped to reach Millwood undetected. However, Jenkins and his cavalry had not occupied the place on Friday night. Rodes wanted to capture intact the eighteen hundred Union forces in Berryville. Rodes then ordered Jenkins to aid him in an encircling move against Berryville.[38] But Union Col. A. T. McReynolds had heard two cannon shots fired from Winchester. This was the signal to abandon Berryville. McReynolds knew the rebels were coming. So he left his tents standing, and gathered just his most important supplies for his wagon train. He headed for Bunker Hill, north of Winchester, leaving 160 men from the Sixth Maryland Infantry, and a detachment of the First New York Cavalry as rearguard. Capt. William H. Boyd used repeating carbines to break up a Confederate flanking movement. North of Berryville, McReynolds led the main column toward Summit Point, passing through land now occupied by the apple orchards of Senator Harry Byrd.

The Confederates slowed up in Berryville. They did not realize the Yankees had gone. Likewise, the stores and supplies were a great temptation. The men sampled and inspected the items Colonel McReynolds left behind. Rodes reported this as "securing the stores."[39] He was very upset to learn that little of value had been left behind, and the enemy had escaped. Valuable time was lost in getting the troops back together.

Jenkins had failed twice in less than twenty-four hours. He had failed to comply with order and occupy Millwood on Friday night. Then he probed the defenses of Berryville, of cutting off the Union retreat. Then somehow during the retreat, Jenkins got ahead of the main body of Union troops, and was pursuing the wagon train. He actually appeared south of Bunker Hill before McReynolds.

Rodes's infantry followed McReynolds to Summit Point. But the day was hot, and they had already marched twenty miles. So they were unable to continue the pursuit.[40]

McReynolds conducted a masterful retreat. From Summit Point he had planned to travel via Smithfield to Bunker Hill, and then head for Winchester. But at Summit Point he learned of another route which Colonel Nye feels is present-day West Virginia Route 632.[41] The alternate route was shorter, along the railroad, thence across the Opequon east of Brucetown, and hit the Winchester road at Clearbrook. After brushing aside some Confederate resistance, he headed south to Winchester, arriving at dark in the midst of the thunderstorm. While his men took shelter, he reported to General Milroy.

Milroy realized that the situation was bad. He tried to send a message to Harpers Ferry, but did not get through. Milroy thought the wires had been cut. But a faint message, too

61

weak to be discerned, got through. Most likely, the wind blew the wires down.[42]

Capt. William H. Boyd, the officer who commanded the skillful rearguard action for McReynolds, volunteered to take the message to Harpers Ferry. He knew the country very well, and was given permission to take his company with him. This constitutes another of the great stories on the Roads to Gettysburg. We cannot cover it here, but for two weeks, Captain Boyd and his small unit was virtually the only company operating in the advance of the Federals. To a large degree, the accurate information Boyd sent to General Couch in Harrisburg, was about the only intelligence coming in on the activities of the Army of Northern Virginia.

Milroy could have escaped during the night. Early was blocking the roads leading south, and Johnson was across or in control of the road leading to Berryville and the east. Rodes was at Summit Point, and Jenkins at Bunker Hill north of Winchester. But there was an eight-mile gap between Rodes and Jenkins. The Confederate net was not that tight. Many experts feel that a skillful commander could have gotten away. In fact, during the thunderstorms would have been a good time. Naturally the men in gray would have been seeking whatever shelter they could find.

But Robert Milroy decided to stick in Winchester. He did not want to be called a coward. And it seems that Milroy actually thought he had defeated the Confederates that June 13. His aide, Capt. Frederick Palmer, writes "we were convinced that the worst was over, and that their attack on Winchester had proved a disastrous failure."[43]

Robert Rodes had his problems on the thirteenth. His cavalry under Jenkins failed him. His men were footsore. They heard that Jenkins was engaged in combat near Bunker Hill. They were sure that morning would bring another long march and possibly combat.

Although McReynolds eluded Jenkins, the Confederate leader was hot on the trail of the wagon train. Sympathetic farmers supplied the gray horsemen with information as to the location of the gray columns. They had gone to Bunker Hill, located on what is now Route 11.

The small town has an interesting history. Most likely it was named after the Revolutionary War battle. Halfway between Winchester and Martinsburg, Bunker Hill often saw the men in blue and gray. The fields around the town were often used by the soldiers. Not only was Bunker Hill on the main road into the Shenandoah Valley, but it was located at the intersection of the road that ran eastward to Harpers Ferry and Charlestown, and westward to Gerrardstown. Incidently, Ward Hill Lamon, Lincoln's friend and bodyguard, is buried in the Presbyterian Cemetery in Gerrardstown.

Two small streams join at the western edge of Bunker Hill, forming Mill Creek which runs through a deep gorge to the Opequon. Bunker Hill was home for two very prominent families. The Boyds lived in a large mansion south of town, two hundred yards west of the main road. To this place General Johnston Pettigrew was brought to die after Gettysburg. A large marker stands at the end of the lane. The other prominent family was the Lamons. John stayed home in the valley and acted as a messenger and guide for the Confederates on the Roads to Gettysburg, while Ward had gone west, entered law practice and became a good friend of Lincoln.

Bunker Hill was and still is a small, lovely place. It had three churches in 1863. But two years of war had turned the houses of worship into barracks, and in mid-June blockhouses. At least two of the churches were used as fortifications that month.

On Saturday night two companies of the Eighty-seventh Pennsylvania Volunteers, and two from the 116th Ohio were on outpost duty. Their task was to keep the road from Winchester to Martinsburg open, a big task for a small unit. They were also supposed to guard the bridge over the Opequon.[44]

The lathered horses of McReynolds' wagon train arrived at 4:00 P.M. on Saturday, forty-two wagons rambled into town escorted by elements of the First New York Cavalry and the Seventy-sixth Pennsylvania Infantry. In addition to the government wagons there were six wagons belonging to the sutler's, and a buggy carrying the wife and children of Capt. William H. Boyd.[45]

Pausing to rest, the wagons were led into a field, and the unhitching process had begun. When suddenly a scout arrived with the news that the rebels were coming fast. The wagon master lived up to his name and got the wagons in line and headed them north.

In his haste he forgot Captain Boyd's wife and buggy. The poor woman struggled to hitch up again. Getting behind, she used the whip to make the tired horse go faster. He took off and the buggy upset. Mrs. Boyd suffered a sprained ankle and the children were scared out of their wits. The brave mother tried to flee with her offspring on foot. However, she was soon captured, sent back to Winchester, thence to Richmond and released.[46]

As the wagon train was moving toward Martinsburg, Major Morris formed a strong line of defense south of Bunker Hill. He tried to make it appear that he had more men than he actually had. Jenkins quickly brushed them aside. But while he rounded up the prisoners, some of the Union men fled to the churches and prepared to give battle from them.

During a lull in the action, Jenkins sent John Lamon into town with a flag of truce demanding the surrender of the Union troops. Morris refused although he was outnumbered about twenty to one.

Rodes was "mortified" at the Union escape from Berryville. He says of the action at Bunker Hill:

> I cannot explain why he (Jenkins) did not intercept at least a portion of the enemy's force. It seems, however, . . . that before the close of the day the general made a fierce attack upon a detachment of infantry and cavalry at Bunker Hill, losing several men in a gallant attack upon a party of the latter, who had thrown themselves into two stone houses, well provided for defense with loop-holes and barricades for that purpose. He captured here about 75 or 100 prisoners and drove the rest toward Martinsburg.[47]

Jenkins made several attacks on the churches turned into fortifications, but accomplished little. Major Morris had a good position. The heavy rain further dampened Jenkins's idea to continue the attack. By midnight he decided that it was not worth the loss involved, and broke off the action. After all, his task was to get across the Potomac. The infan-

64

try, when it came up, could clear out this pocket of resistance. Thus in the wee hours of Sunday morning Jenkins reached a point just south of Martinsburg where he rested until daylight.

Major Morris wondered what was up. After waiting awhile, he concluded that Jenkins had gone away. The major had conducted a gallant stand with a small band of men. But due to the fact that it was a small action, overshadowed perhaps by the fall of Winchester, the action at Bunker Hill has gone relatively unnoticed. While Jenkins was heading north to Martinsburg, Morris and his men left the protection of the churches and headed south for Winchester. On the road, these men who had stood against great odds, joined Milroy's withdrawal and headed for Harpers Ferry.

Today John Hood's division started north from near Culpeper. Instead of Bull Run, they came to the Cedar Mountain Battlefield, the scene of fighting between Jackson and Banks in August of 1862. Grisly scenes awaited the men in gray. There were many unburied skeletons, and one soldier counted forty-nine skulls in one ditch. Animals had gotten into the graves and uncovered many of them.[48]

Sunday, June 14

Robert Milroy had been in command at Winchester since Christmas Day 1862. His actions are hard to describe in June of '63. At first he thought he had repulsed the Rebels and was safe. The forts offered good protection. He had some supplies. But he was very indecisive during this long weekend.

In the last hours of Saturday, Milroy moved his men from Milltown and other outposts into Winchester. At 2:00 A.M. he pulled all units within the fortifications on the ridge north of town. By this time, the telegraph ceased to work. He could not withdraw unless he received orders from his superiors. And with couriers it would take hours for messengers to come through.

"Baldy" Ewell was up at daybreak this Sunday. He didn't have time to go to church, but he would take time the next two Sabbaths. In fact, he would attend church in Greencastle and Carlisle, Pennsylvania. The rain had stopped but it was still cloudy. The general surveyed the situation and conferred with Johnson and Early. Attacks were to be launched on the West Fort, the Star Fort and Bowers Hill. These places witnessed a lot of action this Lord's Day. However, it is not our intent to describe the action. Colonel Nye has done that in *Here Come the Rebels!*

During this hot day, Ewell's command used fire and maneuver to convince Milroy that his position in Winchester was hopeless. We'll turn back to him, for his 10:00 P.M. council of war. But we turn now to the movement of the Army of the Potomac. Hooker moved his headquarters from Falmouth to Dumfries, while the infantry marched and sweated.

By 6:00 A.M. this Sunday morning, the First Brigade of the First Corps was on the road again. About midmorning, they halted at Germantown, the birthplace of Chief Justice John Marshall.[49] After a brief respite the men marched to Warrenton Junction and halted for a coffee break. The day was hot and dusty. Many were exhausted, but had miles to go before they slept. As the day wore on, not only did they crave a Sabbath's rest, but were frantic for water. However, the road continued to Catlett's Station and Kettle Run.

The Twenty-fourth Michigan thought they would be able to make camp. But Dwight Morrow, regimental commander, said, "No, we must go on. We must reach Centreville before the Rebels."[50] So the march continued. The men from the Midwest crossed Kettle Run, stepping from stone to stone. Later in the night they crossed Broad Run in the same fashion. This time they were guided by bonfires from the opposite bank.

Throughout the night the march continued. Before it was over, almost twenty-four hours had been spent on the road. The cooler night air helped to keep some of the men awake. Finally, just before sunrise, "the Iron Brigade" halted for breakfast beside the Manassas Railroad where they were located after Second Bull Run.

We look now at some other reflections and comments on the forced march.

Charles Wainwright and the artillery of the First Corps were unable to move until late Sunday morning. Then they had to move rapidly, and traveled throughout the day until 3:00 this morning.[51] The Third Corps moved at the same time. The land along the railroad was quite open so the men moved in parallel columns. This made a very pretty and inspiring sight. The men of the First and Third corps vied with each other, seeking to see which one could march the best. Wainwright said he never saw men march better. The competition was good.

But all was not roses for Charles. He had trouble with some of his batteries keeping up.

The Sixth Corps hit the ground to rest between three and four o'clock this morning, and rested from the fatigue of the night march until evening. The men watched the immense army trains hurrying by, the mules and horses being lashed by their drivers. George T. Stevens, the Sixth Corps historian, tells us:

> All day long the trains crowded by, four and five wagons abreast; the drivers shouting and lashing their beasts to their greatest speed. No one who has not seen the train of an army in motion, can form any conception of its magnitude, and of the difficulties attending its movements. It was said that the train of the Army of the Potomac, including artillery at the time (June 14), if placed in a single line, the teams at the distance necessary for the march, would extend over seventy miles.[52]

If this figure is correct, then the trains of the Union army would have reached from Hagerstown to Baltimore. We can hardly imagine the horses, mules and forage needed to move such a train. The train was reduced at Fairfax Station, and then later in June George Meade reduced the train even more. Watching the wagons go by, Stevens expressed indignation at those who were always clamoring for the army to move, when they were unaware of what it took to move any army. The trains had to go along because they carried the supplies. They had to be protected, front, rear, and flank. If the wagons got stuck in the mud, or became involved in an accident or roadblock, the entire army was held up. Yet some people thought 75,000 men could be moved as easily as 50. This movement on the Roads to Gettysburg is really remarkable when the reader stops to consider all that was involved.

Throughout the day, Stevens and his comrades watched "the hurrying wagons as they swept by with immense clatter and tumult; and the files of troops to guard the trains, pressing forward, amid the clouds of dust and the rattle and noise of the wagons."[53] As the sun went down in the west, some of John Sedgwick's men gathered on a green knoll, in the shade of some pines, sung some old familiar hymns, and listened while the chaplain offered prayer. The veterans prayed for protection in the upcoming campaign amid the noise of the wagons passing by.

At 9:00 P.M. the Sixth Corps was under way again. Although it was a very dark night, and the roads uneven, the soldiers marched on in good spirits. The news had reached them that Lee was in the Shenandoah Valley heading north. "Maryland, Pennsylvania, and even New York were threatened." The Sixth Corps was anxious for a fight, they would whip the Rebels in an open fight, be it north or south of the Potomac.

Once or twice during the night they passed the campsites of other units of the Army of the Potomac. These men had used cedar boughs to make avenues of shade in the camp. As they moved on, the pines were set aflame.[54]

The terrible all-night march of the Twelfth Corps ended at 7:00 A.M. Sunday.[55] At long last they reached Dumfries, filed into a field, stacked arms, and rested for the day. The historian of the Thirteenth New Jersey says it "was the first and only all night's march we were ever called upon to make."[56]

Unit after unit wheeled onto the roads that day and took some of the initial steps on the Roads to Gettysburg. For some it was a trip of 150 miles or more from the trenches of Fredericksburg to Gettysburg. Yet the longest journey starts with the first step. Hour after hour they tramp, scorched by the sun, and choked by dust. These days comprise the greatest maneuvering ever seen on this continent.

As the Twelfth Corps rested from their night of marching, the First and Third corps marched to Manassas Junction. Howard reached Manassas and pushed on to Centreville. The Second Corps formed the rear guard. The men of the Nineteenth Massachusetts camped at Aquia Creek, "where the men bathed in coffee colored water."[57] This brought temporary relief. We pick up the Third Corps now, looking at Humphreys's division.

Andrew A. Humphreys was from a family of ship builders and naval architects. In fact, his grandfather had drawn the plans for "Old Ironsides."

Andrew graduated from West Point in 1831, being about twenty-one years old at the time. During the next thirty years he served primarily as an engineer, working on river fortifications. When the war broke out, he became an aide to George B. McClellan. Command of a division in the Fifth Corps followed. In June of 1863 Humphreys was switched from the Fifth Corps to the Third.

As the men in blue and gray marched from Fredericksburg, Virginia, through Maryland, to Pennsylvania, each unit seemingly felt that their plight was worse than that of their comrades. Humphreys stated what every man must have felt:

> The loss of sleep, the continued work . . . together with the long marches had not been exceeded by any other division in the army. . . . The Division had never known such service.[58]

He spoke the truth. The long hard marches on the Roads to Gettysburg were the most difficult experienced by the army to that time.

Humphreys, commanding the Second Division of the Third Corps, was assigned the duty of guarding the fords of the Rappahannock River from Kelly's Ford up the river for about eight miles. Rifle pits and other fortification were erected under the direction of the man who had supervised defensive barriers on the Delaware River.

But on Sunday the men of the Third Corps abandoned their positions at the Rappahannock crossings, heading for Catlett's Station on the Manassas Gap Railroad. "There had been no rain, the sun was hot, no wind, and the dust in the road lay several inches thick. . . . Men dropped from exhaustion."[59]

Charles W. Bardeen was very young in 1863. He recorded his experiences in "A Little Fifer's Diary." Quoting his friend McCarthy, he says:

In summer time the dust combined with the heat caused great suffering. The nostrils of the men, filled with dust, became dry and feverish. . . . The grit was felt between the teeth, and the eyes were rendered almost useless. There was dust in the eyes, mouth, ears, and hair.[60]

Night marching was attended with additional discomforts and dangers, such as falling off bridges, stumbling into ditches, tearing the face and injuring the eyes against the bushes and limbs of the trees. . . .[61]

Young Bardeen was attached to the First Massachusetts in June of '63. He and his comrades covered thirty-five miles this sweltering day. The "Little Fifer" was proud of himself. He had a right to be.

I did pretty well to stand that march; a great many grown men didn't. Never . . . did I suffer for water as on this day. I saw men cutting off half a mile to the right where a spring was said to be, and I followed. Whatever it may have been in the beginning, when I got there I found only mud too thick too drink. So I marched an extra mile for nothing.[62]

A comrade-in-arms said, "People at home don't value water. If they saw men . . . with cracked and blackened lips and tongues swollen with the terrible thirst they would value it more."

Humphreys and his division had a right to be tired, thirsty and frustrated. On the twelfth his command had covered twenty-two to twenty-five miles on foot and thrown up rifle pits at the river crossings. The duty required constant vigilance. Then came the order to move out under cover of darkness on Sunday evening.

Through the night Charlie Bardeen and his comrades tramped through the Virginia countryside. Between 7:00 and 8:00 A.M. the command reached Cedar Run where a halt was ordered and the men rested until 2:00 P.M.

Then it was on the road once again. The march continued for some until midnight. General Humphreys, in describing June 15, says:

(The march) . . . was painful in the extreme, for owing to the long-continued drought, streams, usually of considerable magnitude, were dried up, the dust lay some inches deep on the roadway. . . . The suffering from heat, dust, thirst, fatigue and exhaustion was very great.[63]

Joseph Carr, commanding the First Brigade of the division, reports:

This march was one of the most severe in my experience, the air being almost suffocating, the dust blinding, and the heat intolerable. Many men suffered from "coup de soleil," and a large number sank by the wayside, utterly helpless and exhausted.[64]

A. W. Bartlett from New Hampshire said the day brought "weary limbs and blistered feet . . . (our) feet being so badly blistered that some left blood in their tracks."[65] Handkerchiefs, made wet and held over the face, enabled some of the men to keep on going. Without the aid of these more would have fallen out.

We look now at Sykes's division of the Fifth Corps and their activity on June 14. They were up and on the road by 5:00 A.M. Like the rest of the army, the extreme heat was the major problem faced during the day. Survivors of the 155th Pennsylvania said, "the heat was so great and the sun so strong, . . . that ambulances following the troops were frequently filled with sufferers from sunstroke and exhaustion from the heat."[66]

The experience of the Eleventh Corps was much the same this very hot day in June. But on through the heat and dust, plodded 155th Pennsylvania and their comrades until by nightfall the division had reached a point near Catlett's Station.

Sunday was another busy day for the Fifth Massachusetts Battery. The artillerymen tell their own story:

Drove out on the side of the road at 4 a. m. of Sunday the 14th. Ceased raining. We fed our horses, made coffee, and after a halt of half an hour and a scanty meal, we started and pushed on for Brooks Station and Dumfries on the Potomac. The roads were good, though very dusty, and we travelled briskly. Went about two miles on a wrong road; countermarched, and took the right road. Reached Dumfries about noon and made another short halt. After dinner we started again, and with constant halts pushed on till dark. Then for some inexplicable reason, the column halted and remained till nine, moving during that time about a quarter of a mile by fits and starts, then another halt of two hours. All the delay was caused by a hill

71

ahead, up which our Battery went with halting. After passing this hill we kept on at a pretty good jog. We had marched all day and all night, a hard march for man and beast, and were pretty well played out. At 7 p. m. when we had made coffee, we lay down to rest, but before we had rested 15 minutes we were called to "Attention." Not a wink of sleep Saturday night, and but one hour's sleep Sunday night.[67]

Oliver O. Howard, leader of the Eleventh Corps, made his headquarters at Centreville. The Fifty-fifth Ohio, a part of his command, camped at Blackburn's Ford on Bull Run. The dusty, waterless march, exhausted many of the men.[68]

The Sixth Corps faced a repetition of the Twelfth Corps' all-night experience. They started marching in the evening, most of the fellows marched all night. Lt. George Bicknell of the Fifth Maine says this was "the commencement of a long series of hard marches," that were to test the endurance of the men.[69]

The tired men of the Union Sixth Corps rested part of the Sabbath. The three days they spent across the river had been no picnic. It was marked by entrenching, skirmishing and watching the Rebels. In midafternoon, John Sedgwick's men moved to Stafford Court House, getting there about 5:00. Rest was what they needed, and rest was what they hoped they would get. But at 10:00 P.M. they were roused and started with the baggage and artillery trains. A man who took part in the march writes:

> The darkness was intense and a thunder shower prevailed. Our route for a long time lay through a thick woods, where the branches of the trees, meeting over our heads, shut out the little light that might have penetrated the thunder clouds, and the column was shut in perfect darkness. The roads were terribly muddy, and the batteries which were trying to pass over the same route were frequently stuck in the mire. Our men stumbled over stones and fallen trees, often falling beneath the feet of the horses. Men fell over logs and stones, breaking their arms and legs. Thus we continued the hasty and difficult march, while the rain poured in torrents.[70]

That's the way it was in the ranks of the Sixth Corps that Sunday night in mid-June.

The Second Corps, acting as rear guard for the Army of the Potomac, started on the long march to the river and towards Gettysburg. Many of the troops did not leave their bivouac areas until 8:30 P.M. The Fourteenth Connecticut broke camp in silence. The Fifth New Hampshire left Falmouth at 8:30, while the First Delaware did not leave until about 9:00 P.M. Their second religious service of the day was interrupted by the order to "fall in." Everything that could not be taken along was destroyed. Hundreds of blankets were cut or torn into strips.[71]

Early in June, William Harrow was assigned to command the First Brigade of John Gibbon's Second Division. Harrow had been in command of the Fourteenth Indiana. His brigade consisting of the Nineteenth Maine, Fifteenth Massachusetts, First Minnesota, and Eighty-third New York broke camp, marched two miles, and was ordered back to their original spot, waiting to move until 3:00 A.M.

By the morning of June 14, the Army of the Potomac had left the banks of the Rappahannock. During the day, the tents and wagons which had dotted the hillsides since November vanished. Hill sent scouts to look into the situation. But he did not press the issue. He assumed that Hooker was moving to get between Lee and Washington. He was correct.[72]

With Hooker gone, it was time for the Third Corps of the Army of Northern Virginia to get moving. Dick Anderson started on the fourteenth for Culpeper. On the fifteenth Henry Heth and his men took up the march. After Dorsey Pender made sure the Federals were gone, and not playing a trick, he and his men started for Culpeper. Pender wrote to his wife:

> May God in His goodness be more gracious than in our last trial (the invasion of Maryland). We certainly may be allowed to hope as our mission is one of peace altho through blood. The enemy seem to think we have 90,000 men, which will scare them so badly they will be half whipt before they commence the fight. I do not anticipate any fight this side of the Potomac.[73]

The advance of the Third Corps is fairly easy to follow. From Culpeper the long gray column proceeded to Front Royal, Berryville, Charles Town, Shepherdstown, and Boonsboro to Hagerstown. The area is now traversed by Route 340 from Front Royal to Charles Town. A question remains as to the exact route from that city to Shepherdstown. From the Potomac to Boonsboro, the Third Corps marched over what is now Maryland 34. Thence a left turn on the National Road or Alternate Route 40 to Hagerstown. Then it was up Route 11 to Greencastle and Chambersburg. From Chambersburg, the road led to a place called Gettysburg.

J. F. J. Caldwell, a member of Gregg's brigade, later known as "McGowan's Brigade," and composed of the Twelfth, Thirteenth and Fourteenth South Carolina regiments along with other units from that state, describes the march of the Third Corps on June 14:

> We lay behind our works, expecting the enemy, until Sunday, June 14. But they not indulging in anything more hostile than music and cheering, or, on one or two occasions, such a bold display of pickets as to require a few shells at our hands—we moved back, that day, about half a mile, in rear of the works where we had fought the battle of Fredericksburg. We learned this day, that Hooker had abandoned his positions both on this side of the Rappahannock and on the Stafford Hills, and betaken himself higher up the river. Some of the brigade managed to get a peep at the deserted camps.[74]

Richard H. Anderson is the only Confederate commander in the Third Corps to record an itinerary in the Official Records. He states that his command spent Sunday night on the Chancellorsville Battlefield.[75]

This was A. P. Hill's first march as a corps commander. Small but mighty, this Virginian was named after his great-grandfather, a former Indian fighter, pioneer and surveyor. Like Ewell, he had some big shoes to fill.

Ham Chamberlayne, an artillery officer with Hill, rode into Fredericksburg before leaving Caroline County. He was shocked. Ham found words inadequate to describe the desolation. People shrinking from the deserted houses looked to be ghosts of their former selves. Windows were broken, doors hanging open, and the houses gashed and torn with shot. Hugh Mercer's home, a place where Washington had visited, was riddled with shot, and rifle pits dotted the yard. "The town would almost make you weep to see it."[76]

We turn now to Milroy's council of war. He was sure Winchester was surrounded. Therefore, all he could do was to

74

make an effort to escape. Six roads led into Winchester: "the road to Romney, Pughtown, Berryville, Martinsburg, Front Royal and Strasburg." Cavalry and artillery could easily approach the town from any direction. The Confederates had shelled Milroy's position with twenty guns. He was sure the Rebels could open with one hundred guns in the morning. He debated the route of retreat, but then decided on heading for Martinsburg and turning for Harpers Ferry.

The sands of time were running out for Milroy. The general ordered his men to evacuate their positions at 1:00 A.M. But once again something went wrong. The advance guard was late in leaving, and the area was not cleared until after 2:00 A.M. Two hours earlier, Milroy might have gotten away without any difficulty. But now the hour was too late.

At 8:00 P.M. on Sunday evening, Ewell decided that an escape attempt was a very real possibility. Thinking like "Stonewall" Jackson, Ewell concluded that the Martinsburg road would most likely be the route taken. Therefore, he ordered Edward "Alleghany" Johnson to move northward across the fields as quickly as possible to seal the fate of Milroy. Jones's brigade ordered to check any escape attempt by way of Berryville and Front Royal.

Johnson performed admirably in the dark. Walker and Steuart had to leave positions in line of battle, being careful not to give indications of what they were doing, and then move northward. Seven miles had to be covered. The movement should have taken three and a half hours. But it took five. Part of the reason was the darkness. Some of the troops apparently got lost. And there was a big communications problem. A local guide persuaded Johnson to move east on the Berryville Pike, follow a road to Jordan's Springs, and move northwest to Stephenson's Depot.

Mrs. E. C. Jordan, fearing the movement of men meant the Yankees were coming, was overjoyed to find men in gray. She wanted to feed the men. But Johnson said, "Thank you, but there is no time for that now." Mr. Jordan went with Johnson to show him the way to the Depot. He proudly pointed out a railroad cut that would be an ideal spot for an ambush.[77]

It was now about 4:00 A.M. The Twelfth Pennsylvania Cavalry was approaching the fork of the road that leads to Charles Town from the Winchester-Martinsburg Road. The light was beginning to break. The Union horsemen saw figures ahead of them. These were the men of Edward Johnson. Yankee blue and Confederate gray reached the spot at the same time. Then the fire flew. Steuart's Maryland brigade was in the thick of the action. Lt. Randolph McKim describes the action very graphically. Although not a large action in terms of Antietam and the one that was to follow, north of the Potomac, yet the fighting at Stephenson's Depot was very important and quite severe.

Steuart and the Louisiana Brigade, about twelve hundred men in all, met the brunt of Milroy's infantry and cavalry. The men in blue made every effort to break through. Johnson was on the scene directing things in person. He knew he was outnumbered. Ammunition was running low, and he did not know when the rest of his command would arrive. Johnson rode up and down behind his men, shouting encouragement.[78] Once again, Milroy could have made it, but instead of an all-out attack, he committed his brigades one at a time.

In the midst of the action, Milroy's horse was shot from under him. So at the crucial moments of action, his aides had to hunt a mount for him. Actually, he had the upper hand. His troops had overlapped the Confederate flanks, and he had a superiority in numbers. But Milroy was obsessed with the idea that he must escape and "cut his way out." So he gave the order to break off the action and retreat. Colonel Nye says his decision to retreat was sound, but once again the timing and execution was bad. He could have had one unit engage the Rebels, while the rest escaped. Johnson could not have followed quickly. And the men in blue could have gone without hindrance to Harpers Ferry and Hancock.

W. L. Elliott and the First Brigade withdrew via the Martinsburg Road. Milroy did not stay around to supervise the disengagement. He got out of there as quickly as possible. He spurred his horse and caught up with Elliott. The column turned east at Clearbrook and took the back roads to Harpers

Ferry. Milroy, fatigued by physical and mental exhaustion, fell asleep in the saddle.

A signal gun was heard from Winchester. This meant that Early had taken the city. Winchester was back in Confederate hands. Some of the men in blue feared that Early would momentarily fall upon the Union rear.

Then another disaster struck. A thousand government issue mules were following Milroy's Second Brigade. Black refugees and military clerks were riding the mules. They had been told that at the proper moment they were to "take off," and ride en masse through the Confederates.[79] As they approached the field of action, they were met with heavy volleys of musketry and concentrated artillery bursts. The riders felt the moment had come. Now was the time to dash for freedom.

But a mass stampede resulted. It was mass confusion. Panic spread. The riders and the officers nearby lost all sense of direction. Colonel Ely was convinced that he was seven-eighths surrounded. But all around were open fields, avenues of escape.

The concluding action consists of the last Union pockets of resistance falling away. Union regiments just vanished, they were wiped out or disintegrated. General Johnson personally captured thirty Union soldiers at the Opequon Creek. As he was riding across the stream to receive their surrender, his horse fell and General Johnson wound up soaking wet in the middle of the creek.[80] One of the men in blue waded into the water and picked up Johnson's hat, saying "General, here's your hat." Johnson stood dripping wet, speechless. But he says that with nothing but his field glasses he achieved the capture.

By the time "Jube" Early arrived on the scene, the fighting was over. Johnson reports capturing between twenty-three hundred and twenty-five hundred men. Ewell claimed four thousand, but that is high; the figures include those captured prior to June 15 too. Milroy lost half his army. The command was never reorganized. Ewell had done a great job. He performed exceedingly well. Lee had hoped that he would be able to drive the Yankees across the river and inflict some losses. Ewell's achievement exceeded Lee's fondest hopes. Twenty-three spiked guns were among the spoils.

Early received the prisoners. He took them into Winchester, and then shipped them off to Staunton. Ewell sent a message to Rodes, who had pushed on to Martinsburg, urging him to intercept Milroy's fugitives. Rodes said his men were too tired. After all, his men had marched twenty miles on Saturday, and nineteen miles on Sunday. After brushing aside the Union forces on Sunday, Rodes rested his men until 10:00 A.M. on Monday.[81] At that time he received his first news about the action in Winchester.

Colonel Nye feels that Ewell reached the peak of his military career at Winchester.[82] "In a single rapid offensive he had eliminated all the opposition in the valley, and cleared the path for the passage of his own and the other two corps into the North."

While Early and Johnson were maneuvering to capture Winchester, Robert Rodes hurried his infantry north toward Martinsburg to cooperate with Jenkins's cavalry. The latter found a Union skirmish line.[83] Some fighting occurred. That delay, along with the slowness of Jenkins, enabled Col. Benjamin Smith to move more companies of infantry south of town to confront the Rebels. About 10:00 A.M. Smith threw the 106th New York into the fray. That unit, commanded by Col. Edward C. James, had been withdrawn from North Mountain Depot on Friday.

The command situation in Martinsburg was somewhat chaotic. Colonel Smith had been in command in Martinsburg. But Gen. Robert C. Schenck, alarmed over the state of affairs, sent Brig. Gen. Daniel C. Tyler and two aides from Baltimore to assume command. Tyler had been ordered to move the Martinsburg garrison to Bunker Hill to cover Milroy's withdrawal, while Smith had been ordered to go to Harpers Ferry.

The train carrying General Tyler pulled into Martinsburg just as the Confederates struck.[84] Therefore, Tyler and Smith had no opportunity to discuss the placement of the twelve-hundred-man garrison with the escapees from Winchester and Berryville.

About the same time, the courageous Capt. William Boyd rode into town, having ridden all night to avoid Jenkins. He brought news from Milroy and Winchester. Tyler sent the contents via telegraph to Schenck. This was the first word the War Department had of Ewell's attack.

The bulk of the Martinsburg stores and supplies had been shipped out by 11:00 A.M., and were on the road to Harpers Ferry. The Martinsburg wagon train and that of McReynolds was also ready to go. Tyler told the quartermaster to send the wagon train to Williamsport and on to Pennsylvania. Captain Boyd heard the news that his wife was missing and probably captured. He decided to go with the wagon train to Williamsport.

General Tyler decided by noon that the garrison must retreat. However, he wanted action until the wagon train was safely across the Potomac. He thought maybe a retreat under cover of darkness would be best. Tyler had hoped to put the men on the train for Harpers Ferry, but was told that all railroad stock had already been sent east.

Smith saw that he could easily be outflanked, and wished to withdraw to Union Hill near the town cemetery. This would be a good position. A longer route was selected for the movement, because the Union leaders thought the Confederates were anticipating their moves.

Jenkins waited this Sabbath day for Rodes and the infantry to arrive. The foot soldiers were willing, but the flesh was weak. The marching from Culpeper had taken its toll. The last few days had been particularly severe. Their feet were cut, bruised and swollen, and the stone pike was terrible for men already limping. The last of them did not arrive until 9:00 P.M.

Rodes, being mounted, arrived in midafternoon and surveyed the situation. Jenkins had already sent a Capt. W. A. Harris into town demanding the surrender of Martinsburg. The Federals were warned of the consequences. They were told to advise the residents in case they refused to surrender. For one hour, the Rebels used small arms, but then artillery.[85]

Smith, after conferring with General Tyler, sent back the

reply, "Martinsburg will not be surrendered. You may commence shelling as soon as you choose. I will, however, inform the women and children of your threat."[86] When the residents of Martinsburg were informed of the impending action, large numbers left town.

Smith and Tyler agreed to evacuate as soon as darkness fell. They would move north to Williamsport, cross the river and travel down the north bank of the Potomac to Maryland Heights.

The sun was starting to go down when Rodes was ready to attack. Jenkins was moved around to come in from the west. This would also prevent an escape toward Hedgesville. Lt. Col. Thomas Carter came up with a battalion of artillery. This was unlimbered to open up on Maulsby's Union battery which had been holding the Rebels at bay. But the guns opened before all of Rodes's command was in position. The first few shells struck among the Union artillery carriages, sending wood, horses, and debris in all directions, even detonating some of the Union ammunition.[87]

This produced a shock effect on the Union infantry, at least portions of it. Two regiments fled so quickly that Rodes's men could not catch up with them.

In the midst of all of this, retreat plans were changed. The officers thought Shepherdstown offered a closer and better escape route. The men in blue traveled during the night and crossed at Shepherdstown, taking the Chesapeake and Ohio Tow Path to Maryland Heights.

Rodes was somewhat disappointed. He felt that if his infantry could have arrived two hours earlier, giving him time to seize the principal roads leading into Martinsburg, then "I feel certain that I would have captured the whole force."[88]

Jenkins pursued the retreating Union artillery and cavalry, at least some of it, nearly to the Potomac, capturing some prisoners. Rodes says, "the enemy endeavored to burn the stores accumulated at Martinsburg, and to a large extent succeeded in doing so, but left in our hands some 6,000 bushels of fine grain, some commissary stores, about 400 rounds of rifled artillery ammunition, and small arms and ammunition in small quantity."[89]

Ramseur was recalled from pursuit. Doles's brigade was placed in Martinsburg as a provost guard. Officers went to work rooting out the Union soldiers hiding in the houses in Martinsburg.[90]

By nightfall, Rodes was in Martinsburg, 35 miles north of Winchester, and just 15 miles south of the Potomac. Jenkins was given orders to proceed next morning to Chambersburg.

What kind of man was Robert Rodes, the officer who captured Martinsburg? A native of Lynchburg, Rodes was a graduate of Virginia Military Institute, and taught mathematics at his alma mater for two years following graduation. Then he was chief engineer of an Alabama railroad. His military competence was noted by Jackson and Lee and he rose rapidly in rank. His bravery at First Manassas won him a general's star. Severely wounded at Seven Pines, Rodes recovered and was outstanding in the Maryland campaign. At Chancellorsville he was promoted to major general after leading Jackson's flank attack. Only thirty-four years old in June of '63, Rodes met an early death at Winchester on September 19, 1864.

On Saturday evening, Chambersburg was thrown into "a state of great excitement" by the rumor that "the Confederates were approaching." By evening of the next day, the report reached town "that disaster had fallen upon the Union troops at Winchester." Excitement and confusion followed. People left home and headed for their stores and places of business. Even though it was Sunday, there was work to do. Jacob Hoke's firm boxed and shipped part of its stock to Philadelphia. The rest was taken to the Pennsylvania countryside to be hidden on farms. Part was secreted in a fireproof beer vault under an adjoining building. The bank officials and those in charge of the Franklin County Court House packed and hauled precious records away. The railroad brought in all available equipment to begin rail shipment on Monday.[91]

General Jenkins, commanding the advance of the Confederate cavalry, was up early Monday morning. The troopers were routed from their sleep at 2:00 A.M. by the sounds of reveille. Riding from near Martinsburg, he crossed the Potomac into Williamsport, Maryland, meeting no opposition.

Surprisingly, the people of the canal town were happy to see him. The residents set up tables in the streets and filled them with milk, bread, and meat. This was much better than army food.[92]

Jenkins found the people in Hagerstown very cordial also. Perhaps it was a minority of Southern sympathizers making their appearance felt, because later when the infantry passed through town they felt their reception was cold. But ladies and children cheered the cavalrymen. All in all, it was a gay welcome.

Pandemonium prevailed in Pennsylvania. Roads leading to Harrisburg and other points north were choked with wagons and carts of all kinds. Former slaves, fearful of being carried back to the South, were in full flight. Men and women packed what they could carry or haul and fled. Some farmers were driving their cows, horses and sheep northward. Train stations were jammed. Many stores, shops and businesses were closed. War was coming home and the folks did not like it. They were terrified.

Jacob Hoke in *The Great Invasion* and Nye in *Here Come the Rebels!* depict the anxiety of these days. Many were glad to see the Confederates come into Chambersburg. They felt the gray-clad troopers would be able to restore order.[93]

The Rebel column was led by thirty-two-year-old Alfred Jenkins, a graduate of Jefferson College in Canonsburg, Pennsylvania, and Harvard University. Despite his youth, he had served two years in the United States Congress prior to the war.[94]

The Confederate cavalry camped on the grounds of Alexander K. McClure, later editor of the *Philadelphia Times*. Mrs. McClure cooked up a large meal for the officers. But they went scouting and gathering up meat on the hoof.[95]

The *Richmond Examiner* was upset over Jenkins's easy-going and softhearted tactics. The media expected the troopers to make the people in Pennsylvania suffer as the folks in Virginia suffered. The newspaper wanted to see Franklin County burned and devastated. But Lee on moral and psychological grounds did not follow this method of warfare.[96]

To meet the crises caused by the Confederate invasion, President Abraham Lincoln issued a call for 100,000 State Militia. His request stated:[97]

The President's proclamation is as follows: "Whereas, the armed insurrectionary combinations now existing in several states are threatening to make inroads into the states of Maryland, Western Virginia, Pennsylvania and Ohio, requiring immediately an additional military force for the service of the United States.

"Now therefore, I, Abraham Lincoln, president of the United States, and Commander-in-Chief of the Army and Navy thereof, and of the militia of the several states when called into actual service, do hereby call into the service of the United States 100,000 militia from the States following, viz:

"From the state of Maryland, 10,000; from the state of Pennsylvania, 50,000; from the state of Ohio, 30,000; from the state of West Virginia, 10,000, to be mustered into the service of the United States forthwith; to serve for the period of six months from the date of such muster into said service, unless sooner discharged; to be mustered in as infantry, artillery and cavalry, in proportions which will be made known through the War Department, which department will also designate the several places of rendezvous."[98]

Charles Carleton Coffin arrived in Harrisburg on June 15.

The city was a bedlam. A great crowd of people—excited men, women, wringing their hands, and children crying, all with big bundles—were at the railroad station, ready to jump into the cars to escape northward or eastward. Merchants were packing up their goods. There was a great pile of trunks and boxes. Teams loaded with furniture, beds, and clothing rumbled through the streets; wagons were crossing the bridge over the Susquehanna; farmers from the beautiful Cumberland Valley were hurrying their cattle, horses, sheep, and pigs in droves across the river. The railroads were removing all their cars and engines; housewives secreting their silver spoons and candlesticks. The excitement was very wild when a long train of army wagons came thundering across the long bridge driven by teamsters covered with dust—a portion of the train which Milroy had sent from Winchester—all hurrying as if the Confederates were close upon them. The next morning some of the militia began to arrive—farmers and their sons, clerks from the stores in citizens' dress. It was very laughable to see men wearing long linen coats—"dusters" and "stove-pipe" hats, armed with old muskets, mounted as cavalrymen, riding pell-mell through the streets. Hundreds of men were at work throwing up intrenchments.[99]

Coffin left Harrisburg to visit Baltimore. There he found General Schenck in command of the defense of the city.

Large numbers of blacks were at work "building breastworks and barricades on the roads west of the city, using hogsheads of tobacco, filling barrels with earth, piling up old wagons, carts, and boxes; cutting down trees, and placing them in front of the breastworks." Heavy guns were placed on the nearby hills commanding the approaches. Then workers were singing as they shoveled and pounded the earth into place with their mallets.[100]

Charles Coffin was the Ernie Pyle of his day. Strangely little has been written about him. His one biographer calls him "a soldier of the pen and knight of the truth."

Tall and well built, Coffin had blue eyes, and a keen sense of humor. Born and raised in the hills of New Hampshire, Coffin became editor of one of Boston's leading newspapers, a poet, musician, traveler, and journalist.[101]

Born on July 26, 1823, Coffin obtained his education from the famed "New England *Primer*." Leaving home and going to Boston, he was engaged in surveying for a new road, when he received a serious injury. A careless man chopped into his left ankle. The injury kept him from combat in the Civil War.

In the mid-1850s he made his first visit to Washington, D.C., and lamented the fact that he could not find a decent hotel in the entire city. Always a student of great orators, he went to the capitol and listened to the speeches of the senators. He was most impressed with Thomas Benton of Missouri and Robert Toombs of Georgia.

Then it was on to Chicago, a bustling city of 25,000 residents, with mud knee deep in the streets and roads. He attended the Republican Convention in 1860 and watched the proceedings leading up to the nomination of Abraham Lincoln. Coffin also went with the committee to Springfield to tell Lincoln of the nomination. Charles found the two little Lincoln boys on the front yard fence.

When the war broke out, and being unfit for military service, Coffin turned to an old-time friend and did the next best thing. Senator Wilson helped him to become a war correspondent. He talked to generals, privates, and the folks in the war-torn areas. The *Boston Journal* was so impressed with his coverage of First Bull Run that they hired him for the grand sum of twenty-five dollars per week. He was the only writer to serve continuously throughout the Civil War.

In addition to visiting Harrisburg and Baltimore, Coffin was in Frederick when the Army of the Potomac came through. He was present at the change of command. He rode with Hancock and Sykes and members of the Second and Fifth corps on the Roads to Gettysburg. He witnessed Pickett's Charge, and after Gettysburg, Coffin rode twenty-eight miles in a driving rain to file his news story.

He took a brief rest after Gettysburg, and then rejoined the Army of the Potomac. He and U. S. Grant were very close friends. Grant trusted him and allowed him privileges he accorded to few others.

With his sense of history, he had the knack of being in the right place at the right time. Coffin witnessed the raising of the Stars and Stripes over Fort Sumter after an absence of four years. And he was in Richmond as it burned on April 3. He met President Lincoln in the streets of the city.

After the war he traveled around the world and wrote several books, most of them running in series. These included *My Days and Nights on the Battlefield, Following the Flag, Marching to Victory, Drumbeat of the Nation,* and others. Included with his writings were more than two thousand public addresses in the years from 1865 to 1895.

Jacob Hoke looked at Winchester in a philosophical manner. He felt that had Milroy been given an additional twenty-four hours' warning, and fallen back to Harpers Ferry, then disaster at Winchester would never have happened. But the detention of the Rebels around Winchester, "sent a note of warning throughout the entire North, and afford time to raise troops and organize them for effective resistance."[102]

Monday afternoon, Jubal Early moved his division three miles north of town, across the road from the J. Rutherford farmhouse. Here two fine ponds furnished water. Ed Johnson was encamped on the battlefield at Stephenson's Depot. Monday evening a flag raising ceremony was held at Milroy's main fort. A new name was given to the place, Fort Jackson. The ladies and some others wanted Ewell to make a speech but he begged off. Then they turned their attention to Jubal Early. But he fumed and fussed and also declined the invitation.

Ewell asked A. S. "Sandie" Pendleton to prepare a message of congratulations for the troops. General Orders No. 44 read:

> The lieutenant general commanding asks the men and officers of the corps to unite with him in returning thanks to our Heavenly Father for the signal success which has crowned the valor of this command.
>
> In acknowledgment of Divine favor, chaplains will hold religious services in their respective regiments at such time as may be most convenient.
>
> With wonderfully small loss (less than 300 killed, wounded, and missing), we have carried strong works defended by an abundance of superior artillery, capturing over 3,000 prisoners and large quantities of military stores and supplies. Such a result should strengthen the reliance in the righteousness of our cause, which has inspired every effort of our troops.[103]

No wonder they felt that "another Jackson had come." Ewell even sounded like Jackson. However, we must remember that "Sandie" Pendleton wrote orders and messages for Jackson and now had the same task with Ewell. So perhaps some of the wording came from Parson Nelson Pendleton's son.

Some of the victorious Confederates rode into Winchester. Henry Kyd Douglas and "Sandie" Pendleton, both former members of "Stonewall" Jackson's staff, describe their visits:

> I found that the great joy of the people of that faithful town at their release was clouded by their grief at the death of General Jackson; every citizen of the town mourned as for a great personal bereavement. When I left the town I wore a new Confederate cap which a lady had made me during the occupancy of the "Yankees." But a new hat for me always foreboded disaster in the next battle, and I was not mistaken in supposing it would be so again.[104]

"Sandie" Pendleton found the town rejoicing, but its joy toned down by Jackson's death. Writing to his beloved Kate, he said, "If the spirits disembodied can see what goes on in this world, I am sure that General Jackson has felt unfeigned pleasure since yesterday. 'Twas a sight worth seeing, the joy

86

of the good people of Winchester as our men passed by yesterday at daylight. Old men and maidens vied with each other in demonstrations almost frantic."[105]

Douglas and "Sandie" were in Winchester on Monday, but the letter to Kate was written on Tuesday. "Sandie" asked some young ladies to take two captured Union flags and make a set of C.S.A. colors to fly over Fort Jackson, the new name given to the captured Union fort. "Sandie" repaid them by giving them quantities of ladies' shoes seized from sutlers' stores. He also sent some new shoes to his sisters in Lexington.[106]

Robert Rodes allowed his tired men to rest in and around Martinsburg until 10:00 A.M. on Monday. At that time he received dispatches with the news of the victory at Winchester. He also learned that the shattered remanents of Milroy's command was at Smithfield, heading for Harpers Ferry. Leaving Colonel Lightfoot with the Sixth Alabama to guard Martinsburg, Rodes put the division in motion for Williamsport, Maryland. The pioneers of the division were left behind to continue the destruction of railroad property.[107]

It was dark when Rodes arrived at Williamsport. He tells us that it was the most trying march his command had experienced, due to intense heat, the character of the road, and the increasing amount of barefooted men in his division.[108]

Ramseur's, Iverson's, and Doles's brigades, along with three batteries of artillery, were ordered to cross the Potomac at once. The troops had begun to show signs of extreme fatigue. After all, it's a long way from Fredericksburg, across the state to Virginia and north to Williamsport. It is worse yet when the mode of travel is on foot. Rodes was worried. Therefore, a halt was absolutely necessary. Many tramped the road that day from Martinsburg to Williamsport with bruised, swollen and bloody feet. Rodes felt that none but the best of soldiers could have endured such hardship. He felt they all deserved to be called heroes. A guard was placed over the town.[109] And Robert Rodes and his Confederate command spent the next three days in Williamsport. We wonder where the General had his headquarters. This was Monday night, June 15, in

Robert Rodes led the Confederate infantry across the
Potomac at Williamsport.

the Maryland canal town. Confederate infantry were once again across the Potomac River.

The ferry at Williamsport was not operating. But Rodes had Lee's pontoon train. It had been sent by rail from Orange Court House to Culpeper. From there the infantry took it to Front Royal. Then the train was placed with Robert Rodes. So he took it to the Potomac and placed it in operation. Ramseur, Doles, and Iverson marched across and camped in a meadow on the outskirts of town. Daniel and O'Neal remained on the West Virginia shore to guard the approaches to the bridge. There are numerous mentions of the bridge. It was used more for the artillery, wagons, and ambulances than the infantry. Cattle from Pennsylvania were also driven across on it.

Hill's Third Corps was also on the road. Richard H. Anderson, commanding the First Division, moved from the Chancellorsville Battlefield to within four miles of Stevensburg. They were detained for two hours clearing away obstructions leading to the ford on the Rapidan.

The South Carolina troops in Dorsey Pender's division moved up the river, following the plank road between Fredericksburg and Orange Court House. This was the last division of the Army of Northern Virginia to leave the Fredericksburg area. After leaving Chancellorsville, McGowan's brigade turned almost "due west and crossed the Rapidan at Ely's Ford," bivouacking on the hills just west of the river.[110]

Hood's division stayed at Cedar Run but one day, then it was back on the Roads to Gettysburg. Under a blazing sun, the Texans headed north on the east side of the Blue Ridge Mountains toward Ashby Gap. John C. West says the march was conducted "by that unmerciful driver, our beloved General Hood, who simply strikes a trot and is satisfied that the Texas Brigade will at least camp with him at nightfall." Hood must have gone at a good trot, for the men covered twenty-five miles this very hot day. They reached Gaines' Crossroads but paid a dear price. Two hundred men collapsed from sunstroke, five hundred from exhaustion. Several died. One account says fifteen.

On this Monday, Joseph Hooker moved his headquarters

89

from Dumfries to Fairfax Station. The Sixth Corps continued their march which had started the previous evening from Stafford Court House about daybreak to Dumfries, and the Second Corps completed the march it had begun the night before.

The First and Third corps took some time to rest. While Meade and the Fifth Corps marched from Catlett's Station via Bristoe Station to Manassas Junction, Howard's Eleventh Corps arrived at Centreville while the Twelfth tramped from Dumfries to Fairfax Court House.

The Sixth Corps halted briefly at Stafford Court House about daybreak, but the halt was brief. Soon the command was given, "fall in." The soldiers learned to hate that order during the days they tramped on the Roads to Gettysburg. "An all-day march was the next scene in the tragedy of the campaign." Lieutenant Bicknell reports that blistered feet were common as were sunstrokes. The latter put many men out of commission for a long time.[111]

The Second Corps, when it arrived in Stafford Court House, found the place in flames. Frustrated stragglers were thought to have started it. The column halted for two or three hours, before pushing on to Aquia Creek. The day was extremely hot, and the march on dusty roads "proved most fatiguing."[112] Hundreds in the Second Corps fell out. Division commanders reported numerous cases of sunstroke. All the ambulances were brought into service to bring those who could no longer walk to their units. Once they reached their bivouac area, the men were rudely awakened at midnight by a stampede of mules. At first the trouble was blamed on the guerrillas. But the culprit was a soldier yelling in a nightmare and passing his terror on to the poor mules.[113]

In early June, the men of the 106th Pennsylvania, amused themselves in their campsite by stuffing old clothing and setting up dummy guards. From a distance they looked real, and brought many a laugh as those who fixed them watched the reactions of those who came upon the make-believe sentinels.

The fun ended for the 106th on the fourteenth of June. Joseph Ward tells us how it was:

After tattoo or about 9 o'clock, we were ordered in line and soon started. We had gone only about three miles and got safely across a large swamp, wetting ourselves almost to the knees, when we were ordered back to camp, where we arrived about 11 o'clock and told to rest. So, wet as we were, we were soon asleep, but not long to remain so, as at 3 o'clock we were awakened and again ordered in line, and went as far as Division Headquarters, were halted again and kept there until after daylight; we then started in earnest and pushed on rapidly, arriving at Stafford Court House about 10 o'clock, having made ten miles; we halted about an hour and a half and then continued our march. The weather then became very warm, the sun so hot that a great many of the men were sunstruck, and nearly one half of the men gave out, causing heavy straggling, so that when we crossed the Chopawamsic near Aquia Creek, and went into camp about a mile beyond, we had marched about eighteen miles, and there was only about one half of each command present. It was one of the hottest days we had experienced, and then being loaded down with our full accoutrements and three days' rations, and extra ammunition, the men could hardly get along. Over 500 in our Corps alone were sunstruck or overcome with the heat, some dropping in the ranks as they marched along. The writer was one of them; without a moment's notice as he was marching at the head of the Regiment, he dropped in his tracks as though shot down, and unconscious was lifted to one side of the road, placed in the shade, and left, how long he remained there he knew not, but late in the afternoon he regained consciousness and realized his danger of capture, as not a vestige of our troops were in sight, so gathering up his remaining strength he started after the retreating column. Just before dark he reached the Chopawamsic creek and halted long enough to take a good bath, which cooled his heated body and greatly benefited him, so that he continued his lonely march greatly improved. He did not see one of his comrades from the time he dropped in the ranks, until about dark when he caught up with the rear of the army, and about 9 o'clock reached the camp of his regiment and was soon asleep.[114]

Tully McCrea went to West Point from a small Ohio town. For a time he roomed with George A. Custer. After graduating from the military academy in 1862 he joined the Army of the Potomac. June of 1863 found him a young lieutenant with the Fourth Artillery, attached to the Second Corps. Since 1858 when he entered the academy, Tully wrote frequently to a young girl friend, Belle, back home. He continued to write on the Roads to Gettysburg. Writing to Belle on June 15, describing the beginning of the journey, he said:

91

We left Falmouth at sunrise on Monday expecting the Rebs to cross over (the Rappahannock) and follow us up. They did not molest us. . . . Monday's and Tuesday's marches were the hardest I have yet seen. The sun was oppressively hot and the dust was perfectly suffocating. The infantry particularly suffered. A great many died in the road with sunstroke. The ambulance was unable to carry all those that gave out. A great many had to be left on the road, and at night when we got into camp the ambulances were unloaded and sent back again.[115]

Dense woods and thickets of jack pine with scrub oak with occasional clearings, poor roads, and old tumbledown houses, describe "the route of Harrow's Brigade on the 15th."[116]

The men in blue crossed Aquia Creek and marched through Stafford Court House, a smoking ruin. The tramp continued for another six miles, making nearly twenty for the day. The "intense heat and clouds of dust . . . made it one of the most trying days in the whole summer's campaign."[117]

New overcoats, blankets, and changes of underwear were discarded by the side of the road. This was done even though the men didn't know how soon they would need the thrown away items. But when the limits of human endurance are reached, things are thrown away to make the step lighter.[118]

The soldiers of the 140th Pennsylvania, found the fifteenth to be "severely hot, and the march to be the most trying and fatiguing yet experienced. All available ambulances were filled by those unable to walk. . . . The surgeons reported the deaths of fifteen men who had fallen in their tracks from fatigue or sunstroke."[119]

The United States Regulars and the volunteer troops under George Meade covered another twenty miles on this hot Monday. It was a fatiguing march from Catlett's Station to the Plains of Manassas. During the day, the men observed the graves of many of their comrades who had fallen at the battles of Bull Run. Most of the graves were unmarked, and in some instances the "bleached bones of the slain were exposed . . . the weather and the rain having . . . washed away the mounds" of dirt. This was "certainly not a cheerful or encouraging sight to behold."[120] Perhaps the men in blue wondered if a similar fate awaited them at the end of the road. Sadly, many did have a rendezvous with death on up the road at a place called Gettysburg.

The Manassas Junction area had been tramped over, fought over, and camped upon since the summer of 1861. Yet a lot of fences were still standing in June of '63. But they could not withstand the assault of the Fifth Corps. The men had to have their coffee, even in the heat.

The 118th Pennsylvania came upon a spacious mansion, occupied by a single black man who declared his master had set him free and told him to look after the mansion. He begged the men of the Fifth Corps not to take the fence rails. Finally a compromise was reached. The men in blue agreed to take only half a fence rail.[121]

As the dawn broke, the men of the Sixth Corps were near exhaustion. They wanted and needed rest and coffee, but no order was given to halt. Faint and weary with stomachs growling, the men tramped on. The heat became unbearable. Vegetation wilted. Clouds of dust were so thick "that one could not see half the length of a regiment." Men started to fall from exhaustion. Almost every man had a flushed face. Some were panting for breath. The ambulance became full, and those who could no longer march fell by the wayside.[122]

"In every corner of the rail fences, and under every tree and bush, groups of men, with faces glowing with redness, some with streams of perspiration rolling down their cheeks, and others with their red faces dry and feverish strewed the wayside." At one spot was a regimental color bearer, the flag beside him, gasping for breath. At another was a colonel, his horse tied, and the officer using his hat trying to fan a breeze. "Regiments became like companies, and companies lost their identity."[123]

A man can only take so much. Finally at three in the afternoon, the column reached Dumfries. The "tired men, with feet blistered and raw, worn out by seventeen hours' constant march, almost melted and smothered," threw themselves on the ground to rest.[124]

After stumbling along through the night, the Fifteenth New Jersey and other units of the Sixth Corps reached Stafford Court House at sunrise.

Here a halt was ordered. Our regiment came in the road where the dust was inches deep. Muskets were hardly stacked before each man dropped down in his place and was soon asleep. An hour's halt was allowed, when we were ordered to fall in once more, and forced to march ahead. Who can tell what a march it was? None who were on it would ever consent to make it over again. With the previous fatigue, and the dust, and the heat, human nature could not endure it. The men fell out in squads; some fainted, some were sunstruck. The aides came riding back from our division commander, repeating orders to close up the ranks and hurry on the battalions. So the column was forced on and on, until only one man in ten remained with the brigade. There may have been great necessity for haste, but the attempted forced march accomplished nothing. Two miles from Dumfries, General Wright, who was acting under orders to follow the army quickly, was forced to halt, for fear his whole command would leave him. The ambulances were crowded. Stragglers were brought up, forced along at the sword's point. At 6 o'clock, when Dumfries was reached, we stopped for the night. The sleep in a meadow, when the halt had been made, was most delightful, and hot coffee never tasted better.

The marches of the Sixth Corps had been attended with much fatigue on the part of the men. Our brigade formed the rear guard. We witnessed the great extent of property, public and private, that had been destroyed. The corps which had preceded us in the march had been most prodigal. Hundreds of thousands of dollars' worth of property had been destroyed by the flames, or thrown away, to be gathered by the enemy, should they follow. Some of the officers in charge of stores had been most reckless in their waste. Boxes of musket-cartridges and of artillery ammunition were emptied into the streams, to unload the wagons and caissons. We passed some deserted camps where heavy artillery regiments had been posted. Quantities of articles, that would have been luxuries to our men, could they have enjoyed them, were spread on the ground, where they had been abandoned. We were frequently required to burn all property we could, with the view of keeping it from the enemy. All this appeared unseemly and a useless waste of war materials.[125]

About sunrise the Fifth Massachusetts Battery forded the Occoquan River at Wolf Run Shoals. The notes for the day include:

... Halted at 6 o'clock, and unhitched and unharnessed; watered, fed and groomed our horses, made coffee, and rested about an hour. About 9 a.m. hitched up and marched about 3 miles beyond Fairfax Station, and went into park in a large field just at the edge of a fine grove of hard wood, about ¾ of a mile from Fairfax Court House, at 1 p.m. When we arrived we were very dirty, very hungry, and very sleepy. Take it all through it was a pretty good march. We were on the road 44 hours, and marched over 50 miles without sleep or rest of any account. Some of the men went to sleep on horseback, and one sergeant rode quite a distance ahead of the Battery, fast asleep.

On this march, Major McGilvery's wagon got stuck in a mud hole the other side of Dumfries, and the driver got discouraged and left it, reporting to the Major on his arrival in camp. The Major sent back after it, but as several thousand infantry had passed over the same road, nothing was left but a drowned mule and a few fragmentary evidences of the contents. By this accident the Major lost his trunk, clothing, papers, tents, mess stuff, and was in a very destitute condition. On the morning after we reached Fairfax Court House, Captain Phillips found him breakfasting off hard bread and coffee, and insisted on giving him something better, which he was fortunately able to do, as his larder was pretty well stocked.

The night of the 15th all had a good night's rest.[126]

Cumberland, Maryland, is also linked with the Gettysburg campaign. It was the objective of General Imboden and his cavalry. The week of June 7-13 was full of anxiety and excitement. Railroad communication with Baltimore ceased on Sunday the fourteenth. Reports coming from the east indicated that Martinsburg had fallen to the Rebels, that Milroy had been soundly defeated at Winchester. By Monday, government officials in Cumberland decided to evacuate the city and take up positions at New Creek. The railroad line was abandoned, and in a short time droves of "horses, trains of heavily loaded wagons, etc., were in motion, bound for New Creek."[127]

Hundreds were also leaving Frederick, and many more preparing to do so. Free blacks, fearful of being captured and taken South by an invading army, jammed the trains for Baltimore or headed for Pennsylvania.[128]

In preparation for things to come, surplus commissary and quartermaster stores were removed from Frederick. All patients in the military hospitals who could be moved were sent elsewhere.

In the meantime, the Seventh Maryland was able to escape from Hagerstown with fifteen wagons full of government supplies. Thus they were kept from the Confederates. The Seventh Maryland occupied Maryland Heights and felt they held an impregnable position.[129]

95

Jacob Englebrecht lived in Frederick for many years. All this time he kept a diary, filling it with items of local interest as well as personal experiences. He notes that on June 15 "general commotion prevailed in Frederick." He counted thirty cars loaded with government supplies leaving town. Englebrecht also says Milroy was in town getting a train for Baltimore.[130]

VI

HOT AND DUSTY DAYS, JUNE 16-23

The news was not good. Winchester had fallen, along with Martinsburg. Confederate horsemen were riding through Washington County, Maryland, and Rebel infantry were pushing on to the Potomac.

East of the Shenandoah Valley, the Union army was forced to take a rest, at least the bulk of it. The men had to have time to rest their weary feet and bodies, and recover from heat fatigue. However, the Second and Sixth corps, being the last to leave the Fredericksburg area, got no such respite. The Second Corps covered the miles from Aquia via Dumfries to Wolf Run Shoals on the Occoquan. "Uncle John" Sedgwick and the Sixth Corps moved from Dumfries to Fairfax Station.

John Reynolds, commanding the First Corps, had his headquarters in Centreville. Many of the soldiers noticed scenes from First and Second Manassas. However, the 150th Pennsylvania was glad to find no remains of the stench of death on the battlefield. The regiment camped near two beautiful springs. After three days of marching in terrible heat, it seemed like paradise. The water was more precious than gold. After a few hours of rest, the men were ordered to prepare for a dress parade. And at 5:00 P.M. they marched by with polished shoes and glittering arms, and performed the manual of arms for a large crowd of spectators.[1] This was one of the few dress parades on the Roads to Gettysburg. There simply was not time or energy for that sort of thing. The glory of soldiering had to yield to marching and searching for the

97

enemy, in this case a bold opponent who had stolen a march on the men in blue.

Today the regimental sutler arrived in the Thirteenth Massachusetts area. Those who had money or credit "proceeded at once to fill the aching void caused by short rations and hard work."[2]

That evening the band from the Thirty-third Massachusetts came and serenaded the lads from home. Both units wished for some "likker, but there was 'no balm in Gilead.' "[3]

This was the day a nickname was given to the new commander of the First Brigade of the Second Division of the First Corps. The men gave the title of "Apostle" to their leader, Gabriel R. Paul.[4]

The new brigade commander was the grandson of a Napoleonic officer "who is said to have built the first house in St. Louis."[5] "Gabe" graduated from West Point and was given a sword by the citizens of Saint Louis for his bravery in the Mexican War. Then he served as inspector general of the Department of New Mexico. At Fredericksburg he commanded four New York regiments in Doubleday's division. At Chancellorsville he commanded five New Jersey regiments. His new command consisted of the 16th Maine, 13th Massachusetts, 94th and 104th New York, and the 107th Pennsylvania.

Like some others who received promotions and new commands on the Roads to Gettysburg, Paul had a short time to be with his new unit. At Gettysburg, a rifle ball entered his right temple, passed out his left eye, and left him totally blind. His hearing and sense of smell were also greatly impaired.

The Second Corps was back on the road today. Like Monday, the march was one of great effort and fatigue. Many were felled by sunstroke.

The First Delaware halted to replenish its haversacks. Camp was made on the banks of the Occoquan Creek. The march to the stream "proved very exhausting, owing to the intense heat, the long continued drought, and the suffocating dust. The energies of the men gave way before noon each day under the accumulation of this evil."[6]

It seemed as though the provost guard brought in more stragglers than those who limped in with the colors. The most welcome of all commands was "Break ranks, march."[7]

Joseph Ward and the 106th Pennsylvania started the day at 2:00 A.M. They covered nine miles by 7:00, stopping for breakfast in Dumfries. Then it was back in line for the march to the Occoquan at Wolf Run Shoals. Ward says, "It was another very hot day, and large numbers of men were overcome by the heat. . . . When we arrived at the Occoquan Creek nearly all took advantage of the fine opportunity for a bath and a swim."[8]

The Fourth Ohio found the march to be a terrible experience. "Clouds of dust arose; the heat was stifling and oppressive; clothing and blankets were thrown away." News reached the sweating Union soldiers that Ewell was in Chambersburg, and that the Pennsylvania Home Guards had been called out. This was greeted by "Bully for the Home Guards, Bully for Lee."[9]

The subject of the draft and its merits came up in the different Union camps today. Charles Wainwright thought the bounty system was all wrong, whereas drafting was the fairest and cheapest way of getting soldiers. Recruits just were not coming in, and some feared that the War Department might try to raise new regiments instead of filling up the old ones.

The Fourth Ohio also had trouble with the guerrillas. These partisan soldiers hung around the flank of the army seeking whom they could devour. They culled men, material and horses. Anyone who strayed or did not keep up with the column was in grave danger.[10]

The Nineteenth Maine marched twenty miles today, crossing Quantico Creek, passing near Purcell's Mills, continuing through Dumfries to a spot near the Occoquan River. John Smith says, "here we found the first good water since leaving the Rappahannock."[11]

As soon as the order to make camp was given, the men of the 140th Pennsylvania rushed to the stream. "How refreshing it was to plunge into the clear flood of running water after the days march under a burning sun amid the ever present clouds of dust."[12]

The Fifth Massachusetts Battery, part of the Reserve Artillery,

> ...rested in camp all day. At night shelter tents were issued to the men. Inspection of the Battery at 6 p.m. in light marching order by Major McGilvery. News came that the rebels were in Chambersburg. The Rappahannock evacuated. Roll call in the evening at 8 o'clock. Turned out at 9 p.m. Drew two days' rations of coffee, salt pork and bread, and strapped on 4 bags of grain to each caisson and two to each gun, at ½ past 9 p.m., to be ready to march the next day; then turned in again.[13]

The Second Corps resumed their march on the sixteenth. Like the march on Monday, it was one of great effort and fatigue. Quite a few were felled by sunstroke.

The men of the Second New Hampshire, part of the Third Corps, rested from the ordeal of the previous night. They had taken up arms at sunset, but did not hit the road until about 10:00 P.M. In the darkness of the night they were headed for Warrenton Junction. Martin Haynes describes the night:

> Much of the march was along a railroad track, with the unceasing tramp, tramp, tramp of feet. Added to the noise was the clatter of tin cups against bayonets and canteens. At one point this frightened the horses belonging to one of the artillery batteries. The poor animals dashed into the marching columns of infantry. It was everyman for himself. Many headed for the ditches or where ever they could find cover. Some were hurt rather badly though. Officers feared the commotion might waken not only the dead, but any nearby Confederates. The stampede spread from company to company and created havoc in the ranks.[14]
>
> When things quieted down, the men started the difficult task of looking for lost items, guns, hats, haversacks, rations, etc. Alas, many had no luck. And relic hunters had a field day in years to come as they covered the area of the great stampede.[15]

The Fifth Corps spent the sixteenth "halted and resting at Manassas," on the site of the first Battle of Bull Run. The men in blue noticed the Confederate graves. The ground was quite bare.[16]

Near Manassas, George Meade wrote a letter stating, "I think Lee has made a mistake going into Maryland before meeting our army. I hope his movement will arouse the

100

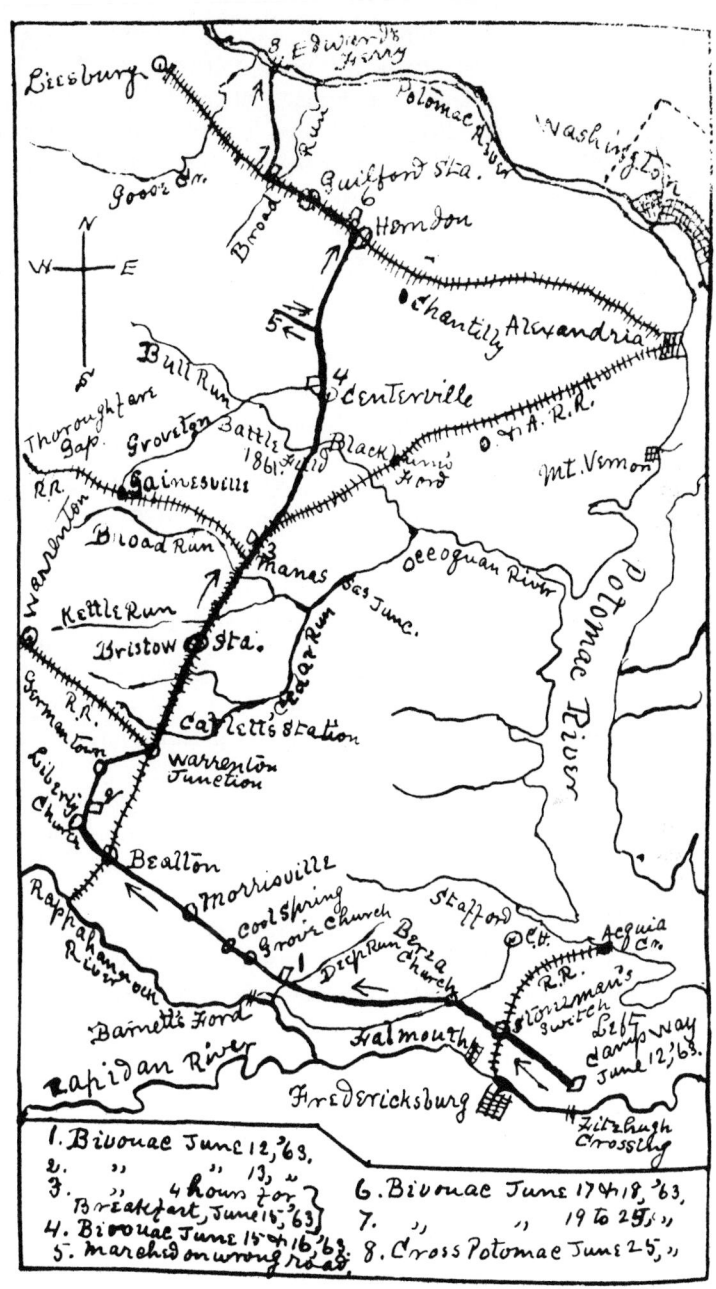

The Union First Corps advances. From
Curtis, *The Twenty-fourth Michigan.*

101

North, and that now men enough will be turned out, not only to drive him back, but to follow and crush him."[17]

We look briefly at the achievements of the Sixth Corps for this Tuesday. James Bowen of the Thirty-seventh Massachusetts tells us that the sun rose as a great ball of fire, bringing a very sultry day. Soon the mud was dried and baked like a great cake. Then it crumbled and suffocating clouds of dust arose. It was like "a choking cloud" settling on every perspiring face and hand. "It penetrated everywhere—eyes, nose, mouth and lungs, all were filled; thirst became intolerable, but water was not to be had. . . ."

The men of the Greek Cross reached Dumfries at noon and fell down to sleep on a sloping hill. There was no shade. The men tried to sleep with the sun beating down on their weary bodies. At midnight the march was resumed, with a brief halt before dawn for coffee. Then it was march, march until noon when finally Wolf Run Shoals on the Occoquan was reached. At this point the column halted for three hours. All the fellows bathed their blistered feet in the cool water.[18] Many jumped in with all their clothes on. Here too were the outer defenses of Washington, garrisoned by Vermont troops. So the men from Massachusetts and the Green Mountain State visited together. Toward evening the Sixth Corps marched a few miles more to Fairfax Station.

Meanwhile, things were bad in Cumberland, Maryland.

On Tuesday there was panic in Cumberland as the news of the fall of Martinsburg reached town. Many folks made hurried preparations to leave town. Stories were told of the destruction of part of the Chesapeake and Ohio Canal. Twenty to fifty thousand Rebels were supposedly invading Pennsylvania. News sources reported Hagerstown and Chambersburg to be occupied. The few Union troops in the area moved on to New Creek, leaving Cumberland virtually defenseless.[19]

Then the folks saw cavalry and artillery drawn up on the hillside. They were not Union men, they were men in gray. A few cannon shots dispersed the meager Union force. Stores were quickly closed and the people went inside. Then two riders in gray rode down Baltimore Street with a flag of truce.

They were met by Acting Mayor Valentine A. Buckey. A short consultation was held. Then the men in gray rode into the streets of Cumberland. Their first task was to round up as many horses as possible. They were not very successful because the resourceful owners had taken them and hidden them on the previous day. The stores and shops were visited next by the Confederate cavalry. Shoes, hats and clothing went quickly. The owners were paid with C.S.A. funds. Naturally they gave a good discount.[20]

The Rebels did not touch the hospitals or the railroad shop. General Imboden himself is said to have put the finishing touches on the destruction of the telegraph office. But otherwise there was little damage and the Confederates behaved as gentlemen. They looked strong and healthy, and left town about 10:30 A.M.

It was also moving day for James Longstreet and the First Corps of the Army of Northern Virginia. As Ewell was putting the finishing touches on the Winchester situation, Longstreet was ordered to move. Lee's order had two purposes: (1) to mislead Hooker, and (2) to protect Hill on his march up the Rappahannock.[21] Therefore, "Old Pete" left Culpeper Court House and advanced along the eastern side of the Blue Ridge Mountains of Virginia, occupying Ashby's and Snicker's gaps. George Pickett and his three brigades of infantry marched with the First Corps. Stuart, with three brigades of cavalry, moved on Longstreet's right, and took position in front of the gaps.[22] Hampton and W. E. Jones remained along the Rappahannock and Hazel rivers, in front of Culpeper. They were to follow A. P. Hill as soon as he passed through.

This day J. B. Kershaw's brigade, part of McLaws's division marched to Sperryville.[23] It was a long day for James Dearing and his artillery brigade. He too marched for Sperryville,[24] and never reached Gaines' Crossroads until 3:00 the next morning. The infantry division to which he was attached had marched by a dirt road. M. W. Henry, commanding another artillery battalion, marched from Culpeper to Little Washington in Rappahannock County. This was a distance of thirty-one miles.[25]

103

Robert E. Lee rode with the First Corps, as did William Nelson Pendleton, commanding the artillery.[26] As the route of the First Corps "lay along the eastern slope of the Blue Ridge, to guard the several passes, . . . its artillery was subjected to serious trial from roads frequently difficult and generally rough, under extreme heat, more than usually long." Most of the First Corps was around Sperryville by nightfall on the sixteenth.[27]

As George Pickett's division started north, Randolph Shotwell hoped that "Stonewall" Jackson's mantle might descend upon Richard S. Ewell. Shotwell realized that "Old Bald Head" had a difficult task, especially in light of the impending invasion. However, the North Carolina soldier hoped that Ewell had served under "the Great Flanker," sufficiently long enough to "get the hang of things!"[28]

On the twenty-sixth, Pickett's division covered twenty miles to Gaines' Crossroads. Shotwell wondered if old Mr. Gaines was a cross man. The young soldier was angry because the roads were not straight. In addition, "our sufferings from heat, dust, and fatigue—and worst of all—lack of drinking water are beyond capacity of tongue or pen to tell."[29]

A few streams crossing the roads helped a little bit. When time permitted, the men sought the source of the water, usually a spring, and surrounded it, struggling to get a few precious drops. Shotwell did not think much of the generals riding in front and sending couriers to the homes to get fresh drinks, when the men in the ranks were "well nigh dead from heat and exhaustion."[30]

Shotwell realized mileage goals were important. But his idea was to move along, take frequent breaks, and take the halts near a spring. Such provisions would have saved a lot of exertion and fatigue. In the evening, the men of George Pickett's command received the joyful news of the fall of Winchester and the utter rout of Robert Milroy.[31]

From his headquarters in Bunker Hill, not far from Ward Hill Lamon's home,[32] Richard S. Ewell sent messages back and forth to his division commanders. Jubal Early was taking care of things in Winchester and sending captured Union prisoners down the valley to Staunton. Robert Rodes was north, across the Potomac in Williamsport, resting and gathering supplies. While Edward Johnson was getting his command on the road to move from Stephenson's Depot to Smithfield, and thence to Shepherdstown to cross the river.

Jacob Hoke tells us what it was like in Chambersburg on June 16:

> Early this morning the Confederates took possession of what is known as Shirk's or Gelsinger's hill. This is a commanding eminence about four miles north of Chambersburg, and on the road leading to Harrisburg. A line of battle was formed along the brow of this hill by a part of the Confederate force, while detachments were sent out in all directions for the purpose of plundering. General Jenkins and staff, after spending the night under the hospitable roof of Colonel McClure, came early in the day into Chambersburg and established his head-quarters at the Montgomery House. One of his first acts was to summon the burgess and town-council to his head-quarters, . . .
>
> General Jenkins also issued an order requiring all arms in possession of our citizens, whether public or private, to be brought to the front of the court-house within two hours; and in case of disobedience all houses were to be searched, and those in which arms were found should be lawful objects of plunder. The pretext for this humiliating order was that his troops had been fired on by a citizen the night before. Many complied with this requisition, and a considerable number of guns, good, bad, and indifferent, were carried to the appointed place, where a committee of our people were ordered to take down the name of each person who brought a gun. This was to secure the houses of all who complied with the order from the threatened search. Some, of course, did not comply, but enough did to satisfy the enemy, and a general search was avoided. Captain Fitzhugh, Jenkins' chief of staff, an ill-natured man—the same person who figured so largely in the burning of the town a year afterward—assorted the guns as they were brought in, retaining those that could be used by their men, and twisting out of shape, or breaking over the stone steps of the court-house, such as were unfit for service.[33]

The Confederate cavalry spent the rest of the day looking for horses, carriages and supplies in Chambersburg. Patrols were sent out ten miles east and west to Caledonia Furnace and Fort Loudon. Many of the horses had already been hidden, but some were found to be sent back to Rodes at Williamsport.

A farmer by the name of Ryder, living in Fort Loudon, thought he would outsmart the Rebels. Hearing that the

Rebels were coming, he took his animals to a large storage room under his barn. The structure was on a slope so the animals entered safely. Then Mr. Ryder piled hay and wood against the entrance seeking to cover it up. But, lo and behold, the Confederates watched all of this with the aid of field glasses. Riding into the farm at the base of the mountains, they ordered the hay removed, and took Mr. Ryder's animals. Thus all his hard work was for nothing.

Confederate cavalry also chased some blacks. Many fled into the fields and jumped up terrified when the Rebel riders drew near. These poor, unfortunate souls were rounded up and sent back to Virginia. A lot of them were free at the time, and even the Confederate officers regretted the experience. There are questions as to the identity of the men engaged in this work. It may have been Jenkins, McNeill's Rangers, or a group of renegades.

Today government wagons and soldiers arrived in Carlisle, increasing the anxiety and tension brought about by the fall of Winchester. Most of the people felt little fear, however. They thought it was just another of Jeb Stuart's antics, a raid like the one in the fall of '62. But different merchants and tradesmen started taking precautionary measures. Some of their best goods were packed and started northward.[34]

A. P. Hill's Third Corps was still in the rear of the Army of Northern Virginia. McGowans's brigade and other units had spent Monday night camped on the hills overlooking Ely's Ford on the Rapidan. On this extremely hot Tuesday they marched to Stevensburg. "The weather was intensely hot and close, and it was with difficulty that the men, fresh from camp, and burdened with unnecessary baggage could be kept up."[35]

Dick Anderson's division marched to Culpeper Court House. This area was home to Ambrose Powell Hill. But this time he was not there on a social visit. He was treading the Roads to Gettysburg.

June 17

Between the two armies were the mountains and the lovely, fertile area known as Loudoun County, Virginia. Much of

106

Gum Springs.

it has changed little since the days of 1863. However, the urban sprawl is reaching out to it.

In the 1700s this virgin wilderness was a part of Prince William County. The cavalier landowners came in from the south and east. Their beautiful plantations can still be seen along Routes 7 and 15, and in many other places in Loudoun County. But others came, the Germans and Quakers and built small family farms and homes. It's a real delight to visit Hillsboro, Waterford, Lovettsville, Leesburg, Aldie, Middleburg, Upperville, and Purcellville.

Eventually there were enough folks to create a new county, and the area was named after John Campbell, Earl of Loudoun, who served briefly as commander in chief of British forces in America.

We hope the reader will want to trace the routes of the Blue and the Gray on the Roads to Gettysburg. Take the time to visit Waterford, a restored Quaker village. It is beautiful. North of the village is Lovettsville, one of Virginia's richest farming areas. Southwest of Leesburg is Middleburg, midway between Winchester and Alexandria. It is the center of Loudoun County horse country. The late President John F. Kennedy had a retreat in the hills near Middleburg. The village, along with Aldie to the east, was the scene of John Mosby's raids and forays. The Aldie Mill goes back to 1807 and remained in operation until just recently.

In Upperville, west of Middleburg, is Trinity Episcopal Church, a gift of Mr. and Mrs. Paul Mellon to the congregation of Mead Parish.[36]

East of Leesburg is Dulles Airport, and Belmont Plantation. The land of the estate was once owned by Francis Lightfoot Lee for whom Leesburg was named.

In Leesburg itself is Courthouse Square. The first building was erected in 1758. Here James Monroe presided as a justice and Patrick Henry spoke with his usual brilliance in behalf of a client. A Confederate monument stands in the courtyard. An old log museum is located on West Loudoun Street, and the earliest known United Methodist property can be found at the corner of Cornwall and Liberty streets.

Nearby is White's Ferry, the last ferryboat still operating
108

on the Potomac River. High on a hill overlooking the Potomac is Ball's Bluff National Cemetery, the resting place for the Union soldiers killed in action at the bluff.

Just as Hagerstown, Maryland, became the objective point of the Army of Northern Virginia, once across the Potomac River, so Loudoun County and the courthouse town of Leesburg became the base of operations for the Army of the Potomac from June 17-26. Leesburg and Edwards Ferry became very important as Hooker tried to stay between Lee and Washington.

On June 17, John Reynolds and the First Corps covered eighteen hot, dusty miles from Manassas Junction to Herndon Station. On the nineteenth, the First Corps moved to Guilford, modern-day Sterling, and stayed there until June 25. The march was a short three miles. Thus the First Corps was east of Leesburg.[37]

Henry Warner Slocum and the Twelfth Corps marched from Fairfax Court House to Dranesville, and the following day came into Leesburg, staying in the area until Friday, June 26.[38]

Meade and the Fifth Corps traveled from Manassas Junction to Gum Springs on the seventeenth, and two days later moved to Aldie, the picturesque village on modern-day Route 50. Units of the corps to Middleburg and Upperville to support the cavalry prior to heading for the Potomac on June 26.

Howard's Eleventh Corps arrived in Loudoun County on June 17 from Centreville. Their area was at Trappe Rock on Goose Creek, southeast of Leesburg.[39]

The Third Corps moved from Centreville to Gum Springs on June 19 and remained in the area until ordered to cross the Potomac.[40]

The Second Corps moved through Loudoun County to support the cavalry at Thoroughfare Gap, then returned to Gum Springs, and took a country road to the Potomac.[41]

Joe Hooker and John Reynolds believed in early starts. This way the men could cover quite a few miles before the sun produced the high temperatures. So at 2:00 A.M. on

109

June 17 reveille was sounded. And by four o'clock the columns of the First Corps were under way.

It was a good thing the march was begun early, because according to some accounts the temperature climbed to 101 degrees. A short halt was made at Guilford Station. Then it was on to Leesburg. During the morning two clerks from a brigade commissary fell into the hands of Mosby's Rangers. In fact, the First Corps entered the streets of historic Leesburg just as Mosby's men were leaving. The guerrillas seemed as thick as blackberries.

Charles Wainwright and the artillery of the First Corps covered fourteen miles today, to a spot on the Loudoun and Hampshire Railroad. It was not a long march but most fatiguing. The commander had never seen so many men played out. They passed through the Chantilly Battlefield in the process. The air was hot and close. For two miles through a woods it was almost intolerable. Some of the officers finally rode out for breath. "The sides of the roads were lined with men who had dropped from exhaustion. There must have been near a thousand of them, many of whom had fainted entirely away."

With the dawn of June 17, the Twenty-fourth Michigan was ordered to move with other units of the Union First Corps toward Leesburg. The day was very hot and humid. The sun seemed like a blazing red ball. It was hot enough to make vegetation and the men in the ranks wilt under its power. To make matters worse, the regiment marched two miles, only to discover they were going in the wrong direction. So they had to do an about face and retrace their steps over the dusty road. Griping seemed to make the men feel better. It always does in the military. Early in the afternoon the men from Michigan reached several springs near Herndon. The sight of water was almost too good to be true. Then men fell out of line for a cool drink. Water was splashed over the face, neck and arms. The springs were like an oasis in a desert.[42]

Somewhere along the line, some of the soldiers left the route of march and obtained a couple of geese. One of the men came up with a rather unique method of carrying the geese until suppertime. A young drummer was called, and requested to take the top off the drum. Then the geese were placed inside. Soon Colonel Morrow rode up and wanted to know why the drum was not being beaten.

"Colonel, Sir," replied the young drummer boy, "I must tell you something."

Colonel Morrow leaned over and said, "Well, what is it?"

"Sir, I have a couple of geese in here."

The commander informed the young man he did not have to play any more that day. When bivouac was made that evening, Colonel Morrow, the drummer boy and numerous others feasted on roasted geese.[43]

June 18 the Twenty-fourth Michigan and other troops of the First Corps spent resting. The army command went over intelligence reports and tried to figure Lee's intentions. That same day, other Union Corps moved to positions west and south of Washington.

James Wadsworth was older than most of the men marching on the Roads to Gettysburg. He was fifty-six years old in the summer of '63. Prior to the war he had managed the large family estate in central New York. But in 1861 he offered himself to the Union cause. Although he had no formal military training, his management of men and supplies on the family farm had been excellent preparation to lead soldiers and keep them supplied. For a time Wadsworth was military governor of the District of Columbia. Then influential friends persuaded him to run for governor of New York. He ran but lost. So it was back to the military and in June he was leading the First Division of the First Corps.

On June 17 orders came to move closer to the Potomac River. Part of the route led through a dense "growth of scrub pine which shut out the breeze but not the sun. The heat was intolerable, the dust an enveloping fog." James Wadsworth had a rough day. So did Rufus Dawes commanding the Sixth Wisconsin, he tells us:

> Our march was terribly severe. The sun was like a furnace, and the dust thick and suffocating. Many a poor fellow marched his last day. . . . Several men fell dead on the road.[44]

111

Joe Hooker had given orders that all excess baggage should be discarded. Wadsworth found an ambulance carrying the personal belongings of his officers. "These the old General ordered thrown out, and the ambulance filled with the knapsacks and muskets of the exhausted soldiers. But the papers of the division headquarters were in these valises and all were sought and gathered up during the night."[45]

Some of the members of the First Corps tell their story of June 17. The Seventy-sixth New York found the day "extremely hot." Their march was through "a dense forest of pine shrubs." The pines provided, as others have said, cover from the rays of the hot sun, but prevented any breeze from getting to the men. The roads were filled with wagons, batteries, cavalry, infantry, artillery, all rushing, halting, sweating.

> The dust arose in suffocating clouds, was inhaled at every breath, and settling upon the faces from which the perspiration flowed at every pore, soon rendered the face of the most intimate friend indistinguishable in the surging crowd. Many fell down in the ranks from sun stroke and exhaustion. Even officers fell from their horses from the effects of the suffocating dust and heat.[46]

Major Chamberlain of the 150th Pennsylvania was placed in charge of the pickets of the First Corps for the night. He was instructed to keep a sharp eye for Mosby. Things were quiet until midnight. There was an alarm. Some animal in the bushes refused to give the countersign and hurried off when challenged.[47]

Naturally the heat and forced marches caused a lot of straggling. Winfield Scott Hancock's Second Corps was the last column in the left wing as the Army of the Potomac moved northward from Fredericksburg. Hancock was a good officer. He took great efforts to round up the stragglers. Those who were exhausted from the heat and lack of sleep were placed in ambulances. The cavalry rode back the road to pick up the men.[48] By June 17, most of the Union army was near Centreville where time was given for a brief respite. Then the blessed rains came, settling the dust, and washing it out of the blue uniforms.

Through the seventeenth, Lee had the advantage, and

Hooker's troops the worst of the deal as the Army of the Potomac marched to counter the Confederate thrust. But by June 18, the shoe was on the other foot. To maintain his advantage the Confederates were going to have to be on the move. Actually they too had been covering a lot of ground in the excessive heat. They too had, and would continue to suffer from "heat, dust, and fatigue." But Lee had another problem, lack of drinking water. In two weeks this problem would help to lose Confederate occupation of Little Round Top. There were few streams near the roads in Virginia on the way to the Potomac. When they did come to a farm spring, "there was always a wall of men around it—struggling to dip a cup or canteen into it." The effort to obtain a drink has been told by a Confederate soldier after marching thirty miles:

> (Men were) crowding you at each elbow, stepping on you from behind, and getting in your way in front; like a flock of sheep, frightened and confused—stirring up a tornado of dust, and making one's eyes ache with the constant motion of surrounding figures.[49]

There were no water wagons or lister bags to accompany the men in June of '63. Likewise the soldier had to endure the weight of his gun, knapsack, blanket, bayonet, cartridge and cap boxes, canteen, mess gear and whatever else he may have been carrying. No wonder they were sweaty and weary.

The first day at football camp or the first day at spring training is always rough. So it was on the first day on the Roads to Gettysburg. The men had had it relatively easy from December to June. Now it was back to long marches in very hot weather. There were many stragglers and ambulances were rapidly filled.

Streams were always a welcome sight. At Wolf Run Shoals the Nineteenth Massachusetts "bivouacked in line of battle, facing the shoals." As soon as possible the men were in the water cooling off. They bathed and washed their clothing at the same time. Some of the men found fence rails. These soon became clotheslines or firewood. The night was filled with campfires and men toasting their hardtack and roasting salt pork on ends of ramrods, bayonets or sticks. The troops were always looking for easier ways to boil water for coffee.

Some placed their cups of water on fence rails propped up on tripods. All went well unless the men forgot their cups and rails burned through. Then the cups and contents went into the fire, and somebody had to look for a new cup.[50]

The Second Corps, like the Eleventh, had trouble with Mosby's Rangers. These Confederate daredevils kept up constant harassing tactics. These made the pickets very uneasy. Many a night's sleep was broken by sentries who thought they saw shadows moving in the darkness.[51]

The Fourteenth Connecticut marched to Fairfax Court House. Sergeant Hirst echoes the feelings of others when in the Army of the Potomac when he says:

> It was a terrible day, the weather being hot and saltry. The roads were ground to powder by the thousands of men who preceded us, which made our progress very slow, and strong men wilted down as though blasted by something in the air. Being on the rearguard, I saw several cases of sunstroke. . . .[52]
>
> The men got rid of any item they felt would be unnecessary. . . . It is strange how generous men become on a march. Do you want a pack of cards, a book, a blanket, a pair of drawers, or perhaps an old iron kettle? No. down they go in the road. All along each side of the road are strewn hundreds of blankets, overcoats, and even pants and vests. The various articles are made into piles and burned by the rear-guard.[53]

Such is the waste of war.

Tully McCrea says the infantry was so footsore that the Wednesday march covered for his unit at least, but six miles. Then the corps rested at Fairfax Station until Saturday when it moved to Centreville.[54]

The 140th Pennsylvania noted the exposed graves at Bull Run. Broken equipment, buckles, cartridge boxes, and other military items littered the ground. "Every tree and house in sight was riddled with minie balls or torn and gashed with shot and shell. It was a sad gruesome and never to be forgotten sight."[55]

John Gibbon, like many others during those tragic days, had interests in the North and the South. He was born in Philadelphia, but early in life was taken to Charlotte, North Carolina. In fact, he was appointed to West Point from the Tarheel State. He graduated in 1847 with A. P. Hill and

114

Ambrose Burnside. Like most of the West Pointers he saw service in Mexico, in Florida against the Seminoles, and then returned to the banks of the Hudson as an artillery instructor. His wife was from Baltimore and three of his brothers went with the Confederacy.

But John Gibbon remained loyal to the Union and soon became a brigadier general. He was assigned to the command of some regiments from Wisconsin and Indiana. These fighting soldiers earned the nickname of "The Iron Brigade" at South Mountain. Gibbon showed great gallantry at Antietam, directing the fire of Battery B as it supported the advance of his troops. He was badly wounded at Fredericksburg, and was on the sidelines for three months. When he returned to duty he was given command of the Second Division of the Second Corps.

Gibbon was one of the men selected by General Grant to receive the surrender of Lee's army at Appomattox. After the war he served on the frontier and did a commendable job leading foot soldiers against the Indians.

But on June 17, 1863, John Gibbon was at Wolf Run Shoals expecting a courier to bring new orders at any moment. One gallopped in and handed a packet of dispatches to General Hancock. The commander of the Second Corps read one of them and then called Gibbon. John expected to receive new orders, but he was in for a sad shock.[56] Gibbon relates the tragic moment.

> The despatch announced the death of one of my children and was accompanied by a note from Gen. Seth Williams authorizing my absence from the army for two days. I know nothing sadder, in the midst of blood and suffering and death, with thousands dying in a few hours, than to hear, unexpectedly, of the death of some loved one far away in a quiet home, and yet mine was probably only one of many thousands of such cases occurring during the four long years of our bloody war.
>
> Hastily mounting my horse, I rode to Fairfax Station and getting on an extra engine reached the Relay House that day and Baltimore the next, where, after remaining a day, I started back, reaching Fairfax station once more and rejoining my command at Centreville that night (the 19th).[57]

Manassas—familiar territory.

Writing to a friend on June 17, David Bell Birney said:

> We may be a little late, but I think we will be up in time. The Third Corps, which I now command temporarily, is here and in position from Manassas Gap to Bull Run, covering the roads and the fords to Centreville. Yesterday was a terrible day, hot and dust; men dropped dead by the roadside. I never can forget the scenes of yesterday. The country is barren of good water, and men would gather on the road side, lapping up like dogs anything like liquid. After the column had halted, I rode some twenty miles to get the men in position and provide for their comfort. I assure you my sleep was deep last night. This morning I am again ready for the tramp, though I do not know where and I do not ask. I am satisfied to obey orders promptly, and still have implicit confidence in the ultimate success of the right. I expect General Sickles back in a few days, and will be glad to see him, for the responsibilities of a command like this, to a temporary commander, are very great.[58]

The next day Birney wrote to alleviate the fears of his friends "we ought to bag all those scamps who are threatening an advance on Harrisburg and Philadelphia. . . . The people in Philadelphia are unnecessarily frightened. The army wishes nothing better than to meet General Lee's men.[59]

June 17 found some troops of the Third Corps encamped near Centreville, and the scenes of Second Bull Run. The wind carried the sounds of battle from Aldie. Edwin B. Houghton of the Seventeenth Maine had close friends in the action, members of the First Maine Cavalry.[60]

Houghton found Centreville "in a very dilapidated condition. The houses and grounds bore unmistakable tokens of ravages and desolations of war. It was completely surrounded by every description of defensive works."[61]

About noon, Carr's brigade crossed Bull Run at Blackford's Ford. The men were given a break and en masse headed for the cool waters of the stream. "It was an abolution long to be remembered, and its effect supplemented by a haversack lunch, was so refreshing."[62]

George G. Meade and the Fifth Corps were back on the road on Wednesday. Reveille sounded early. The weather was cooler, but the roads dusty. The Fifth Corps passed through Centreville.

The soldiers were fatigued and broken down by "continuous and rapid marching." The teamsters and wagoneers came to the aid of the men in the ranks, "by permitting them to throw their knapsacks and rifles into the wagons." At the end of the day, the soldiers obtained their equipment at the wagon parks.[63]

The Fifth Corps encamped at Gum Springs east of Goose Creek, four miles from Aldie on the night of June 17. Leesburg was only ten miles away. This was to be home until June 26, as the infantry supported Pleasonton's cavalry which was assigned to protect the flanks of the Army of the Potomac. The troopers were kept busy, but the foot soldiers had good duty picketing and manning lookout stations.

The farms were nice, and the farmers cordial, although they were very emphatic in stating they were loyal to the Confederacy. The men in blue and the Virginia farmers got along well for the next eight days. Company streets were laid off, drills conducted, and spare time spent in reading, playing cards, sight-seeing or picking cherries.[64] The 146th New York was very much impressed with the quiet charm of the countryside near Aldie.

The historian of the 146th tells us:

> The position of the regimental camp was changed from time to time, each successive location affording some advantage over the previous one. We were called upon frequently to leave our camp and prepare to move out to the support of the cavalry, who were fighting almost daily a short distance to the west of us in the numerous gaps of the Blue Ridge. On none of these occasions did we take part in any real fighting. During the time we were not on picket duty or policing the camp we strolled over the surrounding country and helped ourselves as we pleased of the fruit, especially cherries, which grew in the vicinity. Short walks from our camp brought us to several splendid vantage points along the Bull Run Mountains and as we looked over the Loudon Valley, which lay between those mountains and the Blue Ridge, we all admitted that we had never looked down on a scene of greater beauty.[65]

The 118th Pennsylvania describes the suffering of this hot June day:

> On the 17th, at six o'clock in the morning, the column moved on again over the plains of Manassas, passing the Henry House, famous as the spot where the stalwart regular division held the victorious

118

enemy until darkness permitted the withdrawal of the broken and shattered fragments of Pope's disordered battalions—famous, too, in both the Bull Run battles as a point where the struggle waged the fiercest. Torn and shattered by shot and shell, the residence had still an occupant. A citizen, sullen and uncommunicative, stood in the doorway while the troops passed by. The battle-field was yet thickly strewn with leather accoutrements, shoes, canteens, the skins of dead animals, and all sorts of abandoned military property. Then the route lay by the Warrenton Turnpike, over the stone bridge spanning Bull Run, through Centreville, and thence to Gum Springs, on the Little River, or Leesburg Turnpike, where, at six o'clock, the day's march of twelve hours concluded. The march had exhausted some of the strongest. The heat was intense, and water scarce. Lieutenant-Colonel Gleason, of the 25th New York, overcome by the heat, died from sunstroke, and was buried in the evening in the little village church-yard, with suitable military honors. The men put leaves in their hats and cut boughs as a protection from the fierce rays of the sun. At a little distance, with some appeal to the imagination, there was a faint resemblance to a moving forest, and the well-known passage in Macbeth was recalled, " 'Till Bernam wood do come to Dunsinane," and, for the moment, diverted attention from the re-morseless burning sun, the dry, parched throat, and choking, pene-trating dust.[66]

The Ninth Massachusetts did not make it quite as far. We have to remember that the distance traveled depended upon the starting point in the morning. Thus with several divisions, one regiment or brigade might easily march three miles more or less than another unit. However, the Ninth Massachusetts found the seventeenth to be very hot, "the roads clouded with dust raised by tramping feet, and drinking water was very scarce. Everyone suffered with the heat throughout our[67] marching columns. Many were severely exhausted and several men throughout the division died from the effects of heat and sunstroke. As they tramped through the choking dust the First Division of the Fifth Corps heard the sounds of the cavalry fight at Aldie.

Meanwhile in Frederick, people were talking about the big fire that had hit the northern part of the county, in the little town of Emmitsburg. According to Jacob Englebrecht, thirty-two buildings, including twenty-eight dwellings, were destroyed by the fire that started in Daniel Wiles's Tavern. The fire occurred on Monday night. The folks in Frederick were also concerned about crackers. It seems as though three thousand boxes of crackers, weighing fifty pounds each, had been stored in Frederick for the military. Now to prevent their capture, they were to be destroyed. However, after a "second sober thought" on Monday, it was decided to give the crackers to the local populace. From Monday on into Thursday, crackers were being given to the folks. Some had as high as fifteen boxes. Jacob said, "The town I suppose will be filled with crackers for some time.[68]

Writing from the Eleventh Corps area on June 17, Oliver O. Howard states:

> Goose Creek, near Leesburg. The weather has been hot and dry. We have marched as follows: twelve miles, nineteen, eighteen, rested two days, and then marched seventeen. I was a little feverish at Centreville, but am now quite recovered.[69]

Howard's figures amount to sixty-six miles. That's a lot of walking.

One of the soldiers in the Eleventh Corps has this comment:

> The twenty mile march on Wednesday was not so bad, as Tuesday had been a day of rest, restoring the spent bodies of the soldiers. The Fifty-fifth Ohio camped on Goose Creek at Cow Horn Ford, sometimes called Trappe Rock. The spot was six miles from Leesburg. The stream was clear and cool and provided welcome relief.[70]

The Army of the Potomac hit the Roads to Gettysburg early on those June days. A. S. Williams and his division of the Twelfth Corps left Fairfax Court House at daybreak on Wednesday, June 17. The morning was pleasant, but by 8:00 A.M. it was quite warm. The command halted at Hunter's Mills. There in a shady ravine the men had breakfast. A detachment of the Sixth Michigan Cavalry accompanied the infantry for part of the march.[71]

Original orders called for Williams to move beyond Dranesville. But like so many other times, they were countermanded. The division went into camp two miles from the town. Tents were pitched in the lush grass of a very nice farmhouse. There the men "found the unusual luxury of sweet butter and fresh milk." The march was short, just about ten miles. The campsite was reached by 11:00 A.M. However, despite their fine surroundings, the afternoon was miserable. Even in shade and in the cool grass, the heat was almost unbearable. The men could not get comfortable. To make matters worse the dry grass in the fields and nearby woods caught fire. The air was filled with smoke and additional heat. It was truly an afternoon of "great discomfort."[72]

Noland's Ford, approximately forty-five miles above Washington, seems to have been Hooker's original choice for the crossing of the Potomac. At 12:30 A.M. on the seventeenth, Butterfield, Hooker's chief of staff, sent Slocum a note from Stahel, the cavalry commander, suggesting the Vienna and Freedom Hill route to Leesburg. Headquarters would be taking the Germantown and Ox Road. Gregg and the Second Cavalry Division was ordered to Aldie. By 9:45 A.M. Stahel was saying all roads leading to Leesburg would be marched on by the Army of the Potomac on the morrow. He would be sending cavalry patrols with each corps. According to Stahel, Hooker had one thousand cavalrymen on the Maryland side of the Potomac to protect the pontoon bridges.[73]

At 4:15 P.M. Gregg reported finding one brigade of Rebel cavalry in Aldie. An hour later, Butterfield was saying, "reports from north of the Potomac are uncertain and unreliable." Later in the evening, Dan Butterfield asks Rufus Ingalls in Washington, "Try and hunt up somebody from Pennsylvania who knows something, and has a cool enough head to judge what is the actual state of affairs there with regards to the enemy. Seven or eight thousand men are reported at Williamsport."[74]

Butterfield was upset. "Since we were not allowed to cross and whip A. P. Hill, while Longstreet and Ewell were moving off through Culpeper and Sperryville, we have lost the opportunity of doing a thing which we knew to a certainty we could accomplish. My impression now is that there is not a rebel, excepting scouts, this side of the Shenandoah Valley. . . . We cannot go boggling round until we know what we are going after."[75]

These statements help to substantiate the theory of John

121

Divine, a keen student of the Civil War in his native Loudoun County, that one of the primary reasons Noland's Ford was not chosen was due to uncertainty, and lack of information as to the whereabouts and intentions of Lee.[76]

Before the day was over, Captain Turnbull was ordered to take the pontoons to the mouth of the Monocacy. At 9:10, Stahel reports finding some Rebel guerrillas returning from a raid into Maryland. They brought some horses and mules with them. Butterfield kept late hours, and at midnight, ordered Stahel to prevent E. V. White from crossing the Potomac to cover a possible crossing by Jeb Stuart.[77]

The cavalry was ordered to move toward the Potomac. The First Division was to move by Philomont, Purcellville, and Waterford to Noland's Ferry. Henry Slocum was ordered to move out with the Twelfth Corps to Leesburg and protect all the Potomac River crossings. Once again we can see the darkness in which the Union army was operating.[78]

Colonel Pettes of the Fiftieth New York Engineers was ordered to head for Noland's Ferry in hopes that the pontoon bridge could be laid by noon on the eighteenth. Teams were to be obtained in Washington.[79]

Adding to the confusion of the day was a message from Robert Schenck saying that Imboden, who had been tearing up things in Western Maryland, may be moving on the National Road for Uniontown, Pennsylvania. He was concerned about the protection of Wheeling and Parkersburg.[80]

O. O. Howard and the Eleventh Corps were keeping a close eye on things from their positions at the Trappe Rock milldam and canal lock on Goose Creek.[81]

Today Union and Confederate cavalry skirmished at Aldie. Rebel infantry under George Pickett at Piedmont, and John B. Hood at Upperville acted as a support.

The First Division of the First Corps marched from Sperryville to Mud Run in Fauquier County. The marching of Tuesday and Wednesday were excessively hot, and felled many Confederate soldiers. At Gaines' Crossroads, Kershaw's wagons were sent to Front Royal.[82]

Despite the rough marching in the heat of the day, many Rebel soldiers were nicknamed "Foragers." They left camp under cover of darkness and crossed the mountain into Luray Valley, an area relatively untouched by war. Before daylight the men returned laden with butter, bread, and canteens full of "Mountain Corn" or "Applejack." The men must have been in good shape, because some of their comrades couldn't understand how they could march eighteen miles a day, and then cover another ten or fifteen miles at night in search of food and drink.[83] Henry's Artillery Battalion marched to Upperville today.

The Third Arkansas was a little more clever in their foraging. At one nice farmhouse, a soldier engaged the lady of the house in a conversation, seeming like a perfect gentleman while his buddies pilfered the springhouse. So on Saturday night the men from Arkansas had a banquet.[84]

News from the Third Corps was slack today. Anderson's division moved from Culpeper Court House to the Hazel River and waded across, camping on the left bank.[85]

Randolph Shotwell hardly knew whether he was dead or alive at the end of the day. "Flesh and blood cannot sustain such heat and fatigue as we have undergone this day. It is terrible. All along the roadside since 9 o'clock this morning, I have seen men dropping, gasping, dying, or already dead. . . . Most of our men are just out of winter-quarters, where they were well screened from the Sun; and now under the combined effect of heat, fatigue, thirsty, and intolerable dust they wilt and drop like wax-figures in a fiery furnace."[86] Shotwell continues by saying:

The dust is almost suffocating! Pulverized by sixty thousand pairs of feet of men, and nearly as many of horses and cattle, it forms a fine impalpable powder, sufficiently light to fill the air like smoke; and penetrate the eyes, ears, nostrils, hair, and skin, until its power of annoyance is unbearable. Then, when one's clothing is utterly saturated with perspiration mixing with the dust in a grimy paste; and above all weighs the heavy musket, the muffling blankets, griping waist band and belt (upon which hang the heavy cartridge and cap boxes) and the chafing canteen straps, is it strange that one sees hundreds of men gasping for breath, and lolling out their tongues like mad men? . . . Some of the men say that fully two dozen men were killed today by sun stroke. I saw that number "down" but whether they recovered subsequently I cannot say.[87]

123

Strangely, the men outlasted the horses. Many of the officers had to walk as their horses gave out in the heat and dust. McGowan's brigade covered fifteen to twenty miles. Many of the South Carolina soldiers felt it was the most oppressive heat they had ever felt. Quite a few fainted in the road, and many others fell out by the side of the road. By nightfall the ranks were depleted.[88]

Frederick was excited about a cavalry skirmish near Jefferson between that city and Harpers Ferry. Cole's Rangers had engaged some of Lige White's troopers. The Confederates had crossed the river and destroyed twenty-three empty railroad cars at Point of Rocks, but were unable to destroy a locomotive.[89]

Robert Rodes was busy in Williamsport, Maryland. He was constantly receiving supplies being brought in by the troopers of Jenkins's cavalry. The commissaries and quartermasters were able to replenish their depleted supplies. They were living off the land, primarily Pennsylvania land, and thus relieving the supply officers in Richmond. Capt. Arthur M. Chichester and the division pioneers were very busy trying to destroy the aqueduct over the Conococheague Creek. However, when the C. and O. Canal was built, it was built firmly. They had little success. Five thousand pounds of leather were bought by Maj. J. G. Paxton, probably from the Byron Tannery, an old established Williamsport business. Thirty-five kegs of powder were purchased in Hagerstown and Williamsport and sent to the rear.[90]

The Confederates went on shopping sprees in Williamsport, Hagerstown and Chambersburg. Many useful items were purchased with Confederate scrip and certificates and sent back down the valley. The farmers of Pennsylvania in Franklin County, lost between two thousand and three thousand head of cattle. Some were slaughtered immediately for the men in gray, the rest sent to the rear. The troopers took the horses for themselves. In general, with the exception of some isolated cavalry incidents near Greencastle, the Confederates were well behaved.[91]

Rodes had visitors today, "Sandie" Pendleton and Jed Hotchkiss rode to Williamsport from Bunker Hill to make some maps. It was a warm day with a brisk wind. The dust flew in clouds. Rodes was in excellent spirits. Things were going well. Hotchkiss spent the night with Rodes. Headquarters of the Second Corps moved to Camp Stevens, four miles north of Martinsburg.[92]

John B. Gordon, Harry Hays and William Smith, all brigade commanders in Early's division, left Winchester and headed for Shepherdstown. Once they arrived at the lovely old German town on the banks of the Potomac, they remained in camp until June 22. Again, details of those historic days and events are sketchy.

Shepherdstown is the oldest town in what is now West Virginia. At the outbreak of the war it was western Virginia. Just down the river, the Indians and then the early settlers on their way to the Shenandoah had discovered and used a good ford. Thomas Shepherd came and established a mill and a ferry boat operation. James Rumsey, way back in 1786, made a trial run in his steamboat with supposedly George Washington and other high ranking officials looking on. Old houses dotted the picturesque streets, and Revolutionary War soldiers are buried in the Reformed (United Church) Cemetery. Shepherdstown was, and is a lovely place.

Now for several days Early's Confederate division would be in and around the town, Edward Johnson would pass through on the Roads to Gettysburg. Then as soon as the men of the Second Corps were across, A. P. Hill and the Third Corps would arrive on the scene.

Johnson's division encamped at Shepherdstown. And Henry Kyd Douglas took the opportunity to cross the river and visit his parents at Ferry Hill. The lovely brick mansion built in 1813 and in the Blackford family for many years was now a barren waste. The lawn had been used as an artillery park after Antietam, and the barn burned. It was hard for Douglas to put aside thoughts of retaliation in Pennsylvania.[93]

June 18

For the most part, June 18 was a day of rest for the Army of the Potomac. "Copious showers of rain fell that night and the next day, the first rainfall for six weeks." Somehow the Twenty-fourth Michigan must have escaped the shower of Saturday night, June 13. The men from Michigan had a nice campsite, an open field with springs of clear water.[94]

The Second Corps rested near Centreville. Some excitement occurred when part of Harrow's brigade helped to clean out a sutler. This was a way of getting even for high prices and inferior products. General Hays had to send other troops in to quell the disturbance.[95]

The Sixth Corps moved up from Fairfax Station to Germantown.

Oliver O. Howard described the weather as "almost too hot for campaigning."[96]

At 4:00 P.M. John Reynolds was at the Brady House near Herndon Station. He says that two of his signal stations were within one mile of Leesburg. This was in midmorning. They found nothing but Mosby's men. Slocum was moving up the pike as ordered, but Reynolds feared he would have trouble crossing Goose Creek.[97]

Butterfield reported that the folks in Pennsylvania were getting over their stampede of panic, and starting to report coolly. He was concerned over White's operations at Point of Rocks. The Rebel leader destroyed quite a few cars during the night. But he adds, "We don't exactly settle where Lee is yet. . . . Catch and kill any guerrillas, then try them, will be a good method of treating them."[98]

Meanwhile the pontoon boats were being brought through the C. and O. Canal locks early in the morning. Then teams were hitched to them to haul them overland. Captain Turnbull went through about 6:00 A.M. But the others were tied up for awhile.[99]

Butterfield sent orders from headquarters saying that no more than two days of salt beef was to be carried in the supply wagons. All excess baggage was to be discarded. Wooden benches and bedsteads were to be thrown away. [How sad.] Cooking stoves were also to be thrown out. One spring wagon was to be used for corps headquarters. Sutlers' wagons were to be excluded from the column of march.

Three days of forage had to be carried for the animals and grazing permitted whenever possible.[100]

Late in the day word arrived that Milroy was in McConnellsburg,[101] and some of his men in Bedford,[102] Pennsylvania. They really scattered.

The 118th Pennsylvania[103] camped along the banks of a dry stream.[104] There was little water but a lot of toads. Poor Captain Donegan found enough water for some coffee. He heated the water and waited patiently for it to cool, when kersplash, one of the toads jumped into the hot cup of coffee. He was soon forced out by the heat. But this in no way destroyed the captain's appetite. His only regret was for the precious drops the toad had splashed over the side of the cup.[105]

General Williams of the Twelfth Corps had these memories of June 18:

> I was ordered at 6:00 o'clock to move my division towards Leesburg. The early morning was the hottest we had felt. One perspired freely standing still at sunrise. . . . There was some delay, and it was past 7 o'clock before we were fairly on the road. The pike . . . was . . . rough with unbroken boulders and very hard on the feet of men and animals accustomed to dirt roads. We passed through Dranesville, a small, insignificant village, and made our first halt at Broad Run, over which we found a stout stone bridge. The country along the pike is well cultivated and farmhouses are thick. . . .[106]
>
> About 1 o'clock a brisk shower relieved our tired and over-heated soldiers and we soon reached Goose Creek, where we found a deep and rocky ford, the bridge having been destroyed long ago. My division forded at once, waist deep, with their usual yells and jokes. The storm of rain, hail, thunder, and lightning had become terrific, but the men felt new life from the cool wetting, and we marched directly on (Leesburg), three and a half miles, which my advance reached about 4 P.M. and found no enemy. . . .[107]

Geary's Second Division of the Twelfth Corps was unable to cross until darkness had fallen. The wagon train did not make it on June 18.

Leesburg was not new to Williams. He had been in the prominent Virginia Loudoun County seat the previous autumn. Leesburg had a long and important history, and should be visited by those interested in tracing the Roads to Gettysburg. It lies in a natural bowl, around the rim of which the

127

Confederates had built three or four forts. The Twelfth Corps occupied these positions on June 18.

It was still raining when General Williams arrived in Leesburg. He found a house with two large rooms. About a dozen of his staff joined him with the idea of sleeping in one room, and using the other for headquarters. That night the general slept in a house for the first time in months. His bed was a blanket on the floor of the home occupied by Mrs. Grover.[108]

Reports from the First Corps are scarce for June 18. Mc-Laws, Hood, and Pickett remained in support of the cavalry near Ashby's and Snicker's gaps. Ashby's Gap is west of Upperville on Route 50, east of Winchester. Snicker's Gap is on Route 7 between Leesburg and Berryville.

George Pickett was madly in love with LaSalle Corbell. He wrote to her today from Loudoun County saying, "Each day my darling takes me farther and farther away from you, from all I hold dear. We have been guarding the passes of the Blue Ridge."[109] He continues by saying:

> Today, under orders from Marse Robert, we cross the Potomac. McLaws' and Hood's Divisions and the three brigades of my division follow on after Hill. May our Heavenly Father bless us with an early and victorious return. . . .[110]
>
> As I returned the salute of my men, many of them beardless boys, the terrible responsibility as their Commander almost overwhelmed me, and my heart was rent in prayer for guidance and help. Oh, the desolate homes—the widows and the orphans and heartbroken mothers that this campaign will make! How many of them, so full of hope and cheer now, will cross that other river which lands them at the Eternal Home.[111]

Randolph Shotwell was a member of Pickett's division. He found Thursday evening to be quite a contrast from the hot weather of earlier in the week. "This evening we are positively shivering around our campfires, with hail and sleet falling upon, the ground white with snow. . . . Some of the hail stones were as large as hickory nuts and pelted us fearfully as we toiled up the slopes of the Gap in the Blue Ridge, upon whose summit we bivouac tonight. . . ."[112]

Shotwell was elated. "How fast we are making history! A few days ago we were defending Richmond: now we threaten

Confederate infantry crossing at Williamsburg. From a sketch by C. E. H. Bonwill.

129

Alarm in Harrisburg. From a sketch by George Law.

Washington. . . . Great alarm is said to prevail in many of the large cities such as Washington, Baltimore, Philadelphia and Harrisburg."[113]

John Hood crossed the mountains today, forded the river and camped near Millwood. The river was deep and cold, reaching almost to the armpits of the men. The soldiers had to maintain their balance, and try to hold their rifles and cartridge boxes above their heads as they crossed.

Ambrose Powell Hill and his division commanders continued their movement toward Front Royal and the Shenandoah River. Things were better for McGowan's brigade. Wednesday night's rain had cooled things off, so there was no dust, but the roads were extremely muddy. And they had to make camp on a bare hillside in the midst of a downpour.

On the seventeenth or eighteenth Richard S. Ewell visited Robert Rodes somewhere in Williamsport, giving the young division commander orders to cross the Potomac on the nineteenth. But in the meantime, things were happening downstream from Williamsport.

On the sixteenth, Edward Johnson, another division commander in Ewell's corps, marched from Stephenson's Depot to Shepherdstown. "Jones' brigade was detached to destroy a number of canal boats and a quantity of grain and flour stored at different points."[114]

Edward Johnson was forty-six years old in June of '63. Born in Kentucky, he attended West Point and graduated in 1838. He was honored for bravery in the Mexican War, and became a good friend of Winfield Scott Hancock. In two weeks he would direct vigorous attacks on Culp's Hill at Gettysburg. But on June 18 he is preparing to cross the Potomac River at Boteler's Ford near Shepherdstown.

Sadly there are few accounts available concerning Johnson's march from Stephenson's Depot to Smithfield and Shepherdstown. Henry Kyd Douglas was happy. He was going home, and with other elements of the division he spent the night at Ferry House. General Johnson made his headquarters in the Douglas home. Douglas says:

> We were waiting for Longstreet's and Hill's corps to come up from across the mountain. I could not get over the feeling that an

131

invasion of the enemy's territory, however tempting, was the wrong policy for us. . . . I was conscious of the fact that I was doubting everything since Jackson was gone and was rather ashamed of it.[115]

Jed Hotchkiss spent the day working on maps of Maryland and Pennsylvania for General Rodes. During the day, Richard S. Ewell and Major Sorrell of Longstreet's staff came to the headquarters tent in Williamsport. Together the men discussed strategy. The people of Maryland seemed surprised to see the Confederates in their midst. Hotchkiss notes that it was a pleasant day, although late in the day it rained. Jed mounted his horse and rode from Williamsport back to headquarters of the Second Corps north of Martinsburg.[116]

It was hot and dusty in the Shenandoah Valley. The railroads had been torn up, the bridges destroyed, communications disrupted, and Shepherdstown found itself pretty well isolated. Prior to the war a fine bridge connected Shepherdstown with the Maryland shore. But that had been burned, and now only the massive stone pillars remained. The main river crossing now was a mile and a half south of the old bridge. The road leading to it ran along the face of rocky and steep cliffs.

Almost the entire town had been used as a Confederate hospital after Antietam. Union artillery overlooked the village from the yard of the Reverend Mr. Douglas at Ferry Hill. Jeb Stuart and his cavalry had camped at the Bower, near Leetown. But now it was June of 1863. The men in gray were on the way. The residents, such as Mary Bedinger Mitchell, hoped and prayed they would not see a repeat of Antietam. They had seen enough of the war in September of '62.[117]

Many of the men of the town were away, serving in either the Northern or Southern armies. Edwin Lee, a nephew of Robert E. Lee, had naturally gone with the South. He had served in the "Stonewall" brigade. Colonel Lee had gotten married in 1859, just about the time of the John Brown Raid. His bride was Susan Pendleton, the daughter of the Reverend and Mrs. Nelson Pendleton of Lexington, Virginia. Henry Kyd Douglas and Alexander ("Sandie") Pendleton served as groomsmen at the wedding.[118] We wonder if any

The Potomac at Shepherdstown, near the crossing of Johnson, Early, and A. P. Hill.

Ferry Hill House, the home of Henry Kyd Douglas, the headquarters of Edward Johnson, and the place where Jed Hotchkiss worked on his map.

of the Confederate officers stayed at Leeland while waiting to cross the Potomac.

Randolph Harrison McKim was in the column approaching Shepherdstown. His book tells the plight and the loneliness of the Marylanders in the Confederacy. But Thursday, June 18, was a happy day for him.

> When we reached Shepherdstown . . . on our way to cross into Maryland, it (the Second Maryland Battalion) was given the front of the column. The citizens of the town—especially the ladies—gave us an enthusiastic reception. The general and all his staff had bouquets presented them. It was a gala day for the Maryland men. . . .

We crossed the Potomac . . . about half past two. My chief, Gen. G. H. Steuart, and I rode side by side through the river, and our horses' feet touched the sacred soil of our native state at the same moment; but before I could guess his intention, the general sprang from his horse, and dropping on his hands and knees, kissed the ground. This act was the expression of a feeling of love and loyalty which was deep and strong in the hearts of us all. We loved Maryland. We were proud of her history, of her traditions. We felt that she was in bondage against her will, and we burned with desire to have part in liberating her. . . .

To be a Confederate soldier meant for the Marylander, in addition to hardship and danger, exile from home and kindred. It meant to be cut off from communication with father and mother, brother and sister, and wife. It meant to have an impenetrable barrier of forts and armies between him and all he loved and cherished best in the world.

When we were well over the river, and had gone into camp, the Maryland men had songs and great rejoicings, and Lt. Jas. Franklin made an appropriate address.[119]

Henry Robinson Berkeley was with Ewell's artillery in the Shenandoah Valley. He was just over twenty-two years old in June of '63. The march had been difficult for him. On June 10 he had covered twenty-three miles on a very hot, and dusty day.[120] At Winchester several days later, he threw away his overcoat because he was too hot and tired to carry it. Now he was nearing the Potomac.

Meanwhile things were bad in Harrisburg. A situation of panic prevailed. Horses, wagons, buggies, anything with wheels on headed for the capital city. Most were headed for the train station. There the folks bought tickets for Philadelphia, Reading, or any point north and east just to get away. That's all that mattered. Pictures and records at the State Capitol were hastily packed for shipment to places of safekeeping.

Complicating matters was the presence of the Pennsylvania Democratic party. They were in town for their state convention. Unable to find lodging, many of them slept on the ground in the park around the capitol. The bars were doing a great business, selling alcohol in an effort to ease the anxiety. Prices were up as the city became filled with refugees and soldiers. Coffee was selling for fifteen cents a cup. Colonel

Nye has a great description of the panic in his book, describing the litter along the road, and the huge amount of manure left by the thousands of animals pulling the escape vehicles.

June 19

The First Corps left their bivouac area near Herndon Station and moved to Guilford Springs. John Reynolds found time to write to his sisters, his last letter:

> The Army has moved up so as to cover Washington but we have not yet been able to discern whereabouts the enemy is exactly. Our cavalry has been fighting on our flanks, but no large infantry force of the enemy has been discovered this side of the Blue Ridge. It is possible that Lee is yet in the Shenandoah Valley. Our cavalry drove them back yesterday to Upperville in the direction of Ashby's Gap. We have to move up after them by the gaps or through Harpers Ferry "tho" it is impossible to say where the enemy is with any certainty.[121]

Marsena Patrick, writing from near Fairfax Court House, states his physical and emotional feelings, and agrees with Reynolds.

> Yesterday I was not in condition to write.... The day was the hottest of the Season, I lay panting for breath & weak as a cat. At 3 o'clock orders (came) to move Headquarters to Fairfax Court House.... I had got off but a little way when a violent thunder storm came up.... There are constant Cavalry skirmishes, & heavy fighting in the vicinity of Aldie & Middleburgh. We get a number of prisoners, but our losses are heavy. We get accurate information, but Hooker will not use it and insults all who differ from him in opinion.... He has declared that the enemy are over 100,000 strong—it is his only salvation to make it appear that the enemy's forces are larger than his own, which is all false & he knows it—He knows that Lee is his master & is afraid to meet him in battle.[122]

For the next five days the Guilford Station area was to be home for the First Corps of the Army of the Potomac. General Wadsworth's division encamped beyond Guilford Station on the banks of Broad Run.

During the night of the eighteenth, the first good rain in almost six weeks fell on the area. The men were glad to see the rain. They had a lot of marching to do, and the rain would settle the dust for a spell.

The next morning, June 19, elements of the Union First Corps resumed the march toward Leesburg, Broad Run and Guilford Station. There the command halted and the men stacked arms. Defensive positions were secured. The soldiers were ready to thwart any Confederate movement toward the nearby fords of the Potomac. Heavy firing was heard off in the distance. Union and Confederate cavalry were engaged in a major skirmish at Ashby's Gap.

Lt. Lucius L. Shattuck, of Plymouth, Michigan, had fallen in love with a pretty schoolteacher back home. The night of the nineteenth he wrote to her:

> We are ... habitually turned out at two or three o'clock in the morning, when we fold our blankets and sit down on them to hold our temper and await orders. ... When we heard the firing this morning we thought of course we would be in it before night, but it is now so late in the day that we will probably not move. If we should, it will be much more pleasanter marching than we have had before, as we had a fine shower last night. Give my love to the prettiest girl you find and when the war is over, I'll go and see her.[123]

Shattuck was unable to keep the date with the lovely young girl. On July 1 he fell mortally wounded at Gettysburg. This letter, written on the road to Gettysburg, was his last letter to the girl he loved.

The Eighty-eighth Pennsylvania marched fifteen miles in a heavy rain. They tried to sleep in soaking wet blankets. At midnight the long roll beat. Every man grabbed his rifle and answered the alarm. But the alert was false, and those who could went back to sleep in the rain.[124]

An elderly black man watched the Sixteenth Maine go into camp on June 19. Shouting in a cracked voice he said, "Hebbenly massa bless de Linkum sojers, an show dese yer eyes do golden chariot fo 'I die.' "

With that, a group of blacks who had gathered to watch the men in blue march by, threw hats, jackets, and shoes into the air, and shouted "Glory hallelujah."

The elderly black man wanted to know if Mr. Lincoln was coming too. A corporal in Company F replied, "Yes, he's in his chariot forty miles back the road."[125]

137

The Sixteenth Maine encamped at Guilford Station from June 19-25. They were glad for the break. However, the 266 enlisted men and 32 officers found water to be very scarce. Liquid from the muddy brooks and sluggish runs of Virginia did not make the best drinking water. But nevertheless they had to use it to fill their canteens.[126]

The nineteenth brought the artillery to Guilford Station with good pasture and "an abundance of water." The batteries were just half a mile from headquarters near Broad Run. Wainwright liked being in command and able to take mess at corps headquarters.

The Second Corps was in the Centreville area from June 18-21. On Friday, some of the troops "cleaned out a sutler." This was a common practice during the war. The soldiers picked a sutler they did not like, or one who overcharged them or sold them inferior products. First the guy ropes were secretly cut. Then in the confusion, the men helped themselves to the sutler's wares and disappeared. Most sutler's got the message.[127]

The Fourth Ohio reached Centreville at 9:00 P.M., just as it started to pour down rain. The men could not find fence rails for coffee and campfires. So they leaned against trees for protection or tried to sleep standing up. Some laid down in the mud. Miserable men tramped around through the night hours. Many of them cursed the weather, the military, and the Rebels. By dawn smoking fires were started. But due to the damp, low hanging air, the men were soon coughing.[128]

The day was muggy and close. The country had been very dry. The crops needed rain, and rain was welcome to the troops if they did not get too much.

On this Friday, the Third Corps marched to Gum Springs. This time the march was through mud, not dust. The temperature fell between thirty and forty degrees. The weather took a severe cooling trend.

The Twelfth New Hampshire was not impressed with Gum Springs. "It was a dreary, dismal, swamp-like place to stop in." However, the woods were filled with guerrillas, and a stop was necessary. Several Union soldiers who strolled from the column and bivouac areas later, never returned. Their search for food and water ended in death.[129]

Gum Springs, modern-day Arcola, is just a few miles north of Route 50, the Little River Turnpike. Long ago when erecting a church, the builders tried to locate it near a spring. Thus around 1740 an Anglican Church was built near Gum Springs, a source of water that still bubbles up. Nearby is the site of the old gum tree that blew over in the sixties. In Civil War days less than a hundred people lived here. It is not much bigger today.

We have mentioned so often that the men found marching through the Virginia countryside very depressing. Most of the areas had seen at least one action. Some had not been free of troops moving through or camping. Additionally, most of the able-bodied Virginians were "away," that meant in the army. Therefore, the farms were running down. The women and children were physically unable to maintain them and to repair the damage of war.

Edwin B. Houghton hailed from Maine, but June of '63 found him tramping on the Roads to Gettysburg. His description of Gum Springs is typical of comments about the war torn Virginia countryside. He saw Gum Springs as "a most desolate looking place in a state of complete decay. Some twenty old time worn and weather stained tumble down buildings constituted the village."[130]

Houghton's feelings may have been colored by fatigue and exertion. He and his comrades had marched from Centreville to Gum Springs on the nineteenth arriving in the little village at midnight on the twentieth. Things had started pleasantly. Showers cooled the weather and dampened the dust. But at 6:00 P.M. on the nineteenth it started to pour. Houghton said, "a darker night never settled over the 'sacred soil.' "

> It was with the greatest difficulty that we could distinguish even a faint outline of each other when marching side by side; . . . only by continually shouting could we keep our places in the ranks. It rained in a perfect torrent, and our uncertain course lay over ditches, mudholes, fences, stumps, stonewalls and bushes.[131]

That's the way it was on the way to Gum Springs, June 19, 1863.

On the Roads to Gettysburg, the men marched regardless of the hour or the weather. For instance, the 141st Pennsylvania started marching late in the afternoon of the nineteenth, and marched until 11:00 P.M. They stumbled in the darkness and were soaked by the rain. "Every man was wet to the skin and covered with mud, but the wet blankets were spread upon the wet ground and the men in the wet clothing flung themselves down to rest as best they could."[132]

Major Spaulding described June 20 in one word, "wet." "Every one wet enough this morning having marched half the night in a hard rain storm, and laid upon the ground with nothing but wet blankets for the other half."[133]

Thomas Marbaker and members of the Eleventh New Jersey found the residents of Gum Springs to be "intensely rebel." Some of the men were linked up with Mosby or other partisan groups. "Consequently, but little restraint was placed on the foragers." One evening the lads from New Jersey returned to camp with twenty cows, a large number of sheep, geese, and chickens. They ate good that night.[134]

Members of the 118th Pennsylvania heard the sounds of battle as they arrived in Gum Springs. The cavalry had had a severe tussle at Aldie, and were pressing for the mountain gaps to observe the Rebel movements. Reaching Aldie, they found wounded men lying on litters by the roadside and on the lawns. Dead horses were scattered about. The area was littered with military equipment. They met the remains of Colonel Duffie's First Rhode Island Regiment in the town.[135]

The 118th Pennsylvania described Middleburg as a village of six hundred souls, "two churches and a few stores, in the midst of a well-tilled, productive region." The men had lost their taste for farming and were away in the Confederate army. A feature of the area was the stone fences, dividing fields into picturesque squares of "patch-work green."

Strong Vincent's brigade of the Fifth Corps brought pressure on the Confederate cavalry. The horsemen of the two armies advanced toward each other at a trot. The foot soldiers had a ringside seat for the cavalry charge. "The lines intermingled, sabres flashed, men yelled, horses reared. There

Aldie.

Oliver O. Howard, commander of the Eleventh Corps, and later founder of Howard and Lincoln universities.

was cutting, slashing, cheering, and riderless horses heading for rear." The Confederates withdrew, getting the worst of the deal.

A batch of fifty prisoners walked by the 118th Pennsylvania. They were a talkative group, recognizing the improvement of the Union cavalry by saying, "You'ns will soon be as good as we'ns."[136]

June 19 was a sad day for Gen. A. S. Williams and for many in the Army of the Potomac. On that Friday the Twelfth Corps had the unpleasant duty of shooting three deserters. Two of the men were from the Forty-sixth Pennsylvania. The desertions took place as the Twelfth Corps was marching from Fredericksburg in search of the enemy. The men had bought civilian clothing and tried to escape at Aquia Creek. The third man to be shot was a member of the Thirteenth New Jersey. The man had deserted the previous spring and had taken advantage of a pardon offered by President Lincoln in April.[137]

Joe Hooker approved the court-martial and the sentence of death. The regimental commanders tried to get him to reduce the sentence. However, he refused, thus sealing the doom of the deserters.

The Twelfth Corps was paraded in a large field and "formed the three sides of a square." Because the men belonged to the division commanded by Williams, he was in charge of the execution, although the details fell upon the provost marshal. Three graves were dug some two "apart in a slight depression of the field, and on the gentle swell of the ground the troops were formed so that every man could see the execution."[138]

John de Cheverell of the Twenty-ninth Ohio spent the morning in camp cleaning his gun and equipment. In the afternoon he and his buddies had to quit that task to witness the execution.[139]

At 10:40 A.M. today, Slocum reported arriving in Leesburg at 5:00 P.M. on the eighteenth. Whether he made an inspection of the fords himself, or had one made, it is difficult to tell. But in his dispatch to Butterfield, he states that a "pontoon bridge should be thrown across the river, near Ed-

143

wards Ferry. . . . The material for a bridge, with a party to build it, should be sent at once."[140]

Butterfield wires back asking, "What advantages are to be gained by putting a bridge at Edwards Ferry? Are there reasons why we cannot cross at Noland's and Hauling's Fords?"[141]

To this, Slocum sent the following reply:

> I think the bridge should be built at Edwards Ferry to supply us. I have not force enough to keep the route to Vienna, or to hold many fords on the river in the country filled with guerrillas. Edwards Ferry is most accessible, and is covered by a strong redoubt on this side. Our supplies should be sent from Georgetown, by canal to Edwards Ferry.[142]

So we have the recommendations for the use of Edwards Ferry by the general on the spot.

At 9:30 P.M. Butterfield is on the wire again, saying, "Bridge will be laid at Edwards Ferry in the morning." Forces from Monocacy would be coming. Union detachments were operating freely in the Poolesville-Dickerson area.[143]

Four items led to the bridge at Edwards Ferry: (1) the other fords were impractical in light of existing conditions, (2) the uncertainty as to Lee's whereabouts, (3) the cavalry skirmishes occurring at Aldie and Middleburg, and (4) the sound advice of Henry Warner Slocum.

Longstreet's First Corps remained along the eastern slopes of the Blue Ridge Mountains. This Friday found Lafayette McLaws and his command of Georgia, South Carolina, and Mississippi troops posted in Ashby's Gap. John Bell Hood with Alabama, Texas, and Georgia troops was at Snicker's Gap, and George Pickett guarding points between the two mountain passes.[144] Maffett's Third South Carolina Infantry spent the night on top of the mountain at Ashby's Gap.[145] Dearing's Artillery Battalion headed for Berryville. The day was made tougher by rain.

Randolph Shotwell spent the day at the summit of Snicker's Gap. Throughout the day Pickett's men heard sounds of action coming from Middleburg where Stuart and Buford were at it.[146] In Snickersville the cavalrymen were met with great demonstrations of delight. The infantrymen shouted with glee. Shotwell thought that the shouting of the Rebel infantry scared off the Union cavalry.

The Third Corps moved closer to the Shenandoah River.

Today Richard S. Ewell sent to Leetown to see General Longstreet. Jed Hotchkiss started at an early hour for Shepherdstown. He crossed the Potomac and went to Johnson's headquarters at Ferry Hill. Longstreet was located near Charles Town, while A. P. Hill was close to Berryville.[147] The folks in Shepherdstown were very happy to see the Rebels.

Early and his entire division spent the day in camp on the banks of the Potomac at Shepherdstown.[148] Edward Johnson from bivouac areas located from Ferry Hill to the Dunker Church on the Antietam Battlefield marched up what is now Maryland 65 to Hagerstown. During the march, Henry Kyd Douglas and the Rebel army had an encounter with a tollgate keeper. But we'll get to that in a moment.

Today was moving day for Robert Rodes. He had been in Williamsport since Monday evening. Now on this Friday he headed North to Hagerstown, encamping on the road to Boonsboro near Funkstown.[149]

As Confederate troops marched from Sharpsburg toward Hagerstown the advance was slowed by John Bloom, the tollgate keeper at Tilghmanton. As the gray column drew near, Mr. Bloom put the pole across the road and stood in the middle of the pike to bar the passage of the Rebel army.

"Who's going to pay for the horses and wagons I see coming?"

"I am, Mr. Bloom," Douglas replied. "I'll give you an order on President Davis. Take it to Richmond and get the money."[150]

Bloom preferred to see Davis hung. But one man could not stop a heavily armed division. So the devoted gatekeeper permitted them to continue on the Roads to Gettysburg, with the advice they'd better head back to Virginia.

It had been a busy week for Capt. M. L. Bowie of the Sixth Alabama Infantry. On the eleventh of June, his regiment camped at Flint Hill at the base of the Blue Ridge. Then on:

June 12—Crossed over the Blue Ridge at Chester Gap; passed through Front Royal, Va.; crossed the Shenandoah River, and encamped that night within 16 miles of Berryville. . . .

June 13—Arrived before Berryville at 12:30 p.m., and having formed line of battle, aided in capturing the town, from which the enemy's main force had precipitately fled. The regiment then rested a couple of hours, continued the march and went into camp for the night within 8 miles of Smithfield, Va.

June 14—Continued the march through Smithfield and Bunker Hill . . . and arrived before Martinsburg in late afternoon. Immediately formed line of battle, and assisted in repulsing the enemy and capturing the place. That same night the regiment was taken into town, and placed in charge of prisoners, storehouses, and provisions.

June 15-16—The regiment performed provost duty at Martinsburg.

June 17—Left Martinsburg, and marched to the south bank of the Potomac, and encamped near the river, opposite Williamsport, Md.

June 18—Lay in camp all day.

June 19—Crossed the Potomac at Williamsport, . . . and marching thru Hagerstown, . . . went into camp on the bank of the Antietam Creek, opposite Funkstown, . . . where we remained two days in camp.[151]

Darius Couch, a senior Union corps commander, may have regretted his assignment in Harrisburg. He knew that one task would be to send troops to Chambersburg to block or hinder the Rebel advance. Army headquarters in Washington ordered this in hopes that Hooker would be able to catch up with Lee and whip him. But things were chaotic in Harrisburg. Couch needed good men and time. Therefore, when Jenkins destroyed the railroad bridge at Scotland, north of Chambersburg, he had to do something even if it was wrong.[152]

Herman Haupt was construction chief for the railway system of the military. With repeated Confederate attacks in the early part of the war, he maintained prefabricated bridge trusses at key points. Thus bridges could be repaired quickly. Flatcars and a repair crew were assembled to go to Scotland. But with Rebel cavalry coming and going at will, they needed protection. On June 17 he sent McGowan's company of Invalids to reinforce Lt. Frank Stanwood's company of Regular Army cavalry recruits who had already been sent from the Carlisle Barracks to Shippensburg.[153]

On the eighteenth, the Eighth and Seventy-first New York Regiments arrived in Harrisburg. It was pouring down rain, so they were happy to remain in their cattle cars for the night. The next morning they were given a big breakfast and a big welcome speech by Governor Curtin. Both regiments had fought at First Bull Run, and the men looked and acted like veterans.[154]

Colonel Joshua Varian commanded the Eighth New York. Benjamin Trafford commanded the Seventy-first. Apparently he was not much of an officer. Couch was glad to find another officer to command the brigade. The man was forty-year-old Brig. Gen. Joseph F. Knipe. Having been seriously wounded earlier in the war, Knipe was not on active duty but volunteered his services in this moment of need.[155]

To the eight-hundred-man infantry unit, a battery of naval guns under Lt. Cmdr. Pendleton Watmough was added. On Friday evening in the midst of a tremendous downpour, these men, baggage, tents, and rations were loaded into cars furnished by the Cumberland Valley Railroad and headed south, and arrived in Shippensburg at eleven o'clock. The forty-mile trip required four hours. Knipe had a big job, to check or hinder the advance of the Second Corps of the Army of Northern Virginia.[156]

June 20

Once Hooker decided to cross the Potomac River, the next question was where to cross? At 4:00 A.M. on June 20, Henry W. Slocum, commanding the Twelfth Corps, sent a message to the War Department saying he had occupied three redoubts, one of which covered the approaches to Edwards Ferry, upstream from Washington. In Slocum's opinion, the Chesapeake and Ohio Canal could be used to supply part of the army once across.

Things moved rather rapidly, at 9:00 A.M. on Saturday, June 20, Major Spaulding of the Engineers sent a message to the Navy Yard in Washington, saying:

> The river here (Edwards Ferry) is nearly 1,500 feet wide, and we do not have sufficient material to span it. Please send immediately fifteen boats, completely furnished; also about fifty extra chesses, and some extra lashing in coils, uncut.[157]

147

The construction of a pontoon bridge had not been ordered, but Major Spaulding was sure the order would be forthcoming. Sure enough, at 5:20 in the evening of the twentieth, Captain Turnbull of the Engineers was ordered to lay a bridge at Edwards Ferry. Later in the evening, he was asked to check the width of the Potomac River at Noland's Ford.[158]

At midnight on June 23, General Slocum reported to Washington that Chick's Ford was located one mile below Noland's. It would do for cavalry and infantry, but not for artillery. White's Ford fell in the same category, but had a rough bottom. Seneca Ford, two miles below Goose Creek in Virginia, was thought to be good. After much thought, Edwards Ferry was chosen as the point of entrance for the Union army into Maryland.[159]

From Washington, Edwards Ferry was 30.8 miles. This is the mileage from the eastern terminus of the Chesapeake and Ohio Canal in Georgetown. White's Ferry, where Lee crossed for the Maryland Campaign of 1862, is 35.5 miles from Washington. The Monocacy River Aqueduct is 42.3 miles, and the Point of Rocks Bridge is 48.1 miles. We need to keep these places in mind as we think of the movements of the Union Eleventh and Twelfth Corps on June 25-27. The Confederate crossings at Shepherdstown and Williamsport were 75 and 95 miles from Washington.

Hooker did not enjoy the fording advantages of Lee. The two pontoon bridges at Edwards Ferry were close together. The approach march was long, and unless carefully patrolled, a traffic jam of great proportions was likely to occur. The fords at Shepherdstown and Williamsport were not as deep as the water at Edwards Ferry. Lee's fords were far enough apart to prevent traffic jams. Parallel roads could be used by the Confederate infantry, whereas Hooker's troops had to wait for other detachments to cross.[160]

Officers always had a difficult job on the march. Wagons easily impeded the infantry. Therefore, the officers had to be alert.

Thus the engineers at Monocacy and at Harpers Ferry should report to Captain Turnbull. When Major Spaulding arrived at 9:00 A.M. at Edwards Ferry on June 20, he reported the Potomac River to be fifteen hundred feet wide, or five hundred yards. He did not have sufficient boats and lumber to do his job. He asked for fifteen extra boats, fifty extra chesses, and extra lashing. Still the actual order to lay the bridge had not arrived. Everything was to be held in readiness until orders came from headquarters.[161]

Hooker was desperate for information. He sent a message to John Babcock in Frederick telling him to go to the top of South Mountain for a look. He was to avoid the roads, and take persons who had a clear and intelligent mind. They were to hide in the woods and make an effort to count the Rebels. Only reliable information was to be sent. If John had to spend money to get the job done, he would be reimbursed.[162]

General Stahel broke up his camps, sent all excess baggage and supplies to Fairfax Station, and turned in all sick horses, waiting for fresh mounts. New Burnside carbines were distributed to the Eighteenth Pennsylvania Cavalry.[163] Hooker also directed that one division of the Sixth Corps be sent to Bristow Station.

In the meantime, Dr. H. Seller, a refugee from Williamsport, left Frederick at 2:30 to speak with military authorities in Baltimore. He told John Babcock that only Rodes's command was in Williamsport. Dr. Seller also reported the presence of Jenkins cavalry north of the Potomac. The faithful Babcock reported that he had sent scouts to Elk Ridge.[164]

Finally at 5:20 Captain Turnbull was ordered to build one bridge at Edwards Ferry.

Early in the war, the main job of the engineers was to build trenches for fortifications. But as time passed, it became necessary to master the art of building pontoon bridges for river crossings. One of the great difficulties was that of hauling the boats over land, and at times getting through the underbrush to the river and a good crossing site. Winston Churchill made the remark in the battle for Britain, "never before have so many owed so much to so few." He was referring to the gallantry of the Royal Air Force.

To an extent, the same might be said of the engineer corps

149

as they laid the pontoon bridge at Edwards Ferry. Had they been slower, or done a poor job, who knows what might have happened. But they laid the bridge over a wide span of river. And the bridges held in place, as constantly for three days nearly ninety thousand men crossed over. Along with the men came the horses, mules, wagons, artillery, ambulances, etc. Without the pontoon bridges and the men who built them, the men may never have covered the Roads to Gettysburg.

Charles Turnbull was having his problems at Edwards Ferry. It was now 7:20 P.M. His orders took two hours to arrive. Now he felt he would have to work all night. He had with him sixty-five boats, and twelve hundred feet of bridging. The river though was fourteen hundred feet wide. Also the river had risen two feet since morning due to heavy rains earlier in the week. Benham sent word that extra boats would be arriving, but it would take another twenty-four hours.[165]

At 9:20, Butterfield wanted to know if the river was rising or falling and how good the approaches were to the Edwards Ferry.[166]

About 3:00 Saturday morning, the Ninth New York (the Eighty-third New York Volunteers) were ordered to rise and shine. Four hours later, guarding the wagon train of the First Corps, they marched along the Loudoun and Hampshire Railroad in the direction of Leesburg. They only traveled a short distance to Guilford Station where they went into bivouac. The rain which had started the evening of the nineteenth continued into the twenty-first, making camp life "exceedingly disagreeable."[167]

On the twenty-second a detachment from the Ninth or Eighty-third New York was sent back to Fairfax Station to guard a supply train. When they returned they brought a fresh supply of news from home, the mail. Mosby and the Confederates were annoying the left flank of the Army of the Potomac. The Rebels, knowing the country like the back of their hand, made hit-and-run attacks. They struck, did some damage, and then vanished. In fact, Reynolds was almost captured by one of the guerrilla raids. This made him very angry. He was determined to scour the neighborhood and hunt the attackers down. Naturally, the local people knew nothing about the men in gray. When they were questioned, they replied they had not seen them. Reynolds led the search, but the effort amounted to nothing more than lost energy and time.[168]

Writing from Centreville on the twentieth, Gibbon stated:

> We expect to remain here today, though we may move at any moment. I have heard no news, either of our own movements or of those of the enemy and cannot say I expect a general battle very soon. Each side seems to be watching the other, ready to act according to circumstances. We have, I think, sufficient force to defeat the enemy if it is properly managed. All we want is some competent man to direct matters and I should not be much surprised at any moment to hear of some change.
>
> At noon on that day (the 20th) the 2nd Corps moved from Centreville out on the Warrenton pike, marched through the battlefield of Bull Run, left French's division at Gainesville and reached Thoroughfare Gap late at night.[169]

Tully McCrea says that Centreville was like most Virginia towns, composed of only a few homes. He and his comrades crossed the battlefield today and noticed the sad evidence of the earlier conflicts. "Whole human skeletons lie on the ground uncovered. The dead never have been properly buried, and the rain in many places washed off what little dirt has been thrown over them."[170]

Joseph Ward also noted the bullet ridden trees, carcasses of horses, and hastily dug graves. "From one, the knee of a man was sticking out, another the hand and foot, another the greater part of the head. . . . It seemed hard to give one's life for their country, and harder yet, so long after the battle, not to be decently buried. . . . Our pioneers were finally detailed to fill up the graves and bury the loose bones."[171]

The last part of the march to Thoroughfare Gap was in darkness. The men in the ranks knew the destination, but they were unaware of its location. Finally one lad fell in a big ditch. Someone asked what he was doing down there. He replied, "I've found the gap and stopped it up."[172]

During their stay at the gap, Harrow's men gathered green apples and cooked them. Farm items were scarce. The local people did not want to give or sell to the men in blue. After all, they were their enemies.

This Saturday, the Sixth Corps made a hard march to Bristow Station. "The tower and windmill which had been used for raising water to the tank, remained alone to show where the station had been; all the other buildings being destroyed, except . . . the dismantled ruins of what had once been a hotel."[173]

Along the route and at Bristow Station were the ruins and remains of destroyed railroad cars and their contents. The Sixth Corps found the area delightful. A mile or two south of the campsite of the Seventy-seventh New York was a little church in the midst of a grove of oak trees. This impressed George Stevens. He thought that was better than the Northern custom of setting a church on a hill with no trees of shade around it.

The Sixth Corps stayed in this general area for five days. The weather was delightful. The men enjoyed the rest. They took it easy in the shade of the trees, and strolled along the railroad track looking for usable items. A hospital area was set up in a quiet and lovely woods.

Some newspapers reached the Sixth Corps area telling of the alarm in the North. They read about paintings, books, and records for the State of Pennsylvania being taken from the capital and placed in boxcars to be shipped north if the Rebels appeared on the south shore of the Susquehanna. They laughed about office and businessmen taking shovels and picks to throw up fortifications. The Baltimore and Ohio Railroad was threatened. Bells were ringing throughout the North sounding the alarm and the news of invasion. This was the summer of '63.[174]

Today James Longstreet received a dispatch from general headquarters directing him to be in readiness to move toward the Potomac River, and be ready to cross into Maryland. Longstreet was ready. He had been expecting the order. But first the Shenandoah had to be crossed. Therefore this Saturday was spent in fording the river and occupying the banks on the opposite shore. Sites of ferries, and a spot for cavalry and artillery were selected.

McLaws moved to Berry's Ford and crossed there. From the accounts of Kershaw's brigade we read: "That the river was swollen and the passing most difficult.[175] The Third South Carolina lost 2,370 rounds of ammunition in the crossing. Henry's Artillery Battalion lost 400 rounds of ammunition due to high water."[176]

Shotwell found the day to be very tough. First, the road was winding and narrow, then there were the two branches of the Shenandoah, "each more than sixty feet broad, and fully four feet deep. . . . The hail storm of yesterday chilled the water to winter temperature, . . . the passage was like wading through the same amount of ice water. . . . We were half frozen and dripping with water when we presented ourselves to the fair feminines of Berryville, who, notwithstanding the daily tramp of soldiers through their village, turned out to greet us with bouquets and refreshments. . . . God bless them."[177]

McGowan's brigade spent Friday night at Chester Gap in heavy rain. Saturday they marched into Front Royal, and then crossed both forks of the Shenandoah. The water was deep, hip high, and the current swift. But the men plunged in with cheers, while the band of Fourteenth South Carolina played encouraging music. This was at Christian's Ford. The bridge had been burned. The command continued on toward White Post.[178]

Toward evening, Lt. Col. Arthur James Lyon Fremantle arrived in Culpeper in search of Lee's army. Twenty-eight years old, and a member of the famous Coldstream Guards, Fremantle arrived in Texas three months earlier. He was on leave and had come for adventure and observation. He was sympathetic to the South. He was for the underdog in every situation with the exception of when England was involved. He moved across the South, visiting with and observing the army of Braxton Bragg. Then it was on to Charleston and Richmond.

The North had an abundance of writers, but many feel that Fremantle saw more, and wrote more graphically than any who covered the South. He met most of the leaders, and mingled with the soldiers and the civilians. He kept a journal of his daily activities and had a wonderful knack of describing things as he saw them. He published his adventures in 1863. It sold very well in England because many of the folks were for the South. *The Fremantle Diary* is a fascinating book, and the student of the Civil War should take the time to read it.

Fremantle took the train from Richmond to Culpeper and arrived at 5:30. Lee and Longstreet were gone, having left about the fifteenth. Sergeant Norris, a prosperous Maryland farmer prior to the war, became his escort. The rain was pouring down, but Norris and Fremantle left on two broken-down horses. They both had sore backs, were unfed, and the one was minus a shoe. But despite these difficulties, the two men traveled fifteen miles to Woodville, arriving at 9:30. Shelter was hard to find, but at last they found a man who gave them corn for the horses, and a blanket to use as a bed on the floor.[179]

Henry Kyd Douglas had a sad experience. While visiting some friends, a staunch Unionist stole his pistols from their holsters. One had been given him by a Federal officer at Harpers Ferry. The other was a present from Thomas Jonathan Jackson. Had the thief realized his prize, Douglas would have given a good ransom. Robert Rodes and his division was on the banks of the Antietam at Funkstown.[180] Johnson's division was at Sharpsburg.

On June 20, Lee was able to communicate to President Davis:

> Lt. Col. White of the cavalry has cut the Baltimore and Ohio east of Point of Rocks. General Milroy has abandoned the south side of the Potomac, occupying Harper's Ferry with a picket and holds Maryland Heights. . . . General Ewell's corps is north of the Potomac, occupying Sharpsburg, Boonsboro, and Hagerstown. His advance cavalry is at Chambersburg, Pennsylvania. . . . General Longstreet's corps, with Stuart's cavalry, still occupy the Blue Ridge between the roads leading through Ashby's and Snicker's Gaps, holding in check a large force of the enemy. . . . The movement of the main body of the enemy is still toward the Potomac, but its real destination is not yet discovered.[181]

Jed Hotchkiss spent the day at Ferry Hill, busy drawing maps. The hard rain of Friday night raised the Potomac River and was a factor in keeping "Jubé" Early from crossing into Maryland. More rain fell on Ferry Hill Saturday night.[182]

Robin Berkeley reached the Potomac on Friday. Today he and three comrades obtained a nice dinner at a farm house near Shepherdstown.[183] Robin was pleased to see "four nice ladies."[184]

The Monocacy Aqueduct.

On June 19, Alfred Jenkins sent Col. M. J. Ferguson on an expedition from Greencastle to McConnellsburg. The gray column rode through Mercersburg in the dark, crossed Cove Mountain, and arrived in McConnellsburg at 4:00 A.M. on the twentieth.

They awakened the shopkeepers who were very much surprised. The stores were opened and the Rebels helped themselves to shoes, hats, medicine, food and hardware. The troopers rounded up twelve thousand dollars worth of cattle, 120 horses and several black boys.[185] Although the reception was cool, a few young ladies presented flowers to the men in gray.

Returning to Greencastle, Ferguson's men charged into Mercersburg. They expected to meet some resistance, but there was none. Colonel Ferguson stopped at the home of Dr. Philip Schaff, a noted theologian. The two men had a long discussion. Before departing, the Rebel officer expressed the desire that when they met again it would be in peace.[186]

Poor Joseph Knipe immediately ran into problems in Shippensburg. His command and staff were new. There was paper work to do, and there had been a foul up in rations. Several telegrams were required to correct the problem. Then orders came for him to send troops to Chambersburg. But due to the late hour, 9:00 P.M., he decided to wait. Leaving the Invalid troops in Shippensburg he attached the troopers from Carlisle Barracks to Captain Boyd's First New York Cavalry. The general worked until midnight as the rain poured down outside.[187]

William Boyd is certainly one of the unsung heroes of the Gettysburg campaign. We met him early at Bunker Hill and as he escorted Milroy's wagons to safety. After arriving in Harrisburg, he had to take time to rest and refit his small command. But by the nineteenth he was ready to go again, and reported to General Couch. Wanting to save time and equipment, Boyd loaded his cavalrymen on the train and rode to Shippensburg, reporting on the twentieth. During the night, in the rain, Boyd trotted off to Chambersburg and Mercersburg, learning of Confederate activities, and narrowly missing an encounter with the Rebel raiders. For the rest of June, Boyd sparred with the men in gray, and his reports to Knipe and Harrisburg were the main sources of information on the advance of the Second Corps.[188]

Nathaniel Edward Harris was governor of Georgia after the Civil War, but in '63 he was a member of the Sixteenth Virginia Cavalry, Jenkins's brigade. He tells us what it was like traveling through the Cumberland Valley in June and July.

> I learned the pangs of hunger for I could not eat the bread and apple butter that constituted the larger part of our ration. Every family in Southern Pennsylvania seemed to own a large bakery and kept a supply of apple butter on hand.
> We slept along the fence corners or in open fields or under trees in the forest, if we got any sleep at all. There was a ceaseless call on

all the energies of every soldier. When our horses would give way in forces marches we would swap them for the horses belonging to the citizens. We found these Pennsylvania draft horses of the Percheron-Norman breed to be almost worthless for the cavalry. They could not stand the exposure, and the marches on the pikes soon put them out of the running.

Trooper Harris was fond of his regimental commander, Col. M. J. Ferguson. He was brave and noble. But it seemed like the commander had a bad habit of getting hit in just about every engagement. Jenkins sent Ferguson on an expedition from Greencastle to Mercersburg and McConnellsburg.

The men in gray crossed Cove Mountain at night and rode into McConnellsburg at 4:00 in the morning. We can imagine the shocked surprise of the Pennsylvanians. Routed out of their beds, they were forced to open the stores for the Confederates. Shoes, hats, and all other items they desired were carried away. The men in gray paid for the things they needed with Confederate money. The farmers were not so lucky. They did not have advance warning and thus were unable to drive their cattle and horses away to safe hiding places. Ferguson's men were able to obtain twelve thousand dollars worth of cattle, 120 horses, and several black boys. Colonel Ferguson invited the farmers to submit claims for the return of property. The Rebels had their supporters though, for several young ladies presented bouquets of flowers to the men in gray.

The mission accomplished in McConnellsburg, the men in gray recrossed the mountain and rode into Mercersburg with drawn pistols and sabers. They expected resistance. But there was none. Mercersburg lost less possessions than McConnellsburg, primarily because the Rebels did not have room for more items.

Colonel Ferguson visited with one of the leading citizens of the town, the Reverend Dr. Philip Schaff, a professor of the German Reformed Seminary, and a leading theologian in America. The seminary has since been moved eastward to Lancaster. But in '63 it was a center of theological learning. Schaff and Ferguson had a long philosophical talk on the causes of the war, and the Union Southern views about the same.

Although Ferguson was very kind, Dr. Schaff felt at the mercy of the men in gray. He could not understand why the United States Government was unable to stop the invasion. In his journal he noted that the Rebels were very poorly dressed, and equipped with a variety of arms. Some were so tired that they were asleep in the saddle.

Although Frederick was to see a lot of the men in blue at the end of the week, to their surprise, the residents saw gray-clad troopers on June 20.

> Shortly after six o'clock our citizens witnessed an exciting scene. Four Federal cavalry came dashing into our city from the Hagerstown road at the top of their horses' speed, hotly pursued by about 20 Rebel cavalry who fired at them repeatedly in passing along. One of the Federals effected his escape; the other three being taken prisoners a short distance east of town. None of them were wounded.

> As the Rebels entered our city, John Lambright, a butcher belonging to this place, had several shots fired at him by the Rebels, but fortunately escaped injury. He had on a blue coat at the time and was mistaken for a Federal soldier.

> The Rebels are better looking, better dressed, better fed and better mounted than any of those who visited us last September. By 9 p.m. they had retired from our city and the town again relapsed into its former quietude.

> Yesterday, a small body of Rebel cavalry made their appearance in our city and about 2 p.m. there was an unusual commotion in South Market Street, caused by a squad of about 25 of Capt. George Vernon's Federal cavalry in hot pursuit of about half a dozen mounted Rebels. They dashed through our streets at a furious rate and made the bullets whistle in every direction. One of the Rebels by the name of Carder, from Page County, Va., was wounded twice and captured; the others effected their escape. Capt. Vernon's squad pursued the fleeing Rebels to the top of the hill over looking Battle Town, when observing about six times their own number of Rebel Cavalry about half a mile beyond they prudently withdrew.

> Early this morning two Rebel troopers were seen riding through this city. At about 11 a.m. five Federal cavalry came dashing in and not finding any Rebels, they soon retired. About 2 p.m. a company of 50 of Buford's regular United States cavalry quietly entered the town, remained about an hour and quietly retired again.[189]

Several days after the fall of Winchester, Ed Johnson gave Harry Gilmor roving orders, permitting him to go on his own, as long as he reported at Sharpsburg. He set out with twenty men and captured eight wagons near Harpers Ferry. Captain Davis and ten men were sent to scout in Frederick. Riding in unopposed, they captured some men in blue and then were accosted by a Union cavalry patrol.

The next day, Gilmor and his two-hundred-man battalion rode into Frederick. However, their stay was brief and unwelcome. They encountered by their figures, eighteen hundred blue troopers. The figures were revised downward later. There was a lot of excitement, yelling, and shooting, but not many casualties.

According to Gilmor, he and his men then received a great welcome in Frederick. There was no lack of food, drink, or hospitality. Gilmor feared the men might get scattered, and perhaps surprised by the Union cavalry so he had the bugler sound "recall." Riding on to Monocacy Junction, he was going to try and destroy the bridge but felt it was impossible. A blockhouse guarded the approaches. Gilmor rode back to Frederick, crossed the mountain, and rejoined the army. He was given orders to report to Maryland General George Steuart for a raid on McConnellsburg.[190]

Two days were spent in Fulton County, gathering up all kinds of stock. Then it was on to Fort Loudoun and more of the same. Some bushwhackers were encountered. Gilmor was instructed to leave a pair of plow horses at each farm, and also the milk cows.

Sunday, June 21

When this book was started, it was hoped that we could have at least one page for the seven Union corps and the three Confederate corps for each of the days between June 14 and July 1. However, in many cases, the material is just not there. Sunday, June 21, is one of those days. On the Union side, the days between Saturday, June 20, and Wednesday, the twenty-fourth, were like the lull before the storm. The Second Corps reached Gainesville and Thoroughfare Gap, and the Fifth Corps marched from Aldie and Middleburg to Upperville. Other than the cavalry skirmish at Upperville it was a quiet Sabbath.

Alfred Pleasonton, commanding the Union cavalry, moved

with his command and Barnes's division of the Fifth Corps to Middleburg. Two brigades were left in the town, while with Strong Vincent's brigade, Pleasonton attacked Stuart and drove him back, inflicting heavy losses on the way. The Confederate leader was driven through Upperville into Ashby's Gap.[191]

Strong Vincent says he started in support of Pleasonton at 7:00 A.M., advancing to the left of the Ashby's Gap Road in support of Gregg's cavalry. Rebel troops faced the infantry of the Fifth Corps behind stone walls. But Union cavalry and infantry prevailed. Vincent had never seen cavalry charges before. They "were truly inspiring, and the triumphant strains of the bands, as squadron after squadron hurled the enemy in his flight up the hills and toward the gap, gave us a feeling of regret that we, too, were not mounted and could not join in the chase."[192] Vincent's men were tired and spent the night in Upperville before returning to Middleburg on Monday morning.

The quiet of the June Sabbath was broken for the members of the Union Twelfth Corps by the sounds of cannon fire and volleys of musketry. However, the sound was seven or eight miles away and most of the men continued to rest around Leesburg. General Williams and the troops concluded that it was the cavalry and infantry support meeting the Confederates in Ashby's Gap.

Williams took his Sunday dinner with the corps commander, General Slocum, in a Leesburg hotel. Oddly enough, the hotel was operated by an ex-Rebel officer by the name of Williamson. Williams was very much impressed by the beauty of the fine homes in Leesburg. Equally impressive were the fiery and "explosive Secesh women." He saw very few men. Those he did notice were old. The young ones were away at war.[193]

Although the sounds of cannonading continued in the mountain gap, Williams rode around town and thought back over the years. He had come to the lovely and fertile area for the first time in 1850 or 1851. Forty years earlier Williams had stayed for a while with a farmer and shoemaker in Madison. The man had a son in Leesburg working as a storekeeper.

160

The farmer shared the letters of his son with the little Williams boy. Leesburg therefore had a fond place in his heart. The general writes:

> Strange are the occurrences of our lives. My earliest ideas of Virginia towns were of a peaceful shoestore and here I am as a belligerent, in manhood, dictating terms of ingress and egress to its people![194]

Elements of the Third Corps arrived at a new campsite along Goose Creek on the evening of June 21. Sergeant Marbaker found a cluster of six houses. Company E camped near the home of Widow Miller. She and the other residents were cordial to the men in blue. Therefore the men did not forage, but paid for the items they wanted. Later in the evening, some of the soldiers called on Mrs. Miller. She made a strange request. She wanted to "hear some good Union songs." Naturally, the request was fulfilled. Then Mrs. Miller "favored us with some Confederate songs."[195]

The next morning the soldiers from New Jersey found a scow and a young man to ferry them across the creek. . . . Then it was on to Leesburg. The men were given three days' rations of hardtack, coffee and sugar.

This Sunday, Charles Wainwright wrote that the weather had been unsettled since Thursday. A lot of rain had fallen, but the dust was settled, and streams swollen. Saturday night was cool and the campfire felt good.

Upperville is a pretty little town. But in 1863 the crops and fields were unattended. Once again the men were "away," which meant somewhere in Confederate service. The Union soldiers thought that most of them were probably in the partisan ranger and guerrilla units which operated so effectively in the area.

The cavalry fight at Upperville was severe. The Confederates sought to protect the little town at the base of the mountains. There was street fighting, and shooting from the cover of houses and fences. The dismounted Rebels slowed up the Union cavalry, but finally retired to the hamlet of Paris where they reformed.

Strong Vincent notes, "The charges of cavalry, a sight I

had never before witnessed were truly inspiring, and the triumphant strains of the bands, as squadron after squadron pushed the enemy in his flight up the hills towards the gap, gave us a feeling of regret that we too were not mounted and could not join in the charge."[196]

That June evening the Union infantry and victorious cavalrymen mingled and socialized in Upperville. Colonel Taylor of the First Pennsylvania was a center of attraction.

The men found enough liquid content to mix a drink called "Hooker's Retreat," a beverage that had gained a lot of favor since Hooker pulled back after Chancellorsville.[197]

When the Union cavalry reached the crest of the Blue Ridge at Ashby's Gap, they had a tremendous view of the Shenandoah Valley. But they saw a frightening sight. The valley was filled with "the long lines of gray coated Confederates and their trains as far as the eye could see," all hastening with rapid steps toward the Potomac.[198]

Daniel MacNamara of the Ninth Massachusetts noticed the beautiful large houses along the road to Middleburg and the Little River Turnpike. These surpassed anything the men in blue had seen in Virginia. This area had been relatively untouched by the war.[199]

Looking at some of the correspondence for the day, Slocum reiterated that his position at Leesburg should be held at all cost as it secured the river crossings.

Slocum's command captured a deserter from Pickett's division who told them that Longstreet was near Snicker's Gap. He reported that Ewell was in Maryland and the rest of the army headed that way.[200]

Dan Tyler, reporting from Maryland Heights, said that his signal officers reported three Confederate regiments near Sharpsburg, stacking arms. Their teams were hitched, and a lot of smoke rising. There was a lot of movement.[201]

Confederate cavalry was busy driving off cattle from Sharpsburg and the Valley of the Antietam.

Meanwhile the Tenth Maine Battalion fixed kettles of beans in their ovens. When an order was given to march to Brook Station, there was no time to dig them up. Two years later William T. Dodge remembered the kettles of beans pre-

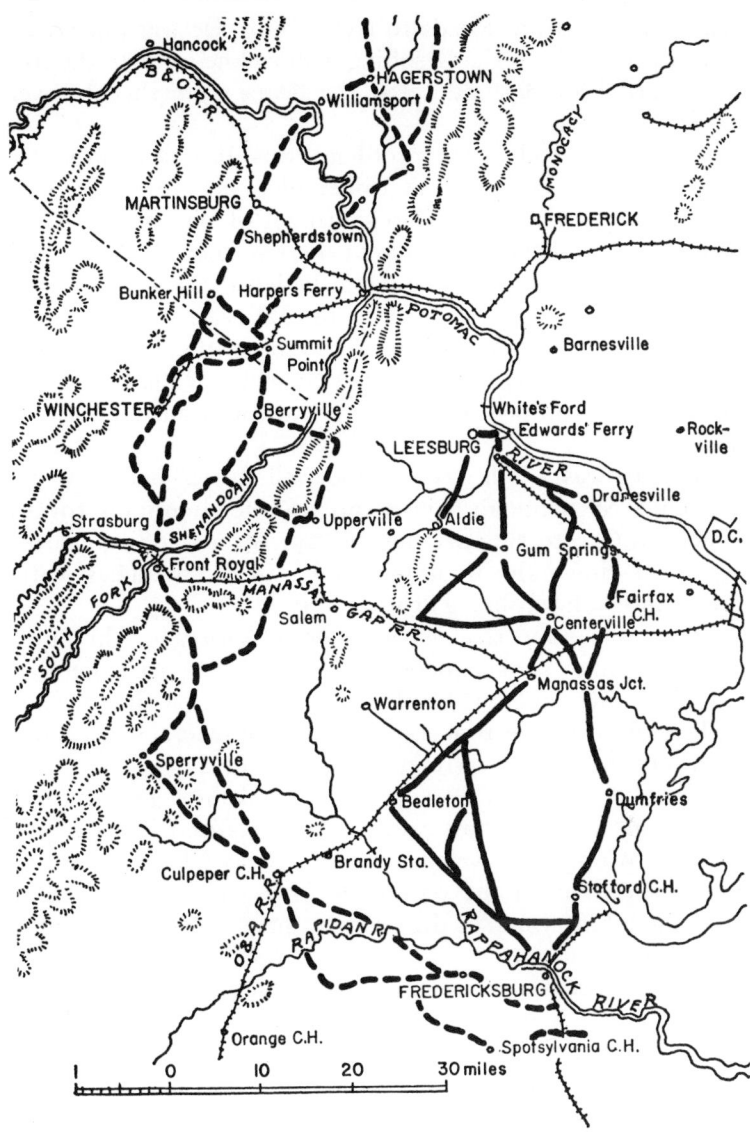

The Confederate march north from Culpeper. Courtesy Louisiana
State University Press from *Here Come the Rebels!*

pared while on the Roads to Gettysburg. He was once again encamped in the area. Grabbing a shovel he went to the spot and started to dig. But alas, the beans were slightly overdone.[202]

Longstreet had some problems this June Sabbath. The Union cavalry hit Stuart at Upperville, and drove him back, nearly through Ashby's Gap southeast of Winchester. Longstreet sent McLaws back across the river near Paris to meet the threat. The infantry apparently led Pleasonton to withdraw, although he got a look at the valley. The infantry had to recross the Shenandoah in the evening, thus making three river crossings in two days. Other elements of the First Corps remained in camp near Snicker's Gap or headed for Berryville.

Sunday was a bad day for Shotwell. It was back into the ice cold Shenandoah River and up the mountain toward Snicker's Gap to support the cavalry. After standing guard it was back down the mountain and into the branches of the river. Shotwell felt like a drowned rat.[203]

But Lee's grand strategy was compensation for the physical exertions. Yankee papers were declaring that Lee had 200,000 men, and forty miles of wagons and artillery. Shotwell rejoiced in the time and millions the federal government would have to spend to repulse the invasion.

While at Snicker's Gap, the Third Arkansas gained a new appreciation of the gray cavalry. They realized that troopers do fight. Constant cavalry skirmishing was taking place, Stuart's men were on the go all the time, galloping to and fro past the infantrymen as they rode to meet some new point of Union penetration.

J. W. Russell was a member of the Eighth Virginia Regiment, Garnett's brigade, Pickett's division as that command marched northward through the western part of Loudoun County to join Longstreet and the main Confederate column.

Evidently the Confederate postal system was not very efficient. His wife Harriett had written to him on May 28 from their home in Waterford. James never received the letter until June 21.

Replying to his wife the next day from Snickersville, Russell said:

> I was very glad to hear from you and to know that you are all well—for I never expected to hear from you again unless I could get home to see you. . . . I wrote to you that I would send you some money . . . but it is not safe to send in a letter. I have nothing but Confederate money and can get no other kind unless I was in Richmond and then I would have to give four dollars for 1 in State Notes.
>
> . . . all the boys are getting permission to go to their homes and stay a day and night. But I think if I got home I can stay longer if the Yankees leave Loudoun.
>
> . . . I think that the South is going to gain her Independence during this Falls campaign. It may be that peace will not be declared for 6 or 9 months after the fighting is over. But I think that the foreign powers will interfere before a great while for they see that the North can never subjugate the South by fighting and therefore I think they will enter into some negotiations for peace. But I hope my prophecy may prove true. For I am getting tired of being away from home any longer.[204]

The next year when James wrote home from the Petersburg area, he sent it "via Point of Rocks, Frederick County, Md."

Colonel Fremantle got his horse shod and left Woodville at 8:15. However, they had barely started when Sergeant Norris's horse lost a shoe. So they stopped at a blacksmith shop in Sperryville. Fremantle observed the natural beauty of the hills and valleys, but the land itself was almost wiped out, being uncultivated, and very few animals. All the fences had been destroyed. After all, the area had seen soldiers coming and going for two years. Some of the farms had been burned.

The colonel saw about thirty blacks on the way to church. They were in wagons and on horseback. Soon Norris and Fremantle caught up with the tail of Lee's army, mostly the sick and broken-down men, trying to keep up the best they could.

At 5:00 P.M. the two men arrived in Front Royal. Fremantle thought it was a beautiful place, the scene of Jackson's campaigns and a battle earlier in the war between two Maryland units. They had trouble finding corn for the horses. Food was another problem. But Fremantle was not bashful.

165

He simply appealed to two nice looking young women. The two could not say "no" to a lieutenant colonel from Her Majesty's army.

Norris and Fremantle did not stay long. At 6:30 they crossed the two branches of the Shenandoah River, "a broad and rapid stream." The bridges having been destroyed, the two had to ford the river. It was deep from the rain, and the two were barely able to make it. At 8:30 Fremantle reached the camping area of Dorsey Pender's division. At last he was with the famed Army of Northern Virginia. The hillsides were dotted with many campfires. It was picturesque. Norris and the colonel rode two more miles and then took refuge in Mr. Mason's hayloft. The hay felt good after a trip of forty-six miles. Before going off to sleep, Fremantle notes, "Stonewall" Jackson is considered a regular demigod in this part of the country.[205]

Spencer Welch wrote to his wife from Winchester today:

> In coming from Fredericksburg here we have taken a much shorter route than the one we took in going from here to that place last fall. Since we left Fredericksburg last week we have not traveled more than one hundred miles, but we traveled 175 miles by the other route. We camped on top of the mountain last night. The night before (19) we did not go into camp until about ten o'clock, and then it began to rain furiously. We were in an open grass field and so we had to stand up and take it. It was a very heavy rain and the night was the worst I ever experienced. I sat up the entire night on a rock and kept dry with an oilcloth. Few men were so fortunate as to have so good place to sit on as a rock. I am willing to endure almost anything, or to be deprived of almost anything, if we can have the pleasure of getting into Pennsylvania and letting the Yankees feel what it is like to be invaded.
>
> Our army is very large now, and if we get into Maryland or Pennsylvania and Hooker engages us you may be certain that he will be severely whipped. General Lee and his army are bent on it. Our troops are in fine health and I have never before seen them get along half so well on a march. Not a man has given out since the rain. I believe they will fight better than they have ever done, if such a thing could be possible. I feel fine and have stood the march admirably. We have had plenty of meat and bread to eat since we started, and I got some good rich milk this morning at Front Royal.
>
> From where I am writing this letter I can look around me and see one of the most beautiful and fertile countries. I do wish you could

see it. My servant has gone to a farmhouse, and he stays so long that I believe he is having something cooked.[206]

Richard S. Ewell arrived in Hagerstown on June 20. On this Sunday, he and Robert Rodes, along with two other generals, attended worship services at the Catholic Church. The troops of Rodes's were still in camp along the Antietam at Funkstown, while Gordon and Early were in Shepherdstown. The troops of Edward Johnson spent the day near the Dunker Church on the Antietam Battlefield.[207]

The Second Corps had maintained these positions for several days waiting "for the other two corps to close up." Sunday afternoon, Ewell received orders from Lee to take Harrisburg. However, the intent of the message is open for debate.[208]

Let's look now at some of the events of the day in the ranks of the Second Corps of the Army of Northern Virginia.

Randolph McKim says that Johnson's men recalled with "intense interest . . . the thrilling story of (Antietam) that tremendous conflict."[209] Sunday morning brought ladies from Shepherdstown to the bivouac area. These were Southern sympathizers who had made a new battle flag for brigade headquarters. The women of Shepherdstown "were always distinguished for their devotion to the Confederate cause. . . ."[210] McKim found the folks of Sharpsburg to be very friendly also.

Jed Hotchkiss was still busy with his maps at Ferry Hill, although he took time to attend a short service conducted by Mr. Lacy. Then it was back to the drawing boards. Jed noted that more rain fell and the Potomac River was high.[211]

McKim led a prayer meeting this June Sabbath, and wrote in his little four-inch square notebook that "Rev. Mr. Patterson of the Third North Carolina held service, preached, and administered the communion."[212]

A. P. Hill and the Third Corps was also getting closer to the Potomac. This Sunday they reached Berryville at the junction of the road running east and west to Leesburg and Winchester, north and south to Charles Town and Front Royal.

Although they were ragged and dirty, and in some cases

barefooted, Hill's men received a great welcome in the Virginia towns and villages. Spencer Welch, surgeon of the Thirteenth South Carolina, noted that "the ladies waved their handkerchiefs from every little farm house." Bands played as they marched through Front Royal. The people were happy to see the men in gray. Meat, bread, and milk were brought to the soldiers.[213]

Daniel Morgan led an outstanding group of "long rifle sharpshooters" during the Revolutionary War. More than once his men turned the tide of battle or saved the day for Washington's army. Morgan was instrumental in the victory at Saratoga. After the defeat of the British army, the conquered Gen. John Burgoyne said to Morgan, "Sir, you command the finest regiment in the world." After the war he built a lovely home about nine miles southwest of Berryville. He called the estate Saratoga. In June of '63, Robert E. Lee encamped about two hundred yards from the stone mansion. His tent is supposed to have stood near a spring at the foot of Saratoga Hill. Lee could have used Dan Morgan on the Roads to Gettysburg.

In the meantime, Jeb Stuart was concluding his third cavalry engagement. The actions at Brandy Station, Aldie, Middleburg, and Upperville certainly did not help him. Indeed, many feel that these events crippled and confused him, making it impossible for him to carry out in detail his mission on the Roads to Gettysburg.[214]

For nearly a week, the Iron Brigade and elements of the First Corps rested near Guilford Station. It was the lull before the storm, quiet "before the terrible event soon to be infolded to history, and many a poor boy wrote his last letter home."[215]

But while men of the First Corps took it easy and splashed and played in the waters of Broad Run, General Wadsworth was busy. He was sure a river crossing would come eventually. Therefore, he built a bridge over Goose Creek, so the army could march by the shortest route to Edwards Ferry.[216]

Nearly all the men in Leesburg were away. This meant in service of the Confederacy. The welcome of the Twelfth

168

Corps was not that great. However, the residents were glad to sell fruit and vegetables in exchange for United States greenbacks. The young ladies of the town did not invite the men in blue to come into their parlors, but seemed glad to talk to them when they strolled in. There was a lot of good-natured kidding. The girls of Leesburg teased the Union soldiers by singing "The Bonnie Blue Flag," "Dixie," and other southern airs.[217]

Fifty members of the Second United States Cavalry reached Frederick today. They rested for a while at the intersection of Church and Market streets. They had ridden into town from the mouth of the Monocacy. They reported sounds of firing from the direction of Leesburg.[218]

On June 22, John Gibbon had the opportunity to visit the Gainesville battlefield. Perhaps riding over the scene of an earlier battle took his mind from the grief over his child, at least momentarily. He speaks of Sugar Plum, a favorite horse.

> As we came along, I rode over the fields and was very much interested in recollecting and recalling different incidents of the battle. The interest was increased when we came to the scene of the Gainesville fight, which you recollect was where my old brigade fought almost entirely alone and behaved so well. I never had had an opportunity of riding over the ground before, and could without difficulty trace the direction of my line by the broken cartridges and the bodies of the men which appear to have been simply covered with earth right where they fell. I saw the very spot where I dismounted from "Sugar Plum" and left him. It will not be very long, however, before most of the traces of the battle will be obliterated and I only wish all marks on the country could be wiped away as easily and as soon.... For a long time yesterday we could hear guns up in the direction of Aldie and Middleburg, and were informed that Pleasanton was having a fight with the enemy's cavalry, so that I think it probable Lee's main force is over in the Shenandoah Valley.[219]

Today, Lieutenant King of the Tenth Maine Battalion rejoined his unit in Leesburg. The men were glad to see him. He brought many letters and packages from friends and relatives in Maine.[220]

The First Corps spent most of Tuesday resting and refitting in and around Millwood and Berryville.

Colonel Fremantle hit the road at 6:15 without food or

Difficulties along the way.

Jubal Early.   John Gordon.

These officers led their men from Shepherdstown to the
banks of the Susquehanna.

corn for his poor horse. He and Sergeant Norris were slowed
down by Pender's infantry. Fremantle's horse lost two more
shoes and there was no opportunity to replace them. The
army was using all the blacksmith shops along the way.

Fremantle was impressed with Pender's men. They looked
like good troops. Most of them had decent clothing and
shoes. However, there was little uniformity in the uniforms.
They were all shades, gray, brown, butternut, you name it.
Many had felt hats. The infantry was armed with Enfield
rifles.

The horses were in poor shape. Their ration was three
pounds of Indian corn per day. The artillery was all kinds—
Parrots, Napoleons, rifled and smooth bores. Many of them
had U.S. letters stamped on them, having been captured
somewhere along the line. The battle flags were generally red
with a blue Saint Andrews cross showing the stars.

Berryville was reached at 9:00. Already Fremantle had
covered eleven miles. That's not much today, but it was a lot
in '63. Lee's headquarters were just beyond the town. Fremantle saw an officer of handsome appearance and realized

171

that it was Lee. But the commander was busy, so Fremantle gave his letter of introduction to a staff member. The colonel met various staff officers who suggested that he ride to Winchester and attach himself to Longstreet's staff. The Englishman also met Captain Schreibert of the Prussian army who was with Lee.[221]

Fremantle ate breakfast with Mr. Lawley, and then rode ten miles to Winchester. The horse without his front shoes had a difficult trip. Fremantle arrived at 5:00 P.M. and was able to get new horseshoes. With Lawley's help he found nice quarters. Two good-looking Winchester girls, relatives of the lady of the house, were also present. This made Fremantle happy. The girls gave a miserable picture of life in the Shenandoah Valley under the Union directives of Banks, Shields, and Milroy.

Milroy was a bad word in Winchester. He was held in utter contempt, almost like Butler in New Orleans. The only item marring the capture of Winchester by Ewell was the escape of Milroy. Many wanted to hang him. Fremantle did not think that even Jefferson Davis could save him if captured.

The Coldstream Guards officer was told that the residents of Winchester could not purchase food and supplies during the Union occupation unless they took the oath of allegiance. A curfew went into effect at 8:00 P.M. Union officers came by from time to time on the pretense of making a search. The ladies were insulted and sometimes bombarded with sexual propositions. Mail from members of the family in the military was withheld from them. No wonder Winchester was happy to see Milroy go.

Isaac Ridgeway Trimble was nearly sixty years old in June of '63. But he wrote to Robert E. Lee offering his services. Trimble was a West Point graduate, a veteran of ten years in the military, and had been a railroad officer in Baltimore. He gave a life of distinguished service to the state of Maryland. His grandsons have followed in his steps, one being a noted doctor in Baltimore, another a career officer in the United States Foreign Service including ambassador to Cambodia, and David, a fine rector of several Episcopalian churches.[222]

Serving with "Stonewall" Jackson, Trimble was seriously

172

wounded at Groveton. But now he was alright and raring to go. Lee could use him. As a railroad engineer he knew Maryland and Pennsylvania very well. So he joined Lee in Berryville, Virginia. Lee was finishing lunch, and said to Isaac, "You must go with us to Pennsylvania."

The Confederate commander was full of optimism. "We have out manuevered Hooker. He doesn't know where we are or what our plans are. Our whole army will be in Pennsylvania day after tomorrow, leaving the enemy far behind and obliged to follow us by forced marches. I hope with these advantages to accomplish some signal result and to end the war, if Providence favors us."

Lee and Trimble then discussed the treatment of the residents of Pennsylvania. They both agreed against the destruction of private property and the mistreatment of nonmilitary persons. Their aims were higher than "to make war on defenseless citizens or women and children."[223]

This was a busy day for Dick Ewell. Early and his troops crossed the Potomac at Shepherdstown and proceeded through Sharpsburg and Keedysville to Boonsboro, or current Maryland 34.[224] Early turned left in Boonsboro and moved three miles west of town where he halted.[225]

Last Monday Robert Rodes marched from Martinsburg to Williamsport. Today they covered thirteen miles from Hagerstown to Greencastle. The march was not so bad as they had tramped less than twenty miles since June 16. Alfred Jenkins and his cavalry reoccupied Chambersburg. For a week the Second Corps had been busy collecting horses and supplies. They had done their job well. Now they were moving northward to bring threats and fear to the Union.

Before Edward Johnson's division took up the march, Randolph McKim had his morning devotions in a woods near Sharpsburg. After reading his Bible and praying, he saw some soldiers looking at graves from the Antietam campaign. With their permission, McKim read the Scriptures to them and prayed with them.[226] These are little items of personal note. Each man must have had more than his share of memories on the Roads to Gettysburg.

Among those crossing the Potomac at Shepherdstown, was

Robin Berkeley. He suffered badly cut and bruised feet. Robin noted, "I shall never try to wade a river again barefooted. Encamped in Sharpsburg."[227]

This morning Alfred Jenkins was patroling the area between Hagerstown and Greencastle. Robert B. Moorman, commanding Company D of the Fourteenth Virginia, was dispatched into the mountains east of Hagerstown. Southern sympathizers had told the Rebels two thousand horses were hidden there. The men trotted off through Leitersburg, the Hughes's Iron Works, and then proceeded to Caledonia, finding very few horses or mules. They had brief skirmish at Monterey with Pennsylvania militia troops, and two days later rejoined Jenkins in Chambersburg.

By 10:00 A.M. Jenkins was a little south of Greencastle. He sent Captain J. A. Wilson with Company I of the Fourteenth Virginia Cavalry on ahead. Captain Wilson was told "that if he met any Yankees he was to simulate panic and thus draw the enemy in a headlong pursuit." The main body of the brigade would be waiting in ambush.

Jenkins rode through Greencastle. A miled north of town they came to the William Fleming house. Down the road was a blacksmith shop. Two Union soldiers, who were having their horses' shoes tightened, ran out. They were quickly taken prisoner. Jenkins saw Union cavalry on a wooded hill nearby. He moved quickly to put the plans for an ambush into action. The rest of Jenkins's force had dismounted and was hidden by the wheat. Rodes was also advancing his infantry. They were tearing down fences on both sides of the road on the Kissecker farm so they could advance unhindered. The Confederates were prepared to commit almost eight thousand troops to the conflict. Their opposition, about thirty-five Union cavalrymen. Rodes and Jenkins were cautious because D. K. Appenzellar, a local farmer, had told the Confederates a tall story. When he was captured for questioning, he told them that George B. McClellan was marching south with forty thousand men. Union newspapers of the day supported the story, so Ewell, riding with Rodes's troops, urged caution.[228]

Captain Boyd was a remarkable officer. He saw through

174

Wilson's trick and halted at the Fleming farm. He saw the infantry moving into line, and sensed the trap. According to William Reach of the First New York (Lincoln) Cavalry, Corporal William H. Rihl came riding out from behind the Fleming house and stopped his horse. At that moment, dismounted Confederates fired a volley of shots. Sgt. Milton Cafferty, riding with Rihl, suffered a severe leg wound. Rihl was hit in the jaw, the bullet passing through the base of his brain. His death was instantaneous. He was the first Union soldier killed in Pennsylvania in the War of the Rebellion. Rihl was just twenty at the time. He stood five feet six inches tall, with light complexion, blue eyes and dark hair. Miss Mary Fleming narrowly escaped injury when a bullet went through an open window near her head. Despite the danger, she ran out into the yard and attempted to care for Rihl.[229]

Boyd withdrew his tiny command in the direction of Marion. The men in gray buried Rihl in a shallow grave near where he had fallen, and left Cafferty in a nearby house. Years later in elaborate ceremonies, Rihl's remains were exhumed and reburied in the cemetery of the Greencastle Lutheran Church. But then the Rihl Post of the Greencastle Grand Army of the Republic reburied Rihl beside Route 11 on the Fleming farm. Those tracing the Roads to Gettysburg must stop north of Greencastle and visit the Rihl monument.

Earlier in the morning, Knipe's Eighth and Seventy-first New York were in the Chambersburg area. The Eighth came into Ben Chambers's city while the Seventy-first halted at Green Village. Then Captain Boyd sent word back that the Rebels were on the way; General Couch to cover the country with scouts. The Seventy-first New York reached Chambersburg at eleven o'clock and received a glorious welcome. The folks came out to cheer. Little boys ran alongside the marching soldiers and offered to carry their packs. Little girls competed to fill canteens. The residents of Chambersburg looked upon them as their protectors. In return they wanted to do all they could for the boys in blue.[230]

The New York unit was assigned the task of covering the Waynesboro Road. Information from that area said the Rebels were there gathering horses.

On June 23, Jubal Early and his men broke camp west of Boonsboro, and proceeded via what is now Maryland 66, going through Mapleville, to Wagner's Crossroads, Beaver Creek, Cavetown and Ringgold. He called the latter hamlet Ridgeville. The troops halted for the night in the Waynesboro, Pennsylvania, area. Rodes was ten miles west of Early in Greencastle.[231]

Ewell's men engaged in hat swapping in Greencastle. Most of their headgear was worn out. Whenever they saw a nice looking hat on the head of a Pennsylvanian, they lifted it, and gave the man who just happened to be at the wrong place at the wrong time, their own faded, wornout piece.

Many of the men walked through the fields and orchards. Soldiers from Longstreet's First Corps and attached elements tramped through the streets in Martinsburg on Tuesday, Wednesday, and Thursday on their way to the Potomac River. Belle Boyd, the sensational lady spy of the Confederacy, greeted many of them. Only twenty years old at the time, the young woman held the soldiers in awe. For some reason she loved buttons and collected them. She made that request of the men in gray as they passed by.

Confederate officers jammed the Martinsburg hotels. Fitzgerald Ross, a British magazine writer, stayed at the home of Col. Charles J. Faulkner, a Virginia congressman whom President James Buchanan had appointed minister to France. Ross observed that the Confederates had colorful blankets. Many of them being made from the carpets of home.

The South Carolinians in Perrin's brigade were impressed with the abundance of the Martinsburg area.

> In every direction yellow fields of grain extended themselves; in every farm were droves of the largest, fattest cattle; gardens thronged with inviting vegetables; orchards gave promise of bounteous fruit yield. . . . The citizens were amazed at our moderation. Many of them bade us help ourselves to poultry, milk, vegetables, fruit, honey, bread, whatever we wanted to eat, provided we spared more valuable property.[232]

By the twenty-fourth, "the progress of Ewell rendered it necessary that the rest of the army should be within supporting distance, and Longstreet and Hill marched to the Potomac. The former crossed at Williamsport, and the latter at Shepherdstown."[233]

The men of Robertson's command spent three days, June 20-23 on top of the mountain at Snicker's Gap. At one time it was called Snickersville after an early farmer. The name of the community today is Bluemont. It was cloudy most of the time, with what seemed like a constant rain and wind. The wind tore the tents down and the men were drenched.

Fremantle and his new friend Lawley rode out to inspect what had been Mr. Mason's nice place. Mason, of course, was the Southern commissioner in London. Mason's home had been beautiful. But it was destroyed earlier. Then in the last seven months, Milroy must have entered a fit of rage. He attempted to destroy even the foundations of the archtraitor (the Union name for Mason). Fremantle tells us that not one stone was left standing upon the other. The debris had been carried away, and all that remained of Mason's home was a hole in the ground.

Folks told Fremantle that Winchester was a charming place with pleasant society, that is, before the war. The men were all away in the military, and the women subject to battle, insults, and hardships. "As many as 5,000 wounded have been accommodated here at one time. All the ladies are accustomed to the bursting of shells and the sight of fighting, and all are turned into hospital nurses or cooks."

Corn was scarce. Fremantle could not find any in Winchester. So he had to take his horse out to graze. Naturally this meant the colonel had to stay with the horse. In the evening Fremantle visited two officers from Louisiana. They had stormed the fort on the fourteenth and were gravely wounded. They had served under Jackson and "venerate his name." They felt Ewell was a worthy successor. They told the British officer that "at no period of the war . . . have the men been so eager for a fight, or so confident of success." Fremantle found time to talk to another pretty young lady who told him that "dancing and horse racing are forbidden by the Episcopal Church in this part of Virginia."[234]

As late as the twenty-third of June, Hooker still had some

ideas about Noland's Ford. At 7:03 A.M., Hooker wanted to know if it was suitable for the passage of the infantry, artillery, and trains of the Twelfth Corps.[235] Slocum said it was not, but sent an officer to double-check. At 9:00 A.M. Slocum reported White's Ford, three miles above Edwards Ferry, as the best ford in the area.[236]

John Babcock in Frederick was asked to take another trip to South Mountain and survey the valley below. He was to ascertain whether or not the Rebels were in Crampton's Gap and Turner's Gap. Oliver Howard was ordered to march to Harpers Ferry via Edwards Ferry, making the march in two days.[237]

At 10:15 P.M. forty pontoons and the items that went with them were started from the Washington Navy Yard for Edwards Ferry. More equipment was to be sent.

A few moments earlier, Slocum sent a message from the Point of Rocks signal officer saying that a large force of Confederates were encamped on the south side of the Potomac River at Shepherdstown. This was A. P. Hill's command.

Now Butterfield wanted to know if Chick's Ford (also called Cheek's) was suitable for infantry. He wanted to know all about that and also White's Ford. At midnight Slocum reported that Chick's Ford was one mile below White's Ford, alright for cavalry, but not for artillery or trains. White's Ford was reported to be in the same condition, with a rough bottom. However, Seneca Ford was reported to be a good one. The approaches were all good. Slocum had his wagon park near Edwards Ferry and said he could get across without delay.[238]

Captain Phillips of the Fifth Massachusetts Battery wrote a letter on Tuesday:

> "Camp near Fairfax Court House,
> Tuesday morning, June 23, 1863.
> As things began to look like a permanent camp, I have taken to drilling, and yesterday I had the camp pitched over again. We have sent on to Washington, and are now living on such luxuries as tomatoes, pease, string beans, squash, asparagus &c., bottled ale for dinner, and oranges and bananas for dessert. I wish our men's fare was as good, but they are at present living very poorly, on hard

bread and salt pork, no soft bread, no vegetables, not even salt beef, and what little fresh beef they get is hardly fit to be eaten. And as if to prevent them from improving the bill of fare the sutlers are not allowed to come out from Washington,—rather aggravating, to be within 15 miles of a good market and not allowed to buy anything."[239]

Men in blue were beginning to arrive in Fredericktown.

Jacob Englebrecht reports seeing Stahel's Cavalry brigade passing through Frederick. He guessed there might be four thousand men with four cannon. Stahel ate dinner at L. J. Brengle's.[240]

Alarming news was arriving at Hooker's headquarters. From Maryland Heights came the report that all the Confederate camps in the vicinity of Sharpsburg were gone. The view was great so Captain Daniels was sure of his information. However, he could not tell where they had gone. The wagon train was headed toward Hagerstown. Long lines of troops and a wagon train was seen coming toward Charles Town from the south. And troops and wagons were on the road to Shepherdstown. The latter column was ten miles long.[241]

Robert E. Lee seems to have been more aware of events. He knew the Union army was clustered in Loudoun County, near Leesburg. He had unconfirmed reports that Hooker was constructing a pontoon bridge, and he suspected that Hooker was about ready to cross the Potomac. He conveyed this message in a letter to President Davis, and also stated that "Hill's corps is moving (from Charles Town) toward the Potomac; his leading division will reach Shepherdstown today."

VII

CROSSING THE RIVER, JUNE 24-25

June 24 and 25 were most important days on the Roads to Gettysburg. During these days, the commands of James Longstreet and Ambrose Powell Hill crossed the Potomac River at Williamsport and Shepherdstown. Meanwhile, downstream, Hooker got things ready to cross on the twenty-fourth, and commenced moving his command across the river on the twenty-fifth.

We can imagine the excitement in the Confederate ranks, one more victory and perhaps the war would be over. On the other hand, there was alarm among the Union soldiers, war was going to their homes and their backyards. We can almost picture the splashing, yelling, and cheers at Williamsport and Shepherdstown, and the shouts of officers at Edwards Ferry as they urged the men in blue forward to the pontoon bridges.

For the Union army the crossing of the Potomac would go down in history as the greatest river crossing in the history of the American Continent. Never before, and never since, has such a large body of men and equipment crossed a major river on the way to combat like the Army of the Potomac did at Edwards Ferry. Therefore, the Union command structure has to be given credit for this major logistical movement.

Hooker initiated the move late on the night of June 23. He ordered Oliver O. Howard to start at daylight with the Eleventh Corps, cross the river and proceed to Harpers Ferry in two days. Then as he so often did, Hooker reversed his decision. When Howard got near Edwards Ferry in the afternoon of June 24, he ordered him to stay as support for Slocum.

His mind was still up in the air. Early in the evening of the twenty-fourth, he ordered Howard to cross the river to guard the bridge and depots on the northern bank.[1] Several hours later he changed his mind again, and directed the Eleventh Corps to march toward Sandy Hook near Harpers Ferry. It's hard to have confidence in a commander who is always changing his mind.

June 24

This Wednesday was full of excitement for the people in Falling Waters, Williamsport, Shepherdstown, and Chambersburg. During the day the infantry of Longstreet and Hill crossed the Potomac River, while Robert Rodes left Greencastle and marched the eleven miles to Chambersburg.[2] From the fields around Greencastle, Rodes put his division in motion. He had five brigade commanders, Junius Daniel, Alfred Iverson, and Stephen D. Ramseur. These men commanded North Carolina troops. George Doles had four Georgia regiments, while Edwin A. O'Neal was in command of five regiments from Alabama.

Stephen Dodson Ramseur was perhaps the most notable. Born on May 31, 1837, he was but twenty-six as he led his men on the Roads to Gettysburg. Ramseur had entered Davidson College, but left the North Carolina school to attend West Point. Severely wounded at Malvern Hill, he became a general on November 1, 1862. He handled his troops gallantly at Chancellorsville and served with distinction until his life was cut short at Cedar Creek October 19, 1864. Married less than a year, he received word the night before he died that his wife had presented him with a daughter.[3]

But what was it like as the men from North Carolina, Georgia, and Alabama entered Chambersburg?

William Nelson Pendleton, the fighting parson, kept his family informed as the gray columns marched northward. Earlier he had written of the grand show, or the cavalry review staged by Stuart. However, he had ridden with Lee six miles at full run, then sat on his horse in the dust as the squadrons of cavalry rode by. Pendleton was very much impressed with Ewell, noting that he rode very well even though

181

he was minus a leg. Ewell even reminded him of Jackson in his disregard for personal safety.

On the twenty-first, the elder Pendleton preached for Mr. Sutor. A good congregation was present, including Generals Lee and Longstreet. After church, the parson turned military commander, rode to Brother Hugh's and got a fine supply of cherries for the northern trip. Some nice lady gave him five lemons. Pendleton sent a supply of cherries and two of the lemons to General Lee. The clergyman's prayer was, "May the Lord go with us to restrain from evil, uphold in duty, strengthen for efficient service, protect from injury, and guide to victory, justice, and peace!"

Pendleton continued with the First Corps from Berryville to Darkesville, and crossed the Potomac on the evening of the twenty-fifth. Camp was made half a mile north of the river. The twenty-sixth found him riding through a most disagreeable rain, searching for Dr. Magill, a southern sympathizer who hopefully would have some road information for General Lee. The stores were all shut, but a group of women walked half a mile through the mud and rain to see General Lee. The Episcopal rector thought Pendleton should renounce the ministry since he had taken up arms. The parson was sure a great battle was in the offing, and it was his hope that it might lead to independence.[4]

About 9:00 A.M. the sound of music was heard on South Main Street in Chambersburg. Some thought it might be the music of the circus that was supposed to come to town. But instead it was the band belonging to Robert Rodes's division of Confederate infantry. As the long gray column reached the hill at the Reformed Church, the band struck up the music of "The Bonnie Blue Flag."[5]

The uniforms were wrinkled and so full of dust that it was hard to distinguish between the Confederate gray and the butternut uniforms. Some were shoeless. Others had shoes that were falling apart. The hot June sun had given them all good tans.

Part of the column marched through Chambersburg and posted a strong position north of town. Jenkins and his cav-

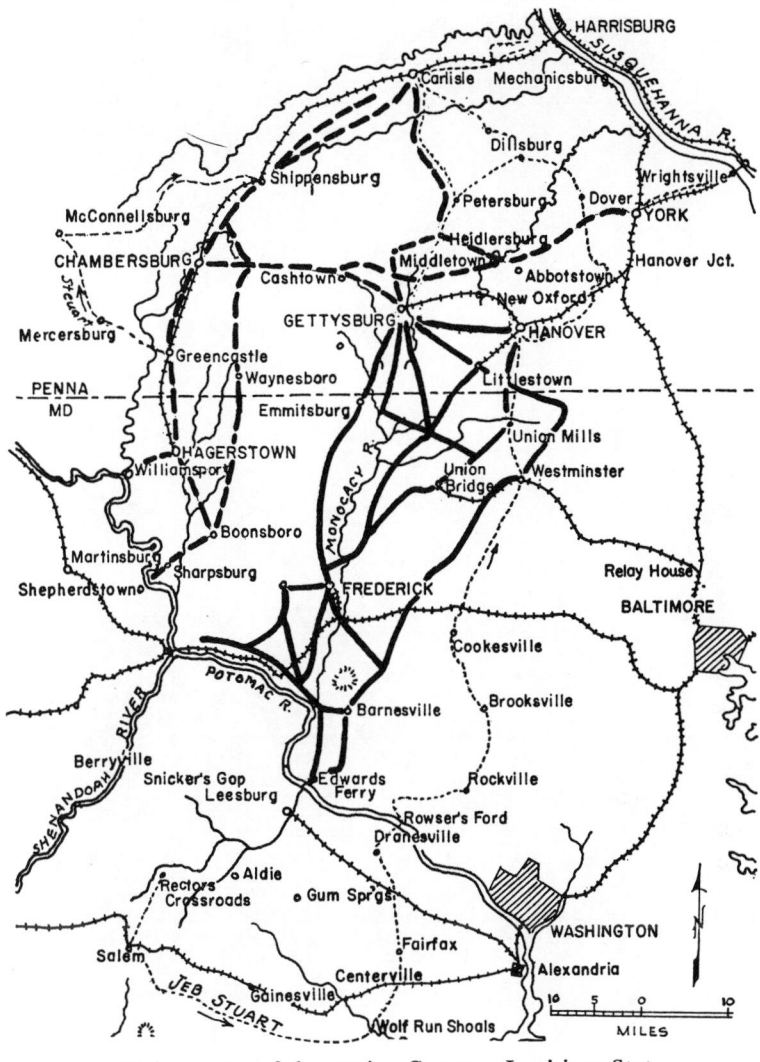

Major routes of the armies. Courtesy Louisiana State
University Press in *Here Come the Rebels!*

alry unit was assigned to guard the approaches from Harrisburg.

Throughout the twenty-fourth, columns of infantry and
artillery with their wagons and ambulances rumbled through

183

Raising the Confederate flag in Chambersburg, June 26. In the square, Lee and Hill conferred and made the decision to turn east.

the streets of Chambersburg. The Confederates also drove the cattle, taken from the farms around Hagerstown and Greencastle, into town. By nightfall, most of the army went into camp between the northern edge of Chambersburg and Shirk's Hill.

About 10:30 that morning, a carriage drawn by two horses and with an escort stopped in front of the Franklin Hotel. It brought the new commander of the Second Corps, Richard S. Ewell. He had some difficulty getting out of the carriage with his artificial limb and his crutch. He had lost his leg at the second battle of Bull Run. Ewell commandeered the parlor of the hotel as his headquarters. "Sandie" Pendleton and others went to work. A flag was run out the window. Thus by midmorning on June 24, the Stars and Bars of the Confederacy flew over Chambersburg. Colonel Willis of the Twelfth Georgia was named provost marshal of the city. He used the courthouse as his headquarters, and flew a Confederate flag from the cupola.

Robert Rodes played a prominent role in the Gettysburg campaign. His command was the first infantry to reach the Potomac, the first to cross into Maryland, the first to cross into Pennsylvania on the twenty-second, and now on the twenty-fourth, he enters Chambersburg, Pennsylvania, operating under the direct eye of Richard S. Ewell.

Jed Hotchkiss was with Rodes's infantry as it entered Chambersburg. Headquarters tents were pitched three miles beyond the town. There was no opposition. Jed had a good dinner at one of the hotels and purchased many valuable supplies. He was able to get some maps and engineering equipment.[6]

While Robert Rodes was occupying Chambersburg, Pete Longstreet was preparing to cross the Potomac River at Williamsport, thirty-one miles away.[7]

George Pickett was a little bit depressed. He did not feel like a conquering hero as he penned a note to his beloved girl friend from a field near Greencastle. He felt he could fight for a just cause and risk his life, but "when we've downed the enemy and won the victory, I don't want to hurrah. I want to go off all by myself and be sorry for them—want to lie down

185

Robert E. Lee crossing the Potomac at Williamsport in the rain. Garnet Jex paints him here with Longstreet and Pickett. Lee is receiving flowers from the ladies of the canal town.[8]

in the grass, away off in the woods somewhere or in some lone valley on the hillside far from all human sound, and rest my soul and put my heart to sleep and get back something—I don't know what—but something I had is gone from me . . . something I never knew I had until I lost it—till it was gone. . . ."[9]

Pickett then goes on to describe the bands marching through Greencastle playing "The Bonny Blue Flag," "My Maryland," and "Her Bright Smile Haunts Me Still." The soldiers were happy and hopeful keeping time to the music. A young girl rushed out and waved a Union flag in their faces.

George Pickett did take off his hat and bowed to her. The Virginians lifted their hats and cheered the little girl who was calling them "traitors." This got to the little miss, she cried out "Oh, I wish, I wish I had a Rebel flag; I'd wave that too."

> The picture of that little girl in the vine covered porch, beneath the purple morning glories (made me) think of you, my darling. For the time, that little Greencastle Yankee girl with her beloved flag was my own little promised-to-be wife, receiving from her Soldier and her Soldier's soldiers the reverence and homage due her.[10]

How would you like to march thirty miles? Well, according to Randolph Shotwell, that's what he and his comrades in Pickett's division did on the twenty-fourth. They were not walking alone, but in ranks. Men on each side, unless you were in the outside column, and men in front of, and in back of you. At times they stirred up a "tornado of dust." After a while the eyes start to swim and the men in front look like a bunch of swaying trees. And how about thirty miles with the musket, blanket, rations, shelter half, ammunition, tin cup, frying pan, etc.[11]

Shotwell compares the difference between the beginning and ending of such a journey. The first five miles are not so bad. By the end of ten you are soaking with perspiration, and starting to get a little sore. Even more discouraging is the fact that it is only 9:00 A.M. There are miles and miles to go before you halt. By noon the fifteenth mile is completed and you are ready to call it quits for the day. The heat, dust, thirst, and fatigue have taken their toll. The next two miles require a full hour.[12]

> Finally the bright officer calls a halt. The nearest spring is half a mile away. So many of the fellows just fall down where they are and pull their cap down over their face. Some might eat a piece of hard tack "as tough as sole leather, and the best thing in the world to provoke intense thirst. Here and there some eat boiled beef or rusty bacon; but generally we eat up our day's ration of meat at breakfast." Then it's time to "Fall in." So they start again, "twice as stiff and sleepy as we were before we halted. By three o'clock we have travelled twenty miles, but now the saltry sun fairly scorches our blistered backs; our brains seem addled; and the weight of the heavy musket has worn first one shoulder then the other into a red heat blister under the saturated jacket and shirt; and our poor legs seem utterly unable to take another step!"

On they trudge with "fainting steps and slow. Men stagger. Many have fallen out. Others straggle. Pain shows on the faces of the men. It's sunset. The sun is still hot. And yet no command to halt. Who is the in humane man keeping the soldiers on the road? Stomachs ache for food. Dusk comes on and campfires are seen in the distance. This is the advance guard." At last comes an aide from General Pickett saying, "General Garnett, your brigade will camp near the big spring.... Ready to move at 6 o'clock tomorrow. So the thirty mile march has been completed, and the footsore, weary, supperless, and half-sick men lie down in their wet clothes and grimy condition to catch seven hours sleep to sustain the same ordeal on the morrow." Who ever said soldering was fun?[13]

Today Ewell's artillery continued their march towards Harrisburg, passing through Hagerstown. Robin Berkeley's unit camped two miles from the Pennsylvania line. He noted, "All the country through which we passed today is beautiful and rich, splendid wheat, hay and corn crops. Nearly all the people are Union."

Many of the Confederates came from small farms. So for some diversion, even though it was against orders, the men from the South went to Washington County farms and held milking contests, seeking to find who was the best at aiming milk into their canteens.[14]

188

Robert Rodes led the first Confederate
infantry into Chambersburg.

Col. William Oates, who later led the assault on Little
Round Top, took his young adjutant and had supper with a
Maryland family. A bright young girl had a thought for ending the war. She thought the best solution was simply to hang
both President Lincoln and Jefferson Davis.

Private John West, hailing from Texas, made kind statements about the barns of western Maryland and Franklin County, saying they were prettier than two-thirds of the homes in Waco. He filled himself with ripe cherries, and even sent some seeds home to his wife.[15]

On this rainy Thursday, Colonel Fremantle, the British observer with the Confederates, noted:

> We took leave of Mrs. —— and her hospitable family, and started to overtake Generals Lee and Longstreet who were supposed to be crossing the Potomac at Williamsport. Before we got more than a few miles on our way we began to meet the first fruits of Ewell's advance into Pennsylvania.[16]

Today Early's division of the Second Corps broke camp at Waynesboro and headed northward through Quincy and Mont Alto to Greenwood at the western base of South Mountain. This was on the road from Chambersburg to Gettysburg. Early says:

> There were no indications of any enemy near us and the march was entirely without molestation. We were now in the enemy's country, and getting our supplies entirely from the country people. These supplies were taken from mills, storehouses, and the farmers, under a regular system ordered by General Lee, and with a due regard to the wants of the inhabitants themselves, certificates being given in all cases. There was no marauding, or indiscriminate plundering, but all such acts were expressly forbidden and prohibited effectually.[17]

Dr. Schaff was in for another surprise today. He had thought that with the disappearance of Colonel Ferguson, Mercersburg would see no more of the men in gray. But as the Schaff family sat down for the Wednesday lunch, a child rushed in saying, "The Rebels are coming, the Rebels are coming."[18]

Soon George Steuart's Confederate infantry marched in from Greencastle. They were two thousand strong with artillery. The fife and drum corps provided march music. Their wagons and equipment bore U.S. markings. Many of the items had been captured at Winchester a week earlier.[19]

Maj. William W. Goldsborough, a Marylander, was appointed provost marshal. He assembled the people and told them all items would be surrendered on demand, but they would be paid for (in Confederate funds). The infantrymen helped

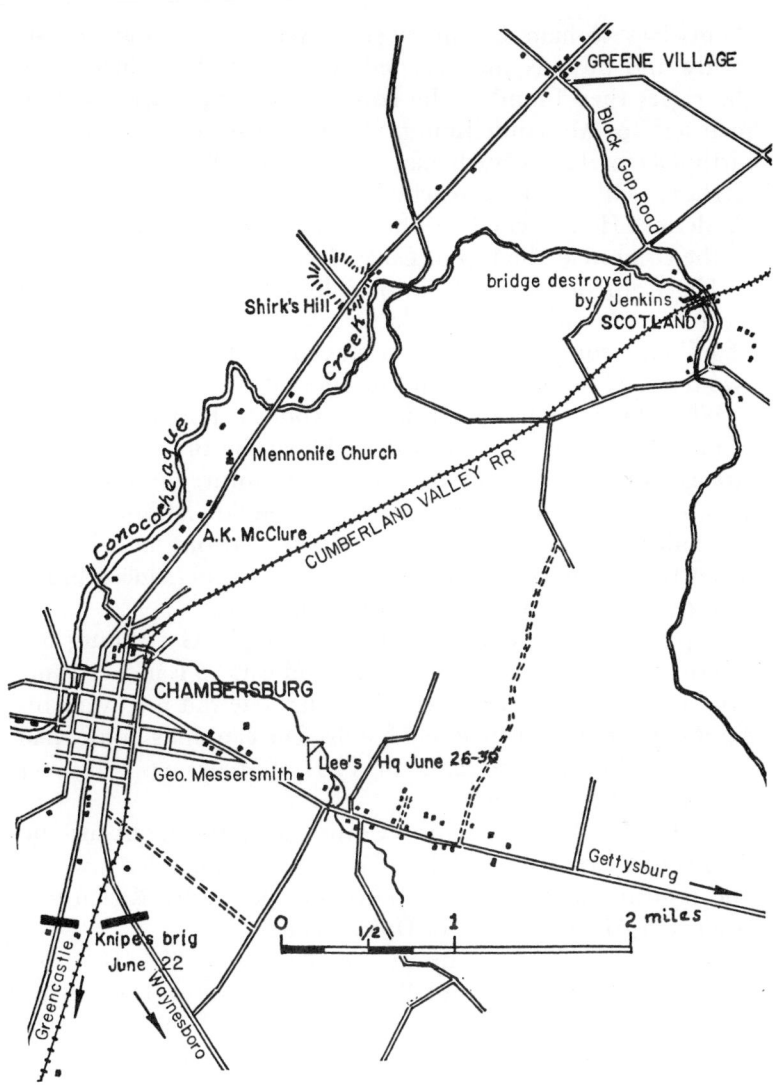

Chambersburg 1863. Jenkins at the McClure residence and Shirk's Hill. The Second Corps at the Mennonite Church, and Lee in Messersmith's woods. Courtesy Louisiana State University Press in *Here Come the Rebels!*

191

themselves to ham, bacon, sugar, molasses, and flour, eating candy and nuts as they carried things out. They lighted up the cigars they found in the store. At sunset, Steuart and his men left for McConnellsburg. On their way, they passed the birthplace of James Buchanan at Cove Gap.[20]

Harry Gilmor had reached Greencastle, traveling from Frederick. He hastened to join Steuart, and reached the rear of the column at the top of Cove Mountain.[21]

The Confederates rode into Fulton County. It was quiet with the exception of the clatter of hoofs, and the clanging of military equipment. Steuart stayed at McConnellsburg for two days, gathering stock and supplies.[22]

When Steuart left on Friday, he rode to Fort Loudon and obtained more horses and cattle. When the brigade left two stragglers remained behind. They were captured in the center of the village and executed in cold blood. Although they surrendered without a fight, they were led out and shot by recently discharged Northern soldiers. Now the American Legion decorates their graves on Memorial Day.[23]

Capt. A. W. Eichelberger, president of the Gettysburg and Hanover Railroad, sent his engines and cars to Hanover Junction as a precautionary measure today. He did not want his equipment to fall into Rebel hands. The captain's family had come to the Hanover area in 1761, purchasing 220 acres southeast of town.[24]

A. P. Hill and the Third Corps spent the night around Shepherdstown. Hill had been a corps commander now for one month. His three division commanders were Richard H. Anderson, Henry Heth, and Dorsey Pender.

Anderson was forty-one in the summer of '63. He came from South Carolina, and West Point, class of 1842. That class furnished twenty-two general officers of the Union and Confederacy from a roster of thirty-seven men. Early in the war he was in command of Charleston, but was then assigned to Longstreet's corps, and after Jackson's death, to the newly formed Third Corps. When Longstreet was wounded in the Wilderness, Anderson took over the command of the First Corps on a temporary basis. At the end of the war he was in charge of the defenses of Richmond. After the war he had a most difficult time trying to exist as his family and his home area had lost so heavily during the war.[25]

Henry Heth was a good, dependable officer. Often he had to bear the brunt of the mistakes of others, or bad situations. Heth came from Chesterfield County, Virginia, and is said to be the only Confederate general whom Lee addressed by his first name. Consistent wherever he served, his career was not marked by distinction. In the Gettysburg campaign, his troops started it all on July 1, and they were involved in the final action at Falling Waters.[26]

William Dorsey Pender is a favorite of the author's. Only twenty-nine in June of '63, Pender was without doubt one of the best brigade commanders in the Army of Northern Virginia. A West Point graduate, class of 1854, Pender served on the Pacific Coast and against the Indians prior to the war. He received command of a brigade in Hill's Light Division in June of 1862.[27] His career was marked by bravery. He kept his wife informed by frequent letters. These should be read by every student of the Civil War. Promoted to major general on May 27, Pender was given a division in the new Third Corps. He and Hill were like brothers, extremely close and full of great respect for one another. Pender had doubts about the invasion. Several days after camping at Shepherdstown, Dorsey was hit in the leg by a shell fragment on the second day at Gettysburg. On the way back to Staunton, an infection set in causing an amputation. He died in Staunton on July 18. "At the time he was perhaps the most outstanding of the younger officers of the army." Pender is buried in North Carolina.

From Shepherdstown on June 24, Gen. Dorsey Pender took time to write to his wife back home in North Carolina.

> Tomorrow I do what I know will cause you grief, and that is to cross the Potomac. The advance of our column is at Chambersburg, Penna. tonight. May the Lord prosper this expedition and bring an early peace out of it. I feel that we are taking a very important step, but see no reason why we should not be successful. We have a large army that is in splendid condition and spirit and the best Generals in the South. Our troops are sending (a) good deal of stock out of Penna. . . .[28]
>
> Hope and pray for the best. This is a momentous time. . . .

Dorsey Pender.

We will get many a horse before we come back. We have the authority and everyone seems determined to have all mounts and transportation well fixed up. I have written very regularly up to this time but of course after this my letters will be exceedingly irregular. I have been handsomely entertained today by a fine family.[29]

The last line from the general raises an interesting question. We wonder where and with whom Pender visited? Often the soldiers on the way to Gettysburg mentioned names or just initials in their letters home. No doubt the loved ones knew of whom they were speaking, but we can only speculate. But then, they were writing to loved ones, not for publication.

When Jenkins left Chambersburg and headed south earlier in the week, the people of Carlisle breathed easier. They thought the worst was over. But this was the lull before the storm. Wednesday brought the news that the Rebels were in Chambersburg, and gray cloud patrols fanning out to Shippensburg and other places. Now it was evident the Rebels were in earnest. This was no mere raid or threat. It was an invasion. The Eighth and Seventy-first New York regiments retreated from Shippensburg to Carlisle. The Eighth took a position on the Walnut Bottom Road, while the Seventy-first placed itself across the main road. A barricade was erected across the road, trenches and rifle pits dug. "Everything indicated that resistance would be offered."[30]

The Carlisle militia was mustered on Wednesday as the threat became more real. Some of the best men of the town were in the local military units. A few of the soldiers were men over sixty-five, anxious to defend their homes to the very last. The Episcopal rector and the pastor of the German Reformed Church were in the ranks too.[31]

Captain Boyd was still roaming the countryside. He had about two hundred troopers of the Second New York Cavalry under him. Picketing the road between Shippensburg and Carlisle, his men were soon driven back, within four miles of Carlisle. Yet his bravery and leadership produced profound admiration. From Bunker Hill to Carlisle, his little command had stood almost alone against the advancing Rebel cavalry and infantry.[32]

About nine o'clock, General Knipe received word that the Rebels were only two miles away. He felt it was useless to offer resistance against overwhelming odds. Therefore he ordered the New York troops and the militia to fall back.

In the Leesburg area, things were astir in the Union camps. Ewell was across the river, and the rest of the Army of Northern Virginia in the process of crossing. Orders and communiques reveal the seriousness of the situation.[33]

Messages were coming in from the signal stations on South Mountain reporting long gray columns approaching Shepherdstown from the southeast. These were the men of Powell Hill heading for "Pack Horse Ford" south of the picturesque

Potomac River town. The ford was also known as Blackford's and Boteler's Ford from local families and ferryboat operators.[34]

Orders flew thick and fast along the Potomac today. At 7:00 A.M. Captain Turnbull at Edwards Ferry was told to meet Oliver O. Howard and his Eleventh Corps on the banks near the bridges. However, Howard was not to cross yet. Captain Turnbull was ordered to build the second bridge as soon as the equipment arrived from Washington. Hooker wanted to know how long it would take once the materials arrived. Benham thought it would take until Monday or Tuesday. Captain Turnbull said that if the heavy wagons kept using the pontoon bridge, more sections of two-inch planks would be needed to save the chesses.[35]

At 1:00 P.M. today, Howard and his men arrived at Edwards Ferry. Hooker was still seeking information on the fords. Slocum reported the river as quite high, and said he would not attempt to cross his trains at night. General Stahel was ordered to take his cavalry unit and cross the river into Maryland.[36]

John P. Shank and Adam Hildebrandt of Smithsburg, Washington County, told Hiram Winchester, president of the Frederick Female Academy, that Jubal Early with twelve regiments of infantry, two of cavalry, and sixteen pieces of artillery, passed through their village yesterday. The two men estimated that eight thousand men tramped through town between 11:00 A.M. and 2:00 P.M. Their wagons were mostly U.S. wagons. Sgt. Alexander Leeds reported that he had seen approximately eleven thousand men under Rodes and Johnson tramp through Hagerstown between the hours of 1:00 to 5:00 P.M.[37]

By evening, Howard was encamped on the south bank of Goose Creek with headquarters near the pontoon bridge. He was ordered to guard the bridge and depots at Edwards Ferry.[38] Howard may have taken the road from Trappe Rock through the Goose Creek Country Club area to Edwards Ferry.

G. K. Warren, the chief engineer of the Army of the Potomac, suggested to Hooker a concentration of the Union

196

army at Harpers Ferry. Lee's army was across the river and threatening an advance upon Harrisburg. From Harpers Ferry, Hooker could protect Washington and Baltimore, and preserve his routes of supply and communication. He would be ideally situated to hinder Lee and threaten his communications and supplies. The South Mountains could be bypassed, thus avoiding a fight. Warren thought the best policy was not to attack Lee but to paralyze his movements by threatening his flank and rear, while gathering information and reinforcements.[39]

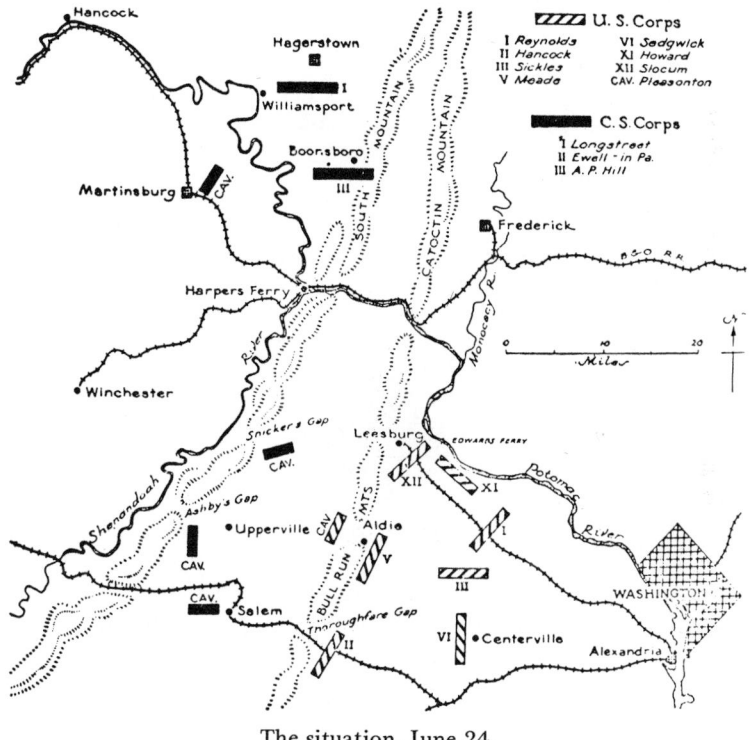

The situation, June 24.

Warren's ideas were sound because Confederate deserters reported Hill and Longstreet across the river with forty thousand men, Ewell in Greencastle with thirty thousand. These

197

figures are not quite correct, but adequate enough for alarm.[40]

Joe Hooker knew by midafternoon on Wednesday that Lee was in earnest, across the Potomac, invading, not on a diversionary mission. Like McClellan, Hooker let precious hours go by before he issued orders to move. When he finally decided to do something, he did it with vigor, but too much time went by in his decision-making process. Thus the Army of the Potomac had to make forced marches in an attempt to thwart the Army of Northern Virginia.

From Charles Wainwright's journal for June 24 are these words:

> There is almost nothing with which to make an entry here tonight. . . . We have lain here in perfect quietness, and a good deal of comfort. My batteries have all got washed up. and their horses are quite refreshed. Have them all out for battery drill each day, there being a tolerable field close by.
>
> The cavalry fight on Sunday was quite a success. Monday morning Butterfield telegraphed an account of it to all corps, closing his dispatch thus: "A disastrous day to the Rebel cavalry."
>
> Army Headquarters are at Gum Spring about six or eight miles from here. . . . All the army is lying somewhere about here; the Eleventh Corps between us and Goose Creek, . . .

II CORPS

Writing from near Aldie Gap on Wednesday, June 24, Alexander Webb, at the time inspector general of the Fifth Corps, told his wife Annie:

> No mail since we left Falmouth. I am getting very anxious to hear from home and have some curiosity to hear from Washington. . . . We set a trap for Mosby yesterday morning and should have caught him. As it had rained the night before some of the muskets did not go off and the Cavalry did not do well. We sent our escort and 100 infantry to catch the fellow & he made right through us without losing a man. Genl Meade is disgusted.
>
> No orders from Genl Hooker for some days. We are "awaiting the

development of the enemy's plan." When R. E. Lee develops them look out for trouble. . . . This country is lovely. All grass . . . a great butter country. No wonder Mosby likes this country to campaign in. As guerillas infest the country we have to send strong cavalry escorts with our mails & trains but we can never tell when to write or when they are going. I began this about ten minutes ago and now they tell me an escort will leave soon, so "so get your letter ready."[41]

Webb lamented the fact that he had no support in Washington. He had hoped to be promoted to brigadier general. Some of his friends had made the grade, but he felt his opportunity had "floated by." Webb ended the letter by saying, "kiss my dear babies for me."[42]

Word traveled slowly at times in that day. And Webb did not know at the moment that he had indeed been promoted to a one star general. Soon he would take command of the second brigade of Gibbon's division of the Second Corps.

Later that day the mail got through. And Webb was able to write a joyous note home.

Dear Old Woman,   (we wonder how much she appreciated this greeting?)

I rec eleven (11) letters from you today. Pretty good haul this time. No news from Washington. . . . Charley Morgain comes by quite often to see me. He is terribly tired of walking along the roads. He wants to be mounted. I will try to get him the position of aide-de-camp.

My eleven letters were a treat to me my dear girls. Tell the children to write again soon. Bessie's letter was sweet. They sent two Brigadiers appointments here today so do not be worried. They have left me out. (He still had not received notification).

They (in Washington) do not see many signs of a coming battle. Yet I pity Maryland and Penna. Nothing seems to comprehend in Washington. All seems at sixes and sevens.[43]

The Second Corps most likely took the Belmont Road from Gum Springs to Route 7 and then headed for Edwards Ferry.

General French left the Second Corps to become commander of the garrison at Harpers Ferry. Alexander Hays was almost forty-four years old in June of '63. In 1844 he graduated from West Point in the same class with Winfield Scott Hancock. He was chosen to command the Third Division of

199

The canal house at Edwards Ferry.

the Second Corps. He was a rough, tough man, and some had doubts about his ability to discipline on June 24. But he soon proved his worth. He was killed in the Wilderness the following May.

Orderlies and aides traveled during those days with great difficulty, and grave danger, through a country infested by Mosby's guerrillas. The Eleventh Corps had been camping for several days at Trappe Rock on Goose Creek. Today, the Reverend R. B. Howard, the general's brother and a member of the Christian Commission arrived in camp. He had ridden forty-five miles and had been exposed to "bushwackers."[44]

> The word "bushwackers" comprehended scouts, spies, and all insurgents who were never really made part of the Confederate army. They penetrated our lines in spite of every precaution, picked off our aids and messengers on their swift journeyings from corps to corps, and circulated every sort of false story that might be made use of to mislead us. In this Goose Creek region we were much annoyed by them. . . .[45]

In fact, Mosby's men almost captured General Howard. The general came riding down the road one day past a thicket where the rangers were hidden. The size of Howard's staff deceived them and they made the decision not to attack.

Howard would soon be rid of the annoyance because Hooker was preparing orders to put the Eleventh Corps on the Roads to Gettysburg.

June 25

XI CORPS

Finally after all the delay, and fluctuating of Hooker's mind, the Army of the Potomac started crossing the river today. Oliver O. Howard got his orders to cross at forty minutes after midnight, and his men hit the pontoon bridge in the dark at the hour of 3:45 A.M. A misstep and a man would go straight down. Reynolds was ordered to assume command of the Third and Eleventh corps in addition to his own. His soldiers were to push on and sieze Crampton's Gap and Turner's Gap in the South Mountain range. Slocum was to be prepared to march at a moment's notice.[46]

So the great crossing that would take three full days had begun. Oliver O. Howard and his men were to be first to cross. His trains and supply wagons did not get across until late morning. Then it was time for the First Corps, and toward evening, the Third Corps hit the bridge. It started to drizzle, then the rains came, so it was a disagreeable day. The humidity was also high.

The Eleventh Corps did alright, making eighteen miles. In spite of a heavy rain, the men received a great welcome in Poolesville. Union flags were all over the little town. Folks were friendly, little children were singing and running after the soldiers. A member of the Fifty-fifth Ohio writes: "The natives gave more than substantial refreshments. The band played in the streets, and all rejoiced at the unaccustomed reception."[47]

Major Chamberlain noticed that General Reynolds seemed preoccupied as the First Corps waited for the Eleventh to complete the crossing. "Doubtless the uncertainty of the military situation worried him, or foreseeing Lee's intentions more clearly than other commanders, he chafed under the inaction which he feared might have ruinous consequences."[48]

I CORPS

At 8:10 A.M. on the twenty-fifth, Hooker sent another message to Reynolds, telling him to hold the mountain passes until further orders, "as their possession may be of great importance in determining the future operations of this army."[49] Reynolds was directed again to march toward

Middletown, midway between Frederick and Boonsboro, on what is now Alternate Route 40. If possible the soldiers were to march in two lines on parallel roads to speed the movement. John Reynolds was told to encamp at Middletown. We wish we could pinpoint the location. Hooker expressed his desire to be kept informed, and to be advised the moment Reynolds was in possession of the mountain passes.

So the First Corps was marching toward the scene of an earlier engagement when they had fought the Confederates under D. H. Hill on Sunday, September 14, 1862. On that occasion some men from the midwest had won the distinction of "The Iron Brigade" for the manner in which they climbed the difficult heights and defeated the men in gray.

But there were problems ahead for Hooker and John Reynolds. There was a mix-up in the orders sent to Major E. O. Beers of the Fiftieth New York Engineers. General Benham had ordered Beers to lay a bridge at the Monocacy River. Captain Turnbull countermanded that order to get the second bridge at Edwards Ferry. As soon as the matter was straightened out, Beers got men and boats to both sides of the Potomac. Turnbull, writing at 11:00 A.M., expected the work to take another three hours. Goose Creek had been bridged, at its mouth, and two bridges were to be in place over the Potomac, and two over the canal. Most of Howard's infantry got across by noon, but the baggage wagons came later.[50]

Howard had gotten his orders at 12:40, was on the road by 3:45 A.M., and by 11:15 was near Point of Rocks. He reported "all quiet at Maryland Heights."[51]

Hooker's staff officers who came to help John Reynolds arrived at Edwards Ferry at 1:45 on June 25.[52] Already Stahel's horsemen were riding towards Frederick. Troops were on the way to Crampton's Gap too. Reynolds had given orders for the First Corps to march via Barnesville, Adamstown and Jefferson, in the direction of Middletown. He was not sure how far they might get, but he hoped at least as far as Barnesville.

The Third Corps under David Birney was to move via the

mouth of the Monocacy River, on the towpath to Point of Rocks, thence to Petersville and Burkittsville.

Things were moving better at Edwards Ferry. The Eleventh and First corps were across the Potomac, although their wagon trains were not. The Third Corps was in the process of crossing.

At 6:00 P.M. on that June Thursday, his last Thursday, John Reynolds wrote a dispatch to Hooker from Poolesville saying, "I am here. The troops are on the march. . . . The trains are not all across the river yet. I don't think the troops can get farther than Barnesville and the mouth of the Monocacy tonight."[53]

What was it like on that June day for the men of the Eleventh, First and Third corps as they crossed the Potomac River into Maryland? Let them tell their story.

The men of the First Corps found the approaches to the pontoon bridges still jammed with the wagons of the Eleventh Corps. So they had to wait awhile before crossing. But

> at last the men of the First Corps felt the bridge sway beneath their tread, and as they took their first steps on the soil of Maryland they broke into cheers. It was a relief to be out of the land of the enemy. . . . Stirring, indeed, was the welcome that met them, and as they marched through Poolesville they found themselves strangely moved by the sight of a large group of school children drawn up to watch them pass.[54]

The rains and the movement of men and wagons made the roads terrible. By evening, the roads or paths to the pontoons were so cut up that the poor mules could hardly pull the wagons. Soldiers had to put their shoulders to the wheels as they became stuck in the mud.[55]

Charles Wainwright found the afternoon warm despite the constant drizzle. The Maryland roads were good and the country quite open in comparison to Virginia. Charles, although he personally liked Oliver Howard, did not have much faith in the men of the Eleventh Corps. He also notes that Hooker seemed to fear that he was behind time, and might come under attack before getting all his army across the Potomac.[56]

The First Corps trudged on through the rain of that June day. Finally they went into camp near Barnesville. One unlucky regiment was assigned a field where the water was three to six inches deep between the rows of corn. But the farmer General Wadsworth was looking for an answer. And he found one. He saw a large straw stack and bought it on sight. In a few moments the straw became the bedding for the men of the First Division.[57]

Major Chamberlain of the 150th Pennsylvania also talks about the heavy rain which hit in the evening. "The troops had a bad night of it—all the more dismal from their inability to cook supper, and the incessant braying of some hundreds of mules belonging to the wagon trains which were parked nearby."[58]

Levin Baker of the Ninth Massachusetts Battery broke camp at 6:00 A.M. and marched to Fairfax Court House where they found everything in motion. At 11:00 A.M. they wheeled into column and headed north of the Roads to Gettysburg.

It was a hard march. Many of the batteries were like ours, having done garrison duty for some time, and were green in marching. The halts were frequent, and the gaps in the column also, and towards night the orders to "close up" came faster and more emphatic. Many men had blistered feet and were giving out; some horses were showing signs of playing out; guns and caissons were separated by casualities; cannoneers were left behind. But we finally arrived in camp, near Edwards' Ferry, about 10 P.M., having covered about thirty-three miles. It was dark and muddy in camp, and we were too tired to get supper. At daylight in the morning officers and sergeants began to look for their guns, caissons and men; we were all there, although our camp was not very orderly. Feed, breakfast, and a few changes of horses, and we were ready to move. We find we are in the reserve artillery of the Army of the Potomac, Gen. Tyler commanding, and the First Volunteer Brigade, Lieut.-Col. F. McGilvery commanding.[59]

Edwards Ferry today.

III CORPS

On the morning of June 25, the Third Corps was on the march, leaving Gum Springs where they had spent five days. About three o'clock the troops sighted the Potomac River at Edwards Ferry. Goose Creek presented a formidable barrier. But a bridge had been placed across the stream, and two across the Potomac. A member of the Seventeenth Maine mentions that the Potomac was eighteen hundred feet wide at this point. Gaily the Third Corps hit the swaying bridges and crossed to Maryland.[60]

Charles Bardeen, like the rest of the men in blue, was glad to shake the Virginia soil from his clothing. After crossing the Potomac, he and many of his comrades thought that would be it for the day. It was almost dark and the rain was falling. But there was no such luck.

> We started on again, and as the Potomac was on one side and the canal on the other it was not easy to straggle far. For a while it was good walking, but soon it became muddy and slippery and by ten o'clock we could appreciate the old problem of the frog in the well who jumped up three feet every day and fell back two.[61]

This was a bad day for Humphrey's division. A fifteen-mile march was made from Gum Springs to Edwards Ferry. Only a few five-minute breaks were allowed. About five o'clock the troops crossed the Potomac. All looked forward to a coffee break. But instead, the infamous "towpath march began."

Every regimental account complains about the march and about General Humphreys. After crossing, the general made his men press on for another ten or twelve miles. His command took the towpath instead of the road on the other side. The men wondered what he was trying to prove.

Those of you who have hiked the Chesapeake and Ohio Canal know how narrow it is. We can imagine the difficulty encountered by an army of several thousand men marching along the towpath. Regimental accounts say that the rains had raised the canal level to the point that in places it overflowed. More than one poor soul in the Third and Twelfth corps fell into the canal.

Captain Bartlett of the Twelfth New Hampshire speaks for many on "the towpath march" as he writes:

> After marching all day, with no time to rest or eat, a slow march on a moonlight night and on a hard wide road would have been severe enough, to say nothing about nature's urgent call for sleep, . . . ; but when the long march ends not with the day but continues mile after mile and hour after hour, through the rain and mud and enveloped in Cimmerian darkness, with no time or place to rest, and no prospect of soon getting a chance to, while the mud that clogs and burdens the already overtaxed limbs gets deeper and deeper, . . . and the rain pours down incessantly from the heavens above, human patience and endurance become exhausted.[62]

Men fell out at first by twos, then by fours, until few were left in companies and regiments. Still General Humphreys kept on, halting about midnight near the mouth of the Monocacy. His command was scattered from Edwards Ferry to the Monocacy. Some slipped or staggered in sleepwalking states into the canal or river and had to be rescued. Several in the Twelfth New Hampshire stuck candles into the muzzles of their guns and served as guides for their buddies. The men of the Second Division never forgot this march, and were slow to forgive their commander.[63]

Warren Cudworth of the First Massachusetts Infantry felt the march from Edwards Ferry to the mouth of the Monocacy River, . . . for length, severity, and discomfort, exceeded anything the army had ever been through before."[64]

It was nearly 5:00 P.M. when the First Massachusetts reached the Maryland side of the Potomac. The pontoon bridge had been slippery, but worse moments were ahead. It was raining heavily, and the wind was blowing.

Cudworth tells us progress was slow. "The rain, which fell in torrents raised the canal so that in some places its waters poured over the embankment into the Potomac River." There was no place to rest. Water, water, everywhere. Water falling, and water on both sides of the narrow towpath. But the men of the First Massachusetts trudged on until 1:00 A.M. Three hundred fifty men started the march from Gum Springs. But at 1:00 A.M. only forty were present to fall down on the wet ground to sleep.[65]

The men were completely drenched, cold and weary. Some had fallen into the canal. Martin Haynes of the Second New Hampshire felt "history would have to judge the wisdom and humanity of the 'towpath march.' Otherwise, . . . General Humphreys can have full credit for the affair."[66]

The historian of the Eleventh New Jersey adds his comments:

> The regiment halted briefly on the Maryland shore. Then the men moved along the towpath of the Chesapeake and Ohio Canal. It was a terrible experience.
>
> Rain was falling heavily, and soon the tramping of many feet made the towpath very insecure footing. Darkness fell; still the tramp continued hour after hour, slipping, sliding,—. . . ; the canal on one side, the steep river bank on the other—no place for halting, nothing to do but worry on through the darkness and dampness, hoping that the canal would soon be crossed and a halt ordered.[67]

But that did not happen until 2:00 A.M. on Friday. The men of the division marched twenty-five miles that day in the rain and slept on sodden ground.

So the Eleventh Corps was across the Potomac and Oliver O. Howard near Point of Rocks. The First Corps was scattered from Barnesville to Poolesville. John Reynolds made his headquarters on this miserable night in the Benson house in Poolesville. In the midst of the driving rain he sent an aide to look for Howard. Birney and the Third Corps was in the middle of their crossing, crossing the bridges in the dark and traveling along the canal. The Second Corps was going into camp at Gum Springs. The rest of the army was prepared to move in the morning.

Dan Butterfield, Hooker's chief of staff, was having his problems too. He couldn't find a map of Frederick County. His sources were unable to find them in Baltimore or Washington, so he had to send to Philadelphia in an effort to get the valuable items.[68]

II CORPS

Turning now to the Union Second Corps, they went into camp for the night at Gum Springs in the midst of a terrific shower. Many of the fellows had covered twenty-five miles today coming from Thoroughfare Gap. It was the longest march for the corps to date, but the record was not to stand very long.

William Kepler of the Fourth Ohio notes that Longstreet and Hill had followed Ewell into "Maryland, my Maryland," where they expected a general uprising in their behalf, a glorious victory, and recognition of the Confederacy by the powers of Europe. While the Rebel forces were now near Chambersburg, the Army of the Potomac began to cross at Edwards Ferry."[69]

Like the rest of the corps, the 106th Pennsylvania marched in the rain, and the men had mud to their knees. When they halted to sleep in the rain, they were too tired to scrape the mud from their clothing. Such is the lot of an infantryman.[70]

The Fifth New Hampshire, Colonel Cross's men, had the misfortune to have guard duty for the night. Despite the twenty-odd miles of marching, they had to remain on the alert because of the proximity of Stuart's cavalry. "It rained in torrents."[71] The red Virginia clay had clogged the feet of men and animals, making progress slow, now came the difficult task of weary soldiers trying to sleep in the rain.

As far as John Gibbon was concerned, the stay at Thoroughfare Gap was uneventful for the Second Corps. He writes:

> We remained in position at Thoroughfare Gap from the 21st to the 25th very quietly and monotonously, undisturbed by anything of interest except the following.
>
> "A little incident which gave us something to talk about will serve to show what active, energetic enemies we have to contend with. No

one, I think, after this war is over, will say that the southern people are wanting in energy. Two Confederate soldiers on horseback and probably acting as spies or scouts were within our lines, two or three miles from here near a place called Haymarket, where they met a wagon loaded with telegraph wire coming up from Gainesville. It had besides the driver, a man (a negro) in charge of it and a sutler. The Confederates had just captured one of our cavalry stragglers. Unhitching one of the mules, they mounted the negro upon it, taking him and the three white men along with them. Shortly after getting up on the Warrenton pike, on their way to Warrenton, they encountered our cavalry pickets, who gave chase. One of the rebels took a horse belonging to one of the prisoners, which was better than his own, and both of them made their escape, leaving their prisoners behind them. In the saddlebags left in the rebel's saddle were a number of letters, including two official notes from Gen. Lee of old dates, referring to the battle of Chancellorsville, which some Maj. Chas. Marshall was sending to a friend—a lady—in order that she might have Gen. Lee's autograph. There was one letter from a poor wife to her husband praying that this cruel war might end and peace come once more. I joined in her prayer. These mounted men are all through this country and such events are of constant occurrence. I only wish our men had one-half their energy and activity, but somehow or other we don't seem to 'do' these kinds of things."[72]

That Thursday, the Nineteenth Maine left Thoroughfare Gap for Haymarket, and there turned north for Gum Springs. As the column reached Haymarket, Confederate artillery placed on a strategic hill started to lob shells into the line of march. Israel D. Jones of Company G was killed, the first man from the unit to die in action. Ten minutes earlier he was talking and joking. Now he was dead. And in a few more minutes his body was buried in shallow grave, hastily dug by the side of the road, a long way from his native Maine and one hundred miles from Gettysburg.[73]

Jeb Stuart describes the affair in this manner:

Moving to the right with my brigades, we passed through Glasscock's Gap without serious difficulty and marched to Haymarket. I had previously sent Major Mosby with some picked men to gain the vicinity of Dranesville, find where a crossing was practicable and bring intelligence to me near Gum Springs on June 25th. As we neared Haymarket we found that Hancock's Corps was enroute through Haymarket for Gum Springs, his infantry well distributed through his trains. I chose a good position and opened with the artillery on his passing column with effect, scattering men, wagons

211

and horses in wild confusion; disabled one of the enemy's caissons, which he abandoned, and compelled him to advance in order of battle to compel us to desist. As Hancock had the right of way on my road, I sent Fitz Lee's Brigade to Gainesville to reconnoitre and devoted the remainder of the day to grazing our horses.[74]

The attack upon the Second Corps and its subsequent movements caused a lot of talk in the ranks. Joseph Ward tells us:

> These sudden changes of position, the long and hurried marches to make them, in different directions, and the haste in which they were made, necessarily provoked anxiety to know why, and rumors as to the cause found rapid transit. Among those, then currently believed, was that the Second Corps was cut off from the rest of the army, by Stuart pushing forward his cavalry and occupying the road between Gainesville and Centreville—that Hancock's orders were to withdraw from Thoroughfare Gap and join the army at Centreville. To have executed that order would have placed him at the mercy of Stuart, who had selected a strong position, covering the road leading to Centreville, and with his whole force well posted and supported by artillery, would have given him a decided advantage over us. But Hancock was equal to the emergency. Knowing that Stuart was so posted, he proposed to keep him there, and knowing also that the objective point of the Army of the Potomac was Maryland and perhaps Pennsylvania, after Lee, if he could not join it at Centreville, he could in Maryland; so he hastily writes a dispatch to General Hooker at Centreville, saying that he would put his corps in motion for that place *via* Gainesville, and would be there that evening; he then sent an orderly full speed in that direction, knowing that he would not go far before he fell into the hands of the enemy, and the dispatch would reveal Hancock's intentions and make them wait there to receive him, and allow him to proceed on his way unmolested; he therefore made direct for the Potomac by taking a small road that branched off to the left of Haymarket, and pushed on rapidly to Gum Spring, where as has been said we arrived about 9 o'clock that night, thus putting a long day's march between his command and Stuart. It was also said that General Hooker did not know what had become of the Second Corps until it turned up in Maryland. As to their full truth the writer is unable to say; but this much was known, that we were making as fast as we could towards Centreville until the attack at Haymarket, when almost immediately the main road was left and the small road taken, even after some of the troops had passed it and they had to come back to it—that with considerable turning and rapid marching, which was kept up till nearly midnight, we reached Gum Spring, a distance of about twenty-three miles.[75]

212

Twenty to twenty-six miles were covered by the Second Corps today. The deep mud made the men as tired as if they had waded through deep snow. They were drenched. And there was no dry wood at Gum Springs. Nothing to do but to lie down on wet ground with wet clothing and wet blankets.[76]

We look now at the accounts of the Fifth Massachusetts Battery:

> June 25, 1863. Reveille and roll call just at sunrise. "Boots and Saddles" at 8 a. m. Broke camp and packed up, and left Fairfax Court House with the Artillery Reserve at about 9 a. m. Marched all day and evening. The Brigades marched in the following order: Ransom, Huntington, McGilvery, DuPeyster, Taft,—
> DuPeyster switched off for Washington. The Ninth Mass. Battery joined our Brigade. We started towards Washington, but changed the direction of our route, and marched towards Edwards Ferry on the Potomac River. Passed Leesburg station at 4 p. m. Roads good, especially the Leesburg turnpike, a macadamized road. We had much halting until the last two hours of our march, when we moved very fast, a good part of the time "double-quick." Upset one caisson about 5 p. m., and broke the stock, but not so badly as to detain us. We righted the caisson and proceeded. At 6 o'clock it commenced raining and rained all night. About half past 6 we passed through Dranesville. Halted for the night a mile from the river about 11 p. m., but did not unhitch. The men made coffee and lay down on the wet ground by the fire without shelter except a rubber blanket. They passed the long, dreary, wet night in misery, being wet to the skin and not a wink of sleep.[77]

Today the Fifth New York Cavalry turned "column north." From beyond Dranesville, near Broad Run, the troopers turned right and struck the Potomac below Edwards Ferry. After crossing the Potomac, the unit was sent to Poolesville, and then via the Monocacy Ford to Licksville.

George G. Meade's wife apparently had more interest in her husband being in command of the Army of the Potomac than he did. On June 25, George told her:

> I see you are still troubled with visions of my being placed in command. I thought that had all blown over, and I think it has, except in your imagination, and that of . . . some . . . of my kinds friends. . . . I do not stand any chance, because I have no friends, political or others, who press or advance my claims or pretensions, and there are so many others who are pressed by influential poli-

213

ticians that it is folly to think I stand any chance upon mere merit alone.[78]

But three days later, George Gordon Meade was in command of the Army of the Potomac. He was much impressed with the lovely land near Aldie. Meade, along with many of the troops, was able to get fresh butter, eggs, milk, and lamb.[79]

He also visited the old home of President Monroe. It belonged to a Major Fairfax on Longstreet's staff. But he was received very cordially by Mrs. Fairfax. She told him her husband was at home visiting when Pleasonton and Stuart got into a fight at Aldie. Major Fairfax barely escaped. But Meade was concerned:

> I hear nothing whatever from headquarters, and am as much in the dark as to proposed plans here on the ground as you are in Philadelphia. This is what Joe Hooker thinks profound sagacity— keeping his corps commanders, who are to execute his plans, in total ignorance of them until they are developed in the execution of orders.[80]

We look now at Hooker's orders for June 26 to the Army of the Potomac.

Slocum's Twelfth Corps was to march at 3:00 A.M. from Leesburg and cross the Potomac on the upper bridge at Edwards Ferry. A detail was to be left behind to hold Leesburg until the Fifth Corps under George G. Meade arrived. Slocum was to cross the Monocacy at its mouth and proceed up the Chesapeake and Ohio Canal towpath to Trammelstown. That was the name of present-day Point of Rocks.[81]

Meade's Fifth Corps was to march from Aldie at 4:00 A.M., they got an hour's grace, crossing Goose Creek at Carter's Mill, cross the Potomac on the upper bridge at Edwards Ferry, the Monocacy at its mouth, (the aqueduct there), and follow the river road in the direction of Frederick City.

The Reserve Artillery was to cross the lower bridge at Edwards Ferry, and then follow the Fifth Corps. Headquarters were to be moved from Hunter's Mills to Poolesville in Montgomery County, Maryland.

Hancock and Sedgwick were also ordered to cross the Potomac with the Second and Sixth corps at Edwards Ferry.

Meanwhile things were happening north of the Potomac between Williamsport and Chambersburg. The Army of Northern Virginia was moving too.

About 10:00 A.M. Colonel Fremantle and his friend left Winchester in an effort to overtake Generals Lee and Longstreet who were supposed to be crossing the Potomac. "Before we got more than a few miles ... we began to meet horses and oxen, the first fruits of Ewell's advance into Pennsylvania."[82]

"The weather was cool and showery, and all went swimmingly for the first fourteen miles, when we caught up M'Laws's Division...."[83] By this time the colonel's horse was again showing signs of fatigue, so he had to stop and let his carrier graze for a while. Fremantle watched Semmes and Barksdale's brigades go by. They were composed of men from Georgia, Mississippi, and South Carolina. The two generals were on their last journey. Barksdale fell before Little Round Top, and Semmes was mortally wounded. ... Some of the knapsacks had Massachusetts, Vermont, and New Jersey names on them, the fruits of victory on other fields. There were about twenty wagons to each brigade. Most of them had U.S. markings on them. It seemed as though the United States was the greatest supplier of items. The men were in good spirits, cheering and yelling. They also seemed to think they were on the way to final victory.

Fremantle reached Martinsburg at 6:00 P.M., having ridden nearly twenty-two miles. The last several miles were on foot because the poor horse had broken down. Martinsburg was supposed to be pro-Union, but some of the women were cheering the men in gray as they marched by on the Roads to Gettysburg. Three miles north of town, Fremantle was forced to seek hospitality from a surly, pro-Unionist. The horse could not take another step.

The advance of Ewell's corps was turning Washington wild and frantic. As Longstreet's men neared the Potomac River, they sensed Union sentiment replacing feelings for the South. The Southern sympathizers had to be discreet for fear of retribution later. But "now and then we would see a window slowly raise in a house by the roadside, or on a hill in the distance, and the feeble flutter of a white handkerchief told of their Confederate proclivities. Generally the doors of all dwellings in the extreme northern portion of Virginia, and in Maryland and Pennsylvania, were mostly closed."[84]

On the morning of the 25th of June we crossed the Potomac at Williamsport. Here was shouting and yelling. Hats went into the air, flags dipped and swayed, the bands played "Maryland, My Maryland," while the men sang "All Quiet Along the Potomac Tonight." We were now in the enemy's country, and scarcely a shot fired. We had lost Stuart. Where was he?[85]

The writer of *Kershaw's Brigade History*, tells us that Stuart had come within sight of the spires of Washington, although not on June 25. People were leaving Washington. "Cabinet officers were running hither and thither.... Lincoln was the only one who seemingly had not lost his head." The Rebel infantry lived in lush fields of clover. Broken down artillery horses and wagon mules were being replaced by Pennsylvania's best.

The Washington Artillery also had a joyous time crossing the Potomac. They crossed on Wednesday in a driving rain, and made camp a mile from Williamsport. The men took off their shoes and trousers and carried them on their shoulders. Carriages from Williamsport came out to see the crossing. Some of them carried young ladies. William Owens was sure the women would never forget the sight of thousands of "Confeds" in the water without their trousers.[86]

According to Randolph Shotwell, Pickett's division made another thirty-mile march today, and passed through Williamsport at 10:30 A.M. The Potomac was forded at Williamsport at 2:30. The passage of the river produced a "novel spectacle." There was a lot of enthusiasm despite the fatigue.

Thousands of rough voices sang, "The Bonny Blue Flag" and "Maryland, My Maryland." Bands of music played their liveliest airs; the musicians, nude as Adam, each with a bundle of clothes on top of his head tooting with "might and main" at their brass horns, being a "sight to behold." ... Many citizens, including women, and negroes of all ages and sexes, occupied the high ground near the river

216

watching us come over. Perhaps they thought the "ragged Rebels" best dressed when entirely undressed.[87]

The joy of the river crossing was chilled by the "ceremonies of a military execution." A soldier of the Fifty-sixth Virginia had repeatedly sold himself as a substitute, and then deserted. He had been caught and tried before. Despite the warnings he continued trying to make money in an easy manner. This time there was no mercy. He was sentenced to be shot.

Pickett's command marched through Hagerstown about 4:30 P.M. and went into camp about two miles north of town (near what is now Rest Haven Cemetery). The brigade was formed and the ceremonies described in the stories of the Union First and Twelfth corps carried out just north of Hagerstown in the rain. The band played the funeral dirge even as the rain descended. It was a gloomy moment.[88]

Yet Shotwell found the people of Hagerstown a little friendlier than before. "Bonnie Blue Flags" waved from some windows. Quite a few were seen in the hotels too. Many took time to visit Dr. McGill—perhaps the most avid Rebel in Hagerstown. Earlier in the war he had been sent to prison. But he was in his glory today. His men had arrived. Tonight young officers and young girls danced the night hours away.[89]

Traffic was heavy. Troops and wagons were going to the front, while droves of cattle and sheep from the farms of Pennsylvania were being sent to the rear.

Ross was greatly impressed with the temperance of the Confederate soldiers. Naturally there were men who drank. But Ross found few of them.[90]

Dick Garnett, commanding one of Pickett's brigades, and Col. Eppa Hunton of the Eighth Virginia, riding north in the Shenandoah Valley, was joined by General Lee. Hunton was not in favor of crossing the river. He feared the ability to get back to Virginia in case of a serious reverse. Lee said he had no alternative. He had to go to Pennsylvania to get supplies.[91]

George Pickett kept his sweetheart in Lynchburg, Virginia, informed as to his travels. Writing on the Roads to Gettysburg, he said:

217

> Each day, my darling, takes me farther and farther away from you, from all I love and hold dear. . . . Today under orders from Marse Robert, we crossed the Potomac. . . . Oh, the desolate homes, the widows, the orphans, and the heart-broken mothers, that this campaign will make.[92]

Like the rest of the men in blue and gray, the Washington Artillery traveled in the rain on that Friday. Headquarters were established in a large farmhouse near Greencastle. A German couple served as hosts. They were being paid one hundred dollars a year by an absentee landlord. When the Southern artillerymen left, they gave the Germans two silver half dollars.[93]

From Greencastle to Chambersburg, the men in gray passed "many fine houses, and large barns full of grain and forage; but 'Massa Robert' won't permit any confiscations, and not a fence rail is disturbed, much to the disgust of the negro cooks, who cannot understand why the army should look so differently from the Federal armies in Virginia."[94]

Most of the people in western Maryland greeted the advancing gray columns with cold stares. Some turned their backs on the Rebels. One woman though was friendly, she cheered Hill's column by saying, "Go it boys! I'm glad to see you coming here again." Lee, Longstreet, and Hill met on top of a wooded knoll near Williamsport. They had a view of the columns wading across the river. Soon they had a visitor. Little Leighton Parks brought them a bucket of freshly picked raspberries. He was thanked and invited to eat with the three Confederate generals. All three of the generals held the lad on their laps. Longstreet seemed especially fond of little Parks. Perhaps it was because he had lost three of his children to the scarlet fever epidemic just a year earlier.[95]

Pender continued to keep his wife informed. "We have a grand race on hand between Lee and Hooker. We have the inside track, Hooker going to Washington and we by Winchester." He urged his wife, "Keep in good spirits, honey, and hope that this summer's work will tend to shorten the war."[96]

The Richmond papers were glad that for once the North was going to feel the brunt of the war. Lee was on serious

218

business. The Charleston *Mercury* clamored for reprisal and destruction. But many of the men in the ranks, although cheering when they crossed the Potomac, had mixed emotions. Pender wrote, "Tomorrow I do what I know will cause you grief, and that is to cross the Potomac. . . . May the Lord prosper this crossing and bring us early peace out of it."[97]

Today McGowans's South Carolinians forded the Potomac at Shepherdstown. Caldwell tells us that most of the men stripped down and crossed with cheering and great expectation of victory. However, he notes that this was not a sight for female eyes. Once across the river, the men pushed on in the rain and marched within eight miles of Hagerstown.

This was A. P. Hill's first march as a corps commander. He had been promoted to lieutenant general "After Chancellorsville" to help take up the void left by Jackson's death.

Hill was from an old Virginia family. Russell Hill came to the Culpeper area in 1740. His youngest son Henry married Ann Powell, daughter of Captain Ambrose Powell, an Indian fighter and pioneer, who helped to survey the Virginia-Kentucky border. Henry and Ann were the grandparents of the lad born to Thomas and Fannie R. Baptist on November 9, 1825.

As he grew, he was called Powell by his mother. From her, he formed a strong fondness for books, including the Bible, biography, and Shakespeare. With his dad he fished and hunted on the Rappahannock and the Rapidan. He enjoyed riding with his father and became a superb horseman. During the war he was described as "the perfect picture in the saddle and the most graceful rider I ever saw."

Five months before his seventeenth birthday, Powell Hill arrived at the United States Military Academy on the banks of the Hudson. His roommate was George B. McClellan. After graduation he served in Mexico, and then against the Seminoles. During a tour of duty in the South he developed yellow fever.

Hill seems to have been a ladies' man. He noted the lovely girls in Mexico and fell deeply in love several times. One of the girls was Ellen Marcy, the daughter of a career army officer. However, her father was not fond of Hill, and he said "no" to their marriage. She wound up with George B. McClellan.

Hill believed in States' Rights and went with Virginia. In May of 1861 he was named colonel of the Thirteenth Virginia Infantry and ordered to report to duty in Harpers Ferry. Although he had feuds with Longstreet and Jackson, Hill became one of the best division commanders in the Army of Northern Virginia, and thus stood near the top of the list for promotion.

Ham Chamberlayne also took time to write home from Shepherdstown. He had been busy taking care of sore backs and shoulders of his horses. He had some sick soldiers, too, and several of the horses needed shoeing. Writing to his mother on the twenty-fifth, he said:

> Yesterday was our eighth day from Fredsbg—Trace the course on the map, about fifteen miles a day to Stevensburg, Culpeper C.H., Front Royal where we crossed the mountain, White Post Millwood, Berryville, & and this place which we reached by 1 p.m. yesterday.[98]

Ham was pretty well exhausted so he spent most of the rest of the twenty-fifth sleeping. Continuing his letter to mom,

> Our course led us by the field of Chancellors where our memory of the great contest was forcibly refreshed by the sight of new made graves, blackened ruins & rotting horses.—Since passing Culpeper C.H. the route lay through a fertile and beautiful country. Specially, Warren, Clarke & Jefferson Counties are covered with the richest green; clover and timothy knee high and thick as the best wheat add to the strictly beautiful features of the scene. . . .
>
> This country enchants me more & more; seeing it now in spring its beauty surpasses even what I had expected from its autum appearance. . . .
>
> I am every moment expecting orders to move—We may reasonably hope, I think, to thrash Hooker and to possess the country— Gen Lee's designs are too deep & far reaching however for guessers to follow, so I have ceased trying.
>
> Ewell is in front, Hill next & Longstreet so far at Berryville guarding Snicker's and Ashby's gaps, Jenkins' cavalry is Ewell's advance, has already sent back considerable horses from & cattle from Pa.

Chamberlayne hoped to stay around Shepherdstown to

meet and talk with the grey-eyed girl he had mentioned in an earlier letter.[99]

The twenty-fifth of June, Early's command spent in bivouac at Greenwood. Early rode in to see General Ewell, the corps commander in Chambersburg.[100] Rodes's and Johnson's divisions were encamped there. Johnson was two miles south of town, and Ewell moved his headquarters from the Franklin Hotel to the grounds of the Mennonite Church.[101]

Ewell instructed Early to move with his division across South Mountain, through Gettysburg to York, for "the purpose of cutting the Northern Central Railroad running from Baltimore to Harrisburg, and destroying the bridge across the Susquehanna River at Wrightsville and Columbia on the branch railroad from York to Philadelphia."[102]

Ewell simply relayed these commands from General Lee to Early. Lt. Col. Elijah White's battalion of cavalry was assigned to the infantry force. The division wagons were to be left behind. And Early was told to rejoin the Second Corps at Carlisle by way of Dillsburg after the mission was accomplished.

When Early got back to camp on the twenty-fifth, he soon had the men up and scurrying about. All the trains with the exception of ambulances, one medical wagon, one ordnance wagon, and one wagon with cooking utensils, for each regiment, and fifteen wagons for getting supplies were sent back to Chambersburg. Officers were permitted to keep just what they could carry with them. When the trains moved out on the evening of the twenty-fifth, heading west toward Chambersburg, they were seen no more until the Confederates crossed the Potomac three weeks later.

To the west, across the mountains in McConnellsburg, residents reported roughly two thousand Rebels, with twenty-four wagons, and a section of artillery.

With the retreat of the small band of soldiers guarding the approaches of Carlisle, many citizens became panicky. Prominent and average citizens started to leave town, using any means of conveyance they could find. Those unable to find wagons or other means of travel, started for Harrisburg on foot. The roads were crowded thus increasing the confusion and alarm. Rumors were a dime a dozen.[103]

But by Thursday night everything seemed to be quiet and peaceful. No Rebel soldiers had entered town as yet. Perhaps it was a false alarm. The day had come and gone and nothing had happened. Some even started to laugh about "the big scare." Scouts bolstered morale by saying there were no Rebels closer than Leesburg, three miles east of Shippensburg.[104]

So the rainy twenty-fifth day of June came to an end, a day of intense excitement and activity along the Potomac and in the Cumberland Valley. Things were worse to the North.

VIII

CHAMBERSBURG AND CARLISLE

Friday, June 26

Today it was "on to Chambersburg" for the men in gray. Hagerstown, Greencastle, Marion, and Chambersburg witnessed the marching of the Army of Northern Virginia.

From the rain-soaked banks of the Potomac, the men in blue continued to cross and move northward into Maryland, heading for a rendezvous in Frederick.

Chambersburg was ready to receive for the first time, the commander of an invading army. As the gray columns headed north, Robert E. Lee also took the road leading to Ben Chambers's city. The Second Corps was moving toward Carlisle and Gettysburg, but Longstreet and Hill were headed for Chambersburg.

With the approach of Hill's corps, Ewell was now free to leave Chambersburg and head north. So his men headed for Shippensburg. It was a short march of eleven miles. Robert Rodes and his men camped at Dykeman's Spring, a half mile south of town. A large fish pond furnished excellent water for the men and animals. Johnson's division and the Second Corps artillery camped on Timber Hill, half a mile west of Rodes.[1] Throughout the day the road from Chambersburg to Shippensburg was lined with soldiers, wagons, and cannons.

About 8:00 A.M. Henry Heth's division of the Third Corps entered the streets of Chambersburg. Instead of following Ewell's command, they turned east toward Fayetteville and Gettysburg. About an hour later, A. P. Hill arrived. He and several staff officers dismounted in the diamond, and hitched

223

their horses in front of a grocery store. Hill remarked that he was expecting General Lee. Mr. Bishop, a local photographer, heard the remark and prepared to take Lee's picture when he arrived. Some soldiers and teamsters got into the act and blocked Mr. Bishop's view. However, Jacob Hoke witnessed Lee's arrival in Chambersburg and gives a description of Hill and Lee:

> General Hill seemed to be a man of splendid physique. Of ordinary height, his figure was slight but athletic, and his carriage erect. His dress was the ordinary Confederate gray, and was plain and without ornament, except the stars upon the collar of his coat, which designated his rank. His appearance indicated a man of robust health, and one who cared not for the tinsel of military trappings, or the honors of his high position.
>
> Returning to the second story of my dwelling, on the north-east corner of the diamond, where I had been to take a look at General Hill, I found there a number of the ministers of the town. They had been in the habit of meeting there to look upon the hosts of invaders, for from the windows of that room an uninterrupted view could be had of Main Street, from the Reformed Church to the Presbyterian, at the lower end. Seeing a group of about fifteen or twenty finely mounted horsemen coming over the brow of the hill, opposite the Reformed Church, I called the attention of the persons present to them, when one of them exclaimed, "That's General Lee and his staff." Snatching our hats we made rapid strides down the stairs and out into the diamond to see them enter. Taking a position in front of the printing establishment of the Reformed Church, then known as the Mansion House, I watched the entrance of these men and the memorable scenes which there transpired. Lee and his staff stopped directly in front of where I stood. General Hill had, upon perceiving the approach of General Lee, mounted his horse, and riding slowly toward him, held his hat gracefully above his head. The two generals—Lee and Hill—then rode a short distance away from the group, and held a short, whispered consultation. As a large part of Heth's division of Hill's corps had already passed through Chambersburg, not following the two divisions of Ewell's corps down the valley toward Harrisburg, but turning eastward and going out on the pike leading to Gettysburg, I concluded that if Lee followed in the same direction, Baltimore and Washington were his destination. With this impression upon my mind, I watched with intense interest the result of the council then taking place, and, observing Mr. Benjamin S. Huber, who resided a few miles from town, standing by my side, and remembering that he had been sent a few days before with a message to Harrisburg, and that he could be relied upon for any

duty, I said to him, "There, Ben, is perhaps the most important council in the history of this war, and the fate of the Government may depend upon it. If General Lee goes on down the valley, then Harrisburg and Philadelphia are threatened; if he turns east, Baltimore and Washington are in danger, and the Government ought to know which way he goes as soon as possible." To this Huber replied, "Well, I have just got back from Harrisburg and I am tired, but as soon as he starts so that I can see which way he goes, I will be off again for Harrisburg." In a short time the council between the two generals ended, and Hill falling back and Lee riding in advance, the whole cavalcade moved forward. Reaching nearly the middle of the diamond, where the road leading to Harrisburg is crossed at right angles by the pike leading to Gettysburg and Baltimore, Lee drew the right-hand rein and his horse turned eastward. Looking around for Huber, I saw him elbowing his way through the crowd of citizens to convey this important information to Harrisburg.[2]

Hoke was very much impressed with the discipline of the Confederate troops. He notes that they were generally better behaved than the Union soldiers. He attributed this to the "no drinking" rule imposed by the officers. Hoke thought the Union army would have been better off if similar orders would have been carried out.

Mr. Hoke describes the headquarters of the Army of Northern Virginia:

General Lee selected for his head-quarters a grove which then stood along the pike leading to Gettysburg, near the eastern edge of Chambersburg. It was once known as "Shetter's Woods," but afterward as "Messersmith's Woods," after the late George R. Messersmith, Esq., who at the time referred to owned it. It was for many years the place where picnics and Fourth of July celebrations were held. The Centennial Anniversary of American Independence, on July 4th, 1876, was held there. The grove has recently been cut down, and the place is now a cultivated field. It was a beautiful location, and from Friday, June 26th, to Tuesday morning, 30th, General Lee and his staff tarried there. There he held his councils of war, there he received reports from the various parts of his vast army, and there he planned and ordered an attack on the capital of our State, and there on the night of Monday, 29th, when Longstreet's scout brought information of the whereabouts of the Army of the Potomac, he recalled that order and decided to cross the South Mountain and fight a battle upon the direct line to Baltimore and Washington. Other acts of importance which transpired upon this historic spot during those memorable four days of General Lee's residence there, will be given in their appropriate places.[3]

Although Hill conferred with Lee in Chambersburg, many of his soldiers did not reach the Chambersburg area today.

McGowan's men resumed the march traveling in the rain and mud to a point near what Caldwell calls "Leitersville." The road itself was good. Provisions were ample. The people of Washington County sold the men various items, and did it at a cheaper rate than that prevailing in Virginia. Some gave the men food due to their own fear. The South Carolinians got a special treat tonight. They were given a liquor ration.

Friday started out as a bad day for Colonel Fremantle. His horse was in terrible shape. Lawley was ill, and the surly Union host was very unhappy at the thought of putting the two men up for another day. But when they gave him real gold instead of Confederate money, he gave them breakfast and warmed up a bit. As Fremantle ate his breakfast, McLaws's division passed by, marching in a heavy rain. Fremantle waited until the weather cleared a bit, and then hit the road at 2:00 P.M. Lawley was so sick he could barely ride. The English colonel walked and rode through the deep mud and gulleys.

By 5:00 P.M. Fremantle was again with McLaws's infantry, covering nine and half miles in three hours. He rode across, finding the Potomac deep and wide. His feet got wet in the stirrups. Once in Maryland he was upset to find that Lee and Longstreet had left town at 11:00, and so it was on to Hagerstown. The houses were shut up, no one on the street, and the few who stared at the soldiers looked sulky. No one in Hagerstown knew the whereabouts of the two generals, and Fremantle was exhausted. At nine o'clock lodging was found with a Dutchman who became friendlier at the sight of gold. Life in the Coldstream Guards was never like this day, a day when a young colonel walked seventeen miles in the rain and mud with a broken-down horse. The Britisher kept his boots on, knowing full well that he'd never get them back on again if he took them off.[4]

William Nelson Pendleton, the fighting parson with Lee's artillery, took the time to write home this Friday. He was located two miles north of the Mason-Dixon Line between Hagerstown and Chambersburg.

226

Day before yesterday (Wednesday) we marched from Berryville and camped for the night at Darkesville,—just where General Jackson had his headquarters two years ago when we were expecting Patterson. Yesterday morning we started at four and proceeded through Martinsburg. Crossed the Potomac at Williamsport last evening and camped half a mile north of the river. This morning we came on through a most disagreeable rain all day, first to Hagerstown, where General Lee got me to see some good Southerner to learn about the roads, etc. I went with George Peterkin to see a Dr. Magill. . . . A number of ladies walked through the mud and rain half a mile to see General Lee. . . . After remaining near Hagerstown some two hours, we marched on and camped, where we are now, in Pennsylvania. Ewell and the cavalry ahead of him have swept along before us, so that we do not see the full harvest of Yankee alarm. . . . Houses are generally shut, and horses, cattle, etc., are missing.

Our men are entirely forbearing. No private property taken by violence, no quiet person molested. A great exhibition of forbearance after all the outrage perpetrated by the Yankees on our soil and our friends. We will take by authority all supplies needed. Everything at old prices here. And we give only Confederate money at par. . . . Stores all shut. No chance of getting anything while Ewell's corps is ahead. We expect a great battle before long. Hooker must of course meet us somewhere in this country. His men will probably fight harder than they have done. It will, I suppose, be the severest struggle of the war. God grant it may help us to independence and peace. . . . The Yankee Episcopal minister in Hagerstown told Perkins he supposed General Pendleton had renounced the ministry. "Noy a bit of it," Perkins told him.[5]

Hood's Texans crossed the Potomac about noon on June 26. The rain was falling. The artillery and wagons took the pontoon bridge. Thus to speed things along, the infantry took to the river and waded across. Many of the soldiers literally stripped and held everything about their heads in an effort to keep dry. However, with the rain, stripping must not have helped very much. Holding their garments aloft the men made their way to the Maryland shore. The regimental bands had crossed first, so they greeted their buddies with stirring military music. It was almost like a carnival. When all were across, General Robertson had them put their clothes back on, and they marched a short distance into Maryland.[6] Then rifles were stacked and the evening meal prepared. John Hood said he had never heard his men sing "Dixie" with more vigor.[7]

During the break, a large cache of federal whiskey, found near Hagerstown, came to Hood's attention. The general was always interested in high morale, and thought a little drink might make them feel pretty good, or perhaps be used to celebrate the return to Maryland. Hood requested and obtained several barrels of the spirits for distribution. One gill per man was to be issued. Those who did not want any had dozens of requests for their share. "The combination of a long march, a hot day, an empty stomach, the excitement of a campaign in Yankeedom, and a few gills of whiskey was disastrous."[8] John Stevens, a member of K Company, Fifth Texas, reports:

> . . . inside half an hour there were more drunk men in Williams-port . . . than I think I ever saw in my life. They were drunk all over. . . . Some laughed, some cried, some hooped and yelled. . . . Some fell by the wayside helpless and were dumped into wagons and ambulances and hauled for the balance of the day. Some others were not seen for fifteen hours afterwards and when they caught up with their commands, they were quite sober but their eyes looked like two burnt holes in a blanket.[9]

J. B. Polley of the Fourth Texas watched the whiskey put more than half of the brigade in "boisterously good humor." John West noted that perhaps one-third got "pretty tight and many of them slipped down and rolled in the mud." Some men got more than a gill, they went to the barrels and got whiskey by the cupful. Some wanted to fight anybody and everybody. One man who was feeling no pain at all and was on cloud nine, grabbed a stack of rifles with bayonets fixed and charged a group of comrades, badly gashing the cheek of an officer. The long roll of the drum broke things up or it's hard to tell what might have happened.[10]

Colonel Manning of the Third Arkansas was a strict officer. He took the men who were feeling good and had them dunked in a nearby stream. If once a round did not do the trick, then the process was repeated, until the man could stand and walk halfway straight. Then it was through Hagerstown and on to Greencastle, Pennsylvania.[11]

Col. Harold B. Simpson, the author of *Hood's Texas Brigade* says the division accomplished a feat achieved by none other during the war. "They had breakfast in Virginia, lunch in the state of Maryland, supper in Pennsylvania and slept that night in the state of intoxication—four states in twenty-four hours."[12] The writer notes that not even Jeb Stuart and his proud troopers could equal that record.

Those who did not get drunk had their own plans. They were more interested in food. Bill Fletcher and others from Company F, Fifth Texas Infantry, bribed the guards and slipped out to scour the rich Pennsylvania countryside. They had to promise to share their loot with the sentries. Fletcher and his buddies had a great experience at the first place they visited near Greencastle. They were entertained and fed by three young ladies.

But the night was young and so were the Texans. They spotted a beehive. A cleverly devised plan was made and a rope thrown around the beehive. A long distance was kept between the two ends. With a yank the hive came down and the men in gray dragged it along the road, tearing it to pieces and scattering the bees. Then the men went to work on the honey. Having no containers, there was nothing left to do but eat it all on the spot. Next came a Pennsylvania milkhouse and the contents of it were sampled. Before going back to camp though, the men wanted to find out if Yankee chickens tasted any different than Southern chickens. So a chicken house was raided and the unlucky birds tossed out to waiting comrades. Now it was time to go back to camp. But the men found they had a big job to do in plucking and dressing the chickens. They were tired. After all, it was a long way from the Virginia side of the Potomac to Greencastle, especially when you are walking. They were full. They had eaten a good supper, had their fill of honey, and milk, so they slipped into camp at another spot and hit the sack.[13]

Hood was in a good mood. After establishing headquarters just south of Greencastle on the lawn of a spacious three-story home, he told the men assigned to guard him for the night, Company K of the Fifth Texas, "Boys, you are now on enemy soil; stack your arms, and do pretty much as you please . . . stay close by and prevent any stranger from coming here to kill me."[14]

That's all the encouragement the men needed. It was off to

the races. The summer kitchen, smokehouse, springhouse, garden and poultry yards were raided. Within five minutes food and supplies had disappeared. The hungry men consumed or took fifteen pounds of butter, about fifteen gallons of milk, everything fit to eat from the garden was taken, and almost three hundred chickens, ducks, and turkeys. The men of K Company were glad they had stayed sober. A good meal was better than getting drunk.

The poor chickens made a terrible noise. The lady of the house came out and begged the men to stop. Then she made the same request to General Hood. John Hood said something to the effect, "Well mam, the men from Texas are very fond of chicken, and I must remind you that the Federal Army in Virginia killed every chicken and nearly everything else. The North ought to be taught a little something about what war means, and what it is like to lose your belongings." John Stevens said he was sure the chickens must have thought they were being raided by a group of hungry Methodist preachers.[15]

K Company also found some honey. Squatting "shoe deep in feathers," they had a banquet with duck, turkey, chicken, fresh vegetables, washed down with fresh milk, and topped off with honey. What a meal.[16] That's the way it was at a nice Pennsylvania farm, just south of Greencastle, June 26, 1863.

By now the entire Confederate army, with the exception of Jeb Stuart's cavalry, was across the Potomac. For the most part, the Confederate infantry was a day or two march ahead of the Union foot soldiers, in some cases, a little more.

At 4:00 P.M. this Friday afternoon, Pickett's division crossed back into the Union between Hagerstown and Chambersburg at State Line or Middleburg. Confederate campfires illuminated many a Pennsylvania road—that "magnificent domain, where shrew . . . and scheming Billy Penn, with a lot of trashy toys, trinkets and tracts, tricked and swindled the simple aborigines." Shotwell called the place of crossing "Muttontown." That was the name given to the place by the local citizens. Shotwell thought this was a good name because the folks seemed "sheepish."[17]

He felt that Pickett's men met a better reception in southern Franklin County than in Maryland. This was strange, but he saw a dozen miniature Confederate flags waving from the windows of Middleburg. Ladies also waved scarves and handkerchiefs. But Shotwell was a suspicious person. He thought maybe the Dutch were trying to appear friendly as they would not be harmed or lose possessions. Behind the outward demonstration, he wondered how they really felt.[18]

One old Quaker demonstrated his feelings. When Ewell's men came to Middleburg, the elderly Quaker drew a line in the middle of the road, and said, "In the name of God, so far thou canst go, but no farther." Like the tollgate keeper at Tilghmanton he tried to hold up the Army of Northern Virginia. But he was outnumbered, and soon retired from the scene, defeated.[19]

It seemed as though George Pickett was homesick, or perhaps lovesick. Or maybe he just wanted the war to be over. Marching through Greencastle, he heard a band playing, "Her Bright Smile Haunts Me Still." In Greencastle he wrote again to his girl friend:

> I want to lie down in the grass, away off in the woods somewhere or in some lone valley on the hillside far from all human sound, and rest my soul and put my heart to sleep and get back something—I know not what—but something I had that is gone from me—some subtle and unexplainable—something I never knew I possessed till I had lost it—till it was gone—gone.[20]

In Greencastle, a young girl rushed out on the porch and waved the Stars and Stripes while the Confederate band was playing "Dixie." She waved it defiantly and called the Rebels "Traitors, Traitors." She dared the men to take her flag. Pickett feared for the safety of the Greencastle Barbara Fritchie. So he took his hat off, saluted her and had the men present arm. This noble act melted the Pennsylvania girl. She stopped her tirade and said she wished she had a Confederate flag too.[21]

As correspondent Ross traveled the dark country road near Greencastle, fires burned alongside the road with a group of soldiers around each. It was "a strange and picturesque sight." The men in gray slept in the fields, in barns, and in strawstacks.[22]

The folks in McConnellsburg had been frightened when the Rebels rode into town. They feared ill treatment. They asked the men in gray to spare their lives and their homes. Finding the Confederates calm and easygoing their fears soon vanished.

Randolph McKim found this a real contrast to the treatment the Southern people received at the hands of the Northern. Indeed, perhaps the admiration of Lee stems in part from the way in which he ordered his men to conduct themselves in Pennsylvania in June of '63.[23] Lee's outlook was much different from that of Phil Sheridan who is supposed to have told Bismark that the correct principle of warfare is to "leave the people nothing but eyes to weep with." Sheridan did just that in the summer of 1864 in the Shenandoah Valley.

From McConnellsburg, a Confederate column turned eastward to Fort Loudon and Saint Thomas. In the little village six miles west of Chambersburg, Major Harry Gilmor "captured sixty head of cattle, forty horses, some mules, and a few militia."[24] The pastor of the United Brethren Church hid his horse in the coal cellar of the house of worship. McKim was surprised to find no opposition of any kind until the appearance of a small militia force in Saint Thomas. They had ridden fifty miles and had been in Pennsylvania for four days.

Hotchkiss reports that Confederate cavalry spent the day scouring the country for horses. The people were fearful of mistreatment. Yet they joked of the Confederates being back in the Union. Rain fell most of the day near Shippensburg. The land was full of everything, and there was plenty, especially of cherries. Jed heard that Early was camping for the night near Mummasburg.[25]

Prior to crossing the Potomac, General Lee had sent, as we have seen, General Imboden to disrupt traffic on the C. and O. Canal, the B. and O. Railroad, and to destroy Union communications. After his visit to Cumberland, Imboden headed east doing all the damage he could to the railroad, depots, tracks, bridges, etc. Then about the twenty-fifth or twenty-sixth, he crossed the Potomac at Cherry Run Ford, about eight miles east of Hancock, Maryland. This is at the very narrowest point in Maryland. Then Imboden headed north into Little Cove in southwestern Franklin County. This is still a very picturesque rural area. He detached some of his men to Webster's Mills, six miles south of McConnellsburg.[26] His men took a lot of stock. Robinson's store at Big Cove Tannery was raided. Some private homes were entered. This command seemingly had little regard for personal belongings, and seems to have been the worst behaved of the Confederates operating in Pennsylvania.

George Steuart thought he would find the Second Corps in Chambersburg today. But on the way he found they had moved on. So he turned northwesterly toward Roxbury, gathering more livestock on the way. When night fell, he camped a half a mile east of Roxbury in a bend of the Conodoguinet Creek.

Early's division broke camp at Greenwood and headed east toward Gettysburg and points beyond. Early was following the orders received from Ewell on the grounds of the Mennonite Church north of Chambersburg on Thursday.

> While on their way across the mountain they burned the Caledonia Iron Works, which belonged to Hon. Thaddeus Stevens. These works were situated about two miles east of Greenwood, at the base of the South Mountain, and about ten miles from Chambersburg. They consisted of a large charcoal furnace, forge, rolling mill, coal house, shops, stables, and other buildings. On Tuesday, June 16th, while Jenkins' cavalry occupied Chambersburg, a marauding party visited these works, and upon the condition that they should be spared, all the horses and mules belonging to the premises were delivered to them. Hon. John Sweeney, Mr. Stevens' business manager, says that he had an interview with General Early, as he sat upon his horse that day, and endeavored to dissuade him from executing his threat to destroy these works. He told him that so far as Mr. Stevens was concerned, he would be better off if his works had been destroyed ten years before, but for the sake of the many poor people who were dependent upon them for support, and would be thrown out of employment if they were destroyed, he should spare them. To this appeal General Early replied, "That is not the way Yankees do business. They do not go on unless they make money. Then, Mr. Stevens is an enemy of the South. He is in favor of

confiscating their property and arming the negroes. His property must be destroyed." General Early then specially detailed Colonel French to apply the torch, and the whole was soon a mass of smouldering ruins.[27]

Years later, "Jube" Early wrote to a Professor Richards describing his reasons for burning the Iron Works:

> No column of our troops was sent to burn the Iron Works of Thaddeus Stevens, near Greenwood, in the campaign into Pennsylvania, in 1863. My division of Ewell's corps was ordered to move along the western base of South Mountain until it came to the road from Chambersburg to Gettysburg, which I did, passing through Waynesborough and one or two smaller villages. I found the iron works above mentioned on the road aforesaid, where it begins to ascend the South Mountain, and they were burned by my order, and on my own responsibility. My reasons for giving the order were founded on the fact that the Federal troops had invariably burned such works in the South. . . . Moreover, in some speeches in congress, Mr. Stevens had exhibited a most vindictive spirit toward the people of the South, as he continued to do to the day of his death. . . .[28]

Early's men crossed the mountain and continued east toward Gettysburg. He heard there were Federal troops in the town. The road through Cashtown was blocked with fallen trees. So part of his command continued while others took a road to the left. Traveling was difficult because the heavy rains of the previous day had made the roads very muddy. Light showers were still falling.[29]

As the news of the invasion spread throughout the North, Gettysburg, like other communities, raised a company of militia. Primarily these were young men from the college and seminary.[30] Designated as Company A of the Twenty-sixth Pennsylvania Emergency Volunteer Militia Regiment, the men were mustered into service under the command of Col. W. W. Jennings.[31]

This Friday the young students had their baptism of fire as they encountered the veteran Confederate soldiers of "Jube" Early three and a half miles west of Gettysburg. Gordon's veterans and White's cavalry soon brushed these willing but untrained troops aside. Most of the twenty-sixth escaped.

However, their rear guard was caught on the Witmer farm and captured.[32]

According to some sources, White's troopers were met on the outskirts of Gettysburg by some shrewd citizens who offered the gray cavalrymen some special brew, resulting in many of them getting high very quickly. But all is fair, or so they say in love and war. The drink, whatever it was, made each man a great hero in his own eyes, and they related tales of how they executed their enemies. Those who provided the drink, now wondered if they had done the right thing.[33]

C. J. Tyson was an eyewitness to the events of Friday afternoon.

> About three o'clock . . . , my wife and I were putting down the last carpet in the front second story bedroom in our little house on Chambersburg . . . (we had just commenced housekeeping—were married April 30, 1863), when we heard an unusual noise. Upon looking out the window toward Chambersburg, we saw the advance of Ewell's corps, consisting of outrages mounted men, some with hats, some without; some in blue and some in gray. On, on they came, and as they dashed past the house and up into the town they rent the air with yells, at the same time discharging their carbines and pistols into the air. Following them came the mass of infantry, which filled the road from side to side, and when they reached our house and passed on . . . the mass extended to the top of Seminary Ridge, and still on they came.[34]

About 3:30 P.M. about two hundred Confederate cavalry rode into Gettysburg. Professor Jacobs says they were "shouting and yelling like so many savages from the wilds of the Rocky Mountains; firing their pistols, not caring whether they killed or maimed man, woman, or child; and rushing from stable to stable in search of horses, the most of which, however, had fortunately been sent forward to Hanover and York a few hours before."[35]

Professor Jacobs describes what occurred next:

> This advance party was soon followed by 5,000 infantry, being General Gordon's brigade of Early's division of Ewell's corps. Most of the men were exceedingly dirty, some ragged, some without shoes, and some surmounted by the skeleton of what once had been a hat, affording unmistakable evidence that they stood in great need of having their scanty wardrobe replenished; and hence the eagerness with which they inquired after shoe, hat, and clothing stores.

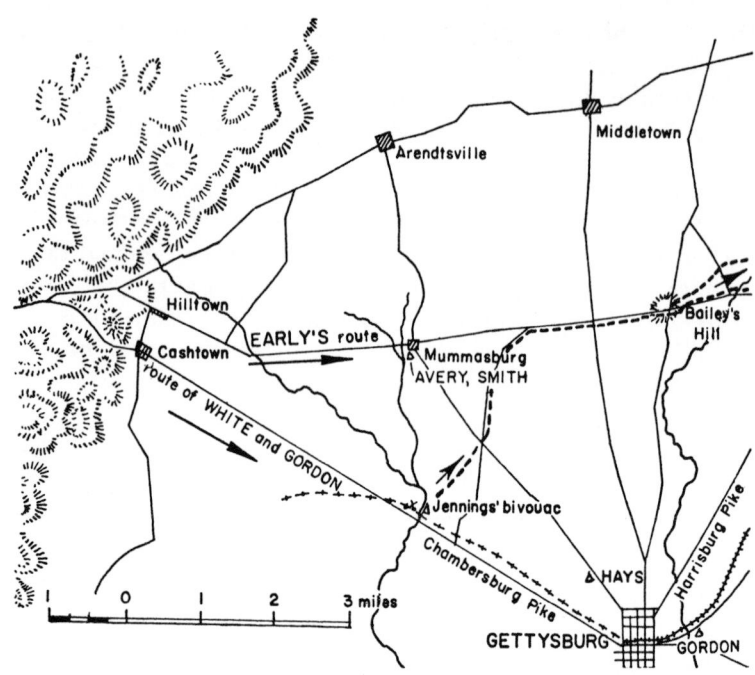

Early's route. Courtesy Louisiana State University
Press in *Here Come the Rebels!*

The gray-clad men were wet and heated and distressed to
learn that hats and shoes were unavailable.[36]

Hugh Scott, a dapper young man with black hair and a
mustache, was at his telegraph office in Gettysburg. This had
been a busy week for him. Every day there were more facts
and rumors to send out about the advance of the Rebels. It
was foggy today, and apparently the fog kept folks from
seeing the advance of Early's men. Scott was unaware of
what was happening until the Confederates were within two
hundred yards of his town. But he was prepared for just such
an emergency. He had a fine horse hitched to a spring wagon
all ready to go. So he and a companion jumped in and galloped off as the Rebels chased him. Although he was shot at,
he was not hit, and Scott reached York safely. Just prior to
leaving, he had dashed off a message to Daniel Trone in

Hanover saying, "The Johnnies are now entering Gettysburg."[37]

Jubal Early sent for the officials of Gettysburg. He demanded that they give him twelve hundred pounds of sugar, six hundred pounds of coffee, sixty barrels of flour, one thousand pounds of salt, seven thousand pounds of bacon, ten barrels of whiskey, ten barrels of onions, one thousand pairs of shoes and five hundred hats or five thousand dollars. That was a pretty big order.

Mr. Kendlehart and Mr. Buehler informed the Confederate general that there was no way they could comply with the request. Such quantities of supplies just were not available in Gettysburg. The money was not on hand either. They told Early they were at his mercy. He could search the town, stores and civilians and take what he could find. But Early backed down and did not force his demands.[38] Two thousand rations belonging to the militia were found in a railroad car and taken. The torch was also applied to about a dozen railroad cars.

During the course of the action, Donald Sandoe, a member of the militia, fell near the slopes of Cemetery Hill, thus becoming the first actual casualty of Gettysburg. He is buried in the Mount Joy Lutheran Church Cemetery on the road to Harney.

After he regrouped his forces, Early ordered Colonel White to proceed to Hanover Junction, burning all the railroad equipment he could find. Gordon was ordered to move the next day on the macadamized road toward York. Early would go with the rest of the command by way of Hunterstown for York.[39] Gordon's brigade camped in and around Gettysburg, while the rest of Early's division bivouacked at Mummasburg.

On Friday afternoon, Robert E. Lee called Isaac Trimble to his headquarters tent. Lee unfolded a map of Pennsylvania, and asked Trimble about the topography east of the South Mountain range. He was very much interested in Adams County and Gettysburg.

Lee felt his army was in good spirits, "not overfatigued, and can be concentrated at any one point in twenty-four

Col. Elijah White led the Confederate cavalry
into Gettysburg and Hanover.

hours or less." Lee felt the Union army would make forced marches to get between his command and the major cities of the east.

Lee continued by saying:

> They will come up, probably through Frederick, broken down with hunger and hard marching, strung out on a long line, and much demoralized when they come into Pennsylvania. I shall throw an overwhelming force on their advance, crush it, follow up the success, drive one corps back on another, and by successive repulses and surprises before they can concentrate create a panic and virtually destroy the army.[40]

June 26

I CORPS

Today John Reynolds and the First Corps took the roads from Barnesville and headed for Jefferson, traveling by way of Adamstown and Mountville. The frustrated men of the Third Corps continued up the canal towpath, and Oliver O. Howard pushed on toward the Middletown Valley and the South Mountain passes. Back at Edwards Ferry, the Twelfth Corps, Meade's Fifth, and late in the day, the Second Corps crossed the Potomac, the Sixth Corps bringing up the rear of the army.

It was sprinkling as the First Corps was under way by 8:00 A.M. Some of the rear elements of the First Corps were greeted by a large group of school children in Poolesville. The sight of the children brought tears to the eyes of the soldiers as they thought of home and their own families. The First Corps was hailed as "protector's from war's devastation."[41]

The path of the Iron Brigade led over Sugar Loaf Mountain via a rough road through thick woods. They crossed the Monocacy River on a 256-foot bridge at Greenfield Mills. The rain kept the men cool but wet. Two miles from the mills, the soldiers halted for dinner. The poor farmer wanted to know who gave permission to burn his fence rails.[42]

General Meredith replied, "By my orders, sir. The men must cook coffee. If you are a loyal man the government will repay."[43]

For General Wadsworth and his men, the eighteen miles seemed much longer in the rain and mud. They were glad to stack arms near Jefferson.[44] The lads had tramped over one hundred miles since leaving the Rappahannock. "The roads between the Potomac and Jefferson completed the destruction of many a pair of shoes," and caused bloody feet.[45]

The soldiers found southern Frederick County "inexpressibly beautiful with its waving grain nestled on the mountain sides, with grand views all around."

Rufus Dawes was typical of the men marching on the Roads to Gettysburg this rainy Friday. Dawes was born at Malta, in Morgan County, Ohio, in 1838. His great-grandfather was William Dawes, Jr., Paul Revere's companion on the eve of the Revolutionary War. After spending his boyhood in Ohio, Rufus attended the University of Wisconsin, and then Marietta College.

In April of 1861, Rufus and his father were on business in Juneau County, Wisconsin. Young Dawes took it upon himself to raise a company of one hundred men. These were known as the "Lemonweier Minute Men." Dawes was elected captain, and a few weeks later the recruits became known as Company K in the Sixth Wisconsin.

Throughout the war Dawes kept a journal and wrote many letters to Mary Beman Gates whom he married in 1864. The journal and the letters became the basis for his book. Rufus and Mary had six children. Among them was Charles G. Dawes, vice-president of the United States, during the Coolidge years.

One of the highlights of the book is the story of a review at Bailey's Crossroads. A lady was watching the troops march by. Sgt. John Ticknor of the Sixth Wisconsin led his comrades in singing "Hang Jeff Davis on a sour apple tree." The entire regiment joined in the chorus, "Glory, glory, hallelujah, as we go marching on." The men were making history.

The lady watching them march by was none other than Julia Ward Howe. That night she was inspired to write new words to the song she heard the men of the Sixth Wisconsin singing. We know it as "The Battle Hymn of the Republic."

While camped near Washington, Dawes went into Washington and on several occasions visited the Presbyterian Church where he saw President Lincoln. In June of 1862, a year prior to the events of this book, Dawes and fifty of his men attended services at the historic Episcopal Church in Fredericksburg.

In military affairs he was greatly impressed with John Gibbon and then General Wadsworth. He felt the latter was a very practical man, looked closely after details, and did all he could for the personal comfort of his command.

Food conditions improved for Rufus Dawes once across the river in Maryland. "We now get butter, eggs, milk, mutton, and almost anything but fruit."

Like many other officers, his home was in the saddle. A pack mule carried provisions and part of a tent. "Everything else Dawes carried on his horse." So you see to lose your horse would be a major disaster.[46]

The Sixth Wisconsin started marching at daylight on the twenty-sixth. Through the rain and the mud they continued all day. The mud was deep by the time they reached their campsite near Jefferson.

Gabe Paul's brigade and the men of the Thirteenth Massachusetts were also under way by 6:00 A.M. They marched eighteen miles from Greenfield Mills to Adamstown, across the Monocacy River to Jefferson. They also note that it was eighteen miles through rain and mud.[47]

The men of the Seventy-sixth New York were to be pitied. Their campsite for Thursday night was a cornfield near Barnesville where the water stood six inches deep between the rows. No soldier was very happy about the spot. So it was almost a welcome relief when camp, if you can call it that, was broken at 9:00 A.M. The wet blankets, now weighing three times their normal weight, were wrung out and placed over their shoulders. Soldiering was no fun that day. Then the men from New York started for Jefferson.[48]

Prior to crossing the river, the men in the Army of the Potomac were warned not to take any livestock or produce in Maryland. They could purchase items if available, but under no conditions were items to be swiped. These orders were heeded. But the fence rails were another matter. Ten thousand men needed a lot of wood to make fires for cooking and coffee. There was a great demand for wood. It was needed to take the chill from their bodies too. One order said that only broken fence rails could be used. The men followed this order, breaking rails to meet the requirements.

The 150th Pennsylvania was moving at the front of the column of march. The men were tired and some were falling by the wayside. Private Rodearmed (better known as Rody), a member of Company B, called out "Captain Jones, we're left in front, aren't we?"

The captain replied, "Yes, Rody, why?"

"Because if we don't soon get a rest, I'm thinking most of us will be left behind."

General Reynolds and his staff was just in front of Company B and overheard the remarks, and almost immediately ordered a halt. Rody was happy and said to his comrades, "Well, boys, the general and I have given you a rest."[49]

The day was disagreeable and hard for Wainwright and the First Corps Artillery. The road over the Catoctin Mountains was "narrow, rough, stony, steep, and muddy pretty much the whole way. The pulling was hard on the horses, for they had no foothold in the slippery clay. I have seldom seen man and beast more tired: never after so short a march (16 miles). The infantry fell out badly all along the road to Jefferson."

There was no sign of war in the Adamstown, Mountville, and Jefferson area. The fields were superb, the wheat ripening fast. But in friendly country and around more people, the men in blue found whiskey. And "today there were a good number of them royally drunk, the hill over which we passed is noted for its distilleries."

William Locke, a member of the First Corps, and attached to the Eleventh Ohio Regiment, says that he crossed the Potomac at 2:00 P.M. on Thursday, and spent the night near Barnesville. But on Friday, "the roads were in the worst possible condition, soft and slippery." However, the sight of Sugar Loaf Mountain brought him inspiration. The peak had stood out since Guilford Station. He also noticed the gap in the mountains at Harpers Ferry. The area was so pretty, the valley "intersected by fields of ripening grain and green, waving corn, looking in the distance like a vast garden. Locke and Chaplain Howell found lodging for the night in Jefferson.[50]

Marsena Patrick ate breakfast at 2:30 A.M. and was in the saddle at 4:30. He was bothered by the rain which made the roads extremely bad. To make matters worse, they were choked with trains. He found the new location of army headquarters in Poolesville to be very disgusting. He was fatigued and fed up with Hooker.

III CORPS

Andrew Humphreys may have had second thoughts as he awakened on a damp Friday morning. His men had pushed on through the night. But the "towpath march" had taken its toll. His command was scattered over a ten-mile stretch of the canal towpath.

Most of the units of the Third Corps were awakened at 5:00 A.M. by the sounds of the bugle. They got up from pools of water. Their first task was to try and wring out their wet clothing. Some were able to get a hasty breakfast in a field near the Monocacy Aqueduct. They felt a little dizzy looking down at the water sixty feet below them. Some of the officers rode their horses on the towpath, and made an effort to take the pack mules by the same route. But the horses and mules weren't sure they liked the elevation either. Quite a few of the horses and mules wound up in the canal and had to swim out.[51]

Young Bardeen was miserable. Everything he had was soaking wet. He was unable to get any breakfast before moving out from Monocacy Aqueduct. His woolen blanket was so heavy from the rain, that he discarded it. Later he was able to grab a handful of cherries, and then in Point of Rocks he obtained some bacon.[52]

Humphreys was unable to get his men under way until the hour of 10:00. The late start was necessitated by the fatigue of the command and by waiting for the stragglers to come up. Seven miles would be the extent of his march today. Cudworth noted that the scenery along the route "brought some refreshment of spirit. The landscape was one of surpassing loveliness."[53]

Regis De Trobriand commanded a brigade in the Third Corps. Married to a New York heiress, De Trobriand became colonel of the Fifty-fifth New York which had been recruited as "The Lafayette Guard." Writing the story of his Civil War years in French, the memoirs were later translated into English. The general tells us about the twenty-sixth and the days following:

> Fourteen hours of forced march brought us to the Monocacy River, where, without shelter, without supper, in a driving rain, we slept in the mud that sound sleep which is known only to soldiers worn with fatigue. Near us was the same aqueduct which I had been ordered to defend with the Fifty-fifth during the first invasion of Maryland. We crossed it the next morning on the footpath, which runs along the canal. . . . We marched towards the enemy at Point of Rocks, Jefferson, and Middletown, where we arrived on the evening of the 27th. . . .
>
> In these small villages we marched by columns of companies, music at the head and flags flying. The National colors were in all the windows; cheers saluted our passage. This part of . . . Maryland was loyally faithful to the cause of the Union, differing in that from the rest of the State, which remained with it only from necessity. In Baltimore they regarded us as enemies; here we were welcomed as liberators. At Frederick our march was almost triumphal. All the houses were draped; all the women were at the windows, waving their handkerchiefs; all the men were at their doors, waving their hats.[54]

V CORPS

Then it was time for the Fifth and Sixth Corps to move. We wish we could go into a lot of detail about each corps, but that is almost impossible when covering ten corps of infantry and trying to present an overall view of the events on the Roads to Gettysburg.

Early on the morning of the twenty-sixth, the Fifth Corps went by way of Carter's Mills, not far from Oatlands, and proceeded by way of historic Leesburg to Edwards Ferry. The soldiers crossed on the upper bridge. They hoped to camp for the night. But no such luck. They pushed on to within four miles of the mouth of the Monocacy. The 155th Pennsylvania marched seven extra miles after crossing the Potomac prior to camping at Poolesville. Like some of the other men, several did not bother to pitch tents for the night. Some of the men had tramped thirty miles. Many recorded a note that was to appear again and again the next few days, "the forced march . . . without doubt the most severe ever experienced."[55] Quite a few fell by the wayside from sheer exhaustion. At the end of this Friday, many were absent from roll-call and the distribution of rations. But this was just a forerunner of things to come for the next five days.

VI CORPS

James Bowen brings us up to date on the activities of the Sixth Corps:

> The Thirty-seventh marched to the vicinity of Centreville, some six miles, on the afternoon of the 24th, and the following day relieved a brigade, now ordered to join the Second Corps, which had

for nearly a year, since entering the service, been very comfortably quartered there, enjoying all the luxuries of soldier life with few of its trials. While they had abandoned great quantities of camp conveniences, which the Thirty-seventh hastened to possess themselves of, it was remarkable to see the enormous knapsacks which the men started out with the intention of carrying on the sweltering marches before them. Their burdens were very much lightened before many miles had been passed. In the course of the day the regiment was comfortably settled with tents pitched near the old earthworks, fitted up in many instances with the equipage abandoned by the departing troops. Every foot of the ground in the vicinity was historic, and the men inspected with much interest the weather-worn intrenchments and the numerous soldiers' graves near by. Despite the rain which fell at night, a feeling of intense satisfaction prevailed. There was every indication that the regiment was to remain for a time in that place on permanent duty—which would be a very agreeable relief from active campaigning.

Alas for the soldiers' expectations! At 2 o'clock that night the familiar tones of Adjutant Colt were heard as he stumbled through the darkness to the different company head-quarters, calling out as each in turn was reached: "Captain, wake up your men, have them pack everything, make their coffee and be ready to march at 4 o'clock!" There was many an exclamation of disgust as the command turned out into the drizzling rain, folded such of their possessions as it seemed best to take upon the march, destroyed everything else that was destroyable, and then waited till near 8 o'clock before the signal for departure was given. Dranesville, 20 miles away, was reached that night, after an exhausting journey; the gentle rain, while saving from the tortures of excessive heat, making the roads exceedingly slippery and difficult.[56]

Alanson Haines and the Fifteenth New Jersey broke camp at 3:00 A.M. today. The brigade marched fifteen miles, passing through Dranesville, and moving on to the Washington-Leesburg Pike.[57] "All the country behind was evacuated and vast stores of public property destroyed."

All good things must end. On the night of June 26, the Sixth Corps left the quiet and beauty of Bristow Station and started on the Roads to Gettysburg again. They had miles and miles to go before they reached their destination. The "darkness was intense," and the drizzle along with an occasional hard shower made it even worse. The march was rapid and some fell behind or like Peter in the Bible "followed at a distance."[58] They were soon set upon by the guerrillas and

246

marched off in another direction—to Richmond as prisoners of war.

XI CORPS

Reynolds asked Howard the condition of the South Mountain passes. He also advised Howard that his headquarters would be set up in Jefferson for the day and night. Howard found no sign of the Confederates in the mountains. Birney and the Third Corps reached Adamstown. Reynolds was having some problems.

The road through the Catoctin Hills very bad.

At 5:10 P.M. on Friday, June 26, Howard communicated with Reynolds saying,

> Fifteen of my headquarters cavalry dashed into Boonsborough, and went about a half mile beyond, chasing out a squad of rebel cavalry. The inhabitants there report that Longstreet encamped between Keedysville and Sharpsburg last night, and moved this morning toward Hagerstown. . . . Yesterday and the day before a part of A. P. Hill's corps passed through; . . . Early himself was with Wright. . . . The whole force which passed through Boonsborough, about 20,000. Lee in person crossed the Potomac last night. His entire force on this side up to yesterday reported to be between 60,000 and 70,000 men.[59]

Howard had placed his troops as follows: one brigade of Barlow's division and a battery in Crampton's Gap; one brigade of Steinwehr's division and a battery in Boonsborough Gap. General Barlow is encamped on the Burkittsville road, General Steinwehr on turnpike, and General Schurz on the old Hagerstown Road, about a mile in front of Middletown. My headquarters at the farm of Mr. Cookerly, first house beyond Middletown, on pike toward Boonsborough.[60]

The Fifty-fifth Ohio led the advance of the Eleventh Corps. Farmers along the way came out to greet them. The drizzle and occasional heavy rain failed to dampen their spirits, or the enthusiasm of the populace. The men of the Fifty-fifth Ohio acted as a provost guard and mingled freely

247

with the citizens of Middletown, most of whom seemed to be retired farmers. "The band played and all rejoiced."[61]

The three mountain passes looked familiar to the many in the Union army. In September of 1862, the entire army crossed South Mountain to fight Lee at Antietam or Sharpsburg. The reader would do well to visit the passes. Each of the three can be easily reached by taking Maryland 67 from 340 which runs from Frederick to Harpers Ferry, or by taking Route 67 from Boonsboro. At Crampton's Pass is the famous War Correspondent's Arch erected by George Alfred Townsend, a noted Civil War writer. Just east of the pass is the quaint town of Burkittsville, already designated as a historic village.

The reader will not want to miss Fox's Gap. This is known as the Old Sharpsburg Road, and was one of the original roads to the west. The Union Ninth Corps traveled by way of this road during the Battle of South Mountain. Their commander, Gen. Jesse Lee Reno, was mortally wounded during the fighting. A monument has been erected to his honor on the mountain top. Troops marched over the road to and from Gettysburg. Then in 1864, Breckenridge's Confederates used the road.

The Fifth New York Cavalry also covered the miles between Adamstown and Jefferson today, reaching Burkittsville, crossing the mountain, and spending the night in Rohrersville on outpost duty.[62]

The Eighteenth Pennsylvania Cavalry moved today also. Earlier in the week they had been on picket duty at Wolf Run Shoals and encamped at Fairfax Court House. On the nineteenth, the men received two months' pay. That made them happy. On the twenty-first they received "Burnside" carbines. On the twenty-third, they covered some of the same roads the infantry had used in their approach to Leesburg. "The roads were strewn with discarded overcoats, winter clothing and blankets. The American soldier will not be hampered with more than absolute necessities, though he must suffer the loss. At 8:40 A.M. today, the Eighteenth Pennsylvania Cavalry crossed the Potomac. As soon as they hit the Maryland shore and were out of the traffic jam, they

248

rested and fed their horses. Then it was on to Poolesville, and many more miles of riding until they reached the regimental campsite at Urbana, just south of Frederick."[63]

Hooker was glad the crossing was going well, for "all the country north of me seemed to be wild and crazy with excitement." The drizzle on the unpaved and heavily traveled roads did not help a lot, but it made marching easier and there was no dust.

During the night Stahel's cavalry crossed the river, guided primarily by the sounds of the mounts in front. There was danger of being swept away. The men did not relax until their horses climbed the steep and slippery banks on the Maryland shore. To make matters worse, it was raining slightly. The guide lost his way, and it was after 2:00 A.M. when the last elements of the column reached a woods near Poolesville. At daylight the march was resumed, and the cavalry soon caught up with the First Corps. Frederick was reached at sunset. For Captain Kidd, it was a great moment.

> The clouds had cleared away, and a more enchanting vision never met human eye than that which appeared before us as we debouched from the narrow defile up which the road from lower Maryland ran, on the commanding heights that overlooked the valley. The town was in the center of a most charming and fertile country, and around it thousands of acres of golden grain were waving and nodding in the sunlight. The rain of the early morning had left in the atmosphere a mellow haze of vapor which reflected the sun's rays in tints which softly blended with the summer colorings of the landscape. An exclamation of surprise ran along the column as each succeeding trooper came in sight of this picture of nature's own painting. But, more pleasing still, were the evidences of loyalty which greeted us on every hand as we entered the village. The stars and stripes floated above many buildings, while from the porch and window, from old and young, came manifestations of welcome. The men received us with cheers, the women with smiles and waving of handkerchiefs. That night we were permitted to go into camp and enjoy a good rest, in the midst of plenty and among friends.

II CORPS

The damp soldiers of the Second Corps greeted the dawn of the twenty-sixth with the hope of drying out. The corps' history has little to say about the day, but the men left Gum Springs and headed for Edwards Ferry. The time of departure was 6:00 A.M., and the march was by way of Farmwell Station and Frankville. The crossing of the Potomac was to be on the lower bridge. Marching helped; the 140th Pennsylvania historian says that body warmth dried the water-soaked clothing in which the men had slept.[64] The Eighth Ohio didn't mind moving in the rain, that was better than lying in it. Frank Sawyer says the drizzle continued all day Friday.[65]

Some units of the Second Corps did not get away from Gum Springs until 10:00 A.M. They reached Edwards Ferry at 5:00 P.M. Soldiers of the Fourth Ohio fixed supper and thought they would spend the night on the Virginia side of the Potomac. But no, it was "hurry up and wait." The soldiers had to stand in line or be ready for the river crossing. Finally between 10:00 and 12:00 P.M., the men of the Second Corps stepped onto the pontoon bridge. Frank Sawyer says:

> We crossed the Potomac on a pontoon bridge about 10 o'clock p.m., and went into bivouac about a mile from the river. The men were wet and tired; the vast number of troops that had preceded us had trod the ground into a complete mortar bed, through which our men floundered along for nearly sixteen hours.[66]

Headquarters was still having map problems. Robert Schenck telegraphed Butterfield from Baltimore at 11:00 P.M. that there were no Frederick County Maps in Baltimore, but at the Coast Survey Office. The Lucas's maps of Maryland were out of print, but the publisher was sending to Philadelphia for the plates.[67]

Even as the tired men of the Second Corps were crossing

250

on the swaying pontoons in the dark of the night, D. N. Couch was sending a message from Harrisburg saying that ten thousand infantry, seven hundred cavalry, and twenty-four pieces of artillery passed through Chambersburg on Wednesday. This was Rodes's command, and the information undoubtedly came from Jacob Hoke and his crew of riding informants.[68]

We can imagine the infantrymen staying close to each other as they crossed, perhaps at arms length. They watched their step because they did not want to fall into the river, weighed down by damp clothing and heavy equipment.

During the evening hours, the men of the Nineteenth Massachusetts gazed upon Ball's Bluff. Here they had received their baptism of fire in the battle that ended as a disaster for the Union. While waiting to cross, some of the soldiers sang and whistled to kill time.[69]

Once across the river, the men of the Nineteenth soon found themselves on the ground of what had been Camp Benton. This was their original bivouac after leaving Massachusetts in 1861. It was both a happy and sad experience. The campsite brought back a lot of memories. The troops from New England thought about the gaiety of the campfires. But they also remembered names and faces of those who were no longer present, friends who had answered the last roll call, and those who were disabled for life from wounds received in action.[70]

Passing by the home of Mr. Williams, a friend from those earlier days, the men found him along the fence. He came to the road and shook hands with as many of his former friends as possible. He was surprised and overjoyed to see his New England friends.

Stahel, the cavalry leader attached to the infantry of the Union army in the Middletown area, lamented the fact on the twenty-sixth that he had no rations for his men. They had gone to Frederick and then headed west for Middletown. Howard gave him rations from the Eleventh Corps' supply. This made the general from Maine fear that his own men might suffer. He wondered if a supply depot was going to be

251

established in Frederick. The telegraph between Middletown and Frederick was also out of order.

Stahel did not realize, nor did Howard, that Rufus Ingalls, the chief quartermaster of the Army of the Potomac, was already ordering food, forage, clothing, and other army materials to Frederick.[71]

Butterfield sent word to General French, commander of the Harpers Ferry garrison, to make a reconnaissance toward the Burnside Bridge over the Antietam Creek.[72]

Alarming news was received in Harrisburg the night of the twenty-sixth. Pennsylvania militia troops reported Confederate troops in Gettysburg. They fired on the men in gray and then retired. The superintendent of the Carlisle Army Barracks reported that large groups of Confederates were near, and he being without adequate defense, he also retired.[73] But Captain Hastings moved all the ammunition and supplies he could. A large Confederate force had been in McConnellsburg west of Chambersburg, taking sheep, cattle, and horses.[74]

The Union cavalry was very busy from June 6 until the moment they crossed the Potomac. A member of the Seventeenth Pennsylvania writes:

> I remember one of the most pitiful scenes of the war during this period. It occurred near Cattlet's Station, on the Orange and Alexandria Railroad. The division had been marching and picketing for almost a week with no rest for man or beast. They had marched all night to reach this point on the railroad for necessary supplies. The column halted before the light of day with orders to "dismount and stand to horse." The ever-vigilant enemy were known to be near. We were covering important movements of Hooker's army, who left dust in the road we stood on not less than eight inches deep. With a fellow-officer I moved to the roadside, and there sat down waiting for orders. An hour passed, and the gray dawn of coming day slowly lighted up a picture I never can forget. The men, who were completely tired out, had slipped the bridle rein over their arms and lay down in front of their horses in a bed of dust that almost obscured them from sight. Their jaded steeds seemed to know they should not move, and, propping themselves with extended necks and lowering heads, stood like mute sentinels over their riders dead in sleep.[75]

John Buford, commander of the First
Union Cavalry Division.

XII CORPS

Friday—It was the Twelfth Corps' turn to cross the Potomac. The men were aroused at 4:00 A.M., and shortly thereafter started to cross the river. To A. S. Williams, the crossing at Edwards Ferry looked to be a quarter of a mile broad, or as broad as the Detroit River.[76]

The Twenty-seventh Indiana and the rest of the troops marched up the river, plodding along on the C. and O. Canal towpath, following in the footsteps of the Third Corps. "It rained all day, a steady drizzle." Brown and his mates camped for the night at the mouth of the Monocacy.[77] All of the regimental journals cover the day with almost these exact words, using not more than two or three lines. So the Twelfth Corps' march wasn't very exciting. "The men," according to George Collins of the 149th New York, "were in good spirits and experienced a sense of relief and pressure in passing from Virginia into the loyal state of Maryland."[78]

Perhaps they thought of a saying prevalent in the ranks of the Thirteenth Massachusetts, "When you see geese flying north, look for good warm weather. When you see rebels marching north, look for warm fighting."[79]

Today William B. French, formerly a division commander in the Second Corps, was named to command the garrison at Harpers Ferry. These men and the troops on Maryland Heights numbered between ten and eleven thousand. For days Hooker had been trying to get them placed under his command. However, Halleck kept saying no. At the same time, Henry Warner Slocum was sent as far as the mouth of the Monocacy River with the idea that the Twelfth Corps and the Harpers Ferry command should operate on the enemy's rear, his line of communications and supply, and harass him in any way possible.[80] Hooker argued that Harpers Ferry should be abandoned for this purpose. But the next day

254

Halleck wired back saying the fortifications on Maryland Heights had been established at great labor and expense, and he could not approve of their abandonment.

Hooker did not like this. He said the garrison at Harpers Ferry was of no earthly good. They were useless as long as they were in camp. He did not think it possible for the Confederates to occupy Maryland Heights. He urged the immediate release of the Harpers Ferry garrison and asked that his letter be presented to Stanton and President Lincoln. Before the wires cooled he sent another wire from Sandy Hook where he had gone himself to view the situation, saying if the troops were not released, he wished to be relieved of command.[81]

Halleck was glad to comply. He had little regard for Hooker, and after Chancellorsville regarded him as unfit to command the Army of the Potomac. We'll pick up the rest of the story later.

John Reynolds was proud of the response of his wing of the army as the soldiers moved toward Middletown. He was able to report that Colonel Othneil De Forest's cavalry brigade was in possession of Crampton's Pass. But somehow these horsemen obtained a supply of some good Maryland whiskey. Several of the troopers became intoxicated and rode around shouting and swinging their sabers. Colonel Leopold von Gilsa's brigade from Barlow's division of the Eleventh Corps was the infantry detached to hold Crampton's Pass. His men became tired of the noise of the cavalrymen. They were also afraid someone was going to get hurt. So they rounded up the drunken troopers at the point of the bayonet, and marched them off for discipline. This and other episodes caused Reynolds to become disenchanted with Stahel. He must have complained loudly enough because on the evening of June 28, Stahel was relieved of command.[82]

As the sounds of taps faded through the bivouac areas of the Army of the Potomac, John Reynolds and the First Corps were strung out along the road from Barnesville to Jefferson; Hancock and the Second Corps were at Edwards Ferry on the Maryland side of the Potomac; Birney and the Third Corps were at Point of Rocks; Meade's Fifth Corps was about four miles from the mouth of the Monocacy River; Sedgwick and the Sixth Corps were still at Dranesville in Virginia; while Howard's Eleventh Corps was at Middletown, with Slocum and the Twelfth at the mouth of the Monocacy.

Saturday would be another big day for the Army of the Potomac as they converged on Frederick. The Army of Northern Virginia would move on toward Carlisle and York, Ewell's Corps that is, while Longstreet and A. P. Hill's men rested near Chambersburg.

Saturday, June 27, was a busy one for Robert E. Lee. Headquarters were in the woods just east of Chambersburg. Lee would have felt better had he known where Stuart was, and likewise the Army of the Potomac. But for the moment he had other things to do. He wanted to make sure the Confederates treated the local people and their property in a proper manner. Thus he issued a strongly worded order, Number 73, saying:

> The commanding general considers that no greater disgrace could befall the army, and through it our whole people, than the perpetuation of the barbarous outrages upon the unarmed and defenseless, and the wanton destruction of private property, that have marked the course of the enemy in our country.
> Such proceedings not only degrade the perpetrators and all connected with them, but are subversive of the discipline and efficiency of the army, and destructive of the ends of our present movement.
> It must be remembered that we make war only upon armed men, and that we cannot take vengeance for the wrongs our people have suffered, without lowering ourselves in the eyes of all whose abhorrence has been excited by the atrocities of our enemies, and offending against Him to whom vengeance belongeth, without whose favor and support our efforts must all prove in vain.
> The commanding general, therefore, earnestly exhorts the troops to abstain with most scrupulous care from unnecessary or wanton injury to private property, and he enjoins upon all officers to arrest and bring to summary punishment all who shall in any way offend against the orders of this subject.[83]

Next came a visit from the handsome Maj. Gen. Isaac Trimble. Lee wanted his advice. Not only was Trimble a West Point graduate, but prior to the war, he had been general superintendent of the Baltimore and Potomac Railroad.

Therefore, Trimble, from nearby Baltimore, had an excellent knowledge of the countryside.

Lee opened a large, detailed map, prepared by Maj. Jed Hotchkiss. For three months, Jackson's chief of engineers had labored to produce a masterpiece of the area from Winchester, Virginia, to the Susquehanna River. Hotchkiss depicted not only the towns, rivers, and mountains, but even the farms, along with them the names of the farmers.

As the two looked at the map, Trimble assured Lee that Adams County was an excellent place for a defensive battle. In fact, said Trimble, "almost every square mile contains good positions for battle or skillful maneuvering."

Gettysburg, of course, is the Adams County seat. Lee is supposed to have placed his hand near Gettysburg and said, "Hereabout we shall probably meet the enemy and fight a great battle. And if God gives us the victory the war will be over, and we shall receive the recognition of our independence."[84]

The curious of Chambersburg came to see the famous Confederate general about whom they had heard so much. They had to be careful of the couriers and the staff officers who were coming and going. Lee was fifty-seven now. His hair had turned white, no doubt due to the strain of the war. Tall and trim, he wore a full gray beard. His eyes were keen and penetrating.[85]

While Lee was mapping strategy in Messersmith's woods, and Early was heading for York, Mr. Huber was riding along back roads seeking to elude the Rebels, and carry messages to Harrisburg. The efforts of Huber and others like him provided Governor Curtin with the only real intelligence as to what was going on. The information was then telegraphed from Harrisburg to the War Department in Washington.

When the Confederate army reached Chambersburg, Mr. Messersmith, cashier of the bank, undertook to ascertain the number, making a tally of each hundred. An officer saw what he was doing and ordered him to stop. Mr. Messersmith bowed, went to his barn, obtained a hundred kernels of corn, holding them in his hand in his trousers-pocket, dropping a kernel for every hundred. When his hand was empty, ten

257

thousand had passed. Then he gathered them up and started again. Through the day he stood upon the steps of the bank counting the passing troops. He estimated the number at sixty thousand. . . .[86]

Saturday afternoon, Lee issued a communique commending his troops for their behavior, saying that he had observed with "marked satisfaction the conduct of the troops on the march. . . . No troops could have displayed greater fortitude, or better performed their arduous marches of the past ten days."[87]

According to many of those living at the time, the behavior of the Confederates, with perhaps the exception of Hood's division, was remarkably good.[88]

On this June Saturday, Robertson's men from Texas and Arkansas camped near Chambersburg. They left camp and went out to the farms and into the streets of the city to purchase food and goodies with Confederate money. However, they obtained much without the use of their funds. When evening came they had a feast with turkeys, chickens, ducks, corn bread, ham, bacon, cheese, bread, crocks of apple butter, pickles and jellies.[89]

Major Stiles saw an elderly woman on the porch of one home and asked permission to water his horse. She granted his wish and invited him in. The major asked her to mail a letter to his sister in Connecticut. The lady wanted to know if he had ever met "Stonewall" Jackson. He replied "yes." Whereupon the old lady said that she expected to see him soon, adding, "If any one ever left this earth who went straight to heaven, it was he." The woman had grown up in Virginia, moved to Pennsylvania, but remained a Virginian at heart.[90]

As the Army of the Potomac stripped the cherry trees in Maryland, so the Army of Northern Virginia raided the trees in Pennsylvania. Even Moxley Sorrel, Longstreet's chief of staff, pulled down "branch after branch." Moxley went shopping in Chambersburg, and bought some material that served as his suit for the rest of the war. He was surprised to hear the Pennsylvania Dutch language being spoken.[91]

Pickett found his men in excellent condition, "bright and

cheerful, singing songs and telling stories, full of hope and courage, inspired with absolute faith and confidence in our success. There is no straggling, no disorder, . . . and there are no desertions. . . . An army of sixty thousand men marching through the enemy's country without the least opposition." But his men found little or no reception in Chambersburg. The place seemed more deserted than Goldsmith's village. Pickett did not want to take advantage of the situation, so he told the bands not to play. However, at the north end of Chambersburg, some young girls came out and requested music. The request was granted. The band played "Home Sweet Home," "Annie Laurie," "Her Bright Smile Haunts Me Still," "Nellie Gray," and "Hazel Dell." The young women wanted to hear "Dixie," but the next band played "The Old Oaken Bucket," "The Swannee River," "The Old Arm Chair," "The Lone Rock by the Sea," and "Auld Lang Syne." So the girls of Chambersburg were treated to a band concert this last Saturday in June. George closed his letter describing the music, "Lovingly and forever, Your Soldier."[92]

Although all seemed to be going well, Lee was beginning to have problems. In Virginia, the people were loyal and reported every move to the men in gray. They would tell the Union soldiers nothing significant. Now the shoe was on the other foot. Lee was in enemy country. Stuart was nowhere to be found, and the loyal people of the Cumberland Valley knew nothing.

Saturday afternoon Randolph Shotwell of Pickett's division passed through Greencastle, a town, according to the North Carolinian, of three thousand, doing a large manufacturing and mercantile business. The people were curious and timid. They stood and eyed the passing Rebels. They did ask some of the tall Texans and Mississippians how many more were coming. The reply was, "There are two hundred and twenty-six thousand more of us, coming on behind."[93]

The Cumberland Valley was to the Confederates "as beautiful a section of country as the State can produce. On to— shall we say Harrisburg? Reports tell of wonderous consternation in the prosperous capital of the 'Keystone State'

259

which has done so much to hound on the war upon the South, and has suffered so little!"[94]

Shotwell had a keen insight into military strategy and diplomacy. He wanted to launch a telling blow at Harrisburg or some place where it would really hurt and cripple the North. He realized the South was the weaker of the two participants, with less manpower and resources. He knew that the blockade was going to bring disaster, and he felt the South had but one hope of success. . . ."a short, sharp, and severe offensive campaign! We cannot afford to stand on our defense. We cannot hope to wear out an enemy who has all the world to draw upon, for men munitions of war! We cannot dream of successful negotiations for peace until we have 'carried the war into Africa' with a vengeance! capturing at least one large northern city and making a show of desperate energy that will dishearten the Northern masses and discourage their leaders."[95]

It sounds as though Shotwell should have been in Richmond in the cabinet. He certainly understood the psychology of warfare and knew what needed to be done.

Colonel Fremantle was an early riser. Lawley was too ill to ride so he borrowed his horse, and by 6:30 reached General Longstreet north of Hagerstown. The general was ready to move, so the introduction was hurried, but arrangements were made to send an ambulance for Lawley. Longstreet invited the English colonel to share his mess during the campaign. "Old Pete" told his new friend that they were now in Pennsylvania, and that he should stay close to the main column because there was the prospect of meeting up with bushwhackers.

Half an hour later, Fremantle returned to the Dutch farmhouse with an ambulance for Lawley. After all the arrangements were made, he set out to rejoin Longstreet on the road to Chambersburg. Once again he encountered McLaws's division. As soon as they entered Pennsylvania, "the troops opened the fences and enlarged the roads about twenty yards on each side, which enabled the wagons and themselves to proceed together. This is the only damage I saw done by the Confederates."

In Greencastle the people just stared. They were cold and indifferent to the men in gray. There was no straggling, no homes were bothered, and no civilians annoyed. Sentries were placed at the doors of the best homes.

It was 6:00 P.M. when Fremantle reached Chambersburg. The houses were closed but the people were on the street. The men in gray were happy singing, "Dixie Land." Some of Longstreet's men marched north and encamped on the Harrisburg Road, others turned right and headed for Fayetteville. At last Fremantle found Lee and Longstreet on the Gettysburg Road, three-quarters of a mile from town. But the British officer was disappointed in the women. They were pretty and well dressed, "but sour and disagreeable in their remarks. Fremantle was told that Ewell was sending great quantities of supplies back from Carlisle. Pennsylvania was now supporting the war and feeding the Rebels. The men in gray were "full of confidence and high spirits."[96]

With regimental bands blaring, Hood's division entered Chambersburg on the twenty-seventh. They had found Greencastle to be a pretty place as they marched through, and were greatly impressed with the farms in the Marion area. It was and is, beautiful country, green hills, nice orchards, productive fields of grain, and sleek cattle. The roads was macadamized, quite a difference from the ruts and the dirt of Virginia. Some of the Texas soldiers felt the barns were built better than many of the houses back home. Mark Smither of Company D, Fifth Texas, thought Chambersburg looked about as big as Houston, and considered it the prettiest place he had seen. The town was laid out in Dutch precision. The girls were real beauties, but they "were Union to the backbone and had capital sport at our shabby and unmilitary appearance." Lieutenant Colonel Fremantle called them "Hood's Ragged Jacks."[97]

The women of Chambersburg did not get too close to the Texans. They stayed behind the yard fences, or looked from upstairs windows. Many of the women hurled insults at the men in gray and taunted them. Some of the ladies wore red, white and blue outfits. One lady said, "Look at Pharoah's Army going to the Red Sea." Another lady looked at John

West and shouted, "Thank God, you will never come back here alive." To the vinegar-faced lady, West replied, "No, we intend to go to Cincinnati by way of New York." The Texas Brigade continued through the town and went into camp a mile north of Chambersburg. Robertson's command stayed in place in the encampment until June 30. They rested and went foraging.[98]

Some returned to town in the afternoon, buying all the food they could, and occasionally getting into private cellars. Hats were a precious commodity. In both Greencastle and Chambersburg, the men left the ranks and grabbed hats from the men watching the march. They helped themselves to the big black-heart cherries in the Franklin County orchards. Apple butter and milk were in abundance.

Early Saturday morning the news was brought to Carlisle that the Rebels were near at hand. But no one believed the report. They had experienced too many false alarms in the last few days. The folks were unwilling to listen to the "cry of wolf." The morning passed and still no sign of Rebels. No one believed the Rebels were close until they were within a quarter of a mile of town. Captain Boyd's cavalry fell back and brought the unwelcome news. But this time there was no alarm. In fact, calmness pervaded the atmosphere. A resigned courage was present. The people of Carlisle were arising to the occasion. If it became necessary to offer the town and the surrounding countryside to save the Army of the Potomac, or to give the commander time to mass his forces, then the sacrifice would be made.[99]

Col. William N. Penrose and Robert Allison, assistant burgess, went out to meet the advancing Rebels. Colonel Penrose stated there were no troops in town and no resistance would be offered. He begged the men in gray not to charge through the streets because it would only hurt innocent women and children. General Jenkins said he did not want trouble and preferred to enter town as quietly as possible. "Accordingly about eleven o'clock on Saturday morning, the rebel advance entered the town from the west end of Main Street. Their horses were at a walk and the general conduct of the soldiers good. They were about four hundred in

262

number, mounted infantry.... They passed down Main Street to the juncture of the Trindle Spring and Dillsburg roads, where a portion of them filed to the left and proceeded to the Garrison. The remainder dismounted for a few minutes, when they again took their saddles, returned to the town, and stopped in the public square."[100]

When the Confederate cavalry entered Carlisle, Mrs. Beetem living on West Pomfet Street, gathered her children from the yard and took them inside. Little Charles and his sister got down on their knees and peeped out under the curtain to see the soldiers. "They were a grim looking set of men, in their thirties and forties, and they and their horses were covered with dust. These troops carried their carbines in hand, the stocks resting on their legs in readiness if anyone fired on them." Another detachment followed and went toward Harrisburg.[101]

Alfred Jenkins, the Pennsylvanian turned Rebel, had ridden all over the Cumberland Valley since June 16. Now he asked for the Borough authorities. Chief Burgess Andrew Ziegler, Esq., and several members of the town council came to talk with the cavalry leader. He demanded fifteen hundred rations to be furnished within the hour and deposited in the Market House. The Burgess and a number of citizens went throughout the town informing people of the demand and asking for assistance. Jenkins said that unless his demands were met, his hungry men would help themselves. "In less than an hour the stalls of the market house were piled with all kinds of eatables, and considerate, secessionists were lining themselves with good food. Their horses were picketed along the pavements faring equally well with their masters, the corn having been procured at the crib of Mr. John Noble. After dinner rebels rode up and down the different streets, and visited the Garrison, Gas Works and other places of note, and conducted themselves, generally speaking, with decorum."[102]

At five o'clock in the afternoon the sound of music announced the entrance into Carlisle of Ewell's Second Corps, Army of Northern Virginia. The invasion had come. This was no raid. It was the real thing. The soldiers came by way of

263

the Walnut Bottom Road, down South Pitt Street to Main Street, "thence to Bedford Street, and thence to the Garrison." The band at the head of the column played "Dixie" as the men in gray marched through the streets of the town. The residents found it to be a humiliating experience. They presented a sorry appearance. "Many were barefooted, others hatless, numbers of them ragged, and all dirty."[103]

No doubt they were tired because many of them had marched twenty-nine miles. Yet they were cheerful. They had reason to be. They were far north of the Rappahannock and the Potomac. They were in Pennsylvania, enemy territory, and if their luck held they might even capture Harrisburg. In fact, orders were being given to General Jenkins to proceed to the Susquehanna River and scout the approaches and defenses of Harrisburg. It was like the little boy beating the big boy, or the underdog turning the tide against the favorite. The war songs of the Confederacy added insult to injury. The men in gray jeered the Union leaders, that is, all but General McClellan. For them it was almost like a picnic.

Robin Berkeley was glad to be there. In fact, he was glad to be alive. On the way to Carlisle, a caisson box of the Third Richmond Howitzers blew up in front of him. The top of the box was blown away. The two riders had just dismounted. The wheelhorses were badly burned by the explosion. The accident was caused by bad packing.

"An hour after their arrival the town was filled with officers, who thronged the hotels, and rode quietly through the town." Some of them described very vividly the suffering their loved ones had endured at the hands of Union occupation. They spoke in a very hateful manner of Butler, Milroy, and several other Union generals. "All asserted that they were tired of war and were only 'fighting to be left alone.' " They were under the conviction that this campaign would end the contest, and they spoke of capturing Hooker's army, Baltimore, and Washington. They had high hopes of marching to the City of Brotherly Love. They seemed to feel invincible. If ever an army had confidence in itself, the Army of Northern Virginia did, and especially the Second Corps. We see this in the letters of "Sandie" Pendleton and others. For the men in gray, this Saturday afternoon in Carlisle was like a holiday. A few more miles, a victory, and perhaps the war would be over. They would emerge on top. No wonder they felt good. And they had right to do so. After all, they had done what everybody said could not be done. Here they were in Carlisle, within twenty miles of Harrisburg, the capital of Pennsylvania. Many of these soldiers expected to be in that city in another day or two. Then came Richard S. Ewell.[104]

Ewell was riding the crest of his command and staff career as chief of the Second Corps. He rode through the town to the garrison or the Carlisle army barracks. Ewell took over the quarters of a Captain Hastings. His staff of over twenty-five occupied the adjacent buildings. Earlier Jenkins had made his demands on the town of Carlisle. Now it was "Old Bald Head's" turn. Soon after establishing headquarters, he sent an aide to demand of the town authorities supplies of food and medicine and medical equipment. The *Carlisle American* stated "this demand was ridiculous in character." Ewell wanted fifteen hundred barrels of flour. There were only two hundred barrels in town. For some reason he wanted four cases of amputating equipment. There was not one set in the Carlisle drugstores. "Immense quantities of quinine, chloroform, and other drugs were called for, far beyond the capacity of the Druggists to supply." Prominent citizens hearing the demands argued the impossibilities of meeting the requests. However, Ewell was very positive, letting the folks know that if the items were not received by a certain hour, then the stores and houses of Carlisle would be searched one by one. The Carlisle authorities, knowing they could not meet the demands, made no attempt to fill them, and decided to take their chances with the search.[105]

Before dark, however, Ewell sent his card, with a note to some of the folks he had known earlier, assuring them that strict discipline would be maintained, and no violence committed. He even offered them protection. This made the folks feel much better.

Richard S. Ewell was a happy man. He sent Jenkins and the cavalry up the Harrisburg Pike, accompanied by H. B. Richardson, his chief engineer. Their assignment was to reconnoiter positions held by Union forces on the West Shore opposite Harrisburg.

Robert Rodes's division took over the Carlisle Military Post. The Thirty-second, Forty-third, Forty-fifth, and Fifty-third North Carolina regiments of Daniel's Brigade; along with the Fifth, Twelfth, Twentieth, and Twenty-third North Carolina of Iverson's brigade; and the Second, Fourth, Fourteenth, and Thirtieth North Carolina regiments of Ramseur's brigade, along with Carter's battery made themselves right at home on the grounds of one of America's oldest military posts.

What had been Rodes's brigade, consisting of Alabama troops, was sent out the Mount Holly Pike for picket and scouting duty. George Doles camped with his Georgia troops on the grounds of Dickinson College. Their presence interrupted graduating ceremonies. Tents were set up over the college grounds. Some trees were cut down for firewood, and the men were loud and noisy. Professors and students trotted off to General Ewell to complain. Having a feeling for the town because of his previous tour of duty, he quickly restored order on the Dickinson campus.

Rodes's men had few tents, so most of them just slept on the grounds of Carlisle barracks. Quite a lot were without blankets as well. Guards were placed on the corners of the principal streets. No one could pass unless they had a written pass. Through the night, Ewell maintained excellent discipline.

Today Steuart and his men marched from Roxbury to Shippensburg, arriving just after Edward Johnson's division had pulled out for Carlisle.[106]

Randolph McKim rode through Chambersburg and Green Village and on to Shippensburg. Another seven miles brought the column to Stoughstown. Camp was made for the night at Big Spring near Springfield. At this place, McKim bought seven copies of the New Testament to give to some of the men. The storekeeper was surprised. He apparently did not believe the Rebels read the Good Book. The week had been difficult on McKim. He was able to get but twelve hours' sleep in five days.[107]

266

Henry Kyd Douglas spent Friday night in Shippensburg on the way north. He stayed with a clergyman who was very kind. The next morning, the twenty-seventh, Douglas went to the stable to check his horse. He found the servants taking a new set of harness, saddles, and other equipment from the straw. These had been hidden to prevent capture. Douglas joked with his host and told him he should not leave such valuables laying around loose.

Later in the day Douglas rode into Carlisle and went to the United States army post now occupied by Ewell and the Second Corps. The general was in a talkative mood and had much to say about his former associations with the place. Douglas, Ewell, and the others were interrupted by a group of townspeople who wanted to know if the general had any objections to prayers for the president of the United States.

"Certainly not," said Old Dick, "pray for him. I'm sure he needs it."[108]

Meanwhile, a farmer came galloping into Hanover with the news that the Rebels were in McSherrystown and would soon be in Hanover.

True enough. In a brief matter of time, Colonel Elijah White and the Thirty-fifth Battalion of Virginia Cavalry came riding down McSherrystown Avenue to Carlisle Street. Four officers led the advance down what is now Third Street.

Back of the officers came the troopers riding four abreast. The men were alert, ready for action. They had their carbines ready, fingers on the triggers. Colonel White rode in the center of the column. He was a big man.

Women and children of Hanover remained in their homes, watching from the corners of the windows. Colonel White ordered guards posted at the ends of all the streets. The rest of the battalion assembled in Center Square. Some of the residents came out in front of the Central Hotel where Colonel White gave a brief speech.

The soldiers wore faded gray suits and looked very dusty. However, they behaved like perfect gentlemen. Colonel White said that noncombatants would not be harmed. They, too, were fighting for a cause, and were not interested in hurting civilians.

267

At the close of White's talk, his troopers dismounted and entered the local stores, searching for shoes and clothing. They were not very successful because most of the merchandise had been hidden.[109]

There was a branch telegraph office in George Grove's store on Frederick Street. The night before White rode into town, the wires were removed and placed in the loft above the old Market House. The Virginia cavalry saw the pole in front of the store, and searched the premises. But they had no luck.

Daniel Trone was in the railroad telegraph office when notified that the Confederate cavalry was coming into Hanover. He took time to send a final message to Hanover Junction saying, "The Confederates are coming, and I guess I will leave."

Dan had to be very careful, sneaking in and out of the alleys. He was afraid Southern sympathizers would turn him over to the gray cavalrymen.

Before leaving the office, Dan pulled up his telegraph instruments and took them up in the attic of a warehouse, hiding them under the floor.[110]

Colonel White's men entered the railroad telegraph office. They grabbed the old keys and sets, but missed the good equipment hidden by operator Trone in the attic. There the telegraph equipment remained safe and sound until brought out for use several days later.[111]

Joseph Leib also left Hanover. He was the freight and passenger agent for the Hanover and Gettysburg Railroad. All the engines and trains were gone, so Leib jumped on a handcar. He and a strong-armed trackman pumped the wheels so they could get away. The Rebels fired at them, but after a brief chase permitted them to get away.[112]

The Virginians spent about an hour in Hanover, then mounted, reformed the column, and rode out York Street toward Jefferson. The *Hanover Spectator,* a weekly tabloid, said the Rebels burned Gulden's Warehouse and several cars of baled hay. They also destroyed some telegraph poles. According to the paper, two thousand dollars worth of jewelry was taken from William Boadenhamer.[113]

About 2:00 P.M. the Virginia Cavalry arrived in Hanover Junction, set fire to the bridge and destroyed the telegraph. Small parties also sought to destroy the bridges between the Junction and Hanover itself.[114]

Saturday night, White and his men bivouacked on the farm of John Weist near Nashville. The next day they resumed their task of destroying communications.[115]

Through the day, with the exception of Gordon's brigade, Early's division tramped through Hunterstown, New Chester, Hampton, and East Berlin. Near the last town, "Jube" Early called a halt so the men could rest for the night.

John Gordon's brigade of twenty-eight hundred men along with Tanner's Battery took the York-Gettysburg Turnpike and marched through New Oxford and Abbottstown, camping for the night in the village surrounding Farmer's Post Office. Gordon stayed at the home of Jacob Altland and enjoyed a Pennsylvania Dutch feather bed.

Among the horses rounded up by the Confederates today was a lovely white horse belonging to Samuel Roth, a Mennonite preacher living near Roth's Church. The horse was saved for Gordon to ride when the Army of Northern Virginia entered York.

McGowan's brigade marched from their campsite near Leitersburg to a place they called Funkstown. However, this must have been Fayetteville. The most likely route was to Waynesboro, Mont Alto, and then the town named after Lafayette. There was great rejoicing when they crossed the Mason-Dixon Line. The Confederates in Hill's corps regarded Maryland as a friendly state and this Pennsylvania was the first invasion of Northern soil. The men were impressed with the beautiful country. They saw great fields of yellow grain, large droves of fat cattle, and lovely gardens. The people of Pennsylvania treated the men from South Carolina in a cordial manner.

Fayetteville was named in honor of General Lafayette. During the last days of June, General Ambrose Powell Hill, commanding the Third Corps of the Army of Northern Virginia, had his headquarters in the house known as "Font Hill."

Somewhere near Fayetteville, east of Chambersburg, Dorsey Pender penned his final letter to his wife Fanny, calling her his dearest wife:

> We are resting today after marching 157 miles since leaving Fredericksburg twelve days ago. (Just think of it, men averaging thirteen miles a day in extremely hot weather.)
>
> Until we crossed the Md. line our men behaved as well as troops could, but here it will be hard to restrain them. . . . They have done nothing like the Yankees do in our country. They take poultry and hogs but in most cases pay our money for it. . . . The people are frightened to death and will do anything we intimate to them. . . .
>
> I hope we can be in Harrisburg in three days. . . .
>
> We are in Adams County, having marched through Franklin. (Here Pender was mistaken.) If we do not succeed in accomplishing a great deal all of us will be surprised. Our men seem to be in the spirit and feel confident. . . . This is a most magnificent country to look at, but the most miserable people. . . . The number of dirty looking children is perfectly astonishing. A great many of the women go barefooted. . . . And such large barns I never dreamt of. . . . We passed through Hagerstown . . . but saw little Southern feeling displayed. The fact is the people in N.W. Md. are as much of the Dutch Yankee as these. . . .
>
> I never saw troops march as ours do; they will go 15 or 20 miles a day without leaving a straggler and hoop and yell on all occasions. Confidence and good spirits seem to possess everyone. . . .
>
> Gen. Hill (A.P.) thus far has managed the march of his Corps and I think will give as much satisfaction as Lt. Gen'l as he did (as) Maj. Gen'l. . . .
>
> Now darling, may our Good Father protect us and preserve us to each other to a good old age. . . .[116]

This last request was not to be granted. Pender fell wounded at Gettysburg, and died in Staunton on the return trip to Virginia. But death was far from his mind that day as he wrote from near Fayetteville.

IX

THE CLUSTERED SPIRES OF FREDERICKTOWN

One by one, coming from the west and the south, the various units of the Union army came in sight of "the clustered spires of Frederick." The spires of Frederick's downtown churches have been immortalized by John Greenleaf Whittier in his poem about "Barbara Fritchie."

Five steeples of four churches comprise "the clustered spires." They are Trinity Chapel, dating back to 1773 and having a 141-foot spire; Saint John's Roman Catholic spire standing 145 feet high, and dating to 1854; the twin spires of the Evangelical Lutheran Church reaching 137 feet, and finally the All Saints Episcopal Church's 134-foot spire. The former rector of the last named church was none other than the Reverend William Nelson Pendleton, D.D., now brigadier general in charge of Lee's Reserve Artillery.[1]

Frederick was laid out in 1745 by Daniel Dulaney. He had acquired some eight thousand acres of almost wilderness land near the Monocacy River. On a wooded knoll south of town, he built himself a brick manor house that stands yet today.

Daniel had a brother Patrick, the main east-west street was named in his honor, and soon became the primary road to the west. The city itself was named after Frederick, the sixth and last Lord Baltimore.

Slowly but surely, German and English immigrants made their way from Philadelphia, to Lancaster, to Hanover, and then down what is Route 194 to Frederick. But the village that was to become a city remained a frontier town until the Revolutionary War.

Frederick was already one hundred years old when the

271

Civil War broke out. Other troops had been there as early as 1755. In that year Benjamin Franklin and Gen. Edward Braddock of the British Grenadiers met in Frederick to plan the expedition against the French and Indians. Frederick was a frontier town then of less than two hundred homes, taverns, and churches. The citizens became upset with the military because the British took the local horses used to haul supplies for the building of the new courthouse. The redcoats needed the horses for their wagons and artillery.

But Frederick gained its revenge in 1765. On November 23 of that year, twelve judges, meeting in what is now Courthouse Square, repudiated the British Stamp Act. They were the first to defy the British in this manner.

North of town is Rose Hill, the home of Thomas Johnson, the first governor of Maryland, and the man who nominated George Washington as commander in chief of the Continental army. Now a modern high school is named after ex-Governor Thomas Johnson and occupies part of what was his lovely estate.

During the Revolutionary War, German prisoners were kept on the grounds of what is now Maryland School for the Deaf. The barracks of that era survive on South Market Street. In June of 1862, the barracks were part of a large Union supply depot.

Francis Scott Key, the writer of the National Anthem, is buried in Mount Olivet Cemetery. The United States flag flies over his grave day and night.

Roger Brooke Taney was from Fredericktown. He was the fifth chief justice of the United States, and administered the oath of office to seven presidents, including Abraham Lincoln. Taney delivered the Dred Scott decision, fanning the flames leading to the Civil War.

When the Civil War started, Frederick remained loyal. In September of 1862, the townspeople gave a great welcome to the Army of the Potomac on the way to Antietam. The gala occasion was to be topic of conversation around campfires for months to come.

Then on September 14, the Army of the Potomac moved west to fight at South Mountain and three days later at

Antietam. On October 4, 1862, "Father Abraham" Lincoln came to Frederick on his way back to Washington after touring the Antietam Battlefield. Lincoln visited the wounded General Hartsuff on Record Street, and then spoke briefly at the train depot. South of Frederick he was greeted by members of the Twenty-fourth Michigan Infantry, camped in a field, on their way to join the Army of the Potomac.

On this June the twenty-seventh, Joe Hooker moved his headquarters from Poolesville and pitched his tents on the Prospect Hill farm. Time was running out for him. But for a few more hours he sent and received dispatches.

I CORPS

The First Division of the First Corps had a short march of six miles, "encamping two miles northwest of Middletown."[2] The spot on the Old Hagerstown Road would be home until Sunday afternoon.

Rufus Dawes notes that he started marching early from the vicinity of Jefferson and reached the regimental campsite about 2:00 P.M. The marches until this Saturday had been long and toilsome.[3]

The 141st Pennsylvania noted the great fertility of the Middletown Valley, and the lovely farms between Middletown and Jefferson. The large wheat fields were either covered with shocks of grain or were waiting for the sickle. Residents of the valley greeted the men in blue as deliverers.

The twenty-seventh was a pleasant day for Charles Wainwright. For once, marching was a pleasure. The weather cleared off fine. The temperature was just about right. The road was good, wide and smooth. Charles, although a farmer and greatly interested in agriculture, notes that he had never seen such rural scenery. "I have never come across its equal in this country. We passed a number of farms which will yield over thirty bushels to the acre, and some of them will go forty. Clover, oats and corn look equally well. The whole of the

273

land is cleared, the farm houses are good, large, and freshly painted, and everything denotes thrift and prosperity. . . . The valley is lovely, lying so quietly between the two ranges of hills, which are a great beauty in themselves. As for fruits, the country is full of the most thrifty trees of all sorts. Cherry trees as big as oaks line the road for a good ways, so that half the corps have been eating cherries all day, and stand a very good show for an attack of stomach ache to-night."[4]

Wainwright continues his vivid description of the Middle-town Valley by saying, "We got into camp by two o'clock this afternoon. My 'brigade is literally rolling in clover.' I parked them on two sides of a fine field of it and turned the horses loose for a couple of hours."[5]

The Twelfth New Hampshire found the weather cooler, and rains had settled the dust of recent days.[6] They went into position near Fox's Gap, close to the spot where Jesse Lee Reno had fallen last September. The New England lads reached their objective just as the golden rays of sunset fell upon the field. H. C. Henney of the Fifty-fifth Ohio, a part of the Eleventh Corps, saw a great rock near Turner's Gap marking the graves of seventeen Confederates killed at the Battle of South Mountain.[7]

II CORPS

Hancock's Second Corps traveled from Edwards Ferry via Poolesville to Barnesville. When Frank Sawyer of the Eighth Ohio got awake this morning, he thought he was surrounded by the entire Army of the Potomac. "Long wagon trains, parks of artillery and dense masses of infantry spread out over the plain."[8] Too bad that Brady was not there to re-capture the moment on film. This was living history in the Edwards Ferry area. The general feeling was that they were on their way to another Antietam. During the morning the soldiers from Ohio received fresh rations and then hit the road for Sugar Loaf Mountain. The Eighth Ohio did not reach camp until ten o'clock.

Thomas Livermore was glad to see Poolesville again. In this quaint Montgomery County town, he had first heard artillery fire, and made friends with members of the First New Hampshire. Two years ago in Poolesville they had shared excellent pipe tobacco with him. Now as he saw the houses of the town where he had his first tour of duty, many memories came back to him. Here in a nearby woods he had first shouldered a musket, and walked guard duty. Now he was an officer, soon to be promoted in the ambulance service of the Second Corps.[9]

The weather had been wet on Thursday and Friday. Some of the men did not bother to take their boots or shoes off. They fared better than those who removed their footwear. They could not get their shoes back on until they dried out and had to walk in their bare feet.[10] They found consolation in the fact that they were back "in God's Country." So the Second Corps continued throughout Saturday on the Roads to Gettysburg. The South Mountain range was on their left, and Sugar Loaf Mountain in their front.

Earlier in the war A. S. Williams, now with the Twelfth Corps, wrote a vivid description of Sugar Loaf Mountain:

> The highest point for signals is Sugar Loaf Mountain, which rises a few miles above Edwards Ferry in the shape of a loaf of sugar, several hundred feet above any surrounding hill. It is a prominent and conspicious point from the whole line of the river. From the station at its top one can plainly see Leesburg on one side and Frederick . . . , on the other. . . .[11]
> The long patches of the Potomac gleam out toward a pleasant sunset, seeming like silver lakes. Everything, of a quiet afternoon . . . looks so peaceful and home like, the cattle grazing on the hillsides, the smoke curling from the many farmhouses, that one can hardly realize that thousands are armed for battle on either side of that pleasant river and amid those quiet valleys. But so it is, and one's heart feels heavy in the thought that it is so.[12]

The letter was written in November of 1861, but the content was true again in '63. But for some, including the men from Maine and New Hampshire, the mountain reminded them of home. The mountains impressed the men of the

275

Eighteenth Pennsylvania Cavalry as they rode through Frederick at 3:00 P.M., trotted on to Middletown, and camped for the night just five miles from South Mountain.[13]

The Sixth New York Cavalry left camp at 6:00 A.M. Two hours later they crossed the river and proceeded to Point of Rocks. For a while they seemed to have followed the Baltimore and Ohio Railroad tracks. John Havey of M Troop captured a Rebel spy who was allowed to go free. He was afterward recaptured by Charles Whitney of F Troop and hanged by order of General Buford.[14]

The Seventeenth Pennsylvania Cavalry describes the march through Western Maryland as "thoroughly enjoyable—good roads, frequent streams of water, fine camping grounds, sympathizing people often crowding villages and country towns as we swept on through them. Mails with letters from home, and newspapers too, met us and were distributed almost every day."[15]

The Fifth New York Cavalry moved from Rohrersville at 4:00 P.M. today. Traveling via Birkinsville (Burkittsville) and Middletown, they rode through Frederick, to a point three and a half miles north of Frederick on the Emmitsburg Road.

At long last, the maps of Frederick County finally arrived for the Army of the Potomac. Now Hooker had a guide. He directed that the cavalry be sent well "to the advance of Frederick, in the direction of Gettysburg and Emmitsburg, and see what they can of the movements of the army."[16]

Today, the Fifth and Sixth Michigan Cavalry, refreshed from a night of rest in Frederick, and with freshly groomed horses and full haversacks, rode to Emmitsburg on the main road. The Seventh Michigan took another route, presumably, the Old Frederick Road.

III CORPS

The Third Corps tramped from near Point of Rocks, to Jefferson and Middletown. The residents of the two farming villages "hailed our coming with unmistakable pleasure." The Sixty-third Pennsylvania and other units marched through in column by company, "with colors unfurled and brass bands and drum corps playing patriotic airs." It was a great day.[17]

The Seventeenth Maine received a great welcome in Jefferson today. They halted near the town for lunch, and then marched into the village "in column by company, with colors unfurled and bands playing." It must have been a lovely sight. Edwin Houghton says:

> Here we witnessed the first expression of Union sentiment that had gladdened our eyes since we joined the Army of the Potomac. The American flag was displayed from most of the houses in the village, and fair ladies greeted us with approving smiles and words of welcome. A thousand handerkerchiefs waved from window and housetop, and on every side we received assurances of sympathy and good will. Such enthusiasm and such a welcome ... was indeed most gratifying. The soldiers cheered the ladies and the flag vociferously and seemed to enjoy the occasion very much.[18]

The welcome in Jefferson made the men feel so good that at least one soldier forgot he had a knapsack on. The men from Maine marched with the rest of the corps about twelve miles on that cloudy Saturday. This made the march easier, and as a result they were not so tired when they reached bivouac near Middletown.

On June twenty-seventh, the Eleventh New Jersey provided guards for the wagon train of the Third Corps. Early in the morning they passed a farmhouse. It stood back from the road, but a group of ladies appeared on the porch waving the Stars and Stripes. This show of loyalty "put new life into each lagging footstep, ... dressing up the ranks, we passed as on review, saluting the ladies with colors, music and three hearty cheers."[19]

Bardeen noted that Jefferson, in his estimation, was "a large and handsome place." His next stop was Burkittsville where the Third Corps was sent to keep the Confederates from coming through Crampton's Gap. Those who had money were able to buy bread from the natives of Burkittsville. The men marched an eighth of a mile on a brick sidewalk and felt "quite at home," almost like New England.[20]

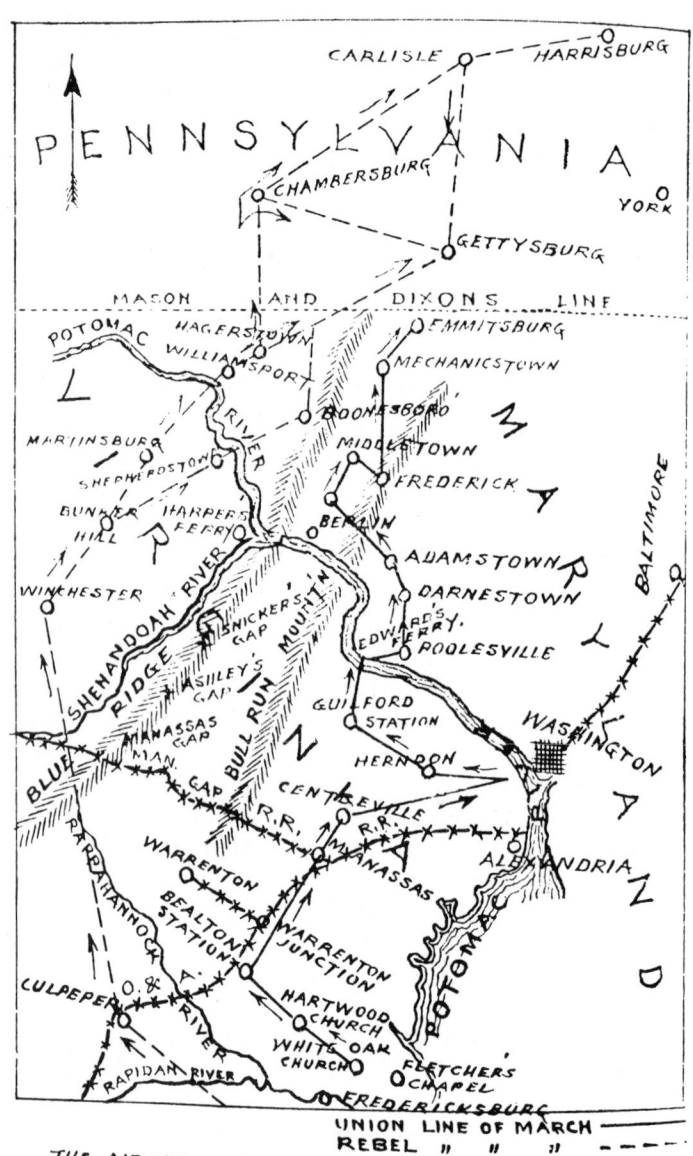

THE AIR LINE DISTANCE BETWEEN THE TOP AND
BOTTOM OF THIS MAP IS ABT. 130 MILES.

Route of Hancock's corps.

Thomas Marbaker was also impressed with the hearty welcome received in Jefferson. The town was decked with flags. And from windows, doorways, and porches, people cheered and young maidens waved handkerchiefs. But the Eleventh New Jersey could not stay in Jefferson. It was on to Burkittsville where camp was made for the night.[21]

The men of the First Massachusetts marched along with the rest of the men in Carr's brigade to Jefferson, Burkittsville, and Crampton's Gap.

V CORPS

While the First, Third, and Eleventh corps were moving into positions or watching the mountain passes in the Middletown Valley, George G. Meade was embarking on his last day as a corps commander. The Fifth Corps moved from campsites between Edwards Ferry and the Mouth of the Monocacy to Frederick and went into camp along the Ballenger Creek Road south of Frederick. The men of the Fifth Corps also noted "the beautiful fields of golden grain almost ready for the reaper and the well laden cherry trees, ripe and ready for the consumer. . . ."[22]

The 146th New York waded the Monocacy River and then rested for a while in the middle of the day. The roads were thronged with soldiers and military equipment. Frederick County, and America had not seen anything like it. All were moving rapidly northward, and congregating near the "clustered spires of Fredericktown." By the time they halted they were four miles from Frederick. Some of the men estimated they had covered fifty miles of marching during the last several days.

Some of the units stopped at a fine gushing spring before crossing the Monocacy. The water just poured out about three feet above the ground, and was ice cold. The tired, hot, thirsty soldiers eagerly and gladly availed themselves of the refreshment it offered."[23]

Clothing was scarce in the Fifth Corps. Sometimes when stopped by a stream, the men hurriedly washed a few items, tied them to their bayonets and let them dry by fluttering in the breeze.

Many of the soldiers had camped in Frederick during the early days of the war. Now they wanted to "do the town." After all, it was Saturday night and they had been marching in the heat, mud and rain. And Saturday night they "did the town." In spite of strict orders and guarded campsites, hundreds of men slipped into Frederick, "made merry with the townsfolk, ate at hotel tables and drank at hotel bars, on the day and evening of the 27th."[24] Some say the Army of the Potomac consumed more liquor that night than any other night in the war. Quite a few obtained hangovers lasting until noon on Monday. Others were of the opinion that the rain on Monday was a blessing, otherwise some of the men would never have made it on the Roads to Gettysburg. The rain brought them back to reality. The merrymaking was to cause a serious problem to an army officer who by afternoon was on his way to Frederick with classified orders.

Jacob Englebrecht also says the streets were full of "wagons & cavalry & infantry." He thought there must be seventy to eighty thousand men in Frederick along with several hundred cannons.[25]

The men in the Ninth Massachusetts Battery could have used a drink. They left Poolesville in the morning, and passed over Sugar Loaf Mountain on an extremely rough road. They passed the wreckages of many ambulances and baggage wagons. They reached Frederick at 9:00 P.M. and were given buckets of cold water. They left their ambulance back on the mountain, broken down. The artillerymen turned in their knapsacks one mile from Frederick, and reduced their baggage "to one change of underwear, an overcoat, one blanket and shelter tent."[26]

VI CORPS

Some men had thoughts of other days as they marched to the river. The chaplain of the Seventy-seventh New York fondly remembered the religious services held along the banks of the Rappahannock. He thought of the services held in the woods, they were God's first temples. Sometimes he conducted services around the campfire, and on other occasions in the rain and storm. Yet with the presence of God, their hearts were warm. In the services, many men of the Seventy-seventh professed faith in Christ. Now as they approached the Potomac, the chaplain thought of those whom he had buried with Christ in baptism. Now they were ready to cross.

One of the chaplain's recollections this June Saturday was that of General Sedgwick standing in the rain at the end of pontoon bridge, yelling at the teamsters to "hurry up." He wore a little round hat and a private's blouse. "There was nothing in his dress to indicate his rank; but when he yelled at a slow teamster, it was apparent that he was a man to be obeyed. Glorious old 'Uncle John!' He was a noble soldier, and of so kind a heart that every man in the corps loved him. He was always mindful of the comfort of his followers, and every wounded man called forth his sympathy."[27]

A member of the Fifteenth New Jersey heard the bands playing "Maryland, My Maryland," as his division stepped off the pontoon bridge. They were hot and tired, but hoping for the best and trusting in God. "The patriotic spirit was not crushed out in this depleted army, torn by unsuccessful conflicts, and worn down with fatigue and privation."[28]

Today was the moment of crossing the Potomac for the Union Sixth Corps, leaving Dranesville, Virginia, the eighteen thousand men crossed at Edwards Ferry and proceeded to Poolesville. The Sixth Corps was in the midst of making perhaps a record for marching mileage in a week. They had covered 25 miles on Friday. But there was no rest for the weary. At 3:00 A.M. Sedgwick's men were under way again. The soldiers marched fifteen miles to the banks of the Potomac River. The weather was cloudy and comfortable. The Thirty-seventh Massachusetts reached the Potomac in early afternoon, and took a break. They saw the columns and the wagons ahead of them crossing the bridges and winding on into Maryland. "The vivid panorama gave to many a beholder a truer realization of the magnitude of that branch of army service. Finally the tired infantry started forward once more, crossed the pontoons on to loyal soil, made some three miles more, and at dusk turned into some vast clover fields, where the weary soldiers were not long in providing themselves with luxurious couches, on which they slept soundly till the sharp notes of reveille broke through the darkness of the waning night."[29] That's the way it was with the Sixth Corps, on Saturday, June 27, 1863.

While the Sixth Corps was crossing the Potomac, Slocum and the Twelfth left the Monocacy Aqueduct and continued up the canal path to a point near Weaverton and Sandy Hook. At noon they stopped for a break at Point of Rocks, "a hamlet of two or three stores and several houses. Two hours were given to rest. The soldiers took the time to look at the piers of the bridge to Virginia, destroyed early in the war. It was a nice march along the river. The mountains were beautiful.[30]

As Saturday wore on, a big decision was made in Washington. That decision was to relieve Joseph Hooker and replace him with George Gordon Meade. Abraham Lincoln made the decision with the concurrence of Secretary of War Stanton.

Orders were drawn up as quickly as possible to facilitate the decision. A copy was made for Meade and another for Hooker. The cabinet was not to be informed until the next day. Secretary Stanton ordered General Halleck to send a letter of instruction to Meade. He assumed that Meade, being a good soldier, would accept the orders without question. The letter contained many of the things Hooker had fought for and wanted but had been denied. The letter from Halleck said in part:

. . . no one ever received a more important command. . . .

You will not be hampered by any minute instructions from these headquarters. Your army is free to act as you may deem proper under the circumstances as they arise. (This is what both Hooker and John Reynolds desired.) You will, however keep in view the important fact that the Army of the Potomac is the covering army of Washington, as well as the army of operation against the invading forces of the rebels. You will therefore manuever and fight in such a manner as to cover the Capital and also Baltimore, as far as circumstances will admit. . . .

All forces within the sphere of your operations will be held subject to your orders.

Harpers Ferry and its garrison are under your direct orders. (Again, this is what Hooker desired.)

You are authorized to remove from command and send from your army any officer or other person you may deem proper; and to appoint to command as you may deem expedient.

In fine, General, you are intrusted with all the power and authority which the President, the Secretary of War, or the General-in-Chief can confer on you. And you may rely on our full support.

You will keep me fully informed of all your movements and the positions of your own troops and those of the enemy, so far as known. . . . [31]

Lincoln was impressed with Meade's reputation. Most of the troops respected him. And Stanton reminded the president that Meade was from Pennsylvania, the state where the crucial battle was likely to occur.

Once the orders and instructions were prepared, a key person had to be chosen to carry the orders and verbally handle the change of command. The officer chosen was Col. James A. Hardie, Stanton's chief of staff. Hardie graduated from West Point in 1840. After a brief stint with the artillery in Maine, Hardie returned to West Point as an instructor. Now forty years of age, Hardie had served on McClellan's staff on the peninsula and then in Maryland. In fact, after Antietam, he was appointed brigadier general of volunteers.

When Hooker replaced Burnside, Hardie was named judge advocate general of the Army of the Potomac. But he was attracting the attention of higher-ups, and was called to be Stanton's staff. His intelligence and common sense were admired and respected in Washington. He was a man who could be trusted.

Colonel Hardie, who gave up his generalship when he came on Stanton's staff, was ordered to start for Frederick immediately. The time was midafternoon. It was hoped that Hardie, being a personal friend of both officers, would make the embarrassing and difficult situation a little easier. For security reasons, Hardie was to dress in civilian clothes. He was not to disclose to anyone where he was going or the purpose of his trip. Everything was top secret. But as personal representative of the president of the United States, Hardie was to find General Meade, take him to Hooker's headquarters and transfer the command of the army.

In the meantime, Meade and the Fifth Corps had reached Ballenger Creek. After the camp was established and secured, George and two staff members rode into Frederick in an effort to find and meet with Joe Hooker. Meade had not seen the commander in chief since June 13. He felt he was traveling in the dark and was anxious to get answers for his questions. However, he had no luck. But in a few hours a more dramatic meeting was to occur.[32]

XI CORPS

Saturday was a quiet day for the Eleventh Corps. The men were quite content in the beautiful Middletown Valley. The eight thousand men mingled freely with the farmers and others as time and duties permitted. Oliver O. Howard remained at his headquarters on the Cookerly farm west of the village along the road to Boonsboro. Steinwehr's men guarded the South Mountain passes. As evening approached they must have stood in awe at the little white pup tents or shelter halves of the First, Third, and Eleventh corps pitched in the Middletown Valley. As the whiffs of smoke went skyward from the campfires preparing supper and coffee, it looked like "a hundred circling camps." Chaplain Locke was encamped within sight of the Mount Tabor Church, having left Jefferson at 8.[33]

During the evening hours Rufus Dawes of the First Corps and General Meredith rode from their campsite west of Middletown over the South Mountain battleground. Here it was that the men from Wisconsin and Indiana were named the "Iron Brigade" for their bravery in assaulting Turner's Gap. The grass had now grown over the graves of their fallen comrades. The wooden headboards had worn with the weather. And the names of the fallen were barely legible. General Meredith pointed out a grave of a lad from the Nineteenth Indiana. Before the war he had been a professor in a western college and a scholarly gentleman. At South Mountain he was a private soldier and gave "the last full measure of his devotion." Returning to camp, Dawes wrote a letter, "What do you think of trudging along all day in a soaking rain, getting wet as a drowned rat, taking supper on hard tack and salt pork, and then wrapping up in a wet woolen blanket and lying down for a sleep, but waked up during the night three or four times to receive and attend to orders and finally turning out at three o'clock in the morning to get the regiment ready to march? Well—that is soldiering, and it is a great deal more comfortable soldiering, than to march through suffocating clouds of dust under a hot sun. In the dust, men are dogged and silent. In the rain they are often even hilarious and jolly."[34]

On a lighter note, Saturday night brought men, women, and children to the campsite of the 141st Pennsylvania. Many brought baskets of food to the men in blue. The citizens were invited to stay. And as the shades of night fell on the Middletown Valley soldiers and civilians joined in singing patriotic songs. And the troopers of the Fifth New York went into cavalry camp three and a half miles north of Frederick.[35]

XII CORPS

By nightfall, the Twelfth Corps was at Knoxville near Brunswick, Maryland. Some of the men camped in Pleasant

285

Valley. Henry Slocum's men had marched by way of Point of Rocks from near the mouth of the Monocacy River. General Williams found the day to be very fatiguing. The Twenty-ninth Ohio had started at 4:30 A.M. and did not pitch camp until after dark. The lads from the Buckeye State camped at Petersville, five miles from Harpers Ferry, about fifteen miles from Frederick. Slocum received orders from Hooker telling him to be ready to march at 4:00 A.M. on Sunday, linking up with the troops at Harpers Ferry. The dispatch was dated 8:00 P.M. Soon another message came countermanding the first order. These were the last orders Hooker issued as commander of the Army of the Potomac. In a few hours he would be relieved.[36]

About the time Slocum was reading Hooker's orders the Fifth Massachusetts Battery was dismounting in an artillery park one mile north of Frederick. They had been on the road fourteen hours and had covered twenty-seven miles. The men were too tired to get supper or fix coffee.[37]

In the minds of the First New Jersey Cavalry, today

> commenced that series of rapid, continuous and exhausting marches which culminated in the junction with the other corps upon the field of Gettysburg, and continued, with scarcely an intermission, until the opposing armies were once again confronting each other across the Rappahannock.[38]

The Eighth Illinois Cavalry crossed the Potomac today, and at nightfall, the tired troopers rolled themselves in blankets and tried to sleep at the base of the Catoctin Mountains near Point of Rocks.[39]

The Fifth New York Cavalry rode through Adamstown, Jefferson, and Burkittsville and occupied Crampton's Gap on Friday. At 4:00 P.M. today they left the mountain, rode back through Burkittsville to Middletown and then into Frederick. They must have passed the artillery park one mile north of the city before going into camp with the rest of the cavalry division, three and a half miles north on the Emmitsburg Road.[40]

As the Second Corps made camp in the shadow of Sugar Loaf Mountain, two friends had a problem.

Joseph Ward and Gustavas Josephs of Company E usually

shared the same tent or blanket. That Saturday night in Barnesville, the two had an experience that almost broke up their friendship. They laid a raincoat on the ground near a rock, fixed a coat as a pillow, and then prepared to sleep under a blanket. But they were in for a surprise. In the state between sleep and being awake, they felt their bodies being bitten, and soon started to scratch. Ward and Josephs came to the conclusion that they had "the soldier's bodyguard," or in other words the grayback lice. Every soldier knew that they came from somebody else. So the two good friends got into an argument. Ward was sure the lice came from Josephs. While Josephs was sure Ward was the carrier. Both were in foul humor and stalked off to sleep alone. But when morning came they went to a campfire together. There their problem was solved. Instead of lice, they found big black ants in their clothing. Most had been killed by their scratching, but the bites left the bodies of the two soldiers from the 106th Pennsylvania looking like a bad case of the measles. The two men went back to the place where they had made their bed, and found to their surprise that the place was full of big black ants. In their blankets many were found dead, partly dead, and alive. Ward and Josephs, thankful that they did not have lice, had a good laugh at themselves and renewed their friendship.[41]

By now things were pretty lively in Frederick. The men in blue were having a great time. Leonard Jordan of the Tenth Maine goes so far as to say that there were more men in the Army of the Potomac drunk than at any other time. He notes happily that "the disgusting scene was never repeated."[42]

Day by day, and step by step, the men in blue were getting closer to a place called Gettysburg, and a train was pulling into the Baltimore and Ohio Railroad Station in Frederick.

During the day elements of the Sixth Corps and the cavalry supply train crossed on the lower pontoon bridge at Edwards Ferry. By 8:35 P.M. Gregg's cavalry was almost across the river.[43] To the north, Stahel was asking if he should send his cavalry toward Emmitsburg and Gettysburg.

Meanwhile, George Gordon Meade was in camp on the Robert McGill farm. This fine country estate was located on the Buckeystown Road near Ballenger Creek, south of Frederick, "Arcadia," as the property was known, had belonged to Arthur Shaff. In the early years of the 1800s cousin Francis Scott Key and his brother-in-law, Roger R. Taney, later Chief Justice Taney, were frequent visitors at the farm.

Hardie arrived about midnight. He was familiar with "the clustered spires of Fredericktown," having been there in September of 1862 on the way to Antietam. Now nine months and two commanders later, he brought the orders to make still another transition.

General Hardie was given the necessary passes and money to buy his way to his destination if he encountered delay or opposition. If met by Stuart and the Confederate cavalry, he was to destroy his papers, endeavor to escape, and deliver his orders verbally.

Hardie was in civilian dress. The trip to Frederick was uneventful. But affairs in Frederick were something else. No one seemed to know where General Meade was located. To make matters worse, it was Saturday night. For some reason, there was no provost marshal, and a carnival-like atmosphere prevailed. The streets of Frederick, and the roads leading to and from the town were filled with drunken, boisterous soldiers. They were having a good time on Maryland whiskey.

General Hardie needed the money given him by Secretary Stanton. By giving liberally, he at last hired a buggy and a driver who knew Meade's whereabouts. He was in haste, but he moved at a turtle's pace. His driver could make but slow progress through the parties of drinking soldiers and the wagon trains along the road. At times, Hardie had to dismount and beg officers to clear the way for him. This was done several times. As the last seconds of June 27 ticked away, Ewell was in Carlisle, Early headed for York, and the rest of the Army of Northern Virginia at Chambersburg. The men in blue were doing the town (Fredericktown) while others were singing and visiting with the folks in Middletown Valley, and still others resting after a weary day. And Hardie was on the way to see Meade.

Hopefully this book will stimulate scholarly work on the advance of each Union and Confederate corps on the Roads

288

to Gettysburg, and of course, the advance of the cavalry. As Lee prepared to cross the Potomac River, the question arose as to where the cavalry would cross. With the infantry advancing through the Shenandoah Valley and concentrating on Williamsport, and Shepherdstown, the roads were filled with men, wagons, and horses. Approaching through the valley, following the infantry might delay Stuart. Jeb had to guard the mountain passes until he was sure of Hooker's intentions. Apparently his idea was to sweep around the rear of the Army of the Potomac, and head northward between Hooker's army and the city of Washington. In the process he could disrupt communications and demoralize the North. Then he could rejoin Lee in Pennsylvania.

Leaving William Jones and Robertson to hold the passes, and then cooperate with Lee, Stuart ordered Wade Hampton, Fitz Lee, and W. H. F. Lee to rendezvous at Salem Church on the night of the twenty-fourth. Then a little after midnight on the twenty-fifth, Stuart's command turned "column north." The men were full of confidence. And on the twenty-sixth the troopers encountered Hancock's Second Corps at Haymarket. They knew Union infantry were in the area from scouting reports sent by Ranger Mosby. Stuart lobbed some shells into the column of marching men, but had to wait and then detour around the rear of the column, and make a swing to the Occoquan. He crossed that stream at Wolf Run Shoals, captured a small force at Fairfax Court House, passed through Dranesville, and finally reached Rowser's Ford on the night of the twenty-seventh. There is some question among scholars as to the spelling of the ford and the exact location. It was a rough crossing with guns and carriages going completely under the water. The cavalrymen carried a lot of the ammunition across the Potomac River. By 3:00 A.M., all were safe and secure on the banks of the Maryland shore.

X

A JUNE SABBATH

June 28

Today the First Corps of the Union army under John Reynolds marched from Middletown to Frederick, crossing the Catoctin Mountain and covering about six miles.

The famed Second Corps under Winfield Scott Hancock marched from Barnesville in Montgomery County to Monocacy Junction south of Frederick. The sabbath journey involved about twenty miles.

The Third Corps marched from Middletown through the streets of Frederick, thence to Ceresville and Walkersville to a bivouac area near Woodsboro.

Sykes and the Fifth Union Corps had a break. They remained in camp near Frederick City.

"Uncle John" Sedgwick and the Sixth Corps marched from Poolesville to Hyattstown. It was a rather grueling march over narrow country roads.

O. O. Howard moved the Eleventh Corps from the lovely Middletown Valley to Frederick and Worman's Mill.

Slocum and the Twelfth Corps left the Knoxville-Brunswick area and proceeded toward Frederick. The corps marched about twenty miles.

Thus when Sunday evening came, the First, Fifth, Eleventh, and Twelfth corps were in and about Frederick. The Second Corps was south of Frederick, while the Sixth was at Hyattstown, and the Third north of Frederick near Woodsboro.

Headquarters Army of the Potomac was also located in Frederick.

Lee and Longstreet were at Chambersburg, A. P. Hill at Fayetteville, with part of Ewell's command in Carlisle and Early's division marching into York and on to Wrightsville. J. E. B. Stuart finally got across the Potomac and made a raid near Rockville.

The clock of Trinity Chapel in Frederick struck two, and then three. Would he never make it? Yes, finally sometime after 3:00 A.M. on Sunday, June 28, General Hardie reached Meade's tent. But now he faced another problem. The guard was not about to let Meade be wakened. However, Hardie prevailed.

Meade was dumbfounded. His first reaction was that he was under arrest. But he could not imagine the charge. When Hardie told him that he had come as a representative of Mr. Lincoln's with an order to assume command of the army, Meade became distressed. It was not right. The command should go to Reynolds. In fact, he insisted, saying such an order was an injustice to his good friend John Reynolds. Besides, he didn't even know the location of the commands of the Army of the Potomac, let alone the Confederates. Meade argued further that he should not go to Hooker's tent to assume command. His superior should send for him. But Hardie said, "You no longer have a superior here. You are in command of the army."[1]

Meade had no recourse but to obey. Horses were prepared and an escort obtained. And in the early morning hours of the Sabbath, several horsemen went to Hooker's headquarters. One look told Hooker what was coming. Hardie broke the news. It was a trying and tense time. Meade, Hardie, Hooker, and his chief of staff, Daniel Butterfield, sat down and went over the maps and other items necessary for the transfer of command.[2]

Meade described what took place in a letter to his wife:

It has pleased Almighty God to place me in the trying position that we have been talking about.... At 3:00 a.m., I was aroused from my sleep by an officer from Washington entering my tent, and after waking me up, saying he had come to give me trouble. At first I thought that it was either to relieve or arrest me, and promptly replied to him, that my conscience was clear, void of offense towards any man; I was prepared for his bad news. He then handed me a communication to read; which I found was an order relieving Hooker from the command and assigning me to it. . . . As a soldier, I had nothing to do but accept and exert my utmost abilities to command success. This, so help me God, I will do, and trusting to Him, who in His good pleasure has thought it proper to place me where I am, I shall pray for strength and power to get through the task assigned me. . . . I am moving at once against Lee, whom I am in hopes Couch will at least check for a few days; if so, a battle will decide the fate for our country and our cause. Pray earnestly, pray for the success of my country.[3]

Hooker and Meade went over troops' dispositions. Pleasonton and the cavalry, or part of it, was at the north end of Harmony Grove along the Emmitsburg Road.[4] General Tyler and the Artillery Reserve were one mile north of Frederick, probably on the grounds of Rose Hill Manor and what is now Governor Thomas Johnson High School. John Reynolds and the First Corps was at Middletown, with part of the First Division near Mount Tabor Church. The Second Corps under Hancock was on the way from Sugar Loaf Mountain to Monocacy Junction. The Third Corps was at Middletown. The Fifth was south of Frederick along the Buckeystown Road, the Sixth was near Barnesville, while the Eleventh was in the Middletown Valley, and the Twelfth on the road from Knoxville to Fredericktown.

John Reynolds had endeavored to ride into Frederick on Saturday evening to call on his relatives. But he was unable to get there at an early hour. So it was back to Middletown, and then into Frederick on Sunday to confer with the new commander in chief.[5]

John Reynolds was gracious and warm, a truly great man. He said, "The command has fallen where it belongs. I am glad that the burden and responsibility did not fall on me. You can count on my earnest support." Meade and Reynolds then discussed the information Hooker had turned over concerning the location and condition of the Army of the Potomac.[6]

After the noon hour, Meade and Hooker drew up the order

formally announcing the change of command to the troops. Toward evening, Hooker left his tent. Many waved and cheered, and said, "God bless you, General."[7] Then Hooker and Hardie got into a spring wagon, to go back into Frederick to the B. and O. Station. When all was ready, Meade walked over to the wagon with his hat off. The old and new commanders shook hands, and talked in low tones. Then the wagon left, and Meade walked into the headquarters tent. The burden of meeting and checking the enemy was now his.[8]

That was the big event on that Sunday, June 28. But throughout the day columns of blue-clad infantry entered the city from the west and the south.

Events were transpiring west of Frederick and in Carroll County as well as in the counties of Pennsylvania along the Mason-Dixon Line.

Church bells were ringing today in Burkittsville, Middletown, Frederick, Westminster, Chambersburg, Carlisle, and York. But today the bells had a new audience, soldiers in the midst. The first three cities were filled with troops on Sunday, September 14, 1862, during the Battle of South Mountain. But the other cities for the first time had visitors, men in blue and gray.

The Eleventh New Jersey of the Third Corps reached Burkittsville at nine o'clock Saturday evening, and spent the night encamped in a field. When the dawn broke, the soldiers from New Jersey found it to be a "pleasant village, beautifully situated at the foot of South Mountain. It contained quite a number of dwellings and two churches."[9] These are the Lutheran and Reformed, now United Church of Christ. As the men from New Jersey marched through on Sunday morning, the church bells started to ring:

> Bells were calling the worshipers to assemble. The sweet tones, vibrating upon the calm morning air, redolent with all the odors of queenly June, and re-echoing from the green mountainsides, seemed sadly at variance with the marching columns, the glittering rifles and frowning cannons. . . . They brought to our mental vision scenes that we had left behind us in our own loved Northland—scenes that many were to look upon never again. For awhile we were oblivious to the

293

instruments of death around us. We heard not the tramping of horses, the rumble of guns and the clanking of sabres. We saw not the dusty roadway filled with a winding column of blue. No! We were again wending our way toward where the village spire peeped above the trees. We saw from every road and footpath friends and loved ones hastening, and we heard the pastor's opening prayer and the sweet tones of the choir as they carried aloft the music of some old familiar hymn. We saw the gray-haired father's reverent bow and the mother's time wrinkled yet tender hands closed in silent devotion. We were awakened from our reverie by the command, "Close up! Close up! The vision had passed; home was far away and war's stern realities around us.[10]

This morning, Charles Coffin made his way from Baltimore to Frederick, arriving before the infantry. However, the cavalry was moving through, stopping for nothing, taking the road leading northward to Pennsylvania. Later the infantry came, and then the Reserve Artillery jarring the ground with the rambling of the carriages. Coffin heard the bells too.

> While the cannon were rolling over the pavements there came the pealing of church bells calling people to worship. The birds were singing in the orchards, the air fragrant with flowers; upon all the surrounding hills the wheat was ripening.[11]

Meanwhile in Carlisle, Pennsylvania, Richard S. Ewell and his staff started the day from the quarters in the Carlisle Army Barracks. A flag raising ceremony was held. But instead of the Stars and Stripes, the colors of the Thirty-second North Carolina Regiment, floated from the flag pole.[12]

After the flag ceremony, "Sandie" Pendleton, William Allan, Hunter McGuire, and Clem Fishburne obtained passes and entered town to attend divine services. Finding the Episcopal Church closed, they went to the Presbyterian Church. A lot of Southern soldiers were in attendance. The minister had a good sermon. He made no mention of the war and asked for divine guidance for all in authority. After the service, the Confederate officers introduced themselves. They found the pastor had lived in Alabama. Some of the soldiers from Alabama who attended the services knew him.[13]

The Thirty-second North Carolina had an important part in the flag raising at Carlisle.

Yes, it was . . . at Carlisle that this regiment was complimented, out of all the regiments in the Confederate army, with the distinguished honor of being presented and entrusted with the first flag or standard made according to the design adopted by the Confederate Congress a few weeks previous. Congress had adopted, conditionally, a new design for the Confederate flag, and an elegant new flag, made according to that design by the ladies of Richmond, had been sent to General Lee for his approval and for him to present to the regiment most worthy of receiving and carrying it. Accordingly General Lee sent it to Lieutenant-General Ewell (who then commanded Stonewall Jackson's old corps), and General Ewell sent it to Major-General Rodes (his favorite division commander) and General Rodes passed it on to his most favored Brigadier, General Daniel, and he ordered it to be presented to the Thirty-second Regiment. The presentation ceremonies were of a most enthusiastic character and were appropriate to the high honor so worthily conferred. The troops, who were encamped at Carlisle, were assembled in the lovely grounds belonging to the United States barracks to witness the presentation, which was attended with much speech-making and enthusiastic rejoicings. Oh! it was a grand occasion—in such striking contrast to the sad scenes witnessed by the same soldiers, two days thereafter, on the blood-stained heights of Gettysburg. Yes, the bright eyes of our brave boys, which then sparkled with joy and hope, were soon glazed with the stony stare of death; and their joyous shouts and cheers, so eagerly and so proudly greeting the new flag of the young Confederacy, were so soon changed to dying groans and expiring gasps.

This flag was then hoisted above the roof of the barracks and unfurled to the breeze. And thus it was that North Carolinians can boast that it was the flag of one of their regiments that waved defiantly on the enemy's soil at a point farther North than any other Confederate flag during the whole war.[14]

Many of the Carlisle churches were in a dilemma. Carlisle was an occupied city and the folks did not know whether to hold services. But a lot of the pastors felt it was their duty to bring comfort, hope, and calm to their parishioners. So the English Lutheran, the German Reformed and the Presbyterian denominations had services the same as always.

The residents of Carlisle were treated kindly by the Confederates. Law and order prevailed. Jacobs says that Rodes's division maintained strict discipline in Gettysburg too. He thought it was because so many of the officers and men were Christians.[15]

Union pickets within two miles of Carlisle found the

Sabbath morning to be very foggy. A captured Confederate prisoner told his captors that the Rebels would be in Harrisburg by Monday.[16]

Although still in shock from the passage of Early's division on Friday, the church bells were ringing in Gettysburg this morning. They greeted the arrival of the Michigan cavalry. R. A. Alger had the honor of leading the Fifth Michigan into the streets of the town, followed by the Sixth Cavalry. Captain Kidd describes the event:

> It was a gala day. The people were out in force, and in their Sunday attire to welcome the troopers in blue. The church bells rang out a joyous peal, and dense masses of beaming faces filled the streets as the narrow columns of fours threaded its way through their midst. Lines of men stood on either side with pails of water or apple butter; others held immense platters of bread. Ladies took the slices, covered them with apple butter, and passed a "sandwich" to each soldier as he passed. At intervals of a few feet were bevies of women and girls, who handed up boquets and wreaths of flowers. By the time the centre of the town was reached, every man had a bunch of flowers in his hand, or a wreath around his neck. Some even had their horses decorated, and the one who did not get a share was a very modest trooper indeed. The people were overjoyed, and received us with an enthusiasm and hospitality born of full hearts.
>
> Turning to the right, the command went into camp a little outside the town, in a field where the horses were up to their knees in clover, and it made the poor, famished animals fairly laugh. That night a squadron was sent out about two miles to picket on each diverging road. It was my duty, with a squadron, to guard the Cashtown pike, and a very vivid remembrance is yet retained of the "vigil long" of that July night, during which I did not once leave the saddle, dividing the time between the reserve post and the line of videttes.[17]

Church bells rang in York too. A lot of people started to church the same as usual. Many unaware of the proximity of Rebel troops. Some received an added sermon, one they had not bargained for from "Extra Billy" Smith, a general in "Jube" Early's division.

Smith was a Virginian, an older gentleman, who had political ties dating back to the days of Monroe and Jackson. He had served as governor of Virginia during the Mexican War, and had just been elected to commence a term as governor beginning January 1, 1864. He had personal magnetism, or as

296

we say today, charisma. However, as a military man he did not rank so high. Early kept him close to John B. Gordon so the Georgian could keep an eye on him. Early must have enjoyed ordering a former governor around.

Then as now, there were political payoffs. Smith had been a mail contractor during the days of Andrew Jackson, being in charge of a run from Washington to Georgia. For extending the route to numerous little places along the main line, Smith had received money. When the situation was investigated, the payments to contractors were called "Smith's Extras." The name was to follow him the rest of his life.

There were no defenses in York. And as Early's division approached, the mayor came out to surrender the city. The band had been playing "Dixie," but Smith ordered them to play "Yankee Doodle." It seemed as though Smith thought he was in the midst of a political parade. With a smile on his face, and his hat off, he rode into York bowing to the crowds on each side of the street. He saluted every pretty girl he saw. The crowd loved it. Their surprise turned into a hearty cheer. In the background the church bells were ringing and people were on their way to church. However, they congregated in the square to see the general and his men. In fact, the dense crowd halted the column. Then it was "Extra Billy's" turn. Leaning forward in the saddle, he started to speak.

> My friends . . . how do you like this way of coming back into the Union? I hope you like it; I have been in favor of it for a good while. . . . We are not burning your houses or butchering your children. On the contrary, we are behaving like Christian gentlemen which we are.

Continuing on, General Smith said:

> We needed a summer outing and thought we would take it in the North, instead of patronizing the Virginia springs, as we generally do. We regret that our trunks haven't gotten up yet; we were in such a hurry to see you that we couldn't wait for them. . . . Look at my men . . . they are such a hospitable, wholehearted, fascinating lot of gentlemen. . . . You are quite welcome to stay here and make yourselves at home, so long as you behave yourselves pleasantly and agreeably as you are doing now.[18]

Billy's fun was about to end. "Jube" Early had arrived. Furious at finding his way blocked, and the things of the military at a standstill, he elbowed his way through the crowd, grabbed Smith by the blouse and shouted, "General Smith, what in the devil are you about, stopping the head of this column in this cursed town!"

"Having a little fun, General," Smith replied.

So the meeting in the square ended and Smith moved on. The church bells were still ringing as the brigades of Gordon and Hoke marched east on Market Street. Gordon, noting the finery of the church people, felt embarrassed at the dirty, ragged appearance of his men. Some even rode double on shaggy horses to rest their bare feet.[19]

In the meantime, Colonel White reached Hanover Junction and succeeded in destroying the depot there as well as several bridges. However, he was unable to hit all the bridges as they were defended by infantry. White was able to destroy the bridge over the Conewago at its mouth and also one over the Codorous south of York.[20]

Early asked the citizens of York for $100,000. But the townspeople were able to raise only $28,600. But they did get the requested hats, socks, and rations. Fifteen hundred pairs of shoes were also given to Early. No more were available. The mayor explained that there was no more money in town. The rest had been taken to Philadelphia. "Jube" Early believed the mayor had done the best he could. The socks and shoes were given to those most in need. The money was used to buy fresh beef, or at least part of it. Early was amazed how fast the beef turned up when the farmers were told they would be paid cash. Money talked even then.[21]

"Old Jube" debated setting fire to York. There were two large railroad car factories, two depots, and other railroad materials. But he did not want to run the risk of setting fire to the town. He did not want to encourage looting, nor did he wish to act as the Union soldiers had acted. In a letter to the citizens of York, Early said:[22]

> I have abstained from burning the railroad buildings and car shops in your town, because, after examination, I am satisfied the safety of the town would be endangered; and acting in the spirit of humanity which has ever characterized my government and its military au-

thorities, I do not desire to involve the innocent in the same punishment with the guilty. Had I applied the torch without regard to the consequences, I would have pursued a course that would have been fully vindicated as an act of just retaliation for the many authorized acts of barbarity perpetrated by your own army upon our soil. But we do not war upon women and children, and I trust the treatment you have met with at the hands of my soldiers will open your eyes to the monstrous iniquity of the war waged by your government upon the people of the Confederate States, and that you will make an effort to shake off the revolting tyranny under which it is apparent to all you are yourselves groaning.[23]

John B. Gordon, one of Early's commanders, was very much impressed with the Pennsylvania countryside as his men marched from Gettysburg to Wrightsville on the Susquehanna. Like so many others, he noted the contrast of the farms and crops. However, he naturally saw it from the Confederate viewpoint.

It was delightful to look upon such a scene of universal thrift and plenty. Its broad grain-fields, clad in golden garb, were waving their welcome to the reapers and binders. Some fields were already dotted over with harvested shocks. . . . It was a type of the fair and fertile Valley of Virginia at its best, before it became the highway of armies and the ravages of war had left it wasted and bare. This melancholy contrast between these charming districts, so similiar in other respects, brought to our Southern sensibilities a touch of sadness. In both these lovely valleys were the big red barns . . . the old fashioned brick or stone mansion . . . and the broad green meadows with luxuriant grasses and crystal springs.[24]

General Gordon, later governor of Georgia, and a great American leader, writes,

One of these springs impressed itself on my memory by its great beauty and the unique uses to which its owner had put it. . . . He had built his dining room immediately over this fountain gushing from a cleft in the underlying rock. My camp for the night was nearby, and I accepted his invitation to breakfast with him. As I entered quaint room, one half floored with smooth limestone, and the other half covered with limpid water bubbling clear and pure, . . . my amazement at the . . . design was perhaps less pronounced than the sensation of rest which it produced. For many days we had been marching on the dusty turnpikes, under a broiling sun, and it is easier to imagine than to describe the feeling of relief and repose which came over me as we sat in the cool room, with a hot breakfast served from one side, while from the other the frugal housewife dipped cold milk and cream from immense jars standing neck-deep in water.[25]

General Gordon describes the Confederates' entrance into York, the city that served briefly as capital of the United States during the Revolutionary War.

> We entered the city of York on Sunday morning. A committee composed of the mayor and prominent citizens, met my command on the main pike before we reached the corporate limits, their object being to make a peaceable surrender and ask for protection to life and property. They returned, I think, with a feeling of assured safety. The church bells were ringing, and the streets were filled with well dressed people. The appearance of these churchgoing men, women, and children, in their Sunday attire, strangely contrasted with that of my marching soldiers. Begrimed as we were from head to foot with the impalpable grat powder which rose in dense columns from the macadamized pikes and settled in sheets on men, horses, and wagons, it is now wonder that many of York's inhabitants were terror-stricken as they looked upon us. We had been compelled on these forced marches to leave baggage wagons behind us, and there was no possibility of a change of clothing, and no time for brushing uniforms, or washing the disfiguring dust from faces, hair, or beard. . . . Halting on the main street, where the sidewalks were densely packed, I rode a few rods in advance of my troops, in order to speak to the people from my horse.[26]

General Gordon was unaware that the dust of the road had been no respecter of rank. Thus he looked as dusty as the rest of the men. His appearance frightened some of the women. But once they heard the calm manner of his voice, they were reassured that no personal harm would come to them. Gordon told the folks that there was no spirit of "vengance or rapine in the breasts of his men."

As the dusty gray column proceeded east through the streets of York, Gordon found he and the Confederate cause had at least one friend. A little girl, about twelve years of age, ran up to his horse, and

> handed me a large bouquet of flowers, in the centre of which was a note, in delicate handwriting, purporting to give the numbers and describe the position of the Union forces in Wrightsville, toward which I was advancing. I carefully read and reread this strange note.

300

It bore no signature, and contained no assurance of sympathy for the Southern cause.[27]

John B. Gordon moved on to Wrightsville. There he encountered opposition from twelve or fifteen hundred Pennsylvania militia. They had a good position. A frontal assault was required. There was no way to launch a flank attack. The artillery unlimbered and commenced fire. Then the Confederate infantry advanced. The militia soon retreated. Gordon, who had marched twenty miles already, pursued as rapidly as possible. However, the Union troops had poured inflammable materials on the bridge and set it on fire.[28]

Gordon's men tried to extinguish the fire, but it was hopeless. The men tried to beat the flames out with their muskets and blankets. That's all they had. Before buckets could be obtained, the bridge was doomed. It was almost a mile long, and water had to be hauled from the river.

The bridge was completely destroyed. Several houses in Wrightsville also went up in smoke. When these residences caught fire, Gordon's men formed a bucket brigade and fought to save the other houses and the town. Early was extremely proud of this. The men involved were Georgia troops under a Georgia general. They were in enemy territory and had to be thinking of how federal troops had just recently burned the town of Darien, Georgia. They could have permitted Wrightsville to burn, but to their credit they fought and extinguished the flames in the northern town.

Gordon was sorry to see the bridge go. He had hopes of marching to Lancaster to levy a contribution on "that rich town, cut the Central Railroad, then move upon Harrisburg linking up with Ewell in a pincers movement. He had plans to mount his infantry division on the fine horses from the York County farms. But the fire at the bridge ended these plans.[29] Early says there was no other means of crossing the river. Gordon was ordered to return to York the next day, the twenty-ninth. Early rode back that evening.

According to the *York Gazette*, it was almost 8:00 P.M. when the fire gained headway. It was a very picturesque scene at twilight. The fire added to the orange of the sunset, and the flames almost danced on the waters of the Susque-

301

hanna. The light could be seen for many miles. The burning timbers fell into the water and drifted downstream. Some thought they looked the infernal boats of hell. By dawn of the next day, only the stone pillars remained.[30]

In Wrightsville, John Gordon saw a white flag flying from Samuel Kauffelt's house at the foot of the hill on Hellman Street. There Gordon gave the town officials word that the city would be spared, and no more damage done. He was invited to use the home of Burgess Magee as his headquarters and lodging for the night.[31]

Tonight, most of Gordon's brigade spent the night in the Detweiler's fields. Some took shelter in the homes of the people who had fled upon news of the Confederate advance. One of the places used was the home of Mr. and Mrs. Samuel Smith. Their son had enlisted in the Union army. As he left, the parents gave him a testament to carry in his pocket. He was captured and died in prison. When the Smiths returned to their home, they found Silas's testament on a table in one of the rooms.[32]

The folks in Westminster, Maryland, went to church as usual on June 28. However, their services were rudely interrupted by the sounds of galloping horsemen. At first the church people thought it might be Confederate raiders. But it turned out to be a portion of the First Delaware Cavalry. One hundred fifteen troopers under Maj. N. B. Knight had ridden into town. Pickets were placed at key locations on the roads leading to and from Westminster. Late Sunday evening, the Union cavalrymen came hurrying back into town. They had been told a large group of Confederates were approaching. It proved to be a false alarm. The First Delaware resumed their picket duty.

Things were hectic in Westminster, the folks had seen residents of the counties closer to Baltimore and Washington fleeing north with their belongings. Westminster had never seen such alarm, and haste. On the streets, and whenever the farmers met, the question was "What's the news now? Where's Lee?"

Like Carlisle, the merchants of Westminster closed their stores whenever a fresh alarm came. The Southern sympathizers were wild with joy. They heard that Lee had already defeated the Union army and was on the way to Philadelphia and New York.

They shared this information with some of those who were fleeing. The frightened teamsters believed the news, laid the whip to horses, and hurried off.[33]

Delaware, like all the other states, furnished troops to the Union. One of the outfits was a cavalry troop from New Castle County. Maj. Napolean Knight and about one hundred men arrived in Winchester about 11:00 A.M. They selected the high hill where Western Maryland College is located as their position. This gave them a good view of the surrounding countryside. The men from Delaware rode in so quietly that many of the residents of Westminster were unaware of their presence. However, martial law was declared, and outposts established on all the major roads. A provost guard of sixteen men was assigned to the town, headquarters being at the Odd Fellows Hall. Things remained rather quiet until late afternoon on Monday.[34]

Charles Corbit, farmer turned soldier, was twenty-five in the summer of '63. Major Knight checked in at the Westminster Hotel. He was not feeling well. Thus Corbit was virtually in charge.

XII CORPS

Things started happening early today for the Twelfth Corps. They broke camp at 6 A.M. at Knoxville near Brunswick and Harpers Ferry. Some of the troops had spent the night at the southern end of Pleasant Valley. Showing the relatively few words to be found on a given day, the first three lines of the paragraph constitute Henry Slocum's report of the day's events.[35] All A. S. Williams has to say is that his division marched from Knoxville to Frederick. The march was one of about eighteen miles, depending again on the location of the previous night's campsite. For instance,

On the banks of the Susquehanna.

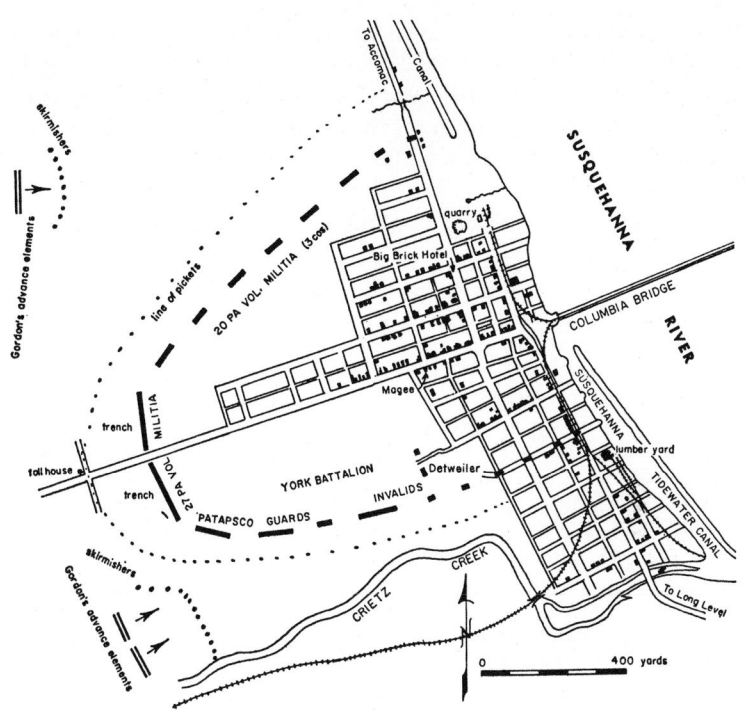

The action at Wrightsville. Courtesy Louisiana State
University Press in *Here Come the Rebels!*

Williams must have been closer as he says he covered but
twelve miles. Several of the regimental histories mention passing through Jefferson.

The Twelfth Corps was located on a circular line with its
left flank resting on the Middletown Road, and the right on
Ballenger Creek Road. Slocum's men arrived at the southwestern edge of Frederick about 2:00 P.M. After setting up
camp they too received the news of the change of commanders.[36]

For the men of the Twenty-seventh Indiana, Frederick was
more like home than any place else. Many of them had been
in Frederick in September of '62. Now once again for a few
brief hours they enjoyed the hospitality of the city and the surrounding farms.[37] George Collins of the 149th New York

305

was impressed with the beauty of Petersville and Jefferson. At the early hour, he noted many Barbara Fritchies hanging from their upstairs windows to see the troops and show their admiration. Many still had their nightcaps on.[38] Men and women brought pails of water and milk to the men in blue. John Boyle of the 111th Pennsylvania recorded his impression of the change of commanders.

George Gordon Meade, who was so suddenly summoned from command of the Fifth Corps to that of the Army of the Potomac, was born of American parents, at Cadiz, Spain, on December 31, 1815. His father was a citizen of Philadelphia, and his mother was from Perth Amboy, New Jersey. They resided abroad for seventeen years, and returned to the United States when their son was a little child. The father died before the boy was thirteen years of age. From a boarding school near Philadelphia the lad was placed under the tuition of Salmon P. Chase, afterward Secretary of the United States Treasury, and through his influence was appointed to the Military Academy in 1831. He graduated number nineteen in a class of fifty-six, and was the only member of his class to attain distinction in the army. He was assigned to the Third Artillery, but resigned the following year and engaged in civil engineering. In 1842 he reentered the army as a topographical engineer, and served with credit during the Mexican War. He subsequently did very important work in a geodetic survey of the Great Lakes as captain of engineers. On August 31, 1861, he was commissioned brigadier general of volunteers and commanded first a brigade and then the division containing the fifteen Pennsylvania reserve regiments. He was twice wounded at Newmarket Crossroads, on the peninsula, but was in the field and on duty during Pope's campaign. At Antietam he commanded the Third Division of the First Corps, and after the wounding of Hooker, the corps itself. On November 29, 1862, he was appointed major general of volunteers. At Fredericksburg he charged the Confederate left with his division in a movement that has been compared to Pickett's celebrated charge at Gettysburg, and for a time secured a foothold upon the enemy's lines. After that battle he was placed in command of the Center Grand Division until this formation was abolished, when he came to the head of the Fifth Corps, which he led at Chancellorsville, as we have seen, and was commanding it at the moment of his promotion.

General Meade was in his forty-eighth year, tall and slender in person, with full dark beard and thin, partly gray hair. His forehead was high and white, his eyes large and expressive, his nose prominent, his manner positive, calm, and reserved, but at times vehement. His mind was highly trained and logical, and his temperament was impetuous. He possessed great natural dignity, an innate and lofty pride, a vigorous conscience, an unyielding will. He lacked the magnetism that excites superficial applause, but embodied the greatness and fidelity that inspire respect and attract worth. It is said that his ear was so well trained that, awakened at night by distant firing, he could tell in an instant whence the sound proceeded and what troops were engaged, and that his eye for topography was so skilled that on looking at a range of hills he could describe the nature of the ground beyond them, and tell where the streams were and in what direction they flowed. He was, without doubt, the third man in the great triumvirate of military leaders that the civil war produced on the Northern side. When the struggle had ended Lee said of him that he feared him more than any man he had ever met in battle. [39]

Meanwhile, the residents of Franklin County were assessing the Confederate invasion.

W. A. Reid of Greencastle estimated that 50,000 Confederates passed through the town. "The Franklin Repository" of Chambersburg gave the figure at 47,000. John F. Glossner was a clerk in the office of the Franklin County prothonotary. Quoting from his diary, he gives us the following figures: "Ewell's corps, fifteen thousand men . . . with sixty pieces of artillery, and over one thousand wagons; A. P. Hill's corps, the same; Longstreet's corps, twenty thousand men, eighty pieces of artillery, and over one thousand wagons. The entire army did not number over forty-eight thousand." [40]

To this we add Early's division which traveled via Waynesboro to Greenwood and Stuart's cavalry. However, the three main sources for the Greencastle-Chambersburg area list the strength of Lee's army from 47,000 to 50,000 men.

According to Jacob Hoke, Longstreet's command was encamped along the east bank of the Conococheague Creek near the Mennonite Church where Ewell had been prior to leaving for Carlisle. John Hood's division encamped on Peter Lehman's farm two and one-half miles northeast of Chambersburg. George Pickett's men were at John Long's farm, and McLaws's on up the creek.

The camp of Robert E. Lee had little pomp and circumstance. He traveled simply and plainly. A Confederate flag marked his headquarters located in several acres of timber. Owen of the Washington Artillery writes, "There are about a

307

half dozen tents and as many baggage wagons and ambulances. The horses and mules for these . . . are tied up to a tree or grazing about the place. The General has a private carriage or ambulance . . . but he never uses it. It formerly belonged to the Federal General Pope."[41]

There was little movement of the Confederates in Chambersburg on Sunday morning. They were content to rest and recover from the hard days of marching. However, Mrs. Ellen McLellan was having problems. The mills and stores were in possession of the Confederates, or at least that's what she thought. She was unable to get flour. Somehow she talked with a captain who informed her that Lee was in Messersmith's woods and that she could see him. The captain offered Mrs. McLellan an escort but said it was perfectly safe for her to go alone. The lady and her young daughter then set out to see General Lee. They encountered no difficulties. Everything seemed in perfect order. Arriving in the woods, Ellen found General Lee and some of his staff at a table. An aide gave her two camp stools. Soon the general came to talk with her. Mrs. McLellan said they were short of food and faced starvation unless he gave them help. Lee was startled by her news and said it seemed impossible in the midst of this lovely and fertile farming area. Lee told her the supplies of food had been turned over to the troops to keep them from ravaging the homes. He told her to send some prominent men to him so he could get an idea of the needs of the people. He requested the services of a miller. Before leaving, Mrs. McLellan asked for his autograph. "Do you want the autograph of a rebel?" Ellen assured him of her loyalty to the Union, but she needed the bread and would like an autograph. Lee replied that having his signature in her possession may be a dangerous thing to possess. But he gave it. Then Robert E. Lee said that war is cruel, and he only wished to go home and eat his bread in peace. Mrs. McLellan was impressed with his strength and sadness. Soon thereafter, several barrels of flour were sent to those in need.[42]

As the dawn broke on the twenty-eighth, Pickett's division was encamped a mile north of Chambersburg. Randolph Shotwell was much impressed with the factories and the well-built homes. He noticed the indifference of the people, feeling that they really didn't care who won as long as they were left alone. The hotels were open on this Sabbath, charging fifty cents a meal. Rebel guests were at Yankee tables, spending Confederate money. Strict orders were in action to prevent harm to private property. A lot of the soldiers were foraging, but paying the asking price.[43]

Shotwell heard the joyous news that Ewell's men were resting in the Carlisle Barracks. "It must be a source of considerable exhilaration for our war worn Rebels to lounge in the comfortable quarters so recently occupied . . . by the Old Army."

The lovelorn George Pickett penned a letter to his sweetheart, saying,

> I wish, my darling, you could see this wonderfully rich and prosperous country, abounding in plenty, with its great, strong, vigorous horses and oxen, its cows and crops and verdantly thriving vegetation—none of the ravages of war, no signs of devestation—all in woeful contrast to the land where we lay dreaming. All the time I break the law "Thou shalt not covet," for every fine horse or cow I see I want for my darling, and all the pretty things I see besides.
>
> At Chambersburg, Marse Robert preached us a sermon . . . taking as his text, "Vengenance is mine, Saith the Lord." I observed that the mourners' bench was not overcrowded with seekers for conversion. The poor fellows were thinking of their own despoiled homes, looted of everything, and were not wildly-enthusiastic as they acquiesced obediently to our beloved Commander's order.
>
> Our whole army is now in Pennsylvania, north of the river. . . . Every tramp-tramp-tramp is a thought-thought-thought of my darling, every halt a blessing invoked, every command a loving caress; and the thought of you and prayer for you make me better, give me courage, give me faith.[44]

Yesterday evening Colonel Fremantle met the members of Longstreet's staff and was very impressed by them. Major Moses, the chief commissary, told him that his orders were to open the stores of Chambersburg by force and take anything that could be used by the army. Some items had been sent away and Ewell's men had helped themselves, but the major had found a good supply of felt hats. These were hidden in a cellar. They did not stay there very long. He was told that

Longstreet and A. P. Hill were now near Chambersburg, "all full of confidence and in high spirits."[45]

Today Fremantle met John Bell Hood. "He is a tall, thin, wiry-looking man, with a grave looking face and a light colored beard, thirty-three years old, and is accounted one of the best and most promising officers in the army. By his Texas and Alabama troops he is adored. . . . His troops are accused of being a wild set and difficult to manage. . . ."[46]

In the afternoon Fremantle rode into Chambersburg and found Lawley at the Franklin Hotel. However, the colonel had trouble getting in. Once in the door, the Pennsylvanians yelled at the officer from the Coldstream Guards and were openly hostile. Once again, though, the sight of real gold made them change their tune. Part of the trouble was that they thought Hood's Texans were Mexicans.

Major Moses had a frustrating day in Chambersburg. He found some items, but had to endure the abuse of the women who called him "a thievish little Rebel scoundrel," and other names that cannot be printed.

Robert Augustus Moore was born on July 2, 1838, so he was not quite twenty-five on the Roads to Gettysburg, but reached that age during the battle. His parents were prosperous farmers in Mississippi prior to the war. They lived eight miles north of Holly Springs. Company G of the Seventeenth Mississippi came from the little town. Ninety-seven of the 150 from the area were farmers. Private Moore joined the outfit and kept his own diary until he was killed at Chickamauga on September 20, 1863. He is one of the unknown soldiers of the tragic war. We pick up his story on the Roads to Gettysburg.

Robert had a tremendous conversion experience during the winter, so on June 14 he went to church services. The brigade was inspected during the day. On the fifteenth he bade farewell to his Culpeper friends and headed over the mountains. The sixteenth brought a twenty-mile march and bivouac near Sperryville. There was a good breeze in the air. The seventeenth was another story. The march of McLaws's division was very fatiguing. Many broke down and a good number had sunstrokes. The heat was oppressive. Yet Robert and his

310

comrades covered eighteen miles. Rain on the eighteenth and nineteenth broke the heat wave. In fact, Robert and the other men in the Mississippi unit had a difficult time keeping their tents up near the top of Ashby's Gap. The wind blew them down. The rain continued most of Saturday. Late in the day, Robert forded the Shenandoah River. It was waist deep. The twenty-third was a nice day. The men were ordered to wash their clothing, and a dress parade was held in the evening. On the twenty-fourth, Robert passed through Berryville, and on the twenty-fifth marched twenty miles to Martinsburg, finding the residents mostly pro-Union. The rain started in the evening, and continued through the twenty-sixth making things most disagreeable. The Potomac at where Robert crossed was just about two feet deep. The night was spent at Williamsport. The next day Moore passed through Hagerstown, "a place of 6,000 inhabitants. . . . This is fine country between the mountains." Camp was made at Marion. Then on Sunday, the men under Lafayette McLaws entered Chambersburg and marched toward Fayetteville.[47] Moore attended prayer meeting.

J. B. Kershaw, commanding a brigade of South Carolina troops in Longstreet's First Corps, gives the following route of advances:

June 16—Sperryville.

June 17—Mud Run in Fauquier County.

These two days were excessively hot, and on the seventeenth many cases of sunstroke occurred.

June 18—Piedmont.

June 25—Martinsburg.

June 26—Crossed the Potomac; encamped near Williamsport.

June 27—Marched by way of Hagerstown, Middleburg, and Greencastle, and encamped five miles from Chambersburg.

June 28—Marched through Chambersburg, and encamped one mile beyond. Remained in camp until the thirtieth, when we marched to Fayetteville.[48]

Ham Chamberlayne had bad luck today. His horses, like many others in the Army of Northern Virginia, suffered greatly from the limestone roads in Maryland and Pennsylvania. The ordnance officer of the Third Corps Artillery made every effort to find shoes. But he had no luck. As a result, twenty horses had to be abandoned, being unfit for service. Ham took a foraging party and went looking for shoes and horses.

He interrupted a service at a little Dunker Church, walking in, flashing his pistol, and telling the congregation that his men needed their horses more than they. To be fair, Chamberlayne gave the folks a receipt, stating they would be paid at the conclusion of hostilities. He and his men then started back to camp. But before they had proceeded very far, they were intercepted by Union cavalry. Perhaps this was their reward for interrupting a church service. Chamberlayne and four of his men were captured, and all the horses taken from the Dunker congregation retaken. His son, as well as the writer, wonders where this little church might have been. Research by John Divine and the author indicates that it might have been the Five Forks Brethren in Christ Church, located between Waynesboro and Chambersburg, or the Price's Brethren Church just a little north of Waynesboro.[49] The men in blue were most likely part of Stahel's patrol, coming over from Emmitsburg.

On Sunday morning, Ewell wanted to know where the supplies were that he had ordered the previous day. When told they were unavailable, he ordered the house-to-house search. Thus an officer and a squad of soldiers went from house to house on a search and seizure mission. All items needed by the Second Corps or the army were taken. The stores were pretty well cleaned out. Yet they did not take items they did not need. From the private homes, only such items that were being stored and not in daily use were taken. This was a far cry from the methods of Sheridan and Sherman. The officers commanding the missions were polite, and the soldiers also behaved in a gentlemanly manner.[50]

The people of Carlisle were upset though by the fact that some of their neighbors led the Confederates to items that had been hidden. Otherwise, the Rebels would have had no way of knowing where some things had been placed. Often the Rebels reached a house and asked for specific items, demanding that it be brought forth. When the *Carlisle American* went to press after the Battle of Gettysburg, the culprits were not known, but the paper stressed the fact these individuals would be caught and dealt with.[51]

R. S. Ewell had a pleasant surprise. A fifteen-year-old boy from Lynchburg, Virginia, arrived, handsome in a new gray uniform looking for his "Uncle Jube." His name was John Cabell Early, anxious to see the war and carry messages for his uncle general.

However, Early was not in Carlisle, but near Wrightsville. Ewell was impressed with the lad and took him under his wing, insisting that he spend the night in his own tent.[52]

Surgeon Welch took up his pen again on Sunday, this last Sunday in June. This seemed to be letter writing day for most of the army.

Franklin County, Pa.,
June 28, 1863.

We are in Yankeedom this time, for certain, and a beautiful and magnificent country it is too. Since we started we have traveled about fifteen miles a day, resting at night and drawing rations plentifully and regularly. We are about fifteen miles over the Pennsylvania and Maryland line and within seven miles of Chambersburg. We are resting to-day (Sunday) and will get to Harrisburg in three more days if we go there.

We hear nothing of Hooker's army at all, but General Lee knows what he is about. This is certainly a grand move of his, and if any man can carry it out successfully he can, for he is cautious as well as bold.

We are taking everything we need—horses, cattle, sheep, flour, groceries and goods of all kinds, and making as clean a sweep as possible. The people seem frightened almost out of their senses. They are nearly all agricultural people and have everything in abundance that administers to comfort. I have never yet seen any country in such a high state of cultivation. Such wheat I never dreamed of, and so much of it! I noticed yesterday that scarcely a horse or cow was to be seen. The free negroes are all gone, as well as thousands of the white people. My servant, Wilson, says he "don't like Pennsylvania at all," because he "sees no black folks."

I have never seen our army so healthy and in such gay spirits. How can they be whipped? Troops have so much better health when on the march. I must say that I have enjoyed this tramp. The idea of invading the Yankees has buoyed me up all the time. Last year when

313

invading Maryland we were almost starved, and of course anyone would become disheartened. My health was never better than it is now, and I feel gay and jovial every way.

My brother Billie is out to-day guarding a man's premises. He was also out last night, and he told me this morning that they fed him splendidly. The reason houses are guarded is to prevent our troops plundering and robbing, which would demoralize them, thereby rendering them unfit for soldiers. Soldiers must have a strict and severe rein held over them; if not, they are worthless.[53]

William Christian wrote home today, revealing the spirit of the army.

Camp near Greenwood, Pa., June 28, 1863.—My own darling wife: You can see by the date of this that we are now in Pennsylvania. We crossed the line day before yesterday and are resting today near a little one-horse town on the road to Gettysburg, which we will reach tomorrow. We are paying back these people for some of the damage they have done us, though we are not doing them half as bad as they done us. We are getting up all the horses, etc., and feeding our army with their beef and flour, etc., but there are strict orders about the interruption of any private property by individual soldiers.

Though with these orders, fowls and pigs and eatables don't stand much chance. I felt when I first came here that I would like to revenge myself upon these people for the desolation they have brought upon our own beautiful home, that home where we could have lived so happy, and that we loved so much, from which their vandalism has driven you and my helpless little ones. But though I had such severe wrongs and grievances to redress and such great cause for revenge, yet when I got among these people I could not find it in my heart to molest them. They looked so dreadfully scared and talked so humble that I have invariably endeavored to protect their property and have prevented soldiers from taking chickens, even in the main road; yet there is a good deal of plundering going on, confined principally to the taking of provisions. No houses were searched and robbed, like our houses were done by the Yankees. Pigs, chickens, geese, etc., are finding their way into our camp; it can't be prevented, and I can't think it ought to be. We must show them something of war. I have sent out today to get a good horse; I have no scruples about that, as they have taken mine. We took a lot of Negroes yesterday. I was offered my choice, but as I could not get them back home I would not take them. In fact my humanity revolted at taking the poor devils away from their homes. They were so scared that I turned them all loose.

I dined yesterday with two old maids. They treated me very well and seemed greatly in favor of peace. I have had a great deal of fun

314

since I have been here. The country that we have passed through is beautiful, and everything in the greatest abundance. You never saw such a land of plenty. We could live here mighty well for the next twelve months, but I suppose old Hooker will try to put a stop to us pretty soon. Of course we will have to fight here, and when it comes it will be the biggest on record. Our men feel that there is to be no back-out. A defeat here would be ruinous. This army has never done such fighting as it will do now, and if we can whip the armies that are now gathering to oppose us, we will have everything in our own hands. We must conquer a peace.[54]

As the soldiers wrote letters home, a man was riding as fast as he could toward Chambersburg. He was a Confederate spy. His name was Harrison, a friend of James Longstreet. Prior to the start on the Roads to Gettysburg, Harrison had been given funds and told to mingle with Union officers and men in Washington and wherever the Army of the Potomac moved. Therefore, he was in Frederick and heard the news of the change of commanders. This bit of intelligence must be gotten to Confederate headquarters. So he left Frederick immediately.

His route and the time he left is a matter of conjecture. Harrison is one of the mysteries, not only of the Gettysburg campaign, but of the Civil War. Even his first name is unknown. He was sent to Longstreet on the personal recommendation of James A. Seddon, the secretary of war. When he heard the news of the change of commanders again is a guessing matter.

It was about 10:00 P.M. this last Sunday in June when a staff officer came to Lee's tent, telling of the arrival of Harrison at Longstreet's headquarters. At first, Lee was skeptical. Then he sent for Harrison and questioned him personally. After a period of discussion, there was no doubt in Lee's mind that Harrison was telling the truth. Drastic steps and changes would have to be made. So in the tent east of Chambersburg the officers in gray huddled around the maps and made new plans.

Many of the soldiers were doing a lot of thinking. A member of the Twenty-sixth North Carolina writes:

Alas, the last Sunday on earth to many a noble soul then beating with such high hopes and aspirations.[55]

As the darkness fell over the area, campfires could be seen on the eastern slopes of South Mountain. They belonged to A. P. Hill's men.[56]

II CORPS

Sunday was not a day of rest for the Union Second Corps. Hancock's men moved from Sugar Loaf Mountain to the Monocacy River just south of Frederick, passing through Barnesville and some little communities on the way. It was a long march of eighteen miles. The men went into camp on the same site they occupied on Saturday, September 13, 1862, just prior to Antietam. Toward evening the supply train caught up with them and the men had the opportunity to change clothing. They took their baths in the Monocacy.[57]

Today, Colonel Cross, a bearded man of thirty-one, was riding on a Maryland road with nineteen-year-old Charles A. Hale, a member of his staff. Sugar Loaf Mountain loomed in the distance. Captain Francis W. Butler of the Signal Corps rode up and traveled with the pair for a time. Cross shared with Butler his joy in receiving a sword, spurs, and watch from the men of his regiment.

The conversation then turned to the impending battle. Colonel Cross paused and said, "It will be my last battle." Young Hale was shocked, but remembered how tense and preoccupied Cross had seemed in recent days. Turning to Hale he said, "Mr. Hale, I wish you to attend to my books and papers. That private box of mine in the headquarters wagon—you helped me to re-pack it the other day. After the campaign is over, get it at once, dry the contents if damp, and then turn it over to my brother Richard."[58]

While marching to Urbana and Monocacy Junction south of Frederick, on Sunday, June 28, the Second Corps received news of the change of command. Artilleryman Tully McCrea, writing from Uniontown on June 30 to Belle McCrea, said:

316

We were all delighted with the news that General Hooker had been relieved and General Meade assigned to the command of the army. This is universally popular and received with great glee. General Meade has for some time past commanded the Fifth Army Corps and has a good reputation. General Hooker leaves the army with scarcely a friend in it. He has always criticized and vilified his superiors and was instrumental in McClellan's removal. His ambition has always aimed at the command of the army. He had his wish satisfied and, instead of accomplishing his boasted plans, he suffered an ignominious and disgraceful defeat at Chancellorsville, . . . His blundering was so apparent that when we returned to Falmouth the army had lost all confidence in him. Hence the general rejoicing at his removal and the total absence of sympathy over his downfall.[59]

John Gibbon, being a general, heard the news while still on the road to Monocacy Junction. Breathlessly he asked, "Who is in command?" When told that the new commander was George C. Meade, Gibbon gave a sigh of relief. Like many others he anticipated a change, but was surprised when it came. John felt it was a hazardous decision, but one that had to be made due to "the total loss of confidence in Gen. Hooker, a feeling I believe, shared by the vast bulk of the army."[60]

There are only four references in the *Official Records* of the Sunday march of the Second Corps. Major Bradley of the Sixty-fourth New York tells us that his brigade left Barnesville at 6:00 A.M. and marched twelve miles to the banks of the Monocacy. The 145th Pennsylvania reached their campsite at 2:00 P.M. The Second Brigade of the Second Division camped on the left bank of the river, and at 5:00 P.M., Alexander Webb assumed command of the brigade. The Fifth New Hampshire concluded its march at 2:00 P.M. also. For the Nineteenth Massachusetts this was a march of nineteen miles. This paragraph contains all the material found in the *Official Records* and in fourteen regimental histories of the Second Corps.[61]

When the Fourth Ohio came in sight of the "clustered Spires of Fredericktown," they were more interested in cool water than pretty scenery. So they stacked arms and ran to the river. After the men had made camp and started supper, Winfield Scott Hancock and John Gibbon rode to headquarters to meet the new commander of the Army of the Potomac, and to learn of any new orders.[62]

V CORPS

While other units of the Army of the Potomac were marching from the west, southwest, and south this day, the Fifth Corps had it easy. They remained in camp south of Frederick, primarily on the Buckeystown Road. The primary topic of conversation was the change in commanders. They were elated that their commander, George G. Meade, was now in charge of the Union army. As a result, George Sykes, a veteran officer, was placed in command of the Fifth Corps while Romeyn B. Ayers took over his division.

VI CORPS

Perhaps John Sedgwick and the Union Sixth Corps had the worst day of all in the Union Army of the Potomac. They were the last infantry to cross on Saturday.[63] Bright and early at 4:00 A.M. the Sixth Corps broke camp at Edwards Ferry and headed east, northeast across Maryland for a distance of at least eighteen miles. From territory between Poolesville and Edwards Ferry, they tramped to Hyattstown.[64] For the Tenth Massachusetts the day took them from Poolesville to Barnesville, around Sugar Loaf Mountain, through Hyattstown to near Monrovia. At Barnesville they heard the church bell ringing. Some left the column and entered the Catholic Church, and were gratified to hear the priest pray for the president and peace. Later in the day the men from Massachusetts received the news of the change of commanders.[65] Tongues wagged far into the night discussing the merits of Hooker and Meade, the wisdom of the move

318

and what it might mean. At last with eyes heavy from a hard day of marching the men fell asleep. The Seventh Massachusetts covered twenty-five miles today.[66]

James Bowen of the Thirty-seventh Massachusetts shares his memories of the day:

> The day which was dawning when the tired column resumed its way at 4 o'clock in the morning of Sunday . . . brought little likeness to the quiet New England Sabbath. . . . The line of march was through a fine agricultural region. . . . Cherries were now ripening, and it was one of the relieving features of the march that the soldiers were occasionally able to spring into a tree loaded with the luscious fruit and gather a few handfuls, adding a delightful relish to the not especially appetizing army rations.[67]

Barnesville was the first town reached by daylight. And the charm of the village was "enhanced by the fact that . . . for the first time since crossing into Virginia the previous November they were greeted by smiling faces and words of sympathy." Once more they were in the land of friends and the heart beat with fresh courage.[68]

Members of the Seventy-seventh New York halted after their march from Edwards Ferry at Barnesville for dinner. The men left the road and occupied a nice little valley. The spreading chestnut trees provided good shade. They had just unslung their knapsacks when the sounds of a church bell came pealing out over the countryside. The soldiers stopped everything. It was Sunday, the Lord's Day. They had lost track of time. Climbing a hill, they saw the lovely little church, half hidden by the trees, and folks gathering for church. It was a joyous sight. It reminded many of the men of their homes and families, and the churches back home. Somehow, the sounds of the church bell and sight of the worshipers infused the men with new inspiration. It brought tears to the eyes of some.

Several of the men in blue went to services. It was a little Catholic Church, and the parish is still in existence. "The parishioners seemed quite devout people, and the pastor a sincere man." The priest prayed for the government, the president, and he asked for peace. He said that due to the confusion and excitement of the hour there would be no sermon. He asked those present to pray for an ailing lady and for the soul of a brother who had passed on.[69]

Then it was on to Hyattstown, where the news was received that Hooker was out and Meade was in. The announcement was received with astonishment, and some were angered. They had nothing against Meade. They were just anxious to recover what had been lost at Chancellorsville. "So they at once transferred hopes and obedience to the new commander. . . . All were willing to try him and hoped for the best."[70]

This afternoon, Alfred Pleasonton had a review of the cavalry troopers north of Frederick. It consisted primarily of the men in Kilpatrick's division, Gregg's and Buford's were on patrol elsewhere.[71]

From the *Official Records* and the mileage indicated by old Frederick County maps, the indication is that the camp and scene of the review was on the historic estate of "RICHFIELD." The farm was probably Thomas Johnson's first home in Frederick County. He named it "Richfield." In 1839 the Schley's lived on the farm. He was a direct descendant of the man who built the first house in Frederick. On October 9, 1839, a son was born to the Schleys. They had house guests at the time. One was a famous man, Gen. Winfield Scott, hero of the Mexican War and in command of the United States Army at the outbreak of the Civil War. In his honor, the baby boy was named Winfield Scott Schley. With a name like that he almost had to enter the military. However, he chose the navy and graduated from Annapolis in 1860. After a distinguished career, his peak of achievement came in 1898 when he was temporarily in command of the United States fleet blocading Santiago, Cuba. When the Spanish fleet attempted to run the blockade, the namesake of the great general destroyed them. Admiral Schley ranks as one of Frederick County's great men. But on June 28, it was horses, guidons, and cavalrymen at Richfield.[72]

The writer of the Fifth New York chronicle says that Pleasonton reviewed the division and "reorganized the entire force. We are now the Third Division of the Cavalry Corps, Army of the Potomac, with the gallant Kilpatrick in command. The first brigade consists of the 1st Vermont, 1st Virginia, First West Virginia, 18th Pennsylvania, and 5th New York, Brig. Gen. Farnsworth commanding."[73]

Jeb Stuart was also busy this last Sunday in June '63. Not only did he cross the river, but he made a raid on the Chesapeake and Ohio Canal, one of the main Union supply arteries. At Edwards Ferry, he captured fifteen barges.

The Washington *National Intelligencer* gives the following report: "On Sunday afternoon a large cavalry force belonging to Stuart's, Lee's and Hampton's Rebel commands, captured at Edwards Ferry 15 barges loaded with government stores and burned the barges with most of their valuable contents, consisting of rations of all kinds. Besides the stores, 150 colored men were taken off by the Rebels."[74]

Several Union officers were taken prisoner and then paroled. However, the private baggage of the officers was carried off by the men in gray. "The depot at Edwards Ferry had a larger amount of government stores than any other in the Army of the Potomac."

All is quiet now at Edwards Ferry. But it was alive and active the last days of June '63. We wonder what vibrations are still there from the days when Edwards Ferry saw one of the greatest troop movements in American history.

The report came to Major Eckert concerning the disaster at 7:20 P.M. The wagon train was still burning at that time. Citizens in Rockville said there were between eight and ten thousand rebels in the area. Communications were also cut.[75]

D. H. Gleason describes the encounter of the First Massachusetts Cavalry with Stuart's men.

> The next morning, June 28, a soldier, going very early to a farmhouse to get food, found a cavalry horse tied at the door, and inside a cavalryman of the 6th Virginia regiment, whom he at once captured and brought in. The man reported himself as one of a small scouting party, who crossed the ford the evening before and camped near. A party sent to capture them ran into a large cavalry camp, in fact all Stuart's cavalry corps, which had just crossed into Maryland.
> After a slight skirmish, Major Frye took the Rockville road, with the column, but soon ran into Stuart's cavalry again—a considerable force, with artillery. Thus cut off from the roads west, Major Frye

retreated to Tenallytown by a country road, but not before a skirmish took place, in which the 1st Massachusetts detachment engaged the enemy, and kept him back until the heterogeneous command could get across the enemy's front into the small road leading east.

Arriving at Tenallytown they brought the first news of Stuart's crossing, who, the same day, captured a wagon train at Rockville.[76]

Middletown is so named because it is midway between Frederick and Boonsboro. The Middletown Valley lies between the Catoctin Mountain and the South Mountain range of the Blue Ridge. The German Lutherans and Reformed Church members erected a house of worship as early as 1755.

Sgt. Lawrence Everhart, a distinguished Maryland soldier, and a man who saved the life of George Washington, was one of the early residents of the area. Later the Lutheran Church became a "landmark church" of the denomination. Wounded from the Maryland Campaign of 1862 were sheltered within its walls until January of 1863.

The Army of Northern Virginia, and the Army of the Potomac marched through Middletown on the way to Antietam in September of 1862. Little girls waved American flags in the face of "Stonewall" Jackson, prompting him to say, "Evidently we have no friends in this town." Seventeen-year-old Nancy Crouse became the Barbara Fritchie of Middletown by wrapping herself in a Union flag and defying the Conferates to take it from her. After the battle of South Mountain, Rutherford B. Hayes, colonel of the Twenty-third Ohio, and later president of the United States, was treated in the home of Jacob Rudy. Hayes had been severely wounded.

The long blue columns of the First, Third, and Eleventh corps marched through Middletown, on the Roads to Gettysburg. Some tramped through the town after Gettysburg as Meade sought to get Lee before he crossed the Potomac. The Confederates were back in Middletown in the summer of 1864 as Early threatened Washington, and made the residents of the farming village pay in order to keep Middletown from being put to the torch.

Middletown, like so many other places on the Roads to Gettysburg, remained a beautiful country farming community, until the development boom of the 1960s. It was

322

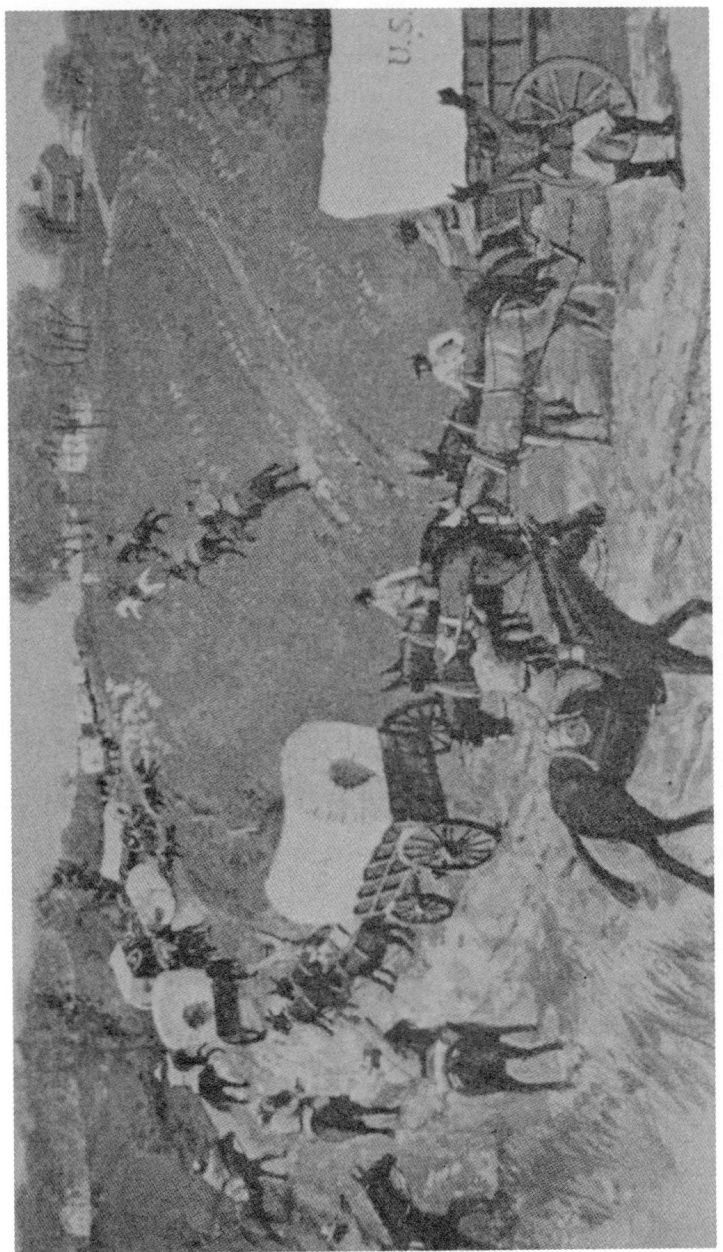

Stuart captures a wagon train. Garnet Jex.

known primarily for Main's great ice cream, and as the home of Charlie "King Kong" Keller, the pride of the New York Yankees.

III CORPS

While the bells were ringing for church services in the beautiful Middletown Valley, the men of the Third Corps started their march for "the clustered spires of Fredericktown," and then the Glade Valley."[77]

Houghton tells us that the reception of the Third Corps in Jefferson was repeated again in Middletown. The long blue lines marched through the thriving farming village in column by company with music and banners unfurled to the breeze. "The stars and stripes were displayed from many buildings, and much enthusiasm was manifested by the inhabitants."[78] Chaplain Cudworth was all eyes in the valley town. He saw the Stars and Stripes flying from every house on Main Street.[79]

Yet a greater welcome awaited the men of the corps as they reached the western edge of Frederick. Once again the troops marched in column by company, with the bands and drum corps playing. Edwin Houghton, along with others, never forgot the moments:

> Frederick is a beautiful city, and was, judging from our reception, thoroughly Union in sentiment. From nearly every house the stars and stripes floated in the breeze, and the windows, housetops, and doorways were lined with ladies in their holiday attire waving their handkerchiefs and American flags. We marched nearly a mile through the streets of the city and our progress was one continued ovation. Nothing since our military career commenced equalled the enthusiasm we received here. The day, the occasion, and the reception we received, will forever be cherished in the memory of the soldiers of the Third Corps.[80]

When the Third Corps reached Frederick, half of the population seemed to be in the streets. Cheer after cheer greeted the men in blue as they stopped briefly on Market Street.

Prospect Hall—where
the command changed.

Burkittsville.

Richfield—the
cavalry camp.

George A. Custer.

Late in the afternoon, the Third Corps forded the Monocacy and reached Ceresville on the eastern bank. They did not have time to visit the famous Ceresville Flour Mills. The mill was as famous in the 1860s as Kellogg's and Battle Creek are today. The road by the mill went to Baltimore. Tomorrow their comrades in the Second and Fifth corps would take that road. But the Third Corps turned left and headed for Walkersville.

Beyond Frederick the Third Corps halted for a rest and for supper. Then it was on the road once again. Six or seven additional miles were covered, depending where the men were in the column. That Sunday evening, the Third Corps camped near Walkersville, the boyhood home of the author. The citizens were really curious. A member of the Seventeenth Maine writes:

> Our course lay through a most magnificent portion of the country. Large and thriving fields of wheat, ripe for the harvest, splendid farmhouses, spacious granaries and storehouses, bespeaking the fertility of the soil. abounded along our route (from Frederick to Walkersville). . . . Our encampment was in a locality which had never been visited by either army, and the inhabitants were very much excited to see so large a body of men, and curious to witness our manner of life in camp.[81]

The Third Corps was stretched out by nightfall from Ceresville to just north of Walkersville. Some of the men were camped on what was known until recently as the Frank Nicodemus farm.

When Meade became commander of the Army of the Potomac, he wished to get rid of Dan Butterfield, Hooker's chief of staff. He offered the post to Andrew Humphreys of the Third Corps. But Humphreys states, "I declined or deferred it." Meade agreed that for the time being, Humphreys could be of greater service in command of the Second Division of the Third Corps.[82]

Regis De Trobriand, marching in Frederick with the Third Corps, had a lovely experience on one of the main streets of the city. We presume it was on either West Patrick Street or North Market Street as the Third Corps came in from Middletown and the west.

A mother and a group of children were standing on the porch of a small house. As De Trobriand came riding by, the mother gave a little girl, about twelve years of age, a bouquet of flowers to take to the officer. Bravely she held out the flowers, and De Trobriand leaned forward to receive the gift of appreciation. As she handed the flowers to him, she said, "Good luck, general." De Trobriand was touched by her gift. He wanted to dismount and hug her, but they had to march on. After she went back to her family, the general turned in the saddle and blew her a kiss. The little girl nodded and blushed.

That's how it was in Frederick. We can almost picture the events and feel the excitement. These encouragements cheered the men in blue. They felt the people were with them, just as a professional team gains confidence from the cheering of hometown fans. The men in blue were back home. The North had been invaded once again. The blue columns felt "Ours the duty to do justice to these hordes of gray-jackets; ours the task to drive them back into their land of slaves. . . ."

Such were the feelings of the army. "We were no longer the defeated of yesterday; we felt our selves predestined conquerors of the morrow. We were on the road to Gettysburg."[83]

But before we end the story of the march of the Third Corps, this last Sunday in June, we turn to the reflections of the Eleventh New Jersey, marching from the defense of Crampton's Gap from Burkittsville to Frederick. Something about the city that was home for Francis Scott Key excited the men from New Jersey. Frederick was the largest Maryland town they had entered on the Roads to Gettysburg. So the troops closed ranks, unfurled their flags, and "with bands playing and colors flying we marched through the city that gave birth to the author of the 'Star Spangled Banner.' "

Like the rest of the Third Corps, the brigade was greeted with demonstrations of delight. The residents of Frederick were surprised at the vast number of men in blue. One old gentleman waved a flag from an upper window exclaiming, "Look at that, look at that. Still they come. Still they come." Yes, that came to Frederick, men in blue, almost 100,000 strong. And on Sunday and Monday, the last of June, they marched beneath the shadows of the "clustered spires of Fredericktown."

Colonel Schoonover was overwhelmed by the reception given to the men in blue by the residents of Frederick County.

> There was enthusiasm in the towns and hospitality in the farm-houses. Cup after cup of water was passed to the thirsty soldiers from the many springs bursting out along the roadside. Up through the beautiful valleys and cozy towns we were welcomed with bright smiles and waving handkerchiefs. . . . A number of big-hearted women . . . provided a large quanity of sandwiches and handed them to the men as they passed by. This act of kindness and generosity brought forth repeated and hearty cheers from the ranks. . . . I am prepared to give my testimony in favor of Maryland sandwiches.[84]

I CORPS

John Reynolds was not around after Gettysburg to make a report. But Abner Doubleday, making the report after the battle, tells us that the First Corps left Middletown and camped at the western edge of Frederick, picketing the roads to the northwest.[85] Most of the First Corps left the Middletown Valley about 3:00 P.M. Part of the Second Division took an old road over the mountain which was very rough. Apparently this was the Old Shookstown Road.[86] For the Ninth Massachusetts the distance was nine miles.[87] It was dusk when the Ninth New York made camp one mile west of Frederick. Rufus Dawes mentions leaving the South Mountain area in great haste, and marching to Frederick "through a drizzling rain as usual."[88] That is all he says about the day although he makes these comments about Meade:

> General Meade as commander of the army was a surprise. Meade lacked the martial bearing and presence of Hooker. Few of our men knew him by sight. He was sometimes seen riding by the marching columns of troops at a fast trot, his hat brim turned down and a

poncho over his shoulders. The only sign of rank was a gold cord on his hat.[89]

The Sixteenth Maine was not as fortunate as some of the other units of the First Corps. The troops of the regiment spent Saturday night on picket near Middletown. They were not given the order to "fall in" until 7:00 P.M. They never reached Frederick until 2:00 A.M. on the twenty-ninth. Their historian says they had to march with but two hours sleep.[90]

As the First Corps headed east from Middletown, the Eighth Illinois Cavalry came in from the east, heading west toward Boonsboro. The riders dismounted and spent most of the day in Middletown, mingling with the people, shoeing their horses and refitting other equipment.[91]

Late in the afternoon a distinguished-looking man rode down West Second Street in Frederick. Dismounting near the intersection of Second and North Market he made a visit.

Catherine Reynolds tells us about it.

> I have been thinking of writing to you for the past three days to tell you how much I enjoyed Cousin John's brief visit. Judging of your feelings by my own, the most trivial circumstance of so dearly beloved a brother will be of interest to you. We have been in such a state of excitement and confusion since our capture and recapture that I do not remember what I wrote Ellie but I think I gave her particulars of the street skirmishes, etc. When we heard the Army of the Potomac was really coming my first and constant thought was, Now I shall see Cousin J.
>
> All day Saturday the Cavalry was passing up Market St. and I enquired of several of the soldiers who stopped to eat the bread and butter the ladies were sending out to them . . . if General Reynolds would be through. All who seemed to know anything about him said that he had gone with the infantry by way of Jefferson . . . so I gave up hope of seeing him for the time, although I had really been so confident that he was coming as to prepare a nice dinner. Saturday night we were kept awake by the noisy wagon trains and such a Sunday I never spent. There was scarcely any possibility of crossing the street for the countless multitudes who were pouring through. Quite unable to read for the noise and wearied after with looking, about 3 P.M. I undressed to try to get a nap. A few minutes after Clara came up and said General Reynolds was downstairs. It really seemed in my hurry as if I never should get ready to go down. I told Ann to set a table for lunch. Cousin looked very well, said he had returned from Jefferson the night before and would have come

329

around then but thought it was too late (but I had a room ready for him and wish so much he had come). He seemed to enjoy the . . . meal of cold roast beef, yellow pickle and cherry pie, said he had eaten nothing that morning being engaged in finding an encampment for his men . . . , promised to return to late tea after he had been to see his new Commander in Chief for orders and spoke as though they expected to be here for some time. . . . We waited for him until ½ past 9 o'clock, meanwhile Ann and I gave supper to 17 soldiers who came in at different times asking to buy bread as all the shops had sold out and they had nothing all day. It was truly a pleasure to supply their wants. One very intelligent old man said he had not eaten a meal at a table for 15 months . . . and would not forget how kind the ladies of Frederick were to them, so different from the Virginia ladies who used to throw stones at them. Another heard the church bells ringing and said, that sounded like home, we've had no Sunday for a year. Ann's gallon of coffee seemed quite to rest and revive them. I forgot to mention that three members of Cousin's staff who accompanied him, remained mounted while he stayed and I sent them a plate of sandwiches which no doubt amused our Secesh neighbors, but no matter.

Cousin did not return to supper, nor have I seen him since. Early next morning he left with his corps. . . .[92]

So it was late when John Reynolds finished his work for the day. It was after 10:00 P.M. when Winfield Scott Hancock and John Gibbon returned to Monocacy Junction after reporting to Meade at army headquarters on Prospect Hill.[93]

Wainwright left Middletown this morning and rode to Frederick to see Henry Hunt, the Union chief of artillery. It was his first opportunity to leave camp since leaving White Oak Church. While in Frederick he learned that the First Corps and his artillery brigade were ordered to Frederick. Charles rode back across the mountain, just in time to see his artillerymen leaving the field and hitting the road for Frederick. John Reynolds pitched his headquarters about a mile north of Frederick, with Wainwright and his batteries close by. Once again, this must have been on the Rose Hill Manor farm, the former home of Governor Thomas Johnson. Seventh Street was about the edge of Frederick at the time, and a mile beyond is Rose Hill.[94]

Wainwright and many others expected Hooker to go, but when he was removed, it took them by surprise. Some were

John Reynolds.

331

very outspoken in their criticism of Secretary of War Stanton. They considered him a dirty, underhanded villain. Meade was Wainwright's choice for a successor. But he did not expect Meade to get it, thinking that the Washington powers would bring in another general from the west. Wainwright met Webb and Stephen Weed at army headquarters during the day. Both were obviously proud of their newly acquired star.

Charles was amused at the way General Birney passed through Frederick with the Third Corps. First, there was a line of orderlies with drawn swords to clear the crowds, then a band, and finally General Birney and his staff with all "the pomp and circumstance of war." But in Frederick, Dan Sickles replaced Birney, so he stepped from the command of a corps back to division command.[95]

Chaplain Locke was enjoying the quiet and beauty of his camp near Mount Tabor Church, getting ready for a worship service with the Eleventh Pennsylvania when "the bugle disspelled delusion." The march to Frederick was completed just as the last rays of the sun went down in the west.[96]

Alfred Pleasonton was a busy man this last Sunday in June. Writing in *Annals of the War*, he states that he arrived in Frederick two days prior to the change of commanders. That would have brought him to Frederick on Friday. When Pleasonton conferred with Meade today, he says:

> I called his attention to a division of cavalry near Frederick City (3½ miles north) which he might place under my command, and I would like to have officers I would name specially assigned to it, as I am expected to have some desperate work to do. The General asserted to my request, and upon my naming the officers, he immediately telegraphed to have them appointed brigadier generals. This was his first dispatch to Washington, and on the day afterward, he received the reply making the appointments, and directing the officers to be assigned at once. They were Custer, Merritt, and Farnsworth; all three young captains, and two of them Custer and Farnsworth, my aides-de-camp.[97]

Thus it would seem that Custer and Farnsworth arrived with Pleasonton in Frederick on Friday, and were with him either in town or at the cavalry camp north of the city.

Throughout the day, detachments of Union cavalry rode

through Frederick, reporting to headquarters and the cavalry campsite three and a half miles northwest of Frederick on the Emmitsburg Road. Some were coming and others going. For instance, John Buford's First Cavalry Division was sent to Middletown after the infantry left. The brigade commanders were Col. William Gamble and Col. Thomas C. Devin. Wesley Merritt commanded the Reserve Brigade.

Gamble commanded the Eighth and Twelfth Illinois, the Third Indiana and the Eighth New York. Devin was in charge of the Sixth and Ninth New York, the Seventeenth Pennsylvania and two companies of the Third West Virginia. The First Division did not enter Frederick. It crossed the Potomac on Saturday using the upper pontoon bridge, traveled over terrible roads, and crossed the Monocacy near its mouth "by a wretched ford, and bivouacked on the east side of the mountains, three miles from Jefferson."[98] Stahel's wagon train blocked further progress. So on Sunday the First Division rode to Middletown where they spent the day shoeing the horses and refitting. In this position they covered the left of the army and protected the road leading to Hagerstown.[99]

Gregg's Second Division was at various points at or near the Baltimore Pike from Frederick to Ridgeville, about sixteen miles away. Col. John McIntosh commanded the First Brigade. One of his regiments, the First New Jersey, was the last unit in the Army of the Potomac to cross the river at Edwards Ferry. The men were in the saddle all of Saturday night, and crossed the river Sunday morning.[100] They then proceeded to Frederick.

Halting for a few hours' rest because of heat and fatigue, the men mounted up and by four o'clock were riding along the turnpike to Baltimore. Their task was to guard the right flank of the Army of the Potomac against any movement of J. E. B. Stuart. Some of Gregg's division spent the night at New Market.[101]

The Third Division under Judson Kilpatrick was in the field three and a half miles northeast of Frederick. This was the day of the big shake-up in the cavalry corps. Three young captains became brigadier generals.[102] Thirty-five hundred comprised this cavalry division. Elon J. Farnsworth, formerly of the Eighth Illinois, was assigned to command the Fifth New York, Eighteenth Pennsylvania, First Vermont, and ten companies of the First West Virginia. The next morning Farnsworth took his command to the Biggs Ford Road, across the Monocacy, and then most likely through Georgetown (now part of Walkersville) and entered the Woodsboro turnpike just north of Walkersville. But toward evening this last Sunday in June, Alfred Pleasonton and Kilpatrick reviewed the troops.

The Tenth New York Cavalry was happy to be in Frederick. They camped on the outskirts of the city and cooked their supper over "fires made from good, dry loyal rails." The area was swarming with men.[103]

We look now at the three new cavalry leaders. There is the possibility that it was in the field near Frederick that Custer received the surprise of his life.

Elon John Farnsworth came from rural America, the hamlet of Green Oak, Michigan. The date was July 30, 1837. Thus he was not quite twenty-six as he traveled the Roads to Gettysburg. He attended the University of Michigan for a brief period. He then joined the expedition against the Mormons as a civilian foragemaster. When the war broke out, he enlisted in his Uncle John's Eighth Illinois Cavalry. Soon he became an officer and served on the staff of Gen. Alfred Pleasonton. Biographical material is lacking on his rapid rise to general. Farnsworth's life would make an interesting study.

Pleasonton was extremely fond of young Farnsworth and supposedly loaned him a blouse with the shoulder straps of a brigadier general. Pleasonton wrote that nature made Elon a general. Commanding a brigade in Kilpatrick's division, Farnsworth battled Stuart in the streets of Hanover.

Then on the last day at Gettysburg, Kilpatrick sought an opportunity to turn the dagger into the remains of Pickett's charge. Ordering a charge over rough terrain into the face of almost certain death, Farnsworth carried out the foolish orders of Kilpatrick and met his death. This was one of the tragedies of Gettysburg and the war.

Fate was more kind to Wesley Merritt. Born on June 16,

1834, Merritt was also in his twenties on the Roads to Gettysburg. One of eleven children who was taken by his parents to Illinois, Merritt was appointed to West Point and graduated in the class of 1860. He was the second captain to be made a general on the eve of Gettysburg. A good officer, Merritt, only thirty years old in 1865, was selected with Philip Sheridan, along with John Gibbon and Joshua Chamberlain, to receive the Confederate surrender. After the war he spent thirty years on the frontier, and in 1895 was made a major general in the regular army. In addition to his service out west, he was superintendent of West Point, and commanded several military districts. Merritt also saw service in the Spanish-American War and commanded the first Philippine expedition. Farnsworth was cut down at Gettysburg, but Merritt survived to have a distinguished military career.[104]

The third youth who was promoted to brigadier general at the end of June was none other than George Armstrong Custer. During much of his boyhood he lived in Monroe, Michigan, and as an eighteen-year-old taught school in Ohio. Custer apparently owed his appointment to West Point to the father of a young lady who wanted to get Custer out of the picture. His career at West Point was not very impressive. Custer seemed to disregard discipline. He accumulated demerits right and left. But he was lucky, showing bravery and leadership at First Bull Run, and then serving on the staffs of McClellan and Alfred Pleasonton. So he knew the brass. He did serve with distinction in the Civil War and cut off Lee's escape route from Appomattox. In 1866 Custer was appointed lieutenant colonel of the newly formed Seventh Cavalry. The rest of his controversial career is history.[105]

When Lee crossed the Potomac, H. H. Lockwood was placed in command of a brigade of Maryland troops along with the 150th New York; moving from Baltimore to Monocacy Bridge to await the arrival of the Army of the Potomac. Soon they saw the long wagon trains, and nightfall brought a sight the men would long remember. From a high hill, perhaps near Jug Bridge, they were amazed to behold the vast number of wagons and cannons. "Thousands of campfires lighted up the region around, and we stood spell bound at the sight of the vast enginery of war that was before us. It was in this camp, inspired by this spectacle, we first imbibed the true spirit of war, and nerved ourselves for the trying scenes we knew we must encounter." Lockwood's command was assigned to Slocum's Twelfth Corps.[106]

Charles Coffin saw Meade and Hooker this memorable Sunday morning. He was present when the command of the Army of the Potomac was formerly transferred.

> It was a surprise. No one thought there could be such an event. It was a position of great responsibility which had come to him (Meade). He knew nothing as to what General Hooker's plans were; he only knew that the army was marching; that before many days there must be a great battle. . . . He was standing with bowed head and downcast eyes, his slouched hat drawn down, shading his features. He seemed lost in thought. His uniform was the worse for wear from hard service; there was dust upon his boots. As a faithful soldier; loyal to duty, he accepted the great responsibility; while General Hooker, shaking hands with him and with his officers, with the tears coursing down his cheeks, bade them farewell. . . .[107]

Assuming command of the Army of the Potomac, not knowing where all the units were, or the Confederates either, must have been a traumatic experience for George G. Meade. We can imagine that he must have felt like Lyndon Johnson when he became president after the death of John F. Kennedy. Meade issued an order on Sunday, June 28, stating:

> By direction of the President of the United States, I hereby assume command of the Army of the Potomac. . . . As a soldier in obeying this order—an order unexpected and unsolicited—I have no promises or pledges to make.
>
> The country looks to this army to relieve it from the devastation and disgrace of a foreign invasion. Whatever fatigues and sacrifices we may be called on to undergo, let us have in view constantly the magnitude of the interests involved and let each man determine to do his duty, leaving to an all-controlling Providence the direction of the contest.[108]

When Lee crossed the Potomac, the Union army with that name received all kinds of abuse for permitting the Confederate crossing to occur. The invasion was the main topic of discussion on the street corners, in the stores, blacksmith shops, and at village crossroads.

Worman's Mill—bivouac for the
Eleventh Corps, June 28.

Center Square in Hanover.

337

As the Confederates penetrated deeper into Pennsylvania, ministers and journalists criticized the Union army all the more, but appealed to the soldiers to throw back the invader.

Theodore Gerrish, a member of the Twentieth Maine, and after the war a distinguished clergyman, said:

> It was the most critical moment in the history of our country. General Lee, with a veteran army . . . flushed with victory, was on Northern soil; behind him was a desperate South, determined to make his campaign successful. Our foreign relations were in a critical condition. England and France were both in active sympathy with the South, and were only awaiting a decisive rebel victory to acknowledge the Confederacy as a nation, and then raise the blockade. A portion of the people had been opposed to the war from the beginning, and our repeated defeats had strengthed their opposition. Some feared that Lee would be able to dictate peace terms.[109]

The Monday morning quarterbacks called for the Army of the Potomac to fight if necessary to the last drop of blood. When the soldiers read these statements they said, "Yes, they want us to shed our blood, but they are not willing to shed theirs." Some of the men in blue advocated sending new units to meet the Army of Northern Virginia comprised of men like Henry Ward Beecher and Horace Greeley.[110]

But Meade was at a point of no return. He was forced to move ahead to meet Lee, who this very night upon hearing that the Army of the Potomac was in Maryland, started to move his army from York, Carlisle, and Chambersburg on the Roads to Gettysburg.[111]

Ever mindful of the possibility of a surprise attack, Meade made the following dispositions "for guarding the approaches to Frederick against any possible dash of cavalry:

"From Monocacy Junction to the bridge above Carroll Creek, near L. M. Thomas's, Second Corps.

"From Thomas's to George Schultz's, on the road to Hamburg, Eleventh Corps.

"From (Schultz's) to the Middletown Road, near D. R. Miller's, First Corps.

"From (Miller's) to Zimmerman's, on the Ballenger Creek, Twelfth Corps.

"From (Zimmerman's), to connect with the Second Corps, by Ballenger Creek and the Monocacy, Fifth Corps."

The corps commanders were instructed to carefully guard their trains and camps on marches and halts. Staff officers from each corps were instructed to bring morning and evening reports. All units were instructed to be ready to move at daylight. In fact, the First, Eleventh, Twelfth, Second, and Third corps were ordered to move at 4:00 A.M. Headquarters and the Fifth Corps would move out at 8:00 A.M.[112]

No time was to be lost. Indeed, time could not be lost. Meade therefore had the following order delivered to the army:

Headquarters Army of the Potomac
Frederick, Md.
June 28, 1863

The army will march tomorrow as follows:

4 a.m. The 1st Corps, Major General Reynolds by Lewistown and Mechanicstown to Emmetsburg, keeping to the left of the road from Frederick to Lewistown, between J. P. Cramer's and where the road branches to Utica and Creagerstown, to enable the 11th Corps to march parallel to it.

4 a.m. The 11th Corps, Major General Howard, by Utica and Creagerstown to Emmetsburg.

4 a.m. The 12th Corps, by Ceresville, Walkersville and Woodsborough to Taneytown.

4 a.m. The 3rd Corps by Woodsborough and Middleburg (from Walkersville), to Taneytown.

4 a.m. The 2nd Corps, by Johnsville, Liberty and Union, to Frizzleburg.

The 5th Corps will follow the 2nd Corps, moving at 8 a.m., camping at Union.

The 6th Corps, by roads to the right of the 5th and 2nd Corps, to New Windsor.

The Reserve Artillery will precede the 12th Corps, at 4 a.m., and camp between Middleburg and Taneytown.

General Lockwood, with his command, will report to and march with the 12th Corps.

The Engineers and bridge-trains will follow the 5th Corps.

Headquarters will move at 8 a.m. and be tomorrow night at Middleburg. Headquarter's train will move by Ceresville and Woodsborough to Middleburg, at 8 a.m.

The Cavalry will guard the left and right flanks and the rear, and give the Commanding General information of the movement and of the enemy in front.

Corps commanders and commanders of detached brigades will report by staff officer their positions tomorrow night and on all marches in future.

339

The corps moving on the different lines will keep up communication from time to time, if necessary. They will camp in position, and guard their camps. Corps commanders will send out scouts in their front. . . .[113]

XI CORPS

Sunday found Oliver O. Howard's Eleventh Corps in Middletown Valley. Barlow's and Schurz's division were near Middletown, while Steinwehr was holding Fox's and Turner's gaps. About 2:00 P.M. orders were received to march to Frederick. The head of the column left Middletown at 3:00 P.M., and moved north of Frederick, going into camp around 8:00 P.M. The historic old mill is still standing at the junction of the Emmitsburg Road and Baltimore Pike.[114]

Steinwehr's brigade had rougher going. Smith's Seventy-third Ohio Infantry and other units did not get under way until 4:40. Instead of a nine-mile march, they had sixteen miles to cover. They did not reach camp until almost midnight, having been held up by the wagon trains of the Eleventh Corps which had preceded them.[115] Thus the rumble of wagons and the tramp of men went on through the streets of Frederick until the end of the last Sunday in June of '63.

With the arrival of the Eleventh Corps the Army of the Potomac was "all present and accounted for," around "the Clustered Spires of Fredericktown." Tomorrow the army would move on three diverging roads, keeping itself between the enemy and the big cities of the east. This was Sunday, June 28, 1863.

XI

THE COMMANDERS

This book is not intended as a critique of military strategy or persons involved. The book was written to describe the Roads to Gettysburg, and what it was like getting there.

However, we must say that Gettysburg was almost Antietam in reverse as far as leadership. Antietam was probably Robert E. Lee's best conducted battle, whereas McClellan threw his units into action on a piecemeal basis instead of one all-out coordinated offensive. At Gettysburg, it seems as though the Confederate troops went into action one unit at a time, while Meade and his leaders made the right move at the right time.

Jackson was at Antietam with Lee, and Longstreet was fighting the defensive battle he loved. At Gettysburg, Lee has two new corps commanders. Richard S. Ewell, commanding the old Second Corps, had been severely wounded earlier in the war, and was definitely a fighter. He had flashes of brilliance. But they were few and far between. At Winchester, the men in the Confederate ranks thought "another Jackson had come." But at Gettysburg on the evening of the first day, and again the next day, they sorely missed "Old Jack." A. P. Hill was one of the best division commanders of the war. But he never showed that promise at the head of a corps. Longstreet, it seems, was opposed to any aggressive action. His method of warfare was "let the enemy come to you." With perhaps two and a half strikes against him in the personages of his corps commanders, Lee confounded matters even more by not making his orders clear. He was too discretionary for his own good.

341

Meade, on the other hand, had excellent lieutenants in Winfield Scott Hancock, John Reynolds, and John Sedgwick. Skyes, a regular army man, was also dependable. Slocum, Howard, and Sickles were not in the same class. But Reynolds led the early fighting, and then for the rest of the battle, Hancock, until wounded, performed in a tremendous fashion.

What kind of men were at the head of the three Confederate army corps as they marched on the Roads to Gettysburg? We have looked briefly at them, but let's take a deeper look. Longstreet, Ewell, and Hill were graduates of West Point. They were brave men, but perhaps not made to be corps commanders.

James Longstreet graduated from West Point in 1842. He served in Florida, was wounded in the War with Mexico, and then served on the frontier and in skirmishes against the Indians.

He failed during the fighting at Fair Oaks and Seven Pines in the summer of 1862. He was dilatory at Second Manassas and prevented even a larger Confederate victory. He was alright at Sharpsburg and Fredericksburg because he held strong defensive positions. This was his idea of warfare. Serving briefly in North Carolina, he showed little ability for independent command.

Longstreet was very much opposed to the second invasion of the North. He favored a strategic offensive in Virginia, reinforcing Bragg in Tennessee, and an offensive under Lee's direction in the West. He was almost like a stubborn child in the Gettysburg campaign. Many Confederates hated him until his dying day for his delays on the second day at Gettysburg, and his failure to support Pickett's charge. A person of lesser stature than Lee would probably have dismissed Longstreet. Perhaps it would have been best. But in June of 1863, Longstreet, with all his faults, was Lee's only experienced corps commander. During the rest of the war, he did little to gain any laurels as a commander.

Longstreet lived until 1904, serving abroad for a time as United States Minister to Turkey. Because of Gettysburg and other failures, he does not go down in history as one of the leading figures of the war.[1]

Richard S. Ewell was another Virginian. He was past forty when the Civil War broke out. Graduating from West Point in 1840 he was assigned to the First Dragoons. Like so many others, he served on the frontier and then against the Indians. He resigned from the United States Army on May 7, 1861. His duties were to instruct the cavalry.

Serving under Jackson, he seemed to be a competent officer. A brave man, he carried out his orders well. Ewell was severely wounded at Second Manassas. In fact, he lost his leg in this engagement. He was unable to return to action until May of 1863. Coming back on the twenty-third of the month, he was given command of Jackson's Second Corps. He had to be lifted into his saddle and then strapped to it.

He led the corps on the Roads to Gettysburg to Carlisle. He had been stationed here earlier, and took great delight in replacing the Stars and Stripes with the Stars and Bars of the Confederacy. He has received much criticism in his failure to follow up the success of his corps on the first day at Gettysburg, and also for failure to attack earlier on July 2. Many feel that he frittered away many precious hours, causing Confederate victory at Gettysburg to go down the drain.

Like Hill, he achieved no notable successes as a corps commander. He was wounded again at Kelly's Ford, and was hurt in a fall from his horse at Spotsylvania. Ewell was then given command of the defenses of Richmond. On the retreat to Appomattox, he was captured at Sayler's Creek on April 2.

Ewell was called "Old Baldy." Like Hill, he suffered a lot of physical distress. Hill's may have been malaria or psychosomatic on the eve of large battles as a corps commander, but Ewell constantly complained of headaches and sleepless nights. At Winchester, early in the Gettysburg campaign, Ewell looked like another Jackson, but never again did he resemble "Stonewall."[2]

Only thirty-five at the outbreak of the Civil War, Hill rose in rank like a meteor flashing across the sky. In ninety days he rose from colonel of the Thirteenth Virginia to the rank of major general in command of the Light Division, one of the best units in the Army of Northern Virginia. He loved combat and was never happier than when in action.

Ambrose Powell Hill was born November 9, 1825. His place of birth is uncertain, though many historians feel it was in the Culpeper, Virginia, area. From his mother, Hill inherited a "small physique and a proud, sensitive nature." As a boy he hunted and fished in the nearby Rapidan and Rappahannock rivers. From his father he learned horsemanship. This later prompted one of his men to say, "He was a perfect picture in the saddle and the most graceful rider I ever saw."

Before he was seventeen years old, Powell Hill was a cadet at West Point. His roommate was George B. McClellan, son of a Philadelphia doctor. George Pickett was in the class and Thomas Jonathan Jackson was still a student on the banks of the Hudson.

While at West Point, Hill was stricken with a disease that caused him to miss several months of classes. This in turn led to a repeat of his second class year. His new classmates were Ambrose Burnside and Henry Heth.

Graduating fifteenth in a class of thirty-eight, Hill was ordered to report to Mexico as an artillery officer. Then it was duty in the South, and service against the Seminoles.

Hill was always fond of lovely women. One who especially caught his eye was Ellen B. Marcy, better known as Nelly. But others were after Miss Nelly, including Hill's former roommate at West Point, George B. McClellan. Father Marcy did not like Hill. He tried hard, and finally successfully to break up the romance. The winner was McClellan. But Hill made him pay on the battlefields of the war.

Hill believed firmly in States' Rights. Slavery was not involved in his thinking. As the war approached he talked to his friend McClellan about his views and the issues at hand. When Virginia passed an ordinance of seccession on April 17, 1861, Hill immediately offered his services to his home state. Like so many other potential Confederate leaders, he was ordered to Harpers Ferry. There he was assigned the command of the Thirteenth Virginia.

He rendered valuable service at Second Manassas. At Antietam, the arrival of the Light Division saved Lee's army

344

from destruction. The command marched seventeen miles in seven hours, forded the Potomac, and struck the Union army in the flank. Hill, picturesque in his red battle shirt, had perhaps his greatest day on the hills above Sharpsburg. He also hurled the Union advance across the Potomac, back to the Maryland shore. This occurred when McClellan tried to follow Lee. Hill was getting his revenge on McClellan for taking Nelly away.

At Chancellorsville he was in the thick of the action, taking command of the Second Corps briefly when Jackson fell. However, Hill was wounded also. Then on May 26, 1863, Ambrose Powell Hill became a lieutenant general and was placed in command of the newly created Third Corps of the Army of the Potomac.

He never quite lived up to expectations as a corps commander. He was plagued with sickness from time to time. Freeman says, "He does not fail beyond excuse or explanation; he does not succeed. . . . It may be because of ill health, or sense of a larger, overburdening responsibility."

Returning to action from a sick bed, Hill was killed near Petersburg on April 2, 1865. When the news was given to Lee, the commanding general shed tears. Later, near death, he, like Jackson, was to mention the name, A. P. Hill.[3]

Joseph Hooker, like his predecessors who commanded the Army of the Potomac, left a lot to be desired. Troop morale dropped very low after Chancellorsville. When Lincoln asked Hooker about future movements against Lee, the replies were vague and almost insulting.

Lincoln at last told Hooker that some of the corps and division commanders had lost confidence in him. This came as a shock to "Fighting Joe." He just could not believe what he was hearing. This revelation made Hooker feel that his days as commander were numbered. He saw the handwriting on the wall. General Webb campaigned for Meade on the basis of his leadership at Fredericksburg, stating too, that Meade had urged Hooker not to withdraw after Chancellorsville.

Governor Andrew Curtin of Pennsylvania carried a great deal of political weight during the Civil War. He was much displeased with Hooker and urged the appointment of a Pennsylvanian to the command of the army. He championed the cause of George G. Meade and John Fulton Reynolds. Curtin liked Reynolds and had succeeded in getting him relieved from army command during the Antietam campaign to take over the Pennsylvania militia in Harrisburg.

Meade confessed that "Hooker has disappointed the army and myself. . . . I am very sorry for Hooker because I like him and my relations have always been agreeable with him." Nevertheless, Meade felt Hooker had missed a golden opportunity at Chancellorsville.

Curtin went to Washington and told all who would listen that the Army of the Potomac no longer had confidence in Hooker. He said this included Meade and Reynolds. Word of the visit and the remarks got back to Hooker. He made a visit to Meade's tent to confront him with the issue. Meade said, "You know we differ in judgement. . . . You have no right to complain about me expressing my views to others."

The *New York Herald* reported that four corps commanders had opposed the retreat from Chancellorsville, including Reynolds and Meade. Slocum and Couch were very outspoken in their criticism of Hooker, In fact, they asked Meade to go with them to see President Lincoln and General Halleck. Meade refused. But Couch went to see Lincoln and asked for the removal of Hooker.

Meade was summoned to visit Lincoln and Halleck. The three men spent two hours discussing the general state of affairs. Little was said about Chancellorsville. It seems as though Mr. Lincoln wanted to get to know what manner of man he was dealing with in the person of George G. Meade.

Reynolds, from past experience, had no time for those in Washington who were trying to run the war. Margaret Meade, the general's sister, echoed this feeling. When she heard George was being considered for top command she said, "Do not accept it—it would only be your ruin."[4]

Rumors got out that if Meade was not the next commander, Reynolds would be. But John Fulton Reynolds was not about to let that happen. He went directly to President Lincoln, talked very freely with him, and told him that he did not want to command the army, and would not accept it unless given free rein. Reynolds felt that the commanders in the field had to be free to move as situations developed, and not on the whims of the folks in Washington.

Many scholars feel that had Reynolds not made the trip, he would have been the next commander of the Army of the Potomac. The visit with the president was made on June 2. A month later his body was on the way to Lancaster for burial.

In the meantime Lee had made a fateful decision. His troops were ready to march northward to the Potomac. Soon 169 infantry regiments, seven cavalry brigades, and thirteen battalions of Confederate artillery would be on the Roads to Gettysburg. Lee believed in himself and in his men. The Army of the Potomac had confidence in themselves, but doubted the leadership ability of Hooker and the folks in Washington.

Relations between Hooker and his corps commanders were strained. An air of suspicion and distrust was in the air. General Couch was transferred. Things were reaching a breaking point, but another three weeks were to pass before that break came.

The man to whom the plight of the nation fell in this dark hour, was born in Cadiz, Spain, on December 31, 1815. His father had been a wealthy American merchant. But when the Napoleonic wars came, the elder Meade's allegiance to the cause of Spain spelled his financial ruin.

George Gordon Meade was able to go to Mount Hope Preparatory School in Baltimore. Then it was on to West Point. Graduating in 1835, Meade had tours of duty in Florida and Massachusetts. But he was never crazy about a military career. So he resigned and became a civil engineer. But this did not bring him happiness either. So he went back into the army.

From 1842 until 1861, with the exception of the Mexican War, Meade engaged in coastal and geodetic work, constructing lighthouses and breakwaters.

On August 31, 1861, Gov. Andrew Curtin of Pennsylvania made Meade a brigadier general of volunteers. He saw continuous service from then until Gettysburg. He was severely wounded on the peninsula, led a division at Antietam and Fredericksburg, and then commanded the Fifth Corps at Chancellorsville. His roll at Gettysburg is described in these pages. He was condemned for not following Lee immediately after Gettysburg. His success after crossing the Potomac was not spectacular either. Then in the spring of 1864, Grant was made commander in chief of all United States armies. Grant made his headquarters with the Army of the Potomac. After the war, Meade was in charge of the military division of the Atlantic. He died in Philadelphia in 1872.[5]

John Fulton Reynolds, now in the prime of life, led the Union First Corps from Frederick to Lewistown, to Mechanicstown, Emmitsburg, and Marsh Creek to the fields of Gettysburg. In a sense he was going home. A native of Pennsylvania, Reynolds had been born and raised in the Lancaster area. In fact, he was going home to stay. Life was running out for Reynolds.

Reynolds was born on September 20, 1820. Twenty-one years later, in 1841, he graduated from the United States Military Academy at West Point. For the next four years he did garrison duty on the Atlantic Coast. Then it was on to the Texas frontier.

In 1860, Reynolds received a high honor. He was named commandant of the Corps of Cadets. His stay at West Point was brief as the terrible Civil War broke out.

During the fighting on the peninsula in the summer of 1862, Reynolds was captured, and held prisoner for several months. He was released in time to return to Pennsylvania in an effort to raise militia forces to fight against Lee's first invasion of the North.

At Fredericksburg he commanded the First Corps. Meade's division of the Corps was the only one to really dent the great Confederate defensive line.[6]

John Reynolds was apparently offered the command of the Union Army of the Potomac after Chancellorsville. However, he declined, feeling there would be too much interference from Washington.

When Meade took command on June 28, he made his good friend Reynolds commander of the left wing of the army, or in charge of the First, Third, and Eleventh corps. Meade wanted someone he knew, someone he could trust, to be in charge.

On July 1 Reynolds received a message from John Buford saying Union cavalry had found the Confederates in force just west of Gettysburg. Reynolds immediately ordered the left wing of the army forward.

About ten o'clock, Reynolds arrived on the field in McPherson's woods west of town and near the Chambersburg Road. While placing the leading regiment, the Second Wisconsin, in position, Reynolds was hit by a Confederate sharpshooter and killed instantly. His death was a stunning blow to Meade and to the army. His body was taken back to the Dobbin house, thence down the Taneytown Road and back to Lancaster for burial. Thus passed one of the best generals of the war.

After Reynolds's tragic death, Meade ordered Winfield Scott Hancock, another Pennsylvanian, to Gettysburg. His orders were to assess the situation and take command of the field. Hancock did so in an excellent manner. In fact, the difference between a Confederate victory at Gettysburg may well have been that Meade had Hancock, while Lee had no one like him.

Three times Hancock saved the day at Gettysburg. When he arrived on July 1, Reynolds was dead, the First Corps had suffered huge losses, and the Eleventh Corps had been routed. Hancock seized control of things and stabilized conditions until reinforcements could arrive. Of course he was aided by the fact that Ewell and Hill did not press their victory. Realizing that Cemetery Hill and Cemetery Ridge were the keys to the battlefield, Hancock ordered a line of defense prepared. When the Confederates did attack, it was too late. The next day, July 2, Hancock, now commanding the left of the Union line, prevented Longstreet from turning the flank. He also helped Sickles in his exposed position. Then on July 3, Hancock commanded the center of the Union line and met the thrust of Pickett's charge. He was painfully wounded during this fighting.

Winfield Scott Hancock, riding at the head of the famed

Second Corps through Frederick and Carroll counties to Gettysburg, was in the mind of the author, the key man at Gettysburg.

Hancock came from rural America. He was born at Montgomery Square, Pennsylvania, on February 14, 1824. Shortly after his birth, the family moved to Norristown; from that city he entered West Point, graduating in 1844.

Tours of duty followed in Indian country. Then he was honored for bravery in the War with Mexico. He saw service in Kansas and Utah, and was then made chief quartermaster for Los Angeles. When the war came he was given a Union command.

At Antietam he was given command of a division of the Second Corps after "Fighting Dick" Richardson was wounded near Bloody Lane. We have already mentioned his bravery at Gettysburg. Throughout the war, he and the Second Corps were conspicuous for gallantry in action.

When the war ended, Hancock remained in the service, and saw duty across the United States. In 1877 he was named commander of the Department of the East, being in command of the United States forces on the eastern seaboard.

Several times Hancock received high numbers of votes at the Democratic National Convention. In 1880 he was nominated as the party's presidential candidate. Running against James Garfield, he lost a very close election.[7]

As we consider the commanders at Gettysburg, "Hancock the Superb" was perhaps the best man on the field at that time.

Commanding the Third Corps of the Union army was the playboy opportunist, Daniel Edgar Sickles of New York City. He attended New York University. Sickles studied law but quickly saw that the way to fame and fortune was in politics with the "in" group.

Hooking up with Tammany group, he advanced quickly and at the age of twenty-eight, Sickles became corporation counsel for the city. He resigned and went to London as the secretary of the legation there. Brief stints followed as a New York State senator and then as a congressman from 1857-1861.

He and his wife became the talk of Washington. Dan was fond of all the women. But he became enraged when he found his wife was playing around too. One day he shot down the son of Francis Scott Key, his wife's boyfriend. This was in the shadow of the White House. A fiery court case followed. Sickles was defended by Edwin M. Stanton. Sickles was freed on the basis that a man has the right to defend his home and his honor.

When the war came, Sickles wanted to be where the action was. He wanted the publicity. He was soon made a brigadier general of volunteers. Although he had no prior military training, he proved to be a good leader of men. He was fearless in combat, and a close friend of "Fighting Joe" Hooker. Naturally his mouth got him into trouble as he was quick to criticize and disagree with others. His advance on Jackson at Chancellorsville left the flank of the Eleventh Corps exposed for "Old Jack's" sudden attack. Meade reprimanded him for not moving quickly enough on the road to Gettysburg, and then Sickles pulled away from the Round Tops and moved to the famous Peach Orchard. This was in direct violation of orders. As a result, the Third Corps was almost wiped out. Only a valiant fight by other units saved Little Round Top, and Sickles himself lost a leg. His movement to the Peach Orchard, contrary to orders from army headquarters, set off a controversy between himself and General Meade. To some, he was the man who almost lost Gettysburg, while to others he was the man who saved the battle.

The loss of his leg meant the end of combat command. After his recovery from the wound, Lincoln sent him to Union held Southern territory for an appraisal of "amnesty, Negro progress, and Reconstruction."

After diplomatic duty in Columbia, Sickles became military governor of South Carolina. He retired in 1869. President Grant appointed him minister to Spain where he became a very close friend of Isabella, former queen of Spain.

When he came back to New York, Sickles served another term as a congressman. For many years he was chairman of the New York State Monuments Commission. He was removed from office in 1912 at the age of ninety-three on speculation charges. However, he continued to speak about Gettysburg, his role there, and about the Civil War. Sometimes he took the leg he lost at Gettysburg with him. On other occasions he went to a museum in Washington to see the leg. Sickles died in 1914.[8]

George Sykes, the commander of the Fifth Corps, was born on October 9, 1822, at Dover, Delaware. He entered West Point in 1838. Sykes was part of a class which gave twelve corps and army commanders to the Union and Confederate causes.

Sykes, like many others, saw service against the Seminoles and on frontier posts. During the Mexican War, he won honors for gallantry. At First Bull Run, he commanded a battalion of the Fourteenth Infantry. This unit covered the Union retreat from the field, rendering perhaps the best service of the day.

When Meade was elevated to the command of the Army of the Potomac, Sykes was selected to lead the Fifth Corps. He led his men on the Roads to Gettysburg and supported Sickles's exposed Third Corps. The Twentieth Maine of his command helped to save Little Round Top.

Later Meade found him too slow and unaggressive. Thus Sykes was sent to Kansas. After the war he commanded the Twentieth Infantry in Texas and Minnesota. He died in 1880, and is buried at West Point.[9]

"Uncle John" Sedgwick commanded the Sixth Corps as the armies marched north to Gettysburg. Not only was he a good general, but one of the best loved officers in the Army of the Potomac. Sedgwick came from the Connecticut Berkshires. He was born at Cornwall Hollow on September 13, 1813.

Graduating from West Point in 1837, John saw service against the Seminoles, the Cherokees, and on various outposts. He served with distinction in the Mexican War. When the Army was enlarged in 1855, Sedgwick was promoted to major of the First Cavalry. The commander was Col. Robert Edward Lee of Virginia.

Leading a division of the Second Corps on the peninsula, Sedgwick was wounded. Again at Antietam, he suffered

352

serious wounds, and was sent back to Cornwall Hollow to recover.

During the Gettysburg campaign, "Uncle John" led the largest unit of the Army of the Potomac, the Sixth Corps. Marching from Manchester, Maryland, to the scene of the action, the Sixth Corps received the well-deserved title of "The Foot Cavalry of the Army." That march will be described in detail later.

Sedgwick continued to lead with skill and devotion until May 9, 1864. Then came that fatal morning when he stepped from his headquarters tent to be struck by a bullet below the left eye. This was a sad day for his command, the army, and the country. His body was returned to Cornwall Hollow and the area where he once said, "Here I would be content to spend the rest of my life."[10]

The commander of the Eleventh Corps was another New Englander, Otis O. Howard. He was born on November 8, 1830, in Leeds, Maine. He worked his way through Bowdoin College, and graduated in 1850. Then it was on to West Point. His classmates were Dorsey Pender, John Pegram and James Ewell Brown Stuart.

Academically inclined, Howard spent most of the 1850s at West Point as an assistant in the math department. When the war broke out he was with the ordnance department.

"Constantly in hot water" is the best way to describe his Civil War record. Howard had a knack of getting in trouble, but then getting out again, often to his advantage. He made numerous tactical errors as well as errors in judgement. Yet he was not demoted or rebuked. His Eleventh Corps broke and ran at Gettysburg as they did at Chancellorsville. However, Howard received the thanks of Congress for his role in the Pennsylvania battle.

Like Sedgwick, Howard was wounded during the Peninsula campaign, losing an arm at Seven Pines. Although a brave man himself, his troops did not stand like a stonewall. They were routed at Chancellorsville. Other soldiers joked and said, "I run with the Germans or with the Eleventh Corps." In fairness we must say that the Eleventh Corps was a victim of Jackson's flanking movement. But because they ran, they received some scorn from their comrades-in-arms. Gettysburg was almost a repeat of Chancellorsville for the Eleventh Corps. Long after the war, the critics talked of the flight from Barlow's Knoll back into the streets of Gettysburg. Loyal members of the corps sought to dispute this. But Howard came out of it all with the thanks of Congress. How lucky can you get?

Howard was sent to the west. William T. Sherman assigned him to the command of the army of Tennessee. When the war ended, Howard became deeply concerned about the plight of the freed Negro. An abolitionist since West Point days, and deeply religious, he felt something had to be done for the blacks. So he was thankful when President Andrew Johnson appointed him the first commissioner of the Freedmen Bureau. But with the hatred and desire for revenge that followed the war, he was powerless to fight the graft in his department.

Next came duty on the plains against the Indians. Then he was named superintendent of the Corps of Cadets at West Point. Retiring after that tour of duty, Howard lived in Burlington, Vermont. He devoted himself to the establishment of Lincoln Memorial University in Harrogate, Tennessee. Howard wanted the poor youth of the mountains to be able to get an education. He died in 1909.[11]

The commander of the Twelfth Corps, Henry Warner Slocum, was born on September 24, 1827, at Delphi, Onondaga County, New York. He attended the local schools, taught school for awhile, and then in 1848 obtained an appointment to the United States Military Academy. He graduated in 1852. Tours of duty against the Seminoles and in Charleston Harbor followed.

He resigned from the service in 1856 to practice law. Slocum moved to Syracuse where he served as county treasurer, as state legislator, and as an instructor of the New York militia. He drilled the artillery.

When the Civil War started, Slocum became colonel of the Twenty-seventh New York and was mustered into service at Elmira. The unit suffered heavy losses at First Bull Run. Slocum was numbered among the wounded.

Returning to duty he was given command of a brigade. In July of 1862 he was promoted to major-general at the tender age of thirty-four. Although never spectacular, Slocum got the job done. He was consistent and dependable on the peninsula, at Second Bull Run and Antietam.

Following the battle of Antietam, Slocum was appointed commander of the Twelfth Corps. His command lost heavily at Chancellorsville. After the battle, he became very outspoken in his criticism of Joseph Hooker.

Coming from Littlestown to Gettysburg, Slocum and the Twelfth Corps occupied the extreme right of the Union line at Culp's Hill and across the Baltimore Pike.

After Gettysburg, Slocum served in the western theater of operations under Sherman. He led the left wing of the army during the march to the sea.

When the war ended, Slocum moved to Brooklyn where he practiced law. He also served New York as a democratic congressman. Slocum was a member of the Gettysburg Battle Monuments Commission. He died on April 14, 1894.

One of the classic accounts of the Gettysburg campaign is that of Frank A. Haskell. Born in Vermont in 1828, he graduated from Dartmouth College in the class of 1854. Moving to Wisconsin he entered law practice. Enlisting in the army in the summer of 1861, Haskell was commissioned first lieutenant in Company I of the Sixth Wisconsin. This regiment soon became a part of the famed Iron Brigade. A man of great ability, Haskell soon became a staff officer, and won the praise of Generals Gibbon and Hancock for his bravery at Gettysburg. Haskell describes the generals of the Army of the Potomac for us.

> Meade is a tall man, with full beard, which with his hair, orginally brown, is quite thickly sprinkled with gray—has a Romanish face, very large nose, and a . . . large forehead, prominent and wide over the eyes, which are full and large, and quick in their movements, and he wears spectacles. His fibres are all of the long and sinewy kind. . . . It would be rather difficult to make him look well dressed.
>
> Sedgwick is quite a heavy man, short, thick-set and muscular, with florid complexion, dark, calm, straight looking eyes, with full, heavish features, which, with his eyes, have plenty of animation when he is aroused. He has a magnificent profile, . . . curly, short,

355

chestnut hair and full beard, cut short, with a little gray in it. He dresses carelessly, but can look magnificently when he is well dressed. Like Meade, he looks and is, honest and modest. You might see at once, why his men, because they love him, call him "Uncle John," not to his face, of course, but among themselves.

Slocum is small, rather spare, with black, straight hair and beard. . . . His movements are quick and angular, and he dresses with a significant degree of elegance. Howard is medium in size, has nothing marked about him, is the youngest of them all . . . has lost an arm in the war, has straight brown hair and beard . . . and on the whole appears a very pleasant, affiable, well dressed little gentleman.

Hancock is the tallest and most shapely, and in many respects is the best looking officer of them all. His hair is very light brown, straight and moist, and always looks well. . . . He wears the moustache with a tuft upon the chin; complexion ruddy, features neither large or small, but well cut . . . deep blue eyes, and a very mobile, emotional countenance. He always dresses remarkably well, and his manner is dignified, gentlemanly and commanding. . . .

Sykes is a small, rather thin man, well dressed and gentlemany, brown hair and beard, which he wears full, . . . feeble blue eyes, long nose, with a general air of one who is weary and a little ill natured. . . . Pleasonton is quite a nice little dandy, with brown hair and beard, a straw hat with a little jockey rim, which he cocks upon one side of his head with an unsteady eye, that looks slyly at you and then dodges.[12]

These, then, were the men who led the Army of the Potomac and the Army of Northern Virginia on the Roads to Gettysburg:

	Birth	Death	West Point Class
Robert Edward Lee	January 19, 1807	October 12, 1870	1829
James Longstreet	January 8, 1821	January 2, 1904	1838
Richard S. Ewell	February 8, 1817	January 25, 1872	1840
Ambrose Powell Hill	November 9, 1825	April 2, 1865	1847
George Gordon Meade	December 31, 1815	November 6, 1872	1835
John Fulton Reynolds	September 20, 1820	July 1, 1863	1842
Winfield Scott Hancock	February 14, 1824	February 9, 1886	1844
Daniel Edgar Sickles	October 20, 1822	May 3, 1914	
George Sykes	October 9, 1822	February 8, 1880	1842
John Sedgwick	September 13, 1813	May 8, 1864	1837
Otis O. Howard	November 8, 1830	October 26, 1809	1854
Henry Warner Slocum	September 24, 1827	April, 1894	1852

From this we can see that Sickles was the only corps commander not to graduate from West Point. Meade, Reynolds, and Hancock were going home to fight on their native soil.

XII

A RAINY MONDAY

Monday–June 29

Today the First Corps of the Army of the Potomac left Frederick and marched northward toward Pennsylvania on what we now know as Route 15. The troops marched through Harmony Grove, Lewistown, Catoctin Furnace, Mechanicstown (now Thurmont), Franklinville to Emmitsburg. Distance covered was about twenty miles.

Hancock and the Second Corps marched out of Frederick to Liberty on Maryland 26. In Liberty the command turned toward Johnsville, and then to the picturesque village of Uniontown where they received a royal welcome.

After a late start which angered Meade, the Third Corps marched from near Woodsboro to Taneytown. Twelve to fifteen miles was the extent of the travel. The Third Corps pitched their tents on the farms of Jacob Null, John Thomson, and Benjamin Shunk.

George Sykes and the Fifth Corps comprised another finger of the Union fist. The Fifth Corps marched northeast on Route 26 through Mount Pleasant to Liberty.

Sedgwick and the Sixth Corps had a long march from Hyattstown to New Market to Ridgeville, and finally to New Windsor in Carroll County. Almost twenty-five miles were covered in the march.

Howard's Eleventh Corps left Frederick and moved to the north on the Old Frederick Road which parallels Route 15. Thus the First and Eleventh corps marched parallel to each other.

Slocum and the Twelfth Corps had another march of

twenty miles from Frederick to Taneytown via what we now know as Route 194. The men marched through Ceresville, Walkersville, Woodsboro, Ladiesburg, New Midway, and Keymar. Army headquarters moved to Middleburg.

It is hard to imagine the excitement and suspense that filled the air in Frederick on June 28. The city was ringed with "a hundred circling camps." Wagons, teamsters, and staff officers filled the streets and the roads leading in and out of Frederick.

Some were sleeping off drunks that Sunday afternoon. Others were polishing and checking equipment. Many took the time to write letters home. Maj. Gen. John Reynolds found time to ride into Frederick to visit Cousin Catherine and her sisters. It was a happy time, a brief time out from the things of war, and also for members of the Reynolds clan, a final reunion. Catherine would have a lot to tell the rest of the family when she got around to writing them on July 1.

Monday morning the tents were struck and the men in the Army of the Potomac started northward on the Roads to Gettysburg. It rained most of the day. Doubleday and units in the First Corps found the march long and toilsome. But at least they were out of war-torn Virginia. The Maryland landscape was fresh and beautiful. Instead of the ravages of war, the Union troops saw fertile fields, with waving fields of grain and green corn growing tall. The orchards looked good, the farmers in Frederick County prosperous. The citizens of Harmony Grove, Hansonville, Lewistown, Catoctin Furnace, Mechanicstown, and Franklinville came out to greet the long blue column. The folks waved flags and cheered. All along the road women offered water, bread, pastries and fresh fruit. The citizens of these rural Maryland towns welcomed John Reynolds's men with open arms. They felt safer now. The Army of the Potomac was in their midst. In the camps at the west edge of Frederick, and at Worman's Mill, the bugles blew, the drums beat, and the First and the Eleventh corps hit the road.

The first cluster of houses to witness the march of the First and Eleventh corps after leaving Frederick and Worman's Mill was Harmony Grove. Then it was "a pretty hamlet . . . situated on the Frederick and Pennsylvania Railroad."[1] The community at the time had a church, a small school, a mill, and a grain store. Harmony Grove has been bypassed in recent years by new Route 15 which has been made a four lane highway. Part of the community was cut up by highway acquisition and right-of-way.

Next came Hansonville, just a cluster of houses, five and a half miles from Frederick. But the community had a tanner, a wagonmaker, and the customary rural services. The Old Frederick Road branched off to the right. At this point, the Eleventh Corps veered to the right and marched on the Old Frederick Road, paralleling the march of the First Corps.

Howard's men came to Utica, eight miles north of Frederick. It is still a picturesque place. The first house in the village was erected about 1770. Nearby is one of Frederick County's covered bridges. Local history says that Hessian prisoners, held in captivity in Frederick, when released after the Revolution, purchased land near Utica and settled. Utica, like Ceresville, had a fine flour mill. Products were sent to New York, Baltimore, and Philadelphia.

The next community in the path of the Eleventh Corps was Creagerstown. This, too, was and is a small German farming community. In the mid-1700s it was a thriving place, and on the main road from Pennsylvania to Frederick. The Lutheran and Moravian churches started near here, at least the history of the denominations in this part of Maryland. The Creagers, Zimmermans, Kolbs, and Cullers were among the first settlers. In fact, in the 1750s Creagerstown seems to have been more important than Frederick. Folks from Graceham, a Moravian community, came down to the Old Frederick Road to watch the Eleventh Corps march by.[2]

I CORPS

Getting back to Reynolds and the First Corps, after Hansonville, Lewistown witnessed the march of the troops in blue. The town lying close to the beautiful mountains, came into existence in 1815. Nine years later a huge gristmill was built. The water of Fishing Creek supplied natural power. The lovely brick Methodist Protestant Church on the hill witnessed the men marching by. When the soldiers reached the top of the hill, they must have been tempted to stop and gaze at the beauty of the valley in front of them. But they had to hurry on to Catoctin Furnace.

In Lewistown and along the road to Catoctin Furnace, the Leathermans, Cramers, Remsburgs, and Snooks, descendants of the original settlers, gave food and drink to the men in blue.

Catoctin Furnace supplied ammunition to troops in another war. In 1774, Thomas Johnson, the first governor of Maryland, and his three brothers obtained seven thousand acres in the area, and erected the furnace. The heavy timber supplied excellent iron ore for the furnace. Local people have recently met with engineers, fearing the construction of dual Route 15 will endanger the old furnaces.

Once again, if the traveler wishes to follow the route of the First Corps, he will have to get off of the main road. Harmony Grove, Hansonville, Lewistown, Catoctin Furnace, Mechanicstown (now Thurmont), Franklinville, Saint Anthony's, and Emmitsburg, all on the road to Gettysburg, have been bypassed by modern highways.

From Catoctin Furnace it was on to Mechanicstown. This area was the western frontier in the 1750s. But brave souls like the Wellers, Creagers, Wilhides and others came anyway. The Weller family came because of the fine large spring. Once when he wanted to entertain guests, he killed seventy-three squirrels, all from the same tree for food.

Mr. Weller was an extremely talented man. He made so many items that he seemed like a mechanic. Thus the name Mechanicstown. He made pumps, chisels, axes, mill irons, etc. He attracted many other artisans who were mechanically inclined. Joseph Weller purchased some French matches in Frederick and soon discovered how to make them himself. So the first match factory in the United States was in Thurmont.[3] The Wellers sold the matches at twenty-five cents a box, along with a piece of sandpaper to ignite them. Many of the farmers were fearful of the matches. They thought the matches were the work of the devil and would lead to the burning of their barns.

The reader might like to circle the second weekend in October. This is the normal date of the Catoctin Colorfest. Mechanicstown, or modern day Thurmont, is the headquarters of this event. Houses, orchards, barns, etc., are open to the public. The visitor can step into the past and witness the boiling apple butter, quilting, and many of the creative arts of days gone by.

The reader can make Thurmont his headquarters while he visits the little villages connected with the march of the First and the Eleventh corps to Gettysburg. The beauty of the area, the lack of congestion, the friendliness of the people, and the sense of history will refresh the spirit.

Charles Wainwright found half the road to Emmitsburg to be turnpike, and most of it good. The men were in fine spirits, marched well and behaved themselves. The people along the road were selling everything they could. Charles found the prices to be high, bargains today though. A large loaf of bread was fifty cents, thirty cents too high; fifteen to twenty-five cents for a canteen of milk, and pies at a higher price. One soldier dumped his three days of rations from his haversack and filled it up with things he bought along the road. Some would not sell, but with eager hands gave all they could to the men in blue. Every village cheered and gave the men of the First Corps "good wishes and pleasant smiles." But whiskey was still present, and some of the artillerymen got drunk. Charles tied his men by the hand to the rear of a gun so they would keep up. As the day wore on, he rode ahead and emptied all the liquor he could find in the taverns so his men could not get it.

Sometime during the march he rode with Reynolds, and the general told him that the command of the Army of the Potomac had been offered him in early June, but he had refused it.[4]

Although, according to Abner Doubleday, the march was rough,[5] yet James Wadsworth was exalted from the welcome

361

in Lewistown, Catoctin Furnace, and Mechanicstown. The welcome blotted out the fatigue. Flags and cheers met the men, along with milk, bread, and cherries.[6] The Iron Brigade was overwhelmed with the reception received in Mechanicstown.[7] The place was "overflowing with patriotism and hospitality." Near the town a farmer and his wife met "Gabe" Paul's brigade with a wagon load of bread. They stood by the side of their vehicle and tossed bread to the soldiers. The wife was in tears saying, "You poor boys don't know what's ahead of you. I'm afraid many of ye'll be dead or mangled soon." So with tears she gave out the bread. The men showed their gratitude by saying, "God bless you, old lady." Cheers were given for the couple.[8]

Emmitsburg had barely recovered from one disaster before being faced with the possibility of another. On June 16, 1863, a great fire broke out in Emmitsburg at 10:00 P.M. Before the flames were brought under control, twenty-eight dwellings had been destroyed and 189 persons made homeless. The fire started at Beam's and Guthrie's Livery Stable. Feeding on the straw and hay, the flames spread rapidly. Daniel Wile's City Hotel and stable were also destroyed. The estimated loss was ten thousand dollars. Eli Smith, a local man, was arrested and charged with setting the disastrous fire.[9]

The residents were at work cleaning up the debris when the news came that the Union Army of the Potomac was concentrated south of Emmitsburg at Frederick. Before the clean up work was completed, the long blue columns of the First Corps were spotted heading for the town square.

The troops were coming to a town that dated back to 1786. The original settlement was called "Silver Fancy." But then the townspeople changed the name to Emmitsburg in honor of William Emmitt, a large landowner. German Lutheran and Reformed churches were erected. Roman Catholic Priests such as Father Ryan and Father Dubois led to the development of Saint Joseph's and Saint Mary's churches, to be followed by centers of academic learning by the same name.[10]

In 1809, the Sisters of Charity had a humble beginning in

362

the home of the Setons. Mother Seton has become famous for her good works and life of prayer. In fact, she was canonized in September of 1975. Those following the Roads to Gettysburg will want to stop in Emmitsburg and see the places related to her life.

The Seventy-sixth New York was detailed as wagon guard on the thirty-mile march to Emmitsburg. Much of the march was through fields on either side of the road so the wagons could proceed normally. The men from New York as well as others took the time to pick all the ripe cherries they could eat or carry.

Ladies in Lewistown and Mechanicstown came out with pails and dippers of fresh milk or cold water. Young maidens held aprons full of ripe cherries, and invited the soldiers to help themselves.

The soldiers responded by shouting, "Three cheers for our friends." Lt. Abram Smith said, "God bless the loyal females of Northern Maryland."[11]

The people of Emmitsburg turned out to welcome the men in blue, even though it was raining. The northern students at Mount Saint Mary's Catholic College were very enthusiastic. Some of the young men marched along with the soldiers for a while. They wanted to see the Union troops "flush the enemy."[12]

After a march of twenty-three miles the Twelfth Massachusetts pitched camp a little north of Emmitsburg, cold, wet, and tired.[13] Paul's brigade and the men of the Thirteenth Massachusetts camped about a mile from town on the Fairfield Road. A lot of his men had marched all day without shoes. In Emmitsburg, all the Union men on horseback received instant promotions. From the cheering people, they were given the name "general."[14] Henry Morrow of the Twenty-fourth Michigan reports the twenty-ninth as "a long march, in which the troops suffered much from fatigue."[15]

A depressing and painful experience of both armies was that of blistered and swollen feet. Many could not wear their shoes. Some had to be hauled in the ambulances. "The man who did not have a limp in his gait was a rare exception."

Chaplain Locke of the Eleventh Pennsylvania was very

much impressed with Mount Saint Mary's "a large, imposing stone edifice at the foot of the Blue Ridge, and surrounded by everything in nature to make it attractive." Opposite the Catholic school, a halt was called. Locke and several others rode through the capacious gateway and, up to the main entrance of the building. We were cordially received by the president, and escorted through several parts of the college." Then it was on to a bivouac spot, a short distance west of Emmitsburg.[16]

The men in blue and gray had a lot to think about as they traveled the Roads to Gettysburg. Thoughts naturally drifted toward home and loved ones. Many wondered whether or not they would survive the next battle. Some thought of comrades, no longer with them. Some had pleasant moments to think about. For instance, no doubt Captain James Stewart, commanding Battery B of the Fourth Artillery was thinking about Lincoln's visit to the camp at Belle Plain in early April. After the artillery officer passed in review, President Lincoln sent for him to take a look at his horse "Tartar." Little Tad was nearby riding on a pony. Tad insisted on trading horses with Captain Stewart. The officer said "No." Whereupon Tad was quick to tell him that his father was president and would give him any horse he wanted. The captain had a terrible time getting away from the persistent little Lincoln boy.

XI CORPS

The Eleventh Corps reached Emmitsburg around 7:00 P.M.[17] The men in blue stacked their weapons east of town and started their search for wood to make the fires for coffee.

The day had been "cold and rainy, the roads heavy, and the march very tiresome." Oliver Howard was weary. But a pleasant surprise was awaiting him. Several of the Catholic fathers from Mount Saint Mary's came and invited him to make his headquarters with them. The general "yielded to the tempting offer of hospitality, and instead of pitching my tent or stretching my 'fly' as usual, I went to enjoy the neat and comfortable bed which was offered me." Howard also spent the thirtieth of June with the kind fathers.

While Howard visited Mount Saint Mary's, Rufus Dawes and the Iron Brigade visited the campus of Mount Saint Joseph's, with the Sisters of Charity in charge. During the war, the sisters were "ministering angels to our sick and wounded comrades."[18]

Howard's Fifty-fifth Ohio did not feel like visiting. The men had left Turner's Gap Sunday afternoon, marched through Middletown, crossed Braddock Mountain, and plodded on to the outskirts of Frederick before going into camp at 1:00 this last Monday in June. Resting but a few hours, they had to march again. In the heavy rain they covered the miles on the Frederick-Emmitsburg Pike, "consisting of good stone, . . . and the march was comparatively easy." They covered thirty-seven miles in twenty-four hours.[19]

As he rode toward Emmitsburg on this rainy Monday, O. O. Howard had his own thoughts about the change of command. We do not know when he got the word. But when he arrived in Frederick on Sunday evening, he found intense excitement and interest in the change. Howard went immediately to see the new commander. The general from Maine shares what transpired.

> I had known Meade before the war, having met him and traveled with him on our northern lakes when he was on engineering duty in that region, and I had seen him frequently after the outbreak of hostilities. But he seemed different at Frederick. He was excited. His coat was off, for those June days were very warm. As I entered his tent, he extended his hand, and said:
> "How are you, Howard?"
> . . . He looked tall and spare, weary and a little flushed. . . . I knew him to be a good, honest soldier, and gathered confidence from his thoughtful face. To him I appeared but a lad, for he had graduated in 1835 at the Military Academy, nineteen years before me. He had served in the artillery among the Indians; in the Topographical engineers on our lakes and rivers; in Mexico, where he was brevetted for his gallantry, and had become favorably known in Washington in the lighthouse service. Then, . . . in the rebellion all

our eyes had been turned to him for the completeness of every work he had thus far undertaken with his Pennsylvania Reserves. He won me more by his thoroughness and fidelity than by any show of sympathy or companionship. To me, . . . he stood in the light of an esteemed, and experienced regular officer, old enough to be my father, but like a father that one can trust without his showing him any special regard. So we trusted and respected Meade from the beginning.

At least, this is the way Howard saw it.

After the 9,500 men of the First Corps filed past the fields near Harmony Grove, Wesley Merritt, now a one star general, led his troopers of the Reserve Cavalry Brigade of the First Division out onto the Emmitsburg Road. His destination was Mechanicstown.[20]

We wonder if the men in blue noticed Auburn, the large mansion built by the Johnson family at the south end of Catoctin Furnace.

Perhaps some of them paid a hurried visit to the General Store in the quaint village. And maybe some of them noticed the Episcopal Church where William Nelson Pendleton, Lee's artilleryman, had ridden from Frederick to conduct services in the 1840s.[21] Since then numerous presidents have worshiped in the little church at the foot of the mountains, including President Gerald Ford on Easter Sunday, 1976.

Merritt's men spent the next two days around Mechanicstown. From the town which is now called Thurmont, Merritt sent detachments as far as Cavetown and Hagerstown.[22]

Ceresville was an important road junction for the Army of the Potomac on the way to Gettysburg. The Third and Twelfth corps, along with the reserve artillery and army headquarters, turned north here on what is now Maryland 194. The Second and Fifth corps continued on what is now Maryland 26 toward Mount Pleasant.

More than six hundred acres comprised the original Ceresville estate. The area was full of choice limestone land. Between 1812 and 1816, General Williams erected a mansion, a sawmill, and flour and grist mills. He did a thriving business. The flour mill is still in operation. The few houses in the area are between the east bank of the Monocacy River and the west bank of Israel's Creek.

One hundred years ago, the products of the Ceresville flour mills were very popular. In the Baltimore-Washington area, the cereals and the grains coming from Ceresville were as popular as General Mills or Betty Crocker today.

The author has looked in vain for regimental descriptions of the mill, or attempts to get the mill products as the men in blue marched by.

Taking the route of the Third and Twelfth corps, Walkersville is the next stop, three miles north of Ceresville. It was a hamlet in 1863, home for a few retired farmers. Until 1950 the population was but 750. But now the overflow of the cities has hit the area. The lovely and productive farms are being sold for development. Challedon and Gallorette, two horses of Kentucky Derby fame, were trained on the Brann farm. Now almost a hundred houses are on the farm. We mention this because part of the Third Corps bivouacked here on June 28. Walkersville was named after farmer John Walker.

Edith Nicodemus was the author's first grade teacher, and a lovely soul. In 1863 her family farmed near Walkersville. According to family tradition, Dan Sickles made his headquarters at one of the Nicodemus farms along the Woodsboro pike. The steps to the farmhouse are supposed to have come from stones at the John Brown fortress in Harpers Ferry.

III CORPS

Some units of the Third Corps were on the road at 5:00 A.M. on June 29. Houghton describes the march as:

... passing through Walkersville to Woodbury (Woodsboro), thence via Middlebury (Middleburg) and Taneytown, about half a mile beyond the village of Taneytown. Our reception in the various places was very enthusiastic. Ladies and young girls distributed beautiful bouquets of flowers to the officers and soldiers; groups of fair damsels ... sang patriotic airs, as the "boys in blue" marched by, and the passage of troops being a novelty, the citizens turned out en masse. Long after tattoo, groups of ladies and gentlemen were promenading through our camps, . . . to see how soldiers really lived in the "tented field."[23]

The welcome greetings and the enthusiastic welcomes from folks along the road, and at every hamlet and town revived the spirits of the footsore members of the Third Corps. They responded with music from the regimental band and drum corps. The smiles, waving of flags, and the "God bless yous" from the older folks "thrilled the soldier's heart anew with patriotic pride and devotion, and made the hours and miles pass more quickly."[24]

The Second Division, the First Brigade moved out with the rising of the sun. The Twelfth New Hampshire led the entire Third Corps during the march of the day. They greatly appreciated that honor. It was always better to be at the head of a column, rather than at the rear. When the men from the Granite State reached Taneytown, they were assigned provost duty. This gave them the opportunity to mingle with the folks of Taneytown, and also the first opportunity to purchase doughnuts, cakes and pies.[25]

The 141st Pennsylvania was detailed as the rear guard of the Third Corps. It was their duty to pick up all the stragglers and help them to find their units. This was a difficult and unpleasant task on June 29. Many of the stragglers were suffering from hangovers, and many others were under the influence from canteens full of whiskey.[26]

At 5:00 P.M., the Third Corps encamped one mile beyond Taneytown. During the day the men in the ranks found that Dan Sickles was back in command. When he arrived and rode through the ranks, he was met with wild cheering. Thomas Marbaker felt there was not a more popular commander to be found. Dan got down from his horse and watched his men march by from the porch of Taneytown's old stone tavern. The men camped on the farms of Jacob Null, John Thompson, and Benjamin Shunk.[27]

Although generally better equipped and supplied than the men in gray, the hard marches took their toll on the Army of the Potomac. By June 29, many of the blue-clad soldiers were just about shoeless. Therefore, the supply wagons reaching the Third Corps area on June 30, carrying a fresh supply of shoes, were a welcome sight.

Farmers from all around Taneytown came to see the Third Corps. This was a new experience. One lady said, "I must run right home and get the children for they will never get the chance to see such a sight again." All were intrigued with the cannons and the stories of their firepower.

The evening of the twenty-ninth was dark and overcast. Among many of the troops there was a feeling of uneasiness. Most felt that a battle was about to occur. They did not know where the Army of Northern Virginia was, but it must be nearby. So there was tension in the air, and all realized there would soon be empty places in the ranks.

XII CORPS

At 2:30 A.M. on June 29, A. S. Williams was awakened by a messenger from Meade's headquarters ordering the divisions of the Twelfth Corps to march toward Taneytown in Carroll County at 5:30 A.M.[28] Williams was encamped in a fine grove of shade trees and hated to leave. After three days of fatiguing marches, his body cried for sleep. The Rebels were in Pennsylvania. They had to be stopped. So he said, "We are bound to go on, cost what of human flesh it may."[29] On the positive side, Williams rejoiced at the change of commanders.

Writing from the office of Dr. Steiner of the Sanitary Commission in Frederick while his troops moved out on the Roads to Gettysburg, Williams jotted a note to his daughters saying:

> I have said very little in my letters, but enough for you to guess that I had no confidence in Hooker after Chancellorsville. . . . I cannot conceive of greater imbecility and weakness than characterized that campaign from the moment Hooker reached Chancellorsville and took command.[30]

Williams was fearful of losing the entire war as a result of Chancellorsville. He had a right to his belief. After all, Lee

369

and the confident Army of Northern Virginia were riding the crest of their war fortunes.

But as the dawn broke, he started to think in a positive manner.

> Still, I don't despair. . . . Now with a gentleman and a soldier in command I have renewed confidence that we shall do enough to preserve our honor and the safety of the Republic. But we run a fearful risk, because upon this small army everything depends. If we are badly defeated the Capital is gone and all our principal cities and our national honor.[31]
>
> Whatever happens, be contented and resigned, and believe it is all for the best. In nations, as in individuals, we must believe there is a "divinity which shapes our ends, rough hew them as we will."[32]

Like many others, Jacob Englebrecht was impressed with general officers. He notes on this Monday that he has seen Generals Stahel, Pleasonton, Buford, Sickles, Patrick and Slocum.

As the Army of the Potomac was marching through the streets of Frederick, two soldiers stopped at his shop. One was George Cronk, an eighteen-year-old member of the 146th New York, and Charles Green, several days short of his fourteenth birthday. Green was born in Chicago on July 4, 1849, and was a drummer boy. He notes that the cavalry and infantry were also using Love Lane and Bentz Street.[33]

While the soldiers were tramping through Frederick, preparations were being made for the evacuation of Maryland Heights. It had been Hooker's wish to have that garrison and the Twelfth Corps strike the Confederate lines of supply and communication at Williamsport. Now the Heights and Harpers Ferry were being evacuated. According to one source it took seventeen hours to haul the supplies and stores away.

Most of the Twelfth Corps got as far as Bruceville and Middleburg this last Monday in June. Meade established army headquarters at Middleburg.

Somehow Meade found time to write to his wife on June 29, saying:

> Yesterday morning, at 3 a.m., I was aroused from my sleep by an officer from Washington entering my tent, and after waking me up, saying he had come to give me trouble. At first I thought that it was either to relieve or arrest me, and promptly replied to him, that my

conscience was clear, void of offense towards any man; I was prepared for his bad news. He then handed me a communication to read; which I found was an order relieving Hooker from the command assigning it to me. . . . It appears to be God's will for some good purpose. . . . I shall pray for strength and power to get through with the task assigned me.[34]

Most of the army moved at 4:00 A.M. Meade, however, did not leave Frederick until about 8:00,[35] riding to Ceresville, Walkersville, and Woodsboro to Middleburg. He sent and received orders as he traveled.

John Sedgwick reported that he could not reach his destination at New Windsor that night. Meade told him to move as early as possible on Tuesday, occupying Westminster and important railroad stores there. He told Sickles to get his wagons moving instead of blocking the way for the Twelfth Corps. He urged Sykes to cover as much ground as he could with the Fifth Corps. The provost marshal was sternly ordered to collect all stragglers and return them to the ranks. He received very little information about the Confederate army. What was given him led Meade to believe the Army of Northern Virginia was moving toward Harrisburg.

But there had been a spy in the ranks, James Longstreet had hired a scout by the name of Harrison. He had mingled with folks in Washington and followed the Army of the Potomac once it got across the river. When Hooker was removed and replaced by Meade, he took off at once for Confederate headquarters. Arriving with the news in Chambersburg, on June 28, the message led Lee to change his plans about Harrisburg, and concentrate instead on the Roads to Gettysburg.[36]

What a day June 29 must have been. Tempers were short. Winfield Scott Hancock wrote to Butterfield at 7:00 A.M., saying his command was just now leaving Monocacy Junction, south of Frederick.[37] The three-hour delay was caused by some irresponsible clerk in his headquarters who failed to deliver the message from higher-ups. But on little things like these swing the fate of battles and campaigns.

Meade expressed the hope the clerk would be punished. Hancock assured him of the discipline. Although he was sorry about the delay, Hancock said, "I shall try to make up the most of it (the march) by shortcuts and rapid marching."

J. B. McIntosh, commanding the First and Second brigades of the Second Cavalry Division, sent regiments to Cooksville, Lisbon, and Popular Springs. He captured a Rebel prisoner who related that the Confederates had spent the previous night at Cooksville.[38] The Rebels cut the telegraph wires. McIntosh was also told that the Confederates had captured a big wagon train at Rockville on June 28. Colonel McIntosh had been delayed too. But his delay was caused by two corps of infantry moving ahead of him from Ridgeville.[39]

Things had gone better for John Reynolds. At 3:15, he reported that he had reached Mechanicsville (now Thurmont). As always, Reynolds had ridden on ahead of his troops. Reynolds was met by Edward Hopkins, a scout, who had just returned from Gettysburg. Hopkins brought the message that Early had passed through that town in the direction of York, with the Confederate cavalry headed for Hancock Junction.[40]

II CORPS

Before daylight on the twenty-ninth of June, reveille was sounded in the tented cities of the Army of the Potomac. North and south of Frederick, the soldiers began to stir. They feared they were in for a long day.

Some of the men threw their muskets over their shoulders like "men starting out on a hunt. Many carried their weapons on the left shoulder, some on the right. They were not too particular."

The Nineteenth Massachusetts led the Second Corps from Monocacy Junction on the June 29 portion of the Roads to Gettysburg. Soon they came to a creek. It had to be forded. And the men hated to do that early in the day. It meant wet feet with dust sticking to the shoes.

It was a hot damp day, or very humid as we would say

now. Sweat ran down the faces of the marching men. It dropped from the nose and chin. Perspiration, "or the salty liquid got into the eyes, causing them to burn and smart, and it ran from under the cap, through the dust and down the sides of the face which was soon covered with muddy streaks, the result of repeated wipings upon the sleeves of the blouse."[41]

Folks in Frederick, Mount Pleasant, and Liberty, and farmers along the way came out to the roadside to greet the men in blue. It might not have been a parade for the men in the ranks, but it was for the people along the road. The dust covered column of boys in blue was indeed a welcome sight. "We're so glad you're here. Chase 'em back to Virginia." These words of welcome inspired the men in blue to keep going.

As we have already mentioned, the Second Corps got a late start due to a foul-up in paper work. Thus it was not until about 9:00 A.M. that Hays's division moved off, moving primarily near the Frederick Fairgrounds and out the Gas House Pike. The men heard rumors that Lee was already near Harrisburg. For Frank Sawyer and the Eighth Ohio, the march on this Monday was "the most severe the regiment ever performed. The day was intensely hot, and we marched over 33 miles with scarcely a halt for dinner and none for supper until two o'clock in the morning when we came to a halt."[42]

The bridges were assigned to the wagon trains and artillery. Thus the infantry had to ford the streams, the Monocacy, Israel's Creek, and others.

The Fourteenth Connecticut hoped to enter Frederick on June 29. The men fondly remembered the kind treatment given them during the Maryland campaign. But alas. No such luck this time. The men went east of Frederick and were not permitted to march through the city itself.[43]

It was a terrible day. Halts were limited to five minutes. Gravel and sand stuck to pants, shoes and socks, gradually finding its way to the sole of the foot where it became very irritating.

When the Second Corps finally started to move from their camp near Monocacy Junction, Webb's brigade stayed behind. No orders came. The men thought they might be in for a "soft snap" of a day. But soon an orderly galloped in with orders for General Webb. Somehow the brigade had been forgotten. Now the assembly was sounded and orders given to move. The brigade of Pennsylvania troops brought up the rear of the Second Corps. The men moved east of Frederick, crossed the Monocacy, and took a secondary road to Liberty. The author feels this was the Gas House Pike connecting with the Old Annapolis and then the Liberty-New Market Road. It is difficult to tell.

Once again, they reached a bend in the Monocacy River. There was no bridge, so the men had to wade the stream. Some stopped to take off their shoes and socks, and roll up their trousers. General Webb saw this was taking too much time. So he soon stopped it. He wanted to make up for lost time. He ordered the men to wade into the river. Webb jumped from his horse and proceeded to the middle of the stream until the entire brigade crossed. The soldiers did not like this. They expressed their feelings in words loud enough for the general to hear. The remarks were far from complimentary.

A man in the Sixty-ninth Pennsylvania, bolder than the rest, said, "It's no wonder you can stand there when ye are leather up to your waist." He was referring to Webb's boots that came above his knees. The comment brought a loud laugh from the men in the ranks. But Webb paid no attention. The general remained in the middle of the stream until all were across.[44]

Then, as now, they had men who will do anything to get out of something distasteful. Captain Breintenback of Company G started across on a log, feeling the order was just for the enlisted men. This incurred Webb's wrath. The good captain trotted off to Dr. McLean, the assistant surgeon of the 106th Pennsylvania, asking for a paper to help get him off the hook. The doctor noted that the captain was subject to rheumatism and that getting his feet wet would not help his health. This did the trick, and after a good lecture from General Webb, the captain rejoined his command.[45]

The Fifth New Hampshire was in Caldwell's division of the

374

Second Corps. Colonel Cross commanded the brigade. And Thomas Livermore was a member of the unit. He remembers leaving Frederick to the left, and turning to the northeast and then moving toward Uniontown. The pace was rapid, and every effort made to keep the regulation twenty-eight inches between the men and their file leader when crossing streams. No one was permitted to stop to remove shoes and stockings. As the day wore on this brought great discomfort to the men and led to an argument between General Hancock and the commander of the First Minnesota.[46]

In the early forenoon, after being on the road for several hours, the Second Division of the Second Corps "came to a considerable creek." The water was knee deep. Someone threw a timber across the water for a bridge. Yet if the soldiers crossed it single file, the column would be backed up and the march impeded. As the soldiers stood in line, some in the rear started to take off their shoes and socks, and roll up their trousers.[47]

They were not afraid of water. But wading a stream in the middle of a hot June day would result in blisters after a while. Staff officers rode back and forth endeavoring to push the regimental commanders to get their men to wade the creek. Colonel Colville of the First Minnesota gave the order. But the men misunderstood. They thought they could go across the log, take their shoes off, or wade. They joined with the Nineteenth Maine and the Fifteenth Massachusetts in hooting at the staff officer. This made him furious and in retaliation, he placed Colonel Colville under arrest.[48]

Lieutenant Palmer had these thoughts about wading the stream:

> On reaching the northern bank of the stream the soldiers intuitively caught the new high step. The sole of the foot was raised to the rear, and the higher the step the better the drainage and the smaller the number of parboiled feet at supper time. There was no opportunity to stop there near the bank to remove the footwear or to use nature's wringers, for an army was upon our backs. We left some more of the stream when deployed in the field and made up our time by the strenuous push that followed. With all the disadvantage of wet clothing and soaked feet, the Regiment made the longest march that day that it ever made.[49]

The men from Minnesota, Massachusetts, and Maine liked the area near Mount Pleasant. It "looked like a beautiful

375

valley, shut in on both sides and settled by prosperous farmers. It seemed like paradise to the soldiers who for so long a time tramped over the desolate and barren soil of Virginia. Cherry trees, loaded with rich cherries, were upon the roadsides, and the hospitable people brought bread and milk to the tired and hungry soldiers."[50]

Robert Stewart says, "through that long, sultry day and a part of the night . . . we tramped over the dusty roads with blistered feet and heavy loads without pausing long enough to make coffee or cook a meal."[51]

The marching and humidity started to take its toll in the ranks of the Second Corps. But General John Gibbon had a temporary solution. As his division neared Liberty, he asked that the "Glee Club" of the Nineteenth Massachusetts would sing as the column marched through town. "Billy McGinnis was orderly sergeant of the right flank company. Col. Devereux told him to drop out of line and get the glee club up front." This was done and some of the infantrymen became singing soldiers in blue. They sang, "March along, we are marching along." "The effect was magical. The division fell into step and the chorus could be heard ringing along the entire line."[52] Hopefully they would take a break in Liberty, but no, the column turned left and headed for Johnsville.

> When the column reached the beautiful town of Liberty, regiment after regiment filed into the fields and groves just north of town and it was supposed that we were going to bivouac for the night. Hardly had the men thrown themselves upon the ground when the order to fall in came, and the men of the Nineteenth stretched their aching limbs, endeavoring to take the swinging gait which they had kept up since morning. Late in the afternoon it was a little cooler. Occasionally stars appeared in the heavens, but still the tramp kept up.[53]

That's the way it was on the road from Liberty to Uniontown, Monday afternoon and evening, June 29, 1863.

Milk, water, and fresh bread and fruit given to the men by the people of Liberty brought temporary help to the bodies and spirits of the men.

To the men from Massachusetts, the Liberty-Johnsville looked like the Garden of Eden, "We are marching through

376

one of the attractive garden spots of the world, . . . a veritable paradise. Crops of every kind and variety (are) hastening forward to maturity, and from the open barns (come) the sweet smell of newly gathered hay."[54]

As the 106th Pennsylvania passed through Johnsville and Union Bridge, the ladies gave them cool water and cold milk. The Glee Club struck up some songs. This amused the townspeople and momentarily helped the soldiers forget their weariness.[55]

The Fourth Ohio had the misfortune to be the rear guard of the Second Corps this last Monday in June. Therefore, it was almost 1:30 P.M. before they left Monocacy Junction. They found the mud, rain, and humidity to be terrible. It would be after midnight before they reached Uniontown.[56]

Then as now, certain men in the ranks became the butt of jokes or the subject of conversation among their comrades. One of these was "the Galvinized Dutchman." He is short and stout, with a big knapsack. He evidently likes to hang on to things, and therefore is considered greedy. Even in the heat, he carries his woolen and rubber blankets, shelter tent and overcoat. It's hard to tell what else he might have inside his knapsack. Tied to his pack is a frying pan, and a black, grimy coffee pot. His uniform is in good shape, and his rifle is spotless. He has a full beard and great beads of sweat are dropping from his brow. Yet he keeps his equipment, and therefore, the men of the Nineteenth Massachusetts call him, "The Galvinized Dutchman."[57]

Now the men turn their attention to another individual. He is tall and slim. His hat is pushed back, and he is taking in all the scenery. He carries a rubber blanket over his shoulder, his firearms, but that's it. A big red handkerchief hangs from a front pocket. He uses it to "wipe the sweat off and rub the dust in."

Next comes a lad of eighteen, a mere boy. He is dressed in the uniform of a private, but carries a sword, and has a lieutenant's bars on his shoulders. Naturally, the men wonder is he an officer, or playing soldier, or what.[58]

The men of the Nineteenth see white socks fluttering from the bayonets of others, their comrades hoping the footwear will dry before long. The men from Massachusetts used this to help pass the time away, and enlighten their feelings on the Roads to Gettysburg, somewhere near Liberty.

Long before night fell most of the men in the Second Corps were dead tired. Only sheer determination kept them going on the Roads to Gettysburg. The officers said, "We must make Uniontown."[59]

Colonel Livermore says:

> The very names of the towns we passed through were reviving, such as Liberty, Uniontown, etc., and they seemed almost like New England in their neatness. . . . We thoroughly enjoyed all these scenes, we never ceased, for a time longer than necessary to rest, to press on, and when night came, we constantly looked ahead to see the column turning into the fields for the bivouac, we still hurried on. . . . Field after field and wood after wood were reached and passed, and at last we realized that it was not a good camping ground that we were marching for, but a position. . . . (We) called up all our determination and hurried on through the shadows. . . . There was little heard in the ranks, but the tread of feet, the clanking of arms and equipment, and an occasional oath or grumble from some tired mortal. I have never made so long a march. . . . I reached camp with perhaps half my company, at two o'clock in the morning, near Uniontown after marching thirty-two miles.[60]
>
> The sun sank below the horizon, evening breezes took the place of its hot breath, bushes by the wayside grew shadowy, and finally faded into dark, irregular masses, taking on fantastic and weird forms as the night settled over the land. The stars came out one by one in a moonless sky, but there was still the incessant tramp, tramp, tramp as the line moved forward without a halt.[61]
>
> The Second Corps, as a result of this forced march, was nicknamed "Hancock's Night Walkers." In silence and with aching bones, they struggled along until nine o'clock (or later) . . . when they halted in the streets of Uniontown, 32 miles from Monocacy Junction. The men dropped where they halted and instantly were asleep.[62]

The Nineteenth Maine was not finished. They had the misfortune to be assigned picket duty. Captains Burpee and Smith, along with Lieutenant Palmer shared the same shelter tent. Captain Smith, like Colonel Cross, had a premonition. He said, "I feel we are on the eve of a terrible battle and I feel that I shall be killed or wounded." Captain Burpee tried to make light of the situation, saying, "Don't you think we all feel this way when we go into battle. We all feel that way."

But Smith was persistent. "I feel something is going to happen to me and I hope I shall be prepared to die."[63] Sadly, three days later, the feeling came true.

Somehow the residents of Uniontown learned of the coming of the Second Corps. Despite the late hour the loyal folks turned out to give the soldiers milk, bread, and cherry pudding.[64]

VI CORPS

It was a long and rough day, too, for the Sixth Corps. They broke camp in the Hyattsville-Monrovia area at an early hour. Marching to New Market, now a leading antique village, the command headed east toward Mount Airy. Then they took parallel roads leading to New Windsor and eventually Westminster. Members of the Thirty-seventh Massachusetts describe an interesting experience in New Market.

A few miles brought the regiment to the village of New Market, where a little incident lightened the spirits of the men wonderfully. Before reaching the place cheers were heard in advance, and on entering the town two or three young ladies were discovered standing in front of their home waving small Union flags. It was an electrifying sight, and the enthusiasm which had pervaded the troops in advance was emphasized from the strong throats of the Thirty-seventh. There was no question now that they were in the land of friends. A little further on the traditional town pump was encountered, but not as had often occurred in Virginia dismantled to prevent the thirsty soldiers from obtaining a drink of water. Its long handle was swung unceasingly up and down by a tall, tattered negro, his homely lineaments beautified by a smile of supreme happiness as he watched the surging throng before the pump, and caught their hurried words of heartfelt thanks. The sweat coursed down his massive features, for he had been thus engaged from early morning, declining all offers of assistance. "No, soldiers," he responded, "I don' wan' no help. Put yo' cup right under there and git some water—I'll gib yo' all you want if I hab to pump up de bottom ob dis yer well!" Bless his kind heart! No man in Maryland did nobler service for the cause of his country that day.[65]

The Seventy-seventh New York tramped the road from Monrovia to New Market, Ridgeville, and Mount Airy Station. Camp was made for the night at Sams Creek.[66]

V CORPS

George Sykes was now in command of the Fifth Corps. Marching through Frederick, they took Route 26 through Ceresville and on to Mount Pleasant. Most of them stopped for the night between Liberty and Unionville. The word "Union" is quite prominent in Frederick and Carroll counties. Unionville was the limit on the Fifth Corps advance on the twenty-ninth. Some of the soldiers marched through the important rail town of Union Bridge, Uniontown was the destination of the Second Corps, and by evening of the next day the Fifth Corps would be at Union Mills.

Staggering is the thought of 175,000 men walking through Fredericksburg, Virginia, to Gettysburg. Yet the roads of Virginia, Maryland, and Pennsylvania witnessed the movement of these troops with their accompanying cannons, ambulances, supply wagons, and implements of war in June of '63.

Never has America seen such a movement of troops. We look at the record of the Twentieth Maine. They tramped twenty miles on June 26, the same distance on the twenty-seventh, rested on the twenty-eighth, walked eighteen miles on this rainy Monday, and covered twenty-three miles on June 30, plus twenty-six miles on July 1. That's a tremendous achievement in any day and age.

We look briefly now at the activities of the Union cavalrymen this last Monday in June. Devin's brigade had traveled from Poolesville to Jefferson on Saturday, and on Sunday rode into Middletown. From the valley they left on a mission on Monday.[67]

The Eighth Illinois remembered Monday as being a dreary day, and riding over two mountains, Turner's Gap to Boonsboro, to Smithsburg, Ringgold, Monterey and the mountain there toward Fairfield. They received word that the Pennsylvania militia had exchanged fire with the Confederates and lost formation. But the men from Lincoln's state were unable to ascertain much else. The natives were either unaware of what was going on or fearful to relay the information.[68]

General Buford states in his report:

> The inhabitants knew of my arrival and the position of the enemy's camp, yet not one of them gave me a particle of information, nor even mentioned the fact of the enemy's presence. The whole community seemed stampeded and afraid to speak or act, often offering as excuses . . . "the rebels will destroy our houses if we tell anything."[69]

Today the Michigan cavalry regiments rode from Gettysburg to Emmitsburg, being replaced by Buford's First Cavalry Division. In the Maryland town, they learned of the command shake-up, and were joined by the First Michigan Cavalry. The brigade from the Wolverine State prepared to move to Littlestown for a meeting with its new commander, George A. Custer.

June 29 was a great day for the men in the Seventeenth Pennsylvania Cavalry:

> June 29th—we crossed the boundary line into Franklin County, Pa. The men of Company G, of this regiment, commanded by Captain Luther B. Kurtz, were natives of this county, and mostly recruited at or near Waynesboro. A trooper of this company, with guidon, stood at the line while the regiment passed, and each squadron lustily cheered him as we hastened on.
>
> The division crossed the South Mountain on a good highway, along which the enemy's cavalry had preceded us some days. The road at some points had been barricaded by home guards and local troops to retard their progress, but these obstructions had mostly been removed. The command bivouacked on the night of the 29th at the foot of South Mountain, with orders to move at sunrise. The camp, as near as we can remember, was some eight or ten miles east of Waynesboro, the home of Captain L. B. Kurtz and the home of the men of Company G. The captain asked Colonel Kellogg for permission to take his company and spend the night in his native village. The request was novel; the orders under which the command was marching were very exacting. The colonel was a West Pointer and a strict disciplinarian. On the other hand, the sympathies of every officer in the command were with Captain Kurtz and his men. The request was granted and Company G went home for the night,

leaving assurances of honor that all would be back at the hour the column would march, and, true to their word and country, they came, and when they reported the next morning, without a man missing or a straggler, they received a warm greeting from their generous, though less fortunate, companions.[70]

Part of Buford's command may have traveled from Middletown to Wolfsville to Ringgold.

Thus Buford and the First Cavalry Division was the nearest to the Rebel Infantry. Buford was near Fountaindale. His men had had a long ride. Merritt, a new general in the division, fared better, having a short, easy ride to Thurmont to guard the trains.

Judson Kilpatrick and Elon Farnsworth left the cavalry camp north of Frederick, and presumably took the Biggs Ford Road across Monocacy to Walkersville, going up Liberty Street and bringing up the rear of the army as it marched on the Walkersville-Taneytown Road. Custer was also on the road to join his command. The official reports have him going to Graceham.[71] He was to have a date with destiny in Hanover. But how did he get there, and where was Alfred Pleasonton this last day in June? Was he with Meade on Route 194 heading for Middleburg?[72]

The Fifth New York Cavalry went through Walkersville and Woodsboro. In Littlestown they were received with great demonstrations of joy. A large group of children appeared on the balcony of a hotel and greeted the troopers with cheers and patriotic songs.[73]

Monday evening, George Custer joined the Michigan Cavalry near Littlestown, Pennsylvania, with his horses and dogs. He obtained two bugler orderlies from the United States Fifth Cavalry. He looked so boyish and young. According to one biographer, "by morning, the Michigan Brigade was thoroughly miserable."

Custer started out to prove himself with stern discipline. This was odd because thus far in life he had exhibited little personal discipline. But as a commander he let it be known he expected the men to "shape up."

The promotion did not sell so well with a lot of the officers. Custer had talked much about his hopes of glory. Those

382

who knew him were afraid the advancement might go to his head. Some laughed about his "girl's hair, his swagger, and West Point conceit." The men would salute, but their respect he had to earn.[74]

David McMurtie Gregg rode at the head of the Second Cavalry Division this humid Monday in June. He was eight years out of West Point, and a captain in the Sixth Cavalry at the outbreak of the war. In January of 1862 he was made colonel of the Eighth Pennsylvania Cavalry, and in November he reached his general's star. Throughout the war he had many skirmishes with his friend from cadet days, Jeb Stuart. After the war he was United States Consul in Prague, auditor general of Pennsylvania, and commander in chief of the Military Order of the Loyal Legion. He was in command of the right flank and Gettysburg and his men assisted by Custer prevented Stuart from gaining the rear of the Union lines. But this day he had other tasks.[75]

His brigade commanders were Col. John B. McIntosh and Col. J. Irvin Gregg. McIntosh was born in Florida, the son of a regular army officer who was killed in the Mexican War. During that conflict, John served in the navy. When the Civil War broke out, a brother entered Confederate service. John looked upon this as a blot upon the family honor, and entered the United States Army to counteract his brother's deed. He rose through the ranks to become colonel of the Third Pennsylvania, and then commanded a brigade at Kelly's Ford.

Gregg's destination for today was New Windsor in Carroll County. One of his brigades was to take Route 26 to Unionville, but the infantry blocked the way, creating some detours.

Maggie Mehring was thirteen years old in June of '63. Her family was eating supper on the night of June 29 when a neighbor came and told them that Union cavalry was on the way. The column proved to be Gen. David Gregg "and cavalry escort." This was just the advance elements. During the evening hours, Maggie estimated that five thousand passed through New Windsor. She says:

They were dressed very nicely and rode handsome horses. It was a beautiful sight, for the moon shone so brilliantly.... The horsemen were riding six and eight abreast with their swords clattering while cheer after cheer. They all said they never felt happier than when they set foot on Maryland soil. They had been in Virginia and enduring all the hardships of patriots. . . . It made them feel at home to be greeted by smiling faces, two of the sixty cavalrymen slept in the church yard. Their names were Mire and Johns. Mire is the clerk of General Greggs. . . . Mr. Mire told us that they had left about twenty-five thousand infantry a few miles back and he thought they would come through about four o'clock (next morning). . . . We girls were afraid we would oversleep ourselves we determined taking it turn about watching. . . . Not any of us slept very much. Isabelle and I had a pleasant time for the pickets came off duty that were on in the first part of the night and as they stopped at the hotel (Dielman Inn) we could see them feeding their horses and hear them chatting. . . . There were fourteen light field pieces with the cavalry. . . . [76]

At 6:40 P.M., Pleasonton instructed Gregg to move toward Hanover Junction, and open communication with Baltimore by the railroad route. On Sunday the objectives of the cavalry divisions had been set forth in Special Orders 99. Buford had carried out his task.[77] Gregg's men were still in the saddle. Kilpatrick's men were to reach Littlestown which they did. Farnsworth took Route 194, while Custer moved via Utica, Cragerstown, and Graceham to Emmitsburg, and then northeast to Littlestown.[78]

While the infantrymen plodded the roads in Frederick and Carroll counties, and the troopers rode in search of the Army of Northern Virginia, things were about to happen in the Carroll County seat of government.

All was quiet in Westminster, but not for long. Some of the men from the First Delaware were having their horses shod at Michael Baughman's blacksmith shop. They were quickly surprised by some men in gray who took them prisoner. Meanwhile, Dr. William Matthias had been out calling on some of his sick patients. He spotted the Confederates and hurried back to town with the news, "The Rebels are Coming." Word was passed to Major Knight and Captain Corbit. The First Delaware formed without delay, and headed east on Main Street.[79]

Lieutenant Clark of Company C was ordered to charge

384

into the head of the Rebel column. This he did and caused momentary confusion. However, Stuart sent a troop around to the rear of the men in blue to cut off their retreat. Corbit led a charge and hand-to-hand fighting occurred at the junction of Main Street and the Washington Road. Corbit's horse was shot and killed, and the captain was standing in the middle of the street, still astride his dead horse. There were many cuts and bruises, and two killed on each side. Corbit and many others from the First Delaware were captured. The dead were sent to F. A. Sharrer, the local undertaker, and prepared for burial. Major Knight listed sixty-seven casualties.[80]

Stuart says that for the first time since leaving Rector's Crossroads, he was able to obtain a full supply of forage. Fitz's Lee Brigade halted at Union Mills, while the rest of the gray troopers encamped a few miles beyond Westminster. Stuart learned that the Union cavalry was at Littlestown.[81] This of course was Farnsworth's command. The Carroll County folks feel that this brief but savage encounter delayed Stuart long enough to permit Union cavalry to block his main route, thus keeping him from bringing information and vital aid to Robert E. Lee. Stuart apparently spent the night in or near Westminster. The daughter of George Sheets was named Eliza Jane. Her grandfather told her that Stuart spent the night straddling a chair on the pavement in front of the house with his bodyguard in attendance.[82] Some of the Rebel officers took tea, and probably something stronger at the home of a John C. Fryese, cashier of the Westminster Bank.

Philip Fisher of Columbus, Ohio, was in Westminster this last Monday in June. He wrote home that Stuart's cavalry came through town eight abreast. This seems a little absurd. Four would be more like it. He counted 175 wagons and noted that most of them bore the U.S. mark. These were the captured wagons. Dr. Hering agrees with Fisher that they passed through until nearly 11:00 P.M. We have to agree with his statement that it is hard to imagine six thousand cavalrymen riding by until you actually see them. Dr. Hering helped to care for the wounded and talked with General Stuart in front of the Shellman house at Main and Sycamore streets.

"He was tall and erect, well proportioned with large bony frame, full beard which was rather sandy and looked every inch a cavalry leader." On the east side of the old City Hotel, Stuart, Fitz Lee and Wade Hampton held a council of war.[83]

According to the Shellman recollections, the people of Westminster were divided in their loyalties. Soldiers from the town entered both armies. Naturally, those in favor of the South were glad to see the men in gray, and from time to time the strains of "The Bonnie Blue Flag" could be heard. A young, rosy-cheeked German girl watched the Confederates with disgust. When she saw a captured United States Flag she could stand it no longer. Gathering an apron full of stones, she shouted, "Go back, you nasty rebels. Go back or I'll throw stones at you." So she stoned the men in gray. A few laughed at her and threw them softly back at her. We have several flag-waving accounts during the war, but this is one of the few where a girl stoned passing soldiers.[84]

Mrs. Neal was surprised to see the Confederates enter Westminster. She had two sons, Henry and Francis, with Jeb Stuart. They were serving as scouts now because of their familiarity with the area. She was reading her Bible when she was told they were in town. The lads passed by on their way up Main Street. They waved to their mother and sister Mary. Mrs. Neal was distressed by their dirty uniforms, and the hot cloud of dust.[85]

Everett Pearson vividly describes the day in Westminster:

> At half-past three in the afternoon the man body of Stuart's command entered the town. (Jeb was aware of the close proximity of the Sixth Corps.) Some of the regiments marched by in silence, others sang familiar ballads as they moved along. A few . . . shrieked, whistled, and cheered. The flags were nearly all folded, the bugles made no sound, the orders were few and short, and there was an entire lack of that pomp and pageantry which all expected to see in an army. It was very evident that the men meant "business" and not play. . . . Most of the men kept up their usual company and regiment formation, and were as particular about their alignment as though on review. . . .
>
> Horses were in demand. Many of the men were mounted on mules, and these received orders to secure for themselves a remount by impressing animals from the citizens. . . .
>
> Stuart came into town about four o'clock, and was greeted with

cheers wherever he was recognized. He rode to the house of a friend, where he remained until a late hour, welcoming with a smile and a shake of the hand the many ladies and gentlemen who called upon him. He seemed to have a heavy load of care on his mind whilst at tea it was noticed that, though at times full of spirits, he occasionally grew abstracted and thoughtful.[86]

Stuart was questioned about the campaign and its intentions. Naturally he was evasive. But he firmly replied that he felt a big battle would soon occur, and that battle would result in Independence for the South. After the tea, his host said, "General Stuart, do you have any doubt about the outcome of the battle of which you spoke?"

"None at all," answered Stuart. "I have the utmost confidence in our men, and I know that if they are given a ghost of a chance they are sure to win." His eyes flashed, full of optimism. He was a positive thinker. He never gave defeat a thought, at least not at this moment.[87]

About midnight Stuart announced that he must go. Even though the hour was late, a large crowd followed him outside and watched him mount. The folks gave him three cheers, and the general responded with a bow. Those present felt history was in the making. A big moment was coming, and that moment would decide the nation's destiny.[88]

John Esteen Cooke remembers leaving Westminster and bivouacking by the side of the road in the rain. They had not captured much in town, an old gun, the Delaware cavalry camp, and a United States Flag taken from the vault of the courthouse. This was a special flag though. The ladies of Westminster had made the flag, and placed their names in the stars representing the various states.[89]

About 4:00 P.M. today, two Union soldiers galloped through Union Mills, yelling, "Pack up and leave, the Rebels are after us." However, the Shrivers and others paid little attention. But at 10:00 P.M. there was a knock upon the door of the Shriver homestead. The residents were told by a gray-clad horseman that the Confederate cavalry was on the way. "In a short time they came, as thick as bees." By 2:00 or 3:00 A.M., the ladies of the house had fed several hundred famished Rebels. They appeared to be gentlemen. General

387

Lee (Fitz) would not take a bed. He slept in Uncle Andrew's orchard.[90]

About daylight on the thirtieth, Jeb Stuart arrived. The Shriver table was filled with majors, colonels, captains, and Stuart and Lee. This thrilled many of the Shrivers as they were pro-Southern. As last the supply of biscuits gave out and some had to leave unfed.[91]

Mrs. Heard came in and started to play the piano. "I wish you had heard General Stuart sing, accompanied by all the rest, 'If you want to be a bully boy, jine the cavalry.' . . . ; his eyes sparkled and he kept time with his spirit; and with it all the elegant gentleman. General Lee joined and Major McClellan played and sang some splendid songs. General Stuart promised to come and see us if he ever got within 25 miles."[92]

Kate Shriver says that Lee's cavalry camped in the orchard back of the house. Many just rode to the door where the black servant Ruth handed out bread and food as long as it lasted. They were almost starving. Kate was a Unionist at heart. The village blacksmith, Bill Tagg, was scared of the Rebels and hid under the old sawmill. It was rather unpleasant because it was also the favorite spot of the pigs. For the ladies who fed the soldiers, the experience was as though a cyclone had hit.[93]

Stuart needed someone to guide him on the Roads to Gettysburg. So as he left the Shriver homestead this morning, he took sixteen-year-old Herb Shriver with him. Feeling the South would win the war, Jeb promised to keep Herb safe, send him to Virginia Military Institute and place him on his staff. After singing "My Old Kentucky Home" and "Annie Laurie," by the Steinway in the parlor, and frolicking all over the house, Stuart took young Herb aside and said, "Young man, I want to know about the dirt or county roads, up yonder leading to Hanover." The general placed a big map on the Shriver's dining room table. As he did he asked, "Are roads wide enough for artillery?"[94]

Herb had not seen artillery, but he told Jeb that big wagons, pulled by four mules could travel the roads. This was adequate. Stuart then took the young man to Mrs. Shriver's room and popped the question. Like any good mother, she was a little apprehensive, but agreed to let him go. By mid-morning after hot coffee, rolls and biscuits, Stuart and Herb Shriver were ready to go.[95]

The Shrivers were impressed with Stuart's magnificent carriage, his superb voice, his gracious thanks. As the column prepared to move, those present would never forget the trampling of the horses, the noise of the caissons and cannons as once again they took the Roads to Gettysburg.[96]

Five miles were covered and they reached the Mason-Dixon Line. Littlestown was just five miles away. Stuart's cavalry watered their horses in a little stream. Scouts were sent out and returned with bad news. They were shaken by the sight of a large force of Union troops near Littlestown. Stuart conferred with some of his officers and decided that an attack was unwise. Young Herb Shriver told the general there was a dirt road leading to Hanover. This was quickly taken. But at noon Stuart encountered Union cavalry in that Pennsylvania town.[97]

Henry Warner Slocum, the Twelfth Corps commander, was upset over some of the problems he faced this Monday. From near Woodsborough (his spelling) he sent a message:

> Owing to the very serious delay I have met with today from trains which I think do not belong on this road, I shall not be able to get beyond Double Pipe Creek to-night with my command. When I left Frederick, there were a great number of men from every corps in the army lying about the streets, beastly drunk. I think it important that a cavalry force should be sent back to bring them up.[98]

The drunken soldiers were a problem for Marsena Patrick, the provost marshal. He agreed that the roads were completely blocked "with trains and troops." Late on the rainy evening of June 29, Patrick sent two squadrons of cavalry "back to Frederick & clean out that town which was reported full of drunken men & Stragglers."[99]

Patrick moved in response to orders from Butterfield which stated:

> The major-general commanding directs that you take immediate and prompt measures to have all the stragglers and drunken soldiers driven out of Frederick and sent to their commands.[100]

Then there was another problem. The wagon train of the Third Corps was at a standstill at Middleburg, delaying all movements in the rear. Sickles was told to get the train in motion.[101]

As the damp, dismal day drew to a close, Meade drafted marching orders for the next day. The Twelfth Corps was to pass the Third and proceed to Littlestown. The Fifth Corps was ordered to the Pipe Creek Crossing between Littlestown and Westminster. The Sixth Corps was directed to go from Westminster to Manchester. Reynolds was told to take the First Corps to Marsh Creek just south of Gettysburg. The artillery was to move to Piney Run Crossing between Taneytown and Littlestown. Headquarters were moving to Taneytown at 8:00 A.M.[102]

The last Monday in June was like the lull before the storm for Pickett's division, encamped one mile north of Chambersburg. There wasn't a ripple of excitement in camp. Some of the bands were playing, and Randolph Shotwell closed his eyes and forgot that he was a soldier, part of a mighty host, "invading an enemy country." In the distance were the steeples of Chambersburg, and the Confederate cavalry was at the gates of Harrisburg. Yet he could not get over the pause and inactivity. News arrived that all able-bodied men were throwing up earthen defenses in Harrisburg. The diggers were groaning, and the "gallant Melish" were nervous and anxious. With all that could be done, here they were taking it easy in Chambersburg as though on picnic. They should be striking fear and terror into the hearts of the Yankees, seeking freedom and independence.[103]

Shotwell did not expect to attack Harrisburg or Philadelphia, but why not hit Baltimore or Washington before the Army of the Potomac was in position. They were wasting precious time, or at least Randolph Shotwell thought so. The North Carolinian was filled with contempt for some in the area who pretended to be Southern friends from the beginning. For two years the Civil War had been something far away, now it was right there in their midst, on their doorstep, in their backyard. "Lee's ragged, sun-burnt, wild, half-starved, half-clad, half-shod, half-armed Rebels" came and blackened every road, filled every field, and startled the people of Chambersburg who so "complacently called for the stripping and destroying of Southern farms, these strange warriors are like a dreadful nightmare."[104]

Shotwell was impressed with the Dutch thrift. "Every farmhouse has its outdoor bake-oven, its big barrel of sauerkraut . . . ; its pile of mighty cheeses, its troops of ducks; its squadrons of turkeys; and brigades of chickens, with skirmish lines of Guinea fowls and peacocks; its orchards and 'Sass' garden; its smoke house, milk house, wood shed, tool house, and a long tier of bee hives; its barnyard full of calves, pigs, sheep and horses. What a feast!"

In contrast was the Confederate infantry with sore and swollen feet, barely existing on six hard crackers a day, and a bite of spoiled meat.

Shotwell found a copy of "Harpers Weekly" which depicted the burning and violent acts of the Rebels north of the Potomac. This was a lie. Folks north of the Mason-Dixon Line were treated much better than the Yankees treated people in Virginia. But Shotwell felt the only way the North could be brought to its knees was to destroy property and let the war in all its horrible reality come home to them.[105]

Soldier Moore had a good meal today consisting of chicken pie, molasses, buttermilk, and pork.

Strange things occurred during the days of June 26-29 in the Chambersburg area. Lee Hoover's grandfather Etter lived on a farm near Red Bridge. He took his horses to Horse Valley, hoping they would be safe. Only an old work horse was kept. But the Rebels came and took it. One lad in gray saw a can of pepper on the shelf of the stove. He took the whole can, saying he had not had pepper for a long time. Then he apologized for his strange behavior.[106]

John B. Hege's grandfather lived near Marion. When the Rebels started taking wheat, he bored a hole through the floor of the granary and ran seventy-five bushels of wheat into the barn cellar. It is said that Lee stopped at this farm for a drink of water.[107]

Beyond Marion was a small house of worship called White Church. Some of the women had just arrived on Friday

391

morning to clean the church when the Rebel column started going by. So the cleaning ladies just stood and watched for awhile.[108]

A Mr. Henry placed his money under the large anvil block in his blacksmith shop. Some of the gray riders shoed their own horses at his anvil but never discovered the money. A Mr. Grossman placed his money in a glass jar and weighing it down, sank it to the bottom of his cistern until the Rebels left.[109]

Some of the Confederates camped on the lawn of what is now Sellers Funeral Home, while one of the family's best horses was kept hidden in the basement. A young black couple was hidden in the attic to escape detection. A lot of the farmers in the Marion area took their four-horse wagons and headed for North Mountain until things quieted down.[110]

On this last Monday in June, Fremantle thought about the conduct of the Confederate army. It was amazing. Virginia had been devastated; Darien, Georgia, burned. And many of the men had lost their own crops and homes. Some wanted to burn Pennsylvania, but they abided by Lee's order. For the most part, the Confederate occupation of southern Pennsylvania remains a model of humane treatment by an invading army. Despite the insults of the residents of Chambersburg, the soldiers did not strike back. The soldiers, however, felt uncomfortable being unwelcome, and many did not bother to go to town. "To anyone who has seen as I have the ravages of the Northern troops in Southern towns, this forbearance seems most commendable and surprising. Yet these Pennsylvania Dutch don't seem the least thankful, and really appear unaware that their own troops have been for two years treating Southern towns with ten times more harshness. . . . (They) openly state that they don't care which side wins as long as they are left alone."[111]

Monday evening, Fremantle and Longstreet had a long talk about Texas. "I complimented him upon the manner in which the Confederate sentries do their duty."[112] The general laughed and said that "after looking at your pass, they might show you another way into town."

Fremantle also saw Generals Pendleton and Pickett. The fighting parson "is Chief of Artillery to the Army, and was a West Pointer," and an Episcopal clergyman from Lexington, Virginia. "He unites the military and clerical professions together, and continues to preach whenever he gets a chance. On these occasions he wears a surplice over his uniform." Pickett wears his hair in "long ringlets, and is altogether rather a desperate looking character."[113]

This might have been the day that could have changed the history of the United States and the history of the world. As the dawn broke, Richard S. Ewell was getting Robert Rodes ready to advance from Carlisle to Harrisburg. Johnson's division, back at the McAllister place, was told to be prepared to move. The Second Corps of the Army of Northern Virginia was poised to march on the capital of Pennsylvania. We cannot imagine the consequences of this in terms of morale and politics had they been successful. As it was, they came within hours of completing this feat, marching from Fredericksburg to within striking distance of Harrisburg.

Shortly after noon, Captain Richardson and two staff officers returned with the news that although there were earthworks and some militia at Harrisburg, they posed no problem, and could be easily brushed aside. Everybody was ready. Perhaps in twenty-four to thirty-six hours, a great northern city would be in Confederate hands, and maybe, just maybe, Lincoln would seek peace.[114]

But Rodes and Johnson never got the opportunity to march on Harrisburg. At 3:00 P.M. a courier came from General Lee with the news that the Army of the Potomac was in Frederick, and that Ewell should move back to Chambersburg. This was a bitter disappointment for the Second Corps. They looked upon themselves as the best soldiers in the Rebel army. They wanted to take Harrisburg. But it was not to be. Instead, Ed Johnson was ordered to turn south. The men were shocked when they took the road. They thought they were going in the wrong direction. The trains of the Second Corps and the Artillery Reserve followed Johnson's infantry. Rodes was to follow, and a courier was sent to contact Early in York. The Army of Northern Virginia had come so far, so close, yet Harrisburg was not to be theirs. One of Johnson's men wrote, "Our disappointment and chagrin were extreme."[115]

Shortly after Johnson's men started south, another message came changing the assembly point from Chambersburg to Cashtown. But it was too late to turn Johnson's division around. Thus Ewell ordered him to turn south at Green Village and take the Black Rock Road to Fayetteville, and then move east to Cashtown. Lee had not ordered a night march, so Ewell permitted the men to rest.[116]

That night, the residents of Carlisle and the men under Robert Rodes mingled together at the Carlisle Barracks and around the campfires. The word had gotten out that the Rebels were leaving. But they had been well behaved, and there was no ill feeling toward the men themselves. So the people of Carlisle chatted as the last Monday in June came to an end. Lads from North Carolina, Virginia, and Georgia talked to the residents of Pennsylvania. All longed for peace and the speedy conclusion of the war.[117] They asked some of the same questions stated during the Vietnam conflict, "How did we get in it? What's it all about? I don't want to fight."

Sadness had come to Carlisle as some of their men had given their all on the fields of battle in the South. They and the gray-clad soldiers to whom they were talking realized a battle was imminent. There would be more sadness, and more family circles broken. So there was apprehension in Carlisle that night. As the hour grew late, gloom set in. Some of the ladies started to weep, and there were tears in the eyes of some of the young men in the springtime of life. When the time came to part, many could not speak. But some said, "Good night. God help us all." But thirty-six hours later, nearly half of the men visited by the folks of Carlisle this June night, would be lying in the fields north of Gettysburg, dead or wounded.

There was sadness in the bivouac areas. Richard Ewell was angry and testy.[118] It seemed as though he was almost in a daze when he was ordered back from Carlisle. He wanted to assault Harrisburg. In his confusion, he forgot to recall

The Old Toll Gate House—Along the path of the Union Third
and Twelfth corps. Boyhood home of the author.

The Eagle Hotel in Gettysburg.

Jenkins and the cavalry. He had to return to the maps and issue new orders.

This morning, John B. Gordon awoke in Wrightsville on the banks of the Susquehanna River. He and his staff were served breakfast by Mr. Magee's daughter, Mrs. Luther L. Rewalt, the great-grandmother of the writer, Gore Vidal. Gordon thought the family was pro-Southern. But he was quickly told otherwise. The hospitality had been extended because he and his men had saved their homes from fire.[119]

It was foggy along the river this morning. Two Union officers rode to the banks of Susquehanna on the Columbia side to see if the Confederates had obtained lumber or timbers to launch a river crossing. Soon the word came that the Confederates were headed back to York.[120]

After their breakfast in Wrightsville, Gordon's command started to retrace their steps to York. While they were marching, "Jube" Early's men were busy in York rounding up food and supplies. Early was walking around town telling folks he was going to put the city to the torch. He wanted to destroy the government buildings, and also make York suffer for Yankee damages inflicted on the South. He planned to burn the railroad shops until told that many homes were nearby and would be endangered. Thus only the switches, tracks, telegraph, and railroad cars were destroyed.[121]

The ladies of York stayed inside. But the men mingled freely with the invaders. They discussed politics and war. Some of the local men denounced the government in Washington. Early posted guards at hotels and shops to protect them and to prevent looting.

York was isolated. There were no papers, and the wires had been cut. Yet John Gall of the Sanitary Commission walked into York without being questioned. The Confederates were in mixed garb, gray, brown, blue, and gray. Many of the trousers had been captured at Winchester.

The Rebels were poorly shod. Most of them had a thin blanket thrown over their shoulder, and a rifle and cartridge box, or between twelve and fifteen pounds of equipment. Gall found men from Louisiana camped at the York fairgrounds. The supply wagons were drawn up in a hollow square. The men were camped by companies in the square. Most of them had no tents.[122]

While the Union infantry tramped through Frederick and Carroll counties, John Gordon continued on toward York, marching westward from Wrightsville. He reached York about 4:00 P.M. and marched on through the city, and camped a mile and a half out on the Carlisle Road. Several hours later, Captain Elliott Johnson of Ewell's staff arrived with orders to concentrate near Cashtown.

At 9:00 P.M. Early withdrew the guards from the shops and the liquor stores in York. Avery's North Carolina troops marched in the direction of Rodes's bivouac.[123]

Meanwhile, A. P. Hill put Henry Heth's division in motion today. It was headed east to Cashtown, not far from Gettysburg. Pender was to follow on Tuesday, and R. H. Anderson on Wednesday.[124]

This was a busy Monday for Eric Dahlgren of the United States Cavalry. Scouring the countryside around Greencastle, with T. S. Paulding as his guide, he captured some Rebel mail, including Lee-Davis correspondence.

The farmers of the Cashtown area suffered a lot as a result of the invasion. Heth's command and others from the Third Corps of the Army of Northern Virginia, spent the twenty-ninth and thirtieth "foraging and gathering provisions for the army."

> They seized beef cattle, flour, and grain, took possessions of the mills near at hand, for the purpose of grinding the stolen grain, and compelled the farmers' wives to bake the flour into bread. They were thus gathering stores, resting, and feeding themselves and their animals and placing themselves in readiness for an encounter with our forces.[125]

In rating the behavior of the Confederate troops, the folks of Adams County felt the Georgians were the mildest and best. Next came those from North Carolina and Alabama. Those from South Carolina, Texas, Louisiana, and Virginia were the worst. They were bitter and filled with hatred. If given an opportunity, they would vent their wrath. After all, the North had ravaged the soil of Virginia.

After dark this evening, Jacob Hoke went up into the steeple of the Reformed Church in Chambersburg.

> From that elevated position we had an uninterrupted view for miles around us. The line of the railroad could be traced by the numerous fires still burning. The sound of the drum was heard in the direction of Pickett's Camp. Along the South Mountain, for miles up and down the valley, innumerable lights were seen. That these lights were used as signals for communicating information, we well knew, but of their occasion and import we were of course ignorant. Perhaps the fact about to be related will solve this problem. Some time in the after part of this night, probably about one or two o'clock, I was awakened by my wife who told me to come to the window for some important movement was going on among the Confederates. Peering cautiously through the half-closed shutters we saw a continuous stream of wagons driven hurriedly through our street. They were coming back from the direction of Harrisburg, and turning east at the Public Square, drove on out the Gettysburg pike. Although these wagons were heavily loaded, as the grinding noise they made indicated, they were sometimes driven at a trot. A low, rumbling noise could be heard which sounded strange in the stillness of the night, as if the whole valley were filled with moving trains. These wagons proved to be part of Ewell's train, and their rapid passage eastward was a part in the great act of the concentration about Gettysburg, which will be fully described hereafter.
>
> But what was the cause of the sudden change in General Lee's plans, and the rapid concentration of his army. . . .[126]

While Hoke was observing things in Chambersburg, an angry and bitter Joe Hooker was thinking over his situation in Baltimore. His number was up. He might just as well resign from the service as to be sent to a small outpost with a token command.

Looking at the Confederate positions this Monday evening, we see Ewell's Second Corps scattered over Pennsylvania. Early was still in the York area. Robert Rodes was in Carlisle, ready to move in the morning, and Ed Johnson at Stoughstown. Jenkins's cavalry was still on the west bank of the Susquehanna, just five or six miles from Harrisburg.

Powell Hill's Third Corps was closer together. Henry Heth had reached Cashtown, east of South Mountain, while Anderson was at Greenwood, and Dorsey Pender around Fayetteville.

James Longstreet had McLaws and Hood near Fayetteville, with George Pickett's men about three miles northeast of Chambersburg.

Imboden's cavalry was at Mercersburg and on patrol at Cove Gap on the road to McConnellsburg. Jeb Stuart was at Union Mills.

Jacob Hoke thinks that perhaps signal fires were used to send messages to the scattered portions of Lee's army. Likewise couriers went out into the night telling of the concentration at Gettysburg. It would take eight or ten hours for a courier to reach "Jube" Early.[127] Early the next morning, Hoke and his friends sent word of Lee's movement to authorities in Harrisburg. Young Stephen W. Pomeroy was the messenger. The word was carried by way of Strasburg and Roxbury to the Amberson Valley, over into Path Valley, to Concord and Port Royal, and the telegraph. Young Pomeroy walked about seventeen miles and rode approximately forty-one on his important mission.

What kind of men were these who tramped the Roads to Gettysburg, enduring the intense heat, the frequent rains? For the most part, according to Ted Gerrish, "they were sober, candid, intelligent, thoughtful men," well aware of "their grave responsibility as defenders of the nation's life."

Their character is seen on the evening of June 29 as they camp after a thirty-mile march in Carroll County. It had been a long, damp day. Supper consisted of coffee and hardtack. But they were thinking of loved ones. Before rolling up in a raincoat on the ground, they look once again at treasured mementos from home, or read once again the last letter received from dear ones. By the dim light of the campfires, "amidst these sacred reminders, and beside the torn and faded battle flags, resolutions were formed that were to be felt on the battlefield—resolutions that sealed the defeat of General Lee. . . ."[128]

XIII

THE LAST DAY OF JUNE

Tuesday—June 30

On this day before the battle of Gettysburg, the First Corps under Reynolds left the bivouac area near Emmitsburg, and marched a relatively short distance to Marsh Creek.

Hancock's Second Corps rested in Uniontown, recovering from several days of strenuous marching. Toward evening they struck their tents and marched for Taneytown, ten miles away.

Sickles and the Third Corps moved from Taneytown toward Emmitsburg. A roadside marker now stands at the location of the corps on June 30.

But there was no rest for the weary men of the Fifth Corps. They left Libertytown and marched via Johnsville to Union Bridge to Union Mills.

Another twenty-mile hike was ahead for Sedgwick and the Sixth Corps. They left New Windsor for Westminster in Carroll County. Then it was on to Manchester, and their position at the right end of Meade's Pipe Creek Line.

Slocum's Twelfth Corps marched ten to fifteen miles from Taneytown, across the Mason-Dixon Line to Littlestown. Meanwhile, Howard and the Eleventh Corps rested near Emmitsburg.

Meade placed his headquarters on the Shunk farm at the north end of Taneytown. He was just about in the center of his Pipe Creek line.

The Union Signal Corps established headquarters in Taneytown also, using the tower of the Lutheran Church as a center of activity. Flags were used by day to send messages, and flares by night.[1]

What a sight a bird flying over Frederick and Carroll counties in Maryland, and over southern Pennsylvania would have seen those last days in June 1863. Long lines of gray and blue could be seen on the country roads. They looked like blue and gray serpents, winding over "hill and dale." Just a few days in history, but what excitement and adventure for those who lived during those memorable hours. Just as we will not forget the attack on Pearl Harbor or V-J Day, so those folks never forgot the experiences along the Roads to Gettysburg.

And so they marched at the rate of two and a half miles per hour. Each commander hoping to get his men across the path of the enemy first, destiny pointing toward a place called Gettysburg.

George G. Meade left the Middleburg area on the morning of June 30 and headed for Taneytown. For two days he would direct his army from this historic Carroll County town.

Meade formulated plans quickly. After receiving the news that the Confederates had withdrawn from near Harrisburg and York, he sent a dispatch to the Union Corps commanders informing them:

> If the enemy assume the offensive and attack, it is my intention, after holding them in check sufficiently long to withdraw the trains . . . to withdraw the army from its present position and form line of battle with the left resting in the neighborhood of Middleburg and the right at Manchester, the general direction being that of Pipe Creek.[2]

Taneytown was much like Sharpsburg a year previous. Both were small towns with a proud history. Both were farming villages located in fertile areas. And neither one dreamed of the events which would link their names forever to the great events of the Civil War.

By June of 1863, Taneytown had sent seventy-five of her five hundred men off to aid the Union cause. When a regular army regiment of cavalry came through the village from Carlisle on the way to Washington, they were received with a

401

great welcome. But as June neared an end, alarm spread among the farmers and the people who lived in Taneytown. Lee was north of the Potomac. The Union army was in pursuit, and somewhere, perhaps near Taneytown, the two would meet. What then?

On June 30 Taneytown became just about the center of the Union line. The new commander, George G. Meade, established headquarters north of town. When the news came that the Army of the Potomac was on the way, many of the prominent citizens of the town, led by the Reverend Levi T. Williams, went out to welcome General Meade and his staff. As the minister and the general neared the town, the women and children lining the streets cheered. Patriotic songs were sung. According to Taneytown history, General Meade made his headquarters in the Lutheran parsonage library. Field headquarters were established a mile outside of town on the Littlestown Road. The farm belonged to Benjamin Shunk.[3]

I CORPS

Thursday the First Corps had crossed the Potomac and pressed on to Barnesville. The next day it was on to Jefferson, and then on Saturday to Middletown and South Mountain. Sunday the men were ordered to Frederick, and on Monday came a twenty-five mile hike to Emmitsburg. The entire distance was covered on foot. Now it was a few more miles this last day in June to Marsh Creek. It was partly cloudy, and some accounts speak of early morning sprinkles.

About midmorning the three divisions with their brigades, regiments, and companies broke camp, and headed for the Mason-Dixon Line. Gettysburg was not far away. The march that started from the trenches near Fredericksburg two weeks earlier was about over.

Coming in from the Fairfield Road at 10:00 A.M., Paul's brigade ran into a roadblock. Elements of the Eleventh Corps were also moving through Emmitsburg. So Paul's men just

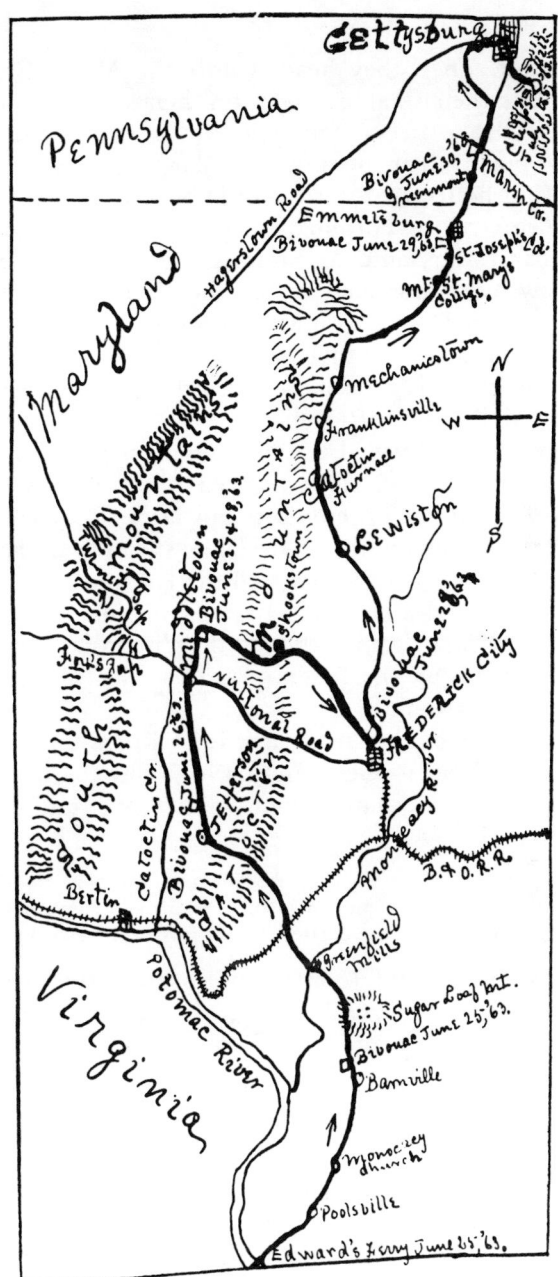

The First Corps moves toward Gettysburg. From
Curtis, *The 24th Michigan.*

403

had to wait. Then they headed north to Marsh Creek. For some it was their final bivouac, and their last roll call. For an example, 284 officers and men of the Thirteenth Massachusetts made their beds along Marsh Creek. In another twenty-four hours, two-thirds would be casualties.[4]

The Army of the Potomac mustered for pay on June 30 in the towns of Maryland. At Emmitsburg part of the Seventy-sixth New York was paid late in the afternoon. The rest of the unit was told to "wait until tomorrow." Major Grover did not sign the muster roll that evening. He never got to the task because the next day, he and one-third of the regiment fell in action on McPherson's Ridge.[5]

Colonel Dawes formed the Sixth Wisconsin for pay at the Emmitsburg campsite. He wondered if the rain would ever stop. "I don't think I ever before saw at this time of the year such a long continued, misty, drizzling storm as we have been marching through since we crossed the Potomac."

When the First Corps left Emmitsburg on Tuesday, and headed for Pennsylvania, the Sixth Wisconsin was the advance regiment and the first to cross the line dividing Maryland and Pennsylvania.[6]

The author can almost picture John Reynolds leading his men on the Road to Gettysburg. No doubt the residents of Lewistown and Mechanicstown could have said with the Comte de Paris:

> Meade intrusted the task of clearing and directing his left to two men equally noted for quickness of perception, promptness of decision, and gallantry on the battlefield—Buford and Reynolds.[7]

Perhaps the sight of John Reynolds made the men of the First Corps feel like O. O. Howard, who said in describing the different types of officers:

> (There were) others . . . who had a steady hand in governing, were generous to a fault, quick to recognize merit, trusted you and sought to gain your confidence, and, as one would anticipate, were the foremost in battle. These generally secured the best results in administration and in active campaigning. To (this) class belonged General Reynolds. From soldiers, cadets, and officers, junior and senior, he always secured reverence for his serious character, respect for his

404

ability, care for his uniform discipline, admiration for his fearlessness. . . .[8]

Today was an easy one for Charles Wainwright. It was a short six-mile trip from Emmitsburg to the place of final bivouac for many members of the First Corps. The artillery commander was engaged in administrative procedures after making camp. The monthly returns had to be completed. The First Division was on Marsh Creek, three miles up the road, while the Second and Third divisions and headquarters were closer to Moritz Tavern or crossroads.

Like some other soldiers, Wainwright found the Pennsylvanians more greedy than the Marylanders, and not as warm and friendly. Prices went up, and the people fussed if fence rails were burned. One man wanted to be paid more than the worth of his farm for a poor field of clover. His wife claimed she had been baking bread and giving them all the butter and milk they could use. What she meant was, upon investigation, that she was selling butter and milk "at from three to ten times their market value."[9]

One of the regiments bivouacked at Emmitsburg and then near Marsh Creek was the Seventy-sixth New York. Before the passing of another day 234 of the 370 who pitched their tents along the Roads to Gettysburg would be casualties.

There was great joy in the ranks of the Eighty-eighth Pennsylvania as they crossed the state line. For many of them it was the first time in two years that they had been home.[10]

The famed Iron Brigade, with the Sixth Wisconsin in advance, crossed the Mason-Dixon Line into Pennsylvania, and moved on nearly to Greenmount in Adams County, . . . "160 miles from the starting point on the Rappahannock, and bivouacked about noon near Marsh Creek."[11]

The soldiers from the Midwest were close to Gettysburg. "The bivouac was but six miles from a field from which their blood will make immortal ere another sunset. Alas, the last campfire for many a weary soldier."[12]

The officers were busy. Not only did the troops have to be mustered for pay, but quartermaster, commissary, ordnance, and regimental returns had to be completed. Then, as now, June 30 was the end of the fiscal year.

General Wadsworth had other things on his mind. He wondered where the Rebs were. He sent Lieutenant Kress to headquarters in an effort to get a map of the area. The aide had no luck.[13]

We can hardly imagine the job the quartermasters had on the Roads to Gettysburg. Every man was entitled to two pounds of rations per day. Multiply that by eighty thousand and we get an idea of the food that was needed in the Army of the Potomac. Besides that, there had to be food for all the horses and the mules. Some of the cavalrymen carried ten-twelve bags of oats for the horses. Once again multiply this by the thousand and you see the problem. And horses pulling supply wagons and artillery pieces got hungry.

Reynolds sent a message to Howard saying that his headquarters were at Moritz Tavern, "one division and a battery on the Gettysburg Road, one ... on the road to Fairfield from here (Moritz Crossroads) and one in reserve on the Gettysburg Road.

The bivouac at Marsh Creek was a welcome relief to the men of the Iron Brigade and to the other members of the First Corps. After the tents were pitched and coffee made, the men took it easy. They did draw some rations.

General Buford's cavalry brigade rode by. As always, there was some good-natured kidding between the horsemen and the foot soldiers. But the cavalrymen had news. They had found the "Johnnies" just ahead and in large numbers. The men of the First Corps realized that they were on the eve of a great battle. For over a week they had been marching and maneuvering to keep between Lee and the great cities of the nation. Now the enemy was in sight. And a struggle was sure to follow.[14]

Some of the men wrote letters to loved ones. Others pinned notes to their clothing to be sent home in case they numbered with the fallen. The campsite was more solemn that night. Some were observed in prayer while others read the Bible. The officers of the Iron Brigade met around a campfire. They were among the last to turn in that night. They would have had a terrible sleep had they known what was ahead. For in twenty-four hours, the Iron Brigade, one of

America's greatest fighting units, would almost cease to exist due to losses at Gettysburg, a little town seven miles away. And so as the campfires faded away on June 30 at Marsh Creek there was a foreboding feeling in the air.

John Reynolds must have been a little anxious. The men in gray were on Pennsylvania soil. His Lancaster home was not far away. Thus far he had been denied the privilege of leading a corps in combat. He wanted to be sure his men were at the right place at the right time. General John established his headquarters in a back room of Moritz's Tavern, close to a crossroads and just south of Marsh Creek. After looking over reports and maps, he took some tea and crackers and chatted with one of Meade's staff officers. Reynolds was in the advance of the left wing of the army. He wanted to confer with O. O. Howard, ten years his junior, but a soldier he remembered well since the days when Howard was a West Point instructor, and he the superintendent of West Point.[15]

About dark on Tuesday, June 30, Oliver O. Howard, resting at Mount Saint Mary's, received a message to come to the headquarters of John Reynolds.

Lt. F. W. Gilbreth, Howard's aide-de-camp, and an orderly, made the six-mile journey in less than an hour. Reynolds was in a little house near the creek. Dismounting, Howard was led to a back room at the south end of the house. Here he met John Reynolds. The room was relatively bare, just a table and a few chairs. The table was laden with dispatches and maps.[16]

After the customary greetings, Reynolds handed Howard Meade's confidential appeal to the army to do its best. The commanders were urged to address the men of their commands urging them to the peak of patriotic fervor to save the Republic.

The two men read the news dispatches of the day. Messages had arrived from Meade at Taneytown, from Buford at Gettysburg, and from local citizens. The reports conflicted somewhat, but they all pointed to the fact that Robert E. Lee and the Confederate Army of Northern Virginia was nearby. Reynolds and Howard pondered over the maps and

407

discussed the possibilities of battle, including what part their commands would play.

Howard thought Reynolds seemed depressed, perhaps having a premonition of death or danger. But then he thought better of it, thinking that the wing commander was anxious over the "scattered condition" of the Army of the Potomac. About eleven o'clock, Howard left Reynolds and rode back to his comfortable bed at Mount Saint Mary's where he soon fell fast asleep.[17]

XI CORPS

Howard and the Eleventh Corps had a relatively easy day. Some of his men experienced the added work of striking camp and moving into spots vacated by the First Corps, but on the whole, they had the opportunity to take it easy, mingle with the folks of Emmitsburg, and partake of generous helpings of country food.

A resident of Waynesboro stopped to visit Howard in the morning. He reported no rebels in his hometown. But Millerstown or Fairfield was occupied. The gentleman also reported that a portion of Hill's corps had spent the night on Wingard farm on the road from Funkstown to Chambersburg.[18]

III CORPS

Meanwhile, the Third Corps, the other unit of the left wing, spent most of the day in and around Taneytown. But then in the afternoon, the soldiers were told to "pack up and hit the road." It was a short march to Bridgeport.

This was in compliance with Meade's order sent at 12:45 P.M. Sickles was told to take three days' rations, sixty rounds of ammunition per man, and his ambulances.[19] Meade related that the enemy was reported in force at Gettysburg. Sickles was to move without delay. Strong forces of pickets were to be thrown out on the roads from Emmitsburg to Greencastle and Chambersburg. Dan did not have to bother too much about an attack from the south as Merritt's cavalry was still at Mechanicstown.[20]

Hancock and Sykes also received orders to have three days of rations prepared, along with sixty rounds of ammunition.

Writing from Bridgeport on the Monocacy at 7:45, Sickles told Meade, "I have gone into camp here. . . . I sent Captain Crocker of my staff to communicate (with) General Reynolds. My First Division and two batteries are farther toward Emmitsburg (across Middle Creek).[21]

Sickles had had problems with the earlier order conflicting with an oral order. Meade and Reynolds had made different requests. Reynolds wanted the Third Corps to take position on Cat Tail Branch "face toward Gettysburg, and cover the roads leading from Gettysburg."[22]

Although the road from Taneytown to Bridgeport was sparsely populated, the Third Corps received a great welcome along the country road. Some of the farmers waved "handkerchiefs and flags as the troops went by, and supplied the hungry with bread, pies, milk and poultry, for a reasonable price."

Near Bridgeport a little girl kept shouting in a shrill voice, "Three cheers for the Union." One of the soldiers smiled and yelled back, "Three cheers for you, little girl." She was a proud and patriotic lass. The unnamed girl had the last word, "Three cheers for you, too, sir."

Fifer Bardeen noted that Taneytown was "a very hospitable place. . . . Here we received our mail. The fellows had a chance to wash up, which was needed as they had got rather lousy." The mail was most welcome. "Many a poor fellow got his last letter here."[23]

For the Third Corps, a source of constant enjoyment and inspiration on the march through Maryland was the band. They always seemed to be in the lead, and when entering a village, the men in the ranks found them on some balcony, front porch, or grouped around the town pump, playing

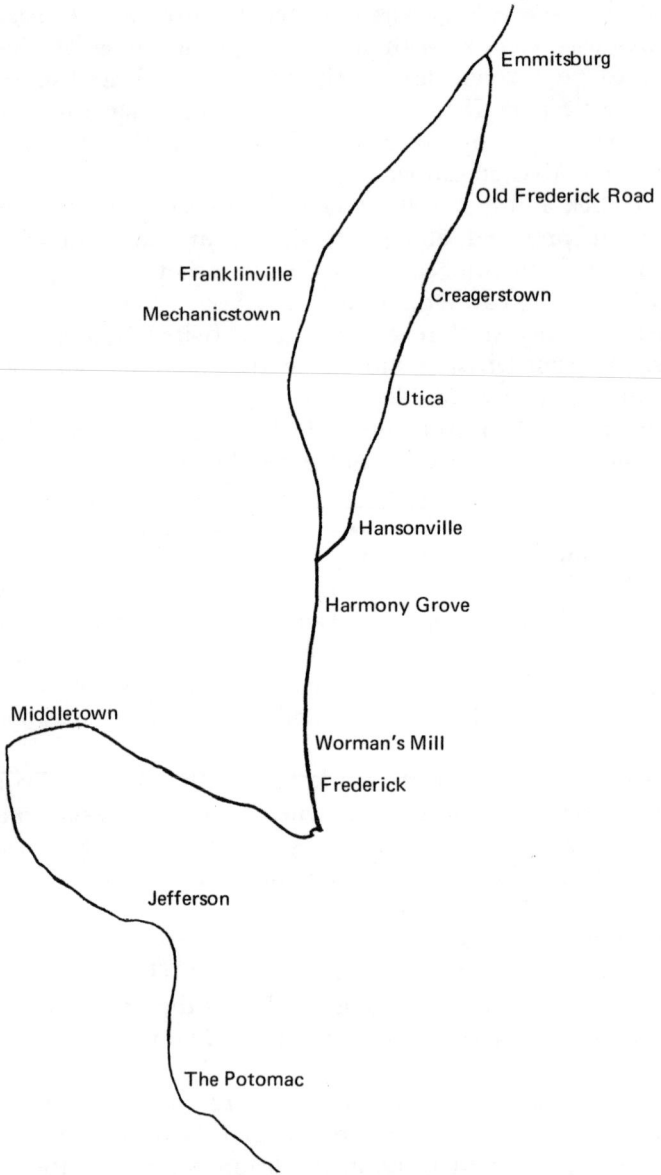

Route of the First and Eleventh corps on the
Roads to Gettysburg.

410

lively military and patriotic music. Often the girls and the children were singing along.

Many men in the Third Corps spent the night of June 30 in wheat fields near Bridgeport. "The grain had been cut and bound, and the sheaves made luxurious beds for the soldiers."[24]

The Third Corps rested in their "tented fields" near Taneytown on Tuesday, June 30. Throughout the morning, large groups of people came to visit the soldiers. A welcome formation took place in the morning, the troops were mustered to receive their pay.

But there was no time for the Third Corps to continue their pleasant moments with the people of Taneytown and nearby areas. Early in the afternoon the troops marched through the village via the plank road, through Bridgeport to positions near Emmitsburg.[25]

As the 105th Pennsylvania marched through Taneytown, their historian spelled it Tawneytown, a young lady, proposed "three cheers for the Stars and Stripes." The color guard held the flag aloft, and everybody cheered, the men in the ranks, and the men and women by the roadside. The noise echoed off the buildings.[26]

According to Charles Bardeen, June 30 was rainy. "An old man brought cakes and bread into Camp, to give to the Soldiers. He would take no pay."

That evening Bardeen and a comrade took supper in a Maryland farmhouse near Emmitsburg. Their host took no pay. The Maryland bread, baked in ovens outside, tasted like manna in the wilderness.[27]

On the evening of June 30, Sickles made his headquarters in a farmhouse east of Emmitsburg on the Taneytown Road. Off in the distance, he could see a place that in two days would link his name in a hot argument, Little Round Top. The Third Corps went into bivouac in the nearby fields. The men were tired. They had been marching for three weeks. They had not marched as far or as fast as some of the other units, but they were tired from continuous marching. The pastoral beauty of the Maryland countryside brought refreshment to their spirits. The area had not been touched by

411

war. Jeb Stuart had brought his cavalry through last October, but there was none of the desolation which marked the Virginia countryside. There was another change. Instead of hostile stares, the folks of Emmitsburg and the nearby farmers cheered the men of the Third Corps and brought them fresh bread, cakes and milk. It proved to be the calm and the rest before the storm.[28]

II CORPS

There were some lighter moments though. The Second Corps was resting in the fields around Uniontown, ten miles from Taneytown. General Hancock and Correspondent Coffin had the opportunity to think about an experience of Monday, as "the two armies were approaching each other like storm clouds." Coffin and Hancock had ridden together for part of the exhausting thirty-two-mile journey.[29]

> We came to a farm-house, where, by the gate-way, with roses in bloom around them and the pinks perfuming the air, stood a mother and her daughters, with loaves of bread in baskets and jars of apple-butter—the mother cutting great slices of bread, the daughters spreading them with the sauce and presenting them to the soldiers.
> "Hurrah for the mother! three cheers for the girls!" shouted the soldiers, as they took of the luscious gifts and hastened on.

One wonders who these folks were and where they lived. The author's great-great-grandmother lived along the route of the Second Corps march. She fed the soldiers, so it might have been relatives.

But Coffin did not stay in one place very long. He had an eye for news and must get as much as possible. So he rode on and joined Sykes's Fifth Corps as it entered Liberty. A farmer rode into town. His wagon was covered with a white cloth.

"What have ye got to sell, old fellow? Gingerbread, eh?" Said a soldier, raising the cloth and peeping in. "What do ye ask?"

"Haven't any to sell."

". . . See here, old fellow, won't ye sell me a hunk of your gingerbread?" said the soldier pulling out his wallet.

"No."

"Well, you are a mean old cuss. It would be serving you right to tip up your old cart. Here we are marching all night and all day to protect your property and fight for ye. We haven't had any breakfast, and may not get any dinner. You are a set of mean cusses round here, I reckon."

The farmer stood up on his wagon seat, took off the table-cloths, and said:

> "I didn't bring any bread here to sell. My wife and daughters sat up all night to bake it for you, and you are welcome to all I've got, and I wish I had ten times as much. Help yourselves."
>
> "See here, my friend, I take back all the hard words I said about you," said the soldier, shaking hands with the farmer, who sat on his wagon with tears rolling down his cheeks.[30]

While the Second Corps was encamped near Uniontown, Frank Haskell had time to think over the area the corps had covered in the last two weeks:

> In moving from Falmouth, Va., the army was formed in several columns, and took several roads. The Second Corps . . . was the last to move, and left Falmouth at daybreak on the 15th of June, and pursued its march through Aquia, Dumfries, Wolf Run Shoales, Centerville, Gainesville, Thoroughfare Gap—this last we left on June 25, marching back to Haymarket where we had a skirmish with the cavalry and horse artillery of the enemy.—Gum Spring, crossing the Potomac at Edward's Ferry, thence through Poolesville, Frederick, Liberty and Union Town. We marched from Frederick to Union Town, a distance of thirty-two miles, from eight o'clock a.m. to nine p.m. on the 28th. . . . I think this is the longest march, accomplished in so short a time, by a corps during the war. On the 28th, while we were near this latter place, we breathed a full breath of joy, and of hope. The Providence of God had been with us—we ought not to have doubted it—General Meade commanded the Army of the Potomac.[31]

Uniontown was indeed a wonderful place. The Second Corps was treated like conquering heroes. The farmers and townspeople came to visit the tenting soldiers, bringing fresh milk, eggs, butter, and garden vegetables. All seemed full of happiness and peace. The thought of war almost escaped, for a time at least.

The little town has been designated a historic district now. The homes on the Main Street are quaint and well kept. There are brick sidewalks, and several places to hitch horses. The treelined streets remind the visitors of another day and another moment, June of 1863, when the famed Second Corps of the Army of the United States, "The Old Guard," was encamped around this beautiful little village.

Thomas Livermore had picket duty as June 30 drew to a close. His picket line was in a wheat field near Uniontown. The wheat was tall and ripe and provided luxurious resting places for off duty. Livermore was at the farmer's house. The man was very cordial although his wheat crop was being ruined. Colonel Livermore was invited to spend the night in the farmhouse, but insisted on sharing some of the privations of his men and slept on the barn floor.

Late that night, Livermore was informed by a staff officer that he had been named chief of ambulances for the Second Corps.[32]

Hancock received word during the day that the Rebels were on the New Windsor Road. Checking this out he found it was false. However, he did find that some of Stuart's men were stealing farm horses within several miles of Uniontown.

V CORPS

Monday had been a bad day for the Fifth Corps because they had been held up by the late departure of the Second Corps. So they got a late start from their bivouac area along Ballenger Creek and spent Monday night in the Liberty-Unionville sector. "The Last Day in June" they made up for the lack of progress on Monday. They were roused early and the corps set in motion from the fields near the roads.

The farmers flocked to their fences as the Fifth Corps

marched through Carroll County on Tuesday. They did not know what to make of the situation. Gazing upon the tanned and dusty veterans, they must have thought the jig was up for the Rebels.

Scenes of contented rural life greeted the Fifth Corps as they marched on the thirtieth. The highlight of the day occurred in Frizzellburg, Maryland, where the weary, footsore soldiers were greeted by one hundred children on the steps of the public school building. They had little flags in their hands and sang the national anthem and other patriotic numbers. This was a great moment. The men needed it because they were to cover twenty-eight rugged miles today.[33]

William Powell of the Fifth Corps tells us that one fine lady stood by her oven all day as the troops marched from Frederick to Union Mills, making hot biscuits. As fast as trays were finished she sent them to the front gate with her children.

The Fifth Corps, Meade's old command, marched through the lush Carroll County countryside. The men tramped by the homesteads of the German and Swiss settlers. Once again we can almost picture the roads crowded with men, wagons, and horses.

The German farmers, like many west of Baltimore, had been drawn to Western Maryland for several reasons: (1) good land, (2) elbow room, and (3) Lord Baltimore's attractive offer. To promote settlement in the backwoods, Lord Baltimore had given the generous terms of one cent per year per acre. An offer like that could not be beaten.

Carroll County in its virgin beauty must have been a delightful place. Of course, it still is. Some of the early grants reflect the nature and characteristics of the area. In the Union Mills vicinity some of the grants were called the Pines, Chestnut Ridge, Piney Creek, Bear Meadow, and Turkey Hill, among others.

The farmers needed mills to care for their crops. The old mills became centers of community activity. Most were built on the banks of streams for water power. One of the mills was erected at a place called Union Mills by Andrew and David Shriver in 1797.

415

Soon a village grew up along the Westminster-Littlestown Road, and about the mill. We now know the road as U.S. 140.

The Shriver house has remained in the same family from 1797 until the present. We wonder what the walls would say to us if they could talk. No doubt they would quote in part from a brochure on the Shriver Homestead:

> A visit here is like walking through a century and a half of American history. It is an old quaint picturesque country home, with 23 rooms planned for comfortable rural living. Located at an important crossroads leading from Baltimore to the West, it was also a stagecoach tavern. An early postoffice, a school, a magistrate's office, and a well known symbol of gracious Southern hospitality.[34]

According to the history of the Shriver Homestead, Washington Irving once was a guest in the house, and relaxed in front of the fireplace.

Americans can step back into those days at the annual Union Mills Corn Roast held about the first weekend in August. One can stroll through the village and visit the old mill and Shriver Homestead.

But on the evening of June 30, Union Mills was being approached by men in blue. The town and the Shriver Homestead were occupied by James Griffin's division of the Fifth Corps. The town became one of the fingers in the hand that Meade was stretching out against Robert E. Lee. Take the time to visit the Shriver Homestead and Union Mills, part of the story of Roads to Gettysburg. But now let's look at how it was for the men in the ranks as they came to and spent the night in Union Mills.

The experiences of the folks in Union Mills, especially those of the Shrivers, illustrate the division brought by the Civil War. Andrew Shriver built the original mill along Pipe Creek. Another Andrew lived on the homeplace and was Unionist. Yet they owned slaves. William Shriver lived across the road, was Southern in his loyalty, yet did not own slaves. Six of William Shriver's sons served in the armies of the South, while Andrew's son Henry served in the Twenty-sixth Emergency Regiment, a unit raised as the invasion occurred, and routed by veteran Confederate troops. The two families

416

visited back and forth, but relations were strained and debates often heated. Stuart made his headquarters at William Shriver's, while Fitz Lee camped at Andrew's place. Louis Shriver remembers seeing the black-bearded Lee rubbing sleep from his eyes on the morning of the thirtieth.

To the people of Union Mills, it appeared as though Stuart's cavalry had hardly disappeared from sight when the Union Fifth Corps arrived. General James Barnes established his camp and headquarters at the mill. This was upon the invitation of Andrew Shriver. Barnes was no spring chicken and gladly took a comfortable bed in the house. The officers of his staff slept on the porch and lawn.

The footsore infantrymen loved Pipe Creek. The cooling waters of the stream felt oh, so good on hot, blistered feet. Many went swimming clad in the "altogether."

Captain Batchelder took a liking to Austin Shriver's dog. It was gladly given as a gift to the Union officer. For years the soldier and the lad corresponded about the health of the dog. Most of the folks in Union Mills agreed that the presence of the Fifth Corps was a most welcome sight. Part of Barnes's division was at Andrew Shriver's, the rest at Sam Erb's and old Myers's. General Sykes established his headquarters at Samuel Erb's, just west of the village at a place called "The Oaks."

George Sykes, the corps commander, reported to Meade that Fitz Lee and Wade Hampton spent the previous night at Mr. Shriver's (who owns the mill). "They left this morning between 4 and 10 a.m., some toward Hanover and some toward Littlestown, but I take it all have gone toward Hanover. Their force is said to be about 5,000 with six guns. They are taking horses."

Sykes continued by saying that Crawford's "men must have marched today in the neighborhood of twenty-five miles. . . . My troops are very foot-sore and tired."[35]

Some of the folks in Union Mills made out pretty good. Stuart paid Andrew Shriver ten dollars for feeding his staff, and they got twenty-five cents each for each trooper they fed in the kitchen. But the main money was from the Union troops. June 30 was payday, and nearly all the men in blue

417

had their money. They were on the way to battle, so they gladly paid for good food. One of the farmers at Union Mills made $165, while Sam Erb made $200. But there was hardship too. The Shrivers had not mowed their hay. They would not have to now. The horses cleaned it up, the horses of the blue and the gray. Andrew's new post and rail fence of which he had been so proud was gone too, used for campfires.

Andrew's family was glad to see the men in blue. The evening of the last day in June, Sis, Fred, and Kate Shriver entertained Barnes's staff with violin, piano, and songs. One number was "When This Cruel War is Over."[36]

Kate Shriver felt it was a miracle that they had anything for the men in blue to eat. The Rebels "had just about eaten us out of house and home." Young Kate was sent to Bankert's for more butter. On the way home she saw, "the old hills covered with tents and lots and lots of camp fires."

XII CORPS

On Tuesday, June 30, the Twelfth Corps marched at daylight from near Middleburg. Their objective was Littlestown, Pennsylvania. Alpheus Williams, in reflecting on the march, said:

> Our whole march from Frederick, as indeed since crossing the Potomac, has been through a very rich and highly cultivated country. . . . It was not easy to find a lot upon which we could encamp, so universal were the cultivated fields by the roadside. On our march today we passed the line (Mason-Dixon) between Maryland and Pennsylvania. The inhabitants are Dutch descendants and quite Dutch in language. (He was referring to the Pennsylvania Dutch as they are called.) . . . They have immense barns . . . full of small windows. . . .[37]

Other troops of the Twelfth Corps remembered the march too.

The writer of the history of the 149th New York saw Littlestown as a place of "about 1,000 inhabitants, and the

418

terminus of the Hanover Branch of the Pennsylvania Central Railroad."[38]

After marching about twelve miles, the Twelfth Corps reached Littlestown about noon. They found great excitement and commotion. There had been a cavalry engagement, which we'll describe in a moment. The residents of Littlestown turned out en masse to look upon and to welcome the soldiers of Slocum and Williams. By now the men were getting used to the shouts of joy. All the way from Frederick to Pennsylvania the people came out along the road to look upon and welcome "Mr. Lincoln's army."

XII CORPS

With the Twelfth Corps in Northern Carroll County on the road to Littlestown was Samuel Toombs of the Thirteenth New Jersey. He writes:

As we neared the Pennsylvania line the spirits of the men grew exultant. There was a novelty in the situation of affairs which affected the troops wonderfully, and increased their anxiety to meet the enemy on loyal territory. On the 30th of June we passed through the small towns of Bruceville and Taneytown, at the latter place receiving a joyful welcome from the inhabitants who cheered us on. Our Brigade was in the advance this day, the Thirteenth being on the extreme right of the line. Just beyond Taneytown we passed part of the Third Corps, and when within two miles of Littlestown, Penn., word was received that the enemy were marching upon that place. Our column at once halted, and the order to load rifles was passed down the line. Skirmishers were deployed, and we moved forward at a rapid pace until we came in sight of the town, where we halted. Other troops came rapidly up, and when Battery "M," First New York Artillery, of our Division, came dashing down the road and into the town, the horses frothing at the mouth, and the sweat streaming from every pore by their violent exercise, the prospect of a battle was greatly heightened. A good deal of amusement was afforded the troops by the actions of a crowd of citizens who fled from the town, on hearing of the approach of the enemy, and took up position on a rail fence along the road. They seemed to fear that the "rebs" would prove too much for us, which accounted perhaps,

419

for the celerity which actuated their movements. Our arrival in the town, however, was the cause of great rejoicing by the inhabitants, and from every house we received tokens of gratitude and delight in the shape of cooked provisions, biscuits, bread and butter, cakes, pies and other luxuries which were keenly relished.[39]

Gregg's Cavalry found the last days of June to be rough ones. The command left Frederick about 4:00 P.M. on June 28, and spent the night between New Market and Poplar Springs scouting for Stuart or other Confederate elements. Monday, the bulk of the day was spent around New Market, Ridgeville, Mount Airy, and Lisbon. The troopers sought to cover the road to Baltimore and at the same time protect the B. and O. Railroad. A supply train was found on the railroad tracks at Mount Airy. McIntosh's famished troopers soon helped themselves to the rations and gave forage to the horses. However, they were unable to tarry and enjoy the food. It had to be consumed while riding. Patrols were sent to the front and soon started after the rear elements of Stuart's column. Throughout Monday night, the men rode over the roads of Carroll County. Men and horses were worn out. Many troopers were asleep and swaying in the saddle. When brief rests were made, the horses fell asleep. The officers resorted to all sorts of things in an effort to stay awake, such as pinching themselves, turning their heads, slapping themselves, and even sticking themselves with pins. Five miles from Westminster it was discovered that part of the column was missing.[40]

About daybreak they reached the outskirts of Westminster.

The column halted momentarily to allow the rear elements to close up. About 7:00 A.M. the Third Pennsylvania Cavalry leading advance, McIntosh and his men charged into the streets of Westminster and drove out the men in gray. A few prisoners were captured. Randol's battery threw a few shells in the direction of Stuart. The people of Westminster were very glad to see the men in blue. "They gave us a most cordial and enthusiastic reception.

The ladies stood on the doorsteps and at the windows, braving the flying bullets, waving flags and handkerchiefs and encouraging us

420

with their smiles and voices. Meanwhile the advance regiment threw a cordon of pickets around the town and the remainder of the column dismounted outside of it to rest and get something to eat.[41]

Like the infantry, the cavalry found repeats of this type of welcome almost everyplace. Almost, but not quite. In a few cases, those whom the soldiers were seeking to protect sought to sell bread and water at top price. The men were glad not to have to worry about Mosby or single Rebel bushwhackers. "The rich farms, the fields of clover and waving grain. . . . " were a sight for sore eyes.

The Tenth New York and the rest of Gregg's cavalry received a cordial welcome in Westminster. Numbers of pretty maidens invited the dirty, sweaty troopers into their homes for food and drink. A detail under Sergeant Mitchell secured "a good supply of corn, oats, and flour from a mill near the village." Then it was back in the saddle again.

Major Avery made a special occasion out of crossing the Pennsylvania border by having the men sing "John Brown."[42]

The Third Pennsylvania Cavalry was a part of Gregg's command. The historian says, "The inhabitants of that beautiful village gave us a most cordial and enthusiastic reception. The ladies stood on the doorsteps and at the windows, . . . waving flags and handkerchiefs. . . . But there was no time to stay in this delightful spot, though the pretty girls of Westminster and its loyal and patriotic citizens promised to make our stay a pleasant one." A detail from the Tenth New York gathered a good supply of corn, oats, and flour from a nearby mill.[43]

The First New Jersey Cavalry found the folks in Westminster "overjoyed to see the dusty, sweaty, blue-clad troopers. They emerged from the cellars where they had gone to hide from the Rebels. Casks of beer and ale were rolled into the street; and as the men marched past, offered to each trooper a brimming glass of the strengthening and refreshing beverage."[44]

Gregg's cavalry was followed by the long lines of the Sixth Corps. All day long, this June 30, the lines of infantry marched through the streets of Westminster, heading for Manchester. There was no straggling.

About 9:00 A.M. today, Dr. Mathias and Hering started down the Orndorff Mill (Liberty Road) to see a patient. They did not get very far. The Sixth Corps was entering Westminster and had the road blocked. The physicians had to turn around.[45]

Dr. Hering says that about five thousand wagons were parked in and around Westminster. There must have been thirty thousand mules. "The army wagons were everywhere, in the streets, in the fields, on the various roads, and a line of them constantly traveling the Gettysburg turnpike. About 10,000 troops were here to guard these trains. Night and day, the noise of the army wagons, the clanking of the cavalry sabres, and the braying of the mules could be heard and general noise and confusion prevailed everywhere."[46]

The Fifth Maine tramped 25 miles through the hills of Carroll County today, making a total of 110 miles in five days. Finally they reached Manchester with sore and aching bodies and blistered feet.[47]

While the Sixth Corps marched through town, the Westminster undertaker, one of its clergymen, and a lady from Virginia were busy. They were preparing for the funerals of those killed in Monday's skirmish.

Thus Rev. James Chrystal had services for four men, two from the South, Lts. St. Pierre Gibson and John William Murray; along with Cpl. William Vandegrift and Private Daniel Welch.[48]

The two Confederate officers were buried in the cemetery of the Protestant Episcopal Church. A Virginia lady was serving as a governess in the home of a local family. After the battle, she recognized the officers; one was a relative, the other a friend. She made the arrangements for their burial.

Philip Fisher and his granddaughter Nellie watched the Sixth Corps pass through the streets of Manchester. Little Nellie collected Union buttons. Poor John Frizell's lovely place had over one hundred wagons parked on it, with one thousand mules and horses in the meadow.[49]

Judson Kilpatrick was one of the younger generals of the war. From New Jersey, he graduated from West Point in 1861. Like Custer, he was dashing and prone to bragging. He

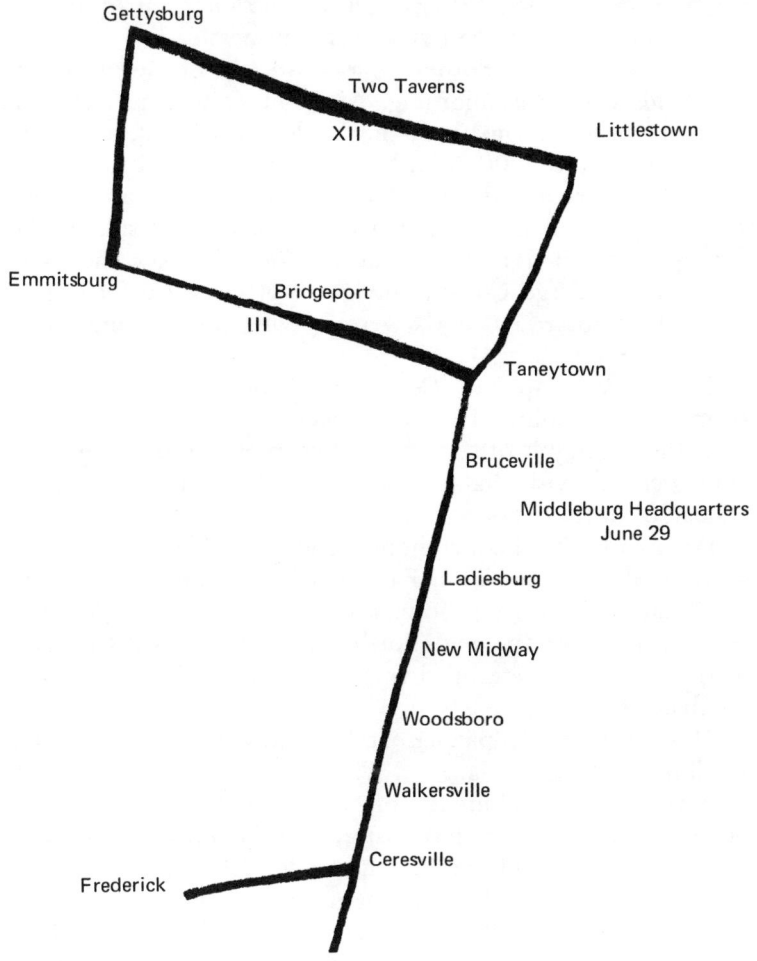

Route of the Third and Twelfth corps, along with Kilpatrick's cavalry, the Artillery Reserve, and Meade's headquarters.

was called "Kill Cavalry" for his treatment of men and mounts. At Gettysburg he was responsible for the death of the brave Elon Farnsworth, one of his brigadiers. After the war he was United States Minister to Chile. In June of '63, he was the first to block Stuart's path, and cause him additional riding, thus adding to Stuart's ineffectiveness.

Samuel and John Forney, Karl Forney's sons, went out in the fields early this morning. After all, it was harvesttime. Samuel's farm was north of the Littlestown Road, adjoining Pennville. About 8:00 A.M. they looked toward Littlestown and saw the road full of soldiers on horseback. Samuel and John stopped their work, tied their horses, and sat on the fence as the men in blue rode by four abreast. They saw Kilpatrick, George Custer, and other officers. Custer rode a lovely bay horse. His curls were flowing and flapping as he rode.

They saw a captured Confederate courier. The man was from North Carolina. He was allowed to chat a few minutes with the Forney brothers about their plowing and crops. He expressed the wish that he might be back home plowing corn instead of in the army.

For two hours the men in blue rode by. Then near the end of the column came Elon Farnsworth. The Forney brothers went back to plowing. Soon they heard a lot of noise and commotion. Soon the fields north of the Littlestown Road and west of Hanover were filled with mounted soldiers engaged in combat.[50]

This morning Kilpatrick and his division moved from Littlestown toward Hanover. The general and his staff were followed by a detachment from the First Ohio, and then the Michigan regiments under Custer. Pennington's battery was between Custer and the brigade under Farnsworth. Elder's battery and the ambulance brought up the rear of the column with the Eighteenth Pennsylvania serving as the rear guard.[51]

About 8:00 A.M., General Kilpatrick entered Hanover. Eyes were riveted upon a young man in a uniform of velvet with the long flowing curls. This was the twenty-three-year-old General Custer. Kilpatrick and Custer entered the home of Jacob Wirt on Frederick Street. They conversed there with

Dr. Emmanuel K. Zieber, pastor of Emmanuel Reformed Church. The generals said their men were in need of food. The announcement was made to the people of Hanover. They immediately went from the streets where they had gathered to look at the soldiers to get food. Coffee, bread, and meat were brought to the men who were still in the saddle. A rest was taken and then Custer's brigade moved out on the road to Abbotstown. On this particular road to Gettysburg, Custer lost his first man. The ammunition chest of one of the artillery caissons exploded, mortally wounding a soldier, killing two horses, and wounding two more.[52]

Then came Farnsworth. The First Vermont and First West Virginia cleared the town by 10:00 A.M. The Fifth New York was partially dismounted, and resting on a line of Frederick Street to the square. They were enjoying the good food provided by the people of Hanover, unaware that men of the Eighteenth Pennsylvania had encountered the enemy near town.[53] While the men in blue rode through Hanover, a group of young girls gathered in front of the Lutheran parsonage and sang patriotic songs.

As the action grew hotter at Hanover, the Forney brothers unhitched their horses and took off for McSherrystown. They stayed at the Geiselman farm until late afternoon. When they returned home, Samuel and John found twenty dead horses along the road in front of their home and their neighbor's, Mr. Keller. Three wounded Union soldiers were in Samuel's living room, along with one Confederate soldier.[54]

The man in gray was Samuel Reddick of the Second North Carolina. He had served two years in the army, but time was running out for him. He had come North to fall in the action at Hanover, far from home. The Forney family tenderly cared for him. He pulled a New Testament from his pocket. Inscribed on the flyleaf was the name of his only sister back home in Carolina.[55]

He asked the Forneys "Please take this book and send it home. My sister gave me this book when I left home two years ago. She asked me to keep it and bring it back when the cruel war was over. It has ended now for me."

The next morning, Samuel Reddick died at the Forney

home. Miss Forney wrote to his sister, and soon a friendship developed through the mail. The letters revealed that Reddick's father was a preacher. He asked that the grave be marked. It was. After the war friends and relatives came and took the body back to North Carolina.[56]

One who fell in the streets of Hanover was Cpl. John Hoffacker of the Eighteenth Pennsylvania Cavalry. John was killed instantly early in the fighting. He was almost home, having been born and raised on a farm in West Mannheim Township. Hoffacker had been in the military but two short months. He is buried beside the grave of his brother who also fell during the war.

Colonel Chambliss was leading the Confederate march toward Hanover. After capturing twenty-five men from the Eighteenth Pennsylvania who were guarding the flanks, he placed two cannons on the farm of Samuel Keller, and the Thirteenth Virginia charged into the ranks of the Eighteenth Pennsylvania. The fighting started in earnest. The men in gray drove through the square to the railroad. Farnsworth by now was in New Baltimore. He quickly ordered the First Vermont and the First West Virginia back to Hanover. Major Hammond led a charge of the Fifth New York and pushed the Confederates back. Farnsworth arrived and took over the direction of the Fifth New York. Hand-to-hand encounters occurred all over town, in the streets and alleys. As Kilpatrick later stated, it was a series of charges and countercharges. But the rattle of sabers, the shots of pistols, the shouts of command, and the blare of bugles were heard in the streets of Hanover.[57]

A sharp fight took place in a vacant lot back of the Methodist Church. Adjutant Gall of the Fifth New York was killed near the church. Captain Forney of Stuart's staff was cut in the head and laid for six hours in a daze in the home of Mr. and Mrs. Forney. Major Hammond was wounded, and Colonel Payne of the famous Rebel "Black Horse Cavalry" was captured.[58]

Kilpatrick, like Sheridan, later in the war, was quite a distance from Hanover. He had just passed through Abbotstown and was heading for York. He had just received a dispatch to be on the lookout for Stuart when he heard the sound of gunfire. Kilpatrick wheeled his horse and galloped toward the sound of the action. When he reached Pigeon Hills, he left the road and galloped through the fields of wheat and corn. He arrived during a lull in the action and took his headquarters in room 24 of the Central Hotel.[59]

Fitz Lee then arrived with four Virginia cavalry units. General Farnsworth climbed to the roof of the Thomas Wirt residence to survey the action. Custer came up with the Michigan troopers. The Union horse artillery went into position on Bunker Hill to the rear of Eichelberger High School. The next arrival was Wade Hampton with the 125 captured United States wagons. Two miles southwest of town, the train was parked in the form of a square and secured with heavy guard.

As soon as the Confederates were driven from the town, the residents of Hanover aided the Union troopers in barricading the streets with boxes, farm wagons, ladders, fence rails, barrels, etc. These served as an obstacle to the Rebel cavalry.

The next event was an artillery duel between the Union and Confederate horse artillery. Some shells passed over the town. A ten-pound shell struck the Henry Winebrenner place, passing through a door shattering a bureau, going through the floor and into the cellar where the family had gone for safety. This was on Frederick Street.

Kilpatrick grilled Colonel Payne. Farnsworth and Custer also asked questions at headquarters in the Central Hotel. Payne had been shot in front of the Winebrenner Tannery at the edge of Frederick Street. His horse was also shot from under him. While trying to escape he fell into a tanning vat which discolored his uniform. He knew the plight of Stuart and his horses. So he stretched the truth more than a little bit, telling the Union generals that Stuart had twelve thousand men. Kilpatrick must have had some doubts. He had climbed the steeple of Saint Matthew's Church earlier to observe, and did not see that many Rebels.

As the artillery duel quieted down, Kilpatrick wrote a dispatch to Pleasonton at army headquarters in Taneytown.

427

Despite his observation from the church steeple, he was unaware of the presence of the captured wagon train guarded by Lee. Stuart's objective was to avoid a serious encounter and protect the precious wagons. Even though the guns cooled, Chambliss and Hampton remained in position until the sun went down. That evening, Stuart gathered 385 horses in the Jefferson-Codorus township area.

Kilpatrick in his official report lists 197 officers and men killed, wounded, and missing. Stuart felt he would have overwhelmed Kilpatrick saying the "cavalry column which we struck near the rear, would have been at our mercy, but owing to the great elongation of the column by reason of the one hundred and twenty-five captured wagons and the hilly roads, General Hampton was a long distance behind us."[60]

Retreating by way of Jefferson, Stuart had additional difficulties. He was about out of ammunition, plus four hundred captured prisoners to guard, and his men and mounts were about exhausted. Had Colonel Payne told Kilpatrick the truth in the Central Hotel, Hanover might have been Stuart's Waterloo. As Stuart's men rode on a very dark road, the last night in June, many fell asleep in their saddles. In fact, Stuart barely eluded capture near Hanover, jumping a stream near Hanover to escape those who were after him.[61]

The chaplain of the Fifth New York Cavalry describes "the last day in June" for the men of Kilpatrick's cavalry:

> June 30th. The column moved early to Hanover, where we were again enthusiastically received by the citizens, who furnished refreshments liberally to the troopers, as each regiment entered and passed through the town. This enjoyable state of things continued until about 10 o'clock; and while the Fifth was receiving the attentions of the people, the sudden report of a cannon was heard from one of the neighboring hills. At first this was taken as a friendly salute for our troops, but the deception was soon removed by a fierce charge of Rebel cavalry under immediate command of Gen. Stuart, upon the unsuspecting column in the street, sending terror to the people, especially to the ladies and children, who were paying their compliments to their defenders. With his accustomed coolness and bravery, Maj. Hammond, in command of the regiment, quickly withdrew from the street to the open field near the rail road depot, ordered the boys into line and led the charge upon the Rebels, who then possessed the town. The charging columns met on Frederick Street,

where a hand to hand conflict ensued. For a few moments the enemy made heroic resistance, but finally broke and fled, closely pursued by our men. They rallied again and again but were met with irresistible onsets, which finally compelled them to retire behind the hills under cover of their guns.

In less than fifteen minutes from the time the Rebels charged the town, they were all driven from it, and were skulking in the wheat fields and among the hills of the vicinity. The dead and wounded of both parties, with many horses, lay scattered here and there along the streets, so covered with blood and dust as to render identification in many cases very difficult. Meanwhile, Gen. Kilpatrick, who was several miles beyond the town, at the head of the column, when the attack was made, arrived upon the field, and took personal charge of the movements. These were ordered with consummate skill, and executed with promptness and success. His artillery, well posted on the hills facing the Rebels, and well supported, soon silenced the guns of the enemy, and compelled him to retire in the direction of Lee's main army. He left not less than 25 dead in the streets and fields, and his wounded by far exceeded this number. We captured 75 prisoners, including Lt. Col. Payne, who commanded a brigade, and one stand of colors, the flag of the 13th Virginia cavalry. This was the trophy of Sergt. Burke, Company A. Our entire loss was nine killed, thirty-one wounded and a few prisoners. Among the killed was Adjutant Gall. . . .[62]

Judson Kilpatrick gives this report of the events in Hanover.

He says that his column was struck and thrown into confusion. But Colonel Douty and the First Maine charged the Rebel flank. Although outnumbered three to one, the men in gray could not withstand the saber blows of the lads in blue. The rest of the morning was a series of charges and countercharges. Kilpatrick's men captured one stand of colors, almost one hundred prisoners and four guns.[63]

He was lavish in his praise of General Farnsworth. The Eighteenth Pennsylvania had been routed by the Rebel surprise. "But the gallant Farnsworth had passed from front to rear ere the shout of the rebel charge had ceased to ring through the quiet street, faced the Fifth New York about, countermarched the other regiments, and with a rush struck the rebel host in full charge. . . . For the first time our troops had met the foe in close contact; but they were on their own free soil; fair hands, regardless of the dangerous strife, waved

429

them on, and bright, tearful eyes looked pleadingly out from every window. The brave Farnsworth made one great effort, and the day was won."[64]

Later Kilpatrick reported Confederate cavalry camped on the Baltimore Road, and also the Littlestown Road. He had word of Early's infantry with fifteen wagons and 113 mules moving toward Gettysburg.[65]

Samuel Althoff was eighty-three years old on June 30, 1863. When he heard that Kilpatrick's cavalry was in the square, he went to watch and help pass out food. Just before 10:00, he was standing in front of Shirk's store when someone gave him a box of cigars to hand to the soldiers. He was busily passing them out when the shooting started. Samuel went to his home on Baltimore Street. His family went to the cellar, but the elderly gentleman climbed through the trapdoor out onto his roof and had a ringside seat for the action. He watched the troops charge back and forth, and observed the smoke of the cannon. An officer of a New York regiment saw him and told him to go in before he got himself killed.[66]

Later in the day, Samuel went to the square to see the debris of battle and gather all the details. He learned that Drs. Smith, Culbertson, and Hinkle, of Hanover, along with Dr. Gardner of the military were tending the wounded.

Althoff learned the sad story of Sergeant Peale of North Carolina. He was shot in the breast during the action, and then fractured his skull when he toppled from his horse. The doctors learned that he was a Catholic and sent for a priest, Father Kittanig of the Conewago Chapel. He gave the last rites of the church to Peale, and when he died, saw that he was buried in the Catholic Cemetery.[67]

Today as one rides through the modern streets of Hanover, it is hard to believe that on the last day of June '63, there was yelling, the clash of sabers, the firing of revolvers and carbines, the clatter of horseshoes on the streets, and the boom of artillery.

As the fighting died down, dead and wounded horses were to be found in the streets and alleys, as well as the men of the blue and the gray. Some prisoners were captured by Stuart. The captured ambulances were started out Frederick Street to the rear. Most of the fighting in the early stages occurred on Frederick and Abbotstown Street and in the Center Square. However, small parties and individuals dueled throughout the town.

The Confederate horsemen were surprised as they rode through the town market in Center Square. The jail was underneath it. The men from the South thought they were riding through a covered bridge, but the hollow sound was produced by the space underneath reserved for prisoners.

While the shooting continued in the streets of Hanover, various buildings were opened as hospitals. The wounded were taken into many private homes by the sympathetic citizens of the town. In most cases, the color of the uniform made little or no difference. Marion Hall was opened as one of the larger hospitals. The Hanover paper states that the women of the town were untiring in their efforts to help the wounded, and added, "God bless the ladies of our town, and forbid that their nerves ever again be shocked by the roar of cannon, the clashing of steel, or the ghostly visage of wounded men."[68]

The next day, Surgeon Gardner came to take charge of the hospital. He brought with him some army nurses and attendants, and soon had everything shipshape. With the aid of some Hanover carpenters, he soon had snug bunks prepared for the wounded. A lot of the wounds were serious and required surgery.

Kilpatrick did not press Stuart. A detachment under Lt. Col. A. J. Alexander followed the gray chieftain as far as Rossville, but the primary purpose was observation.

Stuart tells us that the night march to Jefferson was very rough. The prisoners and the wagons were a great burden. Nearly four hundred men in blue had been captured since paroling others at Cooksville. Some were loaded in wagons, and a few were driving the captured wagons. The mules were starving for food and water and often became downright stubborn. Sometimes the wagon train ground to a halt because a driver near the front fell asleep on his wagon seat. The guards could barely keep their eyes open. The staff offi-

An observation post—Hanover—Saint Matthew's
Lutheran Church.

cers, despite their own fatigue, had the job of their life to
keep the men awake and to watch for the Yankee cavalry.[69]
At Jefferson some of the prisoners were paroled, including

Hanover Junction.

The Central Hotel in Hanover.

433

some local farmers who had been brought along so they would not reveal the Confederates' presence.

About 10:00 this evening, Jeb Stuart called a conference with his brigade commanders, Wade Hampton, Fitz Lee, and John R. Chambliss. The meeting was held at the farm of John E. Zeigler, near Hanover Junction. Like his commander near Gettysburg, Stuart was also in the dark. He did not know where the Yankees were, or his own army. The decision was made to head for Carlisle in the hope that other Confederate units would be there.[70]

Between Jefferson and York New Salem, some of the gray-clad troopers passed Ziegler's stone church. A funeral service was being held in the cemetery. (It must have been early.) The troopers heard the mourners singing "When the Roll Is Called Up Yonder."[71]

The Rebel cavalry was stretched out on the morning of July 1 from York New Salem to Dover. Stuart was about twenty-five miles northeast of Gettysburg. Two hundred captured men in blue were paroled and told to head for York. Even though he was operating in the dark, and had no idea of Lee's need of him, Stuart took the time to have a big breakfast with his staff and other officers at a Dover Hotel. George Dick, the hotel clerk, was pleasantly surprised to be paid in United States greenbacks instead of Confederate money. While in Dover, the Hanover folks who had been brought along to guide the column were released, and residents of Dover taken along.[72]

Meanwhile, Gregg and his men were still riding. They were not permitted to stay in Westminster, but were ordered on to Manchester. Gregg was about to lose part of his command. Pennock Huey's troops were to be detached to Hanover Junction for a few days. Then they would ride back to Winchester and Westminster but not rejoin Gregg until July 9. Gregg was unaware of the cavalry fight in Hanover. In fact, he was expecting to run into Stuart at any moment himself.[73]

Thirty minutes before the end of the last day in June, Pleasonton sent a dispatch to Gregg, telling him to push on to Hanover Junction. If he found no Rebels, then he was to move on to York. If no men in gray were found at that place,

434

Union Mills.

then Gregg was to move on toward Columbia and the Susquehanna River.

Pleasonton, who must have been with Meade and army headquarters, sent a general order to the cavalrymen,

> Our own soil has been invaded, homes, firesides, and all domestic relations are being rudely trampled on. . . .To the cavalry arm of this army, it is only necessary to mention these facts to fire them with the determination of victory so distinguished at Beverly Ford, Brandy Station, Aldie, Middleburg and Upperville. Proud of his confidence in the brave soldiers under his command, every assurance exists that future actions will add luster to their honorable fame.[74]

There was one bright note, John W. Garrett, president of the Baltimore and Ohio Railroad, reported to Secretary Stanton that the road to Frederick was now clear and the mail train running on schedule.

Meanwhile, Buford and his troopers left the Fountaindale-Fairfield area, headed east to the Emmitsburg-Gettysburg Road, and met some units of the First Corps Infantry along Marsh Creek. Heading north, Buford's men rode into Gettys-

435

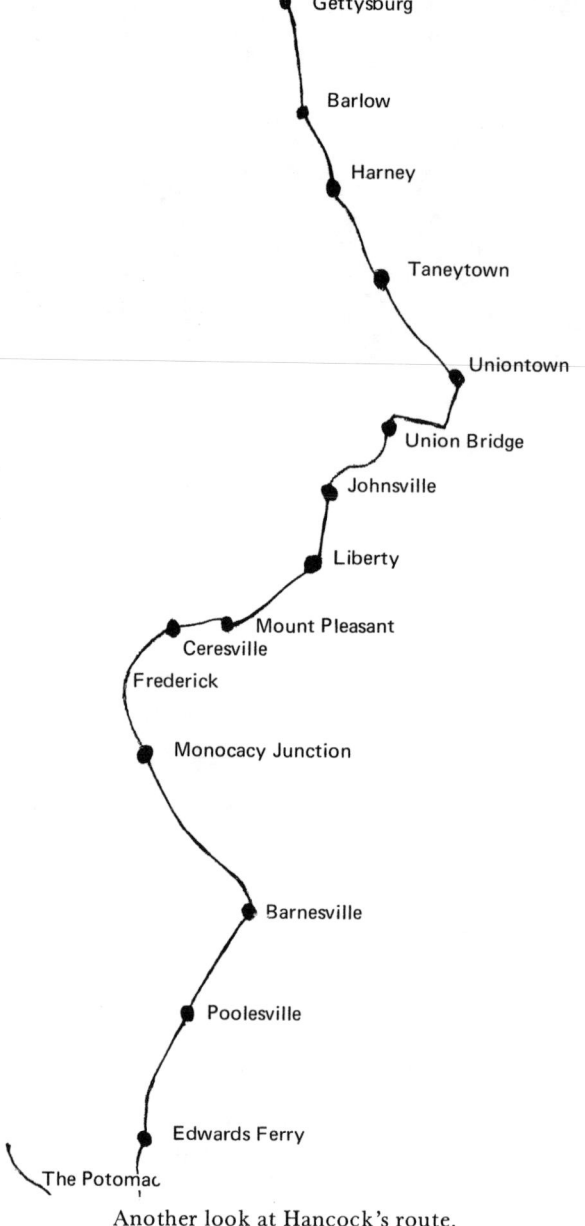

Gettysburg

Barlow

Harney

Taneytown

Uniontown

Union Bridge

Johnsville

Liberty

Mount Pleasant
Ceresville
Frederick

Monocacy Junction

Barnesville

Poolesville

Edwards Ferry

The Potomac

Another look at Hancock's route.

436

burg. They received a joyous welcome. A member of the Seventeenth Pennsylvania Cavalry tells of the moment:

> We reached the town about 2 o'clock p. m. Our arrival was hailed as the advance of the Army of the Potomac, the whereabouts of which for some days previous had been as much of a mystery to the loyal people of the State as it was to the Confederate chiefs. The people of the town lined the streets through which we marched from doorstep to curb, indulged in exclamations of joy and chorused national songs. Passing through the town the division halted and went into camp on Seminary Ridge, the First Brigade on the left of the Cashtown Road and the Second Brigade on the right. The Seventeenth Pennsylvania Cavalry's camp was near the town, and within a few hundred yards of the college grounds. Company F of the regiment was recruited in the Cumberland Valley, mostly at or near Carlisle, but some of the number were former residents of Gettysburg, among them Perry J. Tate, the adjutant, a brother of Dr. Theodore T. Tate, who went into service with this regiment, but was subsequently assigned to duty with the Third Pennsylvania Cavalry.[75]

Newel Cheney of the Ninth New York says the residents of Gettysburg were "profuse in their expressions of gratification at seeing Buford's long column of troopers pass through the village. They were at their doors or on the streets with waving flags and handkerchiefs and hearty words of greeting. . . . One group was singing 'Rally Round the Flag Boys.' This was the first time most of the 'boys' had heard this song and it was wonderfully inspiring. Bread and butter and other luxuries were freely handed out."[76]

The Sixth New York took a different route, but received a warm welcome.

> June 30th.—Left Mowrey Springs at daylight and marched to Fairfield, which was in possession of about 3000 of the enemy. The Sixth New York advanced upon the town and commenced skirmishing with the enemy, while the division marched by another route to Emmitsburg. At 9 a.m. the First and Eleventh Corps passed through and followed the cavalry on toward Gettysburg. The Sixth New York Cavalry reached Gettysburg at 11 a.m., but found the enemy had fallen back from the town. The citizens, already in a state of terror and excitement over the great invasion, gazed with interest and satisfaction as the long column of veteran troopers, with trampling horses and fluttering guidons, moved through their streets. The troops were highly welcomed; such enthusiasm and loyalty were

seldom witnessed. Hundreds of women and children lined the walks and cheered the men with the "Red, White and Blue," which they sang most loyally and charmingly, while handkerchiefs and banners waved most earnestly and gracefully from *stalwart arms* and delicate hands. The rebels had but just disappeared over the hills, and no wonder that the people should manifest such extreme gladness and joy at our coming. A supper was ready for any of the "boys" who desired to eat, and much was done in that line, of course, by the cavaliers. The regiment then marched through the town and encamped in the vicinity of McPherson's farm, a mile and a half to the north of the village. . . . [77]

Lt. John H. Calef of Battery A, Second United States Artillery, was glad to get to Gettysburg. Perhaps there might be action, or something to keep them from moving. On Friday he and his battery had a long and severe march from Aldie to Leesburg. Saturday he brought his guns to Edwards Ferry, crossed the Potomac, crossed the Monocacy Aqueduct, and finally camped near Petersville. Sunday he rode to Middletown. Monday, Calef crossed South Mountain, rode to Cavetown, across another mountain and camped near Fairfield. This was a long and fatiguing march, "The horses were much used up." Then it was on to Gettysburg by way of Emmitsburg on the thirtieth. [78]

Buford must have taken note of the many roads coming into Gettysburg, and probably observed Cemetery Ridge. After a brief stop near the square in Gettysburg, he moved his headquarters to the Lutheran Theological Seminary west of town. He felt that if he established a strong position on Seminary Ridge, he might be able to control or protect the roads until the Union infantry arrived.

June 30 was a big day on Maryland Heights. Edwin Haynes of the Tenth Vermont tells us about it:

> We reached Harper's Ferry on the morning of the twenty-sixth, and went into camp on Maryland Heights. We were halted for the first day upon a narrow plateau half way up the mountain, but were afterwards sent up near the summit, where the ground was so steep that we had to cling to the bushes to keep from rolling down. Here we lay four days, and it rained all the time.
>
> Maryland Heights were very strongly fortified. There were two or three forts and several batteries of large guns; one sat upon the summit, where, like a dog upon his master's doorstep, it guarded the

country for miles around. The garrison consisted of the Sixth New York Heavy Artillery, One Hundred and Fifty-first New York, Tenth Vermont, Sixth Michigan, a part of the Fourteenth New Jersey, and detachments of regiments and fragments of batteries from the unfortunate command of General Milroy—in all perhaps ten thousand troops. Brigadier-General Tyler was in command, but was very soon superseded by Major-General French. While here, General Hooker came to Harper's Ferry,—just then from Chancellorsville, and as he said, fighting the War Department eighteen hours out of the twenty-four, and the rebels the other six. He wanted this force to join his army; General Halleck refused; and just below, at Sandy Hook, is pointed out the place where General Hooker wrote to General Halleck, asking to be relieved from the command of the Army of the Potomac. His request was granted and Major-General George G. Meade assumed command the next day at Frederick.

Maryland Heights were evacuated on the 30th of June. The forts were dismantled, and the ordnance stores sent to Washington. A magazine of one of the forts was accidentally blown up, with a terrific explosion, scattering fragments of shell and the debris of the works far around. A large quantity of ammunition was destroyed, a score of men from the Sixth Maryland were killed; some of them were skinned alive; others were thrown with fearful velocity over the brow of the mountain, and hurled down the cliffs, masses of broken bones and bruised flesh. Pieces of flying timbers, iron and stone, came down among us, as we stood in column ready to move off, near enough to be shaken by the shock, and enveloped in the settling smoke and cinders. An hour later we were off for Frederick.[79]

Through the warm summer night couriers were coming and going over the Roads to Gettysburg. Buford's pickets were along Willoughby Run. John Buford, from the cupola of the seminary, looking westward, could see the glimmering campfires of A. P. Hill's troops, near Cashtown.

Buford felt uneasy. He had less than three thousand men, with only one battery of artillery, Battery A, Second United States, with Lieutenant Calef in command. He placed Devin's brigade north of the Chambersburg Road. Gamble's men were positioned south of the pike. The horses were hidden in the woods, while the men were deployed as dismounted infantry along Willoughby Run. He was sure the attack would come from Cashtown. But he had to be sure. Thus Buford had outposts on Marsh Creek two miles in his front, and men guarding all roads.

John Buford was a good general. With his limited number

439

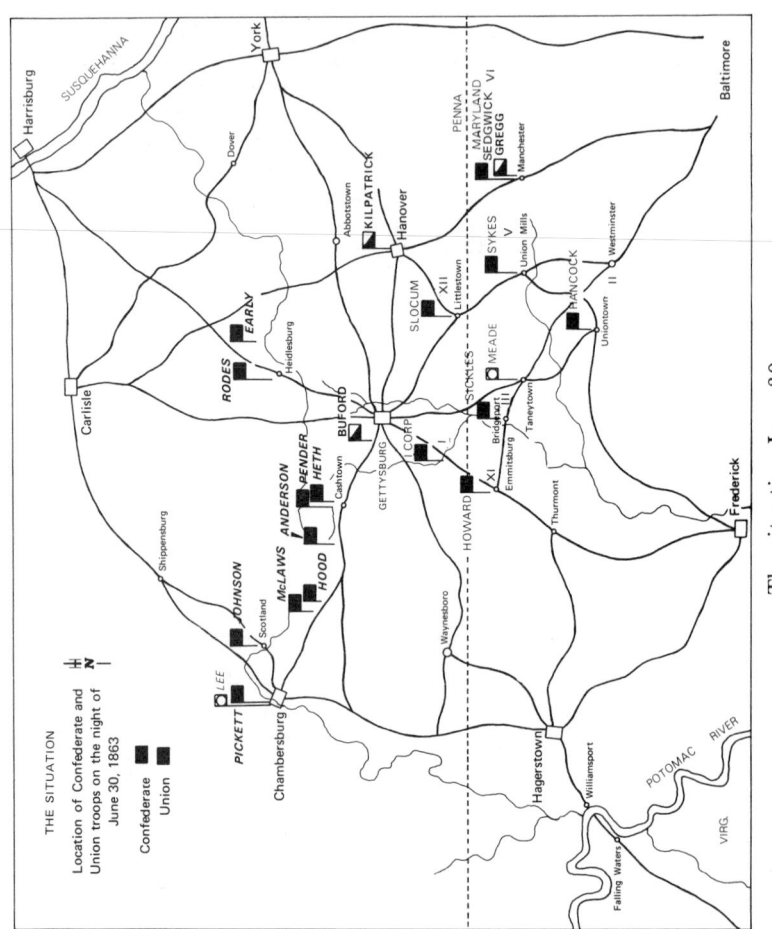

THE SITUATION

Location of Confederate and
Union troops on the night of
June 30, 1863

Confederate

Union

The situation June 30.

of men, he had done all he could. And he sent couriers off to Reynolds and Meade telling them of the buildup in his front.

As John Buford pondered the information brought to him by the cavalry scouts, he was sure Confederate infantry would attack in the morning.

Devin said, "No, I can take care of anything that comes my way for twenty-four hours."

Buford replied, "No you won't. They will attack you in the morning; and they will come booming—skirmishers three deep. You will have to fight like the devil to hold your own until supports arrive. The enemy knows the importance of this position, and will strain every nerve to secure it, and if we are able to hold it we will do well."[80]

> As June ended, George G. Meade and army headquarters were located at Taneytown thirteen miles south east of Gettysburg. John Reynolds and the First Corps is resting at Marsh Run, the men boiling coffee, while the artillery-men water their horses. Reynolds is seven or eight miles from Gettysburg. The Eleventh Corps under Howard is in the fields around Emmitsburg, three miles farther south, near the Pennsylvania-Maryland border. The Third Corps, under Sickles, is at Bridgeport, five miles southeast of Emmitsburg, on the road to Taneytown.

While all of this was occurring in the communities on the Roads to Gettysburg, a great event was taking place in the English House of Commons where Mr. Roebuck was making an impassioned speech favoring the recognition of the Confederate States of America, saying:

> We should acknowledge the South because they have won their freedom, and because it is for our interest. It is not Richmond that is now in peril, but Washington; and if there be terrors anywhere it is in the minds of the merchants of New York.[81]

The debate in the House of Commons continued into the early hours of the morning. Most of the English politicians favored the South. However, they had to wait for a political expedient moment to recognize the South. Although their sympathies were with the South, they decided to wait to see the result of the invasion of Pennsylvania.

French armies are in Mexico. If the South wins in Pennsylvania, perhaps French recognition will come also. So the fate

441

Moritz Tavern—Reynolds's headquarters,
June 30.

of a nation hung in the balance. Will America be one or two nations. The answer hangs in the balance with those men marching on the Roads to Gettysburg.[82]

Meade sent two circulars to the Army of the Potomac.

The Commanding General has received information that the enemy are advancing, probably in strong force, on Gettysburg. It is the intention to hold this army pretty nearly in position it now occupies, until the plans of the enemy shall have been more fully developed.

Three Corps, 1st, 3d, and 11th, are under the command of Major-General Reynolds, in the vicinty of Emmitsburg, the 3d Corps being ordered up to that point. The 12th Corps is at Littlestown. General Gregg's division of cavalry is believed to be now engaged with the cavalry of the enemy, near Hanover Junction.

Corps commanders will hold their commands in readiness at a moment's notice, and upon receiving orders, to march against the enemy. Their trains (ammunition trains excepted) must be placed in the rear of the place of concentration. Ammunition wagons and ambulances will alone be permitted to accompany the troops. The men must be provided with three days rations in haversacks, and with sixty rounds of ammunition in the boxes and upon the person.[83]

442

The next circular directed the corps commanders to address the men on the importance of the upcoming battle and the issues at stake. Part of the circular said:

> The enemy are on our soil; the whole country now looks anxiously to this army to deliver it from the presence of the foe. Our failure to do so will leave us no such welcome as the swelling of millions of hearts with pride and joy, as our success would give to every soldier in this army. Homes, firesides, and domestic altars are involved. The army has fought well heretofore; it is believed that it will fight more desperately and bravely than ever, if it is addressed in fitting terms.[84]

Meade added one more paragraph to the circular. "Corps and other commanders are authorized to order the instant death of any soldier who fails in his duty at this hour."

> It was the crisis of the civil war, and the country was on the verge of a moral panic. Governor Curtin hastily assembled for the defense of his State such emergency militia as he could muster, under the efficient leadership of General Couch. General French, at Harper's Ferry, was ordered to send the government property at that place to the capital, to protect the Baltimore and Ohio Railroad in Meade's rear, and to be ready, in case of necessity, to throw his troops into the Washington fortifications. The newspapers were in hysterics. Business came to a standstill. Treasure was hidden or spirited away. The streets of the great cities were filled with pallid, nervous men who eagerly watched the bulletin boards and anxiously feared for the morrow. Churches were thronged with solemn and tearful worshipers. From a half million homes prayers ascended for the Army of the Potomac, on whose prowess the fate of the nation hung. In his secret chamber, at the capital, Abraham Lincoln was on his knees confessing to God that the burden of his responsibility had become unbearable, and invoking the aid of the Lord of battles with an intensity that brought to him the assurance of the divine favor and approaching victory. Never before in modern times were such stupendous issues intrusted to an army in the field as rested in that hour upon the march-worn, weary Army of the Potomac and its brave, resolute commander, who from the moment he assumed its command, for a whole week, was to permit himself no rest, day or night, until the result was reached. The hopes of nearly thirty million people and the life of the American republic were staked on the strength of Meade's battle line.[85]

Many feel that Harrisburg could have been captured by a small Confederate force on Sunday or Monday. But today, Darius Couch, commander of approximately fifteen thousand

George G. Meade.

militiamen in the Pennsylvania capital, saw the threat vanish as Ewell headed south, and as he got word that Early was moving from Hanover toward Gettysburg.

The Confederates were also moving in Chambersburg, Cashtown, and Carlisle. They were heading south and east on the Roads to Gettysburg.

About three o'clock rumbling was heard in the streets of Carlisle. The men of Robert Rodes were moving out. Carlisle was being vacated. Brigade after brigade filed through the town. It was after eight before the town was cleared. They took the Baltimore Road, heading for Gettysburg. One mile south of Carlisle lived Sarah Moats. She was eight or ten years old at the time. Her father was the tollgate keeper. Sarah saw and admired the gentle Robert Rodes. He sat so tall and straight in the saddle. Then in the middle of the infantry came a carriage carrying Richard S. Ewell. It was a low car-

444

riage with one seat, the rockaway, she called it. She looked at Ewell sitting in the carriage.[86]

By 11:00 the infantry cleared Mount Holly. Two hundred cavalry remained in Carlisle as provost marshals. Ewell left the barracks in good order with the exception of the litter that can be expected from a camp of several days. The local people were more severe on the barracks. After the Confederate army left, many went to the army post to look things over. Ewell had not disturbed any records. But some lower class people and prostitutes made shambles of the place, ripping paper, tearing up ledgers. Clothing, blankets, and anything else that could be carried away was taken. Furniture was also destroyed and carried away. It might have been frustration, or perhaps hostility against the military, but the civilians did more damage than the Rebels.[87]

Jed Hotchkiss notes that he and his friends "started at an early hour and went through Papertown," stopping awhile to examine the large paper mill. Then it was on to Peterstown, and Heidlersburg. He stopped for "awhile on the mountain at a terrified old Dutchman's.... Early was some three miles off. It rained some, but the day was quite pleasant."[88]

At 4:00 A.M. the last of Early's Confederates left York. They marched through with the bands playing and the flags flying. The only Rebels left were the stragglers or the drunks.[89]

"Jube" Early retraced his route through Weiglestown with John Gordon, heading for East Berlin. White's cavalry was out in front with orders to watch the flanks, especially the left one. White learned that Union cavalry and infantry had been spotted near Abbotstown. Early received a message from Ewell stating that with Rodes he was moving toward Heidlersburg. "Old Jube" was to join him there.

It was a hot day, but the men were in good spirits. They had been to the banks of the Susquehanna. Food was plentiful, and they were sure they could beat the Yankees.[90]

Along the way today, the veteran soldiers under Robert Rodes ran into a battalion of school cadets out to protect the sacred soil of Pennsylvania. The men in gray did not take them seriously, scolded them and told them to go on home.

445

However, they relieved the young men of their shoes and socks, saying they could easily get others, while the men in gray could not.

Richard S. Ewell, Robert Rodes, along with "Jube" Early and Isaac Trimble had a conference at Heidlersburg. They debated the wording of Lee's order and dispatches.

Shotwell was impressed with the abundance of everything in the Chambersburg area, and he felt the Confederates should deal harshly with the folks in the occupied areas.

> These people being mostly of Dutch extraction have all the appliances of Dutch thrift. Every farmhouse has its outdoor bake-oven, wherein the weekly supply of bread is baked—(these people eat no warm bread); its big barrel of sauer-kraut—a sweet bouquet for Dutch nostrils; its pile of mighty cheeses; its troops of ducks; squadrons of turkeys; and brigades of chickens, with skirmish lines of Guinea fowls and peacocks; its orchard and "Sass" garden; its smoke house, milk house, wood house, tool house, and a long tier of bee hives; its barnyard full of calves, pigs, sheep and horses. What a feast!—*purely of imagination*, however—is presented by one of these well stocked farm houses, contrasted with past sufferings by one of our poor, emaciated, sweltering, foot-sore soldiers, subsisting on six hard crackers per day, and a morsel of spoilt meat, while at the same time over-loaded and over-marched! It is undoubtedly true that no troops perform such service as we are doing. I, myself, today—sweltering in the sun—must perform all the functions of baggage wagons, ordinance cart, supply train, pack mule, forager, light cavalryman, outpost picket, and general utility man! Yet I am only *one* man and not a dozen!
>
> Many of the citizens express surprise at the civil treatment they are receiving from our men. It is much more than they had expected, and far more than their due! I found an old copy of *"Harper's Weekly"* in which we are depicted as burning, plundering, and outraging the people of Cumberland Valley; when in point of fact we are treating them much more tenderly than we treat our own people down in Virginia. This shows the folly of Davis' and Lee's kid glove policy. We cannot hope to whip the Yankees until we touch their pockets seriously, and this cannot be done by merely killing their men, who are chiefly hirelings—but by destroying their property.[91]

From near Fayetteville, Hill started Pender toward Cashtown. But Henry Heth was up bright and early, and leaving from the town where a tavern owner always demanded cash, he reached Seminary Ridge about 9:30. Staff officers surveyed the town with field glasses. They talked with the folks who lived in the west end of Gettysburg. Heth brought twenty-seven wagons with him, hoping to get supplies. They were accompanied by some cannons.

When Buford arrived, he spotted the Confederate infantry, and dispatched the news to Meade rather than risk an engagement. Pettigrew went back to Cashtown, saying the Union cavalry was in Gettysburg. Heth told Pettigrew to repeat what he had seen to Hill. Powell believed it was a small force. Heth then said to Hill, "If there is no objection, I will march my division tomorrow, go to Gettysburg, and secure the shoes." Hill replied, "Do so." These words determined the encounter at Gettysburg, and the destiny of the nation.

Today Colonel Fremantle had his dream fulfilled. He met Robert E. Lee, commander of the Army of Northern Virginia. Longstreet did the honors prior to leaving Chambersburg. Fremantle was really impressed.

> General Lee is, almost without exception, the handsomest man of his age I ever saw. He is fifty-six years old, tall, broad-shouldered, very well made ... a thorough soldier in appearance; and his manners are most courteous and full of dignity. He is a perfect gentleman in every respect. I imagine no man has so few enemies, or is so universally esteemed. Throughout the South, all agree in pronouncing him to be as near perfection as man can be. He has none of the small vices, such as smoking, drinking, chewing, or swearing; and his bitterest enemy never accused him of any of the greater ones.
>
> He generally wears a well-worn long gray jacket, a high black felt hat, and blue trousers tucked into Wellington boots. I never saw him carry arms, and the only mark of his military rank are the three stars on his collar. He rides a handsome horse, which is extremely well groomed. He himself is very neat in his dress and person, and in the most ardous marches he always looks smart and clean. ...
>
> I believe he has never slept in a house since he commanded the Virginian army, and he invariably declines all offers of hospitality, for fear the person offering it may afterwards get into trouble for having sheltered the Rebel General.[92]

Fremantle found that both Lee and Longstreet longed for a termination of the war. They wanted to retire into obscurity. Some of the Texas troops had a sad chore today. They were sent into Chambersburg to destroy several barrels of excellent whiskey. This was severe discipline, and the only time they were allowed in Chambersburg.

During the evening the English colonel found staff officers saying they thought a battle would occur on the Gettysburg Road instead of in front of Harrisburg. Ewell was ordered to come back to the main body. Everyone was in great spirits and full of confidence. In the South, Fremantle had found great respect for the cavalry. But in the Army of Northern Virginia, the infantry and artillery love to taunt the troopers, jeer at them and insult them.

Today, Hood and McLaws of the First Corps marched from Chambersburg to Greenwood. This was a march of about eleven miles. They went into camp about 2:00 P.M. Lee was with these units. Pickett was left at Chambersburg to guard the rear until Imboden arrived with his cavalry.

McGowan's South Carolina Brigade remained in the Fayetteville area from the twenty-seventh until today. Then the men marched toward Cashtown. The rain continued and Caldwell says that "except for the firm mountain pike, we would scarcely been able to move. That night whiskey was again issued to us."

Caldwell was proud to be part of the Army of Northern Virginia.

> I have little doubt that we had the finest army ever marshalled on this side of the Atlantic, and one scarcely inferior to any Europe has known. Its numbers were not so imposing. . . . But we were veterans—thoroughly experienced . . . willing to encounter the greatest amount of personal danger and moral responsibility. . . . We were in excellent health. . . . A . . . vastly important element in the army was the confidence of the troops in the valor of their comrades and the skill of their officers. . . . Lee . . . was a tower of strength.[93]

As the day ended, Dorsey Pender and Henry Heth were at Cashtown; Anderson's division of Hill's Corps was still at Fayetteville. In the Second Corps, Robert Rodes was at the crossroads hamlet of Heidlersburg, nine miles northeast of Gettysburg; Early's division was about three miles east of Rodes; with Ed Johnson miles away at Scotland.

XIV

THE FIRST DAY OF JULY

On this first day of a new month, the men of the blue and the gray converged on Gettysburg. The march that commenced in early June on the banks of the Rappahannock River was ending over two hundred miles later in Pennsylvania.

Buford and his Union cavalry spent the night west of Gettysburg. But with the dawn came the advance of A. P. Hill's troops from Cashtown, to be joined later by Ewell's men coming south from Heidlersburg and Middletown (Biglerville). Still later Longstreet's men appeared on the field marching from locations between Cashtown and Chambersburg, although many did not arrive on the scene until July 2.

John Reynolds and his wing of the army, located close to Emmitsburg, was the nearest to Gettysburg. So throughout the day the First, Eleventh, and Third corps tramped the Roads to Gettysburg. From the southeast and Two Taverns came Henry Slocum and the Twelfth Corps. At midnight Hancock's Second Corps arrived from Taneytown and Harney, followed later by the Fifth Corps coming from Hanover in the wee hours of the second of July. Like Longstreet's men, the Union Sixth Corps did not get on the field until late in the day on July 2.

During the day, first Buford, then Pettigrew, then Doubleday, and the other commanders of the blue and the gray looked south, west, and north, seeking for signs of the advance of their comrades. The battle and the fate of the nation, hinged on how quickly their comrades covered the Roads to Gettysburg.

449

During the night hours of June 30, and early morning hours of July 1, Devin threw out his picket line to Willoughby Run. Details from the Sixth New York, Ninth New York, Seventeenth Pennsylvania, and Third West Virginia occupied a line from the Chambersburg Pike, northward across the Mummasburg, Carlisle, and Harrisburg roads. Colonel Sackett was in charge.

Cpl. Alphonse Hodges of Company E, Ninth New York and three comrades were at an advanced observation post. As the dawn broke, they saw men coming toward them and immediately sent back a warning. After sending the dispatches, Hodges decided it was time to retire. As he moved, the Confederates of Henry Heth's division, advancing from Cashtown, opened fire. From behind the bridge, the blue-clad troopers opened fire. For a long time, most people thought these were the opening shots. It was just 5:30 A.M. And in a few minutes, Cyrus W. James of the Ninth New York was killed. According to New York sources, "he is said to have been the first Union soldier killed in battle."[1]

However, the Chicago Civil War Round Table has turned up some interesting new material.[2] Regardless of who fired first, or who was the first to fall, the battle was on. Facing the advance of the Rebel infantry was about sixteen hundred Union cavalrymen. However, they were dismounted, meaning that every fourth man was holding the horses.

Then, as now, Gettysburg was a beautiful little town. The Lutherans were proud of their college and seminary, as well as their many churches in the town. Mr. McPherson's well-kept farm was just west of town and the Seminary Ridge. "Then came Willoughby Run and the toll-gate; and then Mr. Herr's tavern. The fields were broad and fertile. Wheat and clover were awaiting the harvest." It was a scene of beauty and a sight to bring joy. But today there was to be a harvest of death and those who tramped the Roads to Gettysburg met in the opening round of a conflict that was to decide the fate of a nation.[3]

Buford got the message of the advance when a courier came galloping from Herr's Tavern. A few moments later the Confederates loudly announced their arrival. Marye's battery of Pegram's command stopped in front of Herr's Tavern, wheeled a cannon and sent a shell toward Gettysburg.

A moment later two of Calef's guns returned the fire from McPherson's Ridge. Charles Coffin writes:

> The great battle had begun. No one had selected the ground. Buford had been ordered to hold Gettysburg and was obeying. Heth had been ordered to advance to Gettysburg, and was also obeying orders.[4]

According to Jacobs, there were clouds in the sky when the day broke. It looked like rain.[5] And rain it would west and north of Gettysburg, there would be showers of shot and shell.

The townspeople got up early and went out in the streets to talk. They were full of anxiety, and talking just might relieve some of the tension.

I CORPS

William Riddle arrived at Moritz's Tavern at 4:00 A.M. on July 1. He hated to waken General Reynolds from a sound sleep, but there was no alternative. When he got awake, Reynolds lay quietly, one hand under his head, staring at the ceiling. He had Riddle read the order three times. He was somewhat puzzled by the contents. He was supposed to lead the First Corps to Gettysburg, and the Eleventh close enough for support. Sickles and the Third Corps was to move to Emmitsburg and be in readiness to move at Reynolds's command. But the rest of the army was being held too far away. It almost seemed as though Meade was unsure of himself. Meade apparently thought he had relieved the threat to Harrisburg and Philadelphia. Now he intended to assume either the defense or an offense, whichever the situation called for.[6]

The Confederates were near Gettysburg. This much Reynolds knew. And he was the nearest to them. Pennsylvania had been invaded. This was almost home to John Reynolds.

451

Meade was ordering him to Gettysburg, and to Gettysburg he would go. The sooner the better.

Leaving Moritz's Tavern, Reynolds went to see General Wadsworth. He wanted the division put on the road at once, the road to Gettysburg. Shortly after 6:00 A.M. a note came from Howard. He and Sickles hopefully would cover the roads to Gettysburg and be in town by evening at the latest.

Before 7:00 A.M., Reynolds visited Abner Doubleday, now commanding the First Corps as he led the left wing of the army. The two men went over the reports and the maps. Reynolds stated he had already started Wadsworth. He wanted Doubleday to call in the pickets, and start the other two divisions plus the rest of the artillery on the road to Gettysburg.[7]

The men of the First Division of the First Corps of the Army of the Potomac were up at dawn on July 1. The men prepared breakfast consisting of hardtack, pork, and coffee. Chaplain Way gathered the men of the Twenty-fourth Michigan together for prayer. But even as they prayed, ammunition was quietly being distributed to the men. About 8:00 A.M. the division hit the road for Gettysburg. Cutler's brigade went first with the exception of the Seventh Indiana which was detached to Emmitsburg to guard the trains. Then came the Second Maine Battery followed by the Second Wisconsin, the Seventh Wisconsin, the Nineteenth Indiana and the Twenty-fourth Michigan. Reynolds was with the First Division. Battle was imminent.[8]

The men of the Iron Brigade were going to their date with destiny with flying colors. Rufus Dawes placed the drums and fifes at the head of the Sixth Wisconsin. The colors were unfurled. Then the musicians struck up "The Campbells Are Coming." We can hardly imagine the pride the men must have felt as they swung into route step on the Emmitsburg Road. Battery B crossed Marsh Creek and then pulled off the road to wait for the other divisions in the corps. The music and sight of the Iron Brigade made a profound impression on one member of the battery.

No one . . . will ever again see those two brigades of Wadsworth's Division—Cutler's and the Iron Brigade—file by as they did that morning. The little creek made a depression in the road, with a gentle ascent on either side, so that from our point of view the column, as it came down one slope and up the other, had the effect of huge blue billows of men topped with a spray of shining steel, and the whole spectacle was calculated to give nerve to a man who had none before. Partly because they had served together a long time, and, no doubt, because so many of their men were in our ranks, there was a great affinity between the Battery and the Iron Brigade, which expressed itself in cheers and good natured chaffing between us as they went by.[9]

Every step brought the men from Michigan and Wisconsin closer to the booming of the cannon and the smoke of battle.[10]

Rufus Dawes started a letter to his wife early in the morning. But he had hardly begun when orders came to "pack up." He stuck the letter in his pocket and carried it with him on the roads to Gettysburg, and into the fields around the town. By the time he finished the letter, he had sad news to send home.[11]

Charles Wainwright ate breakfast soon after sunrise. He was finishing his monthly returns when the order came to move out. The order came from General Doubleday. The Third Division of the First Corps was placed in the lead with the artillery following. Charles rode ahead to see what he could learn. On the way he met General Reynolds who stated that he did not expect a fight today. But from his headquarters at Moritz Crossroads, General John sent the Third Division off to the left, while he moved ahead with the First Division and Hall's battery.

Things seemed so quiet and peaceful as Wainwright threw his saddlebags into a wagon. His horse had lost two shoes and he stopped at a farmhouse with one of his foragers to get it fixed. While they were there a heavy shower came up and Charles waited until it was over before proceeding to the front.[12]

For the writer of these pages, it was a profound experience to visit the campground site of the First Corps at Marsh Creek, and Moritz Tavern, Reynolds's headquarters. One could feel and sense living history, and appreciate the sense of duty in these men.

Around eight o'clock Reynolds and his staff took the road to Gettysburg, some six miles away. They crossed Marsh Creek and headed for their date with destiny. Capt. Edward Baird, riding along with Reynolds, thought the general was more quiet than normal. Others thought him in great spirits. Some felt that despite his visit to Lincoln, he had a fear of being named commander of the Army of the Potomac. But when that command fell upon Meade on the twenty-eighth, he seemed as though a great burden lifted from his shoulders. Some of his staff said that he laughed and joked more than normally during the march from Frederick, Maryland.

About an hour later, a mile south of Gettysburg, Reynolds met a courier sent by John Buford, the cavalry commander located on the Chambersburg pike west of Gettysburg. Buford had an alarming report. He had met the Confederates early in the morning. They were driving toward town. He could hold for a while if ordered to do so.[13]

In that moment, John Reynolds made a fateful decision. Hold the enemy in check as long as possible. The First Corps was on the way, to be joined as soon as possible by the Eleventh and Third. John Reynolds, the Pennsylvanian, made the decision that would link the name of Gettysburg to the great battles of the world.

Orders were given for the First Corps to double-quick the rest of the way to Gettysburg. Reynolds galloped ahead, turned left across town and went to the Lutheran Theological Seminary where Buford had his headquarters.

Buford saw Reynolds coming from the cupola, where he had been watching the development of the A. P. Hill's troops. He had started down the ladder when he was met by Reynolds. "What's the matter, John?" Reynolds asked. Buford shook his head and answered, "The devil's to pay."[14]

Things looked bad for Buford. He was a good general. He devised the idea of cavalrymen fighting as dismounted infantrymen. Using this method, several troopers firing, while one held the horses, he was contesting every step of the Confederate advance. But there were just too many of the gray and butternut-clad men. In addition, his troopers had been on horseback for days with little food or rest. They

454

were tired. Lee's army was on the way. And here he was with just a small cavalry force to stop them.

Reynolds quickly noted that things were not good. He asked Buford if he could hold on until the First Corps arrived. Buford thought he could. Reynolds turned to Capt. Stephen Weld, and instructed him to ride as quickly as possible to Taneytown, and tell Meade: "The enemy is advancing in strong force, and I fear he will get to the heights beyond the town before I can. I will fight him inch by inch, and if driven into town I will barricade the streets, and hold him back as long as possible."[15]

Howard, Hancock, and Doubleday are sometimes given credit for the selection of Cemetery Ridge as the place to rally and establish the Union line. But from these words, the credit belongs to Reynolds.

Reynolds was all action. The adrenalin was flowing swiftly, and John Reynolds was at his best. Aides were sent with messages to Howard, Sickles, and Doubleday, "Make Haste to Gettysburg." Then Reynolds turned and headed for the Emmitsburg Road to meet Wadsworth. He did not bother using the roads, but cut across the fields. His escort knocked down fences so the advancing infantry would not be impeded.[16]

Gettysburg was in a state of alarm. The people were out in the street as curious folks will be, regardless of the danger. Captain Rosengarten, town leaders, and some preachers tried to get the people off the streets. But they continued to mill around like cattle. All sorts of rumors filled the air as well as the sounds of battle west of the town.

But Reynolds had other things to do. He met Wadsworth near the Cordori farm. The pioneers were ordered to take their axes and complete the destruction of the fences. Reynolds channeled all the troops in the direction of the Lutheran Seminary. For a few moments he watched with great pride as the men of the First Corps filed off to the left. His time was running out. He was fighting for time, precious moments to delay the enemy and to give his men time to get into position. Then he rode to rejoin Buford at the seminary.

The two men rode out to the next ridge. It was almost ten

o'clock. The Confederates were trying to cross Willoughby Run. They were driving on the McPherson farm. If they got through the woods, there was no telling what might happen.

Cutler's Union brigade was filing into position. Next came Capt. James Hall with the artillery battery. Reynolds went to Hall and picked out the positions for the guns. Hall said he saw and felt the determination in Reynolds to hold the ground. General John brightened when he saw Doubleday ride up with the report that the Iron Brigade was at the seminary and in a few moments would be in action.

Reynolds said, "I will do what I can. I'll try to hold the Cashtown Road, while you defend the Hagerstown Road." But the Confederates were coming so quickly. The Iron Brigade must get to McPherson's Ridge as quickly as possible. McPherson's Woods had to be held as it commanded both roads. He stopped his horse about two hundred yards from the barn. Doubleday told the Iron Brigade, "That woods where General Reynolds is, must be held." The black-hatted men from the Midwest replied, "If we can't hold it, where will you find men who can?"

Then came the Second Wisconsin up the slope, with the Seventh Wisconsin, Nineteenth Indiana, and Twenty-fourth Michigan following, one of America's greatest fighting units. It was a race between these combat troops and Archer's Confederates. The first lines met and reeled. Reynolds rode behind the first line of infantry, and shouted, "Forward men. Drive those fellows out of there. Forward! For God's sake, forward." He turned in his saddle and looked back to the seminary to see if more troops were on the way. Then he slumped forward. Reynolds had given his last command. His day was done. He had come home to defend his native Pennsylvania. This he had done. As John Reynolds gave his last command, he gave "his last full measure of devotion."

Charles H. Veil, the general's orderly, describes his death:

> He never spoke a word, or moved a muscle after he was struck. I have seen many men killed in action, but never saw a ball do its work as *instantly* as did the ball which struck General Reynolds, a man who knew not what fear or danger was, in a word was one of our very best Generals. Wherever the fight raged the fiercest, there

456

the General was sure to be found, his undaunted Courage always inspired the men with more energy and Courage. He would never order a body of troops where he had not been himself, or where he did not dare to go. The last words the lamented General spoke were *"Forward Men forward for God's sake and drive those fellows out of those woods."* (Meaning the enemy.)

When the General fell the only persons who were with him was Capts. Mitchell and Baird, and myself, when he fell we sprang from our horses, the General fell on his left side, I spread him on his back, glanced over him but could see no wound except a bruise above his left eye. We were under the impression that he was only stunned, this was all done in a flash. I caught the General under the arms, while each of the Capts. took hold of his legs, and we commenced to carry him out of the woods toward the Seminary. When we got outside of the woods, the Capts. left me to carry the word to the next officer in Command of his death. I in the meantime got some help from some of the orderlies who came up about this time, and we carried the body towards the Seminary, really not knowing where to take it to, as the enemy appeared to be comeing in on our right and left. When we arrived at the Seminary I concluded to carry the body to the Emmittsburg Road, and done so. Carrying it to Mr. George's house, (a small stone house) as we were laying him down, I first found the wound in the back of the neck. I then saw that the General was dead—I almost forgot to tell you that in crossing the fields between the woods where he was killed and the Seminary, he moved a little and I thought was comeing to his senses. We stopped a moment and I gave him a drop of water from a canteen but he would not drink, it was his last struggle. I have often wondered why it was that the wound did not bleed. I think now that he must have bled inwardly. When we arrived at Mr. George's house I sent for an ambulance and Mr. Rosengarten and myself went into town to try and get a coffin, but did not succeed—The only thing that we could get was a box from the Marble Cutters this was too short, so we knocked one end of it out and lay the body in this. We left about 1 p.m. I think for Taneytown, from there we went to Union Bridge where we arrived some time during the night. We had a box made there, into which we laid the body with some ice, at an early hour next morning we took the cars for Baltimore where we had the body embalmed—and then took it on to Philadelphia. The burial took place at Lancaster on the 4th—We all mourn the loss of the General very much and I think had he lived the enemy would not have returned to Virginia as safe as they did.[17]

C. J. Tyson awoke on July 1 to find Gettysburg full of soldiers, but the stores were open.

On Wednesday morning, July 1st, I arose to find Gettysburg swarming with Union soldiers, and the stores all open and doing business. I opened the gallery and went to work, and was kept very busy till near ten o'clock. I had made an exposure, and the room was full. I went into the work-room to finish the picture. When I returned the room was empty, excepting the one person. He offered me in pay a note I could not change. I ran down-stairs to get change when, to my surprise, all the stores were closed and no one to be seen. I gave the man his money, and he disappeared. Judge Russell turned the corner just then and I asked, "What does this mean?" He answered, "It means that all citizens are requested to retire into their houses as quietly and as quickly as possible," and off he went, and off I went up-stairs and gathered up a few valuables and started for home. By the time I had reached the opposite side of the square I met my wife, who was coming to see what had become of me. It was then between ten and eleven o'clock. I returned with her to our house. She had a small trunk packed which contained our wedding suits and some valuables.

The cannonading was then going on in good earnest, and the people living on Chambersburg Street were advised to go farther up town. We locked up the house and I put the trunk on a wheelbarrow and started. Going a short distance I met our neighbor, Mr. Boyer, who had a spring wagon, covered, and in it his mother-in-law, who sat upon some trunks. He very kindly permitted me to put my trunk on, which I did and tumbled my barrow over into Mr. Chritzman's yard. We all went up on Baltimore Street and remained there until about two o'clock. In the mean time the churches were being filled with wounded men and the pavements were lined with those slightly wounded. Several blocks of captured rebels passed out Baltimore Street and I concluded to go down home and bring up a basket of fresh bread to distribute to the soldiers (my wife had baked a large quantity the day before or that morning); but when I got nearly down to the square I met one of our officers riding up the street, warning all women, children, and non-combatants to leave the town, as General Lee intended to shell it."[18]

XI CORPS

General Howard had hardly gotten to bed in Emmitsburg when an orderly aroused him. It was early in the morning on July 1. The orderly handed him a packet of materials addressed to General Reynolds. Howard read the contents in the event they were lost in dispatch between Emmitsburg and

Marsh Run. The orders gave the command for the First and the Eleventh corps to proceed to Gettysburg.

> With these orders came a clear indication of Meade's opinion of the location of Hill and Longstreet, as between Chambersburg and Gettysburg, while Ewell was believed to be still occupying Carlisle and York.[19]

Howard went back to sleep, at least for a few hours. Meanwhile with the dawn, Union observers looking westward from the Lutheran Seminary in Gettysburg saw thickening columns of Confederate infantry with their bright red banners. Looking south they also saw the columns of blue coming on the Roads to Gettysburg.

We have read of John Reynolds, now we take a look at Howard. Being nearest to the support of the First Corps, Howard prepared his men to move to Gettysburg. Barlow's division was ordered to march by the main road, following the path of the First Corps. Steinwehr and Schurz were told to follow a road to the east, passing Horner's Mill, and entering the road from Taneytown. Howard felt this road was better than the main route. To a degree, it was hurry up and wait. Although the columns were formed, they did not move forward until the command was received from Reynolds about 8:30 A.M.[20]

Barlow had a difficult day. It was hot, and the road was full of ruts and stones. The road was partially blocked by the wagons of the First Corps. Thus Barlow averaged but two and one-half miles an hour in his march to Gettysburg.

With his staff and a small escort, Howard started forward as soon as his men began stepping off. Like Reynolds, he took to the fields and woods to avoid the congestion of the roads. The officers with O. O. Howard that hot July day, remembered for a long time the rapidity of the ride to Gettysburg. According to Howard, his escort came in sight of Gettysburg about 10:30. A staff officer came from Reynolds to give an initial progress report.[21]

Howard and his staff heard the sound of cannons and rattle of small arms fire. The general from Maine could "see rising smoke, a mile and a half to my left. I could see . . . the divisions of Doubleday, moving along northwesterly across the open fields toward the seminary."[22]

Questioning just where Reynolds wanted him, Howard stopped momentarily at Sherfy's peach orchard along the Emmitsburg Road. He took the time to look over the main features of the nearby terrain, noting particularly Cemetery Ridge. Immediately he and his staff went to look it over.

> Here was a broad view which embraced the town, the seminary, the college, and all the undulating valley of open country spread out between the ridges.[23]

Howard and his adjutant general sat on their horses looking northward. The commander of the Eleventh Corps turned to his aide and said, "This seems to be a good position, colonel." Meysenberg promptly replied, "It's the only position, general."

> After observing the whole sweep of the country, I then made up my mind . . . to use Cemetery Ridge as the best defensive position in sight.[24]

Years afterward, Howard maintained that he and he alone selected Cemetery Ridge as the position for the Army of the Potomac. But that is not for us to argue in this book.

After visiting Cemetery Hill, Howard and his staff rode into Gettysburg. He tried to get into the belfry of the courthouse, but had no luck. Then D. A. Skelly took Howard to Fahnestock's observatory across the street.

> Mounting to the top, I was delighted with the open view. With maps and field glasses we examined the battlefield. Wadsworth's infantry, Buford's cavalry, and one or two batteries were nearest. . . . Confederate prisoners were . . . being sent to the rear . . . from the Seminary Ridge down the street past my post of observation.
>
> We were noting the numerous roads emerging from Gettysburg, and from our charts comparing the location and names, when a young soldier riding up the street below, stopped, and looking up, saluted me and said: "General Reynolds is wounded, sir," and I replied to him: "I am very sorry; I hope he will be able to keep the field."[25]

But soon another officer came, Howard thought it was Captain Hall. The news was sad. "General Reynolds is dead, and you are the senior officer on the field."

We can imagine how Howard must have felt. The Army of the Potomac had less than twelve thousand men present on the field. The First Corps was hard pressed. The Eleventh Corps was still on the road to Gettysburg. The Third Corps was back at Emmitsburg, and the rest of the army scattered at Taneytown, Union Mills, and Manchester. The majority of the army was "too far away—too far for this day's work."

Oliver O. Howard said:

> My heart was heavy and the situation grave indeed! but I did not hesitate.... "God helping us, we will stay here till the army comes."[26]

Quickly dictating orders, Howard assumed command. Schurz was to take command of the Eleventh Corps, Doubleday and Buford were to remain west of Gettysburg. Captain Hall took urgent messages to the division commanders in the Eleventh Corps, telling them to make haste. A description of the action was also sent to Meade in Taneytown.[27]

The Eleventh Corps, marching by the Emmitsburg and Taneytown roads, arrived at Gettysburg, depending on location in column between 11:15 and 1:30. According to the Forty-fifth New York, the town clock said 11:15 when they arrived on the scene. The men were tired. They had made a forced march of over ten miles.[28] The July sun was hot. General Howard kept Steinwehr's division and Weidrich's New York Battery to "hold and fortify Cemetery Hill." Schurz and Barlow were sent immediately to Doubleday's assistance. Howard assumed command of the field by virtue of his seniority and Schurz took command of the Eleventh Corps.

Due to heavy Confederate pressure, the Eleventh Corps found it impossible to continue the line of the First Corps on Oak Ridge. Had the men in gray been coming just from the west, there would have been no problem. But Robert Rodes was advancing from the north. And Carter's Rebel artillery took a position enabling it to enfilade the First Corps line. Thus Barlow's and Schimmelfing's divisions deployed in the fields between Oak Ridge and Rock Creek. Instead of prolonging the line of the First Corps, the Eleventh had to face North to meet Rodes and the Confederate Second Corps under Richard S. Ewell.

Orland Smith's brigade of Steinwehr's division came up.

Three regiments were posted at the northern base of the hill, and occupied some houses at the edge of town. Charles Coster, commanding the First Brigade, was posted on the summit of Cemetery Hill. This was an excellent move, as Howard had the foresight to hold the key to line as a rallying point and also as a line of defense.

When Schurz's two divisions arrived, Barlow and Schimmelfing, the two brigade commanders, leading six thousand men, were ordered to move through the town to the plain north of Gettysburg. They were supposed to connect with Doubleday's right flank on Oak Ridge, and also to guard against the arrival of Confederate reinforcements, namely those of Early's division. Howard rode with Barlow's brigade as it advanced into the fray. He then rode to inspect the lines of the First Corps.[29]

Lt. Bayard Wilkeson had ridden with Battery G, Fourth United States Artillery from Trappe Rock, across the Potomac, the Middletown, Frederick, to Emmitsburg, and was now going into action near the Almshouse. Wilkeson himself took two guns and went into action on Barlow's Knoll.

The position of Barlow's troops was poor. They were exposed to heavy fire with little or no cover. The fields of grain provided some concealment for the Rebels. Heavy fighting followed which will not be covered in these pages. However, the Eleventh Corps, as at Chancellorsville, was struck hard on the right flank by the advancing elements of Rodes and then Early.

It was approximately 3:30 when "Old Jube" arrived with almost sixty-three hundred effective troops. Devin's cavalry had watched his approach march.

As the fighting increased, many of the women and children of Gettysburg went to the cellars for greater protection. Reporters felt the men of Gettysburg should have been at the front. Most of them were in the army, and only the very old men, and the young boys were in Gettysburg in June of 1863.

Shortly after daylight, McGowan's brigade rolled up their blankets and flies. Many of the knapsacks were already discarded. Then the men started on their final march on the

Roads to Gettysburg. The South Carolina veterans smelled battle. The sound of the cannons made them even more suspicious that action was just ahead.[30]

The flag of the First South Carolina was the first Confederate flag raised in Gettysburg. Once the town was occupied, many citizens gave the soldiers food hoping that would cause them to leave them alone. Other than raiding the gardens and hen houses, the men in gray were rather well behaved.

Richard Ewell's blaze of glory was about to end. He had done a great job at Winchester and in leading his troops through Pennsylvania. At sunrise Ewell left Heidlersburg, heading for Middletown (Biglerville). Early's division took a parallel road leading to Gettysburg. A courier was sent to Lee asking for explicit directions.

At 10:00, Ewell reached Middletown. Fifteen minutes later a dispatch came from A. P. Hill asking him to hurry to Gettysburg. Ewell dashed off a note to Lee and received another one. Lee said that if the enemy was in force, he did not want to bring on a general engagement.

Approaching Gettysburg about 11:30, Ewell and Rodes heard artillery fire. Thirty minutes later, Rodes and his men were starting into position on Oak Ridge, coming in on A. P. Hill's flank. His division had completed the Roads to Gettysburg.

Early got a late start. About 11:00 A.M. he received a dispatch from his commander saying that Hill and Rodes were moving to Gettysburg. Early was to do the same.

Early was supposed to move towards Gettysburg by way of Hunterstown, Schrivers, and Mummasburg. But he had learned that the Hunterstown Road was rough. Using digression as a division commander, his division moved to Heidlersburg and took the main road to Schrivers, and then on to Gettysburg.[31]

While things were happening on Seminary Ridge, Robert E. Lee and James Longstreet were riding eastward on the Chambersburg Road headed for Cashtown. Lee expressed some concern over the absence of Stuart, and wonderment about the location of the enemy. Otherwise, he was in good spirits.

Jed Hotchkiss tells of his day in the advance of the Second Corps from Heidlersburg to the fields of Gettysburg.

Wednesday, July 1st. We marched towards Cashtown until we reached Middletown, having heard that the enemy was at Gettysburg. At Middletown we heard that A. P. Hill was approaching Gettysburg, from the mountains, so we turned with Rodes' Division and went on by the Middletown and Gettysburg road until within some 2 miles of Gettysburg when we turned to the right. Early came through Heidlersburg and went directly on to Gettysburg. We pressed forward and soon engaged the enemy on the hills to the west of Gettysburg. A. P. Hill attacked on our right at about the same time. At 11 A.M. firing of artillery by Hill; 11-30 infantry firing by Hill; 11-45 Rodes' line of battle advanced—Iverson being in front. We were moving in column along the crest of the hill. At 12 M. the enemy driven back and Hill advancing; 12-20 Hill's artillery brisk on the right; 2½ P.M. Early's artillery opened on the left; 3¼ P.M. Early's infantry advanced and swept gallantly up to the town; Rodes advanced on our right and had severe fighting with the enemy on the [Emmitsburg ?] road. The enemy shelled our position on the hill and compelled us to retire; but our artillery played on them with effect just before Early advanced. The General was thrown from his horse, the horse being struck by a shell, on the head, and several were wounded near by. Early's line was thrown into some disorder by his advance and he reformed at 4 P.M. and moved into the town at 5 P.M. Heavy firing took place on our right. Rodes entered at about the same hour as Early and we followed into the town, meeting the crowd of prisoners coming back. Gen'l. Lee came up about 4½ P.M.

We supped and [slept] just in the edge of the town. We killed and wounded large numbers of the enemy and took several thousand prisoners. The complete success on our part. The pursuit was checked by the lateness of the hour and the position the enemy had secured in a cemetery. Quite warm in the P.M. and some rain in the A.M. but pleasant. We slept at Spangler's. Our loss was not heavy though the enemy captured most of Iverson's Brigade. We captured most of two Corps of the enemy, the 11th and [I Corps].[32]

Part of Rodes's division of 8,125 men moved to attack what was left of the Second Division of the Union First Corps near the railroad cut. These men were commanded by Gabriel Paul and Henry Baxter. The heat and rough terrain slowed the advance of the Rebels. Again, terrible fighting ensued. Finally, heavier Confederate numbers spelled the dif-

464

ference, and the Union soldiers were forced to withdraw. It was now about 4:15. From midmorning till noon, the First Corps had stood against A. P. Hill's men. Now it was the Second Corps of the Army of Northern Virginia. The Sixteenth Maine was ordered to hold at any cost until the rest could retreat.

The Sixteenth Maine had also traveled from Middletown to Frederick, and up Old Route 15. Now almost all them were gone; 232 of 298 were listed as killed, wounded or missing. The survivors tore the regimental flag to bits and distributed the pieces among themselves to keep it from falling into Rebel hands.

However, Robinson's division had delayed the Confederates two and a half hours on Oak Ridge. They had fought a splendid action. They had inflicted enormous losses on Robert Rodes. Two of his five brigades were shattered. Many who had shared with the people of Carlisle had walked their last mile.

About 3:30 Howard ordered the First and Eleventh corps to withdraw. Somehow, the order never reached Doubleday, and he kept on, hoping for reinforcements. Howard, like Rodes, certainly did not exercise the best control on the field of conflict.

Howard did have some good news. Sickles sent word at 3:15 that he was on the Road to Gettysburg and twenty minutes later a dispatch arrived from Slocum saying he was hurrying to the fields of action.[33]

That was fine, but the Union First Corps was running out of men and ammunition. Before noon Wadsworth's men, commanded by Meredith and Cutler, had repelled Heth's advance and cut down numerous Confederate attacks on McPherson's Ridge. Fresh Rebel troops came up, launched another attack, and at last the valiant First Corps had to give way. Rufus Dawes describes the withdrawal through the streets of Gettysburg.

> The weather was sultry. The sweat streamed from the faces of the men. There was not a drop of water in the canteens, and there had been none for hours. The streets were jammed with crowds of retreating soldiers, and with ambulances, artillery, and wagons. The

cellars were crowded with men, sound in body, but craven in spirit, who had gone there to surrender. I saw no men wearing badges of the first army corps in this disgraceful company. In one case, these miscreants, mistaking us for the rebels, cried out from the cellar, "Don't fire, Johnny, we'll surrender." These surroundings were depressing to my hot and thirsty men. Finding the street blocked, I formed my men in two lines across it. The rebels began to fire on us from houses and cross-lots. Here came to us a friend in need. It was an old citizen with two buckets of fresh water. The inestimable value of this cup of cold water to those true, unyielding soldiers, I would that our old friend could know.

After this drink, in response to my call, the men gave* three cheers for the good and glorious cause, for which we stood in battle. The enemy fired on us sharply, and the men returned their fire, shooting wherever the enemy appeared. This firing had a good effect. It cleared the street of stragglers in short order. The way being open I marched again toward the Cemetery Hill. The enemy did not pursue; they had found it dangerous business. We hurried along, not knowing certainly that we might not be marching into the clutches of the enemy. But the colors of the Union, floating over a well ordered line of men in blue, who were arrayed along the slope of Cemetery Hill, became visible. This was the seventy-third Ohio, of Steinwehr's division of the eleventh army corps. With swifter steps we now pressed on up the hill, and, passing in through the ranks open to receive us, officers and men threw themselves in a state of almost perfect exhaustion on the green grass and the graves of the cemetery. The condition of affairs on Cemetery Hill at this time has been a subject of discussion. If fresh troops had attacked us then, we unquestionably would have fared badly. The troops were scattered over the hill in much disorder, while a stream of stragglers and wounded men pushed along the Baltimore Turnpike toward the rear. But this perilous condition of affairs was of short duration. There was no appearance of panic on the Cemetery Hill. After a short breathing spell my men again promptly responded to the order to "fall in." Lieutenant Rogers brought us orders from General Wadsworth, to join our own brigade, which had been sent to occupy Culp's Hill. As we marched toward the hill our regimental wagon joined us. In the wagon were a dozen spades and shovels. Taking our place on the right of the line of the brigade, I ordered the regiment to intrench. The men worked with great energy. A man would dig with all his strength till out of breath, when another would seize the spade and push on the work. There were no orders to construct these breastworks, but the situation plainly dictated their necessity. The men now lay down to rest after the arduous labors of this great and terrible day. Sad and solemn reflections possessed, at least, the writer of these papers. Our dead lay unburied and beyond our sight or reach. Our wounded were in the hands of the enemy. Our bravest and best were numbered with them. Of eighteen hundred men who marched with the splendid brigade in the morning, but seven hundred were here. More than one thousand men had been shot. There was to us a terrible reality in the figures which represent our loss. We had been driven, also, by the enemy, and the shadow of defeat seemed to be hanging over us. But that afternoon, under the burning sun and through the stifling clouds of dust, the Army of the Potomac had marched to the sound of our cannon.[34]

We can hardly imagine what it must have been like as the First Corps fell back through the southwestern part of Gettysburg, while the Eleventh retreated on Washington and Baltimore streets. Some men hid in cellars, barns, and pigpens to escape capture by the Confederates.

Early and Rodes teamed up to advance and push the Eleventh Corps back to Cemetery Hill. Portions of the Eleventh Corps retreated in disorder. Some hid in cellars and gardens. Many were captured. Gettysburg was chaos and confusion. Fighting men transformed the quaint and quiet town into bedlam.

Ewell rode into town behind his troops who were mopping up. Someone took a shot at him. There was a thud, and Ewell reeled, but then straightened himself in the saddle. He said, "It doesn't hurt to be shot in a wooden leg."[35]

Between 4:00 and 5:00 P.M. he rode into the square, and reined his horse under a tree. There in the saddle he received reports and chatted with his staff and others. Union prisoners and men in gray filled the town square.

Isaac Trimble rode up and said, "Well, General, We've had a grand success. Are you not going to follow it up and push our advantages?"[36]

Ewell replied, "General Lee has instructed me not to bring on a general engagement without orders. I shall await them."

Trimble argued that the way things had gone, he did not feel the order was applicable. Trimble tried to get him to take Culp's Hill. Rodes, Hays, Gordon, and Early all wanted him to press on.

Rodes and Early reported they had been to Cemetery Hill, had seen Little Round Top and wanted to attack it.

The generals were not the only ones to be upset with Ewell. "Sandie" Pendleton and Henry Kyd Douglas were amazed that he did not push on. Douglas carried the message

467

from Johnson saying that his division was in excellent condition. Still Ewell pondered over his discretionary orders. "Sandie" Pendleton, another former Jackson aide, whispered, "O for the presence and inspiration of 'Old Jack' just for one hour."[37]

Harry Gilmor of the Confederate cavalry, along with his friend Welch, claim to have been the first two Confederates to enter Gettysburg. They found mass confusion. Gilmor felt that they could easily have been driven beyond the town or captured. "But unfortunately, this was not done, and they were allowed that night to throw up breastworks and fortifications, which, in the assaults of the next two days, cost us so many brave men." Gilmor blamed Ewell. Early had told his commander that he could take the heights. But Ewell would not consent. "Had Early's advice been followed, nothing could have withstood our legions, flushed with victory, and we should have laid Philadelphia and New York in ashes, or conquered a peace."[38] In Gilmor's mind Ewell's decision not to attack was the turning point of the battle, as well as that of the war.

The next day, Gilmor was ordered to act as provost marshal and search Gettysburg for prisoners, ammunition, and arms. Vast numbers were collected. Twenty-five hundred weapons were piled in the square. They were not collected, and later fell back into Union hands.

Many were taking their final steps today on the Roads to Gettysburg. One of these was Wesley Culp, a native of the town upon which the armies of the north and south were now converging. As a teen-ager, he left home and went to Virginia. When the war came, Wes joined the Confederate army. Now on this hot July afternoon, he was a member of Ewell's Corps marching toward Culp's Hill within yards of the house in which he had been born.

As the broken regiments of the Eleventh Corps fell back to the open ground just north of Cemetery Hill, a colonel, not well versed in English was heard giving commands in German.

General Howard noticed the color sergeant and the color guard of the defeated regiment. He called out, "Sergeant, plant your flag down there in that stonewall!" The young

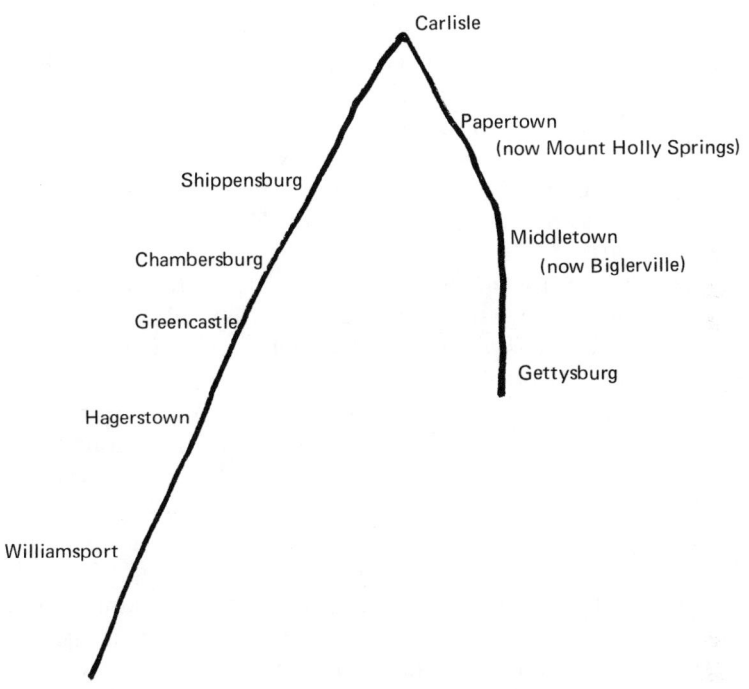

Carlisle

Papertown
(now Mount Holly Springs)

Shippensburg

Chambersburg

Middletown
(now Biglerville)

Greencastle

Gettysburg

Hagerstown

Williamsport

The route of Robert Rodes, the first Confederate infantry to cross the Potomac, the first to reach Chambersburg, and the first to reach Carlisle.

469

man, not recognizing the corps commander, shouted back, "All right, if you go with me, I will." So Howard, Lieutenant Rogers of his staff, the color sergeant and the color guard planted the regimental colors in the stone wall. This act seemed to rally the troops.

Shortly afterwards, Howard, Slocum, and Sickles took their headquarters near the gatekeeper's cottage. Mrs. Peter Thorn and her daughter lived in the cottage while Mr. Thorn was away at war. Howard had been all day without food and was nearly famished. But the desire of his heart was Mrs. Thorn's command. Before the hungry general had the opportunity to ask, Mrs. Thorn had bread and coffee for the generals. "Those refreshments," wrote Howard, "have never been forgotten."[39]

Ed Johnson, Ewell's other commander, started marching at 7:00 A.M., traveling the Black Gap Road to the Chambersburg-Gettysburg Pike. No halt was made in Fayetteville. Johnson's men continued east, passing some of Longstreet's soldiers camped in a woods, cooking their rations. The road was good and the shade of the mountain trees helped with the heat of the day. By midafternoon, they had climbed the mountain and started down into Cashtown. They noticed the orchards, pastures, and fields of grain. They learned that A. P. Hill had spent the previous night in Cashtown. By now they heard a distant rumble, almost like thunder. It was the noise of Hill's men, locked in combat with the Union First Corps at Gettysburg.

Johnson pressed on. His men saw the white puffs of smoke from the shell bursts. Soon walking wounded from Hill's divisions started to pass them. Near Gettysburg, large groups of Union prisoners were being held in a woods. Sweaty, grimy wounded were also seen. They noticed the appalling slaughter in the railroad cut. It was almost dark when the division reached Gettysburg. They rested a bit, then took the York Road, made a turn, and halted for the night near Culp's Hill and the Hanover Road. Ewell and the Second Corps of the Army of Northern Virginia were now present and accounted for at Gettysburg.

It was about 9:00 P.M. It had been a difficult day for

Johnson's men. Despite the heavy rains, water was scarce and guards were posted at the wells to conserve water for the wounded.

Meanwhile down at Manchester, Gregg's cavalry was routed from their sleep at an early hour. By daybreak they were back in the saddle again. The division crossed the Mason-Dixon Line into Pennsylvania. When the men reached Hanover Junction, they found the railroad track had been destroyed and the telegraph wires cut. The main body was halted for awhile, and a scouting party sent out in the direction of York. Orders were flying thick and fast this day. During the halt a message came with the order for a brigade to ride back to Manchester for the purpose of covering the right flank of the Army of the Potomac, and protecting the trains of the army which had been ordered to Westminster. Huey's brigade, not very happy over the situation, had to mount up again. With Fuller's Horse Battery they started back to Manchester. The rest of the division headed for Hanover, but did not reach that place until 1:00 A.M. on Tuesday.

The ride was terrible. The Third Pennsylvania and other regiments in McIntosh's command had been in the saddle about twenty hours a day for three continuous days. They were beat. They and their mounts had gone without food and sleep. They found the heat and dust almost unbearable. Horses fell by the score from exhaustion. The men, especially those in the rear of the column, were scarcely recognizable due to dust and sweat. Some of the cavalrymen were walking, carrying the saddles and bridles of their dead horses, hoping for fresh mounts. The men and their gallant steads had never known such suffering.

III CORPS

Dan Sickles took the Third Corps from Bridgeport to Emmitsburg. So the little mountain town prepared to receive

471

the Third Union Infantry Corps in its streets. The First Corps moved out on Tuesday, and the Eleventh was in the process of moving.

The Third Corps noted the results of the big fire that had hit Emmitsburg. Some thought the Confederates had burned the town, but soon learned otherwise. Halting for a spell, a soldier from the Eleventh New Jersey's B Company went looking for some good food. He found that men of the Eleventh and First corps had already been to most of the places. Finally he was able to get a pan of milk, two pies, and a loaf of bread. The farmer told him to listen to the firing from the north. Soldier Hand heard it and decided he had better get back to the company area. He drank some of the milk, poured the rest in his canteen, placed the bread in his knapsack, and the pies on a big cabbage leaf. His jogging soon broke the pies. Their precious contents started to ooze between his fingers. The poor man had to stop and eat both pies.[40]

Some of the troops from the Third Corps encamped on the grounds of Mount Saint Mary's and some went to see the priests for confession and mass. The bells of the town churches, ringing for mass, reminded the men of home. They thought of Michigan, Maine, and wherever home was.

The rest of the men, until reassembled, fanned out over the Maryland countryside buying bread, ham, eggs, "anything the Dutch farmers could be induced to spare from their larders." Some of the soldiers put in orders for fresh food the next day. Several even paid in advance. But they would not be in Emmitsburg, they had a date with a peach orchard in Gettysburg.

Those who remained in camp to rest, pitched their tents and collected pine cones to serve as mattresses. Some walked into Emmitsburg to see the destructive results of the big fire.

But the Eleventh New Jersey was ordered on the Road to Gettysburg. When the command crossed into Pennsylvania, a German woman came out with a bucket of water, saying, "Here's Pennsylvania water for you, boys." The lads cheered.[41]

There are conflicting weather reports for this first day of

July. But according to the 105th New York, it rained hard early in the morning around Emmitsburg, making the "roads heavy and the marching extremely difficult." Of course, this could have been an isolated shower. Sometimes the regimental historians got their dates mixed. But Professor Jacobs says it was threatening in the morning.[42]

When Dan Sickles received an urgent message from General Howard to "proceed to Gettysburg immediately," the Third Corps struck their tents and took the road for Gettysburg.

However, Burling's New Jersey Brigade, and the brigade under De Trobriand were left behind at Emmitsburg as sort of a rear guard. Two batteries were also left. Orders were "hold the roads in and out of Emmitsburg at all costs . . . stop every turning movement against the rear of the three corps assembled at Gettysburg."[43]

Burling was at the north edge of Emmitsburg, De Trobriand, south. In the event of a Confederate attack the latter, by virtue of seniority, was to assume overall command.

South of Emmitsburg on Route 15 is Saint Joseph's Catholic School for girls. (It is now closed. Hopefully it might become a branch of the University of Maryland.) On the campus of this lovely school De Trobriand deployed his troops to defend against any Confederate move. We can imagine the excitement of the nuns as the artillery wheeled into place, and as they saw the gleam of bayonets. "Nothing like it had ever troubled the calm of this holy retreat."

But let's hear it from De Trobriand:

> When I arrived at a gallop in front of the principal door, the doorkeeper, who had ventured a few steps outside, completely lost her head. She in her fright, she came near being trampled under foot by the horses of my staff. . . . The superior, on the contrary, with whom I asked to speak in the parlor, came down calm and dignified. I had no need to reassure her. Her conversation betrayed neither fear nor even inquietude. She perfectly comprehended the necessities of war. When I asked her to send me up to the belfry, from which the . . . surrounding country was visible, she sent for the chaplain and ordered him to act as my guide.
> The chaplain was an Italian priest. . . . He led us through the dormitories and the classrooms of the boarding school, at that moment deserted, the superior having very wisely sent all the scholars

473

to their relatives. There remained but five or six, belonging to Southern families. . . .

We reached the belfry by a narrow and winding staircase. I went first. At the noise of my boots sounding on the steps, a rustling of dresses and murmuring of voices were heard above my head. There were eight or ten young nuns, who had mounted up there to enjoy the extraordinary spectacle of guns in battery, of stacked muskets, of sentinels walking back and forth, . . . of soldiers making coffee in the gardens, of horses ready saddled eating their oats under the apple trees;—all things of which they had the least idea. We had cut off their retreat, and they were crowded against the windows, like frightened birds, asking Heaven to send them wings . . . to fly away.

This was too much for De Trobriand. He rose to the occasion:

Ah! Sisters. I catch you in the very act of curiosity. After all, it is a very venial sin, and I am sure the reverend father here present will freely give you absolution therefor.[44]

The girls were naturally embarrassed. They were speechless. One brave lass managed to smile. But one thing was on their mind. Escape, get out of the awkward situation as soon as possible.

De Trobriand tried to help "Permit me to make one request of you. Ask St. Joseph to keep the rebels away from here; for if they come before I get away, I do not know what will become of your beautiful convent."[45]

With that the girls made haste. The Confederates did not come. They were busy in Pennsylvania. The night was quiet, and between 2:00 and 3:00 A.M., orders came to march to Gettysburg. Although the distance was short, about eight miles, the road was slippery from rain. The nuns could rest easy now. The soldiers were gone.

On July 1 Andrew Humphreys was examining the ground around Emmitsburg for defensive possibilities in the event of a battle. In his absence, the Second Division of the Third Corps was ordered to the front. The command came from Oliver O. Howard urging the men to "move up with the utmost dispatch." The soldiers took a road about two miles west of Emmitsburg off the present Route 16.

The Second Division marched along Marsh Run almost to Black Horse Tavern on the Gettysburg-Fairfield Road. This just about spelled disaster. In the meantime, Humphreys finished his topographical examination of the Emmitsburg countryside, and rode rapidly to catch up with his command. On the way he encountered Lt. Col. Julius Hayden, inspector general of the Third Corps, with some men to guide the division to Gettysburg.

En route, a message was received from Howard with the warning to watch the left flank. A local citizen reported there were no Union troops west of Gettysburg, only Rebels.

A staff officer told Humphreys to take position on the left of Gettysburg. Colonel Hayden was sure General Sickles said "move by way of Black Horse Tavern." It was evident that the brass did not know the situation.

The maps fooled Humphreys. He felt he was one-half mile from Black Horse Tavern. But in reality, he was just about one hundred yards away. Just imagine, almost midnight, and finding yourself in the rear of Lee's army. What would a Jackson or Hancock have done?

Humphreys talked to the innkeeper and his sons. Then he rode away in an effort to find the rest of the Third Corps. Ten minutes later twenty or thirty Confederates came to Black Horse Tavern and spent the night there. The innkeeper pointed in the direction of a hill, before Humphreys left, saying that at dusk the Confederates had thirty-six cannons on the hill.[46]

The division was beginning to wonder about their commander. They had not forgiven him for the brutal canal march in the rain and mud. Now they had crossed and recrossed Marsh Run. They thought they were on a wild goose chase. Finally the division made an about face and got back on the road. However, it was a tremendous job to get the ambulances and the wagons turned around.

With his staff and Dr. Ana of Emmitsburg, Humphreys headed for the main road to Gettysburg. A company was sent forward to scout. Campfires were seen in the distance. But were they friend or foe? After frustrating moments, contact was made with the outposts of the Army of the Potomac. The sentinels were in doubt. They thought Bobby Lee might be pulling a trick on them. But Colonel Hart, the adjutant

475

Saint Joseph's in Emmitsburg.

general of the Third Corps, arrived and soon paved the way for the missing division to return to Union lines. They got back just in time. By dawn, Longstreet's troops were moving over the ground Humphreys had trod.

The men were beat. They had been on the Roads to Gettysburg since afternoon. It was now well into the wee hours of July 2. They fell in place and soon were fast asleep.

II CORPS

On July 1, Hancock and the Second Corps arrived in Taneytown, covering the distance from Uniontown, and reaching the village about 11:00 A.M. The troops passed through Taneytown and went into camp on Dr. Swope's farm. This was located at the junction of the Harney and Emmitsburg Road. Hancock rode off to visit General Meade at army headquarters.

476

Winfield Scott Hancock was happy to visit Taneytown. He told Maj. St. Clair A. Muhlholland that his grandfather as a Revolutionary War soldier had been to Taneytown to pick up prisoners after Burgoyne's surrender.

Hungry troops were all around Taneytown. Lt. Col. Freeman McGilvery was among them. He wrote:

> The women and young girls of Taneytown were asked to bake pies, bread, and cakes to feed the worn troops and they were told to charge the men for what they took, because these men had just been paid, but they were not to overcharge them. . . . One person alone, the wife of Rev. Levi Williams used up a whole barrel of flour in her baking. . . . (The) commissary wagons were late in getting into town. . . . Four Taneytown citizens were pressed into service as guides and taken to Thompson's meadow on the Littlestown Road. They were Messrs. John W. Jones, James Kridler, John Bishop, and Thomas D. Thompson. At 10:00 o'clock on the night of July 1, the call came ordering them to lead troops to within two miles of Gettysburg at sunrise. . . . Jones and Kridler led General Sickles Third Corps to the Gettysburg area. . . . Bishop and Thompson led the Second Corps. . . . These guides were allowed to come home on the night of July 2, due to the fact that they lost their horses while they were in front of Meade's headquarters . . . when a cannonball smashed into the gabled end of the house and scared them off.[47]

Naturally newspaper correspondents converged on headquarters. Whitelaw Reid of the *Cincinnati Gazette* was one of these. Another was L. L. Crouse of the *New York Times*. He took the wrong road looking for a story and wound up in Cashtown, west of Gettysburg. There he found more than he had bargained for. Crouse found Confederate troops. Thinking the information was vital, he headed for Gettysburg to give the news to General Reynolds. But when he arrived he found Reynolds was dead. So it was off to Taneytown.

Thus the *New York Times* reporter had a sad story to tell when he arrived. The news soon spread through Taneytown. The folks received the news with sadness and shock. Correspondents chatting and drinking together at the Old Stone Tavern, Adam Good Tavern, and the Sauble Inn rushed out to prepare messages to be carried by dispatch riders to the telegraph offices in Frederick for their respective papers.

Not waiting to summon Hancock, Meade rode directly to headquarters of the Second Corps, told Hancock about the death of Reynolds, and gave him orders to turn command of the corps over to John Gibbon. Hancock was to proceed as quickly as possible to Gettysburg and take command of the field.

Hancock had some questions. Caldwell was senior to Gibbon, while both Sickles and Howard, already at Gettysburg or on the road were his seniors in rank. To ease Hancock's mind, Meade showed him the letter from Secretary of War Stanton, authorizing him to make any changes necessary, saying that he had the support of both Stanton and President Lincoln.[48]

Meade has been criticized for not going in person to Gettysburg. But he still felt the main battle would be fought along Pipe Creek. On Hancock's earlier visit the two had discussed the matter, and engineers were planning fortifications. Details were still fuzzy coming from Gettysburg. So instead of going himself, Meade sent his best available officer.

Hancock apparently started his journey of thirteen miles in an ambulance. He had a poor map of Gettysburg. He studied it briefly. Then as the ambulance was making slow progress, he mounted a horse, the fastest one he owned and galloped ahead. Four miles southeast of Gettysburg, near the crossroads community of Barlow, Hancock and his party met the ambulance carrying the body of John Fulton Reynolds to Union Bridge. They took their caps off and proceeded in silence.[49]

It was midafternoon, three o'clock, when Hancock arrived at Gettysburg. Things could not have been much worse. The First and the Eleventh corps were retiring through the streets of the town. The situation was chaotic. Buford and his gallant troopers were still holding on covering the retreat of the infantry. The Third Corps had not yet come up from Emmitsburg.

> Orders were at once given to establish a line of battle on Cemetery Hill, with skirmishers occupying that part of town immediately in our front. The position . . . on the southern edge of Gettysburg, overlooking the town and commanding the Emmitsburg and Taneytown roads and the Baltimore turnpike, was already partially occupied . . . by direction of Major-General Howard.[50]

Howard was not too happy about Hancock being sent to assume command. But the Eleventh Corps had been broken. The Baltimore Pike was jammed with horses, ambulances, wagons, and men fleeing the front. The provost guard of the Twelfth Corps stopped twelve hundred Union soldiers. Buford lamented the fact "there seems to be no directing person."[51]

Hancock was Meade's choice as a "directing person." He had the ability to instill confidence as few other Union officers. Meade made the right choice. And we might say that the Confederates made the wrong choices in attacking his positions or the proximity thereof on the second and third of July.

After a resemblance of order was restored, Hancock looked over the terrain from Cemetery Hill to the Round Tops. It looked good. Howard and Hancock discussed the Pipe Creek line. But Hancock turned to Howard and said, "I think this the strongest position by nature on which to fight a battle I ever saw, and if it meets with your approbation I will select this as the battlefield." Howard agreed. And the choice was made.[52]

Some give Reynolds the credit for selecting the field. Others give it to Howard, and other experts say it was Hancock. All three were graduates of West Point. We can only speculate as to which of the three generals made the original choice. But no doubt Reynolds noted the high ground. Howard fell back to it. And Hancock confirmed the thoughts of the other two. But Hancock acting in behalf of Meade made the final decision to give battle in Pennsylvania rather than Maryland.

Although Howard was miffed, Carl Schurz, one of his division commanders, was glad to see Hancock. He:

> . . . gave the troops a new inspiration. They all knew him by fame, and his stalwart figure, his proud mien, and his superb soldierly bearing seemed to verify all the things that fame had told about him. His mere presence was a reinforcement, and everybody on the field felt stronger for his being there.[53]

The *Philadelphia Times* felt Hancock's presence saved the day. Cemetery Hill was in danger of falling to the Confederates. Then Hancock arrived.

... What a change came over the scene in the next half hour. The presence of Hancock was magnetic. Order came out of chaos. The flying troops halt and face the enemy. The battalions of Howard's Corps that were retreating down the Baltimore pike are called back, and with a cheer go into position on the crest of Cemetery Hill.[54]

William T. Sherman once said,

There is a soul to an army as well as to the individual man, and no general can accomplish the full work of his army unless he commands the soul of his men as well as their body and legs.[55]

Hancock possessed "this mystic appeal." It is good that he did, because it was needed on the afternoon of July 1, 1863, at Gettysburg.

About 4:00 P.M., Hancock sent Maj. William G. Mitchell to tell Meade that he would hold the position until nightfall, and that the position at Gettysburg was a very strong one. Mitchell reached Meade's headquarters at Taneytown at 6:00 P.M. George G. Meade said, "I shall order up the troops."[56]

XII CORPS

Northwest of Westminster was Henry Warner Slocum and the Twelfth Corps of the Army of the Potomac. They were encamped at Two Taverns, midway between Littlestown and Gettysburg. As the sun reached high noon they heard the sounds of battle and awaited orders to move to the front. They soon came and at 1:00 P.M. the Twelfth Corps was under way, making their final steps on the Roads to Gettysburg.

General Slocum sent Major Guindon of his staff and a mounted escort on ahead to find what was happening. Before they returned, a message came from Oliver Howard with orders to push forward.[57]

Farmers along the route came out with buckets of ice water for the men. A. S. Williams and his division moved rapidly up the pike. When they reached a point near Rock Creek, they were directed to cross the Hanover Road and

480

occupy a prominent hill. But it was in Confederate possession, and the orders were countermanded. The First Division spent the night near the Baltimore Pike. At the moment, the Twelfth Corps held the right on the Army of the Potomac's line of battle.[58]

Geary's Second Division had a longer march. It had moved some distance from Littlestown toward Hanover to support the cavalry on Tuesday. So at 5:00 A.M. today, they broke camp and marched for Two Taverns. Geary reports that from the twenty-eighth of June until reaching Two Taverns at 11:00 A.M., his men had covered fifty-two miles.[59] That's a lot of walking. Geary could not find Howard when he arrived in Gettysburg so he reported to Hancock, and took up position on the left flank. Thus by late evening the Twelfth Corps was up. Elements of the Third, and all the Fifth and Sixth corps, along with the Second were on the way.

Hancock placed some of the shattered remnants of the First Corps north of the Baltimore Turnpike. This was Wadsworth's division. The rest of the First Corps was on the right and left of the Taneytown Road, joining Howard's flank. The Eleventh Corps occupied Cemetery Hill.

Then the Twelfth Corps came up. John W. Geary, riding ahead of his troops, reported for duty. Inasmuch as the division was still on the road from Two Taverns, units were ordered to take possession of Round Top. Hancock recognized that this was the key to the Union line, covering the Taneytown and Emmitsburg roads.

Between five and six o'clock, Henry Warner Slocum, commanding the Twelfth Corps, arrived on the field from Two Taverns. Being a senior officer, Hancock transferred command to him. Thus the Army of the Potomac had its fourth commander in eight hours, first Reynolds, then Howard, Hancock, and now for a few hours Slocum.

About dark Hancock started down the Harney Road to army headquarters at Taneytown.[60] He went to report in person to General Meade. Orders had already been given for the Second, Fifth, and Sixth corps to proceed to Gettysburg. Meade was about ready to hit the road himself for his date with destiny.

481

Whitelaw Reid, covering the movement towards Gettysburg for his newspaper, wrote a tremendous description of the march to Gettysburg from Taneytown:

> Riding through the marching columns became more and more difficult as we advanced, and finally, to avoid it we turned off it to a by-way leading to the right. We were told that our . . . path would bring us into the Baltimore pike, certain to be less obstructed. Across the hills to the left we could see the white covered wagons slowly winding in and out through the trees and the blue-coated masses toiling forward. The shades of evening dimmed and magnified the scene until one might have thought the hosts of Xerxes in all the glory of modern armor were pressing on to Gettysburg.
>
> Selecting a promising looking farm-house, with a more than usually impressive barn in the rear, we stopped for supper. Great cherry trees bent before the door under their weight of fruit; the kitchen garden was crowded with vegetables; contented cattle stood about the barn; sleek horses filled the stables; fat geese gave a doubtful hiss of welcome as we came too near, and the farm yard laughed with plenty. To add to our comfort the farmer's hearty welcome was supplemented by a well-spread table.
>
> It was dark when we resumed our journey, but our by-path had now become a road with a full moon casting occasional glances at us from behind the clouds. At last campfires gleamed through the woods ahead and we caught the hum of the camps. We passed in front of a house where all the lights were out, but the family had gathered on the door-step too much interested in the, to them, unfamiliar sounds and sights to go to bed. "If you want to stop for the night," they said, pointing off the road to the right, "turn up by the school-house. Squire Durburrow is such a nice man."[61]

A nice man he was. Correspondent Reid roused the squire who gladly put the horses in the big barn, and gave even better quarters to the men on the road to Gettysburg.

Colonel Fremantle brings us up to date on the activities of the First Corps of the Army of Northern Virginia as it marched toward Gettysburg.

> 1st July (Wednesday)—We did not leave our camp till noon, as nearly all General Hill's corps had to pass our quarters on its march towards Gettysburg. One division of Ewell's also had to join in a little beyond Greenwood, and Longstreet's corps had to bring up the rear.
>
> During the morning I made the acquaintance of Colonel Walton, who used to command the well-known Washington Artillery, but he is now chief of artillery to Longstreet's *corps d'armée*. He is a big

482

man, *ci-devant* auctioneer in New Orleans, and I understand he pines to return to his hammer.

Soon after starting we got into a pass in the South Mountain, a continuation, I believe, of the Blue Ridge range, which is broken by the Potomac at Harpers Ferry. The scenery through the pass is very fine. The first troops, alongside of whom we rode, belonged to Johnson's division of Ewell's corps. Among them I saw, for the first time, the celebrated "Stonewall" Brigade, formerly commanded by Jackson. In appearance the men differ little from other Confederate soldiers, except, perhaps, that the brigade contains more elderly men and fewer boys. All (except, I think, one regiment) are Virginians. . . .

At 2 P. M. firing became distinctly audible in our front, but although it increased as we progressed, it did not seem to be very heavy.

A spy who was with us insisted upon there being "a pretty tidy bunch of *blue-bellies* in or near Gettysburg," and he declared that he was in their society three days ago. . . .

At 3 P. M. we began to meet wounded men coming to the rear, and the number of these soon increased most rapidly, some hobbling alone, others on stretchers carried by the ambulance corps, and others in the ambulance wagons. Many of the latter were stripped nearly naked, and displayed very bad wounds. This spectacle, so revolting to a person unaccustomed to such sights, produced no impression whatever upon the advancing troops, who certainly go under fire with the most perfect nonchalance. They show no enthusiasm or excitement, but the most complete indifference. This is the effect of two years' almost uninterrupted fighting.

We now began to meet Yankee prisoners coming to the rear in considerable numbers. Many of them were wounded, but they seemed already to be on excellent terms with their captors, with whom they had commenced swapping canteens, tobacco, &c. Among them was a Pennsylvanian colonel, a miserable object from a wound in his face. In answer to a question, I heard one of them remark, with a laugh, "We're pretty nigh whipped already." We next came to a Confederate soldier carrying a Yankee color, belonging, I think, to a Pennsylvania regiment, which he told us he had just captured.

At 4:30 P. M. we came in sight of Gettysburg, and joined General Lee and General Hill, who were on the top of the ridges which form the peculiar feature of the country round Gettysburg. We could see the enemy retreating up one of the opposite ridges, pursued by the Confederates with loud yells. The position into which the enemy had been driven was evidently a strong one. His right appeared to rest on a cemetery, on the top of a high ridge to the right of Gettysburg, as we looked at it.

General Hill now came up and told me he had been very unwell

483

all day, and in fact he looks very delicate. He said he had had two of his divisions engaged, and had driven the enemy four miles into his present position, capturing a great many prisoners, some cannon, and some colors. He said, however, that the Yankees had fought with a determination unusual to them. He pointed out a railway cutting, in which they had made a good stand; also, a field in the center of which he had seen a man plant the regimental color, round which the regiment had fought for some time with much obstinacy, and when at last it was obliged to retreat, the color-bearer retired last of all, turning round every now and then to shake his fist, at the advancing Rebels. General Hill said he felt quite sorry when he saw this gallant Yankee meet his doom.

General Ewell had come up at 3:30, on the enemy's right (with part of his corps), and completed his discomfiture. General Reynolds, one of the best Yankee generals, was reported killed. Whilst we were talking, a message arrived from General Ewell, requesting Hill to press the enemy in the front, whilst he performed the same operation on his right. The pressure was accordingly applied in a mild degree, but the enemy were too strongly posted, and it was too late in the evening for a regular attack.[62]

Fremantle observed that the prisoners belonged to the Union First and Eleventh corps. Most officials thought the action was a "brisk little scurry," with a big battle to follow in the morning. Longstreet naturally felt the Union position was quite strong.

The British observer found that Gettysburg was in Ewell's hands, and full of Yankee dead and wounded. Fremantle climbed a tree to see what he could. He immediately noticed Cemetery Ridge.

When the firing ceased about dark, Fremantle rode with Longstreet and his staff to their headquarters in Cashtown. "At that time troops were pouring along the road," marching toward the battle that was certain to resume in the morning.[63]

He may have seen some of Kershaw's men and others belonging to the division of Lafayette McLaws. The First Corps had some problems today. Anderson's division of the Third Corps, and Johnson's division of the Second, along with Ewell's wagon train blocked their advance.[64] The road was jammed. Therefore, it was nearly sunset when Kershaw's brigade arrived on the hills overlooking Gettysburg.[65] From that spot the men could see and hear the smoke and din of battle. However, it would be almost midnight before all the column arrived to take a brief rest on the left of the Chambersburg Pike. In the morning, they tramped to Black Horse Tavern and then on to their position south of the Lutheran Seminary.

Augustus Dickert tells us that he and his comrades in Kershaw's brigade did not hear the guns at Gettysburg due to the distance and the mountains. While his unit enjoyed the shade of the trees, Hill's corps was locked in combat. And there was still no word from Stuart and the cavalry.

Near sundown, Kershaw's brigade received orders to march. So like the Union Second, Fifth and Sixth corps they were in for a night march. Things were going fine until they encountered Ed Johnson and the trains of Ewell's Second Corps. This delayed their march for quite awhile. And at midnight, they encountered the wagon train again, taking three steps, and then standing still. "About three o'clock . . . when we reached the summit of an eminence, we saw in the plain before us a great sea of white tents, silent and still, with here and there a groan, or a surgeon passing from one tent to another relieving the pain of some poor mortal who had fallen in battle on the morning of the day before. We had come upon the field hospital of Hill. . . . Here we first heard of the fight in which so many brave men had fallen, without any decided results." Dickert also learned that a flag from South Carolina was the first to fly over Gettysburg. Finally the command reached Willoughby Run where they fell out to rest for a few hours.[66]

Gradually the details of the first day were pieced together. A. P. Hill, aided by Ewell, had swept the Union army back from Seminary Ridge and Oak Ridge to Cemetery Hill and Cemetery Ridge. Now behind the ridge, Meade was assembling an army, "if not the largest yet the grandest, best equipped of all time, with an incentive to do successful battle. . . ."[67]

Meanwhile, back in Chambersburg, details from Pickett's division were ordered to tear up the railroad track, burn the United States warehouse and destroy other government property. Sledges were used on the turntable. They proved ineffective, so one bright soldier got some firewood and heated the rails, and then twisted them out of place.

Toward evening Pickett's men started for Gettysburg. Shotwell heard the news of Hooker's dismissal. "So 'Fighting Joe' goes up on the shelf with old 'Fuss and Feathers,' 'Little Mac,' 'Braggadocio Pope,' 'Blundering Burnside,' and all the rest. And now comes the new Meade to be soured and spoilt in the thunderclap of 'Uncle Robert's assault.' "[68]

The feeling of the two armies was vastly different as July 1 drew to a close. Ewell's corps and other units of the Confederate army were elated with their success. They boasted about the achievements of the day, their army, and what was going to happen tomorrow. "Their confidence knew no bounds, they felt assured that they should be able . . . to cut up our army in detail—fatigued as it was by long marches and yet scattered, for only two corps had as yet arrived. Resting under this impression, they lay down joyfully for the night."[69]

Jacobs was inclined to believe that the Confederates would be able to carry out their boasting threats. "We were disheartened and amost in despair. But our men, who whilst retreating through the town, seemed to be confused and frightened, coolly and quietly fell into position on the (Cemetery) hill.[70]

> The two armies were being brought together for the bloody work of the succeeding day. The peaceful full moon looked down through a thin canopy of cloud, affording her light as cheerfully as if the hurried movements were all made to save, instead of to destroy life.[71]

Shortly after Hancock had left for Gettysburg, John Gibbon put the Second Corps into a column of march from Taneytown toward Harney. This occurred about 1:30 P.M. Maj. St. Clair A. Muhlholland reports "it was a long and fatiguing march." The distance covered was about ten miles, but the men were being pressed to the front. The Second Corps spent the night in the vicinity of Barlow, just about three miles from Cemetery Hill. Before daylight the men were on the road again, and were rejoined by Hancock who once again resumed command. Now the Second Corps was up. Elements of the Fifth were arriving. Only the Sixth Corps was at a distance, but they too were hurrying on the road to Gettysburg.

What was it like the afternoon of July 1 and the morning of the second for the Second Corps? Brig. Gen. John Brooke says that when they reached Taneytown it was evident "an engagement was in progress with the enemy at or near Gettysburg." He led the fourth brigade of the First Division to within three miles of Gettysburg, arriving at 9:30 P.M. The men took a position on the right of the Taneytown-Gettysburg Road, and established a picket line. The troops were then permitted the opportunity to sleep.

The night was short, because at 3:00 A.M. on the second, his men were on the road again. Once they took position though, they had an easy day until Longstreet's attack about 5:00 P.M.

When George Bruce of the Twentieth Massachusetts saw Winfield Scott Hancock get into the ambulance and disappear on the Gettysburg Road in a cloud of dust, he realized something was brewing. Rumors flew thick and fast. But it was obvious a disaster had occurred, and that Hancock was being sent to correct it. The order to "fall in" quickly confirmed their suspicions.[72]

No one was allowed to leave the column as it marched on the Harney Road. No interval was allowed between the units. "It was the closest marching column that we had ever experienced, and from Taneytown to Gettysburg the world was shut out from our sight. A cloud of dust so dense and all pervading enveloped us that nothing was anywhere visible."[73]

Young Lieutenant Hale thought perhaps Colonel Cross had forgotten his premonition that this battle was to be his last. The colonel was in good spirits. The officers rode through Harney and past the Mount Joy Lutheran Church. Then as the brigade approached the fields of Gettysburg, Cross said in a grave, firm tone, "Mr. Hale, attend to that box of mine at the first opportunity." No more was said. But the words of Colonel Cross convinced Hale "that he was in dead earnest and had a conviction of impending fate."[74]

Winfield Scott Hancock.

As the Second Corps marched from Harney toward Gettysburg:

The step of our well trained soldiers became more solemn and steady, as we heard the booming of the cannon, and saw the smoke of battle rolling up in black columns against the sky. As usual, the conversation in the ranks ceased as we approached, and scarcely a sound was heard except the steady tramp of the moving column.[75]

That's the way it was with the Second Corps just south of Gettysburg.

Hundreds of decks of playing cards were thrown by the wayside. In a day when card playing was considered somewhat evil, the men did not want to be struck down in possession of cards. Someone said, "What if they whip us this time?" A firm reply came, "They won't. I'll die first." The pace quickened. The Second Corps was "ready to go into the jaws of death and compel a victory."[76]

About dark, the brigade met General Hancock along the road. He told them that the First and Eleventh corps had lost heavily, but that the Third and Twelfth corps were coming up to reinforce the positions on Cemetery and Culp's Hill.

Hancock had no doubt but that Lee would attack with his entire army the next day. But for now, the Second Corps was "to stack arms, rest for the night, and go into position early in the morning." General Carroll wanted to know if the Army of the Potomac had a good position. Hancock replied very firmly, "If Lee does not attack before all our forces are up, we can hold the position I have selected against the whole Confederacy.

On that hopeful note, Kepler and his unit pitched their tent near the foot of the Round Tops. "The evening was balmy and beautiful, though somewhat hazy, but with sufficient moonlight to enable anyone to discern any object."[77]

The Eighth Ohio halted on the night of July 1 about three miles from Gettysburg, near Barlow. The men rested in fields, but were roused before daylight and moved up to the front on Cemetery Ridge. As the men waited for the action they knew would come, they kept busy getting their "cap and cartridge boxes in shape."

Somewhere between Harney and Barlow, Colonel Livermore tasted his first "applejack" on the march. He got it from a house by the side of the road.

When the Second Corps halted for the night, or what was

left of it, Livermore was ordered to bring up some ambulances for General Hancock and his staff to sleep in.[78]

For some strange reason, many of the men in blue did not feel their welcome in Pennsylvania was as great as in Maryland, with perhaps the exception of Hanover. Colonel Livermore writes, "The face of the country in Pennsylvania was not as pleasing as in Maryland, and the people were not nearly as friendly toward us in their conduct, and it was said that some of our men paid them for water from their wells."[79]

While the Second Corps was under way, Marsena Patrick was very busy in Taneytown, overhauling wagons and examining prisoners. Orders came at 9:30 to be ready to move at 10:00 P.M. Everything was to be sent to Westminster except the Eighth and Ninety-third. Although Meade left around midnight, Patrick was detained to examine prisoners until 2:00 A.M.[80]

Just after dark, John Gibbon commanded the Second Corps to halt and to go into position where the head of the column was. The Second Division took position between the southeastern base of "Round Top," and the Taneytown Road. The Third Division was posed across the road, to the right of the Taneytown Road, with the First Division in the rear. Arms were stacked "and the men dropped down on the ground to sleep, and to many of them it was their last sleep on earth."

About midnight some were awakened by the horses of General Meade and his staff. Meade stopped briefly to converse with General Gibbon.

It was about one o'clock in the morning on July 2 when George G. Meade arrived on the scene. He was worn from lack of sleep, and the necessity of making so many vital decisions. He had not planned to fight at Gettysburg. General Warren had worked on planning a line of defensive battle along Pipe Creek. General Humphreys had looked over positions near Emmitsburg. But the First and Eleventh corps had met the enemy and suffered defeat. His army was still scattered. But Winfield Scott Hancock assured him Gettysburg was a good place to fight. Meade must see for himself.

490

The moon was shining, and Meade could dimly see the general features of the terrain. The rallied brigades of the First Corps were on Cemetery Hill, in what is now the town and national cemeteries. What was left of the Eleventh Corps was north of the Baltimore Road. The Twelfth Corps was in the pastures and woods on Culp's Hill. The other corps were on the road. Slocum's soldiers were busy putting up defensive works.[81]

George Meade tells his own story of completing the Roads to Gettysburg:

It was too dark to obtain a clear idea of the ground occupied by that portion of the army which had reached the field. General Meade therefore returned to the cemetery, where he addressed himself to the task of making preparations for the next day. Before, however, it had yet become daylight, he mounted his horse, and accompanied by Generals Howard and Hunt, and by Captain Paine, of the engineer staff, rode off to examine the lines. Riding slowly along in the rear of the sleeping line of soldiers around Cemetery Hill, and along its continuation as Cemetery Ridge, and beyond, to where the land dips before it rises abruptly at the base of Little Round Top, he obtained a general knowledge of the features of the ground and of the chief accidents of its surface. As it was still dark when he started along the lines, of course only the most salient features of the ground could be recognized. Before, however, he had finished the examination, day began to break, and he concluded it by an inspection of the right, around Culp's Hill, to the crossing of Rock Creek by the Baltimore Pike. He finally indicated on Captain Paine's sketch of the ground just gone over the position to be held by each corps, and Captain Paine thereupon, by his orders, made from the sketch, and during the morning transmitted to each corps, a tracing showing the positions. The general, after having settled upon the positions to be occupied by the respective corps, sent General Hunt for the second time to examine the lines, in order to make sure that the artillery was everywhere properly posted.

A little farm-house on the western side of the Taneytown Road, directly in rear of Cemetery Ridge, had been selected for permanent headquarters. Near by here, between six and seven o'clock in the morning, as General Meade was seated on horseback in a field on the east side of the Taneytown Road, somewhat below the house, General Gibbon rode up, just in advance of the head of the column of the Second Corps, and reported the presence of the corps.[82]

491

V CORPS

Now only the Fifth and Sixth corps were on the Roads to Gettysburg. For the men of the Maltese Cross this was a rough day. Starting early in the morning from the Schriver Homestead at Union Mills, the men had miles to go before they got to Hanover and Gettysburg. The pace that morning was very rapid. According to the 146th New York, "only the hardiest could endure the gait, and many fell out exhausted."[83]

The spirits of the men of the Eighty-third Pennsylvania were high that July morning. As they left Union Mills, they realized that each step they took brought them closer to Pennsylvania.

Upon crossing the border, Colonel Vincent sent back the word, "We are now on the soil of old Pennsylvania. . . . Hang out the banner and let our march be accompanied by the sound of the earpiercing fife and spirit stirring drum."

Capt. Amos Judson of E Company saw Sergeant Rogers unfurl the flag of the Eighty-third to the wind. The Drum Corps struck up the national air of "Yankee Doodle."

> And as the glorious old banner, shattered and rent by the shocks of a dozen battlefields, floated once more proudly upon the inspiring breezes of the old Keystone State, long and loud shouts of joy . . . broke upon the morning air. The enthusiasm was contagious. In a few moments it had spread from regiment to regiment, and from brigade to brigade, until every banner was flying, every fife screaming, and every drum beating.[84]

The peaceful countryside near Hanover awoke to hear the music and tramping of the armed legions on the way to battle. That's the way it was early on July 1.

Like many others, Thomas Hyde enjoyed the day in Manchester. The weather was nice and he had the opportunity to meet some nice ladies. About 5:00 P.M., General Sedgwick wanted some information. Hyde was standing nearby and was therefore chosen to ride twenty miles to Taneytown. It was a lovely ride, the air was filled with "the scent flowers and new-mown hay."[85]

Near Taneytown, Hyde met General Hancock returning from Gettysburg to report to Meade. Hancock related the gallant story of the First Corps and told the tragic news of the death of General Reynolds. Yet he was confident that the new line in Gettysburg would hold.

In a few moments, Hancock and Hyde reached Meade's headquarters. Hyde reported to General Seth Williams, the adjutant general, who gave him some refreshments. Williams said that important plans were being made in Meade's tent which was next to his. In a few moments, Hyde entered and saw General Meade standing in the center of some staff officers. A table was in front of them, covered with maps. Meade said, "Tomorrow, gentlemen, we fight the decisive battle of the war. Where is the officer from the Sixth Corps?"

As Hyde stepped forward, General Meade handed him orders for the Sixth Corps, written on yellow paper, and another for General Newton to take command of the First Corps. "He told me to commit them to memory and destroy them in case of need." Meade asked him about a cavalry escort, but Hyde said he could make it quicker alone. He then said, "Tell General Sedgwick that I . . . hope he will be up in time to decide the victory for us."[86]

Hyde was very much impressed with Meade, and felt a sense of awe at being present when the decision was being made to concentrate on Gettysburg. He was proud to have an important part in carrying the message to his commander. After all, he was but a lad.

After riding a while, Hyde met some farmers driving their horses to a hiding place. They reported Stuart was nearby. Rumors were all over the place. Hyde took precautions and several times hid in the woods until mounted men passed. However, he met no Rebels. He continued on his way to give the important document to General Sedgwick.

The early orders sent to Sykes and Sedgwick read as follows:

"The major-general commanding directs that you move up

493

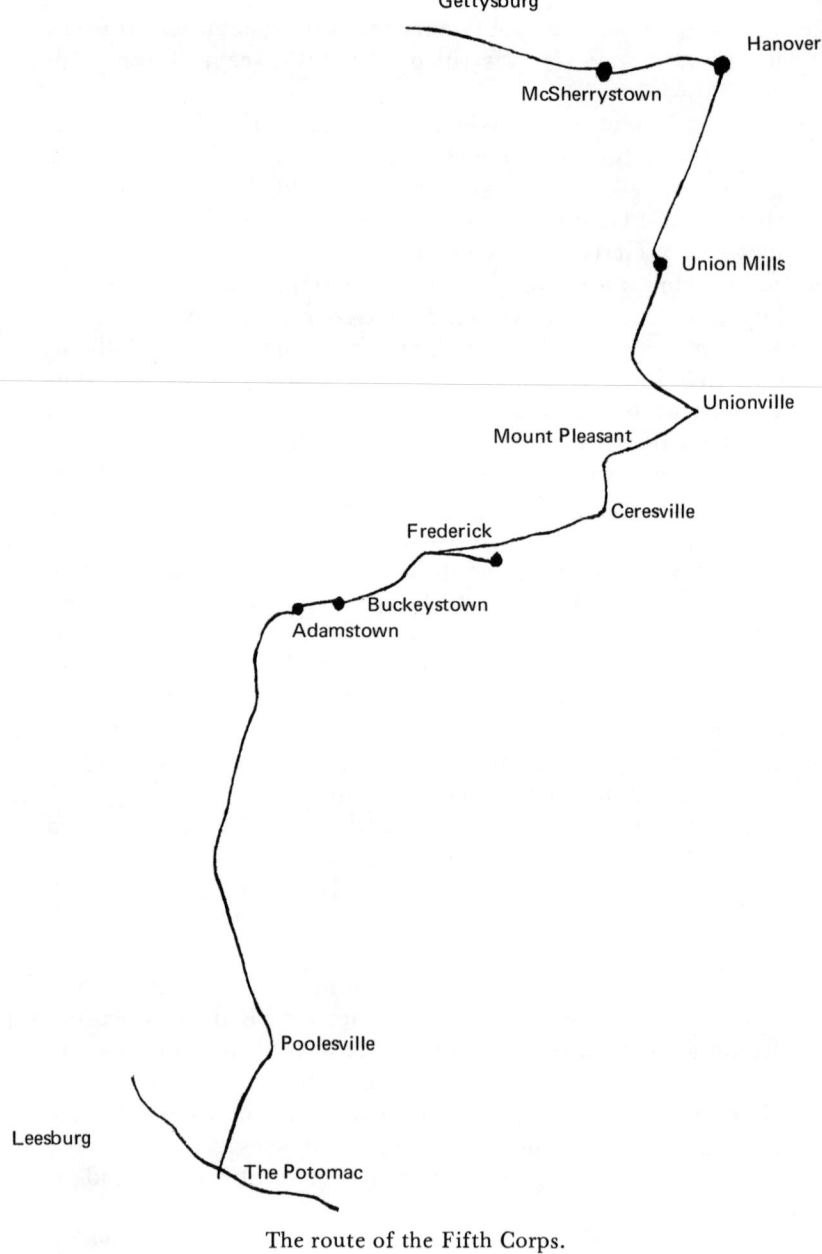

The route of the Fifth Corps.

494

to Gettysburg at once upon receipt of this order, if not already ordered to do so by General Slocum."[87]

The time was 7:00 P.M.

The communique to Sedgwick was sent at 7:30, saying:

> ... a general battle seems to be impending to-morrow at Gettysburg; ... it is of the utmost importance that your command should be up. He directs that you stop all trains that impede your progress, or turn them out of the road. Your march will have to be a forced one to reach the scene of action, where we shall probably be outnumbered without your presence.[88]

These orders set in motion two dramatic marches. The Fifth Corps did not have as far to go, but they had been on the road all day, while the Sixth was to perform a majestic feat. At 11:00 P.M. Meade sent still another message to Sedgwick saying that if he had not started, and if it would not cause too much trouble, take the Littlestown Road to Gettysburg as it was in better condition.[89]

About noon, Ayers's division of the Fifth Corps reached Hanover. The men noted the scenes of yesterday's cavalry skirmish. Dead horses lay in the streets, and buildings bore the marks of artillery shots. Cannonading was heard in the distance, but the men did not know that the First Corps was heavily engaged at a place called Gettysburg.

A few miles beyond Hanover, near sunset, the Fifth Corps received an order "to go into camp and halt for the night." This was a most welcome order to the weary soldiers. Camps were laid out on a hillside. The men prepared to cook coffee and the evening meal. But it was not to be.

Colonel O'Rorke and a courier from General Hancock galloped up with the news of the fighting at Gettysburg. The Fifth Corps was needed to hold the enemy in check.

Within five minutes, "the bugles of each regiment and brigade sounded the orders to pack up." The men lost no time. In ten minutes the regiments of the Fifth Corps were in line. The news from Gettysburg was shared with the men in blue. Although tired, the men knew that the fate of the nation hung in the balance. Therefore, they had to forget their fatigue and press on.

About four o'clock in the afternoon of July 1, General

Barnes, commanding the First Division of the Fifth Corps, arrived from Union Mills. He had traveled just about the same route of Stuart's cavalry from the little Maryland town to Hanover. Then came Ayres's division, and finally the Pennsylvania Reserves commanded by General Crawford. The entire corps made preparations to camp for the night in the fields and meadows southwest of Hanover. In fact, nineteen beef cattle had been killed on the Keller and Sell farms to feed the hungry men. Kettles, pots, and skillets were placed over the open fires. Coffee was brewing and the meat was being prepared. Suddenly a dispatch rider galloped in from Taneytown. He carried an urgent message from General Meade saying, "proceed at once to Gettysburg." The message interrupted the dinner of General Sykes, the division commanders, and six aides seated at the table of Henry Sell one mile west of Hanover on the Littlestown Road when the dispatch arrived.[90]

Sykes read the letter, gave the contents to his division commanders, and told them "Take the road to Gettysburg." The bugles were sounded, tents struck, the campfires extinguished, and the meat that could be carried was taken along as once again the men hit the road. They had a date with destiny. In fact, Colonel Chamberlain and the Twentieth Maine were on the way to help save Little Round Top. Before nightfall of the next day, many of these fine men would march no more. They would pitch their tents in the bivouac of the dead.

The Thirty-second Massachusetts had just completed a ten-mile march. They were congratulating themselves on the prospect of a refreshing sleep after being on the road for sixteen days. They had found a nice, grassy field. But their fond hopes were soon dashed to pieces as they were called to march again. They had miles and miles to go before they slept. Their destination was Gettysburg.[91]

O. S. Barrett of the Fourth Michigan describes his impressions of Hanover:

> We arrived at Hanover, Pennsylvania, on the afternoon of July 1st. Rested and fed; then on to Gettysburg. Marched all night— a beautiful moon-light night. As we passed farm houses, the people

came out with water and refreshments, handed us as we passed along foot-sore and tired. An Aide-de-camp came riding along, saying: "Boys, keep good courage, McClellan is in command of the army, again." Instantly the space above was filled with the hats and caps of the gratified soldiers. They shouted and hollered, and kicked up their heels, and were frisky with the supposed good news. I mention this to show with what veneration Little Mac was held by the Army of the Potomac.[92]

The Ninth Massachusetts shared in the "many welcomes" received in Hanover. However, they could hear the booming of cannons from time to time. Their trained battle-tested ears told them heavy fighting was going on somewhere, and before long they would be in it.

About midnight, the Ninth Massachusetts halted in Bonaughtown, modern day Bonneville. The men filed into the fields to sleep. Fires blazed and coffee was cooked.[93]

The veterans of the 118th Pennsylvania tell us what it was like in Hanover, on July 1, on the Roads to Gettysburg.

Rousing cheers, demonstrative shouts, ringing enthusiasm greeted the good old Commonwealth of Pennsylvania. The unfurling of colors and rolling of drums at one o'clock in the afternoon indicated the crossing of the line. There was a firmer step, better closed ranks, more determined countenances. Beyond there had been some cavalry fighting. The fences were down and the bodies of dead horses scattered about; those branded C. S. A. the more numerous. Rumors were rife of the close presence of the enemy, and stories of a battle to be momentarily expected. Information, none of it of value, was eagerly seized and distributed with frightful exaggeration.

The broad, level acres of York, in Pennsylvania, took the place of the rolling lands of Carroll in Maryland. The rich soil, too productive to permit the timber to stand, was almost entirely cleared of the forests, and patches of woodland were rare. The great red barns, cosey spring-houses, and large, roomy stone mansions were indicative of the successful results of good, substantial tillage.

Hanover, a town of considerable size and of flourishing business, was intended as the destination of the day's march. Its railway depot, extensive warehouses, large stores, substantial dwellings, were the evidence of its enterprise, thrift and comfort. One of the oldest settlements in southern Pennsylvania, it had long been a centre for the gathering and distribution of the prolific yield of the surrounding country. Its broad streets were the terminals of excellent turnpike roads leading to all neighboring important towns. Its main railway outlet, with branches from Gettysburg and Littlestown, was

497

by the Northern Central to Baltimore and Harrisburg, its own branch tapping that line at Hanover Junction. Here, on the outskirts, the column halted at four o'clock in the afternoon, with something of a conviction that it was for an all night's rest. Immediately, in wonder and astonishment at this sudden visitation by such a mass of men, apparently all the people from far and near gathered for a more familiar acquaintance with their uninvited guests—as one of them not inaptly expressed it, for a more intimate association "with these travel-stained, dusty, walking arsenals, licensed to do murder at their chieftain's bidding."[94]

The enlisted men of the 146th New York became very angry near the edge of Hanover. Guards were placed over the camps to permit the men from entering the town and mingling in the shops and among the people. This could be done only as they marched through. However, the officers were granted passes, and were free to go in and get food and drink, especially the latter. "Boy, didn't we swear." That's the way one man in the 146th New York expressed himself. However, the officers were not to have much time. Orders came to move on.

We had inspection and then fell into line quickly just as the sun was setting, one of those large, red, clouded sunsets, and at "quick-step march" we filed out of Hanover to the westward. As we marched along in the bright moonlight people came to the roadside and sang patriotic songs, and waved us forward with cheers that seemed to hail us as their deliverers. We traveled about fourteen miles from Hanover, and it was nearly midnight before we halted, near a village called Bonaughtown, about five miles from Gettysburg.

Only one or two hours' sleep were granted us despite our great fatigue, for at one o'clock the word was passed along the line to resume the march. There was a rustling along the road on the line which marked the bivouac of the Fifth Corps. Dusky forms arose one after another, and fires were quickly lighted. "Make your coffee and fall in," was the word passed along. At early dawn, while it was still almost dark, we were again jogging along the road at a rapid gait. We turned to the left and up the Baltimore pike. To the left from this again, we crossed Rock Creek, and at seven o'clock were massed in the woods a mile back from the Union front. At ten o'clock A.M., having heard no sounds of battle, we moved out in the direction of Cemetery Hill.[95]

Francis Parker tells us:

As we marched toward Gettysburg, we heard in advance the sound of cheering, and soon word came down the line that General

McClellan was again in command of the army. As the news passed along, regiment after regiment sent up cheers, and the soldiers moved with quickened step and joyful hearts. Where this report originated we never knew, yet many went into the battle the next day thinking they were under the command of the general, who, above all others, had won the love and confidence of the Army of the Potomac. Very soon, orders came for the musicians to give the time for the march, and we stepped off quickly to the beat of the drum. This was one of the very few occasions on which we used our music while on the march during the entire service of the Regiment. Our musicians were used, as a general rule, only in camp to sound the various calls that marked the routine of camp duty, and at guard-mountings and parades, and on this occasion we were allowed but a few minutes to enjoy the luxury of marching to the beat of the drum, for it was stopped by orders from an authority higher than our division general, on account of the danger of giving information of our whereabouts to the enemy.

We marched nearly ten miles more that night, and at midnight bivouacked two miles distant from the spot that was to be the field of the battle of Gettysburg.[96]

It had been a bad day at Gettysburg, some eighteen miles away. John Reynolds was dead, the First and Eleventh Corps badly mauled. And the Army of Northern Virginia was moving up. Thus the Fifth Corps could not stay in Hanover. They and the rest of the Army of the Potomac must take the Roads to Gettysburg and move as rapidly as possible.

A member of the First Michigan says, "We will never forget that night and the memory of women and children handing us water and food." They said, "Don't let them come any further, boys." The Fifth Corps replied, "We will not. We will not."[97]

At 9:00 P.M., led by the light of a brilliant moon, the 118th Pennsylvania and the rest of the brigade was under way.

As the army moved forward the bands and regimental drum corps played through the streets of every town through which the corps passed to keep the men awake. As it neared a point of concentration, moving through batteries on one side and infantry battalions on the other, a staff officer approached the colonel, and drawing a paper from his pocket, with the aid of a lantern which he carried, read from it to the effect that McClellan had been restored to the command of the army and would have charge in the next day's battle. This information was evidently intended for publication, but before it was formally announced, the reading having been overheard, the news passed from one to another, until it became known to all the troops in the vicinity. The effect was electric and the result astonishing. So long a time had elapsed since the removal of McClellan it had ceased to be a subject of comment, and the old-time enthusiasm for him it was believed had disappeared forever. The announcement was received with shout and yell and cheer, and as they echoed and re-echoed from battery to battalion and battalion back to battery again, the woods and fields were resonant with the enthusiastic demonstration. It all passed away as suddenly as it came, and was soon lost and forgotten in the startling and thrilling incidents soon to follow.

At 3.30 on the morning of the 2d the column halted in a piece of timber by the roadside for a rest in the little darkness left before the dawn of a day to close big with the fate of the nation. There was little comprehension of the situation beyond the fact that a great battle was likely to be fought, but it was not viewed as in any way different from the many other hot and bloody contests through which the army had already passed. There was no realization of the portentous result of the issue, nor was it remotely conceived that history would record it as the decisive battle of the war. The halt was made some miles southeast of the town of Gettysburg, the distance marched since the early morning of the 1st having been about thirty-seven miles.[98]

July 1 was a lovely evening in Hanover, Taneytown, and Manchester. But the men in blue had "miles and miles to go before they slept." Their comrades had met the enemy at a place called Gettysburg. Reinforcements were needed.

Gerrish describes the Fifth Corps march in the vicinity of Hanover.

> The moon shone from a cloudless sky, and flooded our way with its glorious light. The people rushed from their homes and stood by the roadside to welcome us, men, women, and children all gazing on the strange spectacle. Bands played, the soldiers and the people cheered, banners waved, and white handkerchiefs fluttered from doors and windows, as the blue, dusty columns surged on. That moonlight march will always be remembered by its survivors.[99]

Between ten and eleven o'clock that night, the Twentieth Maine heard the rumor that George B. McClellan was to resume command of the army. The men went wild. They "waved their hats and cheered until they were hoarse." Later some felt the rumor was started to motivate the men to keep going.

About midnight, the Twentieth Maine halted, and the men threw themselves on the ground. They were exhausted.

Amos Judson of the Eighty-third Pennsylvania was grateful to the women along the route of march who brought fresh food and drink to the soldiers of the Fifth Corps.

Strong Vincent took his last journey on the Roads to Gettysburg. Marching under a brilliant moon, on a forced march, the night of July 1, Vincent was stirred by the great welcome received in Hanover. Flags were flying, bands playing, children and adults happy to see the men in blue. Vincent pulled over to observe the citizenry and the marching troops.

A Harvard graduate, Vincent had made the Eighty-third Pennsylvania one of the superior regiments of the Fifth Corps. His military training took place in his father's Erie, Pennsylvania, foundry, and at the famous Ivy League school. His first name was indicative of his courage and character.

He and his wife were skilled horseback riders. She visited her husband in the camps along the Rappahannock River. Their good looks, vim, vigor, and vitality made a big impression on the troops. They had all of life ahead of them. They were so in love. And Strong Vincent observed his twenty-sixth birthday on the Roads to Gettysburg. Near Hanover, on the evening of July 1, he watched the flag of his beloved Eighty-third Pennsylvania unfurled. He remarked to a staff officer, "What death more glorious can any man desire than to die on the soil of old Pennsylvania fighting for that flag." Little did he know, or perhaps he did, that the opportunity to die for the flag was just a few hours away at Little Round Top.[100]

With Strong Vincent in the Fifth Corps was a young colonel from Rochester, New York, Patrick H. O'Rorke, commanding the 140th New York. O'Rorke graduated from West Point in 1861, standing first in his class. His more celebrated classmate, George A. Custer, was last in the class, but now riding the Roads to Gettysburg was a brigadier general of cavalry.

Custer's men and others in Kilpatrick's division had been on the move today also, passing through Abbotstown and

501

Berlin, and then riding back to Berlin to camp for the night. At this point they heard the news of Gettysburg and the rumor that McClellan was back in charge.

This morning, David M. Gregg set out from Manchester with his three brigades. It was a forced march, and Gregg arrived shortly after Wade Hampton, Fitz Lee and Colonel Chambliss had held a conference in the farmhouse of John Ziegler.

July 1 was a terrible day for Huey and his men. Almost twenty hours were spent in the saddle. First it was the trip from Manchester to Hanover Junction. Then they retraced their steps. It seems as though the brass did not know what was taking place. At Manchester, the blue column was directed to deploy on the Baltimore Pike. No sooner was this directive complied with than another one came, saying "return to Manchester, and move toward Gettysburg." Not only was time wasted, but these movements did not help the tired men and horses.

Gregg had found the station house and railroad bridges at Hanover Junction burned by Colonel White. The general had expected to reach York, but with conflicting orders, Huey was detailed, while McIntosh and Irwin Gregg moved northwestward from Hanover Junction to Jefferson and then on to Hanover.

The story of each Union cavalry division is enough to fill a book. However, in Roads to Gettysburg, we have tried to get the high moments. Suffice to say that by midnight of July 1, the Third Pennsylvania Cavalry had lost in four days, about one hundred of its four hundred men and horses due to exhaustion.

One of the men says,

> By this time we had become a sorry-looking body of men, having been in the saddle day and night almost continuously over three weeks, without a change of clothing or an opportunity for a general wash; moreover we were much reduced by short rations and exhaustion, and mounted on horses whose bones were plainly visible to the naked eye.[101]

Rev. W. K. Zieber went to bed the night of July 1, full of apprehension. Hanover was in a state of shock from the engagement of Stuart and Kilpatrick. The folks did not know what minute, men in blue or gray might return. The clergyman retired about 10:00 P.M. But he found it hard to sleep. About midnight he heard the sound of many horses passing his residence on York Street. Leaping from his bed, Mr. Zieber looked out the window and saw a long column heading for Center Square. The night and the dust made it difficult to tell whether they were blue or gray. The pastor, being chairman of the Committee of Safety, yelled out the window, "What force is this?"

"Gregg's cavalry," came the reply from several voices.

The Reverend Mr. Zieber had a hospital flag on his house. Marion Hall, to the rear of his residence, was full of wounded, and a military surgeon was staying in his study. The soldiers wanted to know about the flag. They said, "Was there fighting here?"

"Yes," Pastor Zieber replied, "between Kilpatrick and Stuart."

The man in blue asked, "Did our side win?"

They were delighted to hear that Kilpatrick had been victorious and cheered as they rode into the square.[102]

While Sedgwick's infantry continued their tramp, tramp, tramp on the Roads to Gettysburg, Gregg's cavalry rested in the streets of Hanover. Those who arrived at the head of the column, got a great deal. They were able to rest from 1:00 A.M. until 3:00 A.M. At that time the long blue line started on the Littlestown Road. But Dr. T. T. Tate, a surgeon attached to the Third Pennsylvania, and a native of Gettysburg, advised General Gregg that the shortest and best route to his hometown was by way of Bonaughtown. The horses just turned and were led across the fields by the good doctor to McSherrystown. Colonel McIntosh fell ill, twenty hours a day in the saddle caught up with him. Dr. Tate took him to farmer Geiselman's house, where with medical attention and drink, he was able to continue. Finally they reached the intersection of the Low Dutch or Salem Church and Hanover roads where the command was allowed to rest.

Perhaps the songs they had sung riding through Jefferson were still in the minds of the cavalrymen. They had sung,

"Dear Father, Will You Meet Us," and "We Will Meet You in the Promised Land."

Sleepy and tired, Gregg's cavalry started from Hanover toward Gettysburg at 3:00 A.M. It would be almost noon before they reached the fields of conflict. They halted for a break on the south side of the Hanover Road. Some of them knew folks in Gettysburg. But there would be no time for visiting today.[103]

VI CORPS

Meanwhile, one of the greatest events in American history was under way. We've read about the great feats of Knox taking the cannon to Boston in the Revolution, and "Stonewall" Jackson's great flanking moves. The memory of Patton's Third Army's rapid movement during the Battle of the Bulge is also fresh in our mind. However, the forced march of the Sixth Corps from Manchester, Maryland, to the fields of Gettysburg during the last hours of July 1, and into the afternoon of July 2 has received but little notice. We turn now to that great event.

The Sixth Corps spent the first twenty-one hours of July 1 in relative quiet. They deserved a break. Think of, these men crossed the Potomac on Saturday covering twelve miles, eighteen more on Sunday, twenty-two on Monday, and twenty-three miles on Tuesday.[104]

Yet the men of the Sixth Corps expected to march again on Wednesday. But no one woke them in the dark. The dawn broke. Reveille sounded, the men ate breakfast. But still no order to "fall in." Some were assigned routine army and camp life tasks, but most of the men were free to rest their weary feet and bodies.

The news spread quickly through the hills and valleys of northern Carroll County. "Come and see, there's a whole bunch of Yankee soldiers over at Manchester." Those who could dropped everything. As soon as the livestock was cared for they left their fields and homes to see the men in blue. The women hurriedly packed picnic baskets, putting in some extra goodies for "the poor soldiers." Then they jumped in their spring wagons and carriages and headed for Manchester. History was in the making. They wanted to see it.

Lt. Col. James Latta of the 119th Pennsylvania Infantry said:

> The day at Manchester was a novel one; we had no such experience before or after. . . . Men and maidens, matron and children, afoot and in wheeled vehicles, gathered from far and near for the opportunity to witness the sudden increase of male population.[105]

As he rested in Manchester, George Stevens realized the plot was thickening, "and the hostile forces moving . . . each watching the movements of the other, and each ready to seize any opportunity for rushing upon its enemy to destroy it." He was tired. During the last four days, he and his buddies had traveled over one hundred miles, on foot yet at that.[106]

Stevens noticed that many of the men were getting too many nips of Maryland rye whiskey and were beginning to feel pretty good.

Throughout the day the folks came and visited. Curious children wanted to see the tents and guns. They asked all kinds of questions. Some embarrassed their parents. But the Yankee soldiers who were fathers took the little ones under their wing, substituting perhaps for a few moments, the little children of Maryland for their own youngsters back home.

The teen-age girls were really happy. "My oh, my, so many handsome guys. You didn't know where to look first." The soldiers found themselves to be centers of attraction. They would never forget the bright dresses of calico and pretty bonnets and the faces of the lasses who came to visit. Many of them brought baskets of homemade bread, jelly, and cookies. Soldiering wasn't so bad after all.

The older men showed the children how to roll blankets, and how to fix the haversacks. They yielded to the pleas of the children to touch the guns and bayonets. And they gladly shared hardtack. The boys and girls didn't like it any better than the soldiers.

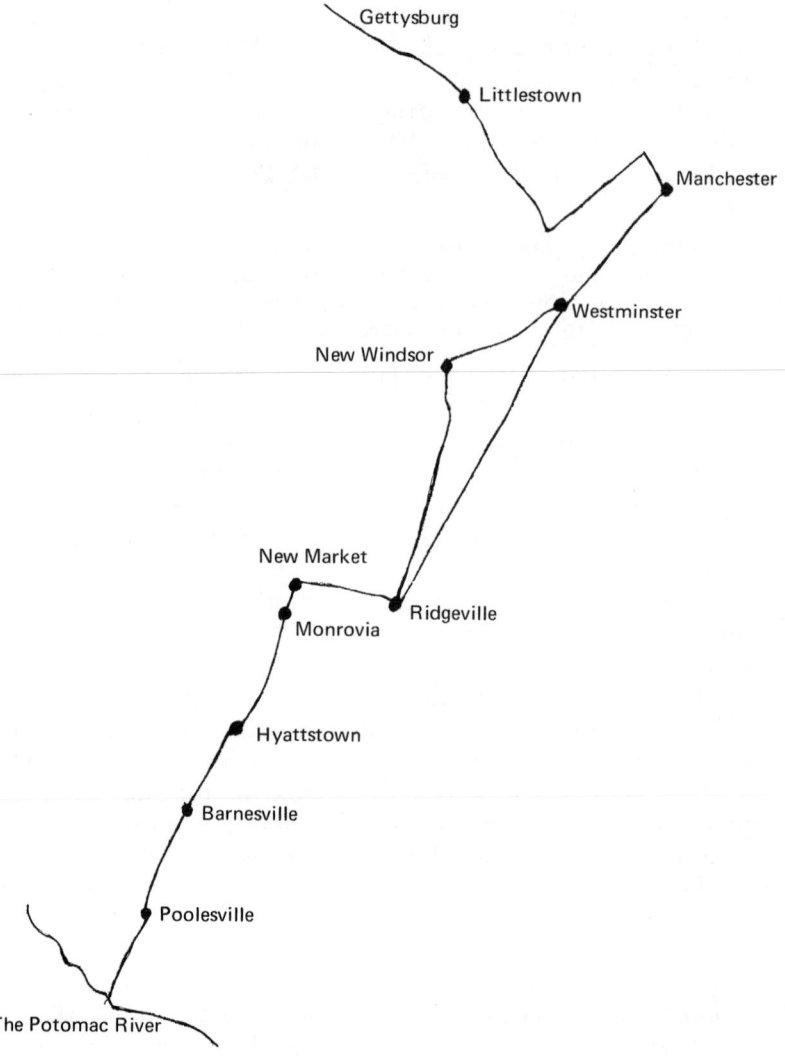

The route of Sedgwick's foot cavalry. Route of the Sixth Corps, from Ridgeville to Westminster, the men moved on two parallel roads. Using what is now Route 27 as well as what was known as the Buffalo Road.

A few showed up with the idea of making money. They offered the soldiers who wanted more than water or coffee some choice apple or peach brandy, or other homemade brew. Then after giving them a taste, they sold jugs to the soldiers. After a while some of them started to feel rather gay, still later they did not have a care in the world. Finally, General Sedgwick had to issue an order, "No more whiskey or homemade brew is to be sold or given to the soldiers."

"Uncle John" Sedgwick was loved and respected by his men. Like Reynolds, he always had the best interest of his men at heart. After their long marches, he wanted them to enjoy themselves. But after all, he might have to move at short notice. Therefore, he did not want his men drunk. But the carnival-like atmosphere continued. Later in the day as the Carroll County folks left to do their milking and other chores, some of the soldiers read the newspapers they had brought. Others played "cat of nine tails." Some played poker. Others wrote letters or visited.

Some of the lads and lasses exchanged addresses, and expressed the fervent hope of meeting again. We often wonder if any marriages developed from this July day in Manchester.

As the day wore on, the soldiers in the Sixth Corps felt good. They were unaware of what was taking place at Gettysburg, thirty-five miles away. It had been a joyous day in that part of Carroll County, a great welcome, all the food you could eat, and home cooked at that, pretty girls, cute children, nice folks. In fact, they had received the best Carroll County could offer. For supper, many of them had chicken sizzling over the campfire, gifts of the Manchester folks. This part of Carroll County had never seen a day like it.

John Sedgwick was pleased too. The Sixth Corps, the largest unit in the Army of the Potomac, had had a good day in the streets and fields of Manchester. The weather was warm. A faint breeze was stirring.

Some of the soldiers were writing letters to little places and big cities scattered from Maine to Wisconsin. They had to tell their loved ones about the long marches and about the day in Manchester. Several were pitching horseshoes.

The corps was traveling light. Meade had ordered all

baggage and personal wagons to be parked in Westminster. Therefore, only the ammunition wagons and ambulances were parked in the fields around Manchester.

In the little brick Fort Hill School,[107] erected in 1803, John Sedgwick checked his morning reports. Fifteen thousand soldiers were "present and accounted for." Lt. Col. Martin T. McMahon, the general's aide and personal friend, checked the reports with him.

But as so often happens this was the lull before the storm. Many times we have a mountaintop experience just before we are plunged into the valley or a crisis situation. The great day in Manchester may have prepared the men of the Sixth Corps for the ordeal that was ahead of them.

As the shades of darkness fell over Carroll County, the Sixth Corps was farthest from Gettysburg. Meade had made a decision. He was going to make a stand, not along Pipe Creek, but on the Pennsylvania hills. Therefore, all troops had to get there as quickly as possible.

"Pappy" Sedgwick was still going over his reports when out of the darkness came the sounds of a galloping rider. "Reynolds had fallen. A crisis was at hand, the Sixth Corps must be in Gettysburg by afternoon of the morrow."[108]

Even the staff officer felt the mission was impossible. "No troops, not even the best can march that far that fast." Sedgwick had other thoughts, "Say to General Meade, my Corps shall be at Gettysburg at two o'clock."

We cannot imagine the excitement that followed. There was no telephone or walkie-talkies, simply aides and orderlies informing division commanders of the situation, and they in turn passing the word down the line or down the chain of command.

But to get fifteen thousand men under way in the dark, that's another problem. However, the Sixth Corps achieved this task. Sadly, they had to leave behind their smoldering campfires and some of the chicken and roast beef. The next day some of the townspeople gathered as souvenirs some of the equipment of war, left behind in the hurried departure. The order was to move by the Taneytown Road.

James L. Bowen gives us an account of the night:

The opening blows of the great conflict were indeed struck while the men of the Sixth Corps were cleaning their weapons, sleeping or eating cherries about Manchester, but the outcome was so different from the anticipation that instead of remaining to fight in the position they had reached by such intense effort, they were called to still greater exertions in order to reach the field—to make, in fact, one of the most famous marches known to military history; and it must be borne in mind that they were not fresh for the effort, but already sadly exhausted by nearly a month of continual skirmishing and marching, having for five days made an average of 25 miles per day through alternate rain and intense heat, followed by 24 hours of comparative rest.

. . . As dusk fell many of the men were asleep, for they were still weary, when the clatter of hoofs, the hurried dash of staff officers, the bustle of preparation at head-quarters, and the vigorous command to "Pack up and fall in!" drove away in a moment all hope of a refreshing night's sleep. Before the slower men are in their places, even, the column is in the road and sweeping back in the direction whence it came the previous evening. There is a hope which is more than half a belief that the destination may be Westminster, which is but ten miles away, and the men move out with cheerful step. Presently a kind-hearted farmer, who is giving each boy in blue a cup of milk, announces that a battle has begun at Gettysburg, nearly 40 miles away, and it is natural to suppose that that to be the destination of the corps.

"*About* 40 miles—he said it was 40 miles—and what did he call the name of the town?" goes from lip to lip, and the step which has been light becomes heavy and mechanical, and the soldiers are transformed into mere machines, to plod on as steadily as possible all the interminable night. There is no moonlight, and only a pale glimmer of the stars, half obscured by clouds; but the long column presses forward and never halts, for if it stops the men will drop into heavy slumber and may be left behind in the darkness. As it is, some of the officers doze in their saddles, and the men as they walk are like those moving in a dream.

The night is well advanced, and the leading brigade has been toiling for miles along a narrow road, when a shouting aide presses through the struggling footmen. "Make way here, make way, for God's sake; you are all wrong!" Then reaching the head of a regiment: "Halt your men, colonel; you are on the wrong road!" Presently the head of the column comes slowly back, those who have dropped to sleep are roused, the regiment countermarches and plods back over the three or four miles that have taken so much of the soldiers' vital force all in vain. Two or three hours have been lost and six or eight miles of ground covered that the general historian will make no account of when he tells the story of the night.[109]

509

The occasion of the rerouting of the corps was the arrival of Thomas Hyde. Riding from Taneytown, he spotted General Sedgwick at the head of the column. Instead of riding to Taneytown, the Sixth Corps was to take the Baltimore Pike through Littlestown to Gettysburg. Hyde felt that his arrival was very important. The orders saved the Sixth Corps from making a triangular move covering fifty-one miles instead of thirty-six. The extra fifteen miles spelled the difference in the arrival of the Sixth Corps at Gettysburg. The orders may have saved the day and perhaps the battle.[110]

Sedgwick gave Hyde a kind word, and then gave the orders to head for the Baltimore Pike. This caused some delay and confusion in the darkness. Regiments went across fields, tramping everything beneath their feet. A member of the Fifth Maine says that some were actually sleepwalking. Many were stumbling along.

Additional problems were ahead for the Sixth Corps. The Westminster-Littlestown-Gettysburg Road was the main supply artery for the Army of the Potomac, and it was blocked with wagons. Instead of a clear, fast road, the Sixth Corps found miles and miles of wagons. "Uncle John" must have wondered whether or not he could keep his promise.

Andrew J. Bennett of the First Massachusetts Light Battery describes his experience:

> It was a typical July night; the sultry air retaining the mid-day heat, there was an uncomfortable closeness.
> The march was made with unflagging energy all night, and there was no relaxation of effort when the scorching sun of the 2d of July appeared to light another day's conflict on that field to which we were hastening. Now was the test of physical vigor,—to keep the ranks and make the requisite time, wipe away the perspiration, grin, and endure. So, for an hour after sunrise, men and horses well stood the test. Then there was a brief rest to answer the calls of nature, after which regiments and batteries were speeding on. . . .
> The next five miles are traversed with scarcely a break in the steady, rapid, forward movement. The sun's rays strike fiercely. Countenances are begrimed with dust and sweat. Now the progress is slower; the road is ascending for a way. We are moving due north.[111]

Along the route, Stevens noted with gratitude, people bringing water to the soldiers, walking along as they filled their canteens. In Littlestown he saw citizens bringing wounded from Gettysburg in their carriages. The tempo picked up. "Our friends were waiting for us" at Gettysburg.[112]

The breeze at dawn was "fresh and bracing," but it gave evidence of being "a scorcher," and the Sixth Corps had miles and miles to go.

Even in the suffering there was humor and comradeship. General Sedgwick, mounted on "Cornwall," pulled over to the side of the road to watch some of his men go by and to observe their physical condition. One of the men said, "Get a fresh horse, Uncle John, and try to catch us." This touched the brave leader from Cornwall Hollow in the Berkshires, he lifted his hand, and smiled in acknowledgment.

With the Sixth Corps on the Roads to Gettysburg was Chaplain James M. McCarter. While serving with the Ninety-third Pennsylvania, he had been severely wounded at Fair Oaks. He was almost an invalid in July of '63, but he stayed in the saddle and traveled with the men. He spoke to his comrades, telling them of the serious situation, and reading Meade's words to them.

The men of the Ninety-third heard but did not respond until they reached the Mason-Dixon Line. Then the colors were unfurled. The sound of the drum was heard. The soldiers perked up. It looked as though they were on parade. They were home. They were in Pennsylvania, the Keystone State. They marched across the line singing, "Home, Sweet Home."[113]

The television and movie people would have had a field day covering the march of the Sixth Corps. What a sight it must have been. We can imagine General Sedgwick and the other officers riding along, near the front of the long blue column, the Stars and Stripes fluttering in the breeze, alongside the Greek Cross, the Sixth Corps flag, and the sun shining on "rows of steel" as thirty-six infantry regiments and eight batteries of artillery continued towards a place called Gettysburg.

The morning wore on. The sun climbed high in the sky. The heat, hunger, and fatigue began to take their toll. Here and there a few dropped, unable to continue. But their comrades kept plodding along, marching around their buddies until the ambulance crews could reach them. Uniforms were soaked with perspiration, and almost white with dust. Yet at times the stout hearts vigorously chanted the corps refrain:

> "The foremost in the conflict,
> The last to say, 'tis o'er.
> Who knows not what it is to yield.
> You'll find the old Sixth Corps."[114]

And on they marched. They did not know when to quit. Near Littlestown, they met the ambulances bringing the wounded back from McPherson's Ridge and Oak Ridge. The ambulance drivers demanded the road. But troops advancing to battle had priority, then the ammunition trains. Everything else had to wait.

The sun grew hotter. By noon the men felt they could see waves of heat, floating from the earth and mingling with the clouds of white dust. Could they get there in time? When they did, would they be in condition to fight? They marched in silence now, or rather plodded along. There was no halt, no dinner, no sound of battle. "Fierce July heat bore down with furious vigor. The sun beat down and the heat came up from the stones of the old Baltimore Pike." It was withering to the point of exhaustion. But the zeal and efforts of the Sixth Corps never slackened.[115]

While the Sixth Corps continued on, Meade and the nation waited. Fortunately, Lee had not renewed the action. Back at the White House, Mr. Lincoln fell to his knees and prayed, "You know I have done all I can. . . . O God, give us victory." With that utterance a sense of peace and well-being came to the president.

Then leading elements of the ten-mile column saw a series of hills, two of them being rather prominent. On the one hill, Little Round Top, a Union signal officer saw the dust and the column of troops. At first he was terrified, thinking it might be Confederate infantry or worse yet, Jeb Stuart in the Yankee rear. But no. No. There was the Greek Cross. It was

John Sedgwick.

The Greek Cross.

not the Rebs. It was "Uncle John" and the Sixth. "Glory Be. Hallelujah. The Sixth Corps is coming. The Sixth Corps is coming."

Men yelled the good news to one another. It was a magic moment. One of the great events of American history. Closer, closer they came. The "rows of steel. The Greek Cross, the Stars and Stripes."

Along Cemetery Ridge the news spread like wildfire. Cheers rocked the air. The Rebels must have wondered what was happening. This had an inspiring effect upon the men of the Greek Cross. Forgetting the pain, the hunger, and the fatigue, the men of the Sixth Corps braced and stiffened with pride. They had a right to be proud. Other units, North and South had made long forced marches on the Roads to Gettysburg. But they had covered thirty-seven miles in seventeen hours. An entire corps . . . made a march that has rarely, if ever, been surpassed in modern warfare. "Uncle John and his men, despite delays, heat, dust, and hunger had kept their promise. They had made it to Gettysburg." Well could they bear the title of "foot cavalry."

The men who made that march from Manchester to Gettysburg could proudly say, as did those who took part in the invasion of France, "I hit the beach on D-Day," "I

513

marched with 'Uncle John' Sedgwick and the Sixth Corps on the Roads to Gettysburg."

At 2:00 P.M., a tired but happy John Sedgwick rode to Widow Leister's house on the Taneytown Road. Reporting to George G. Meade, he said, "Sir, the Sixth Corps is up." We wonder what the two generals must have thought, what their feelings were. The Ninety-eighth Pennsylvania dropped on their knees to lap water from Rock Creek. The Army of the Potomac felt more secure. The entire army had now completed the Roads to Gettysburg.

To the east a train, presumably one belonging to the Western Maryland Railway, was on the tracks heading for Baltimore, carrying the body of John Fulton Reynolds. His sister Jennie and her husband met the train and accompanied the body to Philadelphia. A grieving family had lost a friend and brother. The nation had lost a great man.[116]

Dawn today found Robert Rodes in Gettysburg, occupying Middle Street from the seminary to Stratton Street. Johnson's division was in position across Rock Creek, in front of Benner's and Wolf's Hill. Jubal Early was on the right of Johnson, around to the east slopes of Cemetery Hill.

Robert E. Lee and A. P. Hill's corps were on Seminary Ridge. Most of Longstreet's men were going into position on the ridge getting ready to launch an attack on Little Round Top.

The Twelfth, First and Eleventh corps were guarding Culp's and Cemetery Hill. The Second Corps was in position along the rolling land from Cemetery Hill to Little Round Top. The Fifth Corps was filing into position, some units heading for Little Round Top, with the Sixth, exhausted from their march, in rear of the line.

But all the participants still were not on the fields of Gettysburg. One more had yet to arrive. These were the men of George Pickett. Randolph Shotwell describes the march of the last infantry to cover the Roads to Gettysburg:

July 2d.—Four miles from the Battlefield of Gettysburg.
After a fatiguing march of 30 miles over a very rough turnpike, one has very little energy for note making, and tonight I confess to being as nearly worn out as a man can be without actually breaking

down; yet I will devote the few remaining moments of twilight to recording another day's transactions, as it may be the last that I shall have to note. I say it may be because at this moment as I write, the solemn forest is quivering under the deep reverberations of heavy cannonading, and the stream of gory looking soldiers coming back from the front, tell of the deadly conflict, which must be concluded tomorrow by the work of our own muskets and artillery.

We left camp south of Chambersburg at a very early hour this morning, and marching through town, filed off on the Baltimore turnpike. The townspeople no doubt felt a sensation of relief as our flags fluttered over the hills eastward; tho' any idea they may have had that we were retreating must have been dispelled by the enthusiastic cheers and gratified shouts that went up from the troops when they discovered the head of column tending eastward. "Here we go—right off for Baltimore!"—was the cry that ran along the lines and many companies sang the "Bonnie Blue Flag," or "Way Down South in Dixie."

Indeed, I rarely ever saw the troops more inspirited, which was much of a mystery to the phlegmatic, well-fed "Deutchers" as they could not imagine how any one so poorly fed, clothed, and paid—to say nothing of hardships,—could have any sort of liveliness of spirit.

As the day advanced, the sun took effect on the overladen men (carrying three days' rations, and extra ammunition), and quite a number were prostrated, while all of us suffered most severely. As we approached the Cashtown Gap about noon the vertical rays of the sun seemed like real lances of steel tipped with fire! The broken rock of the McAdamized turnpike and the broad flat flagstones of mountain slate reflected the heat until a perfect steam arose in our faces as we trudged along and the choking dust gathered in throats and eyes causing infinite annoyance. At times the whole line or column seemed to stagger like "men overcome with new wine," as the Good Book mildly describes an attack of "Brandy on the Brain." In the middle of Cashtown Gap we halted for ten minutes' rest, and dinner. There was little shade and less breeze; and the sigh of exhaustion with which the men unshouldered their packs was only exceeded by the groan with which they were resumed, when the so-called rest was over. It was now one o'clock P. M. and we had travelled 20 miles since dawn.

For my own part, having exceedingly sore feet, and not suspecting the proximity of a battle, I had resolved "not to be dragged to death" in this manner, but to take the first opportunity to leave ranks, retire to some shady spot, and "take mine ease" until after sunset; not doubting that the refreshment thus obtained would enable me to catch up with the command by nightfall, as it could hardly make many miles farther. However, before I could put my design into execution, I chanced to overhear General Garnett saying:—*"Pickett says we must go to Gettysburg tonight, at all risks;*

515

the battle is not decided, and if the enemy holds his ground; we must attack him tomorrow ourselves. " Here was news indeed! Of course I could not "fall out of ranks" at such a time, and with feelings akin to despair I strung up my energies to make the nine or ten miles yet before us. In all sincerity I can say that at that moment the thought of the afternoon's march was much more trying than the perils of tomorrow's battle.

To march 30 miles—some say 32—under a broiling July sun—over rocky roads—up hill and down hill—without enough drinking water and loaded down with 120 pounds requires nerves and muscles of iron or gutta percha. Neither of which mine are!

We reached Cashtown at 4 P. M. It is a mere hamlet at the east face of the Gap. Here we found the reserve artillery and wagon trains in park. And here we first learned that there had been heavy fighting for the past two days resulting in a glorious victory for our arms; though the battle was not yet fully decided.

A few minutes ago I was handed a letter from home. It had been nearly three weeks on the way. I wish I had not received it. How strange a contrast between the simple home affairs in the backwoods of North Carolina—of which the letter speaks—and the stirring, exciting situation in which it finds me. *Here* are thousands of weary soldiers lying on the grass, the light of countless camp fires illuminating the grove, the rumble of long trains upon the turn-pike, and the sullen *"Boom!" "Boom!" "Boom!" "Boom!"* of artillery in the distance. *There* the quiet parsonage is calmly bathed in twilight, with only the sound of tinkling cowbells, or the notes of music within hearing. Little did Father imagine the circumstances under which his letter would be read; though he bids me do my duty, and trust in Providence! The one I am doing, the other is rather more difficult. Little Jimmie Bose came to me a few minutes ago, and laid down on the edge of my blanket. Seeing him rather depressed, I asked him what troubled him. Said he:—"I wish you would take my money, and this little Journal and give it to Mother if I get killed tomorrow." I tried to reason him out of his presentiment, but he seems almost certain of death. Says he was barefooted and could have stayed back in Loudon as his Mother wanted him to do, but he told her he wanted to come on with the Army and get himself a pair of new boots in Baltimore. She replied, "I fear you will never live to see Baltimore, Jimmie!" And said Jimmie:—*"I expect she was right."*

Nine o'clock P. M.—The noise of the battle has ceased, but the talking of the men who are cooking rations, prevents sleep. I am nearly dead for a drink of water, and it's fully half a mile to the spring! Alas! Alas![117]

The toils and the hardships of hot and dusty marches were now ended. The Blue and the Gray had marched from Fredericksburg to Gettysburg. Now battle, death, destruction, and suffering were ahead.

516

The story of Gettysburg, in part at least, is the story of the roads that led to the town named after James Getty. For the most part they were unpaved roads in the summer of '63, but white and dusty. These roads leading from the hills of Fredericksburg, through the hills of Maryland and Pennsylvania, linked many towns and villages with the battle. Their names are indeed part of the campaign. Thousands of men tramped these roads in the rain, mud, heat, and dust. Some traveled "the last mile of the way" as they gave "their last full measure of devotion at Gettysburg." But from the men who traveled these roads came one nation, united, and hopefully under God.

Just as my great-grandmother told stories of seeing men in blue on the Roads to Gettysburg, so others have told and retold their stories, in places like Greencastle, Fairfield, New Midway, Adamstown, Berryville, and Emmitsburg, and other places in the path of the two great armies in the summer of '63.

These pages have talked about the roads the men traveled, their reflections, and the things that the men and women experienced in the summer of '63 on the Roads to Gettysburg.

Who were the men who marched on the Roads to Gettysburg? They were farmers and woodsmen, factory workers, teachers, and laborers. They were sons, husbands, fathers, the men of the North and the South.

Where did they come from? They came from the states touching the Gulf Stream waters of the South. They came from the prairies, and the deep woods of Wisconsin and Minnesota. And they came from the pine forests of Maine, and the cities of the industrial states. Now the village churchyards of rural and urban America contain the remains of those who marched on the Roads to Gettysburg in the summer of '63.

517

XV

GLEANINGS

June 1863

Sunday	Monday	Tuesday	Wednesday	Thursday	Friday	Saturday
	1	2	3	4	5	6
7	8	9	10	11	12	13
14	15	16	17	18	19	20
21	22	23	24	25	26	27
28	29	30				

July 1863

1		2		3		4

Today when we go on a journey, the automobile association or some gas company maps out the route for us. In June of 1863, Joe Hooker mapped out the following routes for the Army of the Potomac to cross the river into Maryland.

On June 5, the First Corps was near White Oak Church, while the Second and Third corps were near Falmouth. The Fifth Corps was encamped in the vicinity of Banks', United States and the adjacent fords of the Rappahannock. The Sixth Corps was also near White Oak Church. Howard's Eleventh Corps was near Brooke's Station on the Aquia Creek railroad. Slocum's Twelfth Corps was near Stafford Court House and Aquia Landing. The Cavalry Corps was at Manassas Junction, Warrenton Junction, and Brooke's Station. The Artillery Reserve was near Falmouth.

From these positions, the Army of the Potomac marched west, then northeast until the various units converged on Gettysburg. Now by the interstate highways, the distance from Fredericksburg to Gettysburg is less than 150 miles. But in 1863, the distance was not covered in three hours in modern cars, but by the tramp, tramp, tramp of tired feet on dusty roads in extreme heat.

On June 6 and 7, units of the Sixth Corps crossed the Rappahannock and occupied Confederate rifle pits. The next day, the Cavalry Corps moved to Kelly's and Beverly fords, preparing to make a reconnaissance toward Culpeper. The cavalry and the Sixth Corps were busy the next day crossing the river and fighting the Confederates at Brandy Station, Beverly Ford, and Stevensburg.

Wednesday, June 10, the Cavalry Corps gathered near Warrenton Junction. The infantry supports of the Sixth Corps rejoined their respective commands. Howe's division of the Sixth Corps moved from Franklin Crossing to Aquia Creek.

On Thursday, June 11, the Third Corps marched from Boscobel, near Falmouth to Hartwood Church.

Men and equipment really started to move on June 12. The First Corps marched from Fitzhugh's plantation and White Oak Church to Deep Run. The Third Corps moved from Hartwood Church to Bealeton. The Eleventh Corps under Howard moved from Brooke's Station to Hartwood Church.

That same day, advance elements of the Army of Northern Virginia skirmished with Union troops in the Shenandoah Valley, principally at Cedarville and Middletown.

The itinerary from Saturday, June 13, was:

The First Corps from Deep Run to Bealeton.

The Fifth Corps from near Banks' Ford toward Morrisville.

Elements of the Sixth Corps from Franklin's Crossing to Potomac Creek.

The Eleventh Corps from Hartwood Church to Catlett's Station.

Slocum's Twelfth Corps marched from near Stafford Court House and Aquia Creek toward Dumfries; the Artillery Reserve covered the miles from Falmouth to Stafford Court House.

Fighting broke out in Berryville, along the Opequon Creek, and near Winchester.

Tables and charts are sometimes boring reading. Yet we must list the daily movements and marches of the army to the Potomac and northward. Get out a map and trace the advance, putting the Union line of march in blue, and the Confederate in red.

Hooker moved army headquarters on the Fourteenth from Falmouth to Dumfries. The First and the Third corps marched from Bealeton to Manassas Junction. The Fifth Corps moved to Catlett's Station. Meanwhile the Sixth Corps marched from Potomac Creek to Stafford Court House. Howard and the Eleventh Corps made tracks from Catlett's Station to Manassas Junction, and then moved toward Centreville. Slocum and the Twelfth Corps reached Dumfries, and the Artillery Reserve moved to Wolf Run Shoals. The Eighth Corps was meeting Confederate pressure in the Shenandoah Valley, so they retreated from Martinsburg to Maryland Heights across from Harpers Ferry. Fighting occurred at Martinsburg, Berryville, and Winchester.

On Monday, June 15, Hooker and headquarters moved from Dumfries to Fairfax Station. The other corps proceeded as follows:

Hancock's Second Corps from Falmouth to near Aquia.

The Fifth Corps from Catlett's Station, via Bristoe Station, to Manassas Junction.

The Sixth Corps from Aquia Creek and Stafford Court House to Dumfries.

The Twelfth Corps from Dumfries to Fairfax Court House.

Most of the Cavalry Corps was near Bristoe Station, while the Artillery Reserve was at Fairfax Court House. The Eleventh Corps arrived Centreville. Milroy's division was driven out of Winchester by the Confederates and fell back to Maryland Heights and Hancock.

June 16 was a slow day. Many of the units rested their feet, and tried to escape the oppressive heat. Hancock's Second Corps had no respite. The men marched from Aquia via Dumfries, to Wolf Run Shoals on the Occoquan; Sedgwick marched the Sixth Corps from Dumfries to Fairfax Station.

The Cavalry Corps was active at Manassas Junction and Bull Run.

On Wednesday, June 17, the men were up and at it again. Lee was moving and so must they. The First Corps marched from Manassas Junction to Herndon Station; the Second proceeded from Wolf Run Shoals to Sangster's Station; the Third Corps moved from Manassas Junction to Centreville; the Fifth Corps tramped from Manassas Junction to Gum Springs; Howard's men marched through Virginia hunt club territory heading from Centreville to Goose Creek; while Slocum and the Twelfth, knowing a crossing had to be made, marched from Fairfax Court House to Dranesville. The cavalry moved to Aldie.

Many times one corps occupied the position occupied earlier in the day by another corps. This made it difficult to find wood for camp fires.

June 18 some of the units rested, while others marched. Hooker moved from Fairfax Station to Fairfax Court House. "Uncle John" Sedgwick ordered the Sixth Corps to move from Fairfax Station to Germantown. The Twelfth Corps moved closer to the Potomac as they advanced from Dranesville to Leesburg. Cavalry skirmishes took place at Middleburg and Aldie.

On Friday, June 19, the troops who had marched on Thursday rested, while the First Corps shouldered arms and took the road from Herndon Station to Guilford Springs. The Third took up the march from Centreville, to Gum Springs, while the Fifth Corps moved from that place to Aldie. Again the cavalry skirmished at Middleburg.

On the morning of June 20, Saturday, to be exact, Hancock ordered the "Fighting Second Corps" to move from Sangster's Station to Centreville and thence toward Thoroughfare Gap. Howe's division of the Sixth Corps marched from Germantown to Bristoe Station.

June 21 was Sunday. But it brought no rest to the Second Corps and the Cavalry. They were up and moving. The Second Corps arrived at Gainesville and Thoroughfare Gap. The horse soldiers concentrated around Upperville and Buckland

Mills. The cavalrymen continued to probe and look for signs of the enemy on Monday and Tuesday, June 22 and 23.

Wednesday, June 24, saw the Sixth Corps moving out from Germantown to Centreville. Howard's Eleventh Corps from Goose Creek to the south bank of the Potomac at Edwards Ferry. A skirmish occurred at Sharpsburg, Maryland.

The next day almost the entire army was in motion. The First Corps crossed the Potomac River and proceeded to Barnesville, Maryland. The Third Corps moved out from Gum Springs to the banks of the Potomac at Edwards Ferry, all ready to cross. The Eleventh Corps forded the river and moved to the little town of Jefferson, Maryland, south of Frederick. The Artillery Reserve made a lot of progress and covered the distance from Fairfax Court House to Poolesville.

The Second Corps was kept on the Virginia side of the Potomac near Gum Springs, while the Sixth moved from Bristoe Station to Centreville, where it was joined by additional troops from the defenses of Washington.

Movement of the Union Army to Gettysburg

FIRST CORPS
Maj. Gen. John Reynolds, Commanding

Thursday, June 25—Crossed the Potomac at Edwards Ferry and bivouacked at Barnesville.

Friday, June 26—Marched from Barnesville to Jefferson in Frederick County, Maryland.

Saturday, June 27—Marched a short distance of six to eight miles from Jefferson to Middletown, six miles west of Frederick.

Sunday, June 28—Marched from Middletown to Frederick.

Monday, June 29—Frederick to Emmitsburg along what is Old Route 15. Covered twenty to twenty-five miles.

Tuesday, June 30—Emmitsburg to Marsh Run just south of Gettysburg.

Wednesday, July 1—Marsh Run to positions west of Gettysburg.

SECOND CORPS
Maj. Gen. Winfield Scott Hancock, Commanding

Friday, June 26—Crossed the Potomac in to Maryland near Edwards Ferry.

Saturday, June 27—Marched to Barnesville.

Sunday, June 28—Barnesville to Monocacy Junction, several miles south of Frederick.

Monday, June 29—Via what is now Maryland 26 to Liberty, Johnsville, to Uniontown where the Corps bivouacked.

Tuesday, June 30—In bivouac part of the day. Thence to Taneytown.

Wednesday, July 1—Hurried from Taneytown, through Harney to lines on Cemetery Ridge at Gettysburg.

THIRD CORPS
Maj. Gen. Daniel Sickles, Commanding

Thursday, June 25—Crossed the Potomac at Edwards Ferry and moved to a point near the mouth of the Monocacy River.

Friday, June 26—Marched to Jefferson, Maryland.

Saturday, June 27—From Jefferson to Middletown.

Sunday, June 28—Middletown to Woodsboro, via what is now Route 194 from Ceresville through Walkersville.

Monday, June 29—From near Woodsboro to Taneytown.

Tuesday, June 30—From near Taneytown to Bridgeport on the road from Taneytown to Emmitsburg.

Wednesday, July 1—From near Emmitsburg to Gettysburg.

FIFTH CORPS
Maj. Gen. George Sykes, Commanding

Friday, June 26—Located near the mouth of the Monocacy River.

Saturday, June 27—Marched to Ballenger Creek near Frederick.

Sunday, June 28—Joined by Crawford's Pennsylvania Reserves near Frederick.

523

Monday, June 29—Through Frederick to Mount Pleasant and Liberty, now Maryland 26.

Tuesday, June 30—From Liberty to Johnsville to Union Bridge to Union Mills.

Wednesday, July 1—A long march from Union Mills to Hanover, McSherrystown, Bonneville to Gettysburg.

SIXTH CORPS
Maj. Gen. John Sedgwick, Commanding

Saturday, June 27—Crossed the Potomac at Edwards Ferry. Camped at Poolesville.

Sunday, June 28—Marched to Hyattstown.

Monday, June 29—From Hyattstown to New Market to Ridgeville to New Windsor.

Tuesday, June 30—From New Windsor to Westminster to Manchester.

Wednesday, July 1—After resting near Manchester, made a great forced march of over thirty miles to Gettysburg arriving in the afternoon on July 2.

ELEVENTH CORPS
Maj. Gen. Oliver O. Howard, Commanding

Thursday, June 25—Crossed the Potomac at Edwards Ferry. Went into camp near Jefferson.

Friday, June 26—Marched from Jefferson to Middletown.

Saturday, June 27—Bivouacked near Middletown.

Sunday, June 28—Moved from Middletown to Frederick.

Monday, June 29—From Frederick to Emmitsburg, traveling on the Old Frederick Road from what is now Hansonville, through Utica to the south end of Emmitsburg. This was on a road parallel to the advance of the First Corps.

Tuesday, June 30—Bivouac near Emmitsburg.

Wednesday, July 1—On to Gettysburg.

TWELFTH CORPS
Maj. Gen. Henry Slocum, Commanding

Saturday, June 27—Located near Knoxville, Maryland, not far from Harpers Ferry.

Sunday, June 28—Marched from Knoxville to Frederick along Old Route 340. Covered sixteen to eighteen miles.

Monday, June 29—From Frederick to Bruceville and Taneytown, via Ceresville, Walkersville, and Woodsboro. Marched about twenty miles.

Tuesday, June 30—From Taneytown to Littlestown, Pennsylvania, covering ten to fifteen miles depending where the troops were in column.

Wednesday, July 1—From Littlestown to Two Taverns to Gettysburg. It is ten miles from Littlestown to the battlefield.

HEADQUARTERS ARMY OF THE POTOMAC

Friday, June 26—Poolesville.   Monday, June 29—Middleburg.
Saturday, June 27—Frederick. Tuesday, June 30—Taneytown.
Sunday, June 28—Frederick.   Wednesday, July 1—Gettysburg.

The River Crossings

THE ARMY OF NORTHERN VIRGINIA

Monday, June 15—Jenkins and his cavalry at Williamsport (A.M.).

Monday, June 15—Robert Rodes and his division of Ewell's Corps (P.M.).

Thursday, June 18—Edward Johnson and his division at Shepherdstown.

Monday, June 22—Jubal Early and his division at Shepherdstown.

Wednesday, June 24-Friday, June 26—James Longstreet and the First Corps at Williamsport, and A. P. Hill and the Third Corps at Shepherdstown.

THE ARMY OF THE POTOMAC

June 25—Oliver O. Howard and the Eleventh Corps.
John Reynolds and the First Corps.
David Birney and the Third Corps.

June 26—Henry W. Slocum and the Twelfth Corps.
　　　　George G. Meade and the Fifth Corps.
　　　　Winfield Scott Hancock and the Second Corps.
June 27—John Sedgwick and the Sixth Corps.

BRIDGES ACROSS THE POTOMAC

Point of Rocks, fifty-two miles from Washington.
Berlin, now Brunswick, fifty-eight miles.
Harpers Ferry, West Virginia, sixty-four miles.
Shepherdstown, West Virginia, seventy-six miles.
These bridges had been destroyed by the summer of 1863.

KEY FORDS

G. K. Warren, the chief engineer of the Army of the Potomac, made a report on June 16, saying that the Potomac was full of rocks from Harpers Ferry to Berlin. At the last place there was a good spot for a pontoon bridge, requiring 1,150 feet of bridging. A bridge at Point of Rocks would require 870 feet. He reported that Hauling Ford near the Mouth of the Monocacy was good, likewise Edwards and Conrad's. He stated that the Monocacy was a troublesome river to cross. See *Official Records,* pt. 3, p. 149.

THE ROUTE OF ROBERT RODES

June 14-15—Martinsburg.
June 16—Crossed the Potomac to Williamsport.
June 19-21—Funkstown-Hagerstown Area.
June 22-26—Just north of Chambersburg.
June 27-29—Carlisle.
June 30—Heidlersburg.

THE ROUTE OF JUBAL EARLY

June 22—Crossed the Potomac at Shepherdstown.
June 23—From Beaver Creek to Cavetown, Smithsburg to Waynesboro.
June 24—Quincy to Greenwood.
June 25—In camp.
June 26—In and around Gettysburg.
June 27—Berlin and Farmers Post Office.
June 28—York and Wrightsville.
June 29—Regrouped in York.

June 30—Moved to a point about three miles east of Heidlersburg.

Markers Along the Roads to Gettysburg

POOLESVILLE

Maj. Gen. Joseph Hooker's headquarters were established
here on June 26, 1863, during the Gettysburg campaign.

EDWARDS FERRY (Near Poolesville)

In June 1863, the major part of the Union army crossed
here on the way to Gettysburg.

FREDERICK
(Just south of the Routes 340 and 15 interchange)

Maj. Gen. George G. Meade took command of the Army of
the Potomac under orders from President Lincoln, seven hundred feet north of this marker, June 28, 1863.

U.S. 15 SOUTH OF GREENMOUNT NEAR MARSH CREEK

The Union First Corps camped here on June 30, 1863, on
the way to Gettysburg. Followed by the Eleventh Corps and
Third Corps, they marched next morning to relieve Buford's
cavalry, already in action, west of the town.

PENNSYLVANIA 134 AT BARLOW ON THE TANEYTOWN ROAD

The Union Eleventh Corps, crossing from the Emmitsburg
Road, July 1, 1863, turned north here toward Gettysburg.
The Union Second Corps camped here on the night of July 1.

MEADE'S HEADQUARTERS, MARYLAND 194,
JUST NORTH OF TANEYTOWN

Maj. Gen. George G. Meade, Commander of the Army of
the Potomac, maintained his headquarters at the nearby
Shunk farm from June 30, until the night of July 1, 1863.
From here he directed the initial concentration of the Union
forces at Gettysburg.

BRIDGEPORT, MARYLAND, ROUTE 97 EAST OF EMMITSBURG

As a part of General Meade's screen for Washington as the
Confederates invaded Maryland and Pennsylvania, the Third
Corps of the Army of the Potomac, arrived here on June 30,
1863, from Taneytown. Next day Gen. Daniel F. Sickles
marched this corps to Emmitsburg.

THE WESTMINSTER ROAD, JUST EAST OF UNIONTOWN

Headquarters Second Corps, Army of the Potomac. On and about the nearby Babylon farm. Maj. Gen. Winfield Scott Hancock rested his corps June 29, 1863. On July 1, the corps marched through Taneytown to take part in the battle of Gettysburg.

UNION MILLS, U.S. 140, SHRIVER HOMESTEAD

On June 29, 1863, Gen. J. E. B. Stuart and his cavalry camped here. On June 30, 1863, Gen. James Barnes of the Fifth Corps United States Army spent the night on his way to Gettysburg.

MANCHESTER, MARYLAND

The Second Cavalry Division and the Sixth Corps, Army of the Potomac, camped at Manchester, June 30, 1863. Headquarters for Maj. Gen. John Sedgwick was located on nearby Old Fort School House Road. On night of July 1, the corps left Manchester, and went into battle at Gettysburg the next day.

Markers showing the routes of the Army of the Potomac were located in front of the schools in Emmitsburg and Taneytown. They were also located in Middleburg, Uniontown, and Littlestown.

U.S. 140, TWO MILES SOUTHEAST OF GETTYSBURG

The Union Twelfth Corps arrived here the afternoon of July 1, 1863, and later moved into battle line on Culp's Hill. On July 2, the Sixth Corps arrived by this same road, and the Fifth Corps by the Hanover Road.

PENNSYLVANIA 134, NEAR THE STATE LINE

Gen. George G. Meade, who had replaced Hooker as commander of the Union Army, June 28, 1863, traveled this road from Taneytown to Gettysburg the night of July 1. He made his headquarters just south of Gettysburg.

CASHTOWN, OLD U.S. 30

Crossing South Mountain from Chambersburg, General Hill's Corps of Lee's army assembled here June 29-30, 1863. On July 1, his advance guard moved up from Marsh Creek and met Union troops west of Gettysburg.

U.S. 30, WEST OF GETTYSBURG

The Battle of Gettysburg began here the morning of July 1, 1863, when Union cavalry scouts under General Buford met General Hill's army, advancing from the west. Arrival of General Ewell's army that afternoon drove Union troops to south of town.

HEIDLERSBURG, U.S. 15 NORTH

General Rodes's Confederate troops, returning from Carlisle to join Lee's army, camped here the night of June 30. The next morning, July 1, they marched west toward Biglerville, then known as Middletown.

NORTH TO PENNSYLVANIA
U.S. 11, ONE MILE NORTH OF STATE LINE

Over this route Confederate Gen. R. S. Ewell's Second Army Corps, led Lee's invading forces on June 22, 1863. Next day, Gen. Jubal Early, under Ewell's command, entered the state to the east, near Waynesboro.

U.S. 11, JUST NORTH OF GREENCASTLE,
PENNSYLVANIA

Here on June 22, 1863, the First New York Cavalry attacked the Southern advance force of cavalry under Gen. A. G. Jenkins. Here died the first Union soldier killed in action in Pennsylvania, Cpl. William H. Rihl of Philadelphia, serving in a Pennsylvania unit assigned to the New York regiment.

U.S. 11, SIX-TENTHS MILE SOUTH OF CHAMBERSBURG

Gen. A. G. Jenkins's Southern cavalry raided Chambersburg June 15-17, 1863, prior to the main invasion; and later led the invading army, June 22-24. Gen. R. E. Lee entered Chambersburg on June 26.

CHAMBERSBURG: SOUTHWEST PART OF SQUARE

On June 26, 1863, Gen. Robert E. Lee, and staff, entered this square. After conferring with Gen. A. P. Hill, near the middle of the "Diamond," Lee turned eastward and made his headquarters at the edge of town.

PENNSYLVANIA 33, FIVE-TENTHS
MILE SOUTHWEST OF CARLISLE

June 27, 1863, General Ewell's Confederate army, marching over this road toward Harrisburg, reached Carlisle; Jenkins's cavalry went on to reconnoitre. On June 29, Lee ordered Ewell to join the main army at Cashtown.

Fort Couch, U.S. 11 in Lemoyne, just across the river from Harrisburg. Market and Eighth streets.

Remains of breastworks, at Eighth and Ohio streets, built before the Battle of Gettysburg, to oppose the expected Southern drive on Harrisburg. June 29, 1863, a few Confederate scouts neared here but withdrew.

Fort Couch, U.S. 11 in Lemoyne, just across the river from Harrisburg. Eighth Street and Ohio Avenue.

Remains of breastworks built in June 1863 to oppose an expected attack on Harrisburg by Confederate troops. Site then known as Hummel's Heights. Fort was named for General Couch, commander, Eastern Pennsylvania Military District.

U.S. 11 IN CAMP HILL, MARKET STREET

Farthest advance of a body of Confederate troops toward Harrisburg. Southern units under Gen. A. G. Jenkins of Ewell's Corps reached Oyster Point on June 28, 1863. On the next day, defending militia faced them here in a skirmish in which both sides suffered casualties.

CHAMBERSBURG: LINCOLN WAY EAST
NEAR COLBROOK AVENUE

Name of grove selected by Gen. R. E. Lee for his headquarters, June 26-30, 1863. Here he issued the order for the concentration of troops near Gettysburg. Site of the woods is just south of this point, Messersmith's Woods.

WITH EARLY TO YORK
CALEDONIA. FURNACE JUNCTION U.S. 30 AND
PENNSYLVANIA 233 AT CALEDONIA PARK

Erected in 1837 by Thaddeus Stevens and James D. Paxton. Stevens's antislavery stand led to its destruction by Gen. Jubal Early, June 26, 1863, on his way to York during the Gettysburg campaign.

U.S. 30 EAST AND WEST OF JUNCTION WITH PENNSYLVANIA 94, EAST OF NEW OXFORD

Part of General Early's Confederate army, under Gen. J. B. Gordon, passed here June 27, 1863, to York. Early's main force followed a parallel route through Hampton and East Berlin. Both entered York the following day.

PENNSYLVANIA 394 AT HAMPTON

Gen. Jubal Early's Confederate army, marching by Mummasburg and Hunterstown, passed here June 27, 1863, to York. Returning June 30, they passed a little to the north toward Heidlersburg.

PENNSYLVANIA 116 IN HANOVER

Men of General Early's Confederate army, detached by General Gordon to destroy a bridge at Hanover Junction, passed through Hanover by this route, June 27, 1863. This work done, the detachment rejoined General Gordon west of York.

U.S. 30, WEST OF YORK

June 28, 1863, Confederate General Gordon's brigade of Early's division followed this route through York to Wrightsville. Early's main force remained here until June 30, when it left to rejoin Lee's army.

U.S. 30 IN WRIGHTSVILLE AT THE SUSQUEHANNA RIVER BRIDGE

Confederate troops, sent from York by General Early to cross the river and march on Harrisburg, reached here June 28, 1863. United States militia withdrew, firing the bridge and barring any Southern advance beyond the river.

AT WEIGLESTOWN, NEAR PENNSYLVANIA 74

June 28, 1863, Gen. Jubal Early's Confederates reached York by this route. Here Early sent Colonel French to York Haven to burn bridges. Ordered next day to join Lee's army. Early returned over this road June 30.

PENNSYLVANIA 34, THREE MILES NORTH OF GETTYSBURG

General Rodes's Confederate troops marched down this road July 1, 1863, on their way from Carlisle. At this point

531

they turned right along the ridge to Oak Hill, to attack the Union flank.

U.S. 15 AT HEIDLERSBURG

General Early's Confederate troops, marching from York to join Lee's army, camped June 30, three miles to the east. Arriving here next morning, they turned south toward Gettysburg on orders of General Ewell.

PENNSYLVANIA 34, THREE-TENTHS MILE SOUTH OF CARLISLE

June 30, 1863, General Ewell's Southern army, ordered to retire from Carlisle and rejoin Lee's army, marched over this road to Mount Holly Springs, York Springs, and Heidlersburg, where they camped for the night.

The End of the Road: The Army of the Potomac Arrives at Gettysburg

	George G. Meade	Maj. Gen.*	Midnight, July 1
FIRST CORPS	John F. Reynolds	Maj. Gen.	10 A.M. July 1
	Abner Doubleday	Maj. Gen.	10:15 A.M. July 1
	John Newton	Maj. Gen.	4 P.M. July 2
First Division	J. S. Wadsworth	Brig. Gen.	10 A.M. July 1
Second Division	J. C. Robinson	Brig. Gen.	10:30 A.M. July 1
Third Division	T. A. Rowley	Brig. Gen.	10:15 A.M. July 1
SECOND CORPS	Winfield S. Hancock	Maj. Gen.	4 P.M. July 1
	John Gibbon		About daylight, July 2
First Division	J. C. Caldwell	Brig. Gen.	About daylight, July 2
Second Division	John Gibbon	Brig. Gen.	About daylight, July 2
Third Division	Alexander Hays	Brig. Gen.	About daylight, July 2
THIRD CORPS	Daniel E. Sickles	Maj. Gen.	7 P.M. July 1
First Division	D. B. Birney	Maj. Gen.	5:30 P.M. July 1
Second Division	A. A. Humphreys	Brig. Gen.	1 A.M. July 2
FIFTH CORPS	George Sykes	Maj. Gen.	6 A.M. July 2
First Division	James Barnes	Brig. Gen.	6-7 A.M. July 2
Second Division	R. B. Ayres	Brig. Gen.	6-7 A.M. July 2
Third Division	S. W. Crawford	Brig. Gen.	6-7 A.M. July 2
SIXTH CORPS	John Sedgwick	Maj. Gen.	4 P.M. July 2
First Division	H. G. Wright	Brig. Gen.	4 P.M. July 2
Second Division	A. P. Howe	Brig. Gen.	4 P.M. July 2
Third Division	John Newton	Maj. Gen.	4 P.M. July 2
ELEVENTH CORPS	Oliver O. Howard	Maj. Gen.	11:30 A.M. July 1
First Division	F. C. Barlow	Brig. Gen.	1 P.M. July 1
Second Division	Adolph von Steinwehr	Brig. Gen.	1:30 P.M. July 1
Third Division	Carl Schurz	Maj. Gen.	1 P.M. July 1

TWELFTH CORPS	Henry W. Slocum	Maj. Gen.	7 P.M. July 1
First Division	A. S. Williams	Brig. Gen.	5:30 P.M. July 1
Second Division	J. W. Geary	Brig. Gen.	5 P.M. July 1
CAVALRY CORPS	Alfred Pleasonton	Maj. Gen.	
First Division	John Buford	Brig. Gen.	June 30
Second Division	D. McM. Gregg	Brig. Gen.	July 2
Third Division	Judson Kilpatrick	Brig. Gen.	July 2
Reserve Artillery	H. J. Hunt	Brig. Gen.	About daylight, July 2

*Based on reports in the *Official Records.*

The End of the Road: The Army of Northern Virginia Arrives

Corps	Lieut. General Commanding	No. of Divisions	No. of Brigades	Estimated strength (in round figures)
First—James Longstreet		3	11	19,000
Second—Richard S. Ewell		3	13	23,000
Third—Ambrose P. Hill		3	13	23,000
Cavalry—Maj. Gen. J. E. B. Stuart			7	12,500
Total		9	44	77,500

Lee had 287 guns, each corps having its own artillery reserve; 182 regiments of infantry, 32 regiments of cavalry, and 69 batteries of field artillery.

NORTHERN VIRGINIA	Robert E. Lee	General	1-2 P.M. July 1
FIRST CORPS	James Longstreet	Lieut. Gen.	4-5 P.M. July 1
McLaw's Division	Lafayette McLaws	Maj. Gen.	10 P.M. July 1
Pickett's Division	George E. Pickett	Maj. Gen.	4 P.M. July 2
Hood's Division	John B. Hood	Maj. Gen.	1-2 A.M. July 2
SECOND CORPS	Richard S. Ewell	Lieut. Gen.	About noon, July 1
Early's Division	Jubal A. Early	Maj. Gen.	2:30 P.M. July 1
Johnson's Division	Edward Johnson	Maj. Gen.	Dusk, July 1
Rodes's Division	Robert E. Rodes	Maj. Gen.	11-12 A.M. July 1
THIRD CORPS	Ambrose P. Hill	Lieut. Gen.	About 10 A.M. July 1
Anderson's Division	Richard H. Anderson	Maj. Gen.	4-5 P.M. July 1
Heth's Division	Henry Heth	Maj. Gen.	9 A.M. July 1
Pender's Division	William D. Pender	Maj. Gen.	11 A.M. July 1
CAVALRY CORPS	J. E. B. Stuart	Maj. Gen.	July 2

These are based on reports in the *Official Records.*

A Huge Task

In 1963, Col. A. B. Johnson, a West Point graduate and a career army officer, did some logistical work on the Army of the Potomac tramping through Loudoun County. For instance, he figured that fifteen thousand cavalry in column of fours would cover fifteen thousand yards or eight and a half miles. Seventy-seven thousand infantry in a column of fours would stretch forty thousand yards, or twenty-three miles. Added to this is thirty-five miles for the Union supply trains, and ten miles for the artillery batteries. Thus if the entire Army of the Potomac would line up on one road, it would reach from Gettysburg to the edge of Washington, or cover eighty-three and a half miles.

Colonel Johnson tabulated 15,000 horses for the cavalry, 6,100 for the artillery, 1,948 for the infantry officers, and 12,000 horses and mules for the supply trains, or 35,048 horses and mules. This is a staggering figure. Johnson figures five gallons of water per animal in the morning and five gallons in the evening, or over 350,000 gallons of water per day, plus drinking water for the soldiers.

To supply the Army of the Potomac, there were thirty wagons for every one thousand men. Allowing twenty yards per wagon for the three thousand wagons accompanying the 100,000 troops, thirty-five miles of road would be covered. Twelve pounds of oats or grain were rationed for the animals, plus fourteen pounds of hay. Fifty wagons were needed to carry food for the horses and mules in the supply train, and twenty-five wagons for the horses assigned to the artillery. So it was no easy task moving the troops on the Roads to Gettysburg.

534

EPILOGUE

"Remember the days of old and consider the years of many generations." Deuteronomy 32:8. That's what we have done in *Roads to Gettysburg*. Life moves at a faster pace now. There are cars and trucks instead of horses and wagons. We have radio and television instead of signal flags and couriers on horseback. There are interstate highways instead of dirt roads that served as avenues of travel one hundred years ago. The towns and cities have grown now. Life has changed. But in the summer of '63 Northern Virginia, Western Maryland, and Central Pennsylvania witnessed the move-

Just as the troopers and the civilians pictured above had their memories, so did all who were a part of the Roads to Gettysburg.

ment of the Blue and the Gray on the Roads to Gettysburg. Perhaps as we travel these older roads, we might visualize what it was like then. Maybe we can picture America's greatest military leaders traveling these roads, men like Robert E. Lee, George Meade, Winfield Scott Hancock, and a lot of lesser known officers and men. They are gone now. But we have a new America, a nation whose destiny was changed by those who traveled the Roads to Gettysburg in June of 1863.

NOTES

CHAPTER I (Pages 1-14)

1. William Kepler, *Fourth Regiment Ohio Volunteer Infantry* (Cleveland, 1886), p. 115.
2. Alexander S. Webb to James Watson Webb, May 12, 1863, Webb Papers. Yale University.
3. Augustus Buell, *The Cannoneer* (Washington, D.C.), p. 61.
4. John Gibbon, *Personal Recollections of the War* (New York, 1928), pp. 424-25.
5. George Meade (son) ed., *The Life and Letters of George Gordon Meade* (New York, 1913), vol. 1, p. 373.
6. *Idem.*
7. *Idem*, p. 385.
8. *The War of the Rebellion: A Compilation of the Official Records of the Union and Confederate Armies* (Washington, D.C., 1880-1891), vol. 25, pt. 2, pp. 377-78.
9. Noah Brooks, *Washington in Lincoln's Time* (New York, 1897), pp. 57-58.
10. War Department Records.
11. Meade, p. 372.
12. John Nichols, *Toward Gettysburg* (State College, 1958), pp. 183-84. This is an excellent book on John Fulton Reynolds. The research and documentation give many insights into the life of the great Pennsylvania general.
13. Edmund Brown, *The Twenty Seventh Indiana Volunteer Infantry*, p. 349.
14. *Ibid.*, p. 350.
15. *Ibid.*, p. 351.
16. *Idem.*
17. *Idem.*
18. *Ibid.*, p. 35'/.
19. *Ibid.*, p. 351.
20. Kepler, p. 117.
21. *Idem.*
22. *Ibid.*, pp. 117-18.
23. Orson B. Curtis, *The Twenty-fourth Michigan* (Detroit, 1891), p. 137.
24. *Idem.*
25. *Idem.*
26. *Ibid.*, p. 138.
27. *Ibid.*, p. 139.
28. *Idem.*
29. *Ibid.*, p. 141.
30. *Idem.*

31. John Smith, *The Nineteenth Maine* (Minneapolis, Minn., 1909), p. 54.

32. *Ibid.,* p. 55.

33. Charles D. Page, *Fourteenth Connecticut* (Meriden, Conn., 1906), pp. 129-30.

34. Francis Parker, *Thirty Second Massachusetts* (Boston, 1880), pp. 159-60.

35. Charles S. Wainwright, *A Diary of Battle, the Personal Journal of Colonel Charles S. Wainwright, 1861-1865,* ed. Allan Nevins (New York, 1962), p. 218.

36. Parker, p. 161.

37. Mary G. Green Brainard, *Campaigns of the One Hundred and Forty-Sixth Regiment New York State Volunteers* (New York, 1915), pp. 89-90.

38. Many regimental histories speak of the conduct at headquarters.

39. Earnest Waitt. *History of the Nineteenth Regiment, Massachusetts Volunteer Infantry* (Salem, Mass., 1906), p. 209.

40. *Ibid.,* p. 40.

41. *Ibid.,* p. 41.

42. *Idem.*

43. Waitt, p. 211.

CHAPTER II (Pages 15-26)

1. Robert E. Lee to Jefferson Davis, see the *Official Records,* cited hereafter as *O.R.* For the Lee-Davis correspondence check vol. 25, pp. 783, 842; and vol. 27, pt. 2, pp. 1071, 1074-77. Most of the Gettysburg material is contained in vol. 27, parts 1, 2, and 3.

2. *Ibid.*

3. John B. Gordon, *Reminiscences of the Civil War* (New York, 1903), p. 137.

4. *Ibid.,* p. 138.

5. *Ibid.,* p. 139.

6. *Ibid.,* pp. 139-40.

7. Edwin B. Coddington, *The Gettysburg Campaign: A Study in Command* (New York, 1968), p. 224.

8. *Idem.*

9. Lincoln to Hooker, *O.R.,* vol. 27, pt. 1, pp. 34-35.

10. *O.R.,* vol. 27, pt. 3, pp. 44-45, 54-55, 68-69.

11. Moses Veale, an address delivered at the unveiling of the monument to the 109th Pennsylvania Volunteers on Culp's Hill, September 11, 1889, p. 11.

12. *O.R.,* pt. 1, p. 213.

CHAPTER III (Pages 27-35)

1. John J. Pullen, *The Twentieth Maine* (Philadelphia, 1957), p. 82.

2. Wilbur S. Nye, *Here Come the Rebels!* (Baton Rouge, La., 1965), p. 4.

3. *Ibid.,* pp. 13, 20.

4. Jennings C. Wise, *The Long Arm of Lee* (Lynchburg, Va., 1915), vol. 2, p. 564.

5. Nye, p. 20.

6. *Ibid.,* p. 36.

7. Colonel Nye discussed this in "Lt. Gen. Richard S. Ewell in the Gettysburg Campaign," a paper presented before the Fifth Annual Civil War Study Group at Gettysburg, July 26, 1962.

8. Glenn Tucker, *High Tide at Gettysburg: The Campaign in Pennsylvania* (Indianapolis, 1958), p. 4.

9. Walter Clark, ed., *North Carolina Regiments* (Raleigh, N.C., 1901), vol. 1, p. 717.

10. Henry Heth, "Southern Historical Society Papers," vol. 4, p. 152.

11. The *Richmond Whig,* June 19, 1863.

12. *O.R.,* vol. 27, pt. 2, p. 293.

13. Jed Hotchkiss Diary, June 1863. The Jedediah Hotchkiss Papers are in the Manuscripts Division, Library of Congress.

14. Nye, p. 43.

15. *O.R.,* pt. 3, pp. 12-13.

16. Charles C. Coffin, *Marching to Victory* (New York, 1902), vol. 2, p. 167.

17. *O.R.,* pt. 3, p. 18.

18. Rufus Dawes, *Service With the Sixth Wisconsin* (Marietta, Ohio, 1890), p. 142.

19. *Idem.*

20. Thomas Chamberlain, *History of the One Hundred and Fiftieth Regiment, Pennsylvania Volunteers* (Philadelphia, 1905), p. 111.

21. *Ibid.,* p. 112.

22. Harry Warner, *Generals in Gray* (Baton Rouge, 1959), p. 237.

23. Alanson A. Haines, *History of the Fifteenth Regiment, New Jersey Volunteers* (New York, 1883), p. 69.

24. *O.R.,* pt. 2, p. 305.

25. Hotchkiss Diary, June 7, 1863. Jed was from New York, but settled in Staunton, Va., prior to the war. A civil engineer, he joined Jackson in 1861 and became corps topographer.

26. Daniel Grimsley of the Sixteenth Virginia Cavalry is quoted in John S. Mosby, *Stuart's Cavalry in the Gettysburg Campaign* (New York, 1908), p. 22. Grimsley lived for a long time at Culpeper.

CHAPTER IV (Pages 36-44)

1. *O.R.,* series 27, all in this series unless otherwise noted, pt. 3, p. 27.

2. *Ibid.,* pp. 868-69.

3. John Gibbon was saddened to learn of the death of Grimes Davis. He said, "I regard his death as the greatest loss this army has met with in a long time. He ought long ago to have been promoted, but such men, I am sorry to say, seldom get the positions to which their merit and services entitle them. . . . He would doubtless have risen to high command had he lived, provided his southern birth had not as always stood in his way. See Gibbon, p. 122.

4. For more about Brandy Station, see: The *Official Records,* vol. 27, pt. 2, pp. 679-85, 721-23, 726-38; pt. 3, pp. 902-5, 949-52, 961-62, 965-66, 985-86, 996-97, 1043-48, 1053-54. See also Mosby's writings, as well as Blackford's *War Years With Jeb Stuart,* pp. 263-95.

5. Coffin, p. 173.

6. *Idem.*

7. Coffin, p. 173.

8. Daniel Grimsley, captain, Company B, Sixth Virginia Cavalry, in a letter to John S. Mosby.

9. *O.R.,* pt. 1, p. 440. See also Rodes, p. 546.

10. Hotchkiss Diary, June 10. Nye, p. 71.

11. Levi W. Baker, *Ninth Massachusetts Battery* (South Framingham, Mass., 1888), p. 53.

12. *Ibid.*

13. *O.R.,* pt. 2, p. 546.

14. Hotchkiss Diary, June 11, 1863.

15. *O.R.*, vol. 27, pt. 1, pp. 57-58.

16. *Ibid.*, p. 56.

17. A. W. Bartlett, *History of the Twelfth New Hampshire Volunteers* (Concord, N.H., 1897), p. 113.

18. *Ibid.*

19. Milo M. Quaife, ed., *From the Cannon's Mouth: The Civil War Letters of General A. S. Williams* (Detroit, 1959), p. 212.

20. *Ibid.*, p. 213.

21. *Idem.*

22. Francis A. Walker, *History of the Second Army Corps in the Army of the Potomac* (New York, 1886), p. 258.

23. *O.R.*, pt. 3, p. 64.

CHAPTER V (Pages 45-96)

1. *O.R.*, pt. 3, pp. 67, 69.

2. *Ibid.*, p. 70.

3. *Ibid.*, p. 73.

4. Dawes, p. 151.

5. Curtis, pp. 145-46.

6. John W. Storrs, *The Twentieth Connecticut* (Ansonia, Conn., 1868), pp. 71-72.

7. William Todd, *History of the Ninth New York Regiment* (1889), p. 259.

8. Benjamin F. Cook, *History of the Twelfth Massachusetts Volunteers* (Boston, 1882), p. 97.

9. *O.R.*, pt. 2, p. 546, and Hotchkiss Diary for June 12, 1863.

10. *Ibid.*

11. *O.R.*, pt. 2, p. 547.

12. *Idem.*

13. Hotchkiss Diary, June 12.

14. *O.R.*, pt. 2, p. 188.

15. *Ibid.*, See pp. 189-92.

16. Thomas Marbaker, *The Eleventh New Jersey Volunteers* (Trenton, 1898), p. 85.

17. Curtis, p. 147.

18. Wainwright, p. 219.

19. Meade to his wife, June 16, 1863.

20. Meade to his wife, June 9, 1863.

21. *Idem.*

22. Brown, p. 359.

23. John R. Boyle, *Soldiers True: The Story of the One Hundred and Eleventh Pennsylvania Veteran Volunteers* (New York, 1903), p. 67.

24. *Idem.*

25. Brown, p. 356.

26. *Idem.*

27. *Idem.*

28. *Idem.*

29. Samuel Toombs, *Thirteenth New Jersey* (Orange, N.J., 1878), p. 65.

30. *Under the Maltese Cross, Campaigns of the 155th Pennsylvania Regiment* (Pittsburgh, 1910), p. 146.

31. *History of the Fifth Massachusetts Battery* (Boston, 1902), pp. 612-13.

32. Hartwell Osborn, *Trials and Triumphs: The Record of the Fifty-fifth Ohio Volunteers* (Chicago, 1904), p. 88.

33. Haines, pp. 69-70.

34. *Ibid.,* pp. 70-71.

35. *Idem.*

36. This episode is described in a penciled note in one of Jed Hotchkiss's field survey books. Map Division, Library of Congress.

37. *O.R.,* pt. 2, p. 460.

38. *Ibid.,* p. 547.

39. *Ibid.,* p. 548.

40. *Idem.*

41. When Colonel Nye did his research, local residents said they felt McReynolds took Virginia Road 761 that led to Stephenson's Depot. Some roads and routes are extremely difficult to trace today.

42. Nye, p. 89.

43. *O.R.,* vol. 27, pt. 2, p. 54.

44. Colonel Nye has an excellent description of this action in *Here Come the Rebels!,* pp. 108-23.

45. Nye, p. 128.

46. *Idem.*

47. *O.R.,* vol. 27, pt. 2, p. 548.

48. John C. West, *A Texan in Search of a Fight* (Waco, 1901), pp. 74-75.

49. Curtis, p. 147.

50. *Idem.*

51. Wainwright, p. 221.

52. George T. Stevens, *Three Years in the Sixth Corps* (Albany, New York, 1866), p. 223.

53. *Ibid.,* p. 225.

54. *Ibid.,* p. 226.

55. Toombs, p. 65.

56. *Idem.*

57. Waitt, p. 214.

58. Henry H. Humphreys, *Andrew Atkinson Humphreys: A Biography* (Philadelphia, 1924), p. 186.

59. *Idem.*

60. Charles W. Bardeen, *A Little Fifer's War Diary* (Syracuse, New York, 1910), p. 205.

61. *Idem.*

62. *Idem.*

63. *O.R.,* pt. 1, p. 530.

64. *Ibid.,* p. 542.

65. Bartlett, p. 114.

66. *155th Pennsylvania,* p. 147.

67. *Fifth Massachusetts Battery,* p. 612.

68. Osborn, p. 147.

69. George W. Bicknell, *History of the Fifth Maine Volunteers* (Portland, Maine, 1871), p. 236.

70. Roe, pp. 188-89.

71. Thomas G. Murphy, *The History of the First Regiment Delaware Veteran Volunteers* (Philadelphia, 1866), p. 112.

72. *O.R.,* pt. 2, p. 295.

541

73. William W. Hassler, ed., *The General to His Lady, the Letters of Dorsey Pender* (Chapel Hill, N.C., 1962), pp. 249-50.

74. J. F. F. Caldwell, *The History of the Brigade of South Carolinians Known First as "Gregg's and Subsequently as McGowan's Brigade* (Philadelphia, 1866), p. 91.

75. *O.R.*, pt. 2, pp. 612-13. For the Confederate advance, the route is detailed by the reports of R. S. Ewell, Jubal Early, Edward Johnson and Robert Rodes on pp. 440, 459, 460, 499, and 546. Anderson's day-by-day account of the march of his division is the best *O.R.* description of the route of the Third Corps on the Roads to Gettysburg.

76. C. G. ("Ham") Chamberlayne, *Virginian* (Richmond, 1932), p. 189.

77. Nye, p. 106, and Henry Kyd Douglas, *I Rode With Stonewall* (Chapel Hill, 1940), p. 234.

78. Randolph McKim, *A Soldier's Recollections of the War* (New York, 1910). See pp. 146-49.

79. Nye, p. 115.

80. Douglas, p. 234.

81. *O.R.*, pt. 2, pp. 548-49.

82. Nye, p. 123.

83. *O.R.*, pt. 2, p. 548.

84. *O.R.*, pt. 2, pp. 17-37, 39-40.

85. *Ibid.*, p. 38.

86. *Idem.*

87. *O.R.*, pt. 2, p. 549.

88. *Idem.*

89. *Idem.*

90. *Idem.*

91. Jacob Hoke, *The Great Invasion* (New edition, New York, 1959), p. 97.

92. Herman Schuricht, "Jenkins Brigade in the Gettysburg Campaign: Extracts from the Diary of Lieutenant Herman Schuricht, of the Fourteenth Virginia Cavalry," *Southern Historical Society Papers,* 24 (1896), p. 340. This is a very descriptive account of the brigade during those days in June of 1863.

93. Hoke, p. 107.

94. Harry Warner, *Generals in Gray* (Baton Rouge, La., 1959), p. 154.

95. Hoke, p. 101.

96. Lee's order No. 72 dictated fair and humane treatment.

97. *O.R.*, pt. 1, p. 36.

98. *Idem.* Issued June 15, 1863.

99. Coffin, p. 175.

100. *Idem.*

101. Coffin is one of the great writers of the war. Sadly, only one work has been done about him. See W. E. Griffis, *Charles Carleton Coffin: A Biography* (Boston, 1898).

102. Jacob Englebrecht, Diary, Frederick, Md., June of 1863.

103. *O.R.*, pt. 2, p. 453.

104. Douglas, p. 243.

105. Alexander S. ("Sandie") Pendleton to Kate Corbin, three miles north of Winchester, June 16, 1863. The collection is in the University of North Carolina Library at Chapel Hill. See also W. G. Bean, *Stonewall's Man, Sandie Pendleton* (Chapel Hill, 1959).

106. *Idem.*

107. *O.R.*, pt. 2, pp. 549-50.
108. *Idem.*
109. *Idem.*
110. Caldwell, p. 91.
111. Bicknell, p. 236.
112. Walker, p. 258.
113. *Idem.*
114. Joseph R. C. Ward, *History of the One Hundred and Sixth Regiment Pennsylvania Volunteers* (Philadelphia, 1906), pp. 171-72.
115. Tully, *Dear Belle, Letters From a Cadet Officer to His Sweetheart,* ed., Catherine S. Grary (Middletown, Conn., 1965), p. 202.
116. Smith, *Nineteenth Maine,* p. 56.
117. *Idem.*
118. *Idem.*
119. Robert L. Stewart, *History of the One Hundred and Fortieth Regiment, Pennsylvania Volunteers* (n.p.), p. 84.
120. *155th Pennsylvania,* p. 147.
121. *History of the One Hundred Eighteenth Pennsylvania Volunteers* (Philadelphia, 1905), pp. 220-21.
122. *118th Pennsylvania,* pp. 219-20.
123. Stevens, pp. 226-27.
124. *Idem.*
125. Haines, p. 73.
126. *Fifth Massachusetts Battery,* pp. 612-13.
127. The *Cumberland Union,* June 1863.
128. J. Thomas Scharf, *History of Western Maryland* (Baltimore, 1968. Reprint), vol. 1, p. 270.
129. *Idem.*
130. Englebrecht Diary, June 15, 1863.

CHAPTER VI (Pages 97-179)

1. Chamberlain, p. 113.
2. Charles E. Davis, Jr., *The Story of the Thirteenth Massachusetts Volunteers* (Boston, 1894), p. 213.
3. Andrew J. Boies, *Record of the Thirty-third Massachusetts Volunteer Infantry* (Fitchburg, Mass.), p. 215.
4. Davis, p. 213.
5. Warner, *Generals in Blue,* p. 363.
6. William P. Seville, *History of the First Regiment, Delaware Volunteers* (Wilmington, 1885), p. 78.
7. *Idem.*
8. Ward, p. 172.
9. Kepler, p. 120.
10. *Idem.*
11. Smith, *Nineteenth Maine,* p. 56.
12. Stewart, p. 84.
13. *Fifth Massachusetts Battery,* p. 613.
14. Martin A. Haynes, *History of the Second Regiment, New Hampshire Volunteers* (Manchester, 1865), p. 32.
15. *Ibid.,* p. 133.
16. *155th Pennsylvania,* p. 147.

17. Meade to his wife, June 16, 1863.

18. James L. Bowen, *History of the Thirty-seventh Regiment, Massachusetts Volunteers* (Holyoke, Mass.), p. 164.

19. The *Cumberland Union,* June 17, 1863.

20. *Idem.*

21. See *G.R.,* pt. 2, pp. 293-98.

22. *Ibid.,* p. 306.

23. *Ibid.,* p. 366.

24. *Ibid.,* p. 388.

25. *Ibid.,* p. 427.

26. Susan Pendleton Lee, *Memoirs of William Nelson Pendleton, D.D., Rector of Latimer Parish, Lexington, Virginia: Brigadier General, C.S.A: Chief of Artillery. Army of Northern Virginia* (Philadelphia, 1893). Pendleton's daughter quotes his letters home in the book about her father. The Pendleton Papers are located in the University of North Carolina Library.

27. *O.R.,* pt. 2, p. 348.

28. J. G. de Roulhac Hamilton, ed., *The Papers of Randolph Abbott Shotwell* (Raleigh, N.C., 1929), vol. 1. The writings of Shotwell provide a graphic picture of Roads to Gettysburg, and how a private soldier felt.

29. *Ibid.,* p. 447.

30. *Ibid.,* p. 448.

31. *Idem.*

32. Bunker Hill was the home of Ward Hill Lamon, close friend and bodyguard of President Lincoln. Lamon was master of ceremonies when Lincoln left Springfield, was with him at Antietam and Gettysburg, and was on the funeral train returning to Springfield. Lamon is buried in the Gerrardstown, W.Va., Presbyterian Cemetery.

33. Hoke, p. 106.

34. The Carlisle newspaper, June 19, 1863.

35. Caldwell, p. 91.

36. *O.R.,* pt. 3, pp. 173, 194.

37. *Ibid.,* p. 171.

38. *Ibid.,* p. 173.

39. *O.R.,* pt. 1, pp. 142-43. This gives the itinerary of the Army of the Potomac.

40. *Idem.*

41. When touring Loudoun County, a special effort should be made to see this church. Get a copy of *Loudoun County in the Civil War,* published by the Centennial Committee (Leesburg, 1861).

42. Curtis, p. 149.

43. Donald L. Smith, *The Twenty-fourth Michigan* (Harrisburg, 1962), p. 115.

44. Dawes, p. 153.

45. *Idem,* and Henry G. Pearson, *James Wadsworth of Geneseo* (New York, 1913), p. 197.

46. Abram P. Smith, *History of the Seventy Sixth Regiment, New York Volunteers* (Cortland, N.Y., 1867), pp. 227-28.

47. Chamberlain, p. 110.

48. *O.R.,* pt. 3, pp. 118, 147; and the Letters of A. S. Williams, p. 212.

49. Shotwell Papers, vol. 1, p. 477.

50. Waitt, p. 214.

51. O. O. Howard, *Autobiography* (New York, 1907), vol. 1, p. 390.

52. Page, p. 130.
53. *Idem.*
54. Grary, McCrae Letters, p. 202.
55. Stewart, p. 85.
56. Gibbon, p. 125.
57. *Idem.*
58. Oliver O. Davis, *Life of David Bell Birney* (Philadelphia, 1867), p. 178.
59. *Ibid.,* p. 179.
60. Edwin B. Houghton, *The Campaigns of the Seventeenth Maine* (Portland, 1866), p. 74.
61. *Idem.*
62. Bartlett, p. 115.
63. *155th Pennsylvania,* p. 149.
64. *Idem.*
65. Brainerd, p. 101.
66. *118th Pennsylvania,* pp. 220-21.
67. Baker, p. 310.
68. Englebrecht Diary, June 17, 1863. This is a classic for life in Frederick, prior to and during the war. It has just recently been translated and printed.
69. Howard, p. 385.
70. Kepler, p. 85.
71. A. S. Williams Letters, p. 214.
72. *Idem.*
73. *O.R.,* pt. 3, pp. 171-72.
74. *Ibid.,* p. 174.
75. *Ibid.,* p. 175.
76. John Divine lives in Waterford and is most knowledgeable about the Civil War in historic and beautiful Loudoun County. He helped Colonel Nye with, *Here Come the Rebels!*
77. *O.R.,* pt. 3, p. 176.
78. *Ibid.,* p. 178.
79. *Ibid.,* p. 180.
80. *Ibid.,* p. 184.
81. *Ibid.,* p. 177.
82. *O.R.,* pt. 2, p. 366.
83. Shotwell Papers, vol. 1, p. 228.
84. Calvin L. Collier, *They'll Do To Tie To!* Third Arkansas Infantry Regiment, C.S.A. (Little Rock, 1959), p. 128.
85. *O.R.,* pt. 2, p. 613.
86. Shotwell, vol. 1, p. 479.
87. *Ibid.,* p. 480.
88. Caldwell, pp. 91-92.
89. Englebrecht Diary.
90. *O.R.,* pt. 2, p. 550.
91. *Idem.*
92. Hotchkiss Diary, June 17, 1863.
93. Douglas, p. 243.
94. Curtis, p. 144.
95. Smith, *Nineteenth Maine,* p. 172.
96. Osborn, p. 88.
97. *O.R.,* pt. 3, p. 194.
98. *Idem.*
99. *Ibid.,* p. 196.

100. *Ibid.*, p. 198.
101. *Ibid.*, p. 202.
102. *Idem.*
103. *118th Pennsylvania*, p. 220.
104. Near Bull Run.
105. *118th Pennsylvania*, p. 220.
106. *Idem.*
107. A. S. Williams, *Letters*, pp. 214-15.
108. *Ibid.*, p. 216.
109. Arthur Crew Inman, ed., *Soldier of the South: General Pickett's War Letters to His Wife* (Boston, 1928), p. 42.
110. *Idem.*
111. *Ibid.*
112. Shotwell Papers, vol. 1, p. 717.
113. *Ibid.*, p. 719.
114. *O.R.*, pt. 2, p. 503.
115. Douglas, p. 243.
116. Hotchkiss Diary, June 18, 1863.
117. Mary Bedinger Mitchell, *Battles and Leaders*, eds. Robert U. Johnson and Clarence C. Buel (Boston, 1887), p. 686.
118. Susan Lee, p. 279.
119. McKim, p. 160.
120. Henry Robinson Berkeley, *Hanover Virginia Artillery, Four Years in the Confederate Artillery: The Diary of Private Henry Robinson Berkeley*, ed., William H. Runge, p. 46.
121. John Reynolds to his sisters, June 22, 1863. This was his last letter, written and addressed from Guilford Station where the First Corps encamped, June 19-24. The Lancaster Franklin and Marshall Library in Lancaster, Pa., contains a wealth of Reynolds material and private papers.
122. David S. Sparks, *Inside Mr. Lincoln's Army: The Diary General Marsena Patrick, Provost Marshal General, Army of the Potomac* (New York, 1964), p. 261.
123. Smith, *24th Michigan*, p. 115.
124. John D. Vautier, *History of the 88th Pennsylvania* (Philadelphia, 1894), p. 103.
125. Abner R. Small, *The Sixteenth Maine in the War of Rebellion* (Portland, Maine, 1886), p. 113.
126. *Ibid.*, p. 114.
127. Waitt, pp. 214-15.
128. Kepler, p. 121.
129. Bartlett, p. 115.
130. Houghton, p. 75.
131. *Idem.*
132. David Craft, *History of the One Hundred Forty-first Regiment, Pennsylvania Volunteers* (Towanda, Pa., 1885), p. 109.
133. *Idem.*
134. Marbaker, p. 83.
135. *118th Pennsylvania*, pp. 220-21.
136. *Ibid.*, p. 222.
137. A. S. Williams, *Letters*, p. 216.
138. *Ibid.*

139. John Se Cheverrell, *Journal History of Twenty-ninth Ohio Veteran Volunteers* (Cleveland, 1883), p. 67.
140. *O.R.*, pt. 3, p. 209.
141. *Ibid.*, pp. 209-10.
142. *Idem.*
143. *Idem.*
144. *O.R.*, pt. 2, p. 357.
145. *Ibid.*, p. 371.
146. Shotwell, p. 481.
147. Hotchkiss Diary, June 19, 1863.
148. *O.R.*, pt. 2, p. 464.
149. *Ibid.*, p. 551.
150. Douglas, p. 244.
151. *O.R.*, pt. 2, p. 599.
152. Nye, p. 236.
153. *Ibid.*, p. 237.
154. *Idem.*
155. *Idem.*
156. The *Philadelphia Daily Evening Bulletin*, June 20, 1863.
157. *O.R.*, pt. 3, p. 224.
158. *Ibid.*, pp. 228-29.
159. *Ibid.*, p. 273.
160. *O.R.*, pt. 3, p. 48, offers a graphic description of the Potomac River crossings.
161. *Ibid.*, p. 283.
162. *Ibid.*, p. 272.
163. *Idem.*
164. *O.R.*, pt. 3, p. 289.
165. *Idem.*
166. *Ibid.*, p. 292.
167. *Idem.*
168. *O.R.*, pt. 3, p. 262.
169. Gibbon, p. 169.
170. Grary, McCrae's Letter, p. 202.
171. Ward, p. 173.
172. Smith, *Nineteenth Maine*, p. 57.
173. Stevens, p. 231.
174. *Ibid.*, pp. 235-36.
175. *O.R.*, pt. 2, p. 371.
176. *Ibid.*, p. 428.
177. Shotwell Papers, vol. 1, pp. 481-82.
178. Caldwell, p. 92.
179. Lt. Col. Arthur Fremantle, *Three Months in the Southern States: April-June, 1863* (New York, 1864), p. 177.
180. *O.R.*, pt. 2, p. 251.
181. *Ibid.*, p. 297.
182. Hotchkiss Diary, June 20 and 21, 1863.
183. Early and Johnson of the Second Corps, as well as A. P. Hill and the Third Corps crossed the Potomac at Shepherdstown.
184. Berkeley, p. 48.
185. *Philadelphia Daily Evening Bulletin*, June 20, 1863.
186. Schaff, pp. 22-23.

187. Nye, p. 239.

188. *Ibid.*, pp. 239-40.

189. This was Gilmor's force. He tells about it on page 94 in his book. Jacob Englebrecht mentions the event in his diary account of the day.

190. Gilmor, pp. 93-94.

191. *O.R.*, pt. 1, p. 911.

192. *Ibid.*, p. 614.

193. A. S. Williams, p. 217.

194. *Ibid.*, p. 218.

195. Marbaker, p. 86.

196. *118th Pennsylvania*, p. 226.

197. *Ibid.*, p. 227.

198. Osborn, p. 88.

199. Daniel G. MacNamara, *The History of the Ninth Regiment, Massachusetts Volunteer Infantry. . . . June 1861-June 1864* (Boston, 1889), p. 310.

200. *O.R.*, pt. 3, p. 249.

201. *Ibid.*, pt. 1, p. 21.

202. John M. Gould and Leonard G. Jordan, *History of the First-Tenth-Twenty Ninth Maine Regiment* (Portland, 1871), p. 352.

203. Shotwell Papers, p. 483.

204. Private letters of J. W. Russell, Loudoun County, Virginia.

205. Fremantle, p. 179.

206. Spencer Welch, *A Confederate Surgeon's Letters to His Wife* (New York, 1911), pp. 55-57.

207 *O.R.*, pt. 1, p. 65.

208. *O.R.*, pt. 2, p. 443.

209. McKim, p. 158.

210. *Idem.*

211. Hotchkiss Diary, June 21.

212. McKim, pp. 159-60.

213. Welch, p. 53.

214. Hoke, p. 54.

215. Curtis, p. 150.

216. Pearson, p. 198.

217. Gould, p. 353.

218. Englebrecht Diary, June 21.

219. Gibbon, p. 172.

220. Gould, p. 352.

221. Fremantle, p. 180.

222. Warner, *Generals in Gray*, pp. 310-11.

223. *Idem.*

224. *O.R.*, pt. 2, p. 443.

225. *Ibid.*, p. 464.

226. McKim, p. 160.

227. Berkeley, p. 49.

228. Hoke, p. 124.

229. *Ibid.*, p. 125.

230. See Nye, pp. 245-50.

231. *O.R.*, pt. 2, p. 464.

232. Caldwell, p. 97.

233. *O.R.*, pt. 2, p. 307.

234. Fremantle, p. 181.

235. *O.R.,* pt. 3, p. 216.
236. *Ibid.,* p. 267.
237. *Ibid.,* p. 271.
238. *Ibid.,* p. 273.
239. *Fifth Massachusetts Battery,* pp. 615-16.
240. Englebrecht Diary. This may be read at the C. Burr Artz Library in Frederick.
241. *O.R.,* pt. 3, p. 275.

CHAPTER VII (Pages 180-222)

1. *O.R.,* pt. 3, pp. 289-90.
2. *O.R.,* pt. 2, p. 551.
3. Warner, *Generals in Gray,* pp. 251-52.
4. Susan Lee, p. 279.
5. Hoke, p. 135.
6. Hotchkiss Diary, June 24, 1863.
7. *O.R.,* pt. 2, p. 358.
8. Garnet Jex has an excellent series of paintings of the war along the Potomac River. Most of them can be seen in the Williamsport, Maryland, bank.
9. George Pickett, *Soldier of the South* (Boston, 1925), p. 81.
10. *Idem.*
11. Shotwell Papers, vol. 1, pp. 483-84, 486.
12. *Idem.*
13. *Idem.*
14. William C. Oates, *The War Between the Union and the Confederacy* (New York, 1905), p. 198.
15. John West to his wife.
16. Fremantle, p. 172.
17. *O.R.,* pt. 2, p. 465.
18. Schaff, pp. 22-23.
19. The *Greencastle Pilot,* June 28, 1863.
20. Gilmor, p. 94.
21. Schaff, pp. 22-23.
22. Gilmor, p. 94.
23. McKim, p. 163.
24. The Hanover Chamber of Commerce, *Encounter at Hanover* (Gettysburg, 1962), p. 116.
25. Warner, *Generals in Gray,* pp. 9-10.
26. James L. Morrison, ed., *The Memoirs of Henry Heth* (Westport, Conn., 1974). This is a very good book about Heth, a good commander who always seemed to have bad luck.
27. Warner, *Generals in Gray,* p. 133.
28. Pender to his wife on June 24. See also Hassler's book about Pender and his letters to his wife.
29. *Idem.*
30. Nye, pp. 298-300.
31. *Idem.*
32. *Ibid.,* p. 303.
33. *O.R.,* pt. 3, pp. 298-301.
34. See *Ferry Hill Plantation Journal,* ed. Fletcher Green (Chapel Hill, 1961). This is an excellent book about the events taking place in the early history of

Ferry Hill, the home of Henry Kyd Douglas, and Edward Johnson's headquarters in June of '63. The home has now been purchased to be the headquarters of the Chesapeake and Ohio Canal National Park.

35. *O.R.,* pt. 3, pp. 287, 290.
36. *Ibid.,* p. 286.
37. *Ibid.,* p. 289.
38. *Ibid.,* p. 290.
39. *Ibid.,* p. 292.
40. *Ibid.,* p. 295.
41. The Webb Papers at Yale University.
42. *Idem.*
43. Webb to his wife later that same day in June.
44. Howard, p. 390.
45. *Idem.*
46. *O.R.,* pt. 3, p. 305.
47. Kepler, p. 89.
48. Chamberlain, p. 111.
49. *O.R.,* pt. 3, pp. 305-7.
50. *Ibid.,* p. 310.
51. *Ibid.,* p. 312.
52. *Ibid.,* p. 315.
53. *Ibid.,* p. 317.
54. Pearson, p. 199.
55. Vautier, p. 103.
56. Wainwright, p. 224.
57. Pearson, p. 199.
58. Chamberlain, p. 113.
59. Baker, p. 54.
60. Edwin B. Houghton, *The Campaigns of the Seventeenth Maine* (Portland, 1867), p. 74. Actually the Potomac was closer to fourteen hundred feet wide at the crossing.
61. Bardeen, p. 209.
62. Bartlett, p. 116.
63. *Ibid.,* p. 117.
64. Warren Cudworth, *History of the First Regiment, Massachusetts Infantry* (Boston, 1866), p. 386.
65. *Idem.*
66. Haynes, p. 134.
67. Marbaker, p. 87.
68. *O.R.,* pt. 3, p. 329.
69. Kepler, p. 122.
70. Ward, p. 174.
71. William Child, *A History of the Fifth Regiment New Hampshire Volunteers* (Bristol, N.H., 1893), p. 203.
72. Gibbon, pp. 126-27.
73. Smith, *Nineteenth Maine,* p. 58.
74. *O.R.,* pt. 1, p. 345.
75. Ward, pp. 174-75.
76. *Ibid.,* p. 176.
77. *Fifth Massachusetts Battery,* pp. 617-18.
78. Meade to his wife, June 25.
79. Meade, *Life and Letters,* vol. 1, p. 389.

80. *Idem.*

81. *O.R.,* pt. 3, p. 314.

82. Fremantle, p. 185.

83. *Ibid.,* p. 186.

84. Dickert, *History of Kershaw's Brigade,* is one of the best First Corps accounts of the march.

85. *Ibid.,* p. 230.

86. William M. Owen, *In Camp and Battle With the Washington Artillery of New Orleans* (Boston, 1885), p. 240. Most likely the Confederate infantry advanced on Greencastle after crossing the river, using two roads: first, the main road or what is now U.S. 11 northward through Hagerstown. However, there is good reason to believe that most of the Confederate foot soldiers took the old road to Huyetts Crossroads, or what is now Maryland Route 63.

87. Shotwell, p. 488.

88. *Ibid.,* p. 489.

89. *Idem.*

90. Fitzgerald Ross, while visiting the United States, gives his account of Roads to Gettysburg.

91. Eppa Hunton, *Autobiography* (Richmond, 1933), p. 87.

92. Inman, p. 41.

93. Owen, p. 242.

94. *Idem.*

95. *Century* Magazine, vol. 70, p. 259.

96. Pender to his wife.

97. *Idem.*

98. Chamberlayne, p. 188.

99. *Ibid.,* p. 189.

100. Hoke, p. 150.

101. Hotchkiss Diary, June 25, 1863.

102. *O.R.,* pt. 2, pp. 464-66.

103. The *Carlisle Evening Sentennial,* June 16, 1863.

104. The editions of the *Sentennial* the last two weeks in June are most interesting.

CHAPTER VIII (Pages 223-270)

1. Harriett W. Stewart, *History of Cumberland County,* p. 104; and Hotchkiss Diary, June 26, 1863.

2. Hoke, pp. 161-62.

3. *Ibid.,* p. 169.

4. Fremantle, p. 187.

5. Susan P. Lee, pp. 279-80.

6. *Idem.*

7. John B. Hood, *Advance and Retreat* (New Orleans, 1880), p. 54.

8. *Idem.*

9. Harold B. Simpson, *Hood's Texas Brigade, Lee's Grenadier Guard* (Waco, 1970), pp. 248-56.

10. Joseph B. Polley, *Hood's Texas Brigade* (New York, 1910), p. 147.

11. *Ibid.,* p. 148.

12. Simpson, p. 252.

13. J. B. Polley, *A Soldier's Letters to Charming Nellie* (New York, 1908), p. 121.

14. John W. Stevens, *Reminiscences of the Civil War* (Hillsboro, Tex., published in the *Hillsboro Mirror*, 1902), pp. 105-6.

15. *Ibid.*, p. 106.

16. Polley, *A Soldier's Letters*, p. 121.

17. Shotwell, p. 490.

18. *Idem.*

19. Dickert, p. 288.

20. Inman, p. 43.

21. *Idem.*

22. Ross, p. 35.

23. McKim, p. 163.

24. Gilmor, p. 95.

25. Hotchkiss Diary, June 26, 1863.

26. McKim, pp. 165-66.

27. Hoke, p. 170.

28. Jubal A. Early to Professor J. Fraire Richard, May 7, 1886.

29. Colonel Nye has an excellent description of the advance, pp. 266-77.

30. *O.R.*, pt. 2, p. 465.

31. In the fighting, a Pennsylvania lad fell near Cemetery Hill. He was Cpl. George W. Sandoe. The young man is buried in the Mount Joy Lutheran Cemetery along the Harney Road.

32. For the accounts of the fighting near the Witmer farm, see *Here Come the Rebels!*

33. Nye, p. 275.

34. Noble D. Preston, *History of the Tenth Regiment of Cavalry, New York State Volunteers* (New York, 1892), p. 125.

35. Jacobs, p. 35.

36. *Idem.*

37. *Encounter at Hanover*, p. 115.

38. *O.R.*, pt. 2, pp. 465-66.

39. *Idem.*

40. Isaac Trimble, *The Confederate Veteran*, vol. 25, p. 210 ff.

41. Curtis, p. 150.

42. Davis, p. 219.

43. Curtis, p. 150.

44. Pearson, p. 200.

45. *Idem.*

46. Dawes, p. 156.

47. Davis, p. 219.

48. Abram Smith, *76th New York*, p. 229.

49. Chamberlain, p. 112.

50. William H. Locke, *Story of the Regiment (Eleventh Pennsylvania)* (Philadelphia, 1868), pp. 218-19.

51. Marbaker, p. 87.

52. Bardeen, p. 211.

53. Cudworth, p. 398.

54. Regis De Trobriand, *Four Years in the Army of the Potomac* (Boston, 1889), p. 521.

55. *155th Pennsylvania*, p. 150.

56. James L. Bowen, *History of the Thirty-seventh Regiment Massachusetts Volunteers* (Holyoke, 1884), p. 166.

57. Haines, p. 75.

58. Stevens, pp. 235-36.

59. *O.R.*, pt. 3, pp. 336-38.

60. *Idem.*

61. Osborn, p. 89.

62. Louis N. Benudry (also spelled Boudrye on the title page, hereafter cited as Benudry), *Historic Records of the Fifth New York Cavalry* (Albany, 1868), p. 63.

63. Publication Committee of the Regimental Association, *History of the Eighteenth Regiment of Cavalry, Pennsylvania Volunteers* (New York, 1909), p. 38.

64. Walker, p. 314.

65. Franklin Sawyer, *A Military History of the Eighth Regiment Onio Volunteer Infantry* (Cleveland, 1881), p. 121.

66. *Ibid.*, p. 122.

67. Schenk to Hancock.

68. Hoke, p. 329.

69. Waitt, p. 216.

70. *Idem.*

71. *O.R.*, pt. 3, p. 339.

72. *Ibid.*, p. 341.

73. *Ibid.*, p. 344.

74. *Ibid.*, p. 345.

75. H. P. Moyer, *History of the Seventeenth Regiment, Pennsylvania Volunteer Cavalry* (n.d.), pp. 57-58.

76. A. S. Williams, *Letters*, pp. 217-18. He says the width of the Potomac was a quarter of a mile.

77. Brown, p. 360.

78. George K. Collins, *Memoirs of the 149th Regiment New York Volunteer Infantry* (Syracuse, 1891), p. 128.

79. Davis, p. 215.

80. *O.R.*, pt. 3, p. 292.

81. Gideon Welles Diary, vol. 1, p. 340.

82. *O.R.*, pt. 3, p. 337; and Diary of Newton Heston Mack, Co. K, 153 Pennsylvania, June 27, 1863.

83. *O.R.*, pt. 1, pp. 942-43.

84. Isaac Trimble, *The Confederate Veteran*, vol. 15, p. 200 ff.

85. Sorrel, p. 73.

86. Coffin, p. 197.

87. See Longstreet's Report in *O.R.*, vol. 2 and *From Manassas to Appomattox*.

88. *Idem.*

89. Holley, p. 147.

90. Robert Stiles, *Four Years Under Marse Robert* (New York, 1903), p. 199.

91. Sorrel, p. 177.

92. Inman, *Soldier of the South*, p. 48.

93. Shotwell, vol. 1, p. 491.

94. *Ibid.*, p. 492.

95. *Ibid.*, p. 493.

96. Fremantle, p. 189.

553

97. *Ibid.,* p. 190.
98. John J. West to his wife.
99. The *Carlisle Enterprise,* June 30, 1863.
100. *Idem.* See also the description in *Here Come the Rebels!*
101. Mrs. Belten's notes for June 27, 1863.
102. Stiles, p. 199 ff.
103. Hotchkiss Diary, June 27, 1863.
104. "Sandie" Pendleton to Kate Corbin, June 28, 1863.
105. *Idem.*
106. The *Carlisle Enterprise,* June 30, 1863.
107. McKim, pp. 165-66.
108. Douglas, p. 246.
109. *Encounter at Hanover,* pp. 34-35.
110. *Ibid.,* p. 117.
111. *Ibid.,* p. 116.
112. *Ibid.,* p. 120.
113. From accounts appearing in the *Hanover Spectator* and the *Hanover Citizen,* local papers in 1863.
114. *O.R.,* pt. 2, pp. 465-66.
115. *Encounter at Hanover,* p. 36.
116. Pender to his wife, June 28, 1863.

CHAPTER IX (Pages 271-289)

1. William Nelson Pendleton was born in 1809, and graduated from West Point in 1830. He became a professor of mathematics at the academy, and then resigned to become the headmaster at the Episcopal High School in Alexandria. In 1838, he was ordained and after serving some rural parishes, he became rector of All Saints Church in Frederick, Maryland. The Pendleton family lived in sight of the Clustered Spires from 1846 to 1854. Then it was on to Lexington, Virginia, where Nelson and his son "Sandie" became acquainted with the folks at Washington College and also Virginia Military Institute.
2. Curtis, p. 152.
3. Dawes, p. 156.
4. Craft, p. 110.
5. Sawyer, p. 122.
6. Bartlett, p. 118.
7. Wainwright, p. 225.
8. *Idem,* and Sawyer, p. 122.
9. Livermore, pp. 231-32.
10. Waitt, p. 217.
11. A. S. Williams, p. 32.
12. *Ibid.,* p. 43.
13. *Eighteenth Pennsylvania Cavalry,* p. 38.
14. Hillman A. Hall, *History of the Sixth New York Cavalry* (Worcester, 1908), p. 132.
15. Moyer, p. 58.
16. *O.R.,* pt. 3, p. 349.
17. Hays, *Sixty-third Pennsylvania,* p. 190.
18. Houghton, p. 79.
19. Marbaker, pp. 87-88.
20. Bardeen, p. 211.

21. Marbaker, pp. 88-89.
22. *155th Pennsylvania*, p. 150.
23. *118th Pennsylvania*, p. 231.
24. *Ibid.*, p. 232.
25. Englebrecht Diary, June 27, 1863.
26. Baker, pp. 55-56.
27. *New York at Gettysburg* (Albany, 1900), vol. 2, p. 622.
28. Haines, p. 75.
29. Bowen, p. 167.
30. Collins, p. 128.
31. Harpers Ferry was considered indefensible.
32. Meade, vol. 2, p. 3.
33. Locke, p. 220.
34. Dawes, p. 156.
35. Craft, p. 110.
36. Charles E. Slocum, *The Life and Services of Major General Henry Warner Slocum* (Toledo, 1913), p. 98.
37. *5th Massachusetts Battery*, p. 619.
38. Henry R. Pyne, *The History of the First New Jersey Cavalry* (Trenton, 1871), p. 161.
39. Abner Hard, *Eighth Illinois Cavalry* (Aurora, Ill., 1868), p. 264.
40. Benudry, p. 63.
41. Ward, p. 176.
42. Gould, p. 353.
43. *O.R.*, pt. 3, p. 349.

CHAPTER X (Pages 290-340)

1. Charles F. Benjamin, "Hooker's Appointment and Removal," *Battles and Leaders* (New York, 1884), vol. 3, pp. 239-43.
2. William Henry Powell, *The Fifth Army Corps* (New York, 1896), p. 500. Lt. Col. F. T. Locke, assistant adjutant general of the Fifth Corps, was awakened at 2:00 A.M. It was someone looking for General Meade. It was Colonel Hardie. Locke told the officer that Meade was in the next tent. "Soon I heard loud talking on the part of General Meade. . . . I thought the General had been placed in arrest. Soon I heard him calling for his orderly, his horse, and one of his aides. Soon after the party mounted and rode off. . . . In a few hours Captain Mason returned with the news that Meade was in command of the, Army of the Potomac. . . . I was directed to inform General Sykes that he was in command of the Fifth Corps."
3. *Meade's Life and Letters,* vol. 2, pp. 1-13.
4. Benudry, p. 64.
5. Nichols, p. 190.
6. *Idem.*
7. Meade, vol. 2, pp. 1-13.
8. See B. and L., vol. 3, pp. 238-43.
9. Marbaker, p. 88.
10. *Idem.*
11. Coffin witnessed the change of command, and wrote about it that evening from a home in Frederick.
12. "Sandie" Pendleton to Kate Corbin, June 28, 1863, and Bean, pp. 136-37.
13. *Idem.*

14. *North Carolina Regiments*, vol. 11, pp. 525-26.
15. Jacobs, p. 15.
16. Several soldiers and civilians speak of the fog.
17. *Michigan at Gettysburg* (Detroit, 1889), vol. 1, p. 177. The Michigan Cavalry regiments were on patrol today. Some were with Copeland as he rode into Gettysburg this Sunday. Therefore, Buford was not really the first Union Cavalry to arrive in Gettysburg. It is thought that Custer was inspecting the various cavalry pickets ringing Frederick.
18. Stiles, pp. 202-4.
19. Gordon, p. 141. His description of the entrance to York is very fine.
20. *O.R.,* pt. 2, p. 466.
21. *Idem.*
22. *Idem.*
23. Early felt he treated the folks in York very fairly.
24. Gordon, pp. 140-41.
25. Gordon, p. 141.
26. *Ibid.,* p. 142.
27. *Ibid.,* p. 143.
28. *Ibid.,* p. 147.
29. *Idem.*
30. See the old copies of the *York Gazette.*
31. Nye, p. 293.
32. *Idem.*
33. Klein, p. 46.
34. Klein, pp. 43-54, and Scharf, vol. 1, p. 270.
35. *O.R.,* pt. 1, p. 758.
36. Wilson, p. 252.
37. Brown, p. 361.
38. Collins, p. 129.
39. Boyle, pp. 109-10.
40. Hoke, p. 39.
41. Owen, p. 242.
42. Hoke, p. 197.
43. Shotwell, vol. 1, p. 493.
44. Inman, p. 88.
45. Fremantle, p. 193.
46. *Idem.*
47. Moore, pp. 151-52.
48. *O.R.,* pt. 2, p. 366.
49. Chamberlayne, pp. 167-68.
50. Hotchkiss Diary, June 28, 1863.
51. *Idem,* and the Carlisle newspapers.
52. See Percy Hamlin, *Old Bald Head* (Strasburg, Va., 1940).
53. Welch, pp. 57-58.
54. William Christian to his wife.
55. *North Carolina Regiments,* vol. 2, p. 342.
56. Hoke, p. 199.
57. Sawyer, p. 122, and Kepler, p. 123.
58. The story of Colonel Cross was printed in *Civil War Illustrated,* and is from their files.
59. Grary, p. 204.
60. Gibbon, p. 128.

61. Waitt, p. 217.
62. Gibbon, p. 129.
63. *O.R.*, pt. 1, p. 663.
64. *Ibid.*, p. 669.
65. Roe, p. 204.
66. Hutchinson, p. 150.
67. Bowen, p. 167.
68. *Idem.*
69. Smith, *77th New York*, p. 236.
70. See Roe and Hutchinson for June 28.
71. *O.R.*, pt. 1, p. 961.
72. Thomas J. Scharf, *History of Western Maryland* (Philadelphia, 1882), vol. 1.
73. Benudry, p. 63.
74. *Washington National Intelligencer*, June 29, 1863.
75. *O.R.*, pt. 3, p. 381.
76. D. H. L. Gleason, *A History of the First Regiment of Massachusetts Cavalry* (Boston, 1891), pp. 162-63.
77. Bardeen, p. 211.
78. Houghton, p. 79.
79. Cudworth, p. 390.
80. Houghton, p. 82.
81. *Ibid.*, p. 83.
82. Humphries, pp. 186-87.
83. De Troibrand, p. 525.
84. Marbaker, p. 89.
85. *O.R.*, pt. 3, p. 243.
86. *Ibid.*, p. 295.
87. *Ibid.*, p. 297.
88. Dawes, p. 157.
89. *Ibid.*, p. 158.
90. Small, p. 114.
91. Hard, pp. 254-55.
92. John Reynolds's uncle had four daughters: Mary Catherine, Margareta, Lydia Eleanor, and Sarah. None of the four married. Catherine lived in a two-story L-shaped home, typical of the day, at 9 West Second Street. The home was torn down in 1925. For a while it was the location of the Elks Club. Then it was destroyed by a fire several years ago. Now Maas opticians occupy the site.
93. Gibbon, p. 130.
94. Wainwright, p. 227.
95. *Ibid.*, p. 228.
96. Locke, p. 221.
97. Alfred Pleasonton in *Annals of the War*, p. 452.
98. *O.R.*, pt. 1, p. 926.
99. *Ibid.*, p. 913.
100. Whittaker, p. 161.
101. *Idem.*
102. *O.R.*, pt. 1, p. 991.
103. Preston, p. 103.
104. Warner, *Generals in Blue*, pp. 108-9.
105. There are many books on Custer. For his activity on the Roads to

Gettysburg, check his reports, as well as those of Pleasonton and Kilpatrick in the *O.R.*
106. *New York at Gettysburg*, vol. 3, p. 1039.
107. Coffin had a busy day in Frederick. See *Marching to Victory* and *The Boys of '61.*
108. *O.R.*, vol. 3, p. 375.
109. Rev. Theodore Gerrish, *A Private's Reminiscences of the Civil War* (Portland, 1882), pp. 95-96.
110. *Ibid.*, p. 97.
111. Birney, p. 181.
112. *O.R.*, pt. 3, pp. 370, 374. Using an 1870 map of Frederick, and using the old roads, the mileage stated in regimental histories has been checked as to the location of army units. It seems as though the Artillery Reserve was camped at Rose Hill Manor and on the grounds of what is now Governor Thomas Johnson High School. The cavalry was three and one-half miles north of Frederick on the historic Richfield farm.
113. *O.R.*, pt. 3, p. 400.
114. *Ibid.*, pt. 1, p. 707.
115. *Ibid.*, p. 708.

CHAPTER XI (Pages 341-356)

1. Warner, *Generals in Gray*, pp. 192-93. Longstreet in *From Manassas to Appomattox* has very little to say about getting to Gettysburg. He does make it a point to stress his disagreements with Lee over strategy and the conduct of the campaign.
2. Warner, pp. 84-85.
3. *Ibid.*, pp. 134-35. Two fine books exist on Hill. They are: William W. Hassler, *Ambrose Powell Hill, Lee's Forgotten General* (Richmond, 1957), and Martin Schenck's *Up Came Hill* (Harrisburg, 1958).
4. See the end of vol. 1, *Meade's Life and Letters*, and the beginning of vol. 2.
5. Warner, *Generals in Blue*, pp. 315-17.
6. The Nichols book on Reynolds is a must. The papers of General Reynolds are in the library at Franklin and Marshall College in Lancaster, Pennsylvania.
7. Warner, *Generals in Blue*, pp. 202-4. See Glenn Tucker, *Hancock the Superb*, and note the chapter in Irving Stone's book on Hancock, *They Also Ran.*
8. See W. A. Swanberg, *Sickles the Incredible* (New York, 1956).
9. Warner, *Generals in Blue*, pp. 492-93. There is very little in print about Sykes.
10. See the *Correspondence of John Sedgwick, Major General, and Sedgwick Memorial Association, Spotsylvania Court House, Va.*, May 11, 12, and 13, 1887.
11. Refer to Howard's *Autobiography.*
12. Frank A. Haskell, *The Battle of Gettysburg* (From the Harvard Classics, vol. 43, New York, 1910). A reprint is now in existence, and is sold in most Civil War book stores.

CHAPTER XII (Pages 357-399)

1. Scharf, vol. 1, p. 640.
2. From the records of the Moravian Church, Graceham, Maryland. The reader should make an effort to visit this church and community. The church has an excellent map of the early Monocacy settlements.

3. Scharf, vol. 1, p. 628.
4. Wainwright, pp. 222-24.
5. *O.R.,* vol. 1, p. 243.
6. Pearson, p. 202.
7. Smith, *Twenty-fourth Michigan,* p. 152.
8. Davis, *Thirteenth Massachusetts,* p. 221.
9. Scharf, vol. 1, pp. 593-94.
10. *Idem.*
11. Smith, *Seventy-sixth New York,* p. 232.
12. Dawes, p. 158.
13. Cook, p. 100.
14. Davis, p. 221.
15. *O.R.,* pt. 1, p. 267.
16. Locke, p. 222.
17. *O.R.,* pt. 3, p. 707.
18. Curtis, p. 152.
19. Osborn, p. 89.
20. *O.R.,* pt. 1, p. 914.
21. Susan Lee, p. 99.
22. *O.R.,* pt. 1, p. 943.
23. Houghton, p. 84.
24. Hays, p. 191.
25. Bartlett, p. 118.
26. Craft, p. 111.
27. Marbaker, p. 90.
28. A. S. Williams, p. 220.
29. *Idem.*
30. Williams to his daughters, June 29, 1863, p. 220.
31. *Ibid.,* p. 221.
32. *Ibid.,* p. 223.
33. Jacob Englebrecht Diary, June 29, 1863.
34. Meade to his wife, June 29, 1863.
35. *O.R.,* pt. 2, p. 375.
36. *Battles and Leaders,* vol. 3, p. 395.
37. *O.R.,* pt. 3, p. 395.
38. *Ibid.,* p. 400.
39. McIntosh's report poses a problem. No doubt portions of the Sixth Corps blocked his way. However, it is difficult to see what other infantry corps might have blocked his progress.
40. *O.R.,* pt. 3, p. 397.
41. Waitt, p. 218.
42. Sawyer, p. 122.
43. Page, p. 133.
44. Ward, p. 178.
45. *Ibid.,* p. 179.
46. The incident is mentioned in Tucker's *Hancock the Superb,* and in John Quinn Imholte's *The First Minnesota Volunteer Regiment, 1861-1865* (Minneapolis, Minn., 1963), p. 114.
47. *Idem.*
48. Smith, *Nineteenth Maine,* p. 62.
49. *Ibid.,* p. 63.
50. *Ibid.,* p. 62.
51. Stewart, p. 87.

52. Waitt, p. 221.
53. Smith, *Nineteenth Maine,* p. 62.
54. *Idem.*
55. Ward, pp. 179-80.
56. Kepler, p. 123.
57. Waitt, p. 219.
58. *Ibid.,* p. 220.
59. Seveille, p. 79.
60. Livermore, p. 236.
61. Waitt, p. 61.
62. Smith, *Nineteenth Maine,* p. 63.
63. Page, p. 133.
64. Waitt, p. 222.
65. Bowen, pp. 169-70.
66. *New York at Gettysburg,* vol. 1, p. 234.
67. *O.R.,* pt. 3, p. 398.
68. Hard, p. 255.
69. *O.R.,* pt. 1, p. 926.
70. Moyer, pp. 58-59.
71. *O.R.,* pt. 1, pp. 912-14.
72. Pleasonton says in *Annals of the War* that he was with Meade. Thus it would seem that he might have met Meade at Worman's Mill, riding in from Richfield, and then traveling with him down what is now Route 194 to Middleburg and Taneytown.
73. Benudry, p. 64.
74. Frederick Whittaker, *Complete Life of Gen. George A. Custer* (New York, 1876), p. 170.
75. *O.R.,* pt. 3, p. 400.
76. Frederic S. Klein, ed., *Just South of Gettysburg, Carroll County, Maryland, in the Civil War* (Lancaster, 1974), pp. 211-12.
77. *O.R.,* pt. 1, p. 292.
78. *Ibid.,* p. 400.
79. Klein, pp. 43-46, and *O.R.,* pt. 2, pp. 201-3.
80. *Idem.*
81. *O.R.,* pt. 2, p. 695.
82. Klein, p. 57.
83. *Ibid.,* pp. 64-65.
84. *Ibid.,* p. 81.
85. *Ibid.,* pp. 81-82.
86. *Ibid.,* pp. 71-72.
87. *Idem.*
88. *Idem.*
89. John Esten Cooke, *Wearing of the Gray* (Bloomington, 1959), pp. 239-40.
90. Klein, pp. 183, 186.
91. Klein, p. 186.
92. *Ibid.,* p. 187.
93. *Ibid.,* p. 199.
94. *Ibid.,* pp. 201-2.
95. *Idem.*
96. *Idem.*
97. *Idem.*

98. *O.R.,* pt. 3, p. 398.
99. Patrick, June 29, 1863.
100. *O.R.,* pt. 3, p. 398.
101. *Ibid.,* p. 399.
102. *Ibid.,* p. 402.
103. Shotwell, vol. 1, pp. 493-94.
104. *Ibid.,* p. 495.
105. *Ibid.,* p. 496.
106. *Chambersburg Civil War Centennial Program* (Chambersburg, Pa., 1963), p. 11.
107. *Idem.*
108. *Ibid.,* p. 12.
109. *Idem.*
110. *Ibid.,* p. 15.
111. Fremantle, p. 197.
112. *Idem.*
113. *Idem.*
114. Hotchkiss Diary, June 29, 1863.
115. Nye, p. 346.
116. *O.R.,* pt. 3, p. 943.
117. James W. Sullivan, *Boyhood Memories of the Civil War, 1861-1865* (Carlisle, Pa., 1933), pp. 20-21.
118. Hotchkiss Diary, June 29, 1863.
119. *O.R.,* pt. 2, p. 551.
120. Nye, p. 294.
121. *O.R.,* pt. 2, p. 467.
122. Thomas G. Tousey, *Military History of Carlisle Barracks* (Richmond, 1939), p. 229.
123. *O.R.,* pt. 2, p. 467.
124. *Ibid.,* p. 607.
125. Jacobs, p. 17.
126. Hoke, p. 217.
127. *Ibid.,* p. 222.
128. Gerrish, p. 98.

CHAPTER XIII (Pages 400-448)

1. *O.R.,* pt. 1, p. 201, and the records of the Lutheran Church, Taneytown, Maryland.
2. *Ibid.,* p. 202.
3. Check the Taneytown Bicentennial Program, edited by Charles Buffington, Taneytown, 1956.
4. Davis, p. 223.
5. Smith, *The Seventy-sixth New York,* p. 233.
6. Dawes, p. 158.
7. *O.R.,* pt. 3, pp. 415-22.
8. Howard, p. 402.
9. Wainwright, p. 230.
10. Vautier, p. 104.
11. Curtis, p. 152.
12. *Ibid.,* p. 153.
13. Pearson, p. 202.

14. Smith, *The Twenty-fourth Michigan*, pp. 119-20.
15. *Idem.* The regiment had camped near Saint Joseph's on the twenty-ninth.
16. Howard, p. 403.
17. *Idem.*
18. *O.R.*, pt. 3, p. 421.
19. *Ibid.*, pp. 416, 422.
20. *Ibid.*, p. 422.
21. *Ibid.*, p. 425.
22. *Ibid.*, p. 424.
23. Bardeen, p. 212.
24. Marbaker, p. 91.
25. Houghton, p. 84.
26. Kate M. Scott, *History of the One Hundred and Fifth Regiment of Pennsylvania Volunteers* (Philadelphia, 1877), p. 81.
27. Bardeen, pp. 212-13.
28. Cudworth, p. 390.
29. Coffin, *Marching to Victory*, p. 195; *Boys of '61*, p. 223. Coffin rode with Gregg's cavalry part of today.
30. *Idem.*
31. Haskell, p. 7.
32. Livermore, p. 238.
33. *155th Pennsylvania*, p. 130.
34. Klein, p. 137.
35. *O.R.*, pt. 3, p. 424.
36. Klein, p. 194.
37. A. S. Williams, pp. 223-24.
38. Collins, p. 131.
39. Toombs, pp. 71-72.
40. *O.R.*, pt. 3, p. 425.
41. Edwin G. Longacre, "Alfred Pleasonton, The Knight of Romance," in *Civil War Times* (December, 1974), states that Pleasonton was a man who was prejudiced against men of foreign birth. Longacre says that he practically sacrificed Col. Alfred Duffie, a Frenchman leading the First Rhode Island Cavalry at Aldie on June 17. Duffie obeyed orders, and was not supported when he called for help. Then Pleasonton became upset with Julius Stahel, a Hungarian, and worked to get him replaced.

During the last week in June, Pleasonton placed Captain Elon Farnsworth of Illinois on his staff. He urged the young officer to write to his uncle, Congressman John Farnsworth, in an effort to get himself promoted to major general. Captain Farnsworth wrote, "The Genl. speaks of recommending me for Brg. General. I do not know that I ought to mention it for fear that you will call me an aspiring youth. I am satisfied to serve through this war in the line of my Regt as a Capt on Genl Pleasonton's staff But if I can do any good anywhere else of course. . . . Now try and talk this (Pleasonton's promotion) into the President. . . .
42. Preston, p. 103.
43. Klein, p. 143.
44. Pyne, p. 163.
45. Klein, p. 102.
46. *Idem.*
47. Tobie, p. 175.
48. Klein, pp. 80-81.
49. *Ibid.*, p. 61.

50. *Encounter at Hanover,* pp. 98-100.
51. *O.R.,* pt. 1, p. 992.
52. *Ibid.,* p. 1000.
53. *Idem.*
54. *Encounter at Hanover,* pp. 99-100.
55. *Ibid.,* p. 101.
56. *Idem.*
57. *Ibid.,* pp. 58-59, and *O.R.,* pt. 1, p. 992.
58. *Encounter at Hanover,* p. 59.
59. *Idem,* and *O.R.,* pt. 1, p. 992.
60. The encounter at Hanover may indeed have been the turning point in stopping Stuart from reaching Lee.
61. For Confederate accounts see the works by H. B. McClellan, and W. W. Blackford.
62. Benudry, pp. 64-66.
63. *O.R.,* pt. 1, pp. 986-87.
64. *Ibid.,* p. 992.
65. *Ibid.,* p. 987.
66. *Idem.*
67. *Encounter at Hanover,* pp. 112-13.
68. *Ibid.,* p. 87.
69. *Ibid.,* p. 81.
70. *Ibid.,* p. 97.
71. *Idem.*
72. *Ibid.,* p. 96.
73. *O.R.,* pt. 1, p. 970.
74. *Ibid.,* pt. 3, p. 426.
75. Moyer, pp. 59-60.
76. Cheney, p. 102.
77. Hall, p. 132.
78. *O.R.,* pt. 1, p. 1031.
79. Haynes, p. 135.
80. *New York at Gettysburg,* vol. 1, p. 9.
81. Coffin, p. 196.
82. *Ibid.,* p. 199.
83. *O.R.,* pt. 3, pp. 458-59. A note here in regard to Meade's Pipe Creek line. Meade had prepared for an attack and had looked over a strong defensive line. This was the Pipe Creek line. The position was by road fifteen to twenty miles south and southeast of Gettysburg, stretching from Middleburg to Manchester. The stream was not very deep. Parr's Ridge high ground near Westminster would have given Meade a strong position, and would have enabled him to stand between Washington and Baltimore. It was also close to his base of supplies, and a rail line ran from Baltimore to Westminster.
84. *Idem,* and p. 415.
85. Boyle, pp. 112-13.
86. The Carlisle newspaper accounts.
87. Hotchkiss for June 30, 1863.
88. *Idem.*
89. Nye, p. 296.
90. *Ibid.,* p. 297.
91. Shotwell, vol. 1, p. 496.

92. Fremantle, p. 197.
93. Caldwell, pp. 43-44.

CHAPTER XIV (Pages 449-517)

1. *New York at Gettysburg,* vol. 1, p. 10.
2. The Chicago CWRT.
3. Coffin, p. 200.
4. *Ibid.,* p. 201.
5. Jacobs, p. 19.
6. Nichols, p. 195; and Williams, *Lincoln Finds a General,* vol. 2, pp. 676-77.
7. Pearson, p. 204.
8. *Pennsylvania at Gettysburg,* vol. 1, p. 343.
9. Dawes, p. 164.
10. Curtis, p. 155. Nichols in *Towards Gettysburg* has an excellent description of the advance in the last chapter of his book.
11. Dawes, p. 58.
12. Wainwright, p. 231.
13. Meade, *Letters,* vol. 2, p. 32; Pearson, p. 205.
14. John W. de Peyster, *Decisive Conflicts of the Late Civil War* (New York, 1867); de Peyster quotes from the words of a signal officer who overheard the remark. It must have been Aaron B. Jerome who was on duty that day.
15. Stephen Minot Weld, *War Diary and Letters of Stephen Minot Weld 1861-1865* (Riverside Press, 1912), p. 230.
16. Pearson, p. 205; de Peyster, p. 34.
17. Charles H. Veil in a letter written April 7, 1864, to D. McConaughy. It was in the manuscript collection at Gettysburg College, Gettysburg, Pa. Nichols on pp. 253-54 details the various accounts of the fall of Reynolds.
18. Preston, pp. 126-27.
19. Howard says the orders were received at 3:30 A.M. *O.R.,* pt. 1, p. 701. See also his autobiography, vol. 1, p. 404.
20. *Ibid.,* and Howard, p. 408.
21. *O.R.,* pt. 1, p. 702, and Howard, p. 409.
22. Howard, p. 409.
23. *Ibid.,* p. 410.
24. *Idem.*
25. Howard, p. 412.
26. *Ibid.,* p. 413.
27. *Idem.*
28. The volumes of *New York at Gettysburg* carry stories of the New York regiments approaching Gettysburg.
29. *O.R.,* pt. 1, p. 703, Howard, p. 414. Howard's descriptions in the *O.R.,* and in his *Autobiography* are virtually the same.
30. Caldwell, p. 45.
31. *O.R.,* pt. 2, p. 468. See Nye, p. 362.
32. Hotchkiss Diary, July 1, 1863.
33. *O.R.,* pt. 1, p. 703.
34. Dawes, pp. 178-79.
35. Gordon, p. 144.
36. Trimble, writing in *The Confederate Veteran,* vol. 25, p. 211, very graphically describes the conversation with Ewell and his utter dismay at the failure to press the golden advantage which the Confederates held at the moment.

37. Douglas, p. 247.
38. Gilmor, pp. 97-98.
39. Howard, p. 419.
40. Marbaker, p. 93.
41. *Ibid.*, p. 94.
42. Jacobs, p. 33. Apparently the weather depended on where you were at the time. Some members of the Iron Brigade reported some mud on the roads. Wainwright experienced a shower, and the Twentieth Indiana was drenched. Many reported some morning mist. For the most part it was a hot, cloudy, sultry day. Jacobs reports the 2:00 P.M. temperature at seventy-six degrees.
43. *O.R.,* pt. 1, p. 482.
44. De Trobriand, p. 496.
45. *Ibid.,* p. 497.
46. *O.R.,* pt. 1, pp. 530-31.
47. McGilvery, quoted in the Taneytown Bicentennial Program.
48. Meade, *Letters,* vol. 2; see the first twelve pages.
49. See Tucker's account in *Hancock the Superb.*
50. *O.R.,* pt. 1, p. 368.
51. *Ibid.,* p. 925.
52. *Ibid.,* p. 368.
53. Warren W. Hassler, Jr., in *Crisis at the Crossroads: The First Day at Gettysburg* (The University of Alabama Press, 1970) dwells on the first day.
54. Carl Schurz and others noted the inspiration that Hancock brought to the field.
55. Once again, note Tucker's account of Hancock at Gettysburg in *Hancock the Superb.*
56. *O.R.,* p. 1, p. 369.
57. Wilson, p. 253.
58. *O.R.,* pt. 1, p. 771.
59. *Ibid.,* p. 825. Geary was placed in the Round Top area to anchor the left of the Union line.
60. *Ibid.,* p. 826.
61. Whitelaw Reid was a special correspondent for the *Cincinnati Gazette.* He was in Taneytown when L. L. Crounse of the *New York Times* rode in and reported quite an engagement in Gettysburg. He also told the story of Reynolds's death. Many reporters started to write stories from the porch of a Taneytown tavern. Reid had already covered twenty-seven miles in traveling from Frederick, but he had another twelve or fifteen miles to go. The streets of Taneytown were blocked with army wagons, and he saw the gleam of bayonets as the Second Corps tramped toward Gettysburg. He had just reached Meade's headquarters when Crounse arrived.
62. Fremantle, pp. 201-4.
63. *Ibid.,* p. 205.
64. *O.R.,* pt. 2, p. 366.
65. *Idem.*
66. Dickert, p. 231.
67. *Ibid.,* p. 233.
68. Shotwell, vol. 1, p. 498.
69. Jacobs, p. 25.
70. *Idem.*
71. *Idem.*
72. Bruce, p. 269.

73. *Idem.*
74. Refer again to the CWI files for the story on Colonel Cross.
75. As the men approached the field, they seemed to be filled with more determination to do their duty.
76. Kepler, p. 125.
77. *Ibid.,* pp. 125-26.
78. Livermore, p. 242.
79. *Idem.*
80. Patrick for June 30 and July 1, 1863.
81. *Meade at Gettysburg,* pp. 97-98.
82. *Idem.*
83. Brainard, p. 109.
84. Judson, p. 66.
85. Thomas W. Hyde, *Following the Greek Cross, Or Memories of the Sixth Army Corps* (Boston, 1894), p. 141.
86. *Ibid.,* pp. 142-43.
87. *O.R.,* pt. 3, p. 467.
88. *Idem.*
89. *Ibid.,* p. 469.
90. *Encounter at Hanover,* pp. 124-25.
91. Parker, pp. 164-65.
92. O. S. Barrett, *The Old Fourth Michigan Infantry* (Detroit, 1888), pp. 21-22.
93. Macnamara, p. 315.
94. *118th Pennsylvania,* pp. 235-36.
95. Brainard, pp. 110-11. A very interesting account.
96. The news that McClellan was back in command swept through the ranks both in the march of the Fifth Corps from Hanover and the Sixth Corps from Manchester.
97. The story of the Fifth Corps in Hanover and the later arrival of Gregg's cavalry would be an interesting story for some scholar to pursue.
98. *118th Pennsylvania,* pp. 237-38.
99. Gerrish, p. 99.
100. See Oliver W. Newton, "The Attack and Defense of Little Round Top," *Pennsylvania at Gettysburg,* vol. 1, pp. 285, 462.
101. *Encounter at Hanover,* p. 170.
102. *Idem.*
103. Preston, p. 104.
104. *O.R.,* pt. 1, pp. 666, 669.
105. *Pennsylvania at Gettysburg,* vol. 2, p. 652.
106. Stevens, p. 239.
107. When Glenn Tucker visited Manchester in November of 1957, the old schoolhouse was a tractor shed. Mrs. Celia Showe was ninty-three years of age at that time. Her father had shared with her the story of Sedgwick's headquarters.
108. Bicknell, pp. 241-43.
109. Bowen, pp. 171-72.
110. Hyde, p. 143.
111. Bennett, p. 120.
112. Stevens, p. 240.
113. *Pennsylvania at Gettysburg,* vol. 1, p. 506.
114. See the stories of the forces' march in Hyde and Stevens and their account of the *Sixth Corps History.*

115. *Pennsylvania at Gettysburg,* vol. 2, p. 677.

116. Nichols, p. 211.

117. Shotwell, vol. 1, pp. 498-501. The line has to be drawn somewhere. A book could be made on each Union and Confederate corps on the Roads to Gettysburg as well as the cavalry commands. *Here Come the Rebels!* is certainly the best now in existence. Although we have largely omitted the story of Stuart, and also the battle of Hunterstown, hopefully the overall story of the advance to the fields of Gettysburg will contribute to the knowledge of the campaign.

BIBLIOGRAPHY

Civilian Accounts

Chamber of Commerce. *Encounter at Hanover.* Gettysburg, 1962. This book is filled with eyewitness accounts and the local newspaper coverage.

Coffin, Charles C. Dispatches to the *Boston Journal* "The Boys of '61," "Marching to Victory," Boston, 1886.

Englebrecht, Jacob. Diary covering events in Frederick.

Hoke, Jacob. *The Great Invasion of 1863.* Dayton, 1863.

Jacobs, M. *Notes on the Rebel Invasion of Maryland and Pennsylvania and the Battle of Gettysburg, July 1, 2, and 3, 1863.* Philadelphia, 1864.

Klein, Frederic. *Just South of Gettysburg.* 2nd printing. Lancaster, 1974. Eyewitness accounts of civilians and soldiers.

Nicodemus Family Papers, Walkersville, Md.

Schaff, Philip. "The Gettysburg Week." *Scribner's Magazine,* vol. 16, July, 1894.

The Army of Northern Virginia

The Commanders

Freeman, Douglas S. *Lee's Lieutenants, A Study in Command.* 3 vols. New York, 1943.

———. *Robert E. Lee, A Biography.* 4 vols. New York, 1935.

Hassler, William W. *A. P. Hill, Lee's Forgotten General.* Richmond, 1957.

Lee, Susan P. *Memoirs of William Nelson Pendleton.* Philadelphia, 1893.

Long, Armistead L. *Memoirs of Robert E. Lee.* New York, 1886.

Longstreet, James. *From Manassas to Appomattox, Memoirs of the Civil War.* Philadelphia, 1896.

Dorsey Pender Papers. University of North Carolina, Chapel Hill.

William Nelson Pendleton Papers. University of North Carolina.

Schenck, Martin. *Up Came Hill.* Harrisburg, 1958.

Warner, Ezra. *Generals in Gray.* Baton Rouge, 1959.

First Corps

Alexander, Edwin Porter. *Military Memoirs of a Confederate*. New York, 1907.

Dickert, Augustus. *A History of Kershaw's Brigade*.

Divine, John. *Loudoun County and Civil War Collection*. Waterford, Virginia.

Fremantle, A. J. C. *Three Months in the Southern States: April-June, 1863*. New York, 1864.

Hamilton, J. G., ed. *The Papers of Randolph Abbott Shotwell*. 3 vols. Raleigh, N.C., 1929.

Hood, John B. *Advance and Retreat, Personal Experiences in the United States and Confederate States Armies*. New Orleans, 1880.

Hunton, Eppa. *Autobiography*. Richmond, 1933.

Inman, Arthur Crew, ed. *Soldier of the South, General Pickett's War Letters to His Wife*. New York, 1928.

Owen, William M. *In Camp and Battle With the Washington Artillery of New Orleans*. Boston, 1885.

Polley, J. B. *Hood's Texas Brigade*. Morningside Reprint. Dayton, 1976.

———. *A Soldier's Letters to Charming Nellie*. New York, 1928.

Ross, Fitzgerald. *Cities and Camps of the Confederate States*. Urbana, Ill., 1958.

Russell, J. W. Letters home to Loudoun County.

Simpson, Harold B. *Hood's Texas Brigade*.

Sorrel, G. Moxley. *Recollections of a Confederate Staff Officer*. New York, 1917.

Stiles, Robert. *Four Years With Marse Robert*. New York, 1903.

Second Corps

Bean, W. G. *Sandie Pendleton, Stonewall's Man*. Chapel Hill, N.C., 1959.

Douglas, Henry Kyd. *I Rode With Stonewall*. Chapel Hill, 1940.

Early, Jubal A. *Autobiographical Sketch and Narrative of the War Between the States*. Philadelphia, 1912.

Gilmor, Harry. *Four Years in the Saddle*.

Gordon, John B. *Reminiscences of the Civil War*. New York, 1903.

Jedediah Hotchkiss Papers in the Library of Congress.

McKim, Randolph H. *A Soldier's Recollections, Leaves from the Diary of a Young Confederate*. London, 1910.

Nye, W. S. *Here Come the Rebels!* Baton Rouge, 1965.

Trimble, I. R. "The Campaign and Battle of Gettysburg." *Confederate Veteran*, vol. 25. May, 1917.

———. "The Civil War Diary of General Isaac Ridgeway Trimble." *Maryland Historical Magazine* 17 (March 1922):1-20.

Third Corps

Caldwell. J. F. F. *The History of a Brigade of South Carolinians Known First as 'Gregg's' and Subsequently as 'McGowan's Brigade.'* Philadelphia, 1866.

Chamberlayne, C. G. *Ham Chamberlayne—Virginian, Letters and Papers of an Artillery Officer.* Richmond, 1932.

Christian, William. Letters to his wife.

Morrison, James L. *The Memoirs of Henry Heth.* Greenwood, Conn., 1974.

Thomas, Henry W. *History of the Doles-Cook Brigade.* . . . Atlanta, 1903.

Welch, Spencer Glasgow. *A Confederate Surgeon's Letters to His Wife.* Marietta, Ga., 1954.

The Artillery

Runge, William, ed. *Four Years in the Confederate Artillery: The Diary of Private Henry Robinson Berkeley.* Chapel Hill, 1961.

State Series

Clark, Walter, ed. *Histories of the Several Regiments and Battalions from North Carolina in the Great War, 1861-1865.* 5 vols. Raleigh, 1901.

Cavalry

Blackford, William W. *The War Years With Jeb Stuart.* New York, 1946.

Cooke, John Esten. *Wearing of the Gray.* New York, 1867.

McClellan, H. B., *I Rode With Jeb Stuart.* Burke Davis, ed. Bloomington, 1958.

The Army of the Potomac

The Commanders

Bache, Richard M. *Life of General George Gordon Meade.* Philadelphia, 1907.

Butterfield, Julia L. S., ed. *A Biographical Memorial of General Daniel Butterfield.* New York, 1907.

Carpenter, John S. *Sword and Olive Branch, Oliver Otis Howard.* Pittsburgh, 1964.

Cleaves, Freeman. *Meade of Gettysburg.* Norman, Okla., 1960.

Doubleday, Abner. *Chancellorsville and Gettysburg.* New York, 1882.

Gibbon, John. *Personal Recollections of the War.* New York, 1928.

Hancock, Mrs. W. S., ed. *Reminiscences of Winfield Scott Hancock.* New York, 1887.

Haupt, Herman. *Reminiscences of General Herman Haupt.* Milwaukee, 1901.

Herbert, Walter H. *Fighting Joe Hooker.* Indianapolis, 1944.

Howard, O. O. *Autobiography of Oliver Otis Howard.* 2 vols. New York, 1908.

Humphreys, Henry H. *Andrew Atkinson Humphreys: A Biography.* Philadelphia, 1924.
Meade, George. *The Life and Letters of George Gordon Meade.* Edited by G. G. Meade (grandson). 2 vols. New York, 1913.
Meade, George G. *With Meade at Gettysburg.* Philadelphia, 1930.
Nichols, Edward J. *Toward Gettysburg: A Biography of General John F. Reynolds.* University Park, Pa., 1958.
Quaife, Milo M., ed. *From the Cannon's Mouth, The Civil War Letters of General Alpheus S. Williams.* Detroit, 1959.
John Fulton Reynolds Family Papers. Franklin and Marshall College, Lancaster, Pa.
Sedgwick, John. *Correspondence of Major General John Sedgwick.* 2 vols. New York, 1902-1903.
Slocum, C. E. *Life and Services of Major-General Henry Warner Slocum.* Toledo, Ohio, 1913.
Sparks, David, ed. *Inside Mr. Lincoln's Army: The Diary of General Marsena Patrick, Provost Marshal General, Army of the Potomac.* New York, 1964.
Swanberg, W. A. *Sickles the Incredible.* New York, 1956.
Tucker, Glenn. *Hancock the Superb.* Indianapolis, 1960.
Warner, Ezra. *Generals in Blue, Lives of Union Commanders.* Baton Rouge, 1964.
Williams, Harry. *Lincoln and His Generals,* New York, 1952.

First Corps

I CORPS

Buell, Augustus. *The Cannoneer, Recollections of Service in the Army of the Potomac.* Washington, 1890.
Chamberlain, Thomas. *History of the One Hundred and Fiftieth Regiment, Pennsylvania Volunteers.* Philadelphia, 1905.
Cook, Benjamin F. *History of the Twelfth Massachusetts Volunteers.* Boston, 1882.
Curtis, Orson B. *History of the Twenty-fourth Michigan.* Detroit, 1891.
Davis, Charles E. *The Story of the Thirteenth Massachusetts Volunteers.* Boston, 1894.
Dawes, Rufus. *Service With the Sixth Wisconsin Volunteers.* Marietta, 1890.
Nevins, Allan, ed. *A Diary of Battle: The Personal Journals of Colonel Charles S. Wainwright, 1861-1865.* New York, 1962.
Nolan, Alan T. *The Iron Brigade: A Military History.* New York, 1961.

Pearson, Henry. *James S. Wadsworth of Geneseo.* New York, 1913.

Small, Abner R. *The Sixteenth Maine Regiment in the War of the Rebellion 1861-1865.* Portland, 1886.

Smith, Abram P. *History of the Seventy-sixth Regiment New York Volunteers.* Cortland, N.Y., 1867.

Smith, Donald L. *The Twenty-fourth Michigan of the Iron Brigade.* Harrisburg, 1962.

Survivors Association, *History of the 121st Regiment Pennsylvania Volunteers.* Philadelphia, 1906.

Todd, William, ed. *History of the Ninth Regiment New York State Militia.*

Vautier, John D. *History of the 88th Pennsylvania Volunteers.* . . . Philadelphia, 1894.

Second Corps

II CORPS

Bruce, George A. *The Twentieth Regiment of Massachusetts Volunteer Infantry, 1861-1865.* Boston, 1906.

Child, William. *A History of the Fifth Regiment New Hampshire Volunteers.* Bristol, 1893.

Cray, Catherine S., ed. *Dear Belle, Letters From a Cadet and Officer to His Sweetheart, 1858-1865.* Middletown, Conn., 1965.

Galwey, Thomas F. *The Valiant Hours.* Harrisburg, 1961.

Haskell, Frank A. *The Battle of Gettysburg.* Madison, 1908.

Kepler, William. *History of the Fourth Regiment Ohio Volunteer Infantry.* Cleveland, 1886.

Livermore, Thomas L. *Days and Events, 1860-1866.* Boston, 1920.

Murphey, Thomas G. *History of the First Regiment Delaware Veteran Volunteers.* Philadelphia, 1866.

Page, Charles G. *History of the Fourteenth Regiment Connecticut Volunteer Infantry.* Meriden, Conn., 1906.

Sawyer, Franklin. *A Military History of the Eighth Regiment Ohio Volunteer Infantry.* Cleveland, 1881.

Seville, William P. *History of the First Regiment Delaware Volunteers.* Wilmington, 1886.

Smith, John D. *History of the Nineteenth Regiment Maine Volunteers.* Minneapolis, 1909.

Stewart, Robert L. *History of the One Hundred and Fortieth Regiment Pennsylvania Volunteers.* No place, 1912.

Waitt, Earnest L. *History of the Nineteenth Regiment Massachusetts Volunteer Infantry.* Salem, Mass., 1906.

573

Walker, Francis. *A History of the Second Corps in the Army of the Potomac.* New York, 1886.

Ward, Joseph R. *History of the One Hundred and Sixth Regiment Pennsylvania Volunteers.* Philadelphia, 1906.

Webb, Alexander Stewart. Letters to his wife and family. Yale University.

Third Corps

III CORPS

Bardeen, Charles W. *A Little Fifer's War Diary.* Syracuse, 1910.

Bartlett, A. W. *History of the Twelfth Regiment New Hampshire Volunteers.* Concord, 1897.

Craft, David. *History of the One Hundred Forty-first Regiment, Pennsylvania Volunteers.* Towanda, Pa., 1885.

Crotty, David G. *Four Years of Campaigning in the Army of the Potomac.* Grand Rapids, 1874.

Cudworth, Warren H. *History of the First Regiment Massachusetts Infantry.* Boston, 1866.

De Troibrand, Regis. *Four Years With the Army of the Potomac.* Boston, 1889.

Haynes, Martin A. *History of the Second Regiment, New Hampshire Volunteers.* Manchester, N.H., 1865.

Hays, Gilbert A. *Under the Red Patch, Story of the Sixty-third Regiment, Pennsylvania Volunteers, 1861-1864.* Pittsburgh, 1908.

Houghton, Edwin D. *The Campaigns of the Seventeenth Maine.* Portland, 1886.

Marbaker, Thomas D. *History of the Eleventh New Jersey Volunteers.* Trenton, 1893.

Fifth Corps

V CORPS

Barrett, O. S. *Reminiscences... of the Old Fourth Michigan Infantry.* Detroit, 1888.

Brainard, Mary G. *Campaigns of the One Hundred and Forty-sixth Regiment New York State Volunteers.* New York, 1915.

Gerrish, Theodore. *Army Life. A Private's Reminiscences of the Civil War.* Portland, 1882.

Judson, Amos M. *History of the Eighty-third Regiment Pennsylvania Volunteers.* Erie, Pa., n.d.

Macnamara, Daniel George. *The History of the Ninth Regiment, Massachusetts Volunteer Infantry.* Boston, 1899.

Norton, Oliver Wilcox. *Army Letters, 1861-1865.* Chicago, 1903.

Parker, Francis J. *The Story of the Thirty-second Regiment, Massachusetts Infantry.* Boston, 1880.

Powell, William H. *The Fifth Army Corps, Army of the Potomac,* New York, 1896.

Pullen, John J. *The Twentieth Maine.* Philadelphia, 1957.

Survivors Association. *History of the 118th Pennsylvania Volunteers.* Philadelphia, 1905.

Under the Maltese Cross. Narrated by the rank and file. Pittsburgh, 1910.

Wallace, Willard M. *The Soul of the Lion, A Biography of General Joshua L. Chamberlain,* New York, 1960.

The Sixth Corps

VI CORPS

Best, Isaac O. *History of the 121st New York State Infantry.* Chicago, 1921.

Bicknell, George W. *History of the Fifth Regiment Maine Volunteers.* Portland, 1871.

Bowen, James L. *History of the Thirty-seventh Regiment Massachusetts Volunteers in the Civil War of 1861-1865.* Holyoke, 1884.

Haines, Alanson A. *History of the Fifteenth New Jersey Volunteers.* New York, 1883.

Hutchinson, Nelson V. *History of the Seventh Massachusetts Volunteer Infantry.* Taunton, Mass., 1890.

Hyde, Thomas W. *Following the Greek Cross, Or Memories of the Sixth Army Corps.* Boston, 1894.

Roe, Alfred S. *The Tenth Regiment Massachusetts Volunteer Infantry 1861-1864.* Springfield, 1909.

Stevens, George T. *Three Years in the Sixth Corps.* Albany, 1866.

Woodbury, Augustus. *The Second Rhode Island Regiment.* Providence, 1875.

The Eleventh Corps

XI CORPS

Boies, Andrew J. *Record of the Thirty-third Massachusetts Volunteer Infantry.* Fitchburg, Mass., 1880.

Culp, Edward C. *The 25th Ohio Veteran Volunteer Infantry in the War for the Union.* Topeka, 1885.

Locke, William Henry. *The Story of the Regiment.* Philadelphia, 1868.

Osborn, Hartwell. *The Record of the Fifty-fifth Ohio Volunteer Infantry.* Chicago, 1904.

Twelfth Corps

XII CORPS

Brown, Edmund R. *The Twenty-seventh Indiana Volunteer Infantry in the War of the Rebellion.* No place, 1899.

Boyle, John R. *Soldiers True, The Story of the One Hundred and Eleventh Regiment Pennsylvania . . . Volunteers. . . . 1861-1865.* New York, 1903.

Bryant, Edwin E. *History of the Third Regiment Wisconsin . . . Volunteer Infantry 1861-1865.* Madison, 1891.

Collins, George K. *Memoirs of the 149th Regiment New York Volunteer Infantry.* Syracuse, 1891.

Gould, John M. *History of the First-Tenth-Twenty-Ninth Maine Regiment.* Portland, 1871.

Marvin, Edwin. *The Fifth Regiment Connecticut Volunteers.* Hartford, 1889.

SeCheverell, John H. *Journal History of the Twenty-Ninth Ohio . . . Volunteers, 1861-1865.* Cleveland, 1883.

Storrs, John W. *The Twentieth Connecticut, A Regimental History.* Ansonia, Conn., 1886.

Toombs, Samuel. *Reminiscences of the War . . . Experiences of the Thirteenth Regiment New Jersey Volunteers.* Orange, N.J., 1878.

Veale, Moses. *The 109th Regiment Pennsylvania . . . Volunteers—An Address.* Philadelphia, 1890.

Wilson, Lawrence. *Itinerary of the Seventh Ohio Volunteer Infantry.* New York, 1907.

The Artillery

Baker, Levi. *History of the Ninth Massachusetts Battery*. South Framingham, 1888.

Bennett, Andrew J. *The Story of the First Massachusetts Light Battery*. Boston, 1886.

History of the Fifth Massachusetts Battery. Boston, 1902.

The Cavalry

Beach, William H. *The First New York (Lincoln) Cavalry*. New York, 1902.

Benudry (spelled Boudrye on the title page), Louis N. *Historic Records of the Fifth New York Cavalry*. Albany, 1868.

Cheney, Newel. *History of the Ninth Regiment New York Volunteer Cavalry*. Poland Center, N.Y., 1901.

Hall, Hillman A. *History of the Sixth New York Cavalry*. Worcester, 1908.

Hard, Abner. *History of the Eighth Cavalry Regiment Illinois Volunteers*. Aurora, Ill., 1888.

Moyer, H. P. *History of the Seventeenth Regiment Pennsylvania Volunteer Cavalry*. Lebanon, Pa., 1911.

Pickerill, William N. *History of the Third Indiana Cavalry*. Indianapolis, 1906.

Preston, Noble D. *History of the Tenth Regiment of Cavalry New York State Volunteers*. New York, 1892.

Publication Committee of the Regimental Association. *History of the Eighteenth Regiment of Cavalry Pennsylvania Volunteers*. New York, 1909.

Pyne, Henry R. *History of the First New Jersey Cavalry*. Trenton, 1871.

Tobie, Edward P. *History of the First Maine Cavalry*. Boston, 1887.

Whittaker, Frederick. *A Complete Life of Gen. George A. Custer*. Chicago, 1876.

State Series

Benedict, G. G. *Vermont at Gettysburg*. Burlington, 1870.

Michigan at Gettysburg. Detroit, 1880.

New York at Gettysburg. 3 vols. Albany, 1900.

Nicholson, John P., and Beitler, Lewis E., eds. *Pennsylvania at Gettysburg*. 3 vols. Harrisburg, 1914.

Other Sources

The basic source for *Roads to Gettysburg* was *War of the Rebellion: A Compilation of the Official Records of the Union and Confederate Armies*. Volume 27, parts 1, 2, and 3.

Harper's Weekly. July and August 1863.

Hassler, Warren W. *The First Day at Gettysburg*. Montgomery, 1970.

Johnson, Robert and Buel, Clarence C., eds. *Battles and Leaders of the Civil War.* New York, 1884.

Newspaper Accounts

Baltimore Sun.
Carlisle Evening Sentennial.
Hanover Citizen.
Hanover Spectator.
Richmond Whig.
York Gazette.

INDEX

Aldie, 109, 118, 121, 140-41
Anderson, Richard H., 123, 192
Aquia Creek, 52-53
Arcadia, 20
Arcola, 139
Army of Northern Virginia: Roads to Gettysburg, 18; composition, 19; begins movement, 20; June 21, 165; June 25, 215, 448, 485; river crossings, 525
First Army Corps: starts north, 20, 30; arrival at Gettysburg, 533
Second Army Corps: starts northward, 20, 30-31; June 19, 145; June 21, 165; arrival at Gettysburg, 533
Third Army Corps: leaving Fredericksburg, 73, 105, 106; June 19, 145; June 21, 165-66; arrives at Gettysburg, 533
Army of the Potomac: composition, 19, 109; June 26, 239; June 27, 273, 448; itinerary, 518-24; river crossings, 525-26
First Army Corps: Sunday service, 7; June 17, 109, 112; June 18, 126; June 19, 136-38; June 20, 150-51; June 25, 202-5; June 26, 239-42; June 27, 273; June 28, 328; July 1, 451-57; arrival at Gettysburg, 532
Third Army Corps: 70; June 25, 207-29; June 26, 243; June 27, 276-78; June 28, 324-28; June 29, 367-68; July 1, 471-76; arrival at Gettysburg, 532
Fifth Army Corps: 71; June 17, 109, 112, 117, 119; June 27,

279; June 28, 318; June 29, 380; July 1, 492, 495-501; arrival at Gettysburg, 532
Sixth Army Corps: prayer meeting, 68; Stafford Court House, 90, 93; June 20, 152; June 26, 245-46; June 27, 281-82; June 28, 318; June 29, 379-80; July 1, 504-13
Eleventh Army Corps: 71, 122; June 25, 201-2; June 26, 247; June 27, 284; June 28, 340; June 29, 364-65; July 1, 458-62
Twelfth Army Corps: 55-56, 68; June 17, 109, 120; June 21, 160; June 27, 282; June 29, 369; July 1, 480
Auburn, 366

Babcock, John, 149, 178
Bardeen, Charles, 69-70, 207
Barlow, Francis, 459
Barnesville, 318-19, 402
Barnett's Ford, 10
Berryville, Virginia, 60-61, 169-73
Birney, David B., 117, 332
Black Horse Tavern, 474-75
Bower, 132
Boyd, Belle, 176
Boyd, William H., 63, 156, 174
Brandy Station, 21, 37-39
Brown, Edmund, 4, 5
Buford, John, 333, 381, 435; arrives in Gettysburg, 437-38; Seminary Ridge, 439-41
Bunker Hill, 63, 104
Burkittsville, 248, 276-77
Butterfield, Daniel, 2, 121, 126, 178, 209, 250

Calef, John, 438

579

Calendar for June 1863, 518
Carlisle, 23, 106, 195, 262-65;
    June 28, 294-95, 394
Cashtown, 397
Catoctin Furnace, 360
Cedar Creek, 181
Centreville, 117, 138, 151
Ceresville, 366-67
Chambersburg, 20, 23, 81; occupied
    by Jenkins, 82, 105; arrival of
    Rodes and Ewell, 185;
    June 26, 223
Coffin, Charles, 32; arrival in Harris-
    burg, 83; description of city,
    84-85, 294; observes change of
    command, 336
Couch, Darius, 2, 39, 146
Cove Mountain, 157
Creagarstown, 359
Cross, Edward, 316, 487
Culpeper, 20
Cumberland, 95
Custer, George, 332; sketch, 335,
    382-83

Dawes, Rufus, criticism of Hooker,
    32, 111; sketch, 240, 273,
    465-66
De Trobriand, Regis, 244, 326-27
Doubleday, Abner, 358
Douglas, Henry Kyd, 86, 125,
    131-32, 154, 267
Dover Hotel, 434
Dumfries, 93

Early, Jubal, 23; at Winchester,
    77-78, 145, 173, 176, 190;
    June 27, 233-37, 298, 445,
    468; route of March, 526-27
Edwards Ferry, 23, 143-44, 147,
    180, 196, 203-4, 254, 281,
    321
Emmitsburg, fire, 119-20, 362,
    473-74
Engineer corps, 149-50
Englebrecht, Jacob, 96, 280, 381
Ewell, Richard S., 29; at Winchester,
    60, 65-66, 86, 167; arrives in
    Chambersburg, 185, 221,
    263-69, 341, 393-94, 445,
    463, 467

Fairfax Court House, 178
Fairfield, 381
Falmouth, 5
Farnsworth, Elon, 332; sketch, 334,
    382
Fayetteville, 269-70, 446
Ferry Hill, 134, 154-55
Fleming Farm, 174-75
Fort Jackson, 85
Fort Loudon, 105-6
Fox's Gap, 248, 274
Frederick, June 20, 158-59; June 21,
    169; "clustered spires," 271,
    280, 322, 327, 358
Fredericksburg, description, 74
Fremantle, James, June 20, 153-54;
    June 21, 165; June 22,
    171-72, 190, 215, 226, 260,
    309, 392, 447
Fritchie, Barbara, 271
Front Royal, 75

Gaines' Crossroads, 104
Gettysburg, entered by Early's
    forces, 190; entered by Michi-
    gan cavalry, 296; Buford's ar-
    rival, 437; July 1, 457-58
Gibbon, John, biographical sketch,
    114-15; death of child, 115,
    151, 169, 317, 376, 490
Gilmor, Harry, 158-59, 468
Gordon, John, 18-20, 269, 396
Graceham, 359
Greencastle, 155, 175-76, 187, 190,
    230-31, 259-60
Guilford Station, 110, 138
Gum Springs, 109, 118, 138-40

Haines, Alanson, 34, 58-59
Hancock, Winfield Scott, 13, 40,
    317, 355, 371
Hanover, 267-68, 495-98, 503
Hanover Junction, 269, 298, 502
Hansonville, 359
Harmony Grove, 358-59
Harney, 486
Harpers Ferry, 255
Harrisburg, 82; panic, 135; arrival of
    troops, 147, 265, 398
Haupt, Herman, 146
Haymarket, 211-12

Heidlersburg, 446
Heth, Henry, 193, 223
Hill, Ambrose P., 74, 106, 131; sketch, 219-20
Hoke, Jacob, 82, 85, 105, 224-25, 307, 398
Hood, John B., 65, 131, 227, 229, 261
Hooker, Joseph, entertains, 13; corps insignia, 14, 32; moves base, 52, 90
Hotchkiss, Jed, 31, 42, 124, 132; at Ferry Hill, 145, 167; sketch, 445, 464
Howard, Oliver O., 142, 180, 196, 201, 204, 247, 459-61
Humphreys, Andrew A., 69-70, 207-8, 243, 474-75
Hyde, Thomas, 492-93, 510

Imboden, John, 103, 232-33
Ingalls, Rufus, 252
Iron Brigade, 7, 46-48, 239, 362, 365

Jacobs, Professor, 235-36
Jefferson, Maryland, 277
Jefferson, Pennsylvania, 431-32
Jenkins, Alfred, 79; crosses Potomac, 81; at Williamsport, 82; in Chambersburg, 262-63
Johnson, Edward, 125, 131; sketch, 145, 394, 470-71
Johnsville, Maryland, 377
Jug Bridge, 335

Kemper's Ford, 12
Kennedy, John F., 108
Kettle Run, 66
Kidd, Frederick, 249

Lamon, Ward Hill, 63
Lee, Edwin, 132
Lee, Robert Edward, planning for invasion, 17; begins movements, 20, 104, 168, 172-73; meets A. P. Hill in Chambersburg, 224-25; headquarters in Chambersburg, 225; June 27, 256
Leesburg, 108-9, 160, 169
Lewistown, 359-60
Liberty, Maryland, 357, 376

Lincoln, Abraham, calls for men, 2; confers with Reynolds, 20; letter to Hooker, 21, 273
Littlestown, 381
Livermore, Thomas, 275
Logistics, 25-27, 534
Longstreet, James, 152; sketch, 342-43, 371
Loudoun County, description, 108

McClellan, Ellen, 308
McConnellsburg, 155, 157, 232
McCrea, Tully, 91
McKim, Randolph, 173
Manassas, 118-19
Manchester, 471, 504-9
Marion, Pennsylvania, 311, 390-91
Martinsburg, 77-78
Maryland Heights, 95, 162, 179, 225, 270, 438-39
Meade, George Gordon, 3, 213-14, 306-7, 318, 326; orders for June 28, 336, 338, 342, 346, 370-71, 435, 442-43, 491
Mechanicstown, 360
Mercersburg, 155
Merritt, Wesley, 333; sketch, 334
Middleburg, 140
Middletown, Maryland, 322-24
Millwood, 131
Milroy, Robert, 61, 62, 66, 74
Mitchell, Mary, 132
Monocacy Junction, 316
Monocacy River, 279
Moritz Tavern, 453
Mosby, John, 108, 110, 114, 198-99, 201
Mount Holly, 445
Mount Pleasant, 366
Mount Saint Mary's, 363-64

New Market, Maryland, 379, 380
New Windsor, 379, 383
Noland's Ferry, 122

Pender, Dorsey, 73; sketch, 193; last letter, 270
Pendleton, A. S., 86, 87, 124
Pendleton, William Nelson, 104, 132, 181-82, 227, 271
Pettigrew, Johnston, 63
Pickets, 7

Pickett, George, 185-86, 217-18; in
    Greencastle, 231, 259, 309
Pleasonton, Alfred, 28; reorganizes
    cavalry, 44, 159-60, 332;
    sketch, 334-35
Pontoon bridges, 148-50
Poolesville, 239, 275
Potomac fords, 144, 147-48
Prospect Hall, 325

Ramseur, S. D., 181
Rappahannock River, fords, 36; for-
    mation, 36
Reynolds, Catherine, letter, 329-30
Reynolds, John, 2, 3, 46; last letter,
    136, 151, 204, 242, 328-30,
    346-47; sketch, 348-49, 358;
    July 1, 454-56; death, 456-57
Richfield, 320, 325
Rodes, Robert, 22; Brandy Station,
    40; at Berryville, 50; at
    Bunker Hill, 64; attack on
    Martinsburg, 79-81; crossing
    the Potomac, 87, 88, 124,
    173, 185, 223, 266; July 1,
    464-65
Rohrersville, 248, 276
Rose Hill Manor, 272
Russell, J. W., 164

Sandoe, Donald, 237
Schley, Winfield Scott, 320
Sedgwick, John, 281-82, 318,
    352-53, 357, 371, 507, 511,
    514
Serenading, 11
Shepherdstown, sketch, 125; effects
    of war, 132-34, 178-79,
    192-93
Shotwell, Randolph, 104, 123, 144,
    153, 187, 230-31, 259-60,
    308-9
Sickles, Dan, 350-51
Slocum, Henry W., 178, 354-55, 357,
    389
Smithsburg, 196, 380
Sperryville, 103
Stafford Court House, 5, 72, 90, 92
Stephenson's Depot, 76
Stuart, James E. B., 321, 385-86
Sugar Loaf Mountain, 275
Sykes, George, 352-53, 357

Taneytown, 367, 368
Towpath march, 207-9
Trappe Rock, 122
Trimble, Isaac, 172-73, 237, 256
Troop dispositions, June 28, 338;
    June 30, 400
Twenty-fourth Michigan, 6, 8, 111,
    126, 363, 365
Two Taverns, 480-81

Union Mills, 387-89, 492
Unionville, 380
Upperville, 160, 164
Utica, 359

Vincent, Strong, 27, 160, 161-62,
    501

Wadsworth, James, 111, 168, 240
Wainwright, Charles, 11, 110, 198,
    242; describes Middletown
    Valley, 273-74; rides with
    Reynolds, 453
Walkersville, 326, 367, 382
Warren, G. K., 196-97
Waterford, 164-65
Water problems, 113
Webb, Alexander Stuart, 1, 198-99
Weed, Stephen, 33
Welch, Spencer, 166, 168, 313-14
Westminister, 302-3, 384-87
White, Elijah, 267-68, 298
White's Ferry, 108
Wilkeson, Bayard, 462
Williams, A. S., 5; night march, 43;
    June 18, 127-28; June 19,
    143; June 21, 160-64, 259,
    275, 369-70
Williamsport, 22, 87, 88, 228
Winchester, Ewell's objective, 50-51;
    fall of city, 77
Wolf Run Shoals, 94, 102, 113
Woodsboro, 357, 382
Worman's Mill, 358
Wrightsville, 301-2, 396

York, 296-98, 396